AS CORE Studies
PSYCHOLOGY
OCR

Philip Banyard and

Cara Flanagan

Published in 2006 by Psychology Press
27 Church Road, Hove, East Sussex, BN3 2FA
www.psypress.com

*Psychology Press is part of the Taylor & Francis Group,
an Informa business*

Reprinted 2007
Copyright © 2006 by Psychology Press

British Library Cataloguing in Publication Data
A catalogue record for this book is available from the British Library

ISBN 10: 1-84169-652-8
ISBN 13: 978-1-84169-652-2

Cover design by Hannah Armstrong

Typeset and project managed by
GreenGate Publishing Services, Tonbridge, Kent
www.ggate.co.uk

Printed and bound in Great Britain by
Ashford Colour Press Ltd, Gosport, Hampshire, UK

Contents

Acknowledgements

The authors would most particularly like to thank Rick Jackman, adviser and friend. We also would like to thank Beth Black for providing all sorts of advice, and Dave Mackin and the others at GreenGate for the painstaking care given to producing the complicated layout of this book. Finally we would like to thank Mike Forster, Lucy Kennedy and all at Psychology Press for their confidence in the project and help at a time of need.

Phil Banyard would like to acknowledge the encouragement and support he received from the teachers and examiners of the OCR specification. Their contributions and enthusiasm were the major drivers in the development of the course. He would also like to acknowledge the patience of his co-author, the remarkable skill of the darts players at the Gladstone Hotel, Carrington and the unforgettable piano playing of Mrs Mills.

Illustration credits

Introduction

Page vii: Illustrative page reproduced from E.F. Loftus & J.C. Palmer, (1974). *Journal of Verbal Learning & Verbal Behaviour*, 13, 585–589. Copyright © 1974. Reprinted with permission from Elsevier.

Chapter 1

Page 3 (top): © Louie Psihoyos/CORBIS. Page 3 (bottom): © Royalty-Free/CORBIS. Page 4: © Andy Warhol Foundation/CORBIS. Page 5 (top): From F.C. Bartlett (1932). *Remembering* © 1932 Cambridge University Press. Reproduced with permission. Page 5 (bottom): © CORBIS. Page 6: © Jodi Hilton/Pool/Reuters/CORBIS. Page 10 (top): © MGM/Corbis. Page 10 (bottom): © Chris Coxwell/CORBIS. Page 12: © Royalty-Free/Corbis. Page 15: From J.B. Deregowski (1989). Real space and represented space: Cross cultural perspectives. *Behavioural and Brain Sciences*, 12, 51–119. © 1989 Cambridge University Press. Reproduced with permission. Page 16: From J.B. Deregowski (1972). Pictorial perception and culture. *Scientific American*, 227, 82–88. © 1972 Scientific American. Reproduced with permission. Page 18 (left): © Kazuyoshi Nomachi/CORBIS. Page 18 (right): PETER MENZEL / SCIENCE PHOTO LIBRARY. Page 21: *Tower Bridge* by Stephen Wiltshire © 2005, reproduced with kind permission of the artist. http://www.stephenwiltshire.co.uk. Page 22: © Mika/zefa/CORBIS. Page 23 (left): Reproduced with kind permission of Professor Simon Baron Cohen. Page 23 (right): © Rune Hellestad/CORBIS. Page 26: From S. Baron-Cohen, A.M. Leslie, and U. Frith (1986). Mechanical, behavioural and intentional understanding of picture stories in autistic children. *British Journal of Developmental Psychology*, 4, 113–125. © 1986 British Psychological Society. Reproduced with permission. Page 28: Photo by April Ottey. Reproduced with permission of the Chimpanzee and Human Communication Institute, Central Washington University. Page 29 (top middle): Reproduced from O. Pfungst (1911). *Clever Hans: The horse of Mr von Osten*. New York: Holt. Page 29 (right) © SUNSET BOULEVARD/CORBIS. Page 31: © Bettmann/CORBIS. Page 34 (top): From Savage-Rumbaugh, E.S., & Lewin, R. (1994). *Kanzi: At the brink of the human mind*. New York: Wiley. Page 34 (bottom left): © Bettmann/CORBIS. Page 34 (bottom right): © Reuters/CORBIS. Page 35 (top and middle): © Bettmann/CORBIS. Page 35 (bottom): © Cydney Conger/CORBIS.

Chapter 2

Page 44: © Bettmann/CORBIS. Page 45: © Christophe Calais/In Visu/CORBIS. Page 47: © Bettmann/CORBIS. Page 49 (top left): Reproduced with kind permission of Professor Peter Bryant. Page 49 (top middle): Reproduced with kind permission of Judith Samuel. Page 54: Reproduced with kind permission of Professor Albert Bandura. Page 55 (top): © Steve Prezant/CORBIS. Page 55 (bottom): © Tim Graham/CORBIS. Pages 57 and 58: Reproduced with kind permission of Professor Albert Bandura. Page 60: © Tom & Dee Ann

How to use this book

Each chapter follows the same plan: the chapter opener provides a table of contents; the first double-page spread is an introduction to the area of psychology (cognitive, developmental, etc.).

Each core study is presented following the same format:

- **Starters:** Background material.

- **Core study:** A detailed description of the core study covering an abstract, the aims, method and results of the study plus conclusions or a discussion. There are also questions to answer, activities and biographical notes.

- **Evaluation:** Some themes to consider plus multiple choice questions and short-answer exam questions.

- **Afters:** Research that came afterwards plus links to other studies.

- **Key issue:** Covers various 'themes' identified in the specification such as reductionism, nature–nurture, self-report methods.

Each chapter ends with diagrammatic summaries of the four core studies plus a set of short- and long-answer questions with student answers and examiner's comments.

The chapters are presented in the order they appear in the specification but there is no law that says you have to study them in this order. We have endeavoured to write the book so it can be read in any order. You can do all cognitive core studies first or just one cognitive core study and then a social one. We have tried to make each core study 'standalone' though inevitably this is not exactly possible. There are some concepts that occur all over the place, such as ethics or ecological validity or experiments. You may need to skip around to other sections of the book – it would not be a bad thing to read some of the key issues several times, in the context of different core studies.

The final chapter is entitled 'Psychological research' and provides advice about what to do for the practical investigations folder and how to prepare for the psychological investigations exam. There are four activities that you need to conduct and these can be fitted in at any time during the year. Some of the suggested activities fit with certain core studies, for example there is a questionnaire (Activity A) on dreaming which would fit nicely with the core study by Dement and Kleitman (page 98).

 There is a website associated with this book where you can find suggested answers to all of the questions. See www.a-levelpsychology.co.uk/ocr/ ascorestudies

Introduction

Core studies

The OCR AS specification is based around 20 psychological studies. The studies have been selected either because they are classic studies in psychology or because they illustrate important issues in psychology.

What is a 'psychological study'? When psychologists (and other scientists) conduct research they write a report, published in a magazine or 'journal'. One report might contain details of several investigations. Each core study is one of these reports (also called an article). Journal articles are usually divided up as follows:

Abstract

A summary of the study.

Introduction/Aims

What a researcher intends to investigate. This often includes a review of previous research – theories and studies – which leads up to the aims for this particular study. The researcher(s) may state their research prediction(s) and/or a hypothesis/es.

Method

A detailed description of what the researcher(s) did, a bit like writing the recipe for making a cake. The main point is to give enough detail for someone else to replicate (repeat) the study. Replication is important to be able to check the results – if one repeated the same procedure, one should get the same results and this shows that the results weren't just a fluke.

Writing the procedure includes describing the participants (the sample), the testing environment, the procedures used to collect data, and any instructions given to participants before (the brief) and afterwards (the debrief).

Results

This section contains what the researcher(s) found, often called statistical data, which includes descriptive statistics (tables, averages and graphs) and inferential statistics (the use of statistical tests to determine how significant the results are).

Conclusions/Discussion

In the final section the researcher(s) attempt to indicate what the results mean, for example making generalisations about people based on how the participants behaved in the study and with reference to other research studies. They might propose one or more explanations of the behaviours that they observed. The researchers might also consider the implications of the results and make suggestions for future research.

Read the originals

We have provided fairly detailed accounts of each core study but it is a good idea to read the original articles. These can be obtained if you give the full reference for the study to your local library. They will obtain photocopies through the British Interlibrary loan service for a small fee.

A journal article

JOURNAL OF VERBAL LEARNING AND VERBAL BEHAVIOR 13, 585–589 (1974)

Reconstruction of Automobile Destruction:
An Example of the Interaction Between Language and Memory

ELIZABETH F. LOFTUS AND JOHN C. PALMER

University of Washington

Research methods: Subjects or participants?

In most of the core studies in this book the people in the studies were called 'subjects'. We have changed this in most cases to the more modern 'participants'.

During the 1990s there was a move to use the term 'participant' instead of 'subject' in order to reflect the fact that participants are not passive but are actively involved. They search for cues about how to behave and this may mean that they behave as researchers expect rather than as they would in everyday life. The use of the term 'participants' acknowledges this participant reactivity.

The term 'subjects' also reflects the power relationship in research studies. Typically the researcher holds the power in the research

setting because he/she knows what the experiment is about and knows the procedures to be followed. This often leaves the 'subject' powerless. It is to be hoped that the change of the term from 'subject' to 'participant' is more than just a cosmetic one and that, in more recent studies, the participant isn't quite as powerless. It may not be a good idea to rewrite the old studies and start calling the subjects 'participants', because they weren't. They were treated as passive respondents to the experimental situations set up by psychologists and they were rarely dealt with as collaborators. However, we made a decision to do this in most of the studies.

The AS exam

First of all, you should read the specification – you can download it from the OCR website (http://www.ocr.org.uk).

There are three exams. Each is one hour in duration and each contributes 33.3% to your overall AS grade.

Unit title	Description
2540 Core Studies 1	There are 20 short-answer questions, one question for each core study. You must answer all questions. Each question is worth a maximum of 4 marks. The total marks on the paper = 60.
	This unit examines your knowledge and understanding (AO1) of the core studies, and examines your ability to make evaluative points and ability to see the studies in the wider perspective of psychological concepts and methods (AO2).
	In particular you will be asked questions about: • The information in the studies. • The methods used in the studies. • The way the results are analysed and presented. • The conclusions that can be drawn from the studies. • The context of the studies. • The general psychological issues illustrated by the studies. • Evaluations of all of the above.
2541 Core Studies 2	The paper is divided into Section A and Section B. You must answer one question from each section. Section A (52%): The question you answer must be related to one core study, selected from a list of core studies. Section B (48%): The question you answer must be related to several core studies that are identified in the question. All questions are structured, i.e. split into several parts. The question parts relate to methods, themes and perspectives, which are listed on page x.
2542 Psychological Investigations	This exam is described in chapter 6. It consists of 10–12 questions which are answered in relation to four practical activities conducted by students. You may record details of the activities in a practical investigations folder and take this into the exam with you. Some of the exam questions are directly related to this folder; others are on general issues of methodology.

Assessment objectives

AO1 *knowledge and understanding of psychological theories, terminology, concepts, studies and methods.*

AO2 *analysis and evaluation of psychological theories, concepts, studies and methods.*

AO3 *design, conduct and report psychological investigation(s) choosing from a range of methods, and taking into account the issues of reliability, validity and ethics, and collect and draw conclusions from the data.*

How exam questions are marked

Core Studies 1: Short-answer questions: Examples

In the study by Loftus and Palmer on eyewitness testimony, the participants were shown film clips of car accidents. Outline two differences between witnessing film clips and witnessing a real accident. [OCR AS Psy, Jan 1998, paper 1] [4]

Outline **one** ethical issue raised by Bandura, Ross and Ross's study on aggression. [OCR AS Psy, May 2003, paper 1] [2]

From the study on sleep and dreaming by Dement and Kleitman, outline **one** way in which the study is low in ecological validity. [OCR AS Psy, Jan 2004, paper 1] [2]

Core Studies 2: Long-answer questions: Section A: Example

One of the ethical issues that causes concern in the conduct of psychological investigations is that of deception. It is sometimes argued that the use of deception is an essential part of research, and that, without some form of deception, research would be impossible.

Choose one of the core studies listed below and answer the following questions.

Rosenhan (sane in insane places)
Milgram (obedience)
Piliavin, Rodin and Piliavin (subway Samaritans)

(a) Describe how deception was used in your chosen study. [6]

(b) Give **two** reasons supporting the use of deception in your study and **two** reasons against the use of deception in your study. [12]

(c) Suggest **one** way in which your chosen study could have been conducted without the use of deception and say how this might affect the results. [8]
[OCR AS Psy, May 2003, paper 2]

Core Studies 2: Long-answer questions: Section B: Example

Psychologists often want to make statements about how most people behave or experience the world. These statements are called generalisations. However, such generalisations are often based on a limited range of participants, environments, activity or culture.

Using the core studies below, answer the questions that follow.

Haney, Banks and Zimbardo (prison simulation)
Gould (intelligence testing)
Samuel and Bryant (conservation)
Deregowski (perception)

(a) Describe a generalisation that we can make from each study. [12]

(b) Using examples, discuss **two** advantages and **two** disadvantages of making generalisations about human behaviour and experience. [12]
[OCR AS Psy, May 2003, paper 2]

Core studies 1: Mark scheme for short-answer questions

In most questions on this paper you are required to do one thing for 2 marks or two things for 4 marks. The mark scheme below is used to mark such questions.

0 marks	No answer or totally incorrect answer.
1 mark	Partially correct answer or correct but incomplete, lacking sufficient detail or explanation to demonstrate clear understanding.
2 marks	Correct answer with sufficient detail/explanation to demonstrate clear understanding.

Occasionally a question requires you to name two things for 2 marks, for example

Identify two of the three groups of children in the study by Baron-Cohen, Leslie and Frith in their study on autism. [OCR AS Psy, May 2005, paper 1] [2]

In this case you would receive one mark for each correct answer, no extra detail/explanation is required.

Core studies 2: Mark schemes for long-answer questions

The mark schemes vary with the different styles of question.

Section A part (a)
Question style: Describe XXX in one chosen study. [6]

Marks	Content	Quality of written communication (expression and technical terms)
0	No answers or incorrect	
1–2	One or two general statements, basic and lacking in detail.	Poor, rudimentary.
3–4	Accurate with increased detail.	Good.
5–6	Accurate with appropriate detail. Few omissions.	Competent. For 6 marks must be very good.

Section A part (b) and Section B part (b)
Question style: Discuss **two** strengths and **two** weaknesses of … [12]

For each point (up to 4 points):

1 mark	Point	State the strength/weakness.
1 mark	Example	Give an example from the study.
1 mark	Comment	Provide an evaluation (positive or negative), or an implication.

Section A part (c)
Question style: Suggest **one** other way data could have been gathered for your study and say how you think this may affect the results. [8]

Marks	Alternative	Effect on alternative
1–2	Alternative given but little expansion, or alternative may be only peripherally relevant.	Effect of alternative referred to briefly but not developed. For 2 marks there is some expansion but no analysis.
3–4	Relevant alternative in appropriate detail with understanding of implications	Effect of alternative considered in appropriate detail with analysis. For 4 marks there is clarity of expression and arguments are structured.

1 mark	Point	Identify a point relevant to the question.
1 mark	Description	Brief description OR an extra relevant point.
1 mark	Analysis	Analysis OR a third extra relevant point.

Section B part (a)
Question style: Describe XXX relating to the four named studies. [12]

For each study

The PEC formula

At the end of each chapter in this book there are sample exam questions with student answers and examiner's comments. The long-answer questions for Core Studies 2 Section B require you to describe something (for example strengths or weaknesses) in relation to four named core studies. The trick with these Section B questions is to write FOUR paragraphs. In each one, answer the actual question, trying to stick to the P–E–C formula:

- P(oint) = explain a strength/weakness (which is probably true of all four named studies).

- E(xample) = explain your point further by giving an example from any one of the four named studies.

- C(omment) = expand your point and/or example further. This can be achieved in a number of ways, e.g. explaining the implications further; perhaps saying how such information can by usefully applied to the world, or explaining why it is so difficult to get round a particular problem or weakness without causing yet another weakness. Basically, you need to extend your point/example further for the comment mark (and not just repeat yourself in different words!).

Extra advice

To gain top marks on the part (c) question from Section A, you must write more than one sentence describing the alternative and more than one sentence stating the effect of the alternative on results. You can do this by:

- Describing what you would actually do.

- Being specific about the actual effect on results e.g. 'it might increase obedience' rather than just saying 'the study would be more valid'.

If in doubt, stick it in

In some questions you may not be sure what is required. For example, in one question candidates were asked to describe how data were gathered in a named study – however, they did not gain full marks if they just described how; they also had to include a statement of what data were gathered. The moral of the story is – if in doubt, stick it in.

EVALUATING RESEARCH

An important part of *knowing* about a research article is being able to *evaluate* it. Evaluation is a personal business. We can tell you the facts of the study but *deciding* whether the study is good or bad is up to you. Throughout the book we have provided you with the *tools* to evaluate studies – the **Key Issues**. These are listed in the table below. To help you further, within each study, we have presented a list of possible evaluations for that core study and some points to help you think about the issues. Some suggested answers are available at www.a-levelpsychology.co.uk/ocr

Key issues

Key Issues are covered within the core studies (see page references below or check the index at the back of the book). Each key issue is relevant to lots of other studies and we have indicated some of these with bullets.

The three-point rule

One of the key problems with evaluation is that students fail to elaborate their points. For example they say 'This study was unethical' or 'This study lacked ecological validity'. But, in order to gain marks, these points must be elaborated. One way to do this is to use the three-point rule (a bit like P–E–C on page ix):

1   Name your criticism (which may be a strength or a limitation).

2   Justify it – explain it in context, what is your evidence to support your criticism?

3   Explain why this is a criticism, for example what are the consequences?

So, if the criticism of a study is 'lack of ecological validity' then you have named it. You need to show why this applies to this context ('The study tested memory using a film of a car accident which doesn't reflect how eyewitnesses would actually experience an accident'). Finally you need to state the consequence ('Lack of ecological validity means you can't generalise the findings to everyday life').

Core studies

Key Issues	Loftus	Deregowski	Baron-Cohen	Gardner	Samuel	Bandura	Hodges	Freud	Schachter	Dement	Sperry	Raine	Milgram	Haney	Piliavin	Tajfel	Gould	Hraba	Rosenhan	Thigpen
Behaviourism				35			•						•	•	•					•
Case studies					•			•												203
Children					53	•	•	•								•		•		
Cross cultural studies		19															•	•		
Design and controls	11		•	•	•	•	•		•	•	•	•	•	•	•	•		•		•
Determinism	•	•	•	•	•	•	•	•	•		•	119	•	•	•	•	•	•		•
Ecological validity	•	•	•			•	•	•	•		•	•	137	•	•	•				
Ethics	•		•		•	•	•	•	95	•	•	•	•	•	•	•	•	•	•	•
Ethnocentrism		•	•			•	•	•				•	•		•	161	•			•
Experiments		•	•			•	•	•	•	103	•	•	•	•	•		•			
Generalisation/sampling	•	•	27	•		•	•	•	•	•	•	•	•	•	•	•	•	•	•	•
Individual differences		•	•										•	•	•	•	•	•	•	•
Longitudinal vs. snapshot	•	•	•	•	•	•	69	•				•					•			•
Measurement: qualitative and quantitative	•	•	•	•	•	•	•	•	•	•	•	•	•	145	•	•	•	•	•	•
Nature versus nurture		•	•	•	•	61	•	•	•		•	•	•	•	•	•	•	•		•
Observation		•	•		•	•		•			•				•	•			195	
Personality versus situation	•	•	•		•	•	•		•		•		•	•	153	•	•	•	•	•
Promoting human welfare	•	•	•	•	•	•	•	•	•	•	•	•	•	•	•	•	•	187	•	•
Psychometrics				•		•			•		•	•		•			179	•	•	•
Reductionism	•		•							•	111	•	•			•				•
Reliability					•	•		•						•	•			•	•	
Self reports		•				•	•	77	•					•				•		•
Validity	•	•	•	•	•	•	•	•	•	•	•	•	•	•	•	•	•	•	•	•

This chapter looks at four core studies in cognitive psychology.

1.   *Loftus and Palmer's work on memory for events.*

2.   *Deregowski's summary of cross-cultural work on the differences in the ways we perceive the world.*

3.   *Gardner and Gardner's attempt to teach sign language to a chimpanzee called Washoe.*

4.   *Baron-Cohen, Leslie and Frith's study on the peculiar thought processes of autistic children.*

CHAPTER

1

Cognitive psychology

Introduction to cognitive psychology

The history of cognitive psychology

Computer code: will the study of artificial intelligence produce a code of human thought one day?

What is cognitive psychology?

Cognitive psychology is the study of all mental processes:

- How do we see the world?
- How do we store and recall information?
- How do we communicate?
- How do we think?

Cognitive psychology takes a mechanistic approach, which means that it largely looks at people as if they are machines. Modern research looks at human cognitive processes and compares them to those of a computer. Computers can do several of the things that people can do, and they can do some of them better. They can respond to the environment, store information, calculate and much more.

The first psychology laboratory was set up by Wilhelm Wundt (1823–1920) in Leipzig, Germany in 1879. According to Wundt, psychology was the study of immediate experience – which did not include any issues of culture or social interaction. About half the work in the lab was on the topics of sensory processes and perception, though they also looked at reaction time, learning, attention and emotion. The main method that was used in the laboratory was introspection, which is a form of self-observation.

During the first half of the twentieth century, cognitive psychology was not as prominent as it is today, but we still draw on work from psychologists in that time, for example, Jean Piaget (see the study by Samuel and Bryant, page 48) and Frederick Bartlett (see the study by Loftus and Palmer, page 6).

The cognitive revolution

Cognitive psychology came to the forefront of psychology in the 1950s. George Miller hosted a seminar in the USA in 1956 where Newell and Simon presented a paper on computer logic, Noam Chomsky (see the study on Washoe, page 30) presented a paper on language, and Miller presented his famous paper on 'The magic number seven plus or minus two'. Each of these presentations defined their field and modern cognitive psychology is often dated to this event.

In the UK Donald Broadbent was a strong supporter of the information-processing models of cognition. These models were based on the communication technology of the time and were commonly represented as telephone exchanges to represent the way messages were sorted and distributed.

As technology developed so did the science of how people behave intelligently in the world. The models were now based on computer processes. This brings up a question about whether cognitive psychology is studying the cognitive processes of people or the cognitive processes of computers. It also brings up a much deeper question about what it means to be human and be alive. Can a computer think? Can it be aware of itself? Can it have a theory of mind? (For this last question see the study on autism on page 22.)

Artificial intelligence

One of the key strands of cognitive psychology is artificial intelligence (AI). It is the science and engineering of making intelligent machines, especially intelligent computer programs. The origins of AI can be seen in the work of British scientist Alan Turing in the 1950s on intelligent machines. Turing is particularly famous for his work on code breaking during the Second World War (1939–45) using the Enigma machines he helped to create.

The computer challenge

(a) Make a list of the things that computers and humans can do. To get you started there is:
(i) storing information
(ii) calculating
(iii) recalling.

(b) When you've completed that list try to identify the differences between the ways that humans and computers do these tasks.

(c) Now try to make a list of the things that people can do that computers can't.

When is a robot not a robot?

Several films explore this idea and challenge us to tell the difference between a living person and an intelligent machine. Examples of such films are *Blade Runner, AI, Short Circuit* and *Star Trek*. The robots behave like people and we feel the same way towards them as we do towards human beings.

Deep Blue and Gary Kasparov

Deep Blue is an IBM supercomputer that is programmed to play chess. Deep Blue uses 256 processors working together to calculate between 50 and 100 billion chess moves in less than three minutes. In 1997 Deep Blue defeated chess world champion Gary Kasparov. Real-world applications of computers like Deep Blue include forecasting the weather, drug and genetics research, and powering web servers on the internet.

Cognitive puzzles in everyday life

1. Why do my holiday snaps look so duff?

You were on the beach and saw this giant lizard. It was massive but when you get your photo back you can barely see it. And that giant ship on the horizon has become a dot. Is the camera rubbish? Probably not. Your mind's eye adjusts the size of objects so you perceive them to be bigger. The camera records what is really there, and your mind's eye distorts it to help you concentrate on the important objects.

2. How do children learn language?

I was trying to make excuses for my lack of a foreign language by explaining to a Spanish friend that their language was difficult for English people to learn. My friend commented that this was remarkable because in his country there were many 5-year-olds fluent in it. Children do not need instruction to learn language, and in fact it is almost impossible to stop them developing language. Language is a complex set of sounds and rules that almost defy description yet we have no difficulty in developing them and being understood.

'De primero quiero las gambas, y dos cervezas por favor'

3. How do we tune in to conversations?

You are in a large group of people talking to a friend. You don't know what everyone else in the room is talking about but all of a sudden you hear your name from the other side of the room. Someone is talking about you. You immediately tune out of the conversation with your friend and listen to what is being said about you.

This is remarkable in itself; you don't have movable ears so the tuning in has taken place inside your head rather than outside. Even more remarkable is how you heard your name. If you weren't listening to that conversation how did you hear your name?

Maybe your mind is monitoring all sorts of information below the level of your awareness and selects the important bits for you to attend to. But what is doing this monitoring and how does it decide what is important?

Turing's claim

Turing held that in time computers would be programmed to acquire abilities that rivalled human intelligence.

As part of his argument Turing put forward the idea of an 'imitation game', in which a human being and a computer would be questioned under conditions where the questioner would not know which was which. This would be possible if the communication was entirely by written messages. Turing argued that if the questioner could not distinguish them, then we should see the computer as being intelligent. Turing's 'imitation game' is now usually called 'the Turing test'.

Connections

Cognitive psychology is about understanding how we make sense of our world and communicate within it. It has links to all the other areas of psychology in this text. In Individual Differences we look at the cognitive skill of intelligence; in Developmental Psychology we look at how children think; in Social Psychology we look at how people make social judgements, and in Physiological Psychology we look at how the brain carries out cognitive tasks. One of the fastest growing areas in psychology is cognitive neuroscience which focuses on the connections between brain structures and cognitive abilities.

Research into memory

Memory

Everybody has a tale about memory: how they forgot an important appointment, or the fact that their granny can remember everyone's name in the family over the last 200 years. Sometimes we surprise ourselves by what we can recall when we go back somewhere we haven't been for 30 years, or at an important moment in a quiz. 'How did I know that?' you ask yourself. Mind you, when you are in the exam room trying to answer the questions you are more likely to ask yourself why you can't remember things.

ACTIVITY

Tell family members that you are studying memory and record their reaction. Do they have stories to tell about their own memories or do they just say 'That's nice babe'?

Making adverts work

Advertisers use retrieval cues to help us remember their product. One way of using retrieval cues is to place pictures from television adverts on the packaging of the product. The Campbell Soup Company, for example, reported that sales increased by 15% when their point-of-sales materials (items in the shops) were directly related to their television advertising (Keller, 1987).

Mental mechanisms

The earliest systematic work on the psychology of memory was carried out by Hermann Ebbinghaus at the end of the nineteenth century. He carried out a range of highly controlled experiments most commonly using himself as the sole participant. He measured his ability to remember nonsense syllables. These are three letter syllables that sound like words but mean nothing, for example 'wib', 'fut', 'wol', etc. He used nonsense syllables so that any past knowledge would not affect the results. The studies were methodical, and provided a wide range of findings which had a big influence on how memory research was conducted, and on theories of memory.

Bartlett (see opposite page) criticised Ebbinghaus's work by noting that the use of nonsense syllables created a very artificial situation, and therefore lacked *ecological validity*. He also suggested that Ebbinghaus concentrated too closely on the material that was being remembered, and ignored other important features like the attitudes of the subject and their prior experience.

Later work developed a two-stage model of memory (long-term memory and short-term memory) which became a multi-store model as more boxes were added to the model. Although this research did not use nonsense syllables it commonly used word lists or other tasks that did not have much connection to everyday memory.

ACTIVITY

Try to draw both sides of a £1 coin. Then try to draw a £5 note. How many features can you get right? What does this tell you about memory?

Memory for everyday objects

Our memory of everyday objects is surprisingly bad. Ask someone to draw a coin or a £5 note and they struggle. Even if you ask them to recognise the real coin from a collection of drawings they find it hard to do. In one study researchers found that free recall of a coin was very poor. Of the eight main features of the coin, the average number recalled and correctly located on the drawing was only three, which seems strange given how often the research participants handled these coins (Nickerson and Adams, 1979).

Two traditions

There are two routes to studying memory:

- The study of **everyday experience.**

- The experimental study of **mental mechanisms.**

The most commonly researched of these in psychology is the experimental study of mental mechanisms. This might seem a little disappointing because the interesting bits are the phenomena of everyday life. In fact, the cognitive psychologist Ulrich Neisser (1982) suggested that a basic principle of memory research was:

'If X is an interesting or socially significant aspect of memory, then psychologists have hardly ever studied X.' (p. 4)

Neisser goes on to make a more remarkable claim:

'I think that "memory" in general does not exist.' (p. 12)

This sounds ridiculous because it is obvious that we remember objects and events, but is there really a thing we can call a memory? There does not seem to be any one part of the brain that controls memories, so thinking of memory as a mechanism, like a DVD recorder, is probably not helpful. In fact it would be very misleading because, as we will see later, we do not store and recall exact records of events. Far from it: we recreate our memories and in so doing we distort them.

Everyday experience

In contrast to Ebbinghaus, Bartlett carried out a series of studies into the memory of meaningful material like stories and pictures. One of Bartlett's methods was to ask someone to look at some material and then recall it. This recalled material was then shown to someone else who had to recall what they had seen, and so on. This is called the method of *serial reproduction*.

Bartlett used another method (the method of *repeated reproduction*), where the same person is asked to keep remembering the same material over a period of time. An example of how the recall of an image changed over successive reproductions is shown on the right. The drawing is a representation of the Egyptian 'mulak', a conventionalised reproduction of an owl, which may have been used as the model for our letter 'M'. With each recall of the image the drawing changed and by the tenth version the person believed they had initially seen a black cat.

In his studies Bartlett (1932) found that memories change in a number of ways:

They become more conventional: Drawings became more like common objects such as a cat in the example shown. Also when people were asked to recall stories these memories were also modified to be more conventional.

They are simplified: Stories and pictures become simpler when they are recalled

Labels or names affect recall: For example, in the images shown once a label 'cat' has been used, the recalls become more and more like a common view of a cat rather than the original image.

Elaboration takes place: Some items are introduced into the story or the picture by the person remembering it. In the shown example a tail develops from one of the lines of the mulak but by the last drawing it has no connection to the original.

Emotional distortion takes place: The way someone was feeling during the tests tended to affect the memory of the stories they were told.

Bartlett found that our memories are not exact recordings of events and images. This is obviously important when we look at evidence in court but it was more than 40 years before this idea was looked at again by Elizabeth Loftus (see next page).

Original Drawing

Try the method of successive reproduction to see how much a message or a picture changes as it passes from one person to another.

Flashbulb memories

A flashbulb memory is a memory about what you were doing when you heard about something significant. It is not the memory for the event itself.

Some events have a big effect on us and we are able to say where we were and what we were doing when we heard about the event or when we witnessed it. It is almost as if a flashbulb has gone off in our minds to highlight the scene and fix the image. Flashbulb memories are typically remarkably vivid and seem to be permanent. These memories are usually of very emotional and personal events in your life. Flashbulb memories can also be related to events that are public but affected you emotionally, such as the death of a famous person (like Princess Diana) or a dramatic news event (like the *Challenger* space disaster).

Maybe there is a *flashbulb mechanism* that is responsible for capturing these events and storing them in memory for an indefinite period of time. Maybe these memories are not encoded any differently from others but we remember them because we rehearse them by retelling them often.

A problem with much of the work on flashbulb memories is that data are not checked. If I say I remember I was in the bath when I heard the news that a famous person had died, how would you know this was correct? In fact, how would I know? Neisser doubts whether these memories are any more accurate than our other memories and he carried out a number of studies including one on memories of the *Challenger* space disaster.

In 1986 the *Challenger* space shuttle exploded on take-off killing the entire crew. It was seen live on television and shown repeatedly on newscasts. The next day Neisser and Harsch (1992) asked students to give their recollections of the time when they

first heard of the disaster. They went back to the same students two-and-a-half years later and asked them the same question. They discovered that at least 25% of them were wrong about every major detail. Only 10% gave all the same details. He also discovered that the students' confidence in the memories had no correlation with their accuracy. Students who had inaccurate recall were just as likely to be confident in their memories as students whose memories were unchanged.

The flashbulb moment when the space shuttle blew up

The core study

We are very confident about our own memories: 'I was there, I saw it, I know what happened.' Psychology tells us, however, that this is not the case and memory is far from an accurate record of events. Does this matter? Well, not if you are telling the story of a good night out, but yes if you are giving evidence in a court of law. Perhaps our memories are susceptible to suggestion and if so, the leading questions of barristers and police might have an effect on evidence given to them about a crime.

Elizabeth Loftus and John C. Palmer (1974) Reconstruction of automobile destruction. *Journal of Verbal Learning and Verbal Behaviour*, 13, pp. 585–589.

LOFTUS AND PALMER : EYEWITNESS TESTIMONY

Abstract

This study is concerned with the effect of leading questions on what people remember.

The study consists of two experiments:

Experiment 1

Participants were asked to say how fast a car is going. If the question contained the word 'smashed' ('How fast were the cars going when they *smashed* into each other') their estimates were higher than if other verbs were used (*collided*, *bumped*, *contacted* or *hit*). This shows that estimates of speed were affected by such leading questions.

Experiment 2

Does the critical word (e.g. 'smashed' or 'hit') change a person's subsequent memory of the event they witnessed? Participants were again shown slides of a car accident and asked how fast the cars were going when they smashed or hit each other. A week later they were asked some more questions including one about whether there had been any broken glass. There had been no broken glass but those who thought the car was travelling faster were more likely to say there was.

Elizabeth Loftus

KEY TERMS

A leading question is one that suggests to a witness what answer is desired or leads the witness to give the desired answers.

Biographical notes on Elizabeth Loftus

Elizabeth Loftus is Distinguished Professor at the University of California, Irvine. She was born in Los Angeles, California in 1944 and planned to be a maths teacher but discovered psychology at university. She received her PhD from Stanford University in 1970.

She began her research with investigations of how the mind classifies and remembers information. In the 1970s, she began to re-evaluate the direction of her research. In 'Diva of disclosure' (Neimark, 1996) published in *Psychology Today*, she stated 'I wanted my work to make a difference in people's lives'. She began her research on traumatically repressed memories and eyewitness accounts and suddenly found herself in the midst of sexual abuse stories and defending accused offenders. Loftus has been an expert witness consultant in hundreds of cases on the unreliability of eyewitness testimonies based on false memories, which she believes to be triggered, suggested, implanted, or created in the mind.

Loftus has received numerous awards for her work from psychology and from other disciplines. She has received four honourary doctorates including one from the UK. She received the William James Fellow Award from the American Psychological Society, 2001 for 'ingeniously and rigorously designed research studies ... that yielded clear objective evidence on difficult and controversial questions'. She remains a respected and controversial figure in psychology and in a review of twentieth-century psychologists published by the *Review of General Psychology* she was the top-ranked woman on the list.

'I study human memory. My experiments reveal how memories can be changed by things that we are told. Facts, ideas, suggestions and other forms of post-event information can modify our memories. The legal field, so reliant on memories, has been a significant application of the memory research. My interest in psychology and law, more generally, has grown from this application.'

 Elizabeth Loftus' home page www.seweb.uci.edu/cls/faculty/loftus.uci

CORESTUDY

Experiment 1

Aim

The aim of this study was to investigate the accuracy of memory. In particular it was to see if **leading questions** distorted the accuracy of an eyewitness's immediate recall. People are notoriously poor at estimating the speed of moving cars and therefore they might be particularly receptive to any hints (leading questions) when asked to estimate the speed of a car.

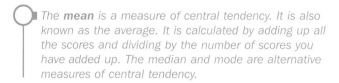

*The **mean** is a measure of central tendency. It is also known as the average. It is calculated by adding up all the scores and dividing by the number of scores you have added up. The median and mode are alternative measures of central tendency.*

Method

Participants: 45 students.

The participants were shown seven film clips of different traffic accidents. The clips were originally made as part of a driver safety film.

After each clip the participants were given a questionnaire which asked them to describe the accident and then answer a series of specific questions about the accident.

There was one critical question: 'About how fast were the cars going when they hit each other?'. One group of participants was given this question. The other four groups were given the verbs 'smashed', 'collided', 'bumped' or 'contacted' in place of the word 'hit'. Thus there were five experimental groups in this lab experiment.

Q_s Experiment 1

1   Identify the independent variable (IV) and dependent variable (DV) in this experiment.

2   Write a suitable hypothesis for this experiment (make sure it is clearly operationalised).

3   Describe **one** strength and **one** limitation of conducting a lab experiment.

4   Why was it a good idea to ask 10 questions rather than just asking the critical question alone?

5   Each group of participants was shown the films in a different order. Why do you think this was done?

6   How might participant reactivity have been a problem in this experiment?

7   Can you think of a way that this problem might have been overcome?

8   Describe a possible sampling method that might have been used in this study.

9   Give **one** strength and **one** limitation of this sampling method.

10   Outline **one** finding from this experiment.

11   State **one** conclusion that can be drawn from this finding.

Results

The **mean** speed estimate was calculated for each experimental group, as shown in the graph below. The group given the word 'smashed' estimated a higher speed than the other groups (about 40 m.p.h.). The group given the word 'contacted' estimated the lowest speed (about 30 m.p.h.).

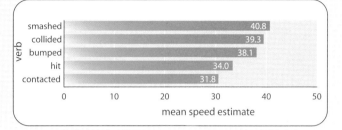

Discussion

The results show that the form of a question can have a significant effect on a witness's answer to the question. In other words, leading questions can affect the accuracy of memory.

Loftus and Palmer propose two explanations for this result:

1.   **Response-bias factors:** the different speed estimates occur because the critical word (e.g. 'smashed' or 'hit') influences or biases a person's response.

2.   **The memory representation is altered:** the critical word changes a person's memory so that he 'sees' the accident differently (more or less severe).

If the second conclusion is true, we would expect participants to 'remember' other details that are not true. Loftus and Palmer tested this in their second experiment which is described on the next page.

ACTIVITY

Try repeating one of the experiments from the study by Loftus and Palmer, using a photograph of an automobile accident and devising a set of questions, one of which will be the critical question.

Each person in your class should give the questionnaire to two people: one has the 'smashed' version, one has the 'hit' version. Make sure they don't know that there are two different versions.

Put all the results together, and calculate the mean speed estimate for all those questionnaires that used the word 'smashed' and the mean speed estimate for all those questionnaires that used the word 'hit'.

Draw a bar chart to illustrate your class results.

Experiment 2

Aim

Loftus and Palmer conducted a second experiment to further investigate the effects of differential speed estimates (leading questions) on memory. In particular they wanted to see if such questions simply create a response-bias (explanation 1) or if they actually alter a person's memory representation (explanation 2).

Method

Participants: a new group of 150 students.

Part 1 Participants were shown a one-minute film which contained a four-second multiple car accident. The participants were asked a set of questions including the critical question about speed. There were three groups:

● Group 1 was asked: 'How fast were the cars going when they *smashed* each other?'

● Group 2 was asked: 'How fast were the cars going when they *hit into* each other?'

● Group 3 was asked no question about the speed of the vehicles. This was a control group.

Part 2 One week later the participants were asked to return to the psychology lab. They were asked some further questions including 'Did you see any broken glass?' There was no broken glass in the film but, presumably, those who thought the car was travelling faster might expect that there would be broken glass.

Q$_s$ Experiment 2

1   Why is it a good idea to have a control group?

2   A possible hypothesis for experiment 2 would be 'Participants are more likely to report seeing broken glass when they are given the word 'smashed' in a previous question than when they have the word 'hit'. Is this a directional or non-directional hypothesis?

3   State a suitable null hypothesis for this study.

4   Describe **two** findings from this experiment.

5   What conclusions can you draw from the probability table on the right?

6   How do the aims for experiment 1 and 2 differ?

What is a 'control group'?

If a **control group** is used in an experiment, they do not receive the IV but their performance is assessed on the DV. We can compare the **experimental groups** (those who receive the IV) with the control group to see if the IV did have an effect. Without the control group we have no record of the baseline.

Results

The results from Part 1 are shown in the bar chart below. Participants gave higher speed estimates in the 'smashed' condition, as before.

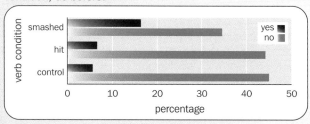

In Part 2 (a week later) they found that participants in the 'smashed condition' were also more likely to think they saw broken glass (see below).

The probability of saying 'Yes' to the question 'Did you see any broken glass?' related to speed estimates

Verb condition	Speed estimate (mile/h)			
	1–5	6–10	11–15	16–20
Smashed	0.09	0.27	0.41	0.62
Hit	0.06	0.09	0.25	0.50

Discussion

The results again show that the way a question is asked can influence the answer given. The results from Part 2 of the second experiment suggest that this effect is not due to a response-bias but because leading questions actually alter the memory a person has for the event.

Loftus and Palmer propose that memory is determined by two sources: firstly one's own perception and secondly external information supplied after the fact (such as leading questions). Over time information from these two sources is integrated in such a way that we are unable to distinguish between them.

ACTIVITY

Draw a bar chart of the table probability above. This may help you understand the results of the study and what to conclude.

EVALUATING THE STUDY BY LOFTUS AND PALMER

(See page x for note on evaluating research studies/articles)

The research method

This study was a lab experiment. *What are the strengths and limitations of this research method in the context of this study?*

The sample

American students were used in this study. *In what way is this group of participants unique? How does this effect the conclusions drawn from the study?*

Ecological validity

To what extent can we generalise the findings from this study to other situations?

Qualitative or quantitative?

What kind of data were collected in this study? What are the strengths and limitations of producing this kind of data in the context of this study?

Representativeness

Eyewitness testimony was tested by showing participants video clips. *To what extent is this like real life?* Real-life eyewitnesses may be feeling scared or anxious. *How do you think this might affect their memory?*

Applications/usefulness

How might you use the findings from the two experiments? How valuable was this study?

DEBATE

What do you conclude about the ecological validity of the study by Loftus and Palmer? Hold a 'mock trial'. One team has the task of arguing that this study has ecological validity and another team has to present the opposite case. You might do some extra research first. What do you conclude?

(?)

What next?

Describe **one** change to this study, and say how you think this might affect the outcome.

Multiple choice questions

1. Which of the following was not a cue word in the experiment by Loftus and Palmer?
   (a) Smashed   (b) Contacted
   (c) Knocked   (d) Hit

2. The DV in the first experiment was
   (a) Estimate of speed.
   (b) The verb 'smashed'.
   (c) The question about broken glass.
   (d) The film.

3. In experiment 1, how many experimental conditions were there?
   (a) 1   (b) 3
   (c) 5   (d) 7

4. In experiment 2, how many experimental groups were there?
   (a) 1   (b) 2
   (c) 3   (d) 4

5. In experiment 2, participants were tested immediately and then asked to return for some more questions. How long afterwards was this?
   (a) 1 day   (b) 3 days
   (c) 1 week   (d) 2 weeks

6. In experiment 2, which group saw the most broken glass?
   (a) The 'smashed' group.
   (b) The 'collided' group.
   (c) The 'hit' group.
   (d) The control group.

7. Which of the following is true?
   (a) Experiment 1 and 2 were both repeated measures.
   (b) Experiment 1 and 2 were both independent groups.
   (c) Only experiment 1 was repeated measures.
   (d) Only experiment 1 was independent groups.

8. The conclusion drawn from experiment 2 was that
   (a) The leading question creates a response-bias.
   (b) The leading question alters memory.
   (c) (a) and (b).
   (d) Memory is not affected by leading questions.

9. The participants in this study were
   (a) Children   (b) Students
   (c) Teachers   (d) Adults

10. A demand characteristic may act as an
    (a) IV
    (b) DV
    (c) Extraneous variable
    (d) All of the above.

Answers are on page 37.

Exam questions

1. In the study by Loftus and Palmer (eyewitness testimony), the participants were shown film clips of car accidents. Suggest **two** ways in which the ecological validity of this study could be improved. [OCR AS Psy, Jan 2002, paper 2]   [4]

2. (a) In their study on eyewitness testimony, Loftus and Palmer suggest that two kinds of information go into a person's memory for a complex event. Identify **one** of these two kinds of information.   [2]

   (b) What does the existence of these **two** kinds of information tell us about memory?   [2]
   [OCR AS Psy, May 2002, paper 1]

3. From the study on eyewitness testimony by Loftus and Palmer outline **two** features of the procedure that were standardised. [OCR AS Psy, May 2005, paper 1]   [4]

4. (a) In the study on eyewitness testimony by Loftus and Palmer, the use of the verbs 'smashed' and 'hit' led to different responses from the participants. Outline **one** of these differences.   [2]

   (b) Give **one** explanation for that difference.   [2]
   [OCR AS Psy, Jan 2004, paper 1]

Mis-identification

Recent experiments have found that people can make errors when asked to identify someone who might have taken part in a crime. People were shown a grainy surveillance video of a man and told them that he had shot a security guard. Then they were presented with five mug shots and asked which one was the perpetrator. It was an impossible task, because none of the five mug shots really matched the man in the video. Nevertheless, every one of the 352 subjects identified one of the mug shots as the man they had seen (Wells and Bradfield, 1998). It seems that people are good at picking a criminal out of a line-up if he or she is there, but they are not good at being able to spot that he or she is not actually in the line-up.

False and recovered memories

Elizabeth Loftus is most famous today for her work on false memory. During the 1980s a number of therapists, mainly in the USA, reported that their adult clients had been recalling traumatic memories of childhood abuse that they had previously been unaware of. Many people were accused of child abuse as a result of these recovered memories and a number ended up in prison. Very few of the recovered memories were backed up with other evidence. Loftus, among others, became concerned about the type of therapy being offered and the quality of the memories. She came to believe that some of these memories were being created in the therapist's consulting room. It will not be a shock to the reader to say that this work is very controversial.

It is a sad fact of modern life that some children suffer abuse. They commonly find it difficult to talk about this and often only deal with it as adults, if at all. What Loftus is challenging is the memories that suddenly appear when the person is an adult and only in the therapist's chair. As she comments, people who suffer traumatic events have problems forgetting not remembering.

Lost in the mall

Can false memories be planted in people? Elizabeth Loftus (1997) believes so and describes one of many cases from the US courts. Nadean Cool was a nursing assistant when in 1986 she received therapy to help her deal with a traumatic event that had happened to her daughter. The therapist used hypnosis among other techniques to dig out any hidden memories. The digging produced a remarkable haul of horrible memories. Cool came to believe that she had been in a satanic cult, that she had eaten babies and had sex with animals. She also came to believe that she had more than 120 personalities including children, angels and a duck. Some years later she realised that none of these events had happened and she sued the psychiatrist for malpractice. She was awarded $2.4 million in an out-of-court settlement.

Loftus also described a study she conducted with her associate, Jacqueline E. Pickrell (1995). They wanted to see if they could demonstrate that memories can be planted. For ethical reasons they could not try to plant memories of childhood sexual abuse. They wanted to plant a memory that would have been distressing but had a happy ending. They decided to use a 'lost in the mall' story. They created a book for each participant that had stories from their childhood. Included in this was one made-up story about being lost in a shopping centre (mall) that was supposed to have been added by a close relative. It was, in fact, false. A quarter of their participants came to believe that this event had happened to them and they could recount features of the incident that were not part of the original planted story. In other words they had started to embellish the story and make it their own. The story was well and truly planted and started to take on a life of its own.

Weapon focus

When people witness an event with a gun involved then they are less likely to be able to describe the characters than if there is no gun. You might well remember this page as the one with the gun.

Loftus (1979) identified the weapon focus. There were two conditions in her experiment. In both conditions participants heard a discussion in an adjoining room. In condition 1 a man emerged holding a pen and with grease on his hands. In condition 2 the discussion was rather more heated and a man emerged holding a paper-knife covered in blood. When asked to identify the man from 50 photos, participants in condition 1 were 49% accurate compared with 33% accuracy in condition 2. This suggests that the weapon may have distracted attention from the man and might explain why eyewitnesses sometimes have poor recall for certain details of a crime.

It might be that the witness focuses his or her attention on the weapon, so not attending to other features of the scene. This might be because of heightened arousal or because it is an unusual event (Wells and Olsen, 2003).

LINKS TO OTHER STUDIES

- The issue of leading questions comes up elsewhere in this text.
- The study by **Samuel and Bryant** looks at the effect of questions on the responses of children to a simple cognitive task.
- The case study by **Freud** on Little Hans contains evidence from the child's father who put some very leading questions to Hans.
- Most controversial is the connection to **Thigpen and Cleckley**'s study on multiple personality. Are the memories and the multiples created by the therapy?

KeyISSUE
Control and design

An experiment aims to show that one variable (the independent variable) causes a change in another variable (the dependent variable).

For example, in Loftus and Palmer's experiment:

- the cue word is the independent variable (IV)

- the estimate of speed is the dependent variable (DV).

They changed the cue word to see if there was any difference in the estimates of speed. Loftus and Palmer found that different cue words attracted different estimates of speed. So we can conclude that the estimates of speed are affected by cue words (leading questions).

But this assumes that the IV was the only thing that was affecting the DV.

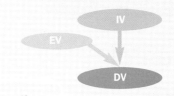

Changes in the dependent variable (DV) may be due to an extraneous variable (EV) rather than being due to the independent variable (IV). Therefore you cannot conclude that the IV affected the DV.

Methods of research design aim to control EVs.

Extraneous variables

Participant variables

Characteristics of individual participants (such as age, intelligence, etc.) that might influence the outcome of a study. For example, in the Loftus and Palmer study, some participants might have more experience estimating the speed of cars and would be less influenced by the IV.

1 Sex
Research suggests that women are more compliant than men because they are more oriented to interpersonal goals (Eagly, 1978). This means that if there are more women than men in one condition of an experiment this might mask the effects of the IV.

2 Age, intelligence, motivation, experience
Any personal variables might act as an extraneous variable – but only if an independent groups design is used because then people in one group may be more intelligent, more highly motivated, etc. than the people in the other group. When a repeated measures design is used participant variables are controlled.

3 Culture and ethnicity
An important feature of many people's identity is the culture or ethnic group which they most identify with. There are remarkably few studies in psychology that directly examine this variable. It is sometimes controlled for by just selecting people from one ethnic group (e.g. Haney, Banks and Zimbardo) to study, or by just ignoring it and pretending it has no effect. Of course some studies don't control for ethnicity but actually investigate it (e.g. Hraba and Grant).

Situational variables

Features of the research situation which influence a participant's behaviour. For example, the way in which the investigator asks a question may lead the participant to give the answer the investigator 'wants'. This is called an *investigator* or *experimenter effect*.

1 Order effects
If a participant did condition A first and then condition B, she might do better on condition B because she had an opportunity to practise. On the other hand she might do worse because she has got tired or bored. These are called practice, boredom and fatigue effects.

2 Investigator effect
For example, research has found that males are more pleasant, friendly and encouraging with female participants than male participants (Rosenthal, 1966). An experimenter might also be more encouraging on one experimental task so this would explain why a participant does better on that task than another task, rather than the IV being responsible.

3 Time of day, temperature, noise
An environmental variable may act as an extraneous variable only under the following conditions:

- It does affect performance on the behaviour tested, e.g. if the task is a cognitive task and people who are tested in the morning always do better than those tested in the afternoon because people are more alert in the morning.

- It varies systematically with the IV, e.g. participants in group 1 are all tested in the morning and those in group 2 are all tested in the afternoon.

- If you test one group of participants in the morning they might do better because people are generally more alert than those tested in the afternoon.

KEY TERMS

An extraneous variable is a variable other than the IV that **may** affect the DV, and thus should be controlled.

A confounding variable is a variable other than the IV that **has** affected the DV, and thus has confounded the findings of the study.

Control by research design

Researchers have to *design* their studies to control extraneous variables. Some techniques:

Repeated measures design offers a means of controlling participant variables because the same participants are exposed to each level of IV.

Independent groups design offers a way to control for order effects. Participant variables can be reduced by randomly allocating participants to different groups. Then you can assume that the same number of males/females, old/young, bright/dim people are in each group.

Single blind prevents participants knowing the aims of the study and altering their behaviour accordingly.

Standardised instructions are a way of controlling investigator effects because they ensure that all participants have the same instructions and no hints can be given.

Exam-style question

When psychologists conduct experiments they need to control certain variables.

Choose **one** core study.

(a) Outline the controls that were used in your chosen study. [6]

(b) Discuss **two** advantages and **two** disadvantages of the use of control in your chosen study. [12]

(c) Describe **one** change to the procedure of your chosen study, and discuss how the change may have affected the outcome of this study. [8]

The puzzles of perception

Sensation and perception

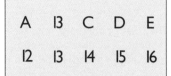

Look at the two rows of characters above. If you read the top row they are clearly all letters, and if you read the bottom row then it is a sequence of numbers. Look again and you will see that the middle figure in both rows is exactly the same. So what is it? The letter 'B' or the number '13'?

It is neither and it is both. You understand the character not just by the shape that you sense but also the meaning you perceive it to have. That meaning is affected by the context you see the character in.

What is the difference between the physical stimuli that hit us (like light and sound) and the images that appear in our minds? The physical stimuli create sensations in our sense organs but we then use these sensations to create our perceptions of the world. We say that 'seeing is believing' but is what we see sometimes the invention of our minds? And are some of our memories also part invention?

Visual illusions show how our minds can be confused by sensations to create a false perception. Look at the images on this page. You may well have seen some of them before but think how they are playing tricks on your mind.

How do we see? Think about these puzzles:

1 Your eyes are moving all the time (stare into a friend's eyes to check this out) but your view of the world is stable.

2 The screen at the back of your eye (the retina) is flat, but you see the world in 3D.

3 The image on the retina is upside down and back to front, but you see things the right way round.

4 Light never reaches the brain. It hits the back of the eye (the retina) and is transferred to your brain as electro-chemical messages.

Perceiving distance

Visual information contains a number of cues which give us hints about how far away things are. Although the image which the retina of the eye receives is two-dimensional, like a picture, we perceive the world in three dimensions, as having depth. Some of the cues are binocular (two eyes) and come from the slightly different view that each eye gets of the world. Other cues are monocular (seen as well with one eye as two) and are the sort of thing an artist uses to give the impression of depth.

Monocular depth cues include:

1 *Relative size* – when one object appears smaller than another.

2 *Shadow* – suggests three dimensions.

3 *Superposition* – when one object partially hides another.

4 *Motion parallax* – when the alignment of different objects changes if we move from one viewing point to another.

5 *Height in plane* – objects which are further away appear to be higher up in a scene.

6 *Gradient of colour* – things which are further away seem greyer, near objects have more vivid colours.

7 *Gradient of texture* – many scenes involve similar textural elements (e.g. grass or pebbles). As these textural elements get farther from us, they appear smaller and closer together.

By combining these cues we are able to make remarkably accurate judgements about how far away things are.

Figure–ground phenomenon

Edgar Rubin (1886–1951) demonstrated the figure–ground phenomenon by creating his classic example of an ambiguous figure–ground situation, called Rubin's vase:

We perceive one part of an event as the figure and the other as the ground. In Rubin's figure, there is no true figure and ground. We can either see the dark piece as background in which case we see the vase, or we can see it as an object in which case we see two faces. We can't see both at the same time. Our perception makes sense of this figure and of the world by deciding what is figure and what is background.

When we see drawings we try to make sense of them. If we give the lines some meaning then they stop being lines and become objects.

Is the eye like a camera?

Yes and no. Look at the diagram of the eye and you'll see it looks like a camera. It has a lens and a screen to collect the light, but if you could capture the images that appear on the retina they would not look like anything you would recognise. The eye is the first strategy in our battle to make sense of the world. It does not just record the information that comes in, it starts to interpret it. You might think of it as a bit of brain on a stick rather than a camera.

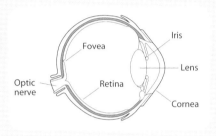

Learning to see: adapting to inverting goggles

G.M. Stratton was interested in whether we can adapt to changes in our visual world. If we can, this would be evidence for how we learn to perceive. Animals commonly cannot adapt, and experiments with distorting goggles showed that chickens kept pecking at empty space rather than grain. They could not learn that the grain was just to the left of where they could see it.

Stratton carried out many studies on himself. In one study (1896) he wore a telescope that turned the world upside down and back to front. Whenever he wasn't wearing the telescope, he spent his time in the dark. He kept the device on for eight days and attempted to act normally. He was largely able to adapt to the reversed world though it never looked right. The impression from Stratton's accounts is that he stopped noticing how odd the world looked rather than fully adjusting his vision to it.

ACTIVITY

The illusory pendulum

Mess with your mind and learn about the eye.

Here's what you need:

- *Two eyes (both your own)*
- *String*
- *White modelling clay*
- *Dark filter (cheap sunspecs split in two will do)*

What to do:

- *With the string and a blob of clay, make a pendulum that swings in a straight arc across your line of sight.*
- *Sit about two metres away to view the swinging blob. Sit so you can see it swinging from side to side.*
- *Now place a dark filter over one eye, and look at the pendulum again. Amazingly, the pendulum will seem to swing in and out, as well as from side to side, in an elliptical orbit.*
- *Put the dark filter on the other eye and the pendulum's orbit will reverse direction.*

So why does that happen?

When you cover your eye with a filter it becomes more sensitive to light. The pupil gets bigger to allow more light in, and the signals to the brain are delayed slightly, to allow more light to enter the eye.

The eye with the filter sees the pendulum movement just a bit earlier and therefore in a different position from the other eye. The brain puts the two positions together, fooling you into thinking the blob is moving in and out in an ellipse.

Illusions

1 The Necker cube

This figure is a flat drawing of two squares joined at the corners but it looks like a cube. And not just any cube. The orientation of the cube appears to change as you look at it. Sometimes the grey spot is at the front and sometimes the 'cube' inverts and you see the grey spot at the back.

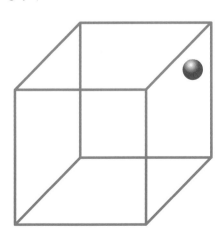

You are seeing something that you know is not really there (a cube) and because it is not really there your mind's eye can not decide which way round it is, so it tries out the different orientations and inverts it. Try keeping the cube in one position and you'll find it can't be done. You cannot stop seeing something that you know is not there.

2 The café wall illusion

The bricks below are parallel and you can check this with your ruler, but try as you might you can not see them this way.

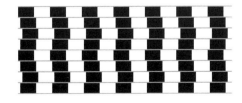

The core study

So do all people in the world see in the same way? If I could see through someone else's eyes would I be surprised by what I saw? Deregowski is asking this question and he does this by collecting the data from a range of studies on cultural aspects of perception. This work contributes to our understanding of which features of perception develop through experience.

Jan Deregowski, (1972) Pictorial perception and culture.
Scientific American, 227, 82–88.

Abstract

To what extent is perception learned rather than innate? If it is innate then we would expect to find the same perceptual abilities in different cultural groups (who have different experiences). Deregowski reviewed six cross-cultural investigations:

1 **Unsystematic reports** suggest that pictorial perception is learned; for example rural African people did not at first recognise a picture of a dog but gradually recognised the features. However, other reports suggest that this only applies to familiar objects.

2 **Hudson** developed a pictorial perception test. African people were shown pictures containing depth cues (such as relative size and overlap). He asked them, for example, 'What object is closer to the man?' Many of the participants could not interpret the cues correctly.

3 **Making models.** African people were shown pictures of two squares connected by a rod which looked three-dimensional (3D). When asked to make a model using sticks and clay, those classified as 3D perceivers (using Hudson's test) were more likely to make 3D models, and 2D perceivers were more likely to make 2D (flat) models.

4 **Ambiguous trident.** African people were shown drawings of an impossible 3D figure (a trident) and a control trident that wasn't impossible. 3D perceivers (classified using Hudson's test) spent longer looking at the impossible figure whereas 2D perceivers spent the same amount of time on both.

5 **Gregory** devised an apparatus to study perceived depth. He found that 2D perceivers set the spot of light at the same depth in all parts of a Hudson-test picture whereas 3D perceivers didn't. This shows that 3D perceivers are actually seeing depth and not just interpreting cues.

6 **Split-style drawings** are used in some cultures and also by children. Perspective drawings are more useful when it comes to constructing models from 2D drawings but the split-style may persist as an art form in societies where communication about relations between objects is not the prime purpose of drawings.

corestudy

Aims

Pictures are a means of representing three-dimensional space in a two-dimensional medium. To do this, pictorial representation has to involve depth cues. Is the ability to interpret these cues universal and innate, or is it learned? If it is learned then we would expect people in different cultures to perceive pictures differently. Jan Deregowski investigated this by looking at various cross-cultural studies of perception.

He also wondered whether, if pictorial representation is universal, it offers a *lingua franca* (universal language) for intercultural communication.

Investigation 1: unsystematic reports of pictorial perception

Participants: Various Africans.

Method: Unsystematic observations.

1 Robert Laws was a missionary in Africa in the late nineteenth century. He showed black-and-white pictures of an ox and dog to rural African people, and found that they would first say he was lying about what he said the pictures showed. However, eventually, they would come to identify recognisable features and agree with him about what the picture showed.

2 Mrs Donald Fraser visited Africa in the 1920s. She said that she showed a picture of a human head in profile to an African woman. The African had difficulty 'seeing' that it was a human head because there was only one eye.

3 In contrast there were also reports that Africans did respond instantly to pictures. When rural African people were shown a picture of, for example, an elephant flashed on a sheet they thought it really was an elephant and ran away. When they eventually looked behind the sheet they found it was only a drawing.

4 A rural African adult was unlikely to choose the wrong toy animal when asked to match a toy to a drawing of a lion. But when shown a photograph of a kangaroo, they chose any toy at random.

Conclusions

The difficulty experienced by some Africans suggests that some form of learning is required to 'read' pictures. A drawing is meaningless until a viewer has learned to organise and interpret the symbolic elements.

However, there is also some evidence that pictorial recognition is independent of learning, provided the pictures show familiar objects. Africans could not make sense of unfamiliar objects (e.g. a kangaroo) when represented pictorially. Therefore it appears that we can innately match pictorial cues to experience but not understand the symbols in the absence of such experience.

Qs

1 Deregowski described the research in Investigation 1 as being 'unsystematic'. What do you think he meant?

2 Suggest a disadvantage with unsystematic research.

3 State Hudson's hypothesis.

4 In what way is Hudson's research more systematic than the research described in Investigation 1?

5 What is suggested as the reason why the Africans found it difficult to interpret the pictures in Investigation 2?

6 How did Hudson know whether or not someone could interpret the picture?

7 In Investigation 3, what depth cue is used to make the drawing of the cube look three-dimensional?

8 State a hypothesis for Investigation 3.

9 How can we explain why some participants might build a two-dimensional model?

10 In Investigations 3 and 4 participants were classified as 2D or 3D perceivers. How was this done?

11 What can you conclude from Investigation 4?

Investigation 2: Hudson's pictorial perception test

Participants: African people from different social and educational levels.

Method

William Hudson discovered, while working with South Africans, that some of them had difficulty interpreting depth cues which meant they found it hard to understand 2D pictures. We use such depth cues when we determine depth in everyday life, and therefore one might think that everyone would naturally use the same cues when looking at pictures. But it seems this isn't true.

Hudson's pictorial perception test.

Which animal is the spear pointing at? Which object is closer?

In order to test his hypothesis, Hudson developed a pictorial perception test. In this test there were a number of pictures (see below left). These used different kinds of depth cues:

- *Size:* objects which are larger are perceived as being close.

- *Overlap:* when one object is in front of another it is perceived as closer.

- *Perspective:* lines converge as they get closer, as with railway lines.

- *Density* or texture gradient: objects which are closer appear to have a denser texture (this powerful cue was only used in one of the pictures).

Participants were shown one picture at a time. They were asked to name all the objects in the picture, and asked about the relation between the objects ('What is the man doing?' 'What is closer to the man?'). If the participant was using the depth cues correctly then they would be able to answer the questions, for example saying that he was spearing the animal.

Results

Both the adults and the children who were tested found it difficult to offer a 'correct' interpretation of the pictures thus suggesting that they could not use the depth cues.

ACTIVITY

Construct your own picture to test depth perception.

Test people on their ability to understand the picture.

Investigation 4: ambiguous trident

Participants: Zambian primary school children.

Method

Participants were classified as 2D or 3D perceivers using the model-building test (investigation 3) and then asked to copy drawings of two tridents: the ambiguous trident (see illustration below) and a control trident which was not impossible. The ambiguous one would be confusing to a 3D perceiver because perspective cues show depth, making it an impossible figure. A 2D perceiver would see the pattern as flat and have no difficulty.

To view the figures participants had to lift a flap and, when finished, had to wait 10 seconds before they were asked to draw the figure.

Results

3D perceivers (classified using the model test) spent longer looking at the impossible figure than the control, whereas 2D perceivers spent a similar amount of time viewing both tridents. This suggests that the 2D perceivers didn't see that the figure was impossible.

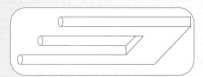

Investigation 3: making models

Participants: Primary school boys and unskilled workers in Zambia.

Method

Participants were shown a drawing of two squares, one behind the other, connected by a single rod (see illustration). They were given sticks and modelling clay and asked to construct a model of what they saw. This is a further test of the ability to use depth cues in perceiving three-dimensional (3D) views because, if someone perceived the drawing to be a 2D shape, they would build a flat model. If they interpreted the drawing as being of a 3D object, then they would build a 3D object.

Results

A few of the participants who were classed as 3D responders (on the basis of Hudson's pictorial perception test) did make flat models but most of them made 3D models, as predicted. In general the results supported the pictorial perception test: almost all 3D perceivers built a 3D object and 2D perceivers tended to build a flat model.

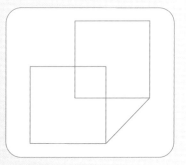

Biographical note on Jan Deregowski

Deregowski has had a long career in the field of culture and perception. He gives his research interests as *'Perception and depiction: cross-cultural studies; object perception, summetry, palaeolithic art, rock art, picture perception.'*

He is Emeritus Professor at Aberdeen University.

Investigation 5: Gregory's measuring apparatus

Participants: Unskilled African workers.

Method

The next question is whether 3D perceivers actually see depth in the pictures or whether they are just interpreting symbols. Richard Gregory designed an apparatus (see below) which enabled participants to view a Hudson-test picture and adjust a spot of light so that it appeared to lie at various depths in a picture. This meant the researcher could determine whether participants were actually seeing depth by asking them to place the spot of light besides a particular object.

Results

2D perceivers set the light at the same apparent depth regardless of which figure they were asked to place it beside. This was not true for 3D perceivers. This shows they were not just interpreting symbols but perceiving depth.

However, if only size was given as a depth cue (and all other cues removed) the 3D perceivers also set the light in the same place for every object. This shows that the size depth cue alone doesn't permit people to interpret a picture three-dimensionally.

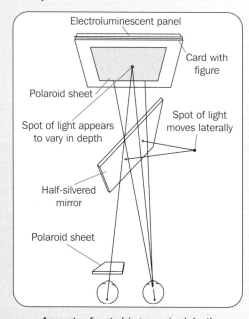

Apparatus for studying perceived depth

A participant can adjust the spot of light so it appears to lie at the same depth as an object in the picture. The spot of light is seen with both eyes (real depth from binocular cues) but the picture is only viewed with one eye because the Polaroid sheets are set to block light (so one relies on monocular depth cues for the picture).

Explaining split-style drawings

Split-style drawing is common in many cultures, such as in cave paintings and primitive art in New Zealand. It can also be found in the drawings of children of all cultures.

It is more difficult to assemble models from split-style engineering drawings than those using perspective cues. So why is the split-style used in some cultures?

Franz Boas, an anthropologist, suggested that the split-style of drawing developed when people wanted to work out the decorations to be placed on three-dimensional objects such as boxes or bracelets. To work out such decoration one first had to work on a flat (two-dimensional) surface. This led to a natural preference for this style of drawing. Claude Lévi-Strauss, another anthropologist, suggested a social explanation, that the split-style was a means of expressing the distress experienced by certain cultures, a kind of split personality.

However, Deregowski argued that neither explanation could account for the fact that the split drawing style is a universal phenomenon. It is suppressed in some cultures (such as ours) because information is not represented as accurately as in perspective drawings. In other societies it is developed to a high artistic level because drawings are not regarded as a means of communication about objects but are primarily ornaments. The artistic styles developed in different cultures are not equally efficient in correctly describing objects.

Investigation 6: split-style drawing

Participants: African children and adults.

Method

Children often produce drawings in the split-style (see illustration). This style of drawing shows an object as if it were viewed from above and includes even those parts of the object which would be hidden from view. Everything is shown as if the object was split to both sides.

Results

When Hudson showed these drawings and other drawings to African children and adults, they almost unanimously preferred those in the split-style.

Participants: Zambian labourers.

Method

Participants were asked to make a drawing of a wire geometric model. They were also shown a geometric drawing and asked to select the appropriate wire model.

Results

Most drew a flat figure of the split-style instead of one with pictorial depth, and most choose a flat wire model that resembled the drawing.

Picture of an elephant drawn in split-style (on left) and normal view from above (on right).

(See page x for note on evaluating research studies/articles)

The research method

There are various ways to describe the research method. This study is an example of cross-cultural research (see page 19). *What are the strengths and limitations of this research method in the context of this study?*

Cross-cultural studies are also quasi-experiments. *What are the strengths and limitations of this research method in the context of this study?*

Control

It might be that the participants couldn't interpret the drawings because they were unused to seeing pictures on paper. *In what way is this a confounding variable?*

What next?

Describe one change to this study, and say how you think this might affect the outcome.

Qualitative or quantitative?

What kind of data was collected in this study? What are the strengths and limitations of producing this kind of data in the context of this study?

Ethnocentrism

If you read the study you might become uneasy that Deregowski appears to present a view of African people as lacking certain abilities, rather than having different abilities as a result of their unique experiences and cultural preferences. If you see the world differently to me it might be me that is lacking rather than you, or neither of us. Deregowski's account can appear ethnocentric. *How can we explain a preference for split-style drawings that is not ethnocentric?*

On the other hand, conducting research into non-Western perceptual abilities balances the usual ethnocentric bias in psychological research. *How does this ethnocentric bias affect psychological theory?*

Nature or nurture?

Some abilities are innate while others are acquired through experience. What evidence is there from this study to support the nature or nurture side of the debate?

DEBATE

Nature or nurture? Divide your class into groups. Some should prepare the case for nature and others prepare the case for nurture. Each group should present their best two pieces of evidence. What do you conclude?

Multiple choice questions

1. Africans could not match a drawing of a kangaroo to a toy kangaroo because:
   (a) The drawing was two-dimensional.
   (b) They had never seen a kangaroo before.
   (c) The kangaroo only had one eye.
   (d) The drawing was too big.

2. Which depth cue was used least in Hudson's pictorial perception test?
   (a) Relative size.
   (b) Overlap.
   (c) Texture gradient.
   (d) Perspective.

3. In Hudson's pictorial perception test which of the following would not be a question that was asked?
   (a) How big is the man?
   (b) Is the man taller than the tree?
   (c) What is the spear pointing at?
   (d) Which animal is closer to the man?

4. In one study participants had to make a model from a drawing of:
   (a) Two circles connected by a rod.
   (b) A cube.
   (c) A circle and square connected by a rod.
   (d) Two squares connected by a rod.

5. In the study that involved making a model, which participants were more likely to make a 3D model?
   (a) The 2D perceivers.
   (b) The 3D perceivers.
   (c) The children.
   (d) The adults.

6. In the study with the ambiguous trident, the 2D perceivers:
   (a) Looked longer at the ambiguous trident than the control figure.
   (b) Looked at the ambiguous trident and the control figure for an equal amount of time.
   (c) Looked longer at the control figure than the ambiguous trident.
   (d) Didn't look at either figure.

7. When Gregory measured depth perception he found that 2D perceivers:
   (a) Placed the light in the same place for all objects.
   (b) Placed the light in different places according to depth cues.
   (c) Placed the light in random positions.
   (d) Refused to take part.

8. Split-style drawings are not produced by:
   (a) Children in rural cultures.
   (b) Adults in rural cultures.
   (c) Children in industrial cultures.
   (d) Adults in industrial cultures.

9. Which of the following is **not** an explanation offered for split-style drawings?
   (a) They reflect a culture with a split personality.
   (b) They developed from a need to work out decorations for 3D surfaces.
   (c) They act as a blue print for building models.
   (d) They are a form of highly stylised art.

10. If different cultural groups interpret drawings differently this is evidence for:
    (a) Nature
    (b) Nurture
    (c) Nature and Nurture
    (d) Neither.

Answers are on page 37.

Exam questions

1. (a) From the study by Deregowski on perception, define the term 'depth cue'. [2]

   (b) Identify **two** depth cues that were used in Hudson's picture of the hunter, antelope and elephant. [2]
   [OCR AS Psy, Jan 2001, paper 1]

2. In his study, Deregowski considers explanations for the origins of split-style drawings. Briefly describe **one** of these explanations and give **one** criticism of it.
   [OCR AS Psy, Jan 2002, paper 1] [4]

3. From the study by Deregowski (perception):

   (a) Give **one** example of anecdotal evidence. [2]

   (b) Outline **one** problem with interpreting the results of cross-cultural studies. [2]
   [OCR AS Psy, Jan 2003, paper 2]

4. From the study on perception by Deregowski outline **two** difficulties in conducting cross-cultural research.
   [OCR AS Psy, Jan 2006, paper 1] [4]

Recent studies in perception

Rock art

In his later work Deregowski (1996) became interested in rock art: the pictures on cave walls drawn by people a long time ago (such as shown below). He noticed that some animals are drawn much more often than others and that drawings of people appear very rarely. This was surprising as the drawings were made by people and were commonly about the things people did. He suggested that one of the reasons for this is that people are very difficult to draw. We change shape a lot in the different positions we adopt whereas a cow is a cow is a cow.

One way to get over this difficulty is to stop using outline shapes and start using diagrams of the central features. This gives us stick men as shown in the bush art found in Australia. Another solution is to put people in impossible positions that show off the key features as found in Egyptian figures.

Synaesthesia

What is the colour of the letter M, the number 6, or a prelude in E-minor? How do red circles taste or sound? If you know the answer to one of these questions you probably enjoy (or suffer from) synesthesia. Most of us, however, do not!

Synesthesia (from the Greek syn = together, and aisthesis = perception) is the experience of a cross-modal association. In other words, the stimulation of one of your senses causes a perception in one or more different sense. According to Baron-Cohen *et al.* (1986) at least 1 in 2000 of the population experiences synesthesia although many suspect it is more common. It is hard to obtain an estimate because many synesthetes are unaware that what they perceive is unusual.

The study of synesthesia helps us to learn more about how the brain processes sensory information and how it makes abstract connections between inputs that seem to be unrelated.

One of the most remarkable demonstrations of synesthesia has been carried out by Ramachandran and Rogers-Ramachandran (1996) on people who have phantom limbs. They investigated patients who had lost one arm and had experience of phantom limbs where the arm had once been. In some of the cases they experienced painful clenching sensations in the phantoms.

Ramachandran and Rogers-Ramachandran created a mirror box so the patients saw their good arm and a reflection of it that looked as if it was the phantom arm. By exercising the good arm the patients felt that their phantom arm was also exercising and they were able to relieve the phantom clenching sensations (see http://psy.ucsd.edu/chip/ramabio.html).

The abstract expressionist artist Kandinsky tried to present his personal experience of synesthesia in his paintings. Kandinsky was one of the painters used by **Tajfel** in his study of ethnocentrism (see page 156).

Eyetracking

Eyetracker devices have been used to investigate how people read. The eyetracker can accurately time-lock the reading event as the eye moves through the text so it records the amount of time the eye spends on each word, if indeed we do look at words one by one.

Eyetracking is being increasingly used for research in psychology, engineering, human factors and education. It is also being used by advertisers to look at how long viewers' eyes remain focused on a particular ad or part of an ad. This information will show designers which parts of a picture viewers show most interest in.

The future for eyetracking is almost limitless. As the technology becomes smaller and cheaper the eyetracker might help us interact with machines, such as computers. Professor Guang-Zhong Yang of the Department of Computing at Imperial College says *'Eye-trackers will one day be so reliable and so simple that they will become yet another input device on your computer, like a much more sophisticated mouse.'*

 http://news.bbc.co.uk/ 1/hi/sci/tech/ 2098030.stm

(Above) Eyetracker equipment. An eye tracker is a camera that records reflections of infrared light off the eye. It is fixed on a frame to a person's head and can show where someone is looking.

LINKS TO OTHER STUDIES

The issue of perception comes up elsewhere in this text.

- The memory study by **Loftus and Palmer** shows how verbal labels affect cognition.

- Social judgements depend on how we make sense of the world so, for example, if we interpret a scene as dangerous we are less likely to help (see the study by **Piliavin, Rodin and Piliavin**).

- An example of how our perception develops with age can be seen in the study by **Samuel and Bryant** on children's perceptual judgements.

DEREGOWSKI : PERCEPTION

KeyISSUE

Cross-cultural studies

Culture refers to all the rules, customs, morals and ways of interacting that bind together members of a society or some other collection of people. We learn all these rules, customs, etc. through the process of socialisation so that we too are able to interact appropriately with the other members of our culture. The term 'culture' doesn't necessarily equate to the term 'country' or even the term 'society', as many different groups, each with their own rules and customs, may co-exist within a country like the UK. The term **subculture** is usually used to refer to a group within a society that, although it shares many of the dominant cultural characteristics of that society, may also have some special, different characteristics.

Who does psychology study?

Most psychology is about Europeans and North Americans. An analysis of introductory text books (Smith and Bond, 1993) found that they mainly cited work by researchers from America. In a fairly standard American text by Baron and Byrne (1991) 94% of the 1,700 studies mentioned were in fact from America. In a British text (Hewstone *et al.*, 1988), about 66% of the studies were American, 32% were European and under 2% came from the rest of the world.

Cross-cultural studies involve making studies of behaviours in one or more cultures in order to make comparisons between cultures. This is a way of seeing whether cultural practices affect behaviour. It is a kind of **natural experiment** (see page 103) because there is an IV and DV. The independent variable (IV) is, for example, perceptual experiences in different cultures. The dependent variable (DV) is some behaviour, such as being able to 'see' a depth using pictorial cues. This enables researchers to see if perception (the DV) is related to experience (the IV).

Do cross-cultural studies exploit people?

It has been suggested that scientists exploit the people they study. They *'enter communities armed with goodwill in their front pockets and patents in their back pockets, they bring medicine to the village and extract blood for genetic analysis ...'* (Smith, 1999, p. 24). You might suggest that studying behaviour can do no harm, but think about how you would feel if you read an account of your behaviour written by someone from, say, Japan, especially if it described your behaviour as backward and unpleasant. And letting someone study your behaviour might actually be harmful. The US military use information from cultural psychologists to better control and fight indigenous peoples (Watson, 1980).

ACTIVITY

Work with a partner.

1 Make a list of 5 cultural groups.

2 Identify ways in which these groups are different and similar.

3 Try to write your own definition for the words 'culture' and 'sub-culture'.

Finding the right language

In cross-cultural studies the people from cultures other than our own are sometimes presented as quite exotic – strange people from strange countries doing strange things. They are often described in a way that compares them against some idea of a Western norm. An example of this is the study on perception by Turnbull (1961) which is commonly cited in text books, where the subjects are referred to as pygmies and characterised as primitive and superstitious.

One of the issues to consider is the language we use to describe people and their behaviour. We might say that someone belongs to a group or a culture or a nation or a tribe. Each of these terms carries a number of assumptions with it. It is hard to imagine a context where we would describe someone from Yorkshire as belonging to a tribe, but we might use that term to describe someone from Africa.

Evaluating cross-cultural studies

- Researchers are often not indigenous (i.e. are foreigners) and may misinterpret local customs and/or not understand what people say.

- Studies are often anecdotal and poorly controlled.

- Participants may not understand what they are expected to do and therefore be more likely to respond to experimenter's cues (demand characteristics).

- Researchers may use tests or procedures that have been developed in their own culture and are not valid in other cultures. For example, using an American IQ test may not be an appropriate way to assess the IQ of children in rural parts of Africa because some of the tasks assume certain educational experiences. This may make the individuals in the other culture appear 'abnormal' or inferior. The term that is used to describe this is an imposed etic – when a technique or psychological test is used in one culture even though it was designed for use in another culture.

- The group of participants may not be representative of that culture and yet we make generalisations about the whole culture – or even the whole country.

- They are natural experiments and therefore can't conclude a causal relationship, for example, that experience has caused different perceptual abilities.

Exam-style question

Some studies in psychology have looked at human behaviour in different cultural settings.

Select **four** core studies that tell us about cultural differences.

(a) Describe the findings of each of these studies.   [12]

(b) Using examples, discuss **two** advantages and **two** disadvantages of making generalisations about human behaviour and experience.   [12]

Autism and a theory of mind

The history of autism

Leo Kanner

In the 1940s Leo Kanner, a psychiatrist at Johns Hopkins University in the USA, recognised that a number of children sent to his clinic displayed similar characteristics which he named 'early infantile autism'. The word autism comes from the Greek for 'self'. Kanner was able to describe the following features that were common to all of the autistic children:

- a lack of emotional contact with other people;
- intense insistence on sameness in their routines;
- muteness or unusual speech;
- fascination with manipulating objects;
- major learning difficulties but high levels of visio-spatial skills or rote memory;
- an attractive, alert, intelligent appearance.

Kanner's pioneering work was slow to catch on but is now the focus of much international research.

Hans Asperger

Asperger was working at the same time as Leo Kanner and published a paper which described a pattern of behaviours in several young boys who had normal intelligence and language development, but who also exhibited autistic-like behaviours and marked deficiencies in social and communication skills. The condition, Asperger syndrome (AS), was named after Hans Asperger. Children with AS are deficient in social skills but, unlike other autistics, have a normal IQ and many individuals (although not all), exhibit exceptional skill or talent in a specific area.

Causes of autism

There is evidence that some people have a genetic predisposition towards autism. The condition appears to have family links but it isn't purely genetic. It is likely that autism develops as a response to environmental hazards though it is not clear at the moment what these hazards are. Currently a lot of research is looking at what happens during pregnancy and just after birth. The likely culprits are diet, hormones or vaccines (other than MMR – see below).

'Reality to an autistic person is a confusing, interacting mass of events, people, places, sounds and sights. There seems to be no clear boundaries, order or meaning to anything. A large part of my life is spent just trying to work out the pattern behind everything.'

A person with autism (www.nas.org.uk)

Theory of mind

'Theory of Mind' is the ability to infer, in other people, a range of mental states, such as beliefs, desires, intentions, imaginations and emotions.

Baron-Cohen argues that having some difficulty in understanding other people's points of view is not the only psychological feature of the autistic spectrum, but it is the core feature and appears universal among individuals with autism. At one extreme, there may be a total lack of any theory of mind, a form of 'mind-blindness'. More frequently, autistics may have some basic understanding, but not at the level that one would expect from observed abilities in other areas.

Animal cognition

The psychologists who first coined the term 'Theory of Mind' (Premack and Woodruff 1978), were interested in animal cognition and believed that primates could read others' intentions. Subsequent research has shown that primates are quite sophisticated in their relationships: they can deceive, form alliances, and bear grudges for days. Chimpanzees can even tell what another chimpanzee can and cannot see. But after decades of studies, no one has found indisputable signs that chimps or other nonhuman primates have a theory of mind. It seems to be a unique human quality.

What are the characteristics of autism?

People with autism generally experience three main areas of difficulty; these are known as the triad of impairments:

- **Social interaction:** difficulty with social relationships, for example appearing aloof and indifferent to other people.
- **Social communication:** difficulty with verbal and non-verbal communication, for example not fully understanding the meaning of common gestures, facial expressions or tone of voice.
- **Imagination:** difficulty in the development of interpersonal play and imagination, for example having a limited range of imaginative activities, possibly copied and pursued rigidly and repetitively.

Other features commonly associated with autism are:

Learning difficulties
Obsessive interests
Resistance to change in routine
Odd mannerisms
Repetitive behaviour patterns

Rising rate of autistic spectrum disorders in UK

For decades after Kanner's original paper on autism was published in 1943, the condition was considered to be rare with an incidence of around 2 per 10,000 children. Studies carried out over the last 100 years have shown an annual increase in incidence of autism in pre-school children. The data below show how dramatic this increase has been:

1966: 1 in 2,222

1979: 1 in 492

1993: 1 in 141

2004: 1 in 110

(Source: National Autistic Society)

No one doubts that the diagnosis of autism is rising dramatically but there is some debate about why. Is this due to more cases and if so what is causing this? Or is it due to changing patterns of diagnosis so people are now receiving the label of autism who would not have done so in the past? There was a scare during the 1990s that the rise might be due to childhood immunisation (the MMR vaccine for measles, mumps and rubella) but there is no evidence to support this and a lot to challenge it (see the evidence at www.bmj.org).

What is it like to be autistic?

There is a surprising lack of first-hand accounts of autism especially as there are so many people with the condition. Frith and Happe (1999) have collected some accounts from autistic people of what it is like to be autistic:

'When I was very young I can remember that speech seemed to be of no more significance that any other sound ... I began to understand a few single words by their appearance on paper.'

'It was ages before I realised that people speaking might be demanding my attention. But I sometimes got annoyed once I realised that I was expected to attend to what other people were saying because my quietness was being disturbed.'

'There are two ways to be a nobody nowhere. One is to be frozen and unable to do anything spontaneously for yourself. The other is to be able to do anything based on mirrored repertoires without any personal self-awareness yet being otherwise virtually unable to do anything complex with awareness.'

Autistic savants

Daniel Tammet is an autistic savant. He can carry out mind-boggling mathematical calculations at fantastic speeds. Unusually for a savant, Tammet can describe how he does it. He speaks seven languages and is even devising his own language.

An estimated 10% of the autistic population (and 1% of the non-autistic population) have savant abilities, but no one knows exactly why. Autistic savants have displayed a wide range of talents, for example the blind American savant Leslie Lemke played Tchaikovsky's Piano Concerto No. 1 after he heard it for the first time and he had never had so much as a piano lesson. And the British savant Stephen Wiltshire was able to draw a highly accurate map of London from memory after a single helicopter trip over the city. Wiltshire's pictures (see right) are world famous and he has had a number of successful art gallery shows.

Last year Tammet broke the European record for recalling pi, the mathematical constant, to the furthest decimal point. He found it easy, he says, because he didn't even have to 'think'. To him, pi isn't an abstract set of digits; it's a visual story, a film projected in front of his eyes. He learnt the number forwards and backwards and, last year, spent five hours recalling it in front of an adjudicator. He wanted to prove a point. 'I memorised pi to 22,514 decimal places, and I am technically disabled. I just wanted to show people that disability needn't get in the way.'

For a review of Daniel Tammet read *The Guardian* 12.02.2005, available online at www.guardian.co.uk

Einstein, Newton, and Asperger syndrome

It is a tradition of psychology to try to diagnose historical figures and explain modern conditions in terms of these people. Baron-Cohen and James (see Muir, 2003) believe Albert Einstein and Isaac Newton may have had Asperger syndrome.

Newton seems like a classic case. He hardly spoke, was so engrossed in his work that he often forgot to eat, and was lukewarm or bad-tempered with the few friends he had. If no one turned up to his lectures, he gave them anyway, talking to an empty room.

As a child, Einstein was also a loner, and repeated sentences obsessively until he was seven years old. He became a notoriously confusing lecturer. And despite the fact that he made intimate friends, had numerous affairs and was outspoken on political issues, Baron-Cohen and James suspect that he too showed signs of Asperger syndrome.

It's fair to say that not everyone is impressed with these diagnoses and suggest that Baron-Cohen and James are being selective with the biographical information they are using. They also wonder about the value of this type of speculation about historical figures.

Drawing from memory by savant Stephen Wiltshire.

The core study

The characteristics of people who receive a diagnosis of autism are varied and puzzling. Does this behaviour all derive from one cognitive deficit? Baron-Cohen *et al.* used a task that would give an insight into the thought processes of young children and establish whether they have a theory of mind. The beauty of this study is that it provides a simple and obvious test of an interesting hypothesis.

Victor: the wild boy of Aveyron

In 1799, a boy was found naked in the Caune Woods in France looking for roots and acorns. He was taken by three sportsmen to a neighbouring town, where he lived with a widow, escaping after a week, but returning back to civilisation of his own accord. He was eventually taken to Paris, where he was cared for by Jean-Marc Gaspard Itard who set about trying to socialise the wild child. Itard was interested to see what were the basic characteristics of human beings and whether he could teach a child to overcome the deprivations of early life. The child, who was given the name Victor, was mute and had probably been isolated from human contact from an early age. Despite a lot of work by Itard, Victor only developed some very basic social skills.

The reason that Victor comes into this text is that modern commentators suggest he displayed a number of characteristics of autistic children. In particular Victor,

- never learned to speak;
- had a 'decided taste for order';
- pulled people towards objects that he wanted to use;
- would not play with toys in a constructive manner.

Itard also noted that whilst he could instruct Victor into how to behave in a social context, when that context was repeated in a different location he would revert to his previous behaviour.

Simon Baron-Cohen, Alan M. Leslie and Uta Frith (1985) Does the autistic child have a 'theory of mind'? *Cognition*, 21, 37–46.

Abstract

Do autistic children lack a theory of mind? In other words, can they can represent the mental states of another person?

Method

Three groups of children (autistic, Down's syndrome and 'normal') were tested using a false belief task: the Sally-Anne test involving two dolls.

Test 1: The child sees 'Anne' take a marble from 'Sally's' basket and place it in her box while Sally is out of the room. The child is asked 4 questions:

1   Naming question: name the dolls.

2   Reality question: where is the marble really?

3   Memory question: where was the marble at the beginning?

4   Belief question: where will Sally look for the marble?

Test 2: This test was repeated a second time, placing the marble in the experimenter's pocket, to check that the child behaved the same on both occasions.

Results

All participants answered the first three questions correctly.

Most of the autistic children answered the belief question by saying that Sally would believe the marble was in the box, demonstrating a lack of theory of mind. Most 'normal' children said Sally would believe it was in the basket. Down's syndrome children behaved like normal children demonstrating that a low intelligence cannot explain a lack of theory of mind.

Discussion

It appears that a lack of theory of mind is a specific deficit in autistic children.

CORESTUDY

Aim

This study sought to find out if autistic children lack a theory of mind. This could explain many of their characteristic behaviours – such as their poor communication skills, lack of pretend play and social impairments – because these behaviours require the ability to see the world from someone else's viewpoint. Most but not all autistic children do poorly on a range of cognitive tasks (which is summarised as low intelligence).

In order to test this a group of autistic children were given a task that assesses theory of mind, and their performance compared to a group of 'normal' children.

The autistic children's performance also needed to be compared to a group of participants with low intelligence to rule out the possibility that poor performance was due to low intelligence rather than a lack of theory of mind. So the performance of autistic children was also compared to a group of Down's syndrome children. Down's syndrome children do not lack pretend play and are socially competent whereas even high IQ autistic children lack pretend play and social competence. This suggests that low intelligence will not explain a lack of a theory of mind.

Method
Participants

The study compared the behaviour of three groups of children on a task that tests theory of mind: autistic, Down's syndrome and 'normal'. The table below gives details of their chronological and mental age. Mental age was measured using a nonverbal and a verbal test. Verbal tests assess intelligence through the use of language.

Down's syndrome is an inherited condition in which children have an extra gene that is associated with a number of cognitive and physical characteristics.

	Number (*N*)	Mean CA (chronological age)	Mean MA (mental age) Nonverbal	Mean MA (mental age) Verbal
Autistic	20	11 years 11 months	5 years 5 months	9 years 3 months
		Range 5,4–15,9	Range 6,1–16,6	Range 2,8–7,5
Down's syndrome	14	10 years 11 months	2 years 11 months	5 years 11 months
		Range 4,9–8,6	Range 6,3–17,0	Range 1,8–4,0
'Normal'	27	4 years 5 months	not tested	not tested
		Range 3,5–5,9		

A quasi-experiment

This study is not an experiment. Three groups of participants were studied, which might appear to be three different levels of the independent variable. Participants were tested on a false belief task which might appear to be the dependent variable.

However, the characteristics of the three groups were not 'manipulated' (i.e. made to change), so it is not a true experiment. It is a quasi-experiment.

When children can appreciate The Three Little Pigs *from the perspective of a misunderstood wolf, they are developing their own 'theory of mind'. This happens, for most children, in the second year of life.*

Baron-Cohen is co-director of the Autism Research Centre (ARC) in Cambridge where he is Professor of Developmental Psychopathology. His first cousin is the comedian Sacha Baron-Cohen, a.k.a. Ali G.

Baron-Cohen is looking to identify the basic mental processes that are common to all cases of autism and that link autistic behaviour to its biological roots. In 1985 he made a breakthrough discovery of one such process. With his advisers Uta Frith and Alan Leslie, he used the Sally-Anne test and demonstrated the unusual thought patterns of children with autism.

In an interview for *Psychology Today* (Kunzig, 2004) he describes his motivation for studying people with mental disabilities. He grew up with an older sister who is severely disabled, both mentally and physically. Today she lives in an institution, is confined to a wheelchair and has a very low IQ. *'Yet despite that,' says Baron-Cohen, 'as soon as you walk into the room, she makes eye contact, her face lights up. Even though she has no language, you feel like you're connecting to another person.'*

Sacha Baron-Cohen a.k.a. Ali G

Procedure

All children were tested individually and were tested using the false belief task or 'Sally-Anne Test'. In this test, children are introduced to two dolls: Sally and Anne.

- Sally puts a marble in her basket.
- Sally leaves the room.
- Anne puts Sally's marble in her own box.
- When Sally returns, the experimenter asks the child 'Where will Sally look for her marble?'(belief question).

If the child says (or points to) 'the basket' they demonstrate that they have a 'theory of mind' because they can perceive that Sally, who was out of the room, still believes the marble is in the basket.

If the child indicates the box, then they have not got a theory of mind because they are assuming that Sally is thinking what they are thinking. The child is unable to accommodate Sally's false (wrong) belief.

Control questions

The conclusions about false belief are justified only if participants can answer three control questions correctly:

- Which doll is Sally and which is Anne? (naming question)
- Where is the marble really? (reality question)
- Where was the marble in the beginning? (memory question)

These questions are asked to check that the child actually knows where the marble is and also can remember where the marble was originally. If the child, for some reason, thinks that the marble is actually in the basket, then saying 'it's in the basket' does not demonstrate a theory of mind.

If the child thinks the marble was originally in the box then saying 'it's in the box' does not demonstrate a theory of mind.

Psycholinguistic and conceptual complexity

All together the children were asked four questions. The researchers claimed that all three questions were equally easy in terms of psycholinguistic difficulty but the 'belief' question ('Where will Sally look for her marble?') is conceptually more difficult. 'Psycholinguistic' refers to whether the language used in the question made the questions more difficult.

Second test

Finally the experiment was repeated for each child, just to make sure the first run wasn't a fluke.

On the second test the marble was moved to the experimenter's pocket instead of the box. The answer to the question ('Where will Sally look for her marble?') should still be 'in the basket'.

ACTIVITY

Draw a cartoon strip to illustrate the Sally-Anne test, or devise some other means to illustrate it.

And/or role play the Sally-Anne test.

Qs

1 Describe some common characteristics of autism.

2 Explain what is meant by a 'theory of mind'.

3 The 'mental age of the autistic children was higher than the controls'. What does this mean?

4 Why was it necessary to include a group of Down's syndrome children in the study?

5 Explain what is meant by a 'false belief'.

6 Give an example of each of the following: the naming question, the reality question and the memory question.

7 What response would you expect the autistic children to give to all three questions?

8 What was the importance of the control questions? What did they control for?

9 Explain why the control questions were the same in terms of psycholinguistic difficulty.

10 One of the questions was conceptually more difficult. Which was it?

11 Why do you think it was necessary to repeat the experiment?

Results

All children answered the control questions correctly, and all children gave consistent responses to the other questions. In other words, they either always answered the false belief question correctly or always answered incorrectly. There was just one exception — one Down's syndrome participant.

Experimental group	Number of correct responders	Percentage (%)
Autistic	4/20	20%
Down's syndrome	12/14	86%
'Normal'	23/27	85%

The four autistic children who responded correctly were not different to the others in terms of their IQ or age, they were average for their group.

Discussion

The fact that all children answered the control questions correctly leads us to conclude that they did all know that the marble was moved after Sally left the room.

The fact that most autistic children answered the critical question, the belief question, by saying the marble was in the box shows they did not have a theory of mind. Their behaviour could not be explained in terms of not knowing which doll was which, nor in terms of not seeing the marble moved, nor in terms of not remembering where it was at the start of the test. Thus they demonstrated an inability to appreciate the difference between their own and the doll's knowledge.

The fact that the autistic children were consistent on both trials shows that their failure can't be explained in terms of a position preference (preferring to say box rather than basket, or pocket rather than basket).

We can also rule out a negativism explanation (deliberately giving the wrong answer) because they always answered the control questions correctly and when providing an answer to the belief question, they did not just give a wrong answer but always answered by stating the actual location of the marble.

The fact that most Down's syndrome children answered the belief question correctly shows that low intelligence cannot be an explanation for failure to cope with this task.

The findings support the hypothesis that autistic children have a specific deficit. They have a 'mind-blindness' because they do not have an ability to represent mental states. This makes it very difficult for them to interact with other people.

What about the autistic children who did cope with the false belief task?

Baron-Cohen et al. suggest that the fact that some autistic children did have a theory of mind deserves further study. It is possible that these children differ in some way to other autistic children, for example they may show evidence of an ability for pretend play. It may also be that they display a different pattern of social impairment to those autistic children who do not have a theory of mind.

Perceptual versus conceptual perspective-taking

It is important to recognise the difference between perceptual and conceptual perspective-taking. The Sally-Anne task involves conceptual perspective-taking. The classic test of perceptual perspective-taking was devised by Piaget – the three mountains task. Piaget tested egocentrism in children. Children were shown a model of three mountains and a set of pictures, and asked to choose which picture showed the doll's perspective. Three- and four-year-old children tended to choose their own perspective, rather than the perspective of the doll. These children are bound by the egocentric illusion, that is they fail to understand that what they see is relative to their own position, and instead take it to represent the world as it really is.

Such perceptual tasks depend solely on visio-spatial skills and do not involve imputing beliefs to others. A study by Hobson (1984) has shown that autistic children cope with this task in line with their mental age.

This shows that the failure to cope with the Sally-Anne task is due to the conceptual skills required rather than perceptual skills.

Piaget's three mountains task.

Qs

1 How would you explain the fact that the Down's syndrome participants performed as well as the 'normal' children?

2 Baron-Cohen et al. explain why it was necessary to use two trials to avoid 'a position preference'. What does this mean?

3 Not all of the autistic children failed the belief task. What can we conclude from this?

4 Baron-Cohen et al. make an important distinction between conceptual perspective-taking skills and perceptual ones. How do they differ?

5 They give the three mountains task as an example of a perceptual perspective-taking task. Can autistic children cope with this task?

6 Briefly state Baron-Cohen et al.'s conclusion.

The research method

This study was a quasi-experiment. *What are the strengths and limitations of this research method in the context of this study?*

Individual differences

The findings clearly show that autistic children were less able to cope with the Sally-Anne task – but some autistic children could cope. *What does this tell us?*

The sample

To what extent do you think the sample was representative of all autistic children?

Qualitative or quantitative?

What kind of data was collected in this study? What are the strengths and limitations of producing this kind of data in the context of this study?

Alternative explanation

The obvious explanation for the poor performance of the autistic children is in terms of the theory of mind. *Can you think of a different explanation? [HINT: think of the problems with language.]*

Representativeness

Theory of Mind was tested using two dolls. *To what extent is this like real life?*

Ecological validity

To what extent can we generalise the findings from this study to other situations?

Applications/usefulness

How might you use the findings from this investigation?

What next? (?)

Describe **one** change to this study, and say how you think this might affect the outcome.

DEBATE

How useful is this study? Take all the criticisms into account when deciding on its usefulness.

(See page x for note on evaluating research studies/articles)

Multiple choice questions

1. Which of the following was not one of the groups of participants involved in this study?
   (a) Autistic children.
   (b) 'Normal' children.
   (c) High IQ children.
   (d) Down's syndrome children.

2. Someone who has a theory of mind can:
   (a) Not see another person's perspective.
   (b) See another person's perspective.
   (c) Lie.
   (d) b and c.

3. Where is the marble at the start of the Sally-Anne task?
   (a) In Sally's basket.
   (b) In Anne's basket.
   (c) In Sally's box.
   (d) In Anne's box.

4. If a person possesses a theory of mind they will expect, at the end of the Sally-Anne test, that the marble is:
   (a) In Sally's basket.
   (b) In Anne's basket.
   (c) In Sally's box.
   (d) In Anne's box.

5. Which of the following are characteristic behaviours of autistics?
   (a) Poor communication skills.
   (b) Poor pretend play.
   (c) Poor social skills.
   (d) All of the above.

6. Which question enabled the researchers to test whether a child had a theory of mind?
   (a) The naming question.
   (b) The reality question.
   (c) The memory question.
   (d) The belief question.

7. Which question enabled the researchers to feel confident that the children had seen the marble being moved?
   (a) The naming question.
   (b) The reality question.
   (c) The memory question.
   (d) The belief question.

8. Which question enabled the researchers to feel confident that the children hadn't forgotten where the marble was at the start?
   (a) The naming question.
   (b) The reality question.
   (c) The memory question.
   (d) The belief question.

9. The conclusion drawn from this study was that:
   (a) Children with low intelligence do not have a theory of mind.
   (b) Autistic children do not have a theory of mind.
   (c) All children do not have a theory of mind.
   (d) All children do have a theory of mind.

10. The participants in this study were aged between:
    (a) 3 and 7
    (b) 5 and 10
    (c) 5 and 17
    (d) 3 and 17

Answers are on page 37.

Exam questions

1. (a) What are autistic children unable to do in the 'Sally-Anne test'? [2]

   (b) What reasons do Baron-Cohen *et al.* give for this failure? [2]
   [OCR AS Psy, June 1996, paper 1]

2. Give **four** behaviours that can be used to identify autism. [OCR AS Psy, June 1998, paper 1] [4]

3. The study by Baron-Cohen, Leslie and Frith (autism) concludes that autistic children do not have a 'theory of mind'.

   (a) What is meant by the term 'theory of mind'? [2]

   (b) Suggest **one** problem autistic children have in everyday life if they do not have a 'theory of mind'? [2]
   [OCR AS Psy, May 2002, paper 2]

4. (a) From Baron-Cohen, Leslie and Frith on autism, identify **two** of the questions the children were asked. [2]

   (b) Outline the findings for **one** of these questions. [2]
   [OCR AS Psy, May 2003, paper 1]

More studies on autism

The Lovaas programme

During the 1970s Ivar Lovaas developed an intensive behaviour therapy for children with autism and other related disorders. The treatment is widely used but remains controversial not least because of its expense but also because of questions about its effectiveness.

What does the programme involve?

Lovaas recommends that treatment should begin as early as possible, and ideally before the child reaches 3½ years. This is believed to be necessary in order to teach basic social, educational and daily life skills. It can also reduce disruptive behaviours before they become established.

The treatment takes place in the home and consists of 40 hours therapy a week. This therapy is on a one-to-one basis, 6 hours a day, 5 days a week, for 2 years or more. Because the therapy is so intense a team of therapists needs to be trained for each child. You can see why it is so expensive.

The intervention programme progresses very slowly from teaching basic self-help and language skills to teaching nonverbal and verbal imitation skills, and then establishing the beginnings of play with toys. Once the child can do these basic tasks, they move to the second stage where they learn expressive and early abstract language and interactive play with peers.

Male brains?

Autism affects far more boys than girls. At the Asperger's end of the spectrum, the ratio is about 10 to 1. The sex difference, says Baron-Cohen, is *'one puzzle that has been completely ignored for 50 years. I think it's a very big clue. It's got to be sex-linked'* (quoted in Kunzig, 2004).

Baron-Cohen suggests that men and women think in different ways due to physical features in the brain. In particular there are two key abilities, empathy and systemising.

- **Empathising ability:** reading the emotional and mental states of other people and responding to them.

- **Systemising ability:** making sense of the world though this can take the form of a seemingly purposeless obsession like plane spotting, or memorising train timetables.

In brief, Baron-Cohen's most recent theory is that autism is characterised by low empathising ability and high systemising ability. Baron-Cohen's theory goes beyond people diagnosed with autism and includes all of us. The essential difference between men and women, according to Baron-Cohen, is that women are better at empathising and men are better at systemising. These are average differences and there are plenty of male brains in

female bodies, and female brains in male bodies. There are even female autistics, but there are many more male ones: in Baron-Cohen's theory, autism is a case of the *'extreme male brain'*.

Facilitated communication

Facilitated communication (FC) is a technique which allegedly allows communication by those previously unable to communicate by speech or signs due to autism, mental retardation, brain damage, or such diseases as cerebral palsy. It involves a facilitator who helps a patient use a keyboard by lightly balancing their hand above the letters; patients who have previously not communicated recite poems, carry on high-level intellectual conversations, or simply chat.

Parents are grateful to be told that their child does not have severe learning difficulties but is either normal or above normal in intelligence. FC allows their children to demonstrate their intelligence by giving them a new technique to express themselves with. But is it really their child who is communicating? Sometimes people using FC make quite startling claims about messages from God or, more worryingly, childhood abuse (see page 10 on false memories). Most scientific observers are sceptical about FC but carers are more willing to believe.

Another study by Baron-Cohen

In order to be able to arrange pictures into simple stories a child has to imagine what the story character is thinking. Baron-Cohen *et al.* (1986) tested the same three groups of children (autistic, Down's and 'normal') on three types of stories; autistic children found most difficulty with the belief story but did better than 'normal' children on the mechanical story.

Mechanical story

Behavioural story

Belief story

LINKS TO OTHER STUDIES

The work on theory of mind is also relevant to the study on Washoe by **Gardner and Gardner**. It is important for our understanding of the 'thought processes' of animals and machines. What do they understand? And what do they think we understand?

This study also illustrates the difficulties of studying children (see the studies in the **Developmental Psychology** section).

Baron-Cohen used the Sally-Anne task with dolls to try to better understand how children think. Another doll study can be found by **Hraba and Grant**.

BARON-COHEN, LESLIE AND FRITH : AUTISM

Key**ISSUE**

Sampling and generalisation

When studying autistic behaviour we can't test all the autistic children in the world. Therefore, when conducting research, psychologists study a sample of a group (called the **target population**).

Psychologists then **generalise** the results from the study sample – assuming that all autistic children would behave in the same way that the sample did.

It is OK to make generalisations about the target population from the sample if the sample is representative of the target population. All sampling methods aim to produce a representative sample.

*Participants are drawn from a '**target population**' (the group of people that the researcher is interested in).*

Target population.

This is a sample of the target population.

ACTIVITY

Sampling

Measure the height of 20 people in your class (alternatively make up 20 heights if you can't find a tape measure). Work out the average height by adding them together and dividing by 20. You now know the average height of your population. The activity is to try out the different sampling methods.

1. Random samples. Pick 10 names out of hat and work out their average height (add them up and divide by 10). Do this 2 or 3 times.

2. Systematic samples. Pick out every other name on the list and work out their average height.

3. Volunteer sample. Look at the heights of the first 10 people to be measured (the keen ones).

Look at the average scores and compare them to the true average (the average of all 20) and see which was the best way to select a sample.

Sampling methods

Opportunity sample
How? Ask people walking by you in the street, i.e. select those who are available.

🙂 The easiest method because you just use the first participants you can find.

🙁 Inevitably a biased method because the sample is drawn from a small part of the target population. For example, if you do an experiment using people in the street then the sample is selected from people walking around the centre of a town – not those at work, or those in rural areas.

Volunteer sample
How? Advertise in a newspaper or on a noticeboard.

🙂 Access to variety of participants.

🙁 Sample is biased because participants likely to be more highly motivated and/or with extra time on their hands (= volunteer bias).

Random sample
How? Put names of the target population into a hat and draw out required number.

🙂 Unbiased, all members of target population have an equal chance of selection.

🙁 It is almost impossible to carry out a random sample unless your population is very small.

Quota sample
How? Subgroups within a population are identified (e.g. boys and girls or age groups: 10–12, 13–14, etc.). Then an opportunity sample (quota) is taken from each subgroup.

🙂 More representative than an opportunity sample because equal representation of subgroups.

🙁 Although the sample represents the subgroups, each quota may be biased in other ways, e.g. just people not at work.

[In a stratified sample the sample from each subgroup is obtained using a random method.]

Systematic sample
How? Selecting every nth person from a list of the target population.

🙂 Sample is spread evenly across the population, avoiding bias.

🙁 The sample may be unrepresentative if e.g. every 10th person is always sitting at the front of the class.

Many students mistake a systematic sample for a random sample.

'You're very special'

Your mother has probably told you at some time or other that you are very special. And it's true, you are. In fact you are unique. There is no one quite like you (even if you are an identical twin).

We have to be careful about making generalisations because although we share common features with other people we are all unique and totally unlike anyone else.

Exam-style question

Many psychological studies use a small sample of participants and then make generalisations about all human behaviour.

Choose **one** study.

(a) Describe the sample and sampling method that was used in your chosen study. [6]

(b) Briefly discuss **two** advantages and **two** disadvantages of conducting research on a limited sample, using examples from your chosen study. [12]

(c) Describe **one** different sample for your chosen study and say how you think this might affect the results of the study. [8]

Animal language

Washoe, the subject of this core study

Language

Communication is inevitable. We can't stop sending messages to other people and interpreting their actions. Humans also have a remarkable way of communicating using symbols which we call language. But what is language and can other animals use it?

Early attempts to teach language to chimps

Vicki

Virginia and Keith Hayes (1952) tried to train a chimpanzee, Vicki, to talk. Their intensive training sessions used rewards to encourage her to make sounds and imitate the lip movements of the trainers. The chimp learned a lot of skills but sadly not the skill of using language. She only learned four sounds, 'Mama', 'Papa', 'cup' and 'up', but her use of them was not very language-like and the sounds were not very convincing either (Hayes and Nissen, 1971).

Sarah

Premack and Premack (1966) raised a chimpanzee, Sarah, and taught her to use different coloured and shaped chips to represent words. She placed these on a board to make sentences. First she learned the symbol for an object (apple), then to string symbols together to form sentences (first Mary + apple, next Mary + to give + apple, and finally Sarah + to give + apple + Mary). At the end she had acquired 130 signs and could make sentences up to eight units long. However, Sarah did not spontaneously ask questions although she would practise sentences on her own.

Language and communication

Language: A small number of signals (sounds, letters, gestures) that by themselves are meaningless, but can be put together according to certain rules to make an infinite number of messages.

Communication: The way in which one animal or person transmits information to another and influences them.

Everyone agrees that animals can communicate with each other, the disagreement is over whether they can use something similar to human language to do this.

Aitchison (1983) suggests there are ten criteria that distinguish communication from language including:

- **arbitrariness** of the symbols (the symbol is not like the object or the action it is describing);

- **semanticity** (the use of symbols to mean objects or actions);

- **displacement** (refers to things that are distant in time and space);

- it is used **spontaneously**;

- it involves **turn-taking**;

- it is **structure dependent** (the symbols are combined according to the rules of grammar).

Animals and humans

What is the difference between animals and humans? Are humans just another animal that is a bit more intelligent or is there a qualitative difference between us and them? This is a question that challenges scientific and religious beliefs.

One of the crucial differences between humans and animals is that we have language, and it is argued that this shows our uniqueness. The work on Washoe is important because if the Gardners can show that Washoe has language then it breaks down one of the last big divides between the species.

Washoe, like many other animals, can communicate and respond to messages but is this the same as language? Linguists argue that a true language is one that can generate novel messages. To do this you need to have a set of rules (a grammar) to combine symbols. One example of a rule is the use of word order to change the meaning of messages. For example, 'the beer is on the table' has a different meaning to 'the table is on the beer'. If Washoe can put words in order she is showing the rule of grammar.

ASL (American sign language)

American Sign Language is the dominant sign language in the United States. American Sign Language is usually abbreviated to ASL though it has also been known as Ameslan. It is a manual language: information is expressed with combinations of handshapes, movements of the hands, arms and body, and facial expressions. Like other sign languages it has rules (syntax and grammar) though these are different to spoken languages. It was developed in the early nineteenth century at the first school for the deaf in America. The first deaf

In 1904 a scientific commission, including a psychologist, assembled to examine the intelligent horse known as Clever Hans. Russian aristocrat Wilhelm Von-Osten claimed to have taught Clever Hans basic arithmetic over a period of two years using skittles, an abacus and a blackboard with carrots for a reward. Hans gave the answers to problems by tapping his hoof on the ground. The commission were convinced by the demonstration. Oskar Pfungst, however, carried out more tests on the horse and discovered that his skills were indeed clever, but not arithmetical. He found that Hans only got the questions right when Von-Osten knew the answer, and could be seen by the horse. Pfungst's studies showed that when Hans was counting with his hoof Von-Osten inclined his head downwards to see the hoof. When

the correct answer was reached he would either straighten up slightly or raise an eyebrow or even slightly flare his nostrils. Pfungst himself was able to get the same level of performance out of Hans using these tricks himself. Von-Osten died a disillusioned man in 1909. It is not recorded what happened to Hans.

Monkey suit

When we look at an ape are we misinterpreting what we see? Do we see an animal or do we treat them as if they are a human in a hairy suit?

Anthropomorphism is the attribution of human characteristics to inanimate objects, animals, forces of nature, and others.

When we say dogs are loyal or foxes are cunning we are treating the animals as if they think and behave like humans. We often take this a step further and attribute human qualities to machines, for example talking to your computer as if it is deliberately messing you about.

When we are anthropomorphic we are assuming that the animals or machines have a theory of mind, that they know what they are doing and they are also responding to us (see the study on autism on pages 22–25).

Examples of ASL signs

ASL consists of handsigns (as on the left) or hand movements which may look like the thing or action they are describing in the same way that some words sound like the thing they are describing, for example 'splash' or 'quack'. Some of Washoe's most common signs looked like the things she was describing. Look at the words below and the description of the signs, for example.

GIVE

The hands move forward to represent giving something away.

BANANA

One hand acting as if it is peeling a banana. The banana is represented by the upright forefinger.

CANDY

A variation of the sign SUGAR. The tip of the index finger and middle finger brush the chin several times.

teacher at the school, Laurent Clerc, came from France: there is a clear French influence in ASL. There has been some debate about whether ASL can be considered as a real language but the work of William Stokoe confirmed it as equivalent to spoken languages.

The fact that ASL uses abstract images is important since this is a crucial characteristic of language. There is a critical difference between learning signs for things and learning signs for abstract ideas.

You can see ASL in action at http://signwithme.com/default.asp. This website is called 'borntosign' for parents to use sign language to communicate with their infants. Infants are capable of communication before they can speak – like primates infants are limited by their immature vocal abilities.

The core study

If only we could speak to the animals, what would they say? If the Gardners can show that chimpanzees have the capacity for language they will have smashed the last great divide between people and other animals. Mind you, if they are successful it begs the question of why chimps don't use language on a daily basis. But then perhaps they do.

R. Allen Gardner and Beatrix T. Gardner, (1969) Teaching sign language to a chimpanzee, *Science*, 165, 664–672.

Abstract

The Gardners set out to teach an animal to use human language. Their subject was a very young female chimpanzee, Washoe, who socially interacted with human tutors using American Sign Language (ASL). ASL was chosen because chimpanzees are good with their hands whereas they are not good at vocalisations.

There was a mixture of training methods:

- *Immediate imitation:* copying a gesture made by a tutor.

- *Imitative prompting:* being reminded of a sign or how to do it correctly.

- *Delayed imitation:* copying a gesture sometime after the sign was demonstrated.

- *Manual babbling:* if a natural gesture was similar to a sign the tutor would demonstrate the sign and the appropriate activity for the sign.

- *Instrumental conditioning (reinforcement):* correct use of signs was rewarded, e.g. by tickling.

- *Shaping:* rewarding behaviours which are progressively closer and closer to the actual sign.

- *Direct instruction:* forming Washoe's hands into correct configuration.

Over a period of 22 months Washoe acquired at least 30 signs. She was able to differentiate meanings (e.g. between 'flower' and 'smell'), to transfer meaning from a specific object to the general group (e.g. use 'dog' to refer to a particular dog or to a dog barking), and to combine two or three words to produce her own novel utterances (e.g. 'open food drink' for a fridge).

COREStudy

Aims

The aim of the project was to see whether it was possible to for a non-human animal to learn to use human language.

The Gardners decided to use a chimpanzee in this study because they are highly intelligent, very sociable and known for their strong attachments to humans. Sociability is especially important because it is probably a prime motivator in the development of language. Therefore it is best to use an animal interested in socialising.

The Gardners decided to teach human language using American Sign Language (ASL), a sign language developed for deaf people. There were several reasons for this. First of all, the vocal apparatus of a chimpanzee is different to a human's, which means it would be difficult for a chimpanzee to produce spoken language. A previous attempt to teach a chimpanzee to use language, by Hayes and Hayes, was unsuccessful. The chimpanzee, Vicki, only learned four sounds in six years – this may well be because she simply couldn't cope with vocal language. Secondly, chimpanzees are good with their hands and make gestures to humans, such as begging gestures. This means that they should cope well with the mechanics of signing. This is especially important when aiming to condition an animal's responses. When planning to train an animal to produce new responses one needs to start with behaviours that are natural to them. For example, Skinner, when training rats to press a lever for food, chose the 'lever pressing behaviour' because he knew this was something rats did naturally.

Biographical notes on Washoe

Full name: Washoe Pan Satyrus (Pan satyrus is an old taxonomic classification used for chimpanzees).

Date of birth: Unknown; Washoe's birthday is celebrated on June 21.

Washoe was born in Africa, around September of 1965 where she was captured by the US airforce. Details of her military service are unknown.

She was taken to the US where Drs Allen and Beatrix Gardner adopted her for their research. Her name sign is formed with the fingers of a 'W' hand flicking the ear on the same side. She was named for Washoe county Nevada where she lived with Drs Allen and Beatrix Gardner until age five. Washoe is a Native American word from the Washoe tribe meaning 'people.' She moved with Roger and Deborah Fouts to the University of Oklahoma in 1970 and went with them to Central Washington University in 1980 where a special facility was built for Washoe and other chimpanzees.

Washoe appears to enjoy spending time in her outdoor area. She spends her free time looking through books, magazines, and catalogues (especially shoe catalogues). Other activities she engages in are brushing her teeth, painting, coffee and tea parties, and checking out the shoes of her human companions. Her favourite foods are oatmeal with onions, pumpkin pudding, split pea soup, eggplant, gum, tea and coffee. (From http://friendsofwashoe.org)

Qs

1. Why do you think it was it important for Washoe to have at least one person with her during her waking hours?

2. What is 'imitative prompting'?

3. Outline the different methods used to teach Washoe to use ASL.

4. If you are familiar with attachment research (from the core study by Hodges and Tizard) you might think how Washoe may have been emotionally affected from being taken away from her natural family. For example, how might this influence her ability to learn?

5. In what way was Washoe's ability to sign 'more' different from her ability to sign 'flower'?

6. Give an example of Washoe's 'babbling'.

7. Explain the process of instrumental learning (operant conditioning – see also page 58).

8. Suggest a reward that a child might get when their first word is uttered.

9. Briefly describe how the Gardners taught Washoe the sign for 'more'.

Method

Washoe

The female chimpanzee was between 8 and 14 months at the start of the study. Chimpanzees are completely dependent until the age of about two years.

Laboratory conditions

Confinement of Washoe was minimal and at least one person was with her during all her waking hours. All carers/tutors were able to sign and restricted all communication to signing, 'chattering' with Washoe extensively as one does with an infant.

Biographical notes on Beatrix Gardner (1933–95)

Trixie Tugendhat Gardner was born in Austria in 1933 and at the age of six left the country for South America to escape the Nazi takeover of her country. Her family later moved to the USA and after studying at university there she moved to Oxford to study for her doctorate. There she worked with Niko Tinbergen on his famous stickleback project. When she returned to the USA she went to Wellesley College in Massachusetts where she was influenced by the comparative psychologist Harry Harlow and where she also met her husband Allen Gardner. In 1963 the Gardners moved to the University of Nevada where, three years later, they first met up with Washoe and started the signing project. Trixie Gardner continued to work on this and similar projects at the University of Nevada until her sudden death in Italy on a lecture tour at the age of 61.

Training methods

Imitation

Chimpanzees are noted for their willingness to imitate others. The Gardners thought that one way to use imitation when training Washoe would be to play a game called 'Do this' (first used by the Hayes when training Vicki) where the trainer says 'do this' and then the chimpanzee is meant to imitate the specified act for the reward of being tickled. Unfortunately this didn't prove very successful with Washoe who readily imitated gestures but not on command.

Imitation was also used as a method of prompting. For example, sometimes Washoe would lapse into poor 'diction' – using a sign rather sloppily. Then she would be shown the correct sign and would imitate this.

Acquiring a vocabulary

Washoe was exposed to a range of signs during her everyday routines (feeding, dressing, bathing and so on) as well as when playing games. Objects and activities were named with the appropriate signs so that she would associate the signs with the objects/activities. In this way Washoe came to have an understanding of a large vocabulary of signs. However, it is true that even dogs can learn to *understand* a large vocabulary.

Delayed imitation

The first example of this was when Washoe produced the sign for toothbrush. She had seen the sign on many occasions but one day (in the tenth month of her training), when about to brush her teeth she made the sign spontaneously. On this occasion, for the first time, Washoe appeared to be using a sign simply for the purpose of communication.

Washoe did the same thing with the sign for 'flowers', a sign that she understood but had not used herself for communication. One day, in the fifteenth month, while walking towards a flower garden she spontaneously made the sign.

Babbling

Infants babble before they speak, for example saying 'ma-ma-ma'. Babbling is a way of rehearsing elements of speech. Washoe did an equivalent kind of thing with her hands, producing various movements that were components of signs; things like clapping and arm waving. The Gardners encouraged this babbling by repeating it back. If the babbled gesture resembled an ASL sign then the correct sign was shown to Washoe as well as the appropriate activity for that sign. Washoe may have learned the sign for 'funny' in this way – it first appeared as spontaneous babble, then the tutors made the sign while laughing and smiling, and repeated the sign when anything funny happened. Eventually Washoe used the 'funny' sign spontaneously.

The same approach was taken with Washoe's begging gesture (open hand, palm up) which is similar to the ASL signs for 'give me' and 'come' except these have a more prominent beckoning movement. Gradually Washoe learned to say 'come–gimme' by modifying her original gesture.

Instrumental conditioning (reinforcement)

The essence of instrumental learning is that if you are rewarded for doing something, it is more likely that you will repeat that behaviour.

Chimpanzees love to be tickled so this was the most effective reward to use with Washoe. When Washoe was tickled she responded by placing her hands where she was being tickled. This gesture of placing her hands together over where she was being tickled resembled the ASL sign for 'more'. If the tutors moved her hands apart and threatened to tickle her again she would quickly put them together again. Her 'sign' would be rewarded with more tickling, reinforcing the learning. At first anything similar to the 'more' sign was rewarded. Later only closer and closer approximations were rewarded. This is the process of 'shaping' (see below).

The 'more' sign was later developed in the context of another game where Washoe was pushed across the floor in a laundry basket. At the end the tutor would sign 'more', prompting Washoe to imitate this sign. Soon, the 'more' sign became spontaneous in the laundry-basket game and then was spontaneously transferred by Washoe to all sorts of activities.

The sign for 'open' was acquired in the same way. The tutors waited for Washoe to produce the response spontaneously, then this was 'shaped' to be like an ASL sign, and gradually the use of the sign was generalised to other situations.

Later Washoe was able to acquire signs more directly. A tutor would shape her hands to make the right gestures and then she would repeat this, a much quicker method of acquiring new words.

Shaping The process of teaching a skill involves more than just rewards. If one waited until a child (or chimp) uttered an actual word, one might have to wait a long time. 'Shaping' is a way to overcome this. For example, in order to train a circus elephant to perform a trick, the animal is initially rewarded for coming into the performing ring, then only rewarded for placing a foot on a stool and so on until a whole routine is learned. If a new behaviour is less like the target behaviour, the animal is not rewarded.

Results

Each new sign that Washoe acquired had to fulfil certain criteria before it could be regarded as a new sign for Washoe:

1. Three different observers had to report seeing Washoe use the sign spontaneously and appropriately (except if she was asked 'What do you want?' or similar).

2. The sign had to be recorded every day over a 15-day period.

Months of training:	7 months	14 months	21 months
Number of signs Washoe could use:	4	13	30

Another four signs were stable but didn't meet the stringent criteria (marked with a *), making 34 signs in total which are shown below, in order of acquisition. The earliest signs were simple demands, the latter ones were mainly names for objects.

come–gimme	out	funny	napkin–bib	pants
more	hurry	please	in	clothes
up	hear–listen	food–eat	brush	cat
sweet	toothbrush	flower	hat	key
open	drink	cover–blanket	*I–me	baby
tickle	hurt	*dog	shoes	*clean
go	sorry	you	*smell	

Concluding observations

Did Washoe have language? The Gardners avoided answering this question because they said it was against the spirit of their research. They argued that the question can only be answered if there is a way of distinguishing between one class of communicative behaviour that can be called language and another class that cannot. However, if it can be shown that animals can acquire language this would have implications for any theory of language because such theories tend to define language in terms of human behaviours.

The Gardners demonstrated that:

*   Chimpanzees can be taught more than a few words (in previous studies chimpanzees had learned only up to four words).

*   Sign language is an appropriate medium of communication for the chimpanzee.

*   More can be accomplished – Washoe's ability to spontaneously transfer the use of signs from specific things to general ones and her ability to combine two or three words both suggest that significantly more can be accomplished in further phases of this project.

There remained a need to develop a method to test Washoe's abilities. One way to do this would be to place an object in a box with a window. A researcher, who doesn't know what the object is, could ask Washoe to say what she sees. However, this would only work for items small enough to fit in a box. The Gardners did this successfully in later work.

Draw a bar chart showing the progress Washoe made (by age and number of signs acquired).

There were three ways that Washoe's language acquisition resembled the process that occurs in human children:

*   *Differentiating* Washoe came to use the sign 'flower' to include reference to odours, for example when smelling cooking or opening a tobacco pouch. The Gardners taught Washoe a new sign for 'smell' using passive shaping and imitative prompting. Washoe learned to discriminate between the two signs though she did continue to occasionally misuse 'flower' in a 'smell' context.

*   *Transfer* Another aspect of learning language is learning to generalise from one particular thing to a general class of objects. Washoe showed this ability early on in being able to apply words like flower to different kinds of flower and also to use the sign 'dog' when she heard a dog barking not just when she saw a dog.

*   *Combining signs* Washoe, like human children, started to combine two or three signs once she had about eight signs in her repertoire, to represent more complex meanings such as 'listen dog' (to refer a barking dog). This may have happened because the researchers combined signs themselves, therefore Washoe was in a sense imitating them. She did, however, produce her own novel combinations such as 'open food drink' (open the fridge) and 'go sweet' (to be carried to raspberry bush). Most famously, and controversially, she signed 'baby in my drink' when a doll was in her cup.

Q~s~

1   Why were there such strict criteria for the signs?

2   What do you think the main difficulty would be in recording sign language in a chimp?

3   Comment on Washoe's rate of learning.

4   In what way did Washoe's language acquisition resemble the way human children acquire language?

5   What evidence is there to support the view that Washoe did learn to use language?

6   What evidence is there against this view?

7   To what extent can the results of this study be generalised to other chimpanzees?

Here is a great website on language in apes: http://www.davidmswitzer.com/apelang.html

(See page x for note on evaluating research studies/articles)

The research method

This study was a case study. *What are the strengths and limitations of this research method in the context of this study?*

Ethical issues

Part of the process of teaching language to an animal is to enculturate them into the human world. *Is it ethical to teach human language to animals?* [You might consider the costs and benefits.]

Nature or nurture?

If animals can learn to use human language, then what can we conclude about the nature of human language?

Validity

Was Washoe spontaneously producing language or was she just responding to cues from her trainers, like Clever Hans (see page 29)?

Applications/usefulness

How can the results be used – for humans? – for animals?

What next?

Describe **one** change to this study, and say how you think this might affect the outcome.

Lloyd Morgan's canon – *suggested by the nineteenth-century British psychologist C. Lloyd Morgan, states that:*

> *In no case may we interpret an action as the outcome of the exercise of a higher psychical faculty, if it can be interpreted as the outcome of the exercise of one which stands lower in the psychological scale.*

In other words don't invent clever explanations if there is a simple one. If you can explain Washoe's behaviour as 'imitation' there is no need to call it 'language'.

Multiple choice questions

1. Washoe is a:
   (a) Female gorilla.
   (b) Male gorilla.
   (c) Female chimpanzee.
   (d) Male chimpanzee.

2. At the start of the study Washoe was about:
   (a) 3 to 9 months old.
   (b) 8 to 14 months old.
   (c) 10 to 20 months old.
   (d) 2 to 3 years old.

3. ASL stands for:
   (a) American Sign Language.
   (b) American Signal Language.
   (c) Automatic Sign Language.
   (d) American Sign Lexicon.

4. A chimpanzee was chosen for this study because chimpanzees are:
   (a) Friendly to humans.
   (b) Good with their hands.
   (c) Sociable.
   (d) All of the above.

5. Washoe lived in:
   (a) Stanford University.
   (b) A laboratory at the Gardners' home.
   (c) A specially made environment with other chimpanzees.
   (d) The wild.

6. One method used to train Washoe was 'imitative prompting', which is:
   (a) Forming her hands into a sign.
   (b) Rewarding her for the correct sign.
   (c) Waiting for a gesture and then shaping it.
   (d) Being reminded how to do a sign correctly.

DEBATE

How ethically acceptable is this study? Divide your class into groups with some groups preparing arguments for the benefits of this research and some groups preparing arguments for the costs.

7. The process of rewarding behaviours which are progressively closer and closer to a target behaviour is called:
   (a) Instrumental learning.
   (b) Babbling.
   (c) Imitation.
   (d) Shaping.

8. The favourite way to reward Washoe was
   (a) Tickling.
   (b) A piece of candy.
   (c) A bath.
   (d) All of the above.

9. How many signs was Washoe able to use fairly consistently after 21 months?
   (a) 25
   (b) 27
   (c) 30
   (d) 34.

10. Washoe used the phrase 'go sweet' which meant:
    (a) Get me a sweet.
    (b) I want to eat the chocolate.
    (c) Carry me to the raspberry bush.
    (d) Give me a kiss.

Answers are on page 37.

Exam questions

1. Some psychologists criticise Gardner and Gardner's work with Washoe by suggesting that the chimpanzee only learned to imitate gestures and did not learn a language as claimed. Give **two** pieces of evidence that suggest that Washoe uses a language. [OCR AS Psy, June 1996, paper 1]   [4]

2. (a) From Gardner and Gardner's study, Project Washoe, outline **one** way in which it was decided whether or not Washoe had added a sign to her vocabulary.   [2]

   (b) Identify **one** way in which Washoe's language differed from that of a human child.   [2]
   [OCR AS Psy, May 2002, paper 1]

3. From the study by Gardner and Gardner (Project Washoe):

   (a) What is meant by the term 'reinforcement'.   [2]

   (b) Give **one** example of how reinforcement was used in this study?   [2]
   [OCR AS Psy, Jan 2003 paper 2]

4. Outline **two** of the training methods that were used by Gardner and Gardner to encourage Washoe to use sign language. [OCR AS Psy, May 2003, paper 1]   [4]

Just monkeying around

More ape studies

Nim Chimpsky

Another study on animal language was carried out by Terrace (1979) on a chimpanzee called Nim Chimpsky (named after the linguistics expert, Noam Chomsky). Nim learnt 125 different signs and put them together in combinations. Terrace recorded, on tape, over 20,000 communications from Nim during a two-year period. When he looked at the data he was disappointed to find a marked difference between Nim's communication and child language.

1   There was no increase in the length of Nim's communications (children show a steady increase).

2   Only 12 per cent of Nim's communications were spontaneous (children initiate more communications than they respond to).

3   Imitation increased (it declines in children) as language developed.

4   Nim made frequent interruptions and did not learn to take turns (very young children learn to take turns).

Terrace concludes his paper by writing:

'Sequences of signs, produced by Nim and by other apes, may resemble the first multiword sequences produced by children. But unless alternative explanations of an ape's combination of signs are eliminated, in particular the habit of partially imitating teachers' recent utterances, there is no reason to regard an ape's utterance as a sentence' (Terrace *et al.*, 1979).

Kanzi and friend

Kanzi

Some apes have developed greater language skills than Washoe. For example, Sue Savage Rumbaugh describes how Kanzi the bonobo has been taught to use an electronic keyboard of symbols (Rumbaugh and Lewin, 1994). Kanzi appears to have a repertoire of 500 words and is able to understand many more. It is claimed she can create novel sentences and shows a clear understanding of complex human sentences. A remarkable aspect of Kanzi's language development was that she actually learned 50 or more symbols simply by watching her adoptive mother Matata being taught to use them.

Koko

The pictures show Koko the gorilla using ASL to sign for 'eat' and then getting her reward. You can see moving images of Koko signing at http://www.koko.org/world/signlanguage.html

Notes from Project Washoe

When the chimps made signs were they like the signs made by human signers? The only native signer on the Washoe Project reported:

'Every time the chimp made a sign, we were supposed to write it down in the log. ... They were always complaining because my log didn't show enough signs.

All the hearing people turned in logs with long lists of signs. They always saw more signs than I did. ...

The hearing people were logging every movement the chimp made as a sign. Every time the chimp put his finger in his mouth, they'd say "Oh, he's making the sign for DRINK," ... When the chimp scratched himself, they'd record it as the sign for SCRATCH. ... When [the chimps] want something, they reach.

Sometimes [the trainers] would say, "Oh, amazing, look at that, it's exactly like the ASL sign for GIVE!" It wasn't' (Pinker, 1994 p. 337–8).

Talking to pets

Millions of pet owners will tell you their animal 'understands every word I say'. Check this out with the dog translation device. It is called the Bowlingual and it claims to be able to interpret about 200 phrases or words – grouped in six different emotional categories: fun, frustration, menace, sorrow, demand and self-expression.

The inventors of the Bowlingual were awarded the 2002 IgNoble Peace Prize (like a Nobel Prize, but not quite) for promoting peace and harmony between species (see www.improb.com).

LINKS TO OTHER STUDIES

In the core study on **autism** the work of Premack and Woodruff on theory of mind is mentioned (page 20); Premack also studied Sarah the chimpanzee.

The Gardners, and the other animal language workers, used behavioural techniques, including reinforcement and imitation to train the chimps. Such techniques are based on the research on imitative learning in the core study by **Bandura, Ross and Ross**.

KeyISSUE

Behaviourism

Behaviourism was one of the great intellectual movements of the twentieth century. The term 'behaviourism' was first used by John B. Watson (1878–1958) in a paper written in 1913 in which he outlined a plan for behaviourism – an approach that was to dominate psychology for the next 50 years. It captured the public imagination because it suggested we are born equal, and the differences between us come from experience rather than breeding. This taps into the USA Declaration of Independence which states:

'We hold these truths to be self-evident, that all men are created equal …'

J.B. Watson and behaviourism

Watson proposed:

- Using experimental and objective techniques.
- Studying behaviour rather than 'mind'.
- We are born with a *tabular rasa* (blank slate), and we develop our personality, intelligence, etc. through our experiences in life.
- Humans are like other animals and we can study animals to find out about human behaviour.
- Psychology should aim to develop techniques that can control and alter human behaviour.

Reinforcement

The various ways that pleasant and unpleasant stimuli can be used to change behaviour are shown below. Skinner suggested that punishment and negative reinforcement should not be used because they were not as effective for long-term learning as positive reinforcement.

Mrs Skinner views her daughter Debbie in a Skinner Box.

	Pleasant Stimulus	**Unpleasant Stimulus**
Given	Positive reinforcement	Punishment
Removed	Omission	Negative reinforcement

In Russia, Ivan **Pavlov** (1849–1936) investigated reflex behaviour and discovered that dogs can learn to produce a reflex response to new stimuli. Most famously, he is reported to have trained dogs to salivate when they heard the sound of a bell because this was associated with food. This type of learning is called **classical conditioning**.

In the USA, B.F. **Skinner** (1904–90) developed the principle of **operant conditioning** showing how behaviour can be shaped through the use of reinforcement. His idea was based on Thorndike's **Law of Effect** which states that if a particular behaviour is successful the consequence is that it is more likely to recur in similar circumstances. This law provided a description of animal behaviour that did not require notions such as consciousness or thought.

Pavlov and his associates at the laboratory

'The major problems of the world today can be solved only if we improve our understanding of human behaviour.'

B.F. Skinner, *About Behaviourism* (1974)

Modern uses of behaviourism

Behaviour techniques are still extensively used today, for example:

Therapies: aversion therapy (classical conditioning) and time outs (operant conditioning). A development of this approach can be seen in cognitive behaviour therapy.

Token economies: used in institutions such as prison to mould behaviour.

Advertising: such as attempts to associate good feelings with an unconnected product.

Pictures of puppies and babies elicit a warm reaction. The Andrex adverts try to associate that good feeling with the product in simple classical conditioning trials.

Cognitive Core Study 1: Loftus and Palmer (eyewitness testimony)

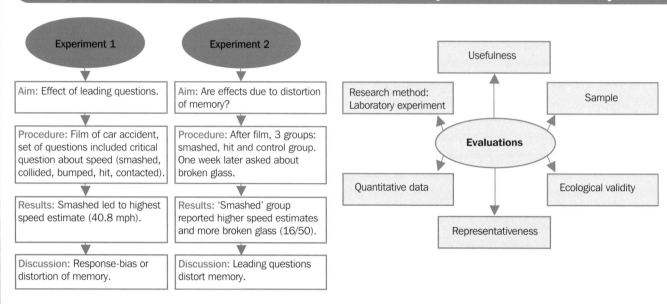

Experiment 1

Aim: Effect of leading questions.

Procedure: Film of car accident, set of questions included critical question about speed (smashed, collided, bumped, hit, contacted).

Results: Smashed led to highest speed estimate (40.8 mph).

Discussion: Response-bias or distortion of memory.

Experiment 2

Aim: Are effects due to distortion of memory?

Procedure: After film, 3 groups: smashed, hit and control group. One week later asked about broken glass.

Results: 'Smashed' group reported higher speed estimates and more broken glass (16/50).

Discussion: Leading questions distort memory.

Research method: Laboratory experiment

Usefulness

Sample

Evaluations

Quantitative data

Ecological validity

Representativeness

Cognitive Core Study 2: Deregowski (perception)

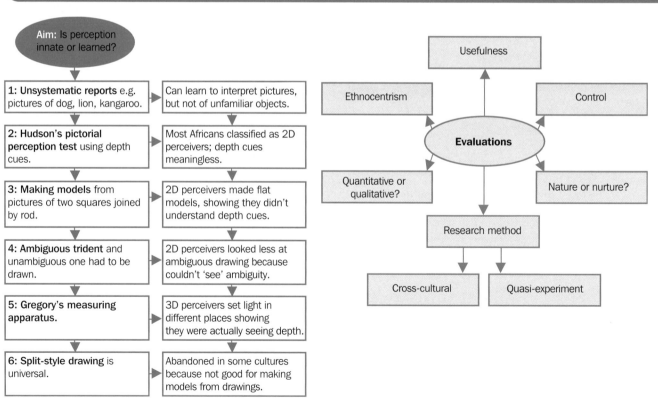

Aim: Is perception innate or learned?

1: **Unsystematic reports** e.g. pictures of dog, lion, kangaroo.

Can learn to interpret pictures, but not of unfamiliar objects.

2: **Hudson's pictorial perception test** using depth cues.

Most Africans classified as 2D perceivers; depth cues meaningless.

3: **Making models** from pictures of two squares joined by rod.

2D perceivers made flat models, showing they didn't understand depth cues.

4: **Ambiguous trident** and unambiguous one had to be drawn.

2D perceivers looked less at ambiguous drawing because couldn't 'see' ambiguity.

5: **Gregory's measuring apparatus.**

3D perceivers set light in different places showing they were actually seeing depth.

6: **Split-style drawing** is universal.

Abandoned in some cultures because not good for making models from drawings.

Ethnocentrism

Usefulness

Control

Evaluations

Quantitative or qualitative?

Nature or nurture?

Research method

Cross-cultural

Quasi-experiment

Cognitive Core Study 3: Baron-Cohen, Leslie and Frith (autism)

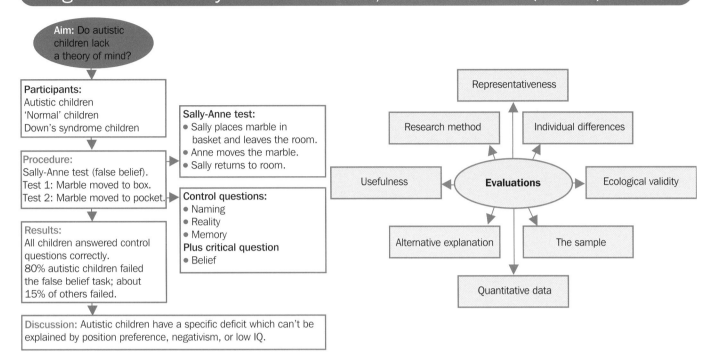

Aim: Do autistic children lack a theory of mind?

Participants:
Autistic children
'Normal' children
Down's syndrome children

Procedure:
Sally-Anne test (false belief).
Test 1: Marble moved to box.
Test 2: Marble moved to pocket.

Results:
All children answered control questions correctly.
80% autistic children failed the false belief task; about 15% of others failed.

Discussion: Autistic children have a specific deficit which can't be explained by position preference, negativism, or low IQ.

Sally-Anne test:
- Sally places marble in basket and leaves the room.
- Anne moves the marble.
- Sally returns to room.

Control questions:
- Naming
- Reality
- Memory
Plus critical question
- Belief

Evaluations
- Representativeness
- Research method
- Individual differences
- Usefulness
- Ecological validity
- Alternative explanation
- The sample
- Quantitative data

Cognitive Core Study 4: Gardner and Gardner (Project Washoe)

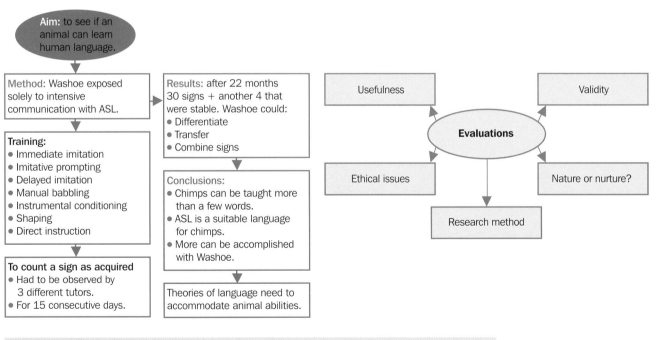

Aim: to see if an animal can learn human language.

Method: Washoe exposed solely to intensive communication with ASL.

Training:
- Immediate imitation
- Imitative prompting
- Delayed imitation
- Manual babbling
- Instrumental conditioning
- Shaping
- Direct instruction

To count a sign as acquired
- Had to be observed by 3 different tutors.
- For 15 consecutive days.

Results: after 22 months 30 signs + another 4 that were stable. Washoe could:
- Differentiate
- Transfer
- Combine signs

Conclusions:
- Chimps can be taught more than a few words.
- ASL is a suitable language for chimps.
- More can be accomplished with Washoe.

Theories of language need to accommodate animal abilities.

Evaluations
- Usefulness
- Validity
- Ethical issues
- Nature or nurture?
- Research method

MCQ answers

Loftus and Palmer (MCQs on page 9)	1c 2a 3c 4b 5c 6a 7b 8b 9b 10c
Deregowski (MCQs on page 17)	1b 2c 3a 4d 5b 6b 7a 8d 9c 10b
Baron-Cohen, Leslie and Frith (MCQs on page 25)	1c 2d 3a 4a 5d 6d 7b 8c 9b 10d
Gardner and Gardner (MCQs on page 33)	1c 2b 3a 4d 5b 6d 7d 8a 9d 10c

1 In the study by Loftus and Palmer, the subjects were shown film clips of car accidents. Identify **two** differences between witnessing these film clips and witnessing a real accident and, for each difference, say how this might affect the results of the study. [OCR AS Psy, June 1998, paper 1] [4]

Stig's answer

One difference is that the film clips weren't real.

Another difference is that people are scared in real life but wouldn't be scared in a lab.

Chardonnay's answer

The first difference is that which means that people don't behave like they do in real life.

Examiner's comments

Don't just repeat the question, Stig. Of course the clips weren't real. Your suggestion about the absence of fear in the laboratory (though not mine – Ed) is a good point.

Chardonnay, your point is OK but you could have made more of it, and you need to at least have a try at making two points. Think about, in real life you would feel the crash, smell it and it would probably make a lot of noise. A full sensory experience rather than just a visual one. More to think about but more to help you remember it.

Stig (0+2 marks) Chardonnay (1+0 marks)

2 The following table appears in the study by Loftus and Palmer on eyewitness testimony. Give **two** conclusions that can be drawn from this table. [OCR AS Psy, June 2000, paper 1] [4]

Table 1. Response to the question 'Did you see any broken glass?'

	Verb condition		
Response	Smashed	Hit	Control
Yes	16	7	6
No	34	43	44

Stig's answer

More people were affected by the word smashed and less people were affected by the word hit.

Chardonnay's answer

Conclusion 1: Leading questions alter what we remember.

Conclusion 2: Even people who are not asked a leading question make mistakes in what they remember.

Examiner's comments

This is not two points, Stig. It is the same point said backwards. You could also be more specific than just saying they were 'affected'. Just look at Chardonnay's answer. She's got the right idea. She makes two good points, especially the second one which is commonly missed when people describe this study.

Stig (1+0 marks) Chardonnay (1+2 marks)

3 The article by Deregowski reports that the split-style of drawing is universal and can be found in the drawings of children of all cultures. However, there are individual and cultural differences in preference for split-style.

(a) Describe **one** explanation of the origin of split-style drawing. [2]
(b) Suggest why most societies do **not** prefer split-style drawings. [2]
[OCR AS Psy, May 2002, paper 2]

Stig's answer

(a) The origin of the split-style drawing could be because children did it.

(b) Split-style drawings are not as appealing to people in most countries.

Chardonnay's answer

(a) Split-style drawings developed because it is the most natural style to use when drawing an object, it shows all parts of the object.

(b) It is not preferred in most societies because it is difficult to construct models from such drawings because they lack perspective.

Examiner's comments

I think you're guessing, Stig. It is true that children use split-style but they probably didn't originate it. Not an outrageous guess though. I don't know what you mean by the second answer.

Theses are two reasonable answers, Chardonnay, to what is a more difficult question than the average. Your answers are clear and precise and would attract good marks.

Stig (0+0 marks) Chardonnay (1+2 marks)

4 From the paper by Deregowski on perception:

(a) Identify **one** cultural difference in perceptual skills. [2]

(b) Give **one** problem with interpreting the results of cross-cultural studies. [2]

[OCR AS Psy, June 2000, paper 1]

Stig's answer

(a) One difference is in depth cues. Some people can't understand the depth cues that are used in pictures.

(b) One problem with such studies is that the methods used are rather uncontrolled and therefore other things may affect the participants' behaviour.

(a) Cultural groups differ in terms of their ability to interpret pictorial cues.

(b) When conducting a cross-cultural study it may be that the participants don't really understand what they are expected to do and this is why they can't do the task very well, not because they lack certain abilities.

Examiner's comments

Better answers, Stig. You're picking up a bit. Depth cues in pictures do seem to be a cultural invention and not all cultures represent the world in the same way. You are also right that there are a number of factors influencing behaviour that might affect results. It would help to be a little more specific and maybe give an example.

Chardonnay is on the case with this question. The first answer is nicely put and in a concise style. The second answer is well-expressed. Cross-cultural results are often presented as one group (usually the non-Europeans) as lacking a skill, whereas they might well just be seeing the world in a different way rather than an inferior one. Also they might not have the study explained to them very well.

Stig (2+0 marks) Chardonnay (2+2 marks)

Chardonnay's answer

---

5 In the study by Baron-Cohen, Leslie and Frith, the autistic children were compared with **two** other groups of children.

(a) Who were the two other groups of children? [2]

(b) Why were the autistic children compared against these two other groups? [2]

[OCR AS Psy, June 1997, paper 1]

Stig's answer

(a) The groups were autistic, normal and Down's syndrome children. The normal children were much younger (about 4 years old). The Down's syndrome children were about the same age as the autistic children but had much lower IQs.

(b) It meant you could see if success/failure on the Sally-Anne task was due to mental retardation rather than lack of theory of mind. The other two groups were socially normal and so acted as a comparison for social competence.

Chardonnay's answer

(a) Children with Down's syndrome and normal children.

(b) You needed to have other groups so you could see if the autistic children were different. They were different because they lacked the ability to get on with other people and this might be because they lacked a theory of mind.

Examiner's comments

You're really doing well now, Stig. Unfortunately you only need to write a couple of phrases to get all the marks.

Autistic children have a number of unusual behaviours. Some of these might be explained by their learning difficulties. To see whether this is an explanation for their behaviour on the Sally-Anne test the experimenters used another group with learning difficulties (Down's). The autistic children performed the same as the others except on the belief question, suggesting a specific problem.

Although both Stig's and Chardonnay's answers could have been clearer they are both sufficient to get the marks.

Stig (2+2 marks) Chardonnay (2+2 marks)

---

6 (a) From the study by Baron-Cohen, Leslie and Frith on autism, explain what is meant by the term 'theory of mind'. [2]

(b) Give **one** problem that arises if a person does not have a theory of mind. [2]

[OCR AS Psy, June 1999, paper 1]

Stig's answer

(a) 'Theory of Mind' is having a theory about what is in someone else's mind, knowing what they are thinking.

(b) If you haven't got a theory of mind you can't engage in pretend play because this requires you to understand what other people are thinking.

Chardonnay's answer

(a) 'Theory of Mind' refers to the ability to represent the mental states of another person and understand what they are likely to be thinking.

(b) One problem that might arise would be you couldn't do the Sally-Anne Task. You would think that Sally knows the marble has moved.

Examiner's comments

Part (a) asks for a simple definition of 'theory of mind'. We can't know what someone else is thinking but we can build up a model in our heads so we can guess what people will think and say. Chardonnay's answer is clear and precise and worth all the marks. Stig has had a good go but maybe will only get 1 mark for part (a).

There are a number of problems that arise if you do not have a theory of mind. They will be a list of the characteristics of autism because Baron-Cohen argues that a lack of theory of mind is the central problem for people with autism. Both answers are therefore correct and provide sufficient detail.

Stig (1+2 marks) Chardonnay (2+2 marks)

7 (a) In Project Washoe, why did Gardner and Gardner use sign language rather than spoken language? [2]

(b) Why did Gardner and Gardner use deaf adults to check Washoe's signs? [2]
[OCR AS Psy, June 1999, paper 1]

Stig's answer

(a) They used sign language because chimps aren't very good vocally whereas they are very good with their hands so they should find signing would come quite naturally.

(b) Deaf adults would be very good at sign language so they would be best for checking Washoe's signs. They would also be more objective than the tutors.

Chardonnay's answer

(a) Because sign language is easy to learn and the chimps don't actually have to speak. Vicki didn't learn much because she had to vocalise.

(b) It would be better to use deaf adults because they wouldn't be distracted by other noises and get muddled.

Examiner's comments

Both Stig's and Chardonnay's answers are fine. Early studies found that chimps can't vocalise very well. They don't have the biology for it. There are, however, very good with their hands, so it was a matter of opportunity.

The original study does not record that deaf signers were recruited to test Washoe. The Gardners report it elsewhere, and we use a quote from a deaf signer on page 34. If you read the quote you will see why it was a good idea to use deaf signers. Both the answers here are fine.

Stig (2+2 marks) Chardonnay (2+2 marks)

---

8 From Project Washoe (Gardner and Gardner):

(a) Describe **one** way that Washoe's signing was similar to human language. [2]

(b) Describe **one** way that Washoe's signing was different to human language. [2]
[OCR AS Psy, June 2000, paper 1]

Stig's answer

(a) It was similar because Washoe combined signs together to make more complex ideas and also invent new words.

(b) It was different because he didn't learn that much in 22 months. Human children learn language very quickly.

Chardonnay's answer

(a) One similarity was that Washoe transferred signs from particular things to more general instances, such as learning the sign for dog and then using it also to describe the sound of a barking dog.

(b) One difference was that Washoe didn't always get the meanings quite right. For example she kept using 'flower' to refer to odours.

Examiner's comments

It is a controversial claim of the Gardners that Washoe combined signs. If she did, this is indeed a feature of human language.

The slow rate of learning is just about worth the marks. But Stig has made one of the most common (though trivial) mistakes in referring to Washoe as 'he'. Washoe is female.

Generalising and transferring signs is an important characteristic of language so Chardonnay gets the marks.

Although Washoe did not get the meanings right all the time this does not challenge the view that she was using language. The lack of consistent word order and the lack of turn taking are much more challenging.

Stig (2+2 marks) Chardonnay (2+0 marks)

---

9 A number of studies take a cognitive approach to the study of psychological processes. This approach is concerned with how people make sense of the world through perceiving it, recalling it and representing it.

Using the four cognitive core studies, answer the questions which follow.

(a) Describe what each study tells us about cognition. [12]
(b) Briefly discuss **two** strengths and **two** weaknesses psychologists may have when they try to study cognition, giving examples from any of these studies. [12]

Stig's answer

(a) Loftus and Palmer's study tells us about how leading questions affect what people recall. In particular this can be used to help us understand the behaviour of eyewitnesses and whether their testimony is likely to be reliable or not. [2]

Deregowski's study tells us about the factors that influence our perception of pictures. It appears that cultural factors are important in determining how people interpret depth cues used in pictures because some of the Africans tested couldn't make any sense from the cues used in pictures and didn't see three dimensional pictures. [2]

Baron-Cohen's study is about the theory of mind. It's possible that autistic children are autistic and lack things like pretend play because they lack a theory of mind. This study showed that autistic children were much less able to cope with the Sally Anne tasks, which tests the ability to understand what is in someone else's mind. 'Normal' children and Down's syndrome children could cope with this. [3]

The study by the Gardner's shows that a chimpanzee can learn human language if taught to do so using sign language. Washoe did acquire a reasonable vocabulary but it is still questionable as to whether he was really using language. [2]

(b) One of the problems with studying cognition is you don't actually know what is going on inside someone's head. [P] Psychologists conduct studies which suggest what people are thinking. For example, in the study of Washoe she might not have been using her mind at all but could have been responding to the experimenter's cues like the talking horse did. [E]

Another problem is that often cognitive research uses lab experiments and so use experimental set-ups which aren't very much like real life. [P] For example it may not be very realistic to ask people what speed cars are travelling at using a film of vehicles. [E] Such research lacks ecological validity.

One good thing about cognitive studies is that they do help us understand how we think and use our memory and this can be very useful for real life applications. [P] For example, in Loftus and Palmer, we know that leading questions affect the reliability of eye witness testimony and police and lawyers can use this information so that they question witnesses carefully without ruining their memory. [E] This research could improve court processes and make sure that people don't get wrongly convicted due to unreliable eye-witness testimony. [C]

Another good thing about cognitive psychology is that they can help us to understand how complex the mind is both when it is working normally and when it is not working normally. [P] For example, Baron-Cohen's study tells us firstly that autistic children tend not to have a theory of mind, and secondly that having a theory of mind is essential for normal social functioning and social interaction. This research helps to shed light on the reasons behind autistic children's behaviour. [E] However, with cognitive psychology you can never be absolutely certain as you cannot directly see into the mind. [C]

Examiner's comments

The trick with these questions is to read the question carefully and respond clearly and concisely. Describe one insight about cognition from each study. This is best done by describing one of the findings and saying what it means. The question is looking for generalistions you can make from the studies. Stig has given four decent answers and has identified one key finding in each study, though he could have fleshed it out a bit more. For example, he could have improved the answer by considering what general point we can make from the study. For example the Deregowski study shows us that perception is not a cultural universal and therefore there are some features that we have to learn to see rather than being born with the skill.

Marks (a) = 2 + 2 + 3 + 2 = 9

We can apply the PEC (point, example, comment) formula to marking this answer (see page ix for an explanation of PEC).

Stig makes two decent points here. We can't know what is going on in someone's head. We can only infer what is happening from our observations of their behaviour. The point about Washoe is well made though Clever Hans (the horse) did not talk. That would have been really remarkable; he could have told me the winner of the 3.30 at Kempton Park.

Ecological validity is another decent point well made and appropriate to this question, expanded with a relevant example.

In both paragraphs so far, Stig has got valid points and examples, but he doesn't get any comment marks. The last sentence of paragraph 2 is just a rewording of the first sentence and Stig cannot get credited twice for the same material.

The third paragraph, on usefulness of cognitive research, is good. Stig has a clearly identified a point, probably true of much cognitive research. He expands the point with a relevant example (NB it is OK to use the same study twice … or even more!); the final sentence gets the 'Comment' mark as it looks at the likely consequences of the application. Stig has taken the line of argument further.

In the last paragraph, Stig just about gives a valid strength. The reference to normal and abnormal workings of the mind helps Stig get the point. The Baron-Cohen example is well expressed and it is a nice touch that Stig has realised that looking at abnormal processes can give psychologists insight into normal processes. Finally, Stig then makes a counterpoint to this and says that all cognitive psychology has some uncertainty to it due to the unobservable nature of the subject matter.

Counting up all the Ps, Es and Cs, Stig has got a very respectable 10/12 for part b – he shouldn't be too down in the dumps!

Marks (b) = 10

Total mark = a+b = 9+10 = 19/24

Chardonnay's answer

(a) The first study is about eyewitness testimony. People were shown a car accident and asked what speed the cars were travelling at when they smashed into each other or hit each other. People said they were travelling faster when the word 'smashed' was used. This is a leading question. In a second experiment participants were asked whether the glass was smashed or not, which was also affected by the leading question. **[2]**

The second study is about perception. Deregowski showed various pictures to African people to see if they could understand the pictures. Quite a lot of people (children and adults) couldn't see three dimensional pictures. He also wrote about split-style drawings which are used in some primitive cultures. He says they aren't used in our culture because they are not good for making models. **[2]**

The third study investigated autistic children to see if they thought the same way that normal children do. All the children had to do the Sally Anne test twice but only the autistic children couldn't get the right answer because they don't have a theory of mind. **[1]**

The 4th study concerns teaching non-human animals to use human language. The Gardners used ASL to teach a chimpanzee called Washoe to use words. Washoe learned to use 30 symbols after 22 months and was able to combine some of these symbols and create new meanings. This was much better than a previous chimpanzee had done, who had only learned about 4 symbols. Washoe probably did better because she was using ASL rather than trying to speak which is difficult for a chimpanzee. **[3]**

Examiner's comments

Chardonnay, like Stig, gives a finding from each study and says what it means. She does not make general points concerning what the studies tell us about cognition and so she hasn't quite answered the question.

What Chardonnay has written about Loftus and Palmer is basically accurate in terms of the results. To ensure the third point in this paragraph gained credit, it would be better if Chardonnay talked about what these results tell us about memory. This study tells us that memories often comprise of two forms of information – information encoded at the time of the event, and information encoded after the event (such as through the use of leading questions) which can contaminate the original memory.

The Deregowski paragraph again is accurate but does not give adequate focus on the question. What does Deregowski tell us about cognition? He tells us that picture perception is not a cultural universal and therefore is not innate or inherent, but learnt through culture.

In Baron-Cohen, Chardonnay has described an aspect of the procedure (which this question did not ask for) and then one conclusion (for which she would get one mark). What more could Chardonnay have said in order to get the three marks? She could have written about what theory of mind means, and how lack of theory of mind causes problems for autistic children.

This is a more detailed paragraph. Chardonnay makes some valid points such as the number of signs Washoe learnt, her creativity, and how and why her language was superior to previous attempts. Although in some respects this paragraph is not perfect, it is enough for three points.

Marks (a) = 2 + 2 + 1 + 3 = 8/12

(b) It is difficult to investigate the mind because it isn't a real thing. **[P]** Studies on memory are often very artificial and not like the real thing. For example psychologists use word lists and nonsense syllables whereas memory is about other things as well.

Another weakness with studying cognition is bias. For example, in Deregowski, some of the experiments conducted were biased against the African participants as the researchers used pencils and paper instead of materials that they were more familiar with. This is not fair on those participants and might have changed the results.

A strength is that in Baron-Cohen, we found out how autistic children lack a theory of mind. This is interesting and psychologists can use this to improve the lives of autistic children. **[E]** Now, Baron-Cohen is working on making software which can help autistic children learn to read different emotions in people's faces. This is very useful. **[C]**

Another strength is that we can compare the cognitive abilities of humans with other animals and this will help us to understand the similarities and differences between the minds of the two species. **[P]** For example, in Gardner and Gardner we can see that monkeys do have some ability to learn a human language. Even if Washoe did not always put signs in the right order, she did seem to use them with the right meanings. **[E]** This study has helped me to understand that monkeys are not so different from humans and also that human language, when you think about it, is really complicated. **[C]**

We can apply the PEC (point, example, comment) formula to marking this answer (see page ix for an explanation of PEC).

Neat idea, Chardonnay. The mind is not a real thing. We talk about it a lot, but we can't define it, weigh it, smell it or find it. We can only make inferences about it. Chardonnay's example of some (unnamed) typical memory experiments and their artificiality is true but (i) it is not an example from a named study in the question and (ii) it is quite vague and not clear how this follows on from the first assumption… so unfortunately, no marks here.

What Chardonnay says in the next paragraph is not incorrect, but it does not answer the question. The issue of (cultural) bias is something specific to Deregowski and not an issue for cognitive research generally. Thus, nil points, Chardonnay.

Again, Chardonnay has gone straight into something specific about a study without relating it to the question (strengths of cognitive research generally). If her first sentence of paragraph 3 had been about the usefulness of cognitive research, then it would have got the point. Chardonnay gets the 'example' point as this could be construed as answering the question. Additionally, Chardonnay takes this further and mentions an actual application of the research and so she gets the 'comment' point.

Chardonnay is now pulling herself back. This is a great paragraph (except she has strangely forgotten that Washoe is a chimp and not a monkey!), with a clear point, example and comment, all of which follow on from each other logically and coherently.

Counting up the Ps, Es and Cs, Chardonnay's part (b) gets 6/12.

Marks (b) = 6
Total mark = a+b = 8 + 6 = 14/24

This chapter looks at four core studies in developmental psychology.

1. Samuel and Bryant's study of children's ability to conserve quantities.

2. Bandura, Ross and Ross's demonstration of how aggression is learned through imitation.

3. Hodges and Tizard's study of the effects of institutionalisation on later social development.

4. Freud's classic study of Little Hans and the Oedipus conflict.

CHAPTER

2

Developmental psychology

Introduction to developmental psychology

What is developmental psychology?

Developmental psychology is sometimes understandably but misleadingly thought of as child psychology: understandably because the major part of the literature in developmental psychology is about children; misleadingly because it gives the impression that psychological development stops as the child enters adulthood. A truly comprehensive developmental psychology should concern itself with the whole lifespan of human development. Having said this, the studies in this chapter reflect the traditional preoccupation with children.

What is a child?

This is not such a silly question as you might think. There have been many views of what childhood is in different cultures and in different periods of history. It is difficult to know how people saw the world 500 years ago but we can have an idea if we look at what they wrote and what they painted. For example, a lot of medieval pictures show children as little adults. They have the proportions of adults only smaller. In reality, children don't have the proportions of adults, for example, their heads are much larger in proportion to their bodies. Maybe the people who produced and looked at those pictures thought of children as being small adults. We know that children took on responsible roles from a young age and were commonly put to work.

What knowledge does a child have when it is born? Can it make sense of the world when it opens its eyes? Does it have a range of instincts that develop as it grows? Alternatively, is it born with a 'blank slate' onto which experience will write the knowledge that gives the child its personality and cognitive skills? This nature–nurture debate has been live for over 300 years in this country and whatever answer is favoured has a significant effect on the social policies of the time for dealing with children.

Today we buy into the idea that children are immature humans and they require support and direction to develop into healthy adults. Although this seems like a modern idea it was proposed by the Greek philosopher Aristotle in the fourth century BC.

Questions for developmental psychologists

Psychologists take a range of different approaches to the study of development.

Similarities or differences: Psychologists can look for the features that all children share and are important to the development of any child, or they can look at the features that are different between one child and another. The work of Freud (see pages 70–71) and Piaget (see pages 46–47) look at the features we share with all other people.

Stages: If children develop bit by bit then we do not need to talk about stages, but if development involves reorganisation and the emergence of new strategies and skills then it is more useful to talk about stages. For example, in everyday speech we commonly refer to informal stages such as the 'terrible twos'. Both Freud and Piaget proposed stages of development. Each stage typically occurs at a particular age and builds upon previous stages.

Theories of development

The various theories of development are commonly grouped under four main headings:

- **Biological theories** point to *maturation* as the best explanation of behaviours such as walking and crawling. Such theories also point to genetics as an explanation of differences between one child and another. For example the current evidence points to a genetic component in autism (see page 20).

- **Learning theories** point to the experience we have in life as the key influence of development. An example of this approach is the work of Bandura, Ross and Ross (page 54).

Oliver and the Dodger

All the world's a stage,
And all the men and women merely players;
They have their exits and their entrances;
And one man in his time may play many parts,
His acts being seven ages. At first the infant,
Mewling and puking in the nurse's arms.
And then the schoolboy, with his satchel,
And shining morning face, creeping like a snail
Unwillingly to school, and then the lover,
Sighing like a furnace, with a woeful ballad
Made to his mistress' eyebrow. Then a soldier,
Full of strange oaths, and bearded like pard,
Jealous in hour, sudden and quick in quarrel,
Seeking the bubble reputation
Even in the cannon's mouth. And then the justice,
In fair round belly with good capon lin'd,
With eyes severe, and beard of formal cut,
Full of wise saws and modern instances;
And so he plays his part. The sixth age shifts
Into the lean and slipper'd pantaloon,
With spectacles on nose and pouch on side,
His youthful hose well sav'd a world too wide
For his shrunk shank; and his big manly voice,
Turning again towards childish treble, pipes
And whistles in his sound. Last scene of all,
That ends this strange eventful history,
Is second childishness, and mere oblivion,
Sans teeth, sans eyes, sans taste, sans everything.

As You Like It, Act II, Scene vii.

ACTIVITY

Make friends with your elderly relatives and ask them what they did when they were children. Try and sort out what was the same as your childhood and what was very different.

Oliver Twist was written by Charles Dickens in 1838. As with most of Dickens' work, Oliver Twist was used to bring the public's attention to various social evils of the time, including the workhouse, child labour and the recruitment of children as criminals.

One of the remarkable aspects of the story is the hidden beliefs about childhood. The central character, Oliver, has upper-class parents but was born in a workhouse and does not know the identity of his parents. He has a punishing childhood being sold by the workhouse to become an undertaker's apprentice. The cruelty he suffers at the hands of an older apprentice makes him run away to London, where he is taken under the wing of the Artful Dodger, a boy criminal.

Throughout the story Oliver's class shines through showing that Victorian readers were happy to believe that a child from the upper class would develop the behaviour of the upper classes despite never having had any experience of that kind of upbringing.

Different images of childhood

Not all childhoods are the same

It is estimated that there are 300,000 child soldiers worldwide (UNICEF website) in at least 18 countries. Although the term 'child soldier' commonly brings up a picture of gun-waving teenage boys the reality is a little different. A number of child soldiers are girls, maybe as many as 40% in some countries, and many of the soldiers are as young as seven or eight.

The effect of being a child soldier

However they came to be soldiers, children suffer from their involvement in military activity. It is an abuse of their right to be protected from the effects of conflict. Not only is their childhood destroyed, but they are also separated from their homes, communities and families. Children's education is brought to a brutal end and military activity damages them physically and mentally as many of them have witnessed or taken part in terrifying acts of violence – even against their own families and communities.

Child labour in the nineteenth century

The exploitation of children was outlawed in the UK by a series of laws including the 1819 Cotton Mills and Factories Act which prohibited children under the age of nine years from working in cotton mills, and restricted those over the age of nine to a 12-hour day. The special status for young people in these laws reflected a changing view of childhood. Now if only all international clothing companies could follow suit today.

- **Psychoanalytic theories** concentrate on the development of emotions and assume that our behaviour is affected by things we are not aware of (our unconscious mind) as well as things we are aware of (our conscious mind). This approach starts with the work of Freud (see page 70) and develops into the work of John Bowlby on attachment (see page 62).

- **Cognitive development theories** concentrate on the development of intelligence and thought, represented in this text by Samuel and Bryant's work (see page 48).

Connections

The studies that are included in this chapter are not the only ones in this book that relate to developmental psychology. In a very real sense all psychology is developmental since it is the study of things (people and processes) which change and develop over time. For too long psychology as a whole has tended to study static snapshots of people, frozen in time and space, and thereby has risked missing some things which lie at the very core of human existence. Elsewhere in the book we look at the development of thought (Baron-Cohen, Leslie and Frith), the development of identity (Hraba and Grant) and the development of ethnocentrism (Tajfel).

Research on cognitive development

How do children think?

Do children think in the same way as adults or do they have their own distinctive ways of seeing and thinking about the world? Jean Piaget started his academic career working on the early IQ tests in Binet's laboratory (see the core study on Gould, page 174). Piaget found the task of devising the test items very dull and he never finished the work. However, during his work he noticed that children of the same age appeared to make the same types of mistake. Piaget wondered whether the IQ testers were asking the wrong kind of questions in their attempts to understand the development of intelligence. Instead of looking at what children get wrong, Piaget asked *how* they get it wrong.

Piaget spent a lot of time watching and listening to children. He would play games with them to find out how they created rules for their play. He found that children don't think like adults. Piaget came to the conclusion that their amusing and apparently illogical thought and talk actually had a logic all of its own. Albert Einstein called it a discovery 'so simple that only a genius could have thought of it'. To Piaget, children are not just little adults but they are *cognitive aliens*: they appear to think like us but in fact there is something very different going on in their minds.

Stages of development

According to Piaget (1954) children develop their ability to think through a series of stages that occur as we mature (age). Children move from one stage to the next when they are 'ready' – which partly results from experiences in the world but is mainly driven by maturation.

- **Sensory motor stage** (birth to around 18 months), during which the child is learning to match their senses (what they see and hear, etc.) to what they can do.

- **Pre-operational stage** (18 months to about 7 years), during which the child is learning to use symbolism (and language in particular), and is developing some general rules about mental operations.

- **Concrete operational stage** (7 to around 12 years), during which the child is able to use some sophisticated mental operations but is still limited in a number of ways; for example, the concrete operational child tends to think about the world in terms of how it is, and finds it hard to speculate on how it might be.

- **Formal operational stage** (12 years and above), which is the most sophisticated stage of thinking and is mainly governed by formal logic.

Piaget said that it is possible to observe these different thought patterns through the errors of reasoning that children make. He devised some ingenious tests to illustrate this different style of thinking. The most famous of these tests relate to the pre-operational stage. In this stage Piaget said that children's thought has the following features:

1 They are unable to *conserve*. For example, they do not appreciate that if you change the shape of an object it keeps the same mass.

2 They are unable to *reverse* mental operations. If they have seen some action take place they can not mentally 'rewind the tape'.

3 They rely on their *intuitions* about what they can see rather than what they can reason.

4 They are perceptually *egocentric*, finding it difficult to imagine a viewpoint different to their own.

ACTIVITY

What is the difference between children and adults?

Make a list of as many differences between children and adults as you can think of. The answers don't have to psychological. You might try using the following three headings for your list: what they think, what they feel, what they do. This will give you a clue as to why it is so difficult to carry out studies on children.

Conservation studies

An example of one of Piaget's tests is carried out with some counters. The child is shown two equal rows of counters.

The adult asks, 'Which one has more counters?' and the child replies 'They're both the same'.

Then, in full view of the child, the adult spreads out one row of counters.

The adult now asks the same question; many pre-operational children point to the bottom row and say, 'This row has more'. Piaget believes that the child does not realise that quantity stays constant (is conserved) even though it may appear to have changed. If children at this developmental stage were able to 'rewind the tape' of the adult spreading out the counters, reversing the adult's actions in their minds, they would realise that the number of counters had not changed.

Because they cannot conserve, or mentally reverse the process, the children use intuition to answer the question. One of the rows *looks* longer than the other, so they answer that it has more.

Biographical notes on Jean Piaget

Piaget grew up near Lake Neuchatel in a quiet region of French Switzerland. His father was a professor of medieval studies and his mother a strict Calvinist. He was a child prodigy who soon became interested in the scientific study of nature. When he was 11 he wrote a short scientific paper on an albino sparrow. This paper is considered as the starting point of his long and brilliant academic career.

In 1923 he married Valentine Chatenay and had three children, Jacqueline, Lucienne and Laurant. Like many developmental psychologists, Piaget studied his own children and reported on their intellectual and language development.

The main theme in Piaget's work is how knowledge develops. How do we come to know what we know and think what we think? His answer was that knowledge develops through our interactions in the world, and we develop through predictable stages.

In the past 20 years Piaget's work has been challenged in a number of ways. For example, experiments have demonstrated that new-born infants already have some of the knowledge that Piaget believed children had to develop for themselves.

There are also many studies that challenge Piaget's description of child thought processes. These new studies challenge the detail of Piaget's theories but not the central theme that children have qualitatively different thought processes to adults – before Piaget's time psychologists thought that children just knew less; Piaget helped us to realise that they don't simply know less, they think differently.

Jean Piaget (1896–1980)

Magic

Magic is the label we give to events we can't explain. To a child, an adult is a magician because they can do all manner of things a child can't.

Because Phil knows the local traffic system quite well, he can say 'abracadabra' just before the lights turn to green and a child will believe that Phil has changed the lights by magic (he knows it's sad but it amuses him). This is the basis of most magic tricks. The magician has more knowledge than you but you don't know how much more so you can't estimate the extent of his powers.

Adults encourage children's belief in magic by telling them about mystical creatures that don't really exist like Father Christmas (sorry if you hadn't heard already) and the Tooth Fairy. Even as adults we believe in magical things such as special medicines or love potions. The practice of homeopathy has no scientific support yet a large number of people continue to purchase homeopathic remedies that have no demonstrably active ingredients.

What makes the wind?

In one of his most famous experiments, Piaget asked children, 'What makes the wind?' A typical conversation went like this:

Piaget: *What makes the wind?*
Julia: *The trees.*
Piaget: *How do you know?*
Julia: *I saw them waving their arms.*
Piaget: *How does that make the wind?*
Julia: *(Waving her hand in front of his face): Like this. Only they are bigger. And there are lots of trees.*
Piaget: *What makes the wind on the ocean?*
Julia: *It blows there from the land. No. It's the waves...*

This is the sort of conversation that delights parents, who then bore you to death telling you about it. Julia is wrong but her answer makes sense. Classifying the answers as 'true' or 'false' misses the point. Piaget was looking for a theory that would show how children come up with answers like this. (Conversation reported in Papert, 1999)

The appearance–reality distinction

This is another characteristic of pre-operational thought, which is related to difficulties with conservation. Pre-operational children are 'overwhelmed' by what they see – how things appear – and let that dominate their thinking. Three-year-olds (pre-operational) were shown Maynard the cat and then watched while the cat went behind a screen and a mask was placed over his head. When they saw the post-transformation 'dog' the children said it was a dog even though they had watched the whole transformation (deVries, 1969).

Animism

Young children readily see psychological characteristics such as consciousness, feelings and motives in physical objects and events. Piaget said that to start with a child will believe that almost anything can be alive whether it moves or not. Later, the child comes to believe that only things that move are alive, but this includes things like trains and clocks. The next step is to see life only in those objects that can move on their own, but this still includes objects such as the sun and the moon. Finally, the child comes to believe that only animals and maybe plants are alive.

Examples of animism:

- *The sun going to bed.*
- *Steam trying to escape from a kettle.*
- *Thomas the tank engine being in a bad mood.*

The core study

The core study directly challenges Piaget's explanation of why children make mistakes in the conservation tasks. It looks at three of those tasks and compares children across different ages. It is asking whether there is something in the design of Piaget's tasks that creates a problem for the children.

Judith Samuel and Peter Bryant (1983) Asking only one question in the conservation experiment. *Journal of Child Psychology*, 22 (2), 315–318.

Abstract

The study aimed to see if younger children would cope better with Piaget's conservation task if they were asked only one question rather than two questions pre- and post-transformation.

Method

About 250 children were involved.

- Four age groups were tested: 5, 6, 7 and 8 years old.

- Each group was subdivided into three groups: standard (two questions asked), one question asked, or fixed array (one question, no transformation).

- Each child was tested 12 times – 4 times on each of 3 materials (mass, number and volume).

Results

Samuel and Bryant found that older children still coped better than younger children (age difference), all children made fewer errors when asked one question (condition difference) and fewer errors on the number task (materials difference).

Discussion

This suggests that Piaget may have underestimated what younger children can do because using two questions confused them. However, the findings continue to support Piaget's theory that there are qualitative changes that occur as children get older.

Matching participants

Another form of control was used to make sure that the three subgroups were the same. If the children in condition 1 happened to be older than those in condition 2 this might explain why they did better on the conservation task. To control for this, the experimenters made sure that the ages of children in each subgroup were the same.

Control group

Control groups are used in experiments to control for extraneous variables, variables other than the IV which may affect the DV. In the case of this experiment, one IV was the number of questions asked and the DV was whether the child gave the right answer. Samuel and Bryant expected that the reason why a child might get the second answer wrong was because they were confused by being asked two questions but it might be because they didn't understand the question at all. Therefore a control condition (fixed array control) was included to exclude this possibility.

corestudy

Aim

The intention of this study was to investigate the question of whether children under the age of 7 or 8 years are able to understand the principle of invariance of quantity i.e. conservation.

Background

Rose and Blank (1974) conducted a variation of Piaget's conservation experiment. In Piaget's conservation experiments, children were asked whether the two displays were the same. This question was asked both before the transformation and again afterwards. In Rose and Blank's experiment children were only asked the question after the transformation took place. The result was that children who failed the traditional task with two questions (one before and one after the transformation) often succeeded when only asked the post-transformation question.

This finding suggests that the reason children fail is *not* because they cannot conserve quantity but because they have been confused by the questions.

Rose and Blank only looked at the number tasks and only tested 6-year-old children, therefore this study aimed to find out if the same results would occur with other conservation tasks and a wider age range of participants.

Method

Participants

252 boys and girls aged between 5 and 8½ years from Devon, England. The children were divided into four age groups, whose mean ages were:

- 5 years 3 months
- 6 years 3 months
- 7 years 3 months
- 8 years 3 months

Procedure

Each group was subdivided into three subgroups, which were closely matched for age.

Condition 1: Standard condition These children were given the traditional conservation task where they were asked two questions.

Condition 2: One judgement condition These children were asked only one question, after the display was changed (i.e. post-transformation).

Condition 3: Fixed array control This group only saw one display, the post-transformation one (i.e. they were just shown the last column in the table (on the right) and asked whether the two were the same mass/number/volume). This was a control condition to check whether children could detect a difference in the post-transformation display. If the control group couldn't cope with the task then failure might be due to problems understanding just the one question.

Each child had four trials with each of the three kinds of material shown in the table (i.e. 12 trials in total). The four trials consisted of two equal and two unequal quantities.

Biographical notes on Peter Bryant and Judith Samuel

Peter Bryant recently retired from the post of Watts Professor of Psychology at the University of Oxford which he held from 1980 to 2004. He is currently involved in a variety of different research projects on how children learn to read and to do mathematics. He is the current editor of *Cognitive Development* which is the official journal of the Jean Piaget Society.

Bryant worked with Piaget and his team of researchers in the 1960s and observed their research firsthand. In his view Piaget completely transformed the subject of child psychology and was an astonishingly gifted experimenter. *'No one in the history of psychology, apart perhaps from Pavlov, has contributed as much as Piaget did to the creation of new, ingenious and highly successful ways of investigating people's behaviour. However .. the actual experimental designs that he and his colleagues adopted were often flawed.'* The flaw was that they failed to have control conditions that would exclude other possible explanations for a child's abilities, such as failure at the conservation task. Other researchers, such as Samuel and Bryant, have been left to do this. *'Our point was that one of the factors that determines the children's success in the conservation task is the context in which the problem is given to them'* (interview with Peter Bryant, 2006).

Judith Samuel is now a Consultant Clinical Psychologist with Oxfordshire Learning Disability NHS Trust. Her main area of research and service development is with people with profound intellectual disabilities (in particular Intensive Interaction). She links this work to her early research *'I have built on my initial interest in the social context of cognitive development and learning'* (personal communication).

	Pre-transformation		Post-transformation
	Equal quantities	**Unequal quantities**	
Mass	Two equal Plasticine cylinders.	Two unequal Plasticine cylinders, one longer than the other.	One cylinder is squashed so it looks like a sausage or a pancake.
Number	Two rows of 6 counters, each arranged identically.	One row of 6 counters and one of 5 arranged to be equal in length.	One row was either spread out or bunched up so the two rows were not of equal length.

Volume	Two identical glasses, with the *same* amounts of liquid.	Two identical glasses, with *different* amounts of liquid.	The liquid from one glass is poured into a narrower or wider one.

Q s

1 How was Samuel and Bryant's study different from Rose and Blank's?

2 What is the 'transformation'?

3 In an experiment there are dependent variables (DV) and independent variables (IV). Which of these is an IV in this experiment: the age of the child or the ability to conserve?

4 There were two other IVs in this experiment – what other conditions were controlled by the experimenters?

5 What is the DV in this experiment?

6 How is ability to conserve measured?

7 Why do you think Samuel and Bryant included both equal and unequal conditions in the pre-transformation display?

8 A longitudinal study tests the same children repeatedly, as they get older, to monitor developmental change. An alternative method is to use a snapshot design where development is seen by comparing the behaviour of children of different ages. Which design was used here?

9 What might be the advantage(s) of using a snapshot design in this study?

10 What might be the disadvantage(s)?

11 The order of the tasks was varied so that each child got them in a different order. Why is this a good idea?

12 How do you think the children's behaviour might be affected by being questioned by a 'strange' adult?

In the standard conservation task a child is first shown two equal quantities and asked 'Are they the same'? Then the display is transformed in front of the child by pouring the liquid from one glass into a taller, thinner one. Then children in all conditions are asked 'Are they the same quantity?' Pre-operational children are likely to say yes.

Pre-operational children base their decisions on current appearance and on their intuition because they cannot 'rewind the tape' to remind themselves what actually happened. They do not use consistent logic – the logic that says quantities can't change.

Results

There were no differences found in the equal and unequal conditions and therefore the results for these two conditions were combined.

The data for the three kinds of material (mass, number, volume) are shown on the right. All kinds of material have been combined in the graph and first table.

There were three IVs in this experiment:

- **Age:** older children made fewer errors.

- **Conditions:** children made fewest errors when shown the transformation and asked only one question.

- **Materials:** children made fewer errors on the number task and most on the volume task.

Children did worse on the control condition which shows that it is the questions and not the arrays that affect performance, but also shows that you need to see the pre-transformation display in order to understand the principle of conservation.

Mean number of errors for each child (rounded to the nearest whole number). An error is a failure to conserve.

Age	Condition		
	Standard	One question	Control
5	8	7	9
6	6	4	6
7	3	3	5
8	2	1	3

Mean errors (out of 4) in each condition. The errors have been rounded to one decimal place.

Material	Standard	One question	Control
mass	1.5	1.2	1.7
number	1.5	1.0	1.5
volume	1.8	1.6	2.5

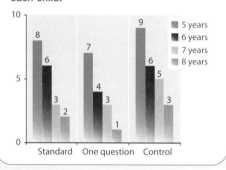

Mean number of errors (out of 12) for each child.

Discussion

The results indicate that children who fail on the traditional two-question conservation task produce the wrong answer because they are asked two questions rather than because they cannot conserve. The experimenter's repetition of the same question makes them think they must change their answer the second time. This is shown by the fact that:

- The children must have been using their knowledge of conservation when they solved the one-question task.

- They must have used their knowledge of the pre-transformation display to do this because they all did much better than the fixed-array control group.

The important lesson is that children may possess certain cognitive abilities (such as conservation) but may not display these when questioned in a certain way.

Q s

1 Describe how performance differed according to age.

2 How did performance differ between the two experimental groups ('standard' and 'one question')?

3 What can we conclude from the performance of the control group?

4 From these results, what can you conclude about the ability to conserve?

5 In what way was the behaviour of the participants in the two-question condition affected by demand characteristics (features of the experiment which 'invite' participants to behave in particular ways)?

6 Did the children find one particular kind of material more difficult to conserve with than the others? Which one?

7 Which was easiest? Why might that be the case?

8 Do you think that any of the children performed perfectly? Explain your answer.

9 Were there non-conservers in all age groups? How can you explain this?

10 In what way do the results still support Piaget?

11 Would it be easy to replicate this study exactly? Why or why not?

ACTIVITY

You could try to draw your own graph for the mass, number and volume table.

You could also try to draw a different version for the graph and organise the bars by age instead of condition.

EVALUATING THE STUDY BY SAMUEL AND BRYANT

The research method

This study was a lab experiment. *What are the strengths and limitations of this research method in the context of this study?*

The study was also a quasi-experiment (because the IV age isn't 'manipulated', it just exists). *What are the strengths and limitations of this research method in the context of this study?*

DEBATE

Are lab experiments useful? Consider any lab experiments that you have studied and construct arguments for and against their validity and usefulness.

Qualitative or quantitative?

What kind of data were collected in this study? What are the strengths and limitations of producing this kind of data in the context of this study?

The participants

In what way do children make good or bad participants?

What next?

Describe **one** change to this study, and say how you think this might affect the outcome.

Ethical issues

What ethical issues should have concerned the researchers in this study, and how might they have dealt with these issues?

Ecological validity

To what extent is this study representative of real life?

Applications/usefulness

Piaget's theory has been used in education, for example, the theory suggests that children should only do certain activities when they are 'ready' for that kind of thinking. *How might you use the findings from this experiment?*

Multiple choice questions

1. This study was a replication of a study by
   - (a) Piaget.
   - (b) Samuel and Bryant.
   - (c) Rose and Blank.
   - (d) Both a and c.

2. What was the age range of participants in this experiment?
   - (a) $4\frac{1}{2}$ to $8\frac{1}{2}$ years.
   - (b) 5 to 8 years.
   - (c) $5\frac{1}{2}$ to 8 years.
   - (d) 5 to $8\frac{1}{2}$ years.

3. What was the IV in this experiment?
   - (a) Children's age.
   - (b) Ability to conserve.
   - (c) The three conditions (one question, two questions, control).
   - (d) Both a and c.

4. Which is the post-transformation question?
   - (a) The question asked before the change was made.
   - (b) The question asked while the change was made.
   - (c) The question asked after the change was made.
   - (d) All of the above.

5. Which of the kinds of material did the children find easiest to conserve?
   - (a) Height.
   - (b) Number.
   - (c) Volume.
   - (d) Mass.

6. Which group of children made most errors on the conservation tasks?
   - (a) 5-year-olds.
   - (b) 6-year-olds.
   - (c) 7-year-olds.
   - (d) 8-year-olds.

7. What were the three kinds of material that were used in the experiment?
   - (a) Height, number, volume.
   - (b) Height, quantity, volume.
   - (c) Mass, quantity, speed.
   - (d) Mass, number, volume.

8. Which of the following were used to control for extraneous variables?
   - (a) Different age groups.
   - (b) Matching participants.
   - (c) Fixed array task.
   - (d) Both b and c.

9. Which of the following is true?
   - (a) This was a repeated measures design.
   - (b) This was an independent groups design.
   - (c) This was a mixed groups design.
   - (d) Both a and b.

10. The results showed that
    - (a) More children can conserve when only asked the post-transformation question.
    - (b) Fewer 5-year-olds can conserve than 8-year-olds.
    - (c) Piaget underestimated what children can do in terms of conservation.
    - (d) All of the above.

Answers are on page 79.

Exam questions

1. From the study by Samuel and Bryant on conservation, identify **two** factors that increase the chance of a child giving the correct answer in the conservation experiments. For each factor explain *why* it increases the chances of a child giving a correct answer. [OCR AS Psy, June 1999, paper 1] [4]

2. From the study by Samuel and Bryant on conservation:

   (a) Briefly describe the standard (two-question) procedure. [2]

   (b) Suggest what can be learned from this procedure that is useful to psychologists when they interview children. [2]
   [OCR AS Psy, Jan 2003, paper 2]

3. Outline **two** conclusions that can be drawn from the results of Samuel and Bryant's study on conservation. [OCR AS Psy, May 2003, paper 1] [4]

4. From Samuel and Bryant's study on conservation:

   (a) Give **one** piece of evidence that supports Piaget's claims about children's ability to conserve. [2]

   (b) Give **one** piece of evidence that challenges Piaget's claims. [2]
   [OCR AS Psy, Jan 2004, paper 1]

Piaget revisited

Naughty Teddy

Another study that revisited Piaget's conservation tests was devised by McGarrigle and Donaldson (1974). In Piaget's test of conservation of number, he showed children two rows with equal number of counters and then spread the counters in one of the rows so the row looked longer. Children in the pre-operational stage tended to say there were more counters in the row that looked longer. There are a number of explanations for this including Piaget's (the child cannot conserve) and Samuel and Bryant's (the second question requires a different answer to the first).

Another possible reason might be in the task itself. Is it the way the counters are moved or even who does the moving that leads the children to make the mistake? To a child an adult has magic powers. Who knows where those powers end? Perhaps the child thinks that the adult can actually change the amount of counters?

McGarrigle and Donaldson used a naughty teddy puppet to mess up the counters rather than get an adult to do this. When Naughty Teddy did the messing up of the counters most of the 4–6 year olds (70%) made the correct judgement about the rows (the quantities in each row are the same).

Very Naughty Teddy

It is not clear why they are more likely to make the correct judgement when the puppet is involved and Moore and Frye (1986) suggested the improvement was because the children were distracted by the naughty teddy antics. Perhaps they were so distracted that they didn't notice the change.

Moore and Frye demonstrated this by getting Naughty Teddy to actually take away a counter as well as messing up the row. The children still said the quantities were the same even though now they weren't.

This all goes to show that it is very difficult to investigate children's thinking, and it also confirms Piaget's basic idea that children appear to have different thought processes to adults.

Cognitive development and culture

Does Piaget's theory describe how all children develop or just those in Western societies? To answer this we have to break down the question and look at three smaller questions:

> Q: *Do Piaget's stages occur in the same order in different cultures?*
>
> A: *Probably yes.*

A cross-cultural study of children in the UK, Australia, Greece and Pakistan found that children developed an ability to complete the conservation tasks in the same order (Shayer *et al.*, 1988).

> Q: *Do children from different cultures go through the stages at the same age?*
>
> A: *Probably no.*

Various studies have found differences of up to 6 years in the age that children reach the third and fourth of Piaget's stages (Matsumoto, 1994). However, there is always an issue about whether the children were just doing badly on the task, even though they have the ability to make the correct judgement.

> Q: *Do all cultures see scientific reasoning as the highest form of thought?*
>
> A: *Clearly no.*

Different societies place different values on styles of behaviour and thought. In the West we appear to think that abstract and hypothetical thought processes are the highest form of intelligence. Many other cultures, however, value thought processes that are more social and take other people into account (Matsumoto, 1994).

LINKS TO OTHER STUDIES

The work of Piaget along with Samuel and Bryant has connections to the work on autism by **Baron-Cohen, Leslie and Frith**. They both use imaginative techniques to explore child thought and they both develop theories about the development of cognitive processes.

In the 1920s Piaget became interested in psychoanalysis and moved to Zurich, where he attended Carl Jung's lectures. This gives us a link to **Freud**'s work.

Piaget's work also gives us an explanation for how children learn right from wrong and that also connects to **Freud**'s and **Bandura**'s studies.

Piaget's work is about intelligence and he started his career working on IQ tests. This provides a link, and a contrast, to the work on IQ described by **Gould**.

Children's drawings

Another illustration of the different way that children see the world to adults is in their drawings of people. The drawings follow a predictable developmental pattern that is nothing like the way adults draw people. Most remarkably, they start off by leaving out the body and draw the arms and legs coming out of a big head. This is like the famous Mr Men, but it is the Mr Men that copy children rather than children copying the Mr Men.

keyISSUE

Practical issues with child participants

The main practical issue to consider is that children are more likely to respond to researcher's cues because they are more uncertain of themselves. Therefore they may unwittingly fulfil the researcher's expectations, leading to findings which are not valid.

The two main types of 'cues' are described below.

1 Demand characteristics

Demand characteristics create participant effects. People always seek cues about how to behave, particularly in a new environment, such as being in an experiment, and particularly if a person knows they are in an experiment. Participants actively look for clues as to how they should behave. The result is that they do not behave as they would usually.

Thus demand characteristics may act as an alternative IV (*confounding variable*) because they explain the change in the DV.

2 Investigator bias

In an interview, leading questions are one way that an experimenter might affect another person's behaviour. In an experiment, an experimenter might unconsciously encourage some participants more than others.

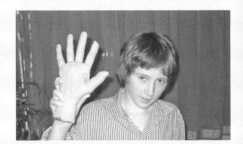

One reason why participants are affected by demand characteristics is that all participants, especially children, want to offer a helping hand. If they know they are in an experiment they usually want to please the experimenter. This sometimes results in them being over-cooperative – and not behaving as they would normally.

The effect of expectations

Rosenthal and Jacobsen (1966) told teachers in a primary school that some of their students were 'bloomers' – children whose IQs suggested they could be doing a lot better than they were. The children identified as bloomers had been identified randomly (i.e. they were actually no different to the other students). However, when all the children were assessed at the end of the year the bloomers had higher IQ gains than their classmates. This has been called the 'self-fulfilling prophecy' – things may turn out as you expected, not because you were right in your expectations but because your expectations altered subsequent events.

In an earlier study Rosenthal and Fode (1963) found the effect even worked with rats! Psychology students were asked to train rats to learn their way around a maze. They were told that one group of rats was bred to be 'fast learners', whilst the others were 'slow learners'. In fact there were no differences between the rats; nevertheless the supposedly brighter rats actually did better.

Ethical issues with child participants

The same ethical issues are important with child participants as with adults. These are described on page 95. But there are some additional issues to consider.

1 Informed consent: researchers cannot obtain the informed consent of children and must seek that of a parent or guardian.

2 Psychological harm: researchers would be even less willing to distress or deceive a child than any other participant. The long-term effects of research on impressionable children should be considered.

Exam-style question

Psychologists investigate developmental processes by studying children.

Using **one** Core Study:

(a) Describe the procedure of your chosen study. [6]

(b) Briefly discuss **two** advantages and **two** disadvantages of using children in research, using examples from your chosen study. [12]

(c) Suggest **one** change to the procedure of your chosen study that would allow it to be carried out on adult participants, and say how you think this might affect the results. [8]

KEY TERMS

Demand characteristics are cues in an experimental situation that may unconsciously affect a participant's behaviour.

Investigator bias is the term used to describe the effects of an investigator's expectations on a participant's behaviour. Any cues (other than the IV) from an investigator that encourage certain behaviours in the participant leading to a fulfilment of the investigator's expectations will act as a confounding variable.

ACTIVITY

Is it acceptable for parents to give consent on their child's behalf? Why or why not?

If parents have given informed consent for their child to be a participant in a longitudinal study, at what age should the child be asked to give his/her own consent?

Can you think of a situation that might not distress an adult but would distress a child?

Learning

*H*ow do we learn? Some of our behaviour is moulded by reinforcement. We do things that bring about pleasant consequences (rewards), such as warmth or praise or money, and we do things to avoid unpleasant consequences, such as cold or disapproval. Some of our learning comes through trial and error, but we also appear to learn by watching other people. It is, after all, safer to let others make the mistakes. When any behaviour appears to have positive consequences, we store it away for an appropriate occasion and then try it for ourselves.

When we are successful we become more confident (*self-efficacy*). As we interact with our environment, it becomes a two-way process: as we change the environment, the environment changes us (*reciprocal determinism*). Learning is therefore a combination of watching, thinking and trying. We learn most from people with whom we identify. When we are very young this is our parents; later it is peers, and later still it is attractive and famous people as well as people in authority.

History

Learning has been one of the key topics in psychology for over one hundred years. It can be defined as:

a relatively permanent change in behaviour (or potential behaviour) as the result of experience.

John B. Watson (1878–1958) was the first to study how the process of learning affects our behaviour, and he formed the school of thought known as *Behaviourism* (see the key issue on page 35). Behaviourists are basically interested in explaining behaviour simply in terms of the stimuli in the environment. Although it can explain some examples of human learning there is a lot of behaviour it cannot explain.

Social learning theory

The behaviourism of Watson took on a more human dimension with the publication of the book *Social Learning and Imitation* (Miller and Dollard, 1941). This approach added imitation to the known principles of learning. The book was written to explain how animals and humans imitate observed behaviours (a process called 'modelling'); in other words you don't just learn because you have been rewarded but because you see someone else rewarded and store this memory for future reference. You then may imitate or model the behaviour given appropriate circumstances and will only continue to repeat it if directly reinforced. Social learning theory explains human behaviour in terms of a continuous interaction between cognitive, behavioural and environmental influences. It is now is most closely associated with Albert Bandura.

Why are people aggressive?

Aggression has a lot of forms. It can be giving someone a funny look, or it can be shouting at them or it can involve physical violence. Sometimes we think aggression is a good thing, such as in sport where we want sportspeople to show controlled aggression. Some people believe it is important to fight and even kill people for your beliefs. Mostly, however, we judge aggression to be a bad thing, though strangely we appear to enjoy watching violence and murder for entertainment.

Biographical notes on Albert Bandura

Albert Bandura was born on December 4, 1925 in the province of Alberta, Canada. He studied at the University of British Columbia and of Iowa. In 1953, Bandura accepted a teaching position at Stanford University, USA where he continues to teach today.

He is most associated with the development of 'social learning theory' which he has recently renamed 'social cognitive theory' to take in further developments of the theory. In 1986 Bandura wrote *Social Foundations of Thought and Action* which outlines his social cognitive theory. Bandura has made a large contribution to the field of psychology, as seen in the many honours and awards he has received including several honorary degrees from universities all over the world.

To introductory psychology students, however, he is still best known for the Bobo studies. Recently he wrote of this,

'In my earlier life, I conducted research on the power of social modeling. … The studies of aggressive modeling were conducted over 40 years ago. But the Bobo doll continues to follow me wherever I go. The photographs are published in every introductory psychology text and virtually every undergraduate enrols in introductory psychology. I recently checked into a Washington hotel only to have the clerk at the registration desk asked, "Did you do the Bobo doll experiment?" I explained that "I am afraid that will be my legacy." He replied, "Hell, that deserves an upgrade. I will put you in a suite in the quiet part of the hotel." So there are some benefits to the wide exposure.' (Bandura, 2004, page 626)

Role models

The idea of role models is one of the most overused concepts in popular psychology. It is often used to criticise people who are in the public eye. For example, the wife of British Prime Minister, Cherie Blair, was blamed by psychologist Sandi Mann for being too successful and so causing stress to ordinary mothers who tried to copy her. *'Whilst Mrs. Blair is a very impressive lady,'* said Dr Mann, *'she may not necessarily be the best role model for women if the perception is that she rarely gets time to take any time out for herself.'* (BBC, 2000). England footballer Wayne Rooney was banned from coaching kids at a schools match because he was not considered a 'good role model' by the English Schools Football Association (*Manchester Evening News*, 2005).

These two examples illustrate the power of the role model and how the idea is used to attack the behaviour of people in the news. It is a common feature to put pressure on women to be less successful in their careers, and on young working-class men not to get above their presumed station in life.

What is aggression?

This is harder to define that you would think. Not least because what one person sees as being aggressive another person might see as a bit of a laugh. One definition is

'any behaviour directed toward another individual that is carried out with the proximate (immediate) intent to cause harm. In addition, the perpetrator must believe that the behaviour will harm the target and that the target is motivated to avoid the behaviour.' (Bushman and Anderson, 2001, page 274)

The important issue is *intention*. If you injure someone accidentally by tripping on the carpet and throwing a cup of coffee on them this would not be seen as aggressive. But if you stood in the middle of the room and deliberately threw it at them, this would be an aggressive act. The action is the same, the injury is the same but the intention is different.

Is aggression learnt?

Perhaps we are born with the potential to be peaceful and calm but learn how to be aggressive as we grow up. This is where the work of Bandura comes in.

Why road rage?

Is aggression a response to frustration?

Dollard, for example, made the assertion that *'the occurrence of aggressive behaviour always presupposes the existence of frustration'* and that the *'existence of frustration always leads to some form of aggression'* (Dollard *et al.*, 1939, page 8).

Is aggression an instinct?

A lot is made of research into animal aggression and one influential book was *On Aggression* by Konrad Lorenz (1966). He defined aggression as 'the fighting instinct in beast and man which is directed against members of the same species' (page ix).

Is aggression cathartic?

Catharsis is the cleansing effect of releasing intense, stored emotion. The term was used by Freud to describe the effect of releasing painful memories during therapy. It is suggested that being aggressive will release the tension and make someone less likely to engage in further violence.

The core study

This study looks at how aggressive behaviour develops in children. It is now over 40 years old but it still attracts a lot of attention and is still quoted in many texts. The study addresses two key questions, first, 'is aggression an innate feature of our behaviour or do we learn it?' Our answer to this question affects how we develop social policies to deal with aggressive behaviour. The second question, which follows on from the first, is 'if aggression is learnt then how is it learnt?'

Cherie Blair: bad role model or just too successful for some people's taste?

Oh Superman ...

In the popular imagination, role models inspire us to do more and achieve more, but is this always the case? What if you think you can't match up to the role model? It seems that Superman is too good a role model. Fans of the man from Krypton seem to compare themselves to the superhero, and realise they can't measure up. And as a result, they are less likely to help other people (Nelson and Norton, 2005).

In a study on decision-making, students were asked to list the characteristics of Superman, or alternatively superheroes in general, as part of a larger questionnaire. Later on the students were given the opportunity to volunteer for a fictitious community programme. Students who had been primed to think about Superman volunteered less often than those who had thought about other superheroes. One explanation for this is that thinking about someone exceptional makes you think about your own shortcomings and think about what you can't do rather than what you can.

Albert Bandura, Dorothea Ross and Sheila A. Ross (1961) Transmission of aggression through imitation of aggressive models. *Journal of Abnormal and Social Psychology*, 63 (3), 575–582.

Abstract

The aim of the study was to see if learning that took place in one situation would be generalised to other situations.

Method

The experiment sought to answer these questions by comparing the behaviour of three participant groups of 24 each, matched for aggressiveness:

1   Observed an aggressive model.

2   Observed a non-aggressive model.

3   No model.

Groups 1 and 2 were further split into four separate groups each: boys with male models, boys with female models, girls with male models and girls with female models.

Procedure

1. Modelling: Children watched a model playing with toys.

2. Aggression arousal: The children briefly played with attractive toys but then had to stop.

3. Delayed imitation: children observed playing with toys.

Results

The children who observed the aggressive model were more likely to exhibit the same specific acts of violence as shown by the model than the other two groups were, and also were generally more aggressive.

The boys were more affected by same-sex models than girls. Both boys and girls were more affected by the male models in terms of physical (but not verbal) aggressiveness.

Discussion

The results showed that children do imitate behaviour of models beyond the specific situation where the behaviour was viewed.

The aggressive models affected behaviour in two ways: they provided information about specific behaviours and also generally increased levels of aggression.

Male models appear to have a stronger influence possibly because aggression is a masculine-type behaviour and therefore boys and girls attend more readily to male models.

A Bobo doll is an inflatable doll about 5 feet tall. There is a weight in the bottom that makes it bob back up when you knock him down. If this experiment was repeated today they might use a Darth Vader doll.

COReSTUDY

Introduction

Previous studies have shown that children will imitate behaviours they observe someone else performing in the immediate setting – but will they repeat such behaviours in a new setting when the model is no longer present? This is a more crucial test of the principles of imitative learning (or social learning theory).

Research predictions

1   Observing an aggressive model will lead a subject to reproduce *aggressive acts* similar to their models, whereas this will not be true of subjects who observed non-aggressive models or who observed no model.

2   Observing an aggressive model will lead a subject to behave in a *generally more aggressive manner*, whereas those who observed a non-aggressive model would be inhibited from behaving aggressively.

3   Subjects will imitate the behaviour of a *same-sex model* to a greater degree than a model of the opposite sex.

4   Boys will be more likely than girls to imitate aggressive behaviour because it is a highly masculine activity.

Method

Participants

The participants were children from a university nursery school (Stanford in California), 36 boys and 36 girls aged between 37 and 69 months (approximately 3 to 5 years). The mean age was 52 months (about 4½ years).

There were two adult 'models', a male and a female, plus a female experimenter.

Procedure

There were two experimental groups and one control group:

Group 1: observed an aggressive model.

Group 2: observed a non-aggressive (and subdued) model.

Control group: no exposure to any model.

Each of the experimental groups was subdivided into four groups: boys watching same-sex model, boys watching opposite sex model, and the same for the two girl groups (making a total of 8 experimental groups each with 6 subjects). There were 24 children in the control group.

This means that there were 3 IVs in this study: the behaviour of the model, the sex of the subject, and whether the model was male or female.

Aggressiveness

In order to ensure that each group contained equally aggressive children (and thus control this potential *extraneous variable*), ratings were done of the children beforehand by an experimenter who knew the children well and one of the children's teachers.

On the basis of these ratings the subjects were arranged in triplets and assigned at random to one of the three groups.

Phase 1: modelling

Each child was taken individually by the experimenter to an experimental room in the main nursery building and the 'model' was invited to join them. The experimenter seated the child at a small table in one corner of the room and encouraged the child to design a picture using stickers and potato prints. Once the child was settled, the experimenter escorted the model to the opposite corner which contained a small table, chair, tinker toy set, a mallet and the Bobo doll. The experimenter then left the room.

1 *Non-aggressive condition:* The model assembled the tinker toys in a subdued manner and ignored the Bobo doll.

2 *Aggressive condition:* The model spent the first minute playing quietly but then turned to the Bobo doll and spent the rest of the time being aggressive towards it. This included specific acts which might later be imitated, namely laying the doll on its side, sitting on it and repeatedly punching it on the nose. Then picking the doll up and striking it on the head with the mallet, throwing the doll in the air and kicking it about the room. This was done three times accompanied by various comments such as 'Hit him down', 'Pow' and 'He keeps coming back for more'.

3 *Control:* The report does not say what treatment these children received.

The experimenter re-entered the room after 10 minutes and informed the subject that it was time to go to another game room.

Phase 2: aggression arousal

Before testing the children's imitation of the models it was necessary to mildly provoke them. This was done partly because observing aggressive behaviour may reduce the probability of behaving aggressively, making it *less* likely that those observing the aggressive model would behave aggressively. It was also done because the children who watched the non-aggressive model might be inhibited from behaving aggressively because of what they observed.

The children were taken to an anteroom in another building that contained some attractive toys (e.g. fire engine, jet fighter plane, colourful spinning top, complete doll set with a wardrobe, and baby crib). The subject was allowed to play with the toys but, after about two minutes the experimenter said that she had decided to reserve the toys for the other children. The experimenter and child then moved to the adjoining experimental room.

Phase 3: test for delayed imitation

This room contained a variety of toys:

*   'Aggressive' toys, that could be used to express aggression, including a mallet, dart gun, tether ball with a face painted on it hung from the ceiling, and a 3-foot Bobo doll.
*   Non-aggressive toys including a tea set, crayons and paper, a ball, dolls, cars and plastic animals.

The experimenter sat quietly in the corner working while the child played for 20 minutes. The child was observed through a one-way mirror by the male model and, some of the time, by another observer. The observers did not know which condition the child had participated in (except if the child had been in one of the sessions with the male model).

The observers recorded what the child was doing every 5 seconds (provides 240 observations). Responses were recorded in the following categories and provided an 'aggression score':

1 Imitative aggression responses
*   *Physical:* Any specific acts which were imitated.
*   *Verbal aggression:* Any phrases which were imitated, such as 'Pow'.
*   *Non-aggressive verbal responses:* Such as saying 'He keeps coming back for more'.

2 Partially imitative responses
*   *Mallet aggression:* uses mallet on toys other than Bobo.
*   *Sits on Bobo doll* but doesn't behave aggressively.

3 Non-imitative aggressive responses
*   *Punches Bobo doll:* strikes, slaps, pushes the doll.
*   *Non-imitative physical and verbal aggression:* aggressive acts directed at toys other than Bobo, saying hostile things not said by the model.
*   *Aggressive gun play.*

A female model kicking Bobo around the room. When Bandura et al. refer to a 'model' they don't mean a fashion model – the term 'model' is used in social learning theory to refer to anyone who is imitated.

Qs

1 Would you anticipate that there would be individual differences in the way people respond to aggressive models? Why or why not?

2 Why is it necessary to have two experimental conditions as well as the control?

3 In what way is this study an experiment?

4 What is the dependent variable (DV)?

5 In assessing aggressiveness, why is 'inter-rater agreement' important?

6 An extraneous variable is a factor that may affect the dependent variable and therefore spoil the experiment (which is why it was controlled). In what way could aggressiveness be an extraneous variable?

7 What kind of design is used in this study (independent, repeated or matched)?

8 What aspects of this experiment might be harmful to a child?

9 What problem(s) might arise from using the male model as the observer? Could he be biased, and if so, in what way?

10 Besides the Bobo doll and the mallet, name a few other toys in the room. Why were they selected?

11 Why was it important that the children were taken to a very different setting for the 'aggression arousal'?

12 Why was it important that the toys were in the same position for every child?

Results

In brief, children imitated the models they saw both in terms of specific acts and in general levels of their behaviour.

Complete imitation Children in the aggressive condition imitated many of the models' physical and verbal behaviours, both aggressive and non-aggressive behaviours – in fact about 1/3 of their imitations were of *non-aggressive* verbal behaviour. In contrast, children in the non-aggressive condition displayed very few of these behaviours; 70% of them had zero scores.

Partial imitation There were differences for partial imitation in the same direction as those found for complete imitation.

Non-imitative aggression The aggressive group displayed more non-imitative aggression than the non-aggressive group, though the difference was small.

Non-aggressive behaviour Children in the non-aggression condition spent more time playing non-aggressively with dolls than children in the other groups.

Gender effects

Same-sex imitation There was some evidence of a 'same-sex effect' for boys but not for girls. The male models had a greater influence in general than the female models.

Gender Boys imitated more physical aggression than girls but the groups didn't differ in terms of verbal aggression.

Was the little girl imitating the model's act of kicking the doll (see previous page)? Or was this behaviour due to demand characteristics – an inflatable doll kind of 'invites' being kicked or punched?

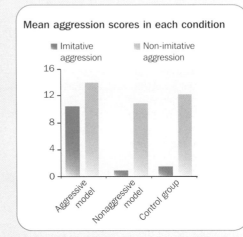

Mean aggression scores in each condition

The graph summarises some of the results, showing that in all conditions children behaved aggressively but children only displayed imitative aggression (physical and verbal) when the model was aggressive.

Discussion

This study shows that people will produce new behaviours that they have observed and generalise these behaviours to other situations. This extends the scope of the principle of *operant conditioning*. According to the principles of operant conditioning we learn through reward and punishment – but this will only work if you produce a particular behaviour. Imitative learning permits a new behaviour to be acquired which may then be rewarded or punished.

The greater influence of the male models might be explained in terms of the fact that physical aggression is a male-type behaviour. Both girls and boys were not surprised by the male model's behaviour, in fact they were quite impressed (saying things like 'Al's a good socker, he beat up Bobo'). Whereas they were surprised by the female models ('That's not the way for a lady to behave.') Thus they may have been more ready to imitate the appropriate behaviour and more prone to ignore the inappropriate behaviour. Imitations were of physical rather than verbal behaviour because that is highly masculine-type behaviour.

It is possible to explain imitative learning in terms of Freud's 'Identification with aggressor' (Freud, 1946). According to this, one deals with aggressive behaviour by adopting the attributes of the threatening person to allay anxiety. This is the process of identification. However, this study suggests that identification may not be necessary for imitative learning to take place because the children imitated the models regardless of the quality of the relationship.

Re-analysis of data from this study

It is interesting to examine the original data more carefully. We have included this data on our website (www.a-levelpsychology. co.uk/ocr/ascorestudies). For example you might note that the children with the aggressive model were sometimes less aggressive than the children with the non-aggressive model. How would you explain that? There were also occasions when boys were more aggressive with a female model rather than the male model.

Qs

1 Why was it necessary for the model to display such extreme and specific acts of violence towards Bobo?

2 Why do you think the acts were repeated three times?

3 Identify three conclusions that can be drawn from the results.

4 This research was conducted a long time ago. Do you think children would behave the same today? Why or why not?

5 What suggestion do Bandura *et al.* offer as to why boys and girls are more likely to imitate the male model in terms of physical aggression?

EVALUATING THE STUDY BY BANDURA, ROSS AND ROSS

The research method

This study was a lab experiment. *What are the strengths and limitations of this research method in the context of this study?*

The sample

The subjects were young children from one middle-class US nursery school. *How much can you generalise the findings to people in general?*

Nature or nurture?

Is aggression biological or learned? Are we born as an aggressive person or do we learn to behave in that way?

Ethical issues

Some issues to consider: witnessing aggressive behaviour (and learning it), mild provocation and covert observation. *Do you think that this study was ethically acceptable?*

Ecological validity

This study involved aggressive behaviour towards a doll. *To what extent is this study representative of real life?*

This study looked at short-term effects. *To what extent can we generalise the findings from this study to other situations?*

Applications/usefulness

How might you use the findings from this study, for example in understanding the effects of media violence on children and adults?

What next? ?

Describe **one** change to this study, and say how you think this might affect the outcome.

DEBATE

'Aggression is in your genes'. Divide your class into groups and let each group decide whether it wishes to argue for or against the statement. Each group should do some research to provide some convincing arguments.

Multiple choice questions

1. What age children were used in this experiment?
   (a) Nursery school.
   (b) Primary school.
   (c) Secondary school.
   (d) A mixture of all three.

2. Which of the following was not one of the research predictions?
   (a) Children will imitate specific acts performed by an aggressive model.
   (b) Children who observe an aggressive model will become generally more aggressive.
   (c) Boys will be more aggressive than girls.
   (d) Boys will be more likely to imitate a same-sex role model than girls.

3. The IV in this experiment was
   (a) Sex of the child.
   (b) Aggressiveness of the model.
   (c) Sex of the model.
   (d) All of the above.

4. Which experimental design was used in this study?
   (a) Single participant.
   (b) Independent groups.
   (c) Repeat measures.
   (d) Matched participants.

5. Which of the following was an ethical issue in this study?
   (a) Deception.
   (b) Right to withdraw.
   (c) Psychological harm.
   (d) All of the above.

6. In the anteroom the children were
   (a) Not allowed to play with the toys.
   (b) Allowed to play with the toys but stopped after 2 minutes.
   (c) Watched while they played with the toys as long as they liked.
   (d) Shown a film.

7. The non-aggressive model was
   (a) Happy   (b) Joking
   (c) Silent   (d) Subdued

8. Observations were made every
   (a) 5 seconds.   (b) 5 minutes.
   (c) 10 seconds.   (d) 10 minutes

9. One of the categories of behaviour that was observed was 'sits on Bobo doll'. Which category did this come in?
   (a) Imitative aggressive responses.
   (b) Partially imitative responses.
   (c) Non-imitative aggressive responses.
   (d) Non-imitative responses.

10. Which of the following is not true?
    (a) Boys imitated more physical aggression than girls.
    (b) Boys imitated more verbal aggression than girls.
    (c) Boys behaved more aggressively than girls.
    (d) Boys were less likely to imitate female models than male models.

Answers are on page 79.

Exam questions

1 The study by Bandura, Ross and Ross is sometimes used as evidence in the argument about the effects of television violence on children. Give **two** differences between the way the children witnessed the violence in the experiment and the way children witness violence on television. [OCR AS Psy, June 1995, paper 1]   [4]

2 The study by Bandura, Ross and Ross into imitation used a number of experimental controls. Identify **two** variables that the researchers controlled for, and for each variable say what they did to achieve that control. [OCR AS Psy, June 1998, paper 1]   [4]

3 (a) In stage two of the Bandura, Ross and Ross study on aggression, outline how the children were subjected to mild arousal of aggression.   [2]

   (b) Why was this necessary?   [2]
   [OCR AS Psy, May 2002, paper 1]

4 From the study on aggression by Bandura, Ross and Ross:

   (a) Identify **two** pf the categories of aggression that were measured.   [2]

   (b) Outline the finding of **one** of these categories.   [2]
   [OCR AS Psy, May 2004, paper 1]

Still kicking ass

Video games

Does watching and taking part in video games make children more aggressive? The video game industry would have you believe that there is no link between video violence and real-life violence. For example, Sacher (1993) reviewed research in this area and found that seven studies did link video games to aggressive behaviour but 19 studies found no link.

A different argument is put forward by ex-US army officer and psychologist David Grossman (1995). He suggests that playing violent video games will *desensitise* people and make them emotionally disengaged from violence. Grossman points out how difficult it is to get soldiers to fire guns. The history of warfare shows that fewer than one-fifth of soldiers fire their guns at another human being. To counteract this and improve their 'kill rate' the US army used psychological techniques to train shooting response in their soldiers. Part of the training uses video combat simulations. The 'kill rate' had been increased to 90% by the time of the American War in Vietnam.

Today the US army has made its own video game, 'America's Army', that you can download for free. In the game, you get to kill people with cool weapons that look and respond like the real things. You get to ambush terrorists and, when caught in a firefight, you can hear bullets whistle past your ears. The game has been downloaded more than 16 million times since the original version was launched in 2002.

For a different point of view there is 'Special Force' produced by the Islamic group Hezbollah in which you can be a Palestinian fighter attacking Israeli soldiers and settlers (Ryan, 2004).

Observing violence at home

All children with a TV observe aggressive behaviour every day on the screen. Most, however, do not see real-life aggression. One exception to this is children who witness, or are victims of, domestic violence.

In the UK it is estimated that 13% of women and 9% of men experience domestic violence (abuse, threats or force) in the course of any one year (British Crime Survey, 2004). Of the people who experience domestic violence women are much more likely to receive a serious injury than men (6% women, 1% men) and experience far more incidents on average than men (women 20, men 7). No other crime has such a high repeat victimisation rate.

Violence is a family affair. For every parent experiencing domestic violence there will often be children who are also suffering. It

is estimated that in 90% of incidents involving domestic violence, the children are in the same or the next room (Hughes, 1992). During violent assaults on a parent children might well intervene to protect the parent or their brothers and sisters.

Effect on children

The jury is out on the effect on children of observing domestic violence. Some children show a range of responses such as poor school performance, aggression to peers, and rebelling against adults. Some children don't show any negative effects at all and may even show signs of improvement such as better school work. There is no clear pattern of response to observing domestic violence (Women's Aid, 2002).

Violence on terrestrial television

An analysis of two weeks' prime-time viewing on UK terrestrial television looked at the levels of violence in a range of programmes (BSC, 2002). It found an increasing trend towards violence in programmes compared with previous years.

The study found that on average there were 5.2 acts of violence per hour in 2001 whereas in 1997 the figure was 4.1 acts per hour. The programmes containing the most violence were films (8.4 scenes per hour), the news (8.3 scenes per hour), and drama (6.6 scenes per hour). There is a common belief that programmes before the watershed (9pm) are less violent that those after it. Although this used to be the case it is no longer true and in 2001 there were more scenes of violence before the watershed than after it.

The most common context for violent scenes was crime and police action which accounted for 31% of all violent scenes. And the most common reason for violence was shown as anger or frustration (16% of scenes). Although 83% of the programmes were made in the UK, the programmes from the USA accounted for 35% of the violent scenes. The analysis also found that there is a growing trend to show violence in a realistic way. In the two weeks of prime-time programmes there were 335 deaths of which 35% were shown as murders. Over half of the deaths occurred as the result of gunshots.

In brief, the average viewer in the UK watches a regular diet of violence and murder. Two questions come from this: first, does this violent wallpaper have an effect on levels of violence in our communities, and second, why is watching violence an essential part of our daily entertainment?

LINKS TO OTHER STUDIES

This study gives an explanation of how our social behaviour develops and so links to social psychology studies such as **Haney, Banks and Zimbardo** and **Piliavin, Rodin** and **Piliavin**.

The study extends the theory of behaviourism (see page 35) and so links to the studies that use behaviourist methods such as **Gardner and Gardner** (Washoe).

The sophisticated method used has a tight experimental design and uses observational techniques to collect the data. Observation is also used in **Rosenhan**'s study.

key**ISSUE**

Nature and nurture

KEY TERMS

Nature Those characteristics determined by your genes. These may be present at birth or appear later as you mature.

Nurture The view that everything is acquired through interactions with the environment – the physical and social world. May be more widely referred to as 'experience'.

The nature–nurture debate looks at the relative importance of genetics (nature) over experience (nurture) in the development of behaviour. It is often thought to be a relatively recent discussion starting with Francis Galton at the end of the nineteenth century (Fancher, 1996) but it is possible to find much earlier references to it. For example, in *The Tempest* written by William Shakespeare, Prospero refers to Caliban as: *'A devil, a born devil, on whose nature Nurture can never stick'*.

Nature AND nurture

The extreme positions of believing a behaviour is completely due to genetics or completely due to experience are impossible to support. Without our bodies there can be no behaviour so genetics clearly has an effect and without being cared for as an infant we will not survive so nurture is also essential.

The nature–nurture debate sometimes looks at behaviours we all share (universals), and sometimes it looks at the differences between individuals. If you think of a complex behaviour like *language* then it seems to be a cultural universal. All known societies have some form of language. It is not unreasonable to argue that we have a genetic predisposition to develop language and, in fact, it is possible to identify key language areas in the brain. Although all people can learn language we can't always understand each other because everyone learns their own language. So nurture has a clear effect on our language but can only work if the genetic structures are present in the first place.

It is possible to go a step further and look at why some people are good with language and some are poor. The debate then centres on whether these differences are due to genetic variation or early experience.

ACTIVITY

Write a list of the behaviours and characteristics that you think you inherited.

To what extent do you think that any of these have been affected by your experiences?

David Beckham and son. *If you believe that ability is inherited then place your bets now that the boy will play for England or sing in a band.*

Exam-style question

To what extent is behaviour inherited (nature) or learned (nurture)? The nature–nurture debate is concerned with this question.

Using **four** Core Studies:

(a) Describe what each study tells us about how behaviour is learned or inherited.   [12]

(b) Briefly discuss **two** advantages and **two** disadvantages of conducting research on the nature–nurture debate, using examples from these studies.   [12]

Doing research on nature–nurture

Infant studies We might presume that the behaviour of an infant demonstrates what people can do innately.

Twin and family studies. An obvious way to make comparisons between nature and nurture is to look at identical and non-identical twins. Any differences in behaviour between identical twins must be due to environment. There are cases of twins brought up in different homes. In this instance any *similarities* are presumed to be due to nature.

Adopted children can be compared to their biological parents (to see the influence of nature) or their adoptive families (to see the influence of nurture).

Gene-mapping studies investigate the effects of specific genes on behaviour.

Difficulties of nature–nurture research

- Even in the womb nurture affects development.

- Children and parents who do not live together nevertheless often share similar environments.

- Identical twins aren't completely identical. From birth we each affect the people around us and the experiences we have, creating a microenvironment that influences us.

- It is very controversial.

- Most behaviours are not caused by a single gene, and the expression of genes depends on environmental factors (nature and nurture).

Let's have a heated debate

Although people don't commonly use the terms nature and nurture in everyday speech they use the concepts in a whole range of conversations. For example, think about the arguments on why some young people engage in violence or substance abuse. Are young people bound to behave violently or self-destructively because of their genetics or how they were brought up? Are people born to be aggressive and selfish and is that why we have the economic system we have? Why are some people more successful at cognitive tests than others?

It doesn't take a rocket scientist to recognise that the answers to these questions are very political. They will shape social policy and affect the lives of all of us. At its most extreme, people have argued that if, for example, the differences in IQ performance are due to genetics then we should encourage people with high IQs to have more children and people with low IQs to have less (see the study by Gould, page 174).

Attachment and social development

Attachment

John Bowlby and James Robertson described a syndrome of distress that children go through when they are separated from their parents. First they *protest*, then they show *despair* and finally they become emotionally *detached* (called the PDD cycle).

Make a list of other events, besides separation, that might bring about this syndrome of distress.

The term 'attachment' refers to a strong emotional bond between two people. In developmental psychology, the term attachment is often taken to mean the emotional tie between a child and its adult caregiver. It is a popular belief in this culture that the emotional experiences we have in our early years will have a critical effect on our adult behaviour and experience. This belief has been supported by Freud and also by John Bowlby.

John Bowlby

The social disruption caused by the Second World War (1939–45) created thousands of orphans across the world and prompted concern about the effects of bringing up children in institutions. In 1951, Bowlby produced a report for the World Health Organisation (WHO) in which he suggested that:

'mother love in infancy and childhood is as important for mental health as are vitamins and proteins for physical health'. (see Bowlby, 1953, page 240).

In the WHO report Bowlby put forward the concept of 'maternal deprivation' which occurs when a child does not receive a *'warm, intimate and continuous relationship with his mother'*. Although many children might experience mild deprivation, Bowlby was most concerned with those who experience severe deprivation. He argued that research from orphanages and hospitals showed that this deprivation will have a dramatic and lifelong effect on the child's emotional health and ability to form relationships. Bowlby claimed that such effects would occur when a child under three was deprived of its mother (or permanent mother substitute) for frequent or prolonged periods *if* there was not adequate substitute care.

Mothers

The clear implication of Bowlby's account is that mothers are a crucial part of a child's development and that many problems of later life can be traced back to inadequate mothering. One effect of this was to change the way that judges awarded custody in divorce cases. Until this time custody was often given to fathers but now the importance of the mother and 'mothering' was recognised.

Fathers

There is no reason why a father can't assume the role of 'permanent mother substitute'. *Mothering* is a collection of activities that can be carried out by anyone. There is some evidence that women are biologically more suited to this role, for example one study found that fathers were less sensitive to infant cues than mothers (Heerman *et al.*, 1994). However, in a classic study on attachment in the 1960s Schaffer and Emerson (1964) found that fathers were often a child's primary attachment figure.

Impact

Although Bowlby's work has been challenged over the years there is an acknowledgement that it led to a change in the way that children are cared for in institutions and helped to raise the standards of child care in this country (Tizard, 1986).

Severe childhood deprivation

There are a few famous case studies of children brought up in conditions so bad that their survival must have been threatened. If they can recover from their experiences it shows that early experiences may be important but children can be resilient; if they cannot recover it suggests there is a critical period for emotional development and that, after that time, full recovery is not possible.

These cases attract a lot of popular attention and they remain both fascinating and controversial. We have referred to Victor, another of these famous cases, in the material on autism (page 21).

Koluchová and the twin boys

One of the most detailed case studies was described by Jarmila Koluchová (1976, 1991) and concerns twin boys born in central Europe in 1960. Their mother died shortly after birth and they were fostered for the first 18 months of their life during which time they developed normally.

When their father remarried and took over the care of the boys his new wife was excessively cruel to them and kept them in a cellar for the next five and a half years. When they were discovered at age 7 the boys were small for their age, couldn't speak, had rickets and could not understand pictures.

The medical staff who examined the boys predicted that the boys would be permanently disabled both physically and mentally. They were sent to a school for the severely disabled but were then adopted by two exceptionally dedicated women. They made remarkable progress over a number of years and caught up with their peers intellectually and emotionally. Both were drafted for national service and later married and had children. They are said to be entirely stable and enjoy warm relationships (Clarke and Clarke, 1998).

The twin boys show that severe emotional deprivation can be overcome but, sadly, they are not a typical case. One reason may be that they had each other – and provided each other with some 'mothering'.

HODGES AND TIZARD : SOCIAL RELATIONSHIPS

Do babies from different cultures behave differently?

Brazelton *et al.* (1976) studied the behavioural differences between a group of urban Zambian newborns, and urban American newborns. They made extensive structured observations of 10 newborn babies from each culture. The babies were measured in a variety of ways on the first, fifth and tenth days of their lives. On day one the Zambian infants scored lower on a number of measures, mostly to do with alertness and activity. The researchers put this down to the relatively stressed intra-uterine environment of the Zambian babies, resulting in early dehydration and an overall lack of energy. By the tenth day, however, the Zambian group had started to score more highly than the US group on measurements of social interaction (for example, social interest and alertness).

The reason for this turnaround might be to do with the differences between the environments of the two groups of children. Due to the good health and diet of their mothers the US infants had a good physiological conditions in the womb but after birth they experienced a 'relatively nonstimulating environment' (page 106). The US babies were less likely to be handled than the Zambian infants and their mothers followed the 'cultural emphasis in the United States on quieting the infant and protecting him from external stimulation' (page 106). In contrast, the Zambian infants improved as they began to be rehydrated and to receive nutrition by feeding from their mother. The increased social responsiveness of the Zambian babies may have been influenced by the more active, contact-oriented, stimulating child-rearing practices of the Zambian women.

What this study again shows us is that healthy emotional and social development depends not only on the presence of a 'mother' but also the responsiveness of that mother. The study also should warn us that European studies of attachment may not apply equally in other cultures where child-rearing practices are quite different.

Genie

Another example of severe deprivation is the well-reported case from the USA of a girl called Genie who had been kept in a back room strapped to a chair until she reached her teens (Rymer, 1993). Sadly Genie's suffering did not come to an end when she was discovered, but continued at the hands of the scientific community. After her discovery researchers struggled for access to the disturbed child and some were given the task of fostering her in order to help her development and also to facilitate the scientific observation. Distressingly, when the research money ran out, the fostering ended, and Genie then experienced a number of poor foster placements where she was again abused and regressed to her non-communicative condition. Later, her mother was able to take more responsibility for her and sued the psychologists for excessive experimentation on the child.

Genie never recovered from her early deprivation; she lacked social responsiveness and was never able to use language fully. It is difficult to draw firm conclusions from this case because we cannot be sure that she was not mentally retarded from birth. Brain scans showed that her brain was not normal, but this may be either a cause or an effect of her retarded development.

 Read more about these and other case histories at http://kccesl.tripod.com/genie.html or http://www.feralchildren.com/en/children.php?tp=2

What is love?

And how do we develop our bonds of affection? Freud argued that cupboard love (affection for the one who provides the food) was the beginnings of the mother–child love but comparative psychologist Harry Harlow (1959) suggested a different explanation.

A monkey clings to a cloth-covered wire 'mother'.

Harlow was studying learning using rhesus monkeys as his subjects and for health reasons, he raised them in isolation in sterile cages. He observed that the monkeys became quite attached to the gauze nappy pads that were placed on the floor of their cages. They showed some distress when the pads were removed once a day for cleaning; their attachment seemed similar to a human baby's attachment to a teddy or a blanket. Harlow used this observation as a starting point for experiments on the importance of body contact in the development of attachment.

Harlow made two models to act as *surrogate mothers*. One was a bare wire frame with a wooden head and a crude face. The other model had a covering of terry cloth over the frame and a more monkey-like face. Harlow placed eight newborn monkeys in individual cages with equal access to both 'surrogate mothers'. Four of the infants received their milk from the cloth model and four from the wire model. The milk was provided via a nursing bottle with a nipple protruding through the frame. The baby monkeys thrived whether they got food from the cloth or the wire model. However, regardless of which model provided food, all the monkeys spent more time clinging to the cloth model, to which they appeared to have developed an attachment.

Harlow believed he had found the crucial factor in the development of attachment: body contact, and he proudly presented his results in to the American Psychological Association (Slater, 2005).

Unfortunately the story does not end there because when the monkeys matured they showed some very strange behaviours. They engaged in repetitive behaviour patterns such as clutching themselves and rocking constantly back and forth and they exhibited excessive and misdirected aggression. Most dramatically, they were unable to interact with their peers and were unable to have sex. Clearly, the contact comfort of the cloth mother was not enough for healthy psychological development. Healthy development requires a *reciprocal* attachment relationship – more than an unresponsive though cuddly wire mother.

The core study

One of the questions which developmental psychologists have studied is whether or not there is a **critical period** in the first stages of human development, and, if there is, how long it extends after birth. This study looks at children who spent the first two years of their lives in institutional care, before being either adopted or returned to their biological parents. A comparison of these children with a matched group who had been with their families throughout their lives may help our understanding of the critical period issue.

Jill Hodges and Barbara Tizard (1989) Social and family relationships of ex-institutional adolescents. *Journal of Child Psychology and Psychiatry*, 30 (1), 77–97.

Abstract

The aim of the study was to see if early disruption of attachments had long-term effects on social and family relationships.

The participants in the study were 65 children who had spent their early years in a children's institution. They were less than four months when they arrived and left sometime after their second birthday.

There were two groups: 'adopted' and 'restored' (went back to their families).

The children were assessed at 4, 8 and 16 years, and their families, peers and teachers were also interviewed.

Family relationships

The institutional children appeared not to have any consistent relationships before age 4. When assessed at 8 and 16 more of the adopted children were attached to their mothers than the restored children; by 16 none of the institutional children had any attachments. Restored children had greatest problems with siblings.

This suggests that early emotional privation does not necessarily lead to a later inability to form close attachments – it may depend on the degree to which later attachments are encouraged or discouraged.

Peer relationships

There were no significant differences between the restored and adopted children but there were significant differences between the ex-institutional children and matched comparisons in terms of peer relationships. This was supported by scores on the Rutter 'B' scale and teacher reports of bullying. Those who were more closely attached to mothers at age 8 had better peer relationships.

This suggests that early privation does have long-term effects on social relationships when the other person isn't going to work at the relationship (a transactional explanation).

There are other possible explanations, for example ex-institutional children lag behind their peers in emotional development.

ACTIVITY

Some people have suggested that day care may have similar harmful effects to those caused by institutionalisation. Do some research on day care yourself. A useful website to try: www.whyfiles.org/087mothers/5.html (have a look at some of the related websites too).

Method

Participants

The participants were 65 children who had been placed in institutional care in London when they were less than four months old.

These participants were selected because, before the age of four months, they would not yet have formed attachments. It was unlikely that they would subsequently form attachments, while in the institution, because there was an explicit policy in the institution against the 'caretakers' forming attachments with the children and there was also a high turnover of staff. By the age of four the children had had an average of 50 different caretakers for at least a week. This meant that the children had little opportunity to form a close, continuous relationship with an adult.

All of the children remained in the institution until they were at least two years of age. After that time some children left the institution. These 'ex-*institutional*' children were either returned to their natural families or were adopted. They were called the 'restored group' or the 'adopted group' respectively.

Follow-up study at age 4 and 8

The children were assessed regularly throughout their childhood. This study was a longitudinal study because the children were assessed at various times during their development.

At age 4 all 65 children were still involved; 15 had been returned to their natural homes ('restored'), 24 had been adopted, and 26 remained in the institution.

CORE STUDY

Aims

Previous research (as reviewed on the last spread) found that children who experienced early institutional care and experienced a lack of early attachments later appeared to be incapable of forming deep human relationships.

The aim of this study was to follow a group of children through their childhood and early adolescence to observe the effects of such experiences on family and non-family social relationships.

Another study also by Hodges and Tizard (1989a) focused on the behavioural and intellectual development of this group of children.

At age 8, only 51 children remained in the study. The others could not be contacted or declined to take part. There was a home-reared comparison group.

Follow-up up study at age 16

The main focus of this study was on the children at age 16. At this time there were 39 participants remaining: 13 in the restored group, 23 in the adopted group and 5 left in institutional care. Only the restored and adopted children were studied, as well as two new comparison or *control* groups:

- *Control 1:* 16-year-olds matched with the ex-institutional children on sex, position in family, being in a one- or two-parent family, and occupation of main breadwinner.

- *Control 2:* Same-sex friend of each ex-institutional child.

Collection of data

Data were collected in various ways:

- Interviews with the adolescent.

- Interviews with mothers (sometimes with father present).

- Questionnaire asking about 'social difficulties'.

- Questionnaire given to the adolescents' school teachers asking about their relationships with their peers and teachers.

- The Rutter 'B' scale which provided information about their mental health.

Institutional care refers to places set up to specifically care for children or elderly people. It is not the same as a nursery school or hospital care. Today, in Britain, there are few child institutions or orphanages like this but that was not the case in the 1950s and 1960s when this study took place. The work by psychologists such as John Bowlby contributed to their disappearance because it showed the devastating long-term consequences of such care for social and emotional development.

What research method was used in this study?

The study used a **longitudinal approach** – the children were studied over a number of years (see page 69 for a discussion of this). The study can also be described as a **natural experiment** because use was made of naturally occurring IVs rather than IVs manipulated by an experimenter.

Biographical notes on Jill Hodges and Barbara Tizard

Jill Hodges is Consultant Child and Adolescent Psychotherapist at the Great Ormond Street Hospital for Sick Children and Senior Research Fellow at the Anna Freud Centre. Besides clinical work she is currently working on another longitudinal research study of adopted children who were removed from severe abuse or neglect before being placed for adoption.

'I enjoyed the research interviews, and the extraordinarily wide range of children and of parents who shared such a lot about their family lives. Later, I did a clinical training as a child psychotherapist, and have always felt grateful that I'd had that background of learning so much about so many "ordinary", generally unproblematic children and families. In addition I greatly admired Jack Tizard's and Barbara Tizard's work, and this was an opportunity to work with them and in a very lively research unit.' (Jill Hodges, personal communication, 2005).

Barbara Tizard is Emeritus Professor at the Thomas Coram Research Unit, University of London.

What did you learn from the study? *'We learnt that even good quality institutional care had some adverse effects on about half the children, at least until the age of 16. Those children who were adopted were less likely to have problems, probably because the others, including those who had returned initially to their parents, tended to come in and out of care, or to move from one foster home or institution to another. This suggests that children do best in families, whether natural or adoptive, where they had really been wanted, and where they had a stable upbringing.'* (Barbara Tizard, personal communication, 2005).

Barbara Tizard

Results: family relationships

A large number of results were reported in the journal article, only some of which are highlighted here and on the next spread.

Early attachments

An early study of the children (before age four) found that 70% were described as not able 'to care deeply about anyone', i.e. had not developed attachments to anyone.

Attachment to parents

All of the ex-institutional children were less closely attached than the home-reared comparison group. More of the adopted children were attached to their mothers than the restored children at age 8 to 16. Hodges and Tizard explain this:

Adopted group: The majority of these children went to families who very much wanted a child and put a lot of time and energy into building up a relationship.

Restored group: Their parents were often ambivalent about having their child back, and had other children and material difficulties which competed for their attention. At age 8 and 16 they showed less affection for their parents than any other group, and their parents also found difficulty showing affection to them.

Relations with siblings

The restored group got on particularly poorly with their siblings at both age 8 and 16 (as reported by the children themselves and their mothers). This was less true for the adopted group.

Taken as a whole the ex-institutional children had more difficulties with siblings than the matched comparison group.

Discussion: family relationships

We can conclude that most, if not all, of these children had experienced early emotional privation (a lack of attachment rather than a loss of attachment).

The later results (at age 8 and 16) suggest that recovery is possible, whereas Bowlby predicted that recovery from such deprivation/privation was difficult. This study suggests that the effects of deprivation/privation occur mainly when a child remains in an emotionally deprived environment.

Qs

1. The original sample was reduced in subsequent follow-ups. This is called attrition and is a problem in longitudinal studies because particular kinds of participants are likely to be the ones who 'drop out'. Suggest the likely characteristics of those who drop out.

2. Why might some children be chosen for adoption rather than others?

3. How might this affect (or have affected) the outcome of this study?

4. It was found that the children who were more attached to their mothers at age 8 were more likely to have close peer relationships. How would you explain this relationship?

5. Why might it be likely that the adopted children would form closer attachments with their parents than the restored children?

6. In the follow-up study at age 16 there were two experimental groups and two control groups. What were they?

7. This study is a natural experiment. At the final follow-up, at 16 years, what was the naturally occurring independent variable?

8. Name at least three of the dependent variables.

Results: peer relationships

Differences between restored and adopted children

There were no significant differences between the restored and adopted children in terms of peer relationships according to themselves, their mothers and their teachers.

Differences between ex-institutional and comparison children

There were significant differences between the ex-institutional children and their matched comparisons, for example:

- Overall the teachers rated the ex-institutional children as less popular than average with peers, i.e. had fewer friends – though there were more ex-institutional children than matched comparisons who were more popular than average.

- Teachers also rated the ex-institutional children as more quarrelsome, less often liked by other children and more likely to bully.

- Scores on the Rutter 'B' scale indicated that the ex-institutional children had greater peer difficulties.

- Mothers and adolescents reported ex-institutional adolescents were less likely to have a close friend.

Peer and family relationships

Those ex-institutional children who were closely attached to their mothers at age 8 had better peer relationships at 16 than those who had not been attached at age 8 (according to the adolescents' own ratings).

Discussion

Here the picture is quite different than outlined in the discussion on page 65. There were major differences between the ex-institutional group and their comparisons, rather than differences within the ex-institutional group (i.e. between the restored and adopted children). This suggests, in contrast, that early attachment *does* have a special importance in social development.

The findings at age 16 suggest that early privation had a negative effect on the ability to form relationships when the relationship involved someone who wasn't going to work hard at it, i.e. in peer relationships and relationships with restored parents. This has been called a *transactional explanation*, one that emphasises interactions between people.

The fact that ex-institutional children who were closely attached to their mothers at age 8 had better peer relationships at 16 suggests that successful peer relationships depend on successful family relationships (attachments).

What other explanations are possible?

Hodges and Tizard suggest that the findings, at age 16, might be explained in other ways. For example, it could be that the adopted children suffered from poor self-esteem

Gross (2003) reports that attrition may not be an issue in this study. He quotes Hodges and Tizard: *'the data do not suggest a systematic loss of children who, as eight-year-olds, presented fewer or more problems at home than those who remained and were studied at home.'*

Can attachments be formed at any age? Bowlby suggested that this would not be possible after the age of five and difficult after the age of three years – yet some of the children in this study formed attachments later in childhood.

Do you think that lack of attachments does or does not have an effect on the development of social relationships?

Qs Is there an 'ex-institutional syndrome'?

The results suggest that, as a group, the ex-institutional adolescents show a pattern of social relationships that is different to that of matched comparisons. The five key characteristics are:

1. More often adult-oriented.

2. More likely to have difficulty in peer relations.

3. Less likely to have a special friend.

4. Less likely to turn to peers for emotional support when anxious.

5. Less likely to be selective in choosing friends.

The graph shows how many of these five characteristics were found in ex-institutional children and their matched comparisons.

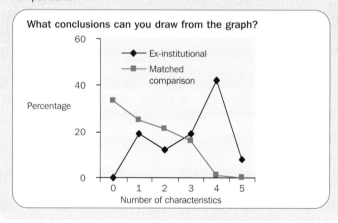

What conclusions can you draw from the graph?

stemming from being adopted, which would explain their problems outside the home.

Another explanation could be that the ex-institutional children lag behind their peers in emotional development and this would explain their poor peer relationships – they are simply not yet ready to cope.

It was also true that the adopted families were better off, so another explanation might be related to having better resources.

EVALUATION OF THE STUDY BY HODGES AND TIZARD

The research method

This study was a natural experiment. *What are the strengths and limitations of this research method in the context of this study?*

The research design

This study used a longitudinal design. *What are the strengths and limitations of this research design in the context of this study?*

The study also used self-report techniques (interviews and questionnaires) as a means of collecting data. *What are the strengths and limitations of this research design in the context of this study?*

Ethical issues

What ethical issues should have concerned the researchers in this study, and how might they have dealt with these issues?

Ecological validity

To what extent can we generalise the findings from this study to other situations?

The sample

The original sample was reduced in subsequent follow-ups (called 'attrition'). *In what way might attrition affect the findings from this study?*

The children in the 'restored' and 'adopted' groups might be different because, for example, the children chosen for adoption might be more likeable. *In what way might this affect the findings from this study?*

Applications/usefulness
How valuable was this study?

DEBATE

Does emotional care matter? Should employers give parents time off work to attend to sick children at home or in hospital?

What next?

Describe **one** change to this study, and say how you think this might affect the outcome.

Multiple choice questions

1. Data in this study were collected using:
   (a) Questionnaires.
   (b) Interviews.
   (c) Psychological tests.
   (d) All of the above.

2. Which of the following was a dependent variable in this study?
   (a) Age.
   (b) Attachment.
   (c) Peer relationships.
   (d) Both b and c.

3. How many children remained in the study at age 16?
   (a) 65.   (b) 51.
   (c) 39.   (d) 23.

4. At age 16 which group of children had more attachments to their mothers?
   (a) Restored.   (b) Adopted.
   (c) Ex-institutional.   (d) Institutional.

5. 'Restored' children were those who were
   (a) In the institution at age 8.
   (b) Adopted by the age of 4.
   (c) Went back to their natural families.
   (d) Had special treatment so they didn't experience privation.

6. The word used to describe the 'loss' of participants during a study is:
   (a) Attention.   (b) Attrition.
   (c) Attribution.   (d) Attenuation.

7. The Rutter 'B' scale assessed:
   (a) Educational attainment.
   (b) Mental health.
   (c) Maternal attachment.
   (d) All of the above.

8. At age 16 which group of children had least difficulty with their peers?
   (a) Restored.   (b) Adopted.
   (c) Ex-institutional.   (d) Comparison.

9. Which of the following is *not* one of the criteria of the ex-institutional syndrome?
   (a) Less likely to have a special friend.
   (b) Less often adult-oriented.
   (c) Less likely to turn to peers for emotional support when anxious.
   (d) Less likely to be selective in choosing friends.

10. The results of this study suggest that:
    (a) Early privation does not have an effect on social relationships.
    (b) Early privation does have an effect on social relationships.
    (c) Both a and b.
    (d) None of the above.

Answers are on page 79.

Exam questions

1. (a) From their study on social relationships, outline **one** of the differences that Hodges and Tizard found between the restored and adopted children. [2]

   (b) Give an explanation for this difference. [2]
   [OCR AS Psy, May 2003, paper 1]

2. From the study by Hodges and Tizard (attachment) one conclusion was that the problems of disruption in early life can be overcome. From the study, outline **two** pieces of evidence that challenge this conclusion. [OCR AS Psy, June 2000, paper 1] [4]

3. (a) Hodges and Tizard's study on social relationships is an example of a natural experiment. What is a 'natural experiment'? [2]

   (b) What was the independent variable in this study? [2]
   [OCR AS Psy, June 2001, paper 1]

4. From Hodges and Tizard's study on the social relationships of adolescents, outline **two** characteristics of the behaviour of ex-institutional adolescents. [OCR AS Psy, Jan 2003, paper 1] [4]

Not all families are the same

New families

Bowlby started his work on family relationships over 50 years ago. Families are now very different in this country. At least one in three children will experience parental separation before the age of 16. Most of these children go through a period of unhappiness; many experience low self-esteem, behaviour problems, and loss of contact with part of their extended family. Children are usually helped by good communication with both parents, and most settle back into a normal pattern of development (Dunn and Deater-Deckard, 2001). Many children have experience of being in a step-family. Becoming part of a step-family seems to be helpful for younger children but is harder for older children to adapt to (Hawthorne et al., 2003). Older children seem to appreciate step-parents more when they act in a supportive and friendly way rather than being involved in discipline or control.

There is relatively little research on step-families and it has become a very controversial area. There are also controversial issues around the role of fathers in successful parenting and some fathers argue for greater access to their children. The group called 'Fathers 4 Justice' is a new civil rights movement campaigning for a child's right to see both parents and grandparents in cases where courts have denied access. One of the consequences of John Bowlby's research (see page 62) was that, in divorce cases, courts in the 1950s started to give custody to mothers rather than the traditional placement with fathers. Bowlby's work led to the understanding that mothers played a critical role in child development. The result was that fathers (and grandparents) often got cut out.

Cinderella: is it all true?

One of the strongest themes in fairy tales is of the wicked stepmother. The story of Cinderella has been around in many cultures for centuries. It is estimated that over 350 versions of it exist starting with one recorded in the ninth century in China. In this version Cinderella doesn't have a fairy godmother but is helped by a magical fish (a glass kipper perhaps?). The story has developed over the centuries but the role of the wicked stepmother remains constant.

Is the story so powerful because it relates to a truth we know but daren't speak about? There is an uncomfortable line of research developing that points to the negative effects of being in a step-family. We'll put in the usual caveats and say that many children in step-families have a perfectly acceptable life though Bowlby is recorded as saying *The myth (of the wicked step-parent) has some validity to it. A step-parent is a very unsatisfactory parent for a child to have. It is nobody's fault. It's a fact'* (Maddox, 1998).

Evolutionary psychologists go a step further and suggest that we are going against thousands of years of evolution when we try to nourish and support our partner's children as if they were our own. On the front cover of their book *The Truth about Cinderella*, Daly and Wilson (1998) state *'having a step-parent is the most powerful risk factor for severe child maltreatment yet discovered.'* You can see why this work is controversial.

Romanian orphanages

It is now more than 15 years since the world found out about the thousands of children locked away in Romania's state institutions. When British teacher Monica McDaid first came across the orphanage in Siret she was horrified.

'One thing I particularly remember was the basement. There were kids there who hadn't seen natural light for years. I remember when they were brought out for the first time. Most of them were clinging to the wall, putting their hands up to shield their eyes from the light.' (BBC website, 2000).

Many children were adopted by families across Europe and the USA, but did they manage to adapt and recover? A group of adoptees in this country have been studied by Michael Rutter from the Institute of Psychiatry. When they arrived in the country as babies, more than half the 165 children he studied showed severe delays in development compared with British children. Later he found that, even at the age of 11, many of these children had not caught up.

'Contrary to popular opinion at the time, we found there were definite long-term effects from being in an institution' (Rutter, 2000) and the effects were more damaging the longer the child had spent in institutionalised care.

 To read more about these orphans go to the BBC news website and search for Romanian orphan

Black, white or mixed race?

Racially mixed couples are no longer a rare phenomenon. It is estimated that a third of British people of Afro-Caribbean origin under the age of 30 who are currently married or co-habiting have white partners. Tizard and Phoenix (2002) explored the issue of mixed race identity by interviewing young people from a range of social backgrounds, all of whom had one white and one African or Afro-Caribbean parent. They found that many young people have very positive dual identities, as both black and white, and resist demands from others about the kinds of identities they should have.

LINKS TO OTHER STUDIES

There are some links in the methods that Hodges and Tizard used. They used a range of psychometric tests, like for example **Thigpen and Cleckley,** and they also used a longitudinal design, like for example **Gardner and Gardner** (Washoe). Their study is of real-life situations and therefore it is much more difficult to produce precise measures and make sharp comparisons. Other studies, for example **Rosenhan,** also benefit from this approach while having to deal with the issues of interpretation that arise.

keyISSUE

Longitudinal versus snapshot designs

In developmental psychology researchers are often interested in observing the effects of experience.

> For example, Hodges and Tizard were interested to see if the experience of institutional care would have an effect on later social relationships.

One way to conduct such research is to use a longitudinal design: the same people are studied over a period of time. This is a kind of repeated measures design. The same people were tested at age 4, 8, 16.

Another way to conduct such research is snapshot studies (cross-sectional design). This is a kind of independent groups design. Two or more groups of people of different ages are compared.

> For example, Samuel and Bryant were interested in the conservation abilities of children of different ages. They compared the performance of children ages 5, 6, 7 and 8.

	Longitudinal studies	**Snapshot studies**
Time	Longitudinal studies take a long time, which makes them more expensive and also requires patience because you have to wait a long time for the results.	Snapshot studies can be done much more quickly (in a few months instead of many years).
Attrition	Attrition is a problem for longitudinal studies because some of the participants inevitably drop out. The problem is that they may be certain kinds of participants (the ones who are less motivated or more unhappy or who have done less well), which leaves a biased sample.	
Participant variables	In longitudinal studies participant variables are controlled. Participant variables are characteristics such as IQ, sociability, interests and so on.	The groups of participants may be quite different. The participant variables in a snapshot design are not controlled in the same way that they are not controlled in an independent groups design. This means that differences between groups may be due to participant variables rather than the independent variable.
Cohort effects	Cohort effects – occur when a group of people are all the same age. They share certain experiences, such as children born just before the war having poor diets in infancy due to rationing. We may not be able to generalise the findings from a study that looks at only one cohort because of the unique characteristics of that cohort.	Cohort effects may produce spurious results, for example one snapshot study compared IQs of 20-somethings with those of 80-somethings and found the IQs of the latter group were much lower, concluding that ageing led to a decreased IQ. The reason, however, might well be because the 80-somethings had lower IQs when they were 20-something (due to e.g. poorer diet). This is also a cohort effect.

Some longitudinal studies are not experimental; they may be case studies which take place over many years. For example the case study of Little Hans spanned two years as did the study of Washoe.

Exam-style questions

1 Psychologists sometimes study a 'snapshot' of human behaviour instead of spending months or even years conducting a study. Take **one** core study and:

   (a) Describe the results of your chosen study.   [8]

   (b) Briefly discuss **two** advantages and **two** disadvantages of snapshot studies, using examples from your chosen study.   [12]

   (c) Suggest how a longitudinal approach could be used in your chosen study, and say how you think this might affect the results.   [8]

2 In some studies psychologists follow a group of participants over a long period of time. This is called a longitudinal study.

   Using **four** core studies:

   (a) Describe the longitudinal approach taken in each study.   [12]

   (b) Using examples, discuss **four** problems psychologists may have to consider when they study behaviour over a long period of time.   [12]

People (like Phil and Cara) who grew up in the 1960s have many shared experiences and attitudes which makes them different to, say, people who were teenagers in the 1990s. This means that a study of adolescents in the 1960s might have different findings to a study conducted today because of cohort effects.

Psychoanalysis

You can't get more interesting or more controversial than this. Basically it's about sex and death, two topics that we obsess about but find it difficult to discuss in a sensible way. The name of Sigmund Freud will always get a reaction. Many people seek to dismiss his work and many others will argue that he was the greatest thinker of the last century. Love him or hate him, you can't ignore him.

It is nearly 70 years since Sigmund Freud died in London but he is still one of the most influential thinkers in the Western world. Type his name into Google and you'll get more than 2 million hits. Site after site gives summaries of his work, interprets it, applies it to life, the universe and everything, and carries on arguments with other sites about what the theory means. In this text it is only possible to hint at the importance of the theory so if you are interested then check out the many websites.

The unconscious mind

Perhaps Freud's most important contribution to the way we think about ourselves has been the unconscious mind. He didn't invent the concept but developed the idea and applied it to a wide range of events. Freud proposed that our awareness is in layers and there are thoughts occurring below the surface. He suggested that the power of the unconscious can be seen in dreams which he called the 'royal road to the unconscious'. Dreams may appear to be nonsense but they are meaningful and reveal your hidden thoughts, feelings and desires. We hide the true meaning of the dream in symbols. The trick is to interpret the symbols and find the cause of the dream.

Psychic structure

Freud developed the idea of the unconscious by proposing a 'psychic structure'. This structure is divided into the id, ego and superego.

You are born with a mass of pleasure-seeking desires (I want it, and I want it now!). This is the *id*. As you become socialised your *ego* develops and controls the desires of the id. Finally you take on the ethics of other people and these appear in your mind as the *superego*. One way to think of the superego is as your conscience or maybe as the voice of your mother, which you can hear even when she isn't there. The task of the ego is to maintain a balance between the id and the superego. Too much id and you get in all sorts of trouble, too much superego and you get consumed by guilt. Much of the id is in the unconscious because if you had half an idea of what your desires are telling you to do you'd die of shock.

The talking cure

Freud believed that the answer to a number of psychological and physical problems lay deep in the unconscious mind. The task of the therapist was to help the patient get access to these unconscious thoughts and feelings. After he studied with Charcot in Paris, Freud briefly used hypnosis to achieve this. He later moved on and developed the method of free association, which is one of the techniques used in psychoanalysis – commonly called 'the talking cure' – to get people to say whatever is going through their minds. He believed that if he could guide his patients to a relaxed mental state their thoughts would automatically drift towards any areas of conflict and pain.

The couch

When Freud carried out psychoanalysis on his patients he got them to lie on a couch. In fact, Freud's original couch can be seen at the Freud Museum in London. Many psychoanalysts still use a couch with their patients. They believe it is useful because when lying down the patient will focus less on objects in the environment and more on images and feelings that come from their own minds. Also they are unable to see the reaction of the analyst which prevents them playing the game of trying to guess what the analyst is thinking or feeling. Maybe the lack of eye contact also helps the patient to relax and be less concerned by the reaction to what they are saying (Ross, 1999).

Ego defence mechanisms

We can protect ourselves from a full awareness of unpleasant thoughts, feelings and desires with 'defence mechanisms'. They are ego defences because the ego (our rational, conscious mind) uses them to protect itself from anxiety. For example:

Denial is the refusal to accept reality and to act as if a painful event, thought or feeling did not exist.

Displacement is the redirecting of thoughts feelings and impulses from an object that gives rise to anxiety to a safer, more acceptable one. For example, being angry at the boss and kicking the dog.

Projection means placing your undesired impulses onto someone else. For example, an angry spouse accuses their partner of hostility.

Repression is the blocking of unacceptable feelings or memories from consciousness. However, things which are placed in the unconscious mind are expressed through, for example, dreams or neurotic behaviour such as phobias. This is a key theme in the study of Little Hans – he repressed his anxieties about his mother, father and sister; this anxiety was then attached to something else (horses) which made him fearful of horses.

Biographical notes on Sigmund Freud (1856–1939)

Sigismund Schlomo Freud (later shortened to Sigmund by himself) was born to a middle-class Jewish family in Freiberg in central Europe. When he was four years old the family moved to Vienna where he stayed until 1938 when he was forced to leave the city to escape the Nazi regime. During

Andy Warhol's portrait of Freud

his childhood Freud had some hostility towards his father but was very close to his mother. This family dynamic is thought by some to have influenced his later theories of, for example, the Oedipus complex.

He studied medicine and became a respected neuropathologist. One condition that interested him was hysteria, where patients would exhibit extreme physical symptoms such as paralysis without an obvious physical cause. A visit to the French neurologist Jean-Martin Charcot convinced him that hysteria was caused by mental events rather than physical ones. He started to explore the mental reasons for hysteria and developed his techniques of free association. With Joseph Breuer he published *Studies in Hysteria* in 1895.

Freud continued to develop and publish his theories for the next 40 years. *The Interpretation of Dreams* (1900) and *Three Essays on the Theory of Sexuality* (1905) made Freud famous. They also made him very controversial especially because of his views on infantile sexuality. He developed his theories from his clinical work and some of his case studies are published, including the story of Little Hans. He also engaged in a lot of self-reflection and analysis.

Freud tackled the big questions about life and came up with many uncomfortable answers. He attracted devoted followers though there were many splits in the community of psychoanalysis. Wider society recognised the extraordinary contribution Freud made to our understanding of the human mind and in 1935 he was appointed Honorary Member of the Royal Society of Medicine. The anti-Semitism that he had lived with all his life finally drove him out of Vienna. Four of his sisters were subsequently unable to get out and died in the death camps.

The Oedipus complex

Stages of development

Freud believed that children are born with powerful emotions and drives. As a child develops, the drives focus on different parts of their body. After birth, the focus is on the mouth and children explore the physical and emotional world through it (this is called the *oral stage*). As children start to gain control of their bodily functions they move into the *anal stage* where they get pleasure from retaining or expelling faeces. Then comes the *phallic stage* where the focus is on their genitals. Between the ages of 7 to 11 Freud suggested children go through a *latency period* where sexual feelings are repressed before moving into the adult *genital stage* at puberty.

The part of this theory most relevant to the study of Little Hans is the phallic stage and, in particular, the Oedipus complex:

'I want a girl, just the girl that married dear old dad.'

Part of the Greek myth of Oedipus refers to a child who is brought up not knowing who his parents are. As a man he goes to the city of Thebes where he kills the tyrant king and marries the queen. Unfortunately for Oedipus he then discovers that the king was his father and the queen, now his wife, is also his mother. Well it would upset anyone.

Freud saw the story as describing a childhood drama for all little boys. Their mother is their first source of affection and is the focus of their erotic feelings. During the phallic stage of development the boy wants to possess his mother and recognises a competition with his father. He fears he will be punished for such wishes by castration but resolves the conflict by 'identifying the aggressor' and taking on the values and behaviour of his rival.

Book burning

It's difficult to imagine in the UK today that a government would organise events to burn the books of people they believed had degenerate views. This is what happened to Freud among others during the 1930s in Germany.

Freud (1933) commented: *'What progress we are making. In the Middle Ages they would have burned me. Now they are content with burning my books.'*

Anti-Semitism

'My language is German. My culture, my attainments are German. I considered myself German intellectually, until I noticed the growth of anti-Semitic prejudice in Germany and German Austria. Since that time, I prefer to call myself a Jew.' (Freud, 1925)

The core study

Freud used case studies as evidence for his theories. Much of his theory on children was based on the recollections of adults which are, of course, coloured by their subsequent experiences. Little Hans is one of the few children that Freud had direct experience of, and even then most of the contact is made indirectly through interviews with Hans's father. The full study is the length of a short novel and we recommend that if you enjoy reading you look it out.

Sigmund Freud (1909) Analysis of a phobia in a five-year-old boy. In J. Strachey (ed. and trans.) *The Standard Edition of the Complete Psychological Works: Two Case Histories* (vol. X), pages 5–147. London: The Hogarth Press.

Abstract

The case study of Little Hans is divided into three parts.

Part I. Introduction: Hans's early life

Hans's father recorded Hans's early childhood and used Freud's theory of psychoanalysis to analyse events.

Part II. Case history and analysis

This section blends evidence and analysis of that evidence.

- The *source of his anxieties*, mainly his parents and sister.

- The *development of his phobia* about horses, which changed from being a concern about white horses biting him to a fear of horses with laden carts. The phobia was related to his anxieties.

- The *fantasies* which represented his anxieties, including the 'two giraffes' and the origin of babies.

- The final fantasies which enabled him to *resolve his anxieties*, including one about his own make-believe children.

Part III. Discussion

Freud offered a discussion of the case dealing with three major issues:

- Support for Freud's theory of sexuality.

- The nature of phobias and how they develop.

- Views on life and the upbringing of children.

core STUDY

Aims

Freud spent his time treating adult patients and using their recollections as the basis for his theory of child development. The case study of Hans gave him the opportunity to test his theory about infantile sexuality and the Oedipus conflict on a 'real' child.

There was a second aim for this study. During the period when Hans's father was recording observations, Hans developed an intense phobia of horses. This provided Freud with an opportunity to also test his explanation of the genesis of phobias.

Method

Participant

The participant in this case study is a boy called Little Hans who was aged between three and five during the period of this case study.

Procedure

Hans's father recorded events and conversations with Hans and sent these regularly to Freud. Both Freud and the father offered interpretations of Hans's behaviour. On one occasion Hans was taken to meet Freud. Hans's father was one of Freud's closest 'followers' and was keen to put Freud's ideas of psychoanalysis into practice. Psychoanalysis involves the interpretation of a patient's thoughts and fantasies so that the patient can come to understand them himself.

Part I. Introduction: Hans's early life

Little Hans and his 'widdler'

Just before he was three, Hans started to show a lively interest in his 'widdler'. Hans observed that animals had big ones, especially an animal like a horse. He assumed that both his parents must have big ones because they were fully grown.

He got pleasure from touching his widdler and also from excretion. Later, when he imagined having his own children, he imagined he would help them widdle and wipe their bottoms – performing those things which had given him much pleasure. He kicked about when weeing/defecating showing the pleasure associated with such activity.

His mother found him playing with his penis: 'If you do that, I shall send for Doctor A. to cut off your widdler'. This led to acquiring a *castration complex* (fear of having his penis removed) which meant he had to *repress* his feelings of pleasure. Hans also felt sexual desire for his mother, which was *repressed* and expressed as an interest in other girls and wanting to kiss them.

Death wish towards his father and baby sister

During his summer holiday at Gmunden, Hans spent much time alone with his mother while his father returned to work in Vienna. Back home, Hans had to share his mother once again with his father and wished his father to be permanently away.

Hans expressed his conflicting aggression and love towards his father by hitting him and then kissing the spot.

When Hans was $3\frac{1}{2}$ his baby sister Hanna was born (October 1906), further separating him from his mother and reminding him of the attentions he used to receive from his mother when he was a baby. Hans admitted that he had watched his sister having a bath and wished his mother would let *her* go. This unconscious desire to see his sister drown became translated into a fear that his mother might equally let Hans go. Baths were womb-like and so also related to the process of being born.

Sources of his anxieties

In summary, Hans felt anxious about his:

Mother He had sexual fantasies about her but these resulted in anxieties, for example she had threatened that his penis would be cut off and that led to castration anxiety.

Father Hans saw his father as a rival for his mother, and wished him dead. But at the same time he loved his father and this created conflict and feelings of anxiety.

Sister He wished Hanna would drown, which led to anxiety and a fear that his mother would drop him.

Part II. Case history and analysis

The phobia starts (January 1908)

When Hans was 4½, he developed a fear that a white horse would bite him in the street – Hans referred to his fear as *'my nonsense'*. Freud felt that Hans's real fear was that he would lose his mother; his anxieties had been repressed into his unconscious mind and eventually expressed as a phobia. Freud explained the links between his anxieties and horses:

1 It was partly based on a real event. Hans heard a father warn his daughter that a white horse might bite her if she touched it.

2 This was linked to his mother telling him that it would not be proper if she touched his penis – Hans had asked to her to touch his widdler once when she was drying him after a bath. The link was: if you put your finger on a white horse it will bite you, if someone put their finger on your widdler this was not proper.

3 This created a sense of anxiety because his mother might leave him because she disapproved of his request. Hans's desire for his mother was a product of his sexual libido (his sexual drive). His sexual desire was now linked to a sense of anxiety. A coping mechanism would be to transfer his anxiety from his libido to the horses and therefore he became afraid of a white horse biting something that touched it.

4 Horses also represented his father (see Hans's visit to see Freud) and the anxiety associated with his father.

5 His anxiety was exacerbated because his father told him that women have no widdlers. Freud reasoned that this would lead Hans to think – 'My mother had a widdler before and now she hasn't. It must have been cut off. She said mine might be cut off if I touched it. She obviously wasn't joking because it happened to her'. This would lead to castration anxiety.

Hans visits Freud (March 1908)

Freud proposed that a horse might be symbolic of Hans's father because the black around the horses' mouths and the blinkers in front of their eyes might be symbols of his father's moustaches and glasses – symbols of manhood (i.e. things that Hans might envy because he wanted to be grown up and able to have his mother's love).

Freud told Hans that he was afraid of his father because he was so fond of his mother. Freud's revelation appeared to release Hans and enable him to deal more directly with his phobia. He started to be able to go out into the street again and to the park. However, soon another phobia developed, the fear of horses pulling heavy carts.

A conversation recorded by Hans's father

I: Did you often get into bed with Mummy at Gmunden?

Hans: Yes.

I: And you used to think to yourself you were the Daddy?

Hans: Yes.

I: And then you felt afraid of Daddy? Can you remember the funeral at Gmunden? You thought then that if only Daddy were to die you'd be Daddy.

Hans: Yes.

[From page 90]

Further horse anxieties

A new fear developed of horses pulling heavily laden carts or a bus. This again was related to an actual event: Hans recalled an occasion when he was walking with his mother and they saw a horse pulling a bus fall down and kick its legs about. This terrified Hans because he thought the horse was dead. However the fear also represented many repressed anxieties:

- Hans secretly wished his father would fall down dead. Seeing the horse fall over increased his anxiety about this death wish.

- Hans had become preoccupied with bowel movements ('lumf'). A laden cart was like a body full of faeces. Lumf falling in the toilet made a noise similar to the noise of a horse falling.

- A heavily laden cart was also like a pregnant woman and babies are also lumf-like. Therefore all the laden vehicles represented pregnancy. When they fall down it represents giving birth. This was linked to Hans's repressed feelings about his sister.

- Hans was particularly concerned about the horse 'kicking about' when it fell over which was linked to his own behaviour when defecating.

The phobia also served a real purpose of keeping him at home with his mother.

Hans played with dolls and had one that he named 'Lodi', the word for 'sausage'. His father pointed out that a sausage is like a lumf. *'When you sat on the chamber and a lumf came, did you think yourself you were having a baby?'* Hans said yes *'You know when the bus–horses fell down? The bus looked like a baby–box, and when the black horse fell down it was just like …'* Hans finished the sentence *'…like having a baby'*. And the noise of the horses' hooves was like Hans's noise he made with his feet when on the chamber.

[Conversation from page 95]

Qs

1 Briefly outline Hans's feelings towards his sister, mother and father.

2 Give an example of a 'leading question' from the conversation between Hans and his father.

3 Give **two** explanations for Hans's castration anxiety.

4 Explain why Hans came to fear having baths.

5 Give **two** reasons why Hans developed a fear of being bitten by a horse.

6 Suggest **one** reason why Hans might have been afraid of a horse pulling a laden cart.

7 Give an example of Freud's search for 'deep meanings' (i.e. the hidden meaning for something).

8 What is the link between anxiety and phobia?

Part II. Case history and analysis continued

Fantasies

Hans reported many fantasies or 'dreams' which each expressed different aspects of his anxieties

The dream about giraffes A week or so before they visited Freud, Hans told his father the following 'dream' of two giraffes – *'In the night there was a big giraffe in the room and a crumpled one; and the big one called out because I took the crumpled one away from it. Then it stopped calling out; and then I sat down on top of the crumpled one.'* Hans's father perceived that he (or his penis) was the big giraffe and the crumpled one was his wife's genital organ. The scene is a replay of what happened on recent mornings – Hans came into their bed in the morning, welcomed by his mother but his father warns her not to do this (this is the big giraffe calling out). Hans stays a little while (sits on the crumpled one). In the night Hans experiences a longing for his mother and comes to see her for that reason. The whole thing is a continuation of his fear of horses.

Origin of babies When Hanna was born Hans was told that the stork brought her but he didn't believe this and made up his own story that she had been like a lumf (faeces) inside his mother and giving birth was like defecating (pleasurable).

The resolution

Hans had several fantasies which enabled him to express his repressed feelings and finally fully recover from his phobias.

1 The plumber Hans related the following to his father *'I was in the bath, and then the plumber came and unscrewed it. Then he took a big borer and stuck it in my stomach.'* Hans's father interpreted this to mean: 'I was in bed with Mummy. Then Daddy came and sent me away. He pushed me away with his big penis.'

Hans also had another fantasy: *'The plumber came and first he took away my behind with a pair of pincers, and then he gave me another, and then the same with my widdler.'* Presumably both the new backside and widdler were bigger, like Daddy's.

These fantasies showed that Hans was becoming more conscious of his feelings about his father and resolving those feelings.

2 Knowing where babies came from Hans's continued fear of baths represented an unconscious understanding of where babies come from, and his interest in laden carts represented his own answer – he called them 'stork carts' because his parents told him a stork brought the baby. Hans's parents finally explained where babies really came from – from inside 'Mummy'. This meant he no longer had a need for the cart analogy. After this he played outside, not fearing the carts.

3 Becoming the mummy instead of the daddy Hans had always had an ongoing fantasy about his own children and how he was going to look after them. One day he was playing a game with these imaginary children and his father asked 'are your children still alive?' Hans replied that boys couldn't have children, he had been their mummy but now he was their daddy. This led Freud to conclude that Hans had at last overcome his Oedipus complex and was able to identify with his father.

Part III. Discussion

I. Support for Freud's theory of sexuality

There are two criticisms: (1) If Hans was 'abnormal' we can't draw conclusions about normal development, (2) The analysis was conducted by his father and lacked objective worth. Freud's response was (1) that such neuroses in early childhood are relatively normal and (2) that, even if a response is triggered by suggestion, it is not arbitrary. In any case Hans did sometimes disagree with his father's suggestions, and there were benefits of the close relationship (more intimate details would be revealed).

Freud concluded that the case study of Hans provided support for his ideas about infant sexuality, for example Hans's interest in his 'widdler'. He also was a perfect example of a 'little Oedipus'. Hans had a wish to be close to his mother and to engage in sexual relations with her. His father was his rival whom he wished dead, but also loved deeply.

II. Understanding phobias

Freud explained phobias as the conscious expression of repressed anxieties. Hans's case fitted this well. In order to help Hans, Freud's task was to throw out hints so that Hans could obtain a conscious grasp of his unconscious wishes.

This enlightenment enabled Hans to delve deeper into his other fears – the fear of horses falling down and a new fascination with 'lumf' which was variously associated with pleasure in defecation, pregnancy, understanding where babies come from and laden carts.

III. Views on life and the upbringing of children

Hans's conflicts were relatively 'normal' and therefore the same could be said of the phobias. It might be generally useful to apply the same principles of psychoanalysis to all children to free them of repressed wishes that inevitably arise during childhood.

Postscript

Hans was interviewed much later, when he was 19. At that time he appeared entirely normal and had experienced no difficulties during adolescence. He had no recollection of the events of his childhood.

Qs

1 In what way were Hans's fantasies important?

2 What might have led both Freud and Hans's father to draw biased conclusions?

3 How did Freud respond to the **two** criticisms of the study?

EVALUATION OF THE STUDY BY FREUD

(See page x for note on evaluating research studies/articles)

The research method

This study was a case study. *What are the strengths and limitations of this research method in the context of this study?*

The research technique

Hans's father collected data by observation and interview. *What are the strengths and limitations of these techniques in the context of this study?*

DEBATE

Prepare arguments for and against the usefulness of this study, taking validity into account. What do you conclude?

The sample

In what way is the participant in this sample unique? How does this affect the conclusions drawn from the study?

Ethical issues

What ethical issues should have concerned the researchers in this study, and how might they have dealt with these issues?

Qualitative or quantitative?

What kind of data were collected in this study? What are the strengths and limitations of producing this kind of data in the context of this study?

Validity

Hans's father may have influenced the information Hans provided by using leading questions. *Explain how this might affect the validity of this study.*

Hans's father and Freud explained Hans's behaviour. *In what way were these explanations biased and thus might lack validity?*

Applications/usefulness

How valuable was this study?

What next? ?

Describe **one** change to this study, and say how you think this might affect the outcome.

Multiple choice questions

1. How old was Hans when his father started recording the case study?
   (a) 2 years old.   (b) 3 years old.
   (c) 4 years old.   (d) 5 years old.

2. When Hans was 3½ what important event occurred?
   (a) He developed a phobia.
   (b) His sister Hanna was born.
   (c) He had to start sleeping on his own.
   (d) All of the above.

3. In the dream of the giraffes, Hans dreamed that the big giraffe called out because:
   (a) He sat on the big one.
   (b) He sat on the crumpled one.
   (c) He took the crumpled one away.
   (d) He hit the big one.

4. What animal represented his father?
   (a) Horse.   (b) Giraffe.
   (c) Lion.   (d) Both (a) and (b).

5. What is a 'castration complex'?
   (a) Fear of becoming a man.
   (b) Fear of having one's penis removed.
   (c) Fear of sexual rejection.
   (d) All of the above.

6. What kind of horse was Hans afraid of?
   (a) Large horse.   (b) White horse.
   (c) Spotted horse.   (d) Police horse.

7. Hans used his own word for his phobia, which was his
   (a) Troubles.   (b) Illness.
   (c) Babble.   (d) Nonsense.

8. What did a laden cart represent?
   (a) His father.
   (b) A full stomach.
   (c) A pregnant woman.
   (d) All of the above.

9. The term 'lumf' referred to
   (a) Faeces.   (b) Horses
   (c) Mountains   (d) A penis

10. The final fantasy Hans had was about:
    (a) Giraffes.
    (b) Breaking into a train.
    (c) A plumber.
    (d) His pretend children.

Answers are on page 79.

Exam questions

1. Outline **two** pieces of evidence used by Freud to suggest that Hans's fear of horses was symbolic of his fear of his father. [OCR AS Psy, May 2005, paper 1]

2. From the study by Freud, briefly describe **one** of Little Hans's dreams or fantasies. [OCR AS Psy, May 2003, paper 1] [2]

3. The study by Freud contains the following extract of a conversation between Hans and his father:
   Father: When the horse fell down did you think of your daddy?
   Hans: Perhaps. Yes it's possible.

   (a) What was Hans's father trying to find out with this questioning? [2]

   (b) Give **one** problem with this type of questioning. [2]
   [OCR AS Psy, June 1998, paper 1]

4. (a) In the study by Freud, Little Hans is referred to as a 'little Oedipus'. Briefly describe the Oedipus complex. [2]

   (b) Outline **one** piece of evidence from the study that is used to support the claim that Hans is a 'little Oedipus'. [2]
   [OCR AS Psy, Jan 2001, paper 1]

The legacy

Since Freud first published his theories whole forests have been destroyed printing what people have to say about them. Bookshop shelves still groan with texts about Freud and by people following his ideas. In mainstream psychology, however, Freud does not feature very highly in UK university courses and many psychologists would not cite Freud as an important influence on the modern subject. Having said that, he still has the greatest recognition of any psychologist and when students were asked to identify the most important psychologist in a recent survey (Banyard and Kagan, 2002) they gave Freud twice as many votes as his nearest rival.

Freud's influence is massive both in psychology and beyond. Most obvious is the effect on therapy. Although traditional psychoanalysis is relatively rare in this country, the ideas about the importance of the first five years, the role of the unconscious and the power of defence mechanisms influence many therapists. Freud is commonly cited in texts on critical theory and his influence is seen in literature and the arts.

Freud's family continue to be prominent in British life and the diversity of their work perhaps reflects the enduring influence of the man.

Freud merchandise

Can't afford a therapist but want someone to talk to? You can get the Sigmund Freud Beanbag Doll ('Soft, squeezable, and oh so smart! Great gift for anyone in the mental health field'), or maybe the Freud and Couch finger puppet, or the ever popular movable Freud action figure ('captures Freud in a pensive pose, holding a distinctly phallic cigar. Put him on your desk or nightstand to inspire you to explore the depths of your unconscious and embrace the symbolism of your dreams').

The Freud dynasty

The only one of Freud's children to continue his work as a therapist was *Anna* who came to the UK with him in 1938. Famous in her own right, her legacy is the Anna Freud centre in Hampstead, London dedicated to the well-being of children and their families.

Of Freud's grandchildren, *Lucian* Freud is one of Britain's most famous (and expensive) living artists. His daughter is the fashion designer *Bella* Freud.

Lucian's brother is *Clement* Freud who has been a broadcaster for 40 years. He was a Liberal Party MP for the Isle of Ely between 1973 and 1987. His daughter *Emma* Freud is a British broadcaster and cultural commentator. She is married to the writer Richard Curtis which therefore gives us a link from Freud to The Vicar of Dibley. He'd be so pleased.

Emma's brother *Matthew* Freud is one of the most powerful PR men in London. He has close connections to the Labour Government and his clients include companies like Pepsi, BT, and BskyB. He is married to Elizabeth Murdoch (Rupert's daughter) who is a media executive.

Farting as a defence against unspeakable dread

Psychoanalyst Mara Sidoli was famous for her willingness to deal with difficult cases. She took on a severely disturbed 'latency boy' (named from Freud's latency period between the ages of 7 and 11 years) called Peter who frankly didn't smell too good.

According to Sidoli (1996) *'Peter held loud conversations with imaginary beings and made loud anal farts as well as farting noises with his mouth whenever he became anxious or angry.'* He also tended to soil himself when anxious. Sidoli describes this behaviour in terms of Freud's defence mechanisms and suggested he was testing his parents' commitment to him.

After a year of therapy that seemed to be having little effect Sidoli took the nuclear approach and started to make farting noises herself. This so surprised Peter that it finally broke through the defences and he was able to express his dread, affection and humour in a less noxious way.

For this report and for her courage and tenacity Mara Sidoli was awarded the 1998 igNoble Prize (like the Nobel Prize but not really) for literature.

The careers of the family members reflect the areas of life that continue to be influenced by Freud: therapy, broadcasting, the arts, advertising and public relations.

Behaviourist explanation of phobias

Freud's explanation of Little Hans's phobia is not the only possible explanation. The behaviourist Hobart Mowrer (1947) analysed the same situation using the learning theory concepts of association and reinforcement. According to this behaviourist view a fear is learned when something that was previously neutral (such as a horse) is paired with something that provokes fear (the experience of watching the horse fall down dead). Once this association has been learned other things reinforce it. In this case the fact that Hans's phobia meant staying away from horses and thus spending more time at home with his mother was reinforcing.

LINKS TO OTHER STUDIES

Such is Freud's influence that there are links all through this text. The work of Elizabeth **Loftus** looks at repressed and false memories; the case study of **Thigpen and Cleckley** deals with the unconscious mind. Freud contributes to our understanding of moral development in children and offers an opposing view to the social learning theory of **Bandura**. **Hodges and Tizard**'s study investigated Bowlby's theory of attachment which was much influenced by Freud – Bowlby trained as a Freudian psychiatrist.

keyISSUE

Self reports

Experiments or observational studies provide insights into behaviour but they can't tell us what people are thinking or feeling. For this we need self-reports: questionnaires or interviews.

Questionnaires: Respondents record their own answers.

Structured interview: Pre-determined questions, i.e. a questionnaire that is delivered face-to-face in real-time (e.g. over the telephone).

Unstructured interviews: New questions are developed as you go along, similar to the way your GP might interview you. He or she starts with some pre-determined questions but further questions are developed as a response to your answers. For this reason this unstructured or semi-structured approach is sometimes called the clinical interview.

KEY TERMS

Social desirability bias A tendency for respondents to answer questions in such a way that presents themselves in a better light.

Reliability A measure of consistency both within a set of scores or items and also over time such that it is possible to obtain the same results on subsequent occasions when the measure is used.

ACTIVITY

How daring are you? Try the questionnaire below.

- Would it be better to do this as an interview rather than a questionnaire?
- If you wanted to find out about attitudes towards dieting, why would it be preferable to conduct an interview rather than use a questionnaire? Why might it be better to use a questionnaire than conduct an interview?

Try another questionnaire or try writing one yourself (see page 216).

:)	:(

Questionnaire

- Can be easily repeated so that data can be collected from large numbers of people relatively cheaply and quickly (once the questionnaire has been designed).
- Respondents may feel more willing to reveal personal/confidential information than in an interview.

- Answers may not be truthful, for example because of leading questions and social desirability bias.
- The sample may be biased because only certain kinds of people fill in questionnaires – literate individuals who are willing to spend time filling them in.

Structured interview

- Can be easily repeated.
- Requires less skill than unstructured interviews.
- More easy to analyse than unstructured interviews because answers more predictable.
- In comparison with unstructured interviews, the data collected will be restricted by a pre-determined set of questions.

- The interviewer's expectations may influence answers the interviewee gives (this is called interviewer bias). This may especially be true because people don't always know what they think.

Unstructured or semi-structured interview

- Generally more detailed information can be obtained from each respondent than in a structured interview.
- Can access information that may not be revealed by predetermined questions.

- More affected by interviewer bias than structured interviews.
- Requires well-trained interviewers, which makes it more expensive to produce reliable interviews.
- Interviews may not be comparable because different interviewers ask different questions (low inter-interviewer reliability). Reliability may also be affected by the same interviewer behaving differently on different occasions.

Exam-style question

One way to collect information about human behaviour and experience is to ask people what they think or feel. This technique is called a self-report measure.

Using **four** core studies answer the following questions:

(a) Describe the self-report measure that was used in each of these studies. [12]

(b) Using examples from these studies, discuss **two** strengths and **two** weaknesses of using self-report measures. [12]

Developmental Core Study 5: Samuel And Bryant (conservation)

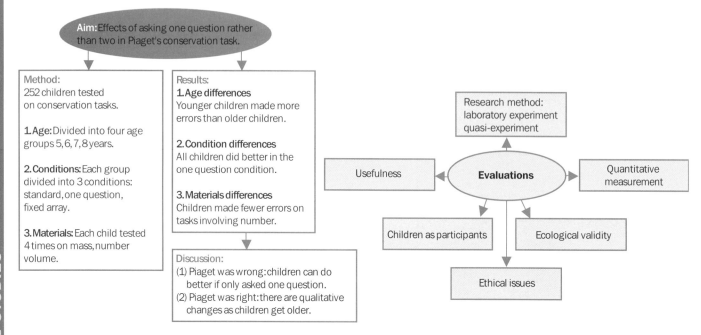

Aim: Effects of asking one question rather than two in Piaget's conservation task.

Method:
252 children tested on conservation tasks.

1. **Age:** Divided into four age groups 5, 6, 7, 8 years.

2. **Conditions:** Each group divided into 3 conditions: standard, one question, fixed array.

3. **Materials:** Each child tested 4 times on mass, number volume.

Results:
1. **Age differences**
Younger children made more errors than older children.

2. **Condition differences**
All children did better in the one question condition.

3. **Materials differences**
Children made fewer errors on tasks involving number.

Discussion:
(1) Piaget was wrong: children can do better if only asked one question.
(2) Piaget was right: there are qualitative changes as children get older.

Research method: laboratory experiment quasi-experiment

Usefulness

Evaluations

Quantitative measurement

Children as participants

Ecological validity

Ethical issues

Developmental Core Study 6: Bandura, Ross And Ross (aggression)

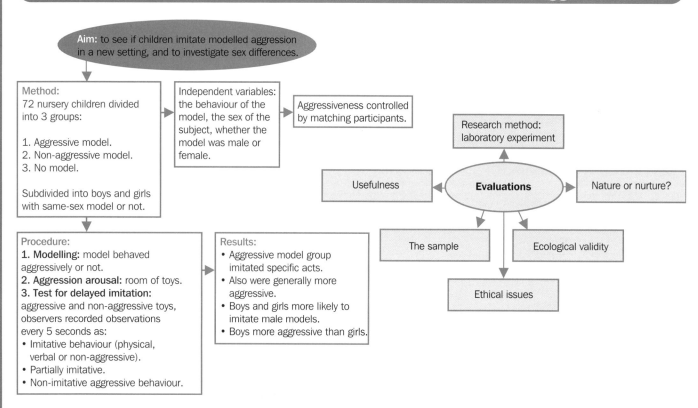

Aim: to see if children imitate modelled aggression in a new setting, and to investigate sex differences.

Method:
72 nursery children divided into 3 groups:

1. Aggressive model.
2. Non-aggressive model.
3. No model.

Subdivided into boys and girls with same-sex model or not.

Independent variables: the behaviour of the model, the sex of the subject, whether the model was male or female.

Aggressiveness controlled by matching participants.

Procedure:
1. **Modelling:** model behaved aggressively or not.
2. **Aggression arousal:** room of toys.
3. **Test for delayed imitation:** aggressive and non-aggressive toys, observers recorded observations every 5 seconds as:
• Imitative behaviour (physical, verbal or non-aggressive).
• Partially imitative.
• Non-imitative aggressive behaviour.

Results:
• Aggressive model group imitated specific acts.
• Also were generally more aggressive.
• Boys and girls more likely to imitate male models.
• Boys more aggressive than girls.

Research method: laboratory experiment

Usefulness

Evaluations

Nature or nurture?

The sample

Ecological validity

Ethical issues

Developmental Core Study 7: Hodges And Tizard (social relationships)

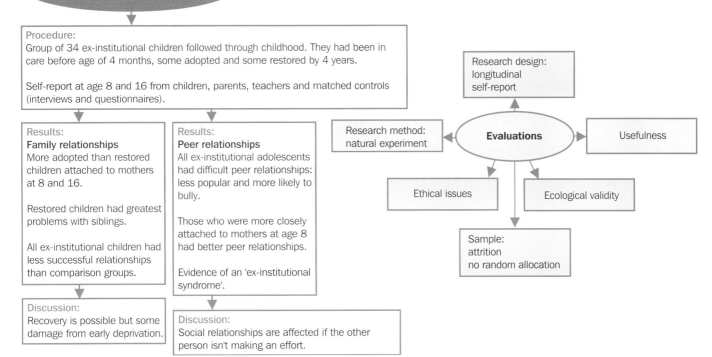

Aim: Observe effects of a lack of early attachment on later social relationships.

Procedure:
Group of 34 ex-institutional children followed through childhood. They had been in care before age of 4 months, some adopted and some restored by 4 years.

Self-report at age 8 and 16 from children, parents, teachers and matched controls (interviews and questionnaires).

Results:
Family relationships
More adopted than restored children attached to mothers at 8 and 16.

Restored children had greatest problems with siblings.

All ex-institutional children had less successful relationships than comparison groups.

Results:
Peer relationships
All ex-institutional adolescents had difficult peer relationships: less popular and more likely to bully.

Those who were more closely attached to mothers at age 8 had better peer relationships.

Evidence of an 'ex-institutional syndrome'.

Discussion:
Recovery is possible but some damage from early deprivation.

Discussion:
Social relationships are affected if the other person isn't making an effort.

Evaluations
- Research design: longitudinal self-report
- Research method: natural experiment
- Usefulness
- Ethical issues
- Ecological validity
- Sample: attrition no random allocation

Developmental Core Study 8: Freud (Little Hans)

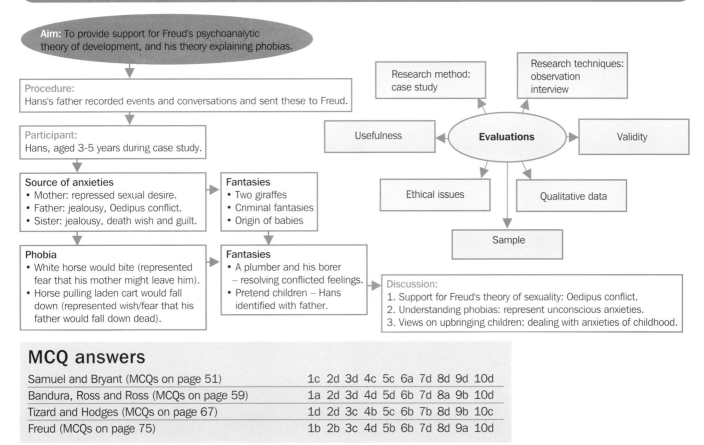

Aim: To provide support for Freud's psychoanalytic theory of development, and his theory explaining phobias.

Procedure:
Hans's father recorded events and conversations and sent these to Freud.

Participant:
Hans, aged 3-5 years during case study.

Source of anxieties
- Mother: repressed sexual desire.
- Father: jealousy, Oedipus conflict.
- Sister: jealousy, death wish and guilt.

Fantasies
- Two giraffes
- Criminal fantasies
- Origin of babies

Phobia
- White horse would bite (represented fear that his mother might leave him).
- Horse pulling laden cart would fall down (represented wish/fear that his father would fall down dead).

Fantasies
- A plumber and his borer – resolving conflicted feelings.
- Pretend children – Hans identified with father.

Evaluations
- Research method: case study
- Research techniques: observation interview
- Usefulness
- Validity
- Ethical issues
- Qualitative data
- Sample

Discussion:
1. Support for Freud's theory of sexuality: Oedipus conflict.
2. Understanding phobias: represent unconscious anxieties.
3. Views on upbringing children: dealing with anxieties of childhood.

MCQ answers

Samuel and Bryant (MCQs on page 51)	1c 2d 3d 4c 5c 6a 7d 8d 9d 10d
Bandura, Ross and Ross (MCQs on page 59)	1a 2d 3d 4d 5d 6b 7d 8a 9b 10d
Tizard and Hodges (MCQs on page 67)	1d 2d 3c 4b 5c 6b 7b 8d 9b 10c
Freud (MCQs on page 75)	1b 2b 3c 4d 5b 6b 7d 8d 9a 10d

1 In the study by Samuel and Bryant:

    (a) What do the psychologists mean by the term *conservation*? [2]

    (b) Describe **one** of the ways in which the psychologists tested for conservation. [2]
       [OCR AS Psy, June 1994, paper 1]

Stig's answer

(a) They mean that children are able to work out that something stays the same even if it looks like it is different.

(b) You can test for conservation using mass, volume or number – counters in a row. You show a child two identical rows of counters and then space the counters out in one row so it looks longer and see if the child says they are the same or different.

Chardonnay's answer

(a) The same quantity of water may look more or less in a shorter or taller glass but it doesn't actually change.

(b) One way to test for conservation is using volume – a liquid in two beakers.

Examiner's comments

Stig, you are showing off now. These are two sound answers. Although part (a) could be more tightly phrased, it is accurate. Part (b) is very clear.

Chardonnay, you talk about conservation of water … which is actually conservation of volume. You're a bit confused. You're not wrong, but you're not totally right either. In part (b) you need to describe and not just identify.

Stig (2+2) Chardonnay (1+1)

2 (a) From the study on conservation by Samuel and Bryant, outline the main difference between the children's responses to the 'one-question condition', compared to the 'two-question condition' (Piaget's original design). [2]

    (b) Suggest **one** reason for this difference. [2]
       [OCR AS Psy, June 1996, paper 1]

Stig's answer

(a) In Samuel and Bryant's study young children did less well when they were asked only one question than when they were asked two questions.

(b) One reason is that they might have been confused. Being asked two questions could be confusing.

Chardonnay's answer

(a) In Piaget's original experiment (with two questions) he found that younger children did less well than those over the age of 7. In the one-question experiment more of the younger children got the question right but there were still differences.

(b) The reason why more younger children did better with only one question might be due to demand characteristics. They might have thought that when they were asked a second question they were supposed to give a new answer.

Examiner's comments

Hmm, you have got it the wrong way round. Children did better in the one-question condition, making fewer errors on the conservation task. Despite getting part (a) wrong, you strangely are on the right lines for part (b). You would need further explanation – why *does* asking two identical questions cause confusion?

Chardonnay's turn to show off now. Part (a) is a very full answer and you also talk about one-question/two-question in terms of another IV – age. This is almost surplus to the requirements for 2 marks for this question. Part (b) is also very strong!

Stig (0+1) Chardonnay (2+2)

3 All studies present some ethical issues to consider. Outline **two** ethical issues raised by the study by Bandura, Ross and Ross into the imitation of aggressive behaviour. [OCR AS Psy, June 2000, paper 1]   [4]

Stig's answer

The children should not have experienced harm and there were two ways they could have been psychologically harmed. First the children who watched the aggressive model might have been stressed and they also learned to be violent. They also were made to feel aggressive because the toys they were playing with were taken away.

Chardonnay's answer

One issue is of informed consent. The younger children couldn't give their own informed consent. Their parents must have been asked and they might not have wanted to take part. A second issue is that they might have felt distressed because of the frustration of having the toys taken away from them.

Examiner's comments

This is all true Stig, but you have, sadly, not identified two separate ethical issues as both stress and mild aggression arousal relate to the same issue – protection from harm.

Chardonnay has outlined two different ethical issues. However, informed consent is not strictly speaking, according to the ethical guidelines, a problem here. As the parents and carers gave consent, the guidelines indicate this is acceptable. The second issue is fine – identified and outlined.

Stig (2+0) Chardonnay (1+2)

---

4 (a) Explain how **one** control was used in the study on aggression by Bandura, Ross and Ross.   [2]

(b) Suggest **one** reason why it is difficult to generalise from the findings of this study to aggression outside the laboratory.   [2]
[OCR AS Psy, Jan 2006, paper 1]

Stig's answer

(a) One control that was used in Bandura's study was that the children were matched for their aggressiveness.

(b) It's difficult to generalise from Bandura's findings because the study was done in a lab and children might not behave like that in everyday life.

Chardonnay's answer

(a) Bandura had a control group who did not observe any aggression. This controlled for the fact that the children may have behaved aggressively even if they didn't see any aggression.

(b) One reason why it might be difficult to generalise from this study is because the children were American children and they might be more aggressive than other children.

Examiner's comments

Stig, you have identified a control used in the study, and this automatically gets you one mark. However, the question asks you to 'explain how', so you are required to give a brief (1–2 sentence) description of how they were matched. In part (b) you have provided enough for two marks as you have identified the reason and given some explanation.

Chardonnay, in part (a) you have identified a control and explained how it was used. So, 2 marks. In part (b) you have identified that they were American, so limiting generalisability to other cultures. Another point you could have made is that the nursery was for the children of university staff, who were probably middle-class, thus limiting generalisability to other groups. Anyway, you have written enough for 2 marks.

Stig (1+2) Chardonnay (2+2)

---

5 Hodges and Tizard describe a number of differences between the 'ex-institutional' children and the control groups. Outline **two** of these differences. [OCR AS Psy, June 1997, paper 1]   [4]

Stig's answer

The ex-institutional children were less likely to have formed an attachment to their mothers, because they had no caretakers in the institution so they weren't able to form relationships. The ex-institutional children also had problems making friends with their peers. This was for the same reason.

Chardonnay's answer

One difference between the 'ex-institutional' children and the control groups was that the ex-institutional children were less popular than their matched comparisons. This was in general, because in fact more of the ex-institutional children than comparison group were voted most popular. Another difference was that the ex-institutional children were more likely to be bullies, according to their teachers.

Examiner's comments

Stig, you make a common mistake. For this question, you need to describe differences between the controls and the ex-institutional group as a whole. Actually, it was only the restored group who had lower rates of attachment to their mothers. The controls and the adopted group were pretty similar. Your second point is a valid one as the mothers certainly reported that the ex-institutional group were less likely to have a special friend.

Chardonnay, I am not sure what you mean by popularity. Perhaps you are talking about special friends? Or you are talking about being part of a crowd of people who go round together. Certainly, these were differences, but you need to be more precise. Your second point is spot on.

Stig (0+2) Chardonnay (1+2)

6 Outline **one** practical and **one** ethical problem with the Hodges and Tizard study on social relationships. [OCR AS Psy, May 2002, paper 1] [4]

Stig's answer

One practical problem with this study is that they couldn't find all the children when they were 16 (called attrition).

One ethical problem is that the children might feel their privacy was invaded by all the questions.

Chardonnay's answer

One practical problem is that the researchers used questionnaires to collect some of the data and people don't always answer these honestly.

An ethical issue is that the participants were children and therefore couldn't give their informed consent; their parents would give informed consent and the children might not like to be the subjects in a study especially when they got older.

Examiner's comments

Stig, attrition was a problem and you have outlined this fairly minimally, but just enough for 2 marks as you have named it and explained it. Your ethical problem is correct about the potential for violating privacy. I think you would need to be a bit more specific to get the second mark here – instead of referring to 'all the questions asked' could you think of some specific questions which violate privacy?

Chardonnay, your practical problem is true though you could give more marginally more detail to secure a second mark (e.g. how will this alter the findings?). The ethical problem you outline is a true and I am glad to see that you have not just said 'there is no informed consent' and left it at that. You show your understanding that, while BPS guidelines might be met, it may still cause some resentment.

Stig (2+1) Chardonnay (1+2)

7 (a) In Freud's case study of Little Hans, how did Hans respond to the birth of his sister? [2]

(b) According to Freud, what was the connection between Hans's sister and his fear of death? [2]
[OCR AS Psy, June 1994, paper 1]

Stig's answer

(a) Hans did not like his little sister. He wished she hadn't been born and was dead.

(b) The connection was that his wish that his sister was dead made him fear that he might die too.

Chardonnay's answer

(a) Hans had mixed feelings about his sister. He loved her but also wished her dead because she was a rival for his mother's affections.

(b) I think it might be due to the bath and Hans's worries that his mother would let him go and he would drown. This was because he wished that she would let his sister go.

Examiner's comments

A bit too simple, Stig. Hans did appear to have a bit of a 'deathwish' thing going on with his little sister, but it wasn't necessarily a conscious wish. We do not know if Hans liked his little sister or not. Chardonnay has provided the examiner with a fuller picture and brought in the important theme of jealousy and rivalry for his mother's affections.

Part (b) for both Stig and Chardonnay is good enough to attract full credit.

Stig (1+2) Chardonnay (2+2)

8 From Freud's study of Little Hans, outline **one** strength and **one** weakness of the way in which the data was gathered. [OCR AS Psy, May 2004, paper 1] [4]

Stig's answer

One strength is that this was a study about a normal child rather than Freud's usual work with patients who were mentally ill. One weakness is that there were lots of different ways the data could be interpreted. Freud's way is only one possibility, not necessarily the right one.

Chardonnay's answer

One strength about the way the data was collected is that Hans knew his father well and therefore felt freer to tell him everything. On the downside his father talked to him a lot and often gave 'leading questions' about the meaning of what Hans did or said, and this might have led him to give answers that were what his father expected.

Examiner's comments

Stig, I don't really think that you were concentrating on the question. The key phrase here is 'the *way in which data was gathered*' and this is different from the sample or the interpretation. The question is interested in how the data was collected from Hans.

Chardonnay is more on the right lines. A key issue in this study (though Freud was in denial about this!) was that the person collecting the data (Hans's dad) was biased, being instilled with Freudian ideas, and this is apparent in his use of leading questions.

Stig (1+0) Chardonnay (2+2)

9 A number of studies take the developmental approach to the study of behaviour and experience. This approach looks at how people change as they get older. Using the **four** core studies from this chapter:

(a) Describe what each study tells us about development. [12]

(b) Briefly discuss **four** problems of studying development, using examples from the named studies. [12]

Stig's answer

(a) Samuel and Bryant's study was about conservation. They found out that young children were in fact confused by being asked two questions and if you don't ask them two questions more of the younger children can work out the correct answer to conservation questions. However the study still shows that older children did better. **[2]**

The study by Bandura, Ross and Ross was about aggression. It shows that children will learn by imitation. The children watched an aggressive model or a non-aggressive model. If they watched the aggressive model they were more likely to repeat what the model did and they behaved more aggressively. This shows that behaviour can be learned. **[2]**

The third study was by Hodges and Tizard about social relationships. In this study it was found that children who had spent their early lives in an institution had suffered privation and had difficulty forming social relationships later in life. Some of the children did form relationships with their mothers but all of the children had problems making friends at school. **[3]**

The fourth study was by Freud about a little boy called Hans. This study illustrated his Oedipus complex and showed that children of a certain age (about 4) have a thing about their mothers which makes them resent their fathers and wish they were dead. This makes them guilty and to relive their guilt they eventually identify with their father. The result is the superego develops. **[3]**

Examiner's comments

Stig, you have written accurate and reasonably detailed paragraphs about each of the developmental studies, and this will certainly attract credit. But for the first two studies, you have answered the question 'describe the findings of each study', rather than 'describe what each study tells us about development'.

What do they each tell us about development? Samuel and Bryant: that conservation ability (i.e. an aspect of cognitive skills) does indeed increase with age, but that age 7 is not the magic age when children begin to think more logically (with 'operations'). By disposing of the two-question format we can see that even younger children can conserve.

Bandura suggests how children learn much behaviour (through social learning) as they grow up and that children are more likely to imitate the behaviour of a same-sex role model. So, Stig, you were more likely to have copied your dad when you were little!

Your paragraphs on Hodges and Tizard and then Freud have better question focus.

If you feel more comfortable starting each paragraph identifying the study, that is fine – but be aware that saying 'Bandura, Ross and Ross was about aggression' won't get you any marks as it is really just repeating information in the question.

Part (a) = 2+2+3+3 = 10

(b) There are many problems when psychologists study development. First of all working with children is difficult both practically and ethically. Practically children are just more likely to do what the experimenter wants (experimenter bias) **[P]** and so you are not testing what they really know but what they think they ought to do. **[C]** Ethically you obviously have to be a lot more careful with children than you would with adults. For example you shouldn't really cause any psychological harm. **[P]**

A second problem with studying development is finding suitable participants. It's hard to get a group of children who are right for what you want to do. They may not have had the right experiences. **[P]**

A third problem is that the sample may be biased so you can't generalise from the sample to other children in other cultures.

A fourth problem is demand characteristics. Children may respond to the wrong cues.

Examiner's comments

We can apply the PEC (point, example, comma) formula to marking this answer (see page ix for an explanation of PEC).

Oh dear, Stig, you are petering out – perhaps you were running short of time in the exam? Remember to keep the P–E–C structure for each paragraph. Where are your Examples from the studies??!

Your first paragraph is actually two separate problems. Your discussion about the implications of a bit of experimenter bias is just enough to get you the comment mark, even though you don't relate your points to examples from the studies.

Your next paragraph is not exactly clear, but I can see how this point might have related to Hodges and Tizard.

Your 'third' problem is no truer of developmental studies than any other kind of study – so nothing here, and your 'fourth' problem is not sufficiently different from your first…

Part (b) = 4

Total = a + b = 14/24

Chardonnay's answer

(a) In Bandura's study they found that children did imitate the aggressive behaviour of the model – they imitated specific acts and also became generally more aggressive. This tells us something about development. It tells us that aggressive children may have learned this behaviour because they have seen others behave like that. **[3]**

The study on conservation found that younger children are less likely to be able to conserve than older children. This shows us that there are differences in the way that children of different ages think. **[2]**

Hodges and Tizard investigated the development of social relationships from the point of view that children who are in an institution early in life then are less able to have good relationships with other people, which is what they found. This shows us that early experiences – particularly emotional ones, are important for being able to have adult social relationships. **[2]**

Freud's study of Little Hans supported his concept of the Oedipus conflict and showed that children may develop their gender identity and also moral development by identifying with their same-sex parent. **[3]**

(b) One problem with studying children is that ethical issues are trickier. You would not want to cause harm to a child, whereas you might feel it was acceptable to distress an adult. So psychologists need to be more sensitive. **[P]** For example, in Bandura, children watched an adult behaving aggressively towards a Bobo doll. This exposure to an aggressive adult may have distressed the children. **[E]** However, some people might say this was justified as Bandura discovered important things about aggression in children. **[C]**

There is also the ethical issue of informed consent. Children can't give informed consent so their parents might agree whereas the child didn't really want to take part. If the child is in a longitudinal study they might not consent when they get older.

This brings us to practical problems when doing research with children. They are probably less easy to get them to sit still and pay attention to what they are supposed to do, especially because they haven't actually agreed to take part. **[P]** For example, in Samuel and Bryant, the children, some of whom were only 4 years old, may have been 'bored' by the conservation tasks which were repeated lots of times and just said anything to the questions so they could go off and do something more interesting. **[E]** This would mean the results are not trustworthy and do not really tell us about children's conservation skills. **[C]**

They also may be more affected by demand characteristics and experimenter bias, so their behaviour may not be 'real' but affected by the experimenter's expectations. **[P]** Like in the study on Little Hans, there were leading questions and this may have affected what Hans said. **[E]** This means there are demand characteristics and the behaviour is not 'real'.

Examiner's comments

Chardonnay, I like how in the first paragraph you describe a finding and then move on to talk about what this tells us about development more generally.

Samuel and Bryant – a bit brief and oversimplistic. You could have said a bit more about these 'differences' in thinking between children of different ages, i.e. how children become more logical with age and less swayed by appearance.

Hodges and Tizard, for the third point in this paragraph Chardonnay, you could expand the idea of 'social relationships' e.g. attachment with mum, special friends, being part of a large group etc, or perhaps suggested why institutionalisation in childhood impacts upon such relationships. A bit more is needed here.

For Freud, you are short and sweet here. You have packed a lot of concepts into a couple of sentences. A touch more detail would really guarantee 3 marks here, but I will give you them anyway as I was still impressed.

Part (a) = 3 + 2 + 2 + 3 = 10

Examiner's comments

We can apply the PEC (point, example, comma) formula to marking this answer (see page ix for an explanation of PEC).

Chardonnay, a perfect first paragraph, your point, example and comment all link together logically and coherently. Your comment ('however, the ends may justify the means' type thing) is an interesting counterpoint and a nice way of 'discussing the problems' as commanded by the question. Many students struggle with the comment bit and one useful little tip is to start with either 'However' or 'Therefore'.

Sadly, your second paragraph does not score. The reason for this is that you cannot get credited for two ethical points or problems in the same essay.

The third paragraph does point out a valid problem when studying children and development – that researchers need to carefully design their procedures to engage and interest little minds which may not have such powers of concentration. You have kept to the P–E–C format nicely.

Demand characteristics are probably more of an issue for kids than for adults. You could have explained why this is the case. Also, you could have said how the leading questions affected Hans's answers, or given an actual example. The last sentence may *look* like a comment, but really Chardonnay you are just trying to hoodwink the examiner into that comment mark – you have written nothing different from your 'Point' sentence … so nothing here!

Counting up all the Ps, Es and Cs…

Part (b) = 8

Total marks = a + b = 18/24

This chapter looks at four core studies in physiological psychology.

1. Schachter and Singer's study of the relative contribution of physiological and cognitive factors to the experience of emotion.

2. Dement and Kleitman's research into the link between REM sleep and dreaming.

3. Sperry's investigation of what happens when you deconnect the two hemispheres of the brain.

4. Raine, Buchsbaum and LaCasse's study of the brains of murderers who plead 'not guilty by reason of insanity'.

Physiological psychology

Introduction to physiological psychology

What is physiological psychology?

Physiological psychology explores human behaviour and experience by looking at people as if they are biological machines. This idea has some value because it is clear that our biology affects our behaviour and experience. On a simple level we know that certain foodstuffs, such as coffee or alcoholic drinks, will affect the way we see the world and the way we behave. Also, it has been observed for a long time that damage to the brain and nervous system can have an effect on behaviour and experience. So the structure of the nervous system and the action of chemicals are the two main themes of physiological psychology. However, the question that arises is *how much* does our biology affect us and what *other* factors intervene to affect the response.

An artist's impression of Phineas Gage's skull

Don't try this at home

The case of Phineas Gage is often cited as an example of the effects of the brain on personality. Phineas was a US railway worker in the nineteenth century who had an industrial accident that blew a hole through his brain. His behaviour changed dramatically after the event but the question remained as to whether this was a result of losing some of his brain or the result of the shock of the experience. Whatever the explanation the case shows how the brain can continue to function even when some parts are damaged.

A more recent version of this was reported recently when Isidro Mejia of Los Angeles had a nail gun discharged into his head. The incident was an accident and fortunately he survived and made a good recovery (BBC, 2004).

The history of brain science

Brain science goes back centuries and there is evidence that people were doing simple brain operations thousands of years ago. For example the technique of trepanation (scraping a hole in the head) was carried out in Africa, Europe and South America. There is evidence of South American people doing this using surgical tools made of bronze and sharp-edged volcanic rock 4000 years ago. It is believed that trepanation was used for both spiritual and magical reasons, as well as to treat headaches, epilepsy and mental illness. As techniques became more sophisticated people would have the 'stone of madness' removed from their skulls by the travelling barber.

The story of the biological approach in psychology starts with the French scientist and philosopher René Descartes (1596–1650). At the time he was writing, a number of scientists were studying the human body as if it were a machine. Descartes suggested that we are made up of two principle components, a body and a soul. He argued that a body without a soul would be an automaton that was completely controlled by external stimuli and its internal chemistry. According to Descartes we are a ghost in a machine, and he set about trying to understand how the machine works.

It was not until the demonstrations of Franz Josef Gall (1758–1828) that we realised the brain is the control centre of this machine. Unfortunately, Gall went on to develop the bogus science of phrenology which attempted to read a person's personality though an analysis of the shape of their skull. Phrenology was based on the idea that the shape of the skull exactly matched the shape of the brain, which is sadly not true. Brain research was moved on by French scientist Pierre Flourens who systematically removed parts of animals' brains in order to observe the effects.

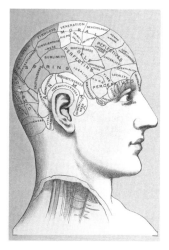

An example of phrenology

If there are areas of the brain that control specific movements then maybe there are also areas for cognitive functions. One of the early examples of evidence for this came from the work of Paul Broca (1824–1880) who was able to show that a small area of the brain is responsible for the production of speech. Damage to this area renders a person speechless even though they can still understand the spoken word. This area is still referred to as Broca's area.

Applications of the physiological approach

Serotonin and prozac

There is currently a widely held theory that depression is caused by lowered levels of the neurochemical serotonin. The basic idea here is that depression is mainly a biological condition and can be alleviated by chemicals that boost the levels of serotonin. The most common class of drugs to do this is SSRIs (selective serotonin reuptake inhibitors); the most commonly known is Prozac.

In the UK in 2002 there were over 26 million prescriptions for anti-depressants (costing nearly £400 million) of which around 60% were for SSRIs (DoH statistics). The number of antidepressants taken in the UK has trebled in ten years. There is little difference in the effectiveness of the many different anti-depressant drugs though there is a difference in price as the SSRIs are much more expensive, so the cost to the NHS has gone up by 20 times in the same ten years.

Between 60% and 80% of people report improvement in their mood or behaviour when taking anti-depressants.

Among the problems with SSRIs are the side effects of which the most worrying is the evidence linking the drug to suicidal thoughts. The UK government recommends that SSRIs are not given to under-18s for this reason.

The biggest issue is the idea that a single chemical in a complex structure like the brain will bring about changes in complex emotions like depression.

The brutal history of psychosurgery

Psychosurgery can be dated to a research report given at a talk in London by Jacobsen and Fulton in 1935. They had been training two chimpanzees to carry out a memory task. One of them, called Becky, was particularly temperamental and became very distressed when she failed the task. She would fly into a tantrum and refuse to try again. Fulton and Jacobsen surgically removed part of the frontal lobes of her cerebral hemispheres which have a lot of connections with the *limbic system*. They reported that Becky no longer became distressed during the memory task.

Egas Moniz was at the talk and speculated whether it would be possible to reduce anxiety states in people by a similar operation. Within a year, Moniz had started to carry out frontal lobotomies on distressed patients. By 1950 over 20,000 people around the world had been treated in this way, including prisoners and children.

Was the operation effective? As with many forms of treatment, the effectiveness was assessed by the people carrying out the operations. Surprisingly enough, they thought that the operations were very successful. However, it eventually became clear that the benefits of this sort of gross destruction of brain tissue were often very small, and sometimes the consequences were disastrous. Moniz himself, who won the Nobel prize in 1949, was shot in the spine by one of his own lobotomised patients. This operation is relatively rarely used today, but it is worth reflecting on how the report of one chimpanzee's behaviour could lead to so many people having their brains mashed.

Biological machines

If we think of people as biological machines then it suggests certain solutions to everyday problems. Look at the following quote from physiological psychologist Peter Milner:

'I am interested in organisms as pieces of machinery, and I would like to know much the same about them as I once wanted to know about the gadgets I saw around me: first, what happens when the controls or inputs are manipulated and, a little later, how it happens' (Milner, 1970, page 1).

This quote has a strange irony to it. If I went to my doctor and said 'I feel like a machine. I am a gadget. One of my bits is going wrong, could you fix it please', the doctor might regard this statement as a sign of my mental instability and immediately send for the straight-jacket. If, on the other hand, I make this statement to a conference of psychologists, and make it not about myself but about 'people', then I can be hailed as a scientific genius.

The idea that we can regard people as objects in science means that people might be treated as objects in everyday life. When objects breakdown we fix them by the use of spare parts (brain surgery) or by throwing them away (murder). It is difficult not to be shocked at such a brutal approach to people and to such a pessimistic vision of human behaviour and experience.

Physiological research

An international team of brain scientists used the EEG technology (see page 96) to look at the effects of chewing different flavours of chewing gum (Yagyu et al., 1997). Twenty volunteers had to chew three different flavours of gum while being attached to an EEG machine. The three flavours were plain (with no sugar or favourings), Relax Gum (a popular Japanese brand) and Relax Extra (with added green tea). Each chewing session went through a strict routine of chewing to strict time, opening and closing eyes when told and strict rest periods. They found two things: first it is possible to measure brain waves while someone is chewing gum and second that the EEG showed different patterns for the three flavours.

Connections

Many psychologists will argue that all psychology will eventually be physiological psychology. They believe that concepts such as free will or consciousness will be found to be controlled by simple biological processes when we have unlocked more secrets of the brain. Other psychologists are more sceptical about what we are able to discover about the brain. Elsewhere in this text Piaget (page 46) and Freud (page 70) both look to biological explanations of behaviour and Milgram (page 132) argued that being obedient is our destiny because it is part of our nature. The physiological approach also gives us explanations for unusual behaviours such as autism and mental illness and for other individual differences such as intelligence or personality. There is no doubt that physiological explanations have contributed to our understanding of a range of conditions but if we follow the argument too far we arrive at biological solutions for all our social problems.

Feelings

How does it feel?

'I just wanna feel' croons Robbie Williams in a song about the most popular theme in music. As a country we have something close to an obsession about how people feel. 'How do you feel?' says the reporter to the footballer who has just lost in a cup final, to the accident victim in hospital, to the winner of an acting award. What can we answer? 'I'm gutted', says the footballer, and 'I'm overwhelmed' gushes the winning actress. We are often at a loss to describe our strong feelings and so we have to use clichés.

William James

In 1884 William James proposed that the bodily changes that happen during emotions occur as a *response* to a stimulating event, and our experience of these changes is what we call emotion. The Danish psychologist, Carl Lange, suggested a similar idea around the same time, and so the theory is referred to as the James–Lange theory of emotion.

The theory suggests that we are afraid because we run, and we are angry because we hit out. This seems to be the wrong way round, but it is easy to think of instances where the recognition of emotion does come after the bodily responses. If you trip on the stairs you automatically make a grab for the banister before you have a chance to recognise a state of fear. After the crisis is over, the emotion you feel includes the perception of a pounding heart, rapid breathing, and a feeling of weakness or trembling in your arms and legs.

Walter Cannon

In 1927 Cannon produced a critique of the James–Lange theory. Among other things he pointed out that:

- The same changes occur in many emotions and this would be a problem if you identify how you feel from the changes in your body. If you describe fear, or sexual attraction or starting to get the flu you will use very similar words.

- We are relatively unaware of changes in our internal organs. We only tend to hear our heart beating because it presses against the chest wall. If somebody asks how your kidneys are today you won't have a clue.

- Artificial changes in the internal organs by drugs ought to produce emotions according to the James–Lange theory but this does not appear to be the case (see 'What if ....' below).

Psychological research into emotion started with this debate and this big question: 'What is the relationship between bodily changes and our experience of emotion?'

What if ...?

... you can't feel the changes in your body?

What if you can't feel your body and therefore can't feel butterflies in your stomach or a tingling in your legs? People who have severe back injuries sometimes lose all sense of feeling. Hohmann (1966) investigated the emotional experiences of 25 people with spinal injuries, finding that all patients had reduced levels of emotion; the higher up the spine that the injury occurred (and therefore the greater the loss of feeling) the greater the loss of emotion.

The exceptions to the loss of emotion were sentimental feelings, which increased in the patients who reported crying and feeling choked up. Most of this evidence seems to support the James–Lange theory but it is important to add that Hohmann's patients still reported feeling emotion; just a bit less of it than they had had before their injuries.

More recent attempts to replicate Hohmann's findings have found that some spinal patients continue to experience a full range of emotions (Chwalisz *et al.,* 1988). These results seem to contradict the James-Lange theory though it has been noted that most spinal cord injuries are incomplete so the patients are still getting some bodily sensations (Damasio, 1999).

What if ...?

... you have body changes for no reason?

Marañon (1924) tested the effects of physiological arousal in the absence of cognitions. He gave participants injections of adrenalin (which creates a feeling of physiological arousal – heart beats faster, slightly sweaty). Seventy-one per cent of the 210 participants reported only their physical symptoms, 29% described some emotional experiences 'as if I was afraid' or 'as if I was awaiting great happiness'. In other words they didn't have an emotional experience but felt it was similar to one.

In a very few cases participants did report an emotional experience but in all of these Marañon had provided an appropriate cognition, such as reminding the participant of a sick child.

False feedback

If we judge our emotions from how we think our body has changed, what if we misread those changes? Valins (1966) suggested that what you think the changes in your body are is more important than what they really are. Valins asked male college students to view a series of slides of semi-nude women. The subjects were wired up with dummy electrodes and heard pre-recorded sounds that were described either as their own pulses or as random sounds. For half the subjects in each group the rate of sounds increased during the presentation of the slides; for the other half it decreased. After the slide show, the subjects were asked to give attractiveness ratings for the women they had seen. As expected, subjects in the pulse condition rated the women as more attractive when the rate increased, believing that they had been aroused by the slides; this belief affected their judgement of attractiveness. This effect has been replicated several times.

Brains, bulls and murders

Emotion in the brain: the limbic system

There are a range of brain structures that are associated with emotions. Perhaps the most researched is the series of small structures hidden deep in the brain called the *limbic system*. It is this system that is the difference between mammals (us) and reptiles (crocodiles), well that and the teeth of course.

The discovery of the importance of these structures in emotion was made by Papez (1937) by looking at the brains of people and animals that had suffered emotional disorders.

Bulls

Two structures are particularly important; the *hypothalamus* which controls the bodily changes associated with emotion and the *amygdala* which has an effect on aggression (see diagram of the brain on page 114). This has been demonstrated by a range of experimental and case study evidence. For example, the Spanish psychologist, José Delgado, is a pioneer in the implantation in the brain of radio activated electrodes. His ability to find an exact spot in an animal's brain is so precise that he has trusted his life to it in dramatic demonstrations. He implanted an electrode in the amygdala of a bull and then got into the bullring with it. When the bull started to charge, Delgado activated the electrode and the bull halted its charge. After repeated experiences of this, the animal became permanently less aggressive. Not many people would put their science on the line in his way.

No need to fear a charging bull – if its amygdala is disabled.

Murders

We can consider the tragic case of Charles Whitman, who murdered his family, then climbed a tower at the University of Texas with a high-velocity rifle. For several hours he shot at everything he saw, killing 14 people and wounding 31 before he was gunned down by police. After the tragedy it was found that Whitman had sought psychiatric help for bad headaches and violent feelings. In a diary he requested an autopsy to be carried out after his death to see if there was a physical cause to his mental anguish. This autopsy discovered a tumour the size of a walnut pressing on the *amygdala*.

The case illustrates the difficulty in making connections between biological changes and behavioural changes. The more you read about the Whitman case the more confusing it gets (if you are interested just Google his name). Whitman had been experiencing a depressed mood over a long period of time and had even told his therapist of his dreams of shooting people from the tower. On the day of the murders he was observed to be very calm and left long diary entries describing the reasons for his actions. It is easy to see how a problem with the brain might make you have a strong emotion and so behave out of character but this can't fully explain Whitman's behaviour. The tumour didn't make him climb the tower and shoot people; ultimately he did have choices – biology alone cannot explain behaviour.

Love on a suspension bridge

In one psychological study male participants who were interviewed on a narrow, wobbly, footbridge suspended high above a scenic canyon (making them experience strong physiological arousal) expressed greater interest in a female interviewer than those interviewed on a bridge over a small stream. This study by Dutton and Aron (1974) shows how we try to interpret the arousal in terms of available cues; the men who felt aroused (on the suspension bridge) interpreted this as love interest whereas the men on the low bridge had no arousal and therefore no need to seek an explanation.

ACTIVITY

Try to describe how you feel (a) when you are afraid, and (b) when you are physically attracted to someone. When you've done this (and don't show it to anyone) look at the comment in the 'Afters' section of this study.

Psycho-trekkies

The Star Trek team represent the conflict between emotion and reason. The doctor (Bones) is the heart of the argument and the science officer (Spock) is the voice of reason. Captain Kirk has to resolve the conflict. The message is that neither reason nor emotion is enough. We have to combine them to be successful (and rule the galaxy). Of course, this is fiction but the conflict between emotion and reason is a common theme in our stories.

There is a link to Freud's theory of personality – some people have suggested that the three Star Trek characters represent the ego, superego and id.

The core study

Schachter and Singer considered the conflicting evidence about emotion from previous research and tried to make sense of it. They combined what was known about the physiological responses in emotional states, and also the cognitive approach of Cannon. They proposed a two-factor theory of emotion and set out to test it in this innovative experiment. The issues for them were how to create a state of arousal and how to measure the emotion in their participants.

Stanley Schachter and Jerome E. Singer (1962) Cognitive, social and physiological determinants of emotional state. *Psychological Review*, 69, 379–399.

KEY TERMS

What is 'cognition'? In chapter 1 you studied cognitive psychology, which was concerned with the influence of mental processes on our behaviour. 'Cognition' refers to mental processes.

Abstract

The study aimed to see if a participant who is in a state of physiological arousal which has no immediate explanation would 'label' this state in terms of the cognitions available to him.

Method

128 male students were exposed to three independent variables:

1   *State of physiological arousal*: given an injection of 'Suproxin' (a new vitamin), which was either adrenalin or saline.

2   *Available explanation*: informed, kept ignorant or misinformed about the effects of the injection.

3   *Environmental cue*: a euphoric or angry confederate.

A summary of the seven conditions:

Euphoria	Anger
(1) Epi Inf	(5) Epi Inf
(2) Epi Ign	(6) Epi Ign
(3) Epi Mis	
(4) Placebo	(7) Placebo
(Epi = epinephrine i.e. adrenalin)	

The participants' emotional state was assessed by:

- **Observation:** two experimenters watched participant's interaction with confederate through a one-way mirror, providing activity index or anger units.

- **Indirect:** (1) self-rating scales of anger and happiness to produce a happiness score, (2) open-ended questions.

- **Pulse rate** before and after injection.

Results

The happiness gradient in the euphoria condition was:

Epi Mis > Epi Ign > Placebo > Epi Inf

The anger condition reflected the same pattern in reverse because happiness = less anger (Epi Ign < Placebo < Epi Inf).

The placebo condition should have been lowest but some participants in this condition did experience arousal and thus had 'evaluative needs'.

Discussion

This shows that, where evaluative needs exist, emotional experience is influenced by environmental cues. Evaluative needs were created by having physiological arousal without any appropriate explanation. If an appropriate explanation was available (the informed condition) then the environmental cues had no effect, as predicted.

CORESTUDY

Aim

The aim of this study was to investigate Schachter's two-factor theory of emotion. He proposed that emotional experience results from a combination of internal and external factors: the internal state of physiological arousal suggests that there has been an emotional event. We use external cues to inform us what the emotion is.

Schachter (1959) proposed that if you slipped someone a pill containing adrenalin (which creates physiological arousal) the subsequent state would lead to 'evaluative needs' – the person would seek to understand and label their bodily feelings. For example, if a beautiful woman is present a man might interpret the feelings as physical attraction, or if he was arguing with his wife the man might interpret the arousal as hatred. The attractive woman and the wife are external (environmental) cues.

Propositions

1   If a participant is in a state of physiological arousal which has no immediate explanation, he will 'label' this state in terms of the cognitions available to him.

2   If a participant is in a state of physiological arousal (e.g. from an injection of adrenalin) which has a completely appropriate explanation, no evaluative needs will arise and an individual is unlikely to label his feelings in terms of the cognitions available.

3   In the same cognitive circumstances an individual will only describe an emotional experience if he happens to be experiencing some physiological arousal.

Method

Participants

These were 184 American male college students taking an introductory course in psychology who received extra points on their final exam for taking part.

Procedure

Prospective participants were told

'In this experiment we would like to make various tests of your vision. We are particularly interested in how certain vitamin compounds and vitamin supplements affect the visual skills. In particular, we want to find out how the vitamin compound called "Suproxin" affects your vision'.

Participants who objected (and one did) could opt out.

The independent variables

1 The injection All participants were told that they were given Suproxin but in reality it was either:

- *Adrenalin* (epinephrine). The adrenalin would make them feel physiologically aroused (increased heart beat, blood pressure and breathing, flushed face).

- *Saline*, a placebo – no physiological effect.

2 Manipulating an appropriate explanation There were three further conditions. The experimenter described the effects of the injection to the participant:

- *Informed:* told correct effects of injection (*Epi Inf* condition).

- *Ignorant:* told nothing (*Epi Ign*).

- *Misinformed:* told incorrect effects, that they would possibly experience a slight headache, itching all over their body and numbness in their feet (*Epi Mis*).

- *Placebo:* given the 'ignorant' instruction, i.e. told nothing about any side effects.

3 Producing an emotion-inducing cognition Each participant was placed in a situation where a confederate provided environmental cues (cognitions). Immediately after the injection the confederate was introduced as another participant and both were told to wait 20 minutes for the experiment proper in order for the injection to take effect. During this time the confederate was trained to behave according to one of the following scripts:

- *Euphoria:* The confederate engaged in a series of slightly manic activities: for example he flew a paper plane around the room, ending by throwing it at the participant.

- *Anger:* Both participant and confederate were given a five-page questionnaire to fill in. The confederate started by passing innocent comments but grew increasingly annoyed (e.g. 'How ridiculous can you get?') as the questions became more personal (e.g. 'How many times a week do you have sexual intercourse?') and ended up in a rage, stomping out.

Participants in the misinformed conditioned were only exposed to the euphoric confederate because it was felt that this would be a sufficient control for the informed condition.

Confederates

A confederate is an individual in an experiment who is not a real participant and has been instructed how to behave by the experimenter. A confederate often acts as an independent variable.

ACTIVITY

1 Write the names of each of the seven conditions on a slip of paper and place in a hat. Students take turns drawing out a slip of paper. They must then describe the condition and predict a participant's response. Keep a score of correct answers.

2 Make a mobile to represent this study in some way.

The dependent variables: measurement of emotional state

1 Observation The participant's interaction with the confederate was scored by two observers watching through a one-way mirror. A score was obtained for euphoria and for anger (activity index or anger units) by categorising the participant's behaviour in each of the parts of the confederate's pre-set routine, e.g. whether the participant was joining in or not with the confederate.

2 Self-report The participants were asked to fill in a questionnaire which included two questions about mood: 'How irritated, angry or annoyed would you say you feel?' (4 = I feel extremely irritated and angry) and 'How good or happy would you say you feel?' (4 = I feel extremely happy and good).

A happiness score was calculated by subtracting the angry score from the happy score.

The questionnaire also contained questions about the physical effects experienced: 'Did you feel any palpitation (consciousness of your own heart beat)? Any tremor (involuntary shaking of the hands, arms or legs)? Did you feel any numbness in your feet? Any itching sensation? Any headaches?' These were rated on a four-point scale.

Finally there were two open-ended questions about other physical or emotional sensations.

3 Pulse rate The participant's pulse rate was measured both before the injection and at the end of the study as a measure of physiological arousal.

Debriefing

After filling in this questionnaire the participants were informed in detail about the true nature of the experiment. Then they were given a further questionnaire about the experiment which asked, most importantly, whether they had any suspicions about the experimental procedures. Eleven of the participants were so suspicious of some features of the experiment that their data were discarded.

Qs

1 Schachter and Singer proposed a 'two-factor theory of emotion'. What are the two factors?

2 Which participants would experience 'evaluative needs'?

3 The *epi mis* was a 'control' condition. What was it controlling for?

4 Why was it necessary to have an anger and a euphoria condition for the environmental cue?

5 Why might participants in the placebo condition have been physiologically aroused?

6 How might demand characteristics affect the results of this experiment?

7 Why was it a good idea to use two independent observers to record the participants' behaviour?

Results

Effects on physical state

Participants in the epinephrine conditions showed more physiological arousal than those in the placebo condition as measured by pulse rate and as indicated by self-ratings.

However, there were individual differences – five participants in the adrenalin condition reported no effects.

Effects on emotional state

Euphoria Participants in the ignorant and misinformed conditions rated their emotional state as significantly more euphoric and behaved in a more active manner than those in the informed condition (see graph).

The effect may be greatest for those in the misinformed condition because in the ignorant condition participants had no explanation for their arousal and thus decided for themselves that it was due to the injection.

Anger The informed group showed more happiness (i.e. less anger) and behaved less angrily than the ignorant group (see graph) thus showing again the effect of 'evaluative needs'.

Placebo The data from the placebo group fell between the ignorant and informed condition.

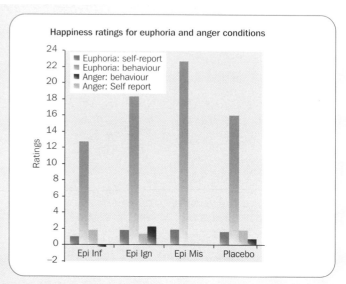

Happiness ratings for euphoria and anger conditions

Legend:
- Euphoria: self-report
- Euphoria: behaviour
- Anger: behaviour
- Anger: Self report

(y-axis: Ratings, –2 to 24; x-axis: Epi Inf, Epi Ign, Epi Mis, Placebo)

Evaluation of the experimental design

There were several problems:

1 The participants in the placebo condition may have experienced some physiological arousal because the experiment was fairly dramatic. This would explain why the scores for the placebo condition were higher than the informed condition.

2 Some of the *Epi Ign* and *Epi Mis* participants did attribute their physiological state to the injection (e.g. reporting that 'the shot gave me the shivers') which means they would not be affected by the confederate.

3 Participants were less willing to behave in an angry than a euphoric manner because the experimenter (who they knew) was present some of the time.

Discussion

The expectation was that mood should vary in the following fashion: Epi Mis> Epi Ign > Epi Inf = Placebo

When the inconsistent data are excluded the results strongly conform to the expectations. This reliance on excluding some of the data means the conclusions are tentative but further studies (e.g. Schachter and Wheeler, 1962) support the original propositions.

This study explains why, despite the fact that we have a limited range of states of arousal, we experience such a range of different emotions. The results indicate that emotional states may be considered as a function both of physiological arousal and of cognition appropriate to this state of arousal.

Biographical notes on Schachter and Singer

Stanley Schachter (1922–1997) investigated many aspects of social behaviour aside from his research on emotion, such as looking at the basis of nicotine addiction and investigating miserliness and obesity (obese individuals eat more because they are more affected by external cues whereas non-obese people tend to respond to internal cues of hunger). He also was involved in a memorable study of a religious cult who believed the world was to end on a particular date (see page 195).

Jerome E. Singer is now an Emeritus Professor at the University of Uniformed Services, Maryland, US. When we contacted him for this short biography he said that the *'only research I now do is anecdotal: what are the most effective and efficient ways to spoil grandchildren. If your biographical piece turns up anything interesting about my later life, I would appreciate if you could tell me.'* (personal communication).

Jerome E. Singer.

Qs

1 Identify **one** apparently inconsistent finding and try to explain it.

2 Link each of the **three** initial propositions to a finding from the study.

3 In what way does the study provide evidence counter to William James' view?

4 How could Schachter and Singer use their theory to interpret the results of Marañon's study (see page 88)?

The research method

This study was a lab experiment. *What are the strengths and limitations of this research method in the context of this study?*

The sample

In what way are the participants in this sample unique? How does this affect the conclusions drawn from the study?

Data collection

Behaviour was measured by observation and by using self-report methods. *Give* **one** *advantage and* **one** *disadvantage of each of these methods in the context of this study.*

Ethical issues

What ethical issues should have concerned the researchers in this study?

Qualitative or quantitative?

What kind of data were collected in this study? What are the strengths and limitations of producing this kind of data in the context of this study?

Validity

It was difficult to control the physiological arousal experienced by the participants. How do you think this would affect the validity of the results?

Applications

How valuable was this study?

A curious outcome was that the placebo effect, which doctors sometimes rely on when treating psychological illnesses, can sometimes backfire. For example, insomniacs have trouble sleeping because they feel in a state of arousal when trying to sleep. Their doctor gives them a placebo pill which purports to help them sleep. If they continue to feel arousal the placebo may have the opposite effect – they can only surmise that, since the drug is proving ineffective, they must be particularly distressed, so greater insomnia results.

What next? ?

Describe **one** change to this study, and say how you think this might affect the outcome.

DEBATE

Was this study really unethical? Divide your class into groups and let each group decide whether they think you would allow this study to be repeated today.

Multiple choice questions

1. Schachter and Singer proposed that:
    (a) Physiological arousal alone is sufficient for an emotional experience.
    (b) Cognitive cues alone lead to an emotional experience.
    (c) Cognitive cues and physiological arousal are both needed for an emotional experience.
    (d) None of the above.

2. Adrenalin causes:
    (a) Faster heart beat.
    (b) Slower breathing rate.
    (c) Hallucinations.
    (d) All of the above.

3. Epinephrine is another word for:
    (a) Placebo.   (b) Saline solution.
    (c) Noradrenaline. (d) Adrenalin.

4. A placebo is:
    (a) The Spanish word for IV.
    (b) A drug which slows down metabolism.
    (c) A drug that mimics adrenalin.
    (d) A drug that has no physiological effect.

5. Which instructions were given to the placebo group?
    (a) Informed.   (b) Ignorant.
    (c) Misinformed.   (d) All of the above.

6. In which condition should participants experience 'evaluative needs'?
    (a) Epi informed.   (b) Epi ignorant.
    (c) Epi misinformed. (d) Both (b) and (c).

7. Which of the conditions was not used with the angry confederate?
    (a) Epi informed.   (b) Epi ignorant.
    (c) Epi misinformed. (d) Placebo.

8. According to the two-factor theory, what will be the response of a participant in the misinformed condition?
    (a) Affected by confederate's behaviour.
    (b) Seek cognitive cues to explain arousal.
    (c) Unaffected by the confederate's behaviour.
    (d) Both (a) and (b).

9. What should be the response of a participant in the informed condition?
    (a) Affected by confederate's behaviour.
    (b) Seeks cognitive cues to explain arousal.
    (c) Unaffected by the confederate's behaviour.
    (d) Both (a) and (b).

10. The participants' behaviour was assessed using:
    (a) Observation through a one-way mirror.
    (b) Self-report questionnaire.
    (c) Measuring pulse rates.
    (d) All of the above.

Answers are on page 121.

Exam questions

1. In Schachter and Singer's study on emotion, one variable was manipulated using an injection. What were the **four** conditions of this variable? [OCR AS Psy, Jan 2001, paper 1]   [4]

2. Explain what the study by Schachter and Singer tells us about emotion. [OCR AS Psy, May 2005, paper 1]   [4]

3. From the study by Schachter and Singer (emotion):

    (a) Identify **two** ways in which the researchers measured the emotion of the subjects (participants).   [2]

    (b) Give **one** problem with each type of measurement.   [2]
    [OCR AS Psy, June 1998, paper 1]

4. From the Schachter and Singer study on emotion:

    (a) Give **two** effects that adrenalin (epinephrine) has on a person.   [2]

    (b) Give **one** explanation for the behaviour of the epi-ignorant group.   [2]
    [OCR AS Psy, Jan 2004, paper 1]

Show some emotion

Emotional intelligence

The expression *emotional intelligence* or EI describes a kind of intelligence or skill that involves the ability to perceive, assess and positively influence your own and other people's emotions.

John D. Mayer and Peter Salovey introduced the term in a series of academic papers. They divide emotional intelligence abilities into four areas:

- the capacity to accurately perceive emotions;
- the capacity to use emotions to facilitate thinking;
- the capacity to understand emotional meanings;
- the capacity to manage emotions.

The idea of EI was popularised (some say hijacked) by Daniel Goleman in his 1995 book *Emotional Intelligence* (Mayer and Salovey argue that he has left out key features). Goleman suggests that there is not a strong relationship between IQ and success in life, but instead success depends on emotional intelligence (EI).

Unfortunately although this sounds appealing it does not have much evidence to back it up.

After the publication of his book, Goleman founded the *Emotional Intelligence Consortium* in order to promote his research. He has developed his framework of emotional skills which you can check out at his website. Some schools in the USA have actually implemented programmes to develop emotional abilities in children and claim to have produced good results.

On the fiddle

If we can control our bodily changes can we control our emotions?

This was tested in an experiment by Ian James (1988) with six young violinists. The musicians were filmed and assessed in conditions designed to increase stress. They played one piece in the morning and another in the afternoon. Before the afternoon recital half of the musicians were given a drug while half were given a placebo. The drug was a beta-blocker which stops the action of adrenalin. There are two types of receptor sites for adrenalin – alpha and beta. When the beta sites are stimulated the heart accelerates, blood vessels dilate in the skin and muscles, and the muscles of the intestine and bladder are relaxed. Many of our responses to danger or stress are switched on through such receptors. The beta-blocker blocks the beta receptors and stops adrenalin having its usual effect.

The violinists who were given the beta-blocker gave a noticeably better performance in the afternoon. The drug also reduced the feeling of anxiety as well as the symptoms. The violinists noticed this; one reported that in the afternoon '*I was less nervous both physically and mentally*', and another said '*...the beta-blockers made you relax more, mentally and physically.*'

Comment (follow up to the activity on page 89)

You will probably find that you have mainly used descriptions of bodily changes, for example, 'my legs turned to jelly' or 'I felt warm' or 'I had butterflies in my stomach'. We experience various bodily changes when we experience emotion and there is clearly a strong connection between the reactions of our body and our feelings. In fact it seems to be the easiest way to describe our feelings to someone else.

Selling emotion

One of the most expensive commodities is emotion. Films can make you sad or scared or uplifted. So can music. This is so powerful that film makers test the final version on a selected audience using *people meters* before they release them to the general public. These meters measure the slight changes in emotion that a viewer feels during the movie. You watch it and you know it's rubbish but it still makes you feel good because they have all the tricks of matching music to images that manipulate your emotions.

This type of research is also used in the design of products. For example Pieter Desmet (Delft University of Technology) created the *Product Emotion Measurement Instrument* (PrEmo) to measure emotional responses. He reasoned that people are very good at interpreting emotional expressions. In the face-to-face encounters of daily life we are always monitoring the emotions of others – is she annoyed with me? Was my joke funny? In some cases facial expression gives us a way of communicating emotion that is even more effective than verbal expression. The PrEmo uses this skill to measure 14 emotions that people often report:

Pleasant emotions	Unpleasant emotions
Desire	Indignation
Pleasant surprise	Contempt
Inspiration	Disgust
Amusement	Unpleasant surprise
Admiration	Dissatisfaction
Satisfaction	Disappointment
Fascination	Boredom

People use the PrEmo by clicking on a puppet (such as those below) that best describes their feelings about the product they are reviewing.

LINKS TO OTHER STUDIES

The obvious links are to the other **physiological psychology** studies because of the attempt to explain behaviour using our knowledge of the brain and the nervous system. This line of argument leads you to consider how to stimulate or reduce emotion by biological means. The other set of links is to **cognitive psychology** because we have to make sense of our feelings to be able to describe the emotion. The Schachter and Singer theory is a bold attempt to bring together the cognitive and the biological. One study that makes use of the concept of arousal is also found in one of the social core studies, the subway samaritans (**Piliavin, Rodin and Piliavin**).

Key**ISSUE**
Ethics

Many studies are criticised for lack of ethics. It is not acceptable for participants to be harmed during the course of any study. However, what constitutes 'harm'? Is it harmful for a person to experience mild discomfort or mild stress? Is it acceptable to lie to participants about what an experiment is about? Such deception may be necessary so that participants' behaviour is not affected by knowing what the aim of the experiment is.

Ethics is a topic which has no straightforward answers. Psychologists have to weigh up various factors when deciding whether a study is ethically acceptable. Professional organisations such as the British Psychological Society (BPS) produces ethical guidelines or 'codes of conduct' to help do this.

ACTIVITY

1 Before you read this page consider what is ethically acceptable in psychological research. Draw up your own list of ethical guidelines.

2 In a small group rank the ethical issues below in order of importance.

'I want to find out important things about human behaviour, which means I need to design my experiment in this way'.

'I have rights, you can't do that'.

Ethical issues are like a see-saw.

The BPS code of conduct

On deception

Intentional deception of the participants over the purpose and general nature of the investigation should be avoided whenever possible. Participants should never be deliberately misled without extremely strong scientific or medical justification.

On protection from harm

Investigators have a primary responsibility to protect participants from physical and mental harm during the investigation. Normally the risk of harm must be no greater than in ordinary life.

KEY TERMS

An ethical issue is a conflict between what the researcher wants and the rights of participants.

Ethical guidelines (ethical principles, code of conduct) are instructions to guide professional conduct and practice. They aim to resolve ethical issues.

Ethical committee A group of people within a research institution who must approve a study before it begins.

Debriefing A post-research interview conducted for ethical and practical reasons: (1) to inform participants of the true nature of the study and ensure their well-being, (2) may be used to gain important feedback about procedures used in the study.

Exam-style question

Ethical issues arise because of conflicts between the requirements of research and the rights of participants. Ethical guidelines are produced to help protect participants.

Using **four** Core Studies answer the following questions:

(a) Describe how each study may have caused psychological harm to its participants.   [12]

(b) Briefly discuss the arguments for and arguments against the deception of participants.   [12]

Ethical issue	How to deal with it	Problems
Deception [Deception isn't always objectionable, e.g. Loftus and Palmer]	The need for deception should be approved by an ethical committee, weighing up benefits (of the study) against costs (to participants). Participants should be fully debriefed after the study and offered the opportunity to withhold their data.	Cost–benefit decisions are flawed because both are subjective judgements. And the costs are not always apparent until after the study. Debriefing can't turn the clock back – a participant may still feel embarrassed or have lowered self-esteem.
Informed consent	Ask participants to formally indicate their agreement to participate and this should be based on comprehensive information concerning the nature and purpose of the research and their role in it.	If a participant knows such information this may spoil the study. Even if researchers have obtained informed consent, that does not guarantee that participants really do understand what they have agreed to.
The right to withdraw	Participants should be informed at the beginning of a study that they have the right to withdraw at any time during the study.	Participants may feel they shouldn't withdraw because it will spoil the study.
Protection from harm	Avoid any situation that may cause psychological or physical damage.	Researchers are not always able to accurately predict the risks of taking part in a study.
Confidentiality	Do not record the names of any participants, use numbers instead or use false names.	It is sometimes possible to work out who the participants were, for example knowing the geographical location of a school.
Privacy	Do not observe anyone without their informed consent unless it is in a public place.	There is not universal agreement about what constitutes a public place.

Sleep and dreams

Stages of sleep

Sleep does not mean switching off and closing down the body's activity. Far from it. Sleep is a very active state, both physically and mentally. Our bodies move frequently and, more interestingly for psychologists, our brain activity is even more varied during sleep than it is during the normal waking state.

Measuring sleep

Sleep researchers commonly look to three measures to describe the stages of sleep. First, *gross brain wave activity*, as measured by an *electroencephalogram (EEG)*. This machine provides the summary of electrical activity from one area of the brain. Second, *muscle tone* is measured with an *electromyogram (EMG)*. Third, *eye movement* is recorded via an *electro-oculogram (EOG)*.

Awake

When we are awake our brain wave patterns (measured by EEG) can be classified into two types, beta and alpha. *Beta waves* are associated with day-to-day wakefulness. During periods of relaxation, while still awake, our brain waves become slower and more regular. These types of waves are called *alpha waves*.

Asleep: stages one and two

In this stage the brain shows *theta waves*, which are even slower in frequency and greater in amplitude than alpha waves. The difference between relaxation and stage 1 sleep is gradual and subtle. As the sleeper moves to stage 2 sleep theta wave activity continues. Stages 1 and 2 are relatively 'light' stages of sleep. In fact, if someone is awoken during one of these stages, he or she will often report not being asleep at all.

Asleep: stages three and four

During a normal night's sleep a sleeper passes from the theta waves of stage 1 and 2, to the *delta waves* of stage 3 and 4. Delta sleep is our deepest sleep, the point when our brain waves are least like waking brain waves. It is the most

difficult stage during which to wake sleepers, and when they are awakened they are usually sleepy and disoriented. Interestingly, delta sleep is when sleepwalking and sleeptalking are most likely to occur.

REM sleep

REM sleep gets its name from the darting eye movements that accompany it (rapid eye movement), as indicated by the EOG. It is also characterised by a sudden loss of muscle tone, which is measured by the EMG. In fact during REM sleep a person is effectively paralysed. This stage is also associated with a unique brain wave pattern – fast, desynchronised EEG activity resembling the awake state.

The puzzle of dreams

Dreams have puzzled people for centuries. Why do we dream, and what do they mean? Some people believe that dreams can prophesy the future, some think they tell us about our emotions and some think they are just random firing of the brain that mean nothing.

Perchance to dream

In perhaps the most famous speech from a Shakespeare play, Hamlet considers whether he should take his own life or not. To be or not to be is a question about whether to go on or not. But as he muses about this he starts to consider what death is like. Is it an extension of sleep? But what if our nightmares persist in this endless sleep?

…To die, to sleep;
To sleep: perchance to dream: ay, there's the rub;
For in that sleep of death what dreams may come
When we have shuffled off this mortal coil,
Must give us pause: there's the respect
That makes calamity of so long life;

Hamlet *(III. i)*

Normal night

In a normal night's sleep, a sleeper begins in stage 1, moves down through the stages, to stage 4, then back up through the stages, with the exception that stage 1 is replaced by REM, then the sleeper goes back down through the stages again. One cycle, from stage 1 to REM takes approximately 90 minutes. This cycle is repeated throughout the night, with the length of REM periods increasing, and the length of delta sleep decreasing, until during the last few cycles there is no delta sleep at all.

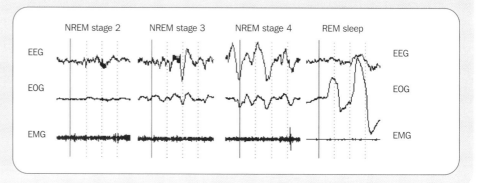

Dream worlds and real worlds

When I am dreaming then I feel as if I am there. I get scared or I get happy depending on what is happening in my dream world. But it is not real and when I wake up I know that. But do I really know that? Maybe this is all a dream and one day I will wake up from this. What is the difference between the awake world and the dream world? When I'm awake I use the sensations I get and my experience of the past events to create a perception of the world. This 'real' world is as much in my head as my dream world. So how do I tell the difference?

Shakespeare had a lot to say about dreams in his plays and he ponders on this idea in *The Tempest* (IV, i) when Prospero says

We are such stuff
As dreams are made on, and our little life
Is rounded with a sleep.

'Do androids dream of electric sheep?'

If dreams are just the random thoughts of a mind that is switched off then do computers dream? The little red light is on and it sometimes whirrs and gurgles. Is it dreaming and if so what is it dreaming of? Possibly the best ever title for a science fiction book asks the question, *Do Androids Dream of Electric Sheep?* The book was adapted to make the cult film *Blade Runner*.

Famous dreams: the discovery of the benzene ring

One of the most famous dreams in science was reported by the German chemist Kekulé. He was puzzling over the properties of benzene which did not fit into the theories of chemical structure that existed at the time. He describes what happened next:

'...I turned my chair toward the fire place and sank into a doze. Again the atoms were flitting before my eyes. Smaller groups now kept modestly in the background. My mind's eye sharpened by repeated visions of a similar sort, now distinguished larger structures of varying forms. Long rows frequently rose together, all in movement, winding and turning like serpents; and see! What was that? One of the serpents seized its own tail and the form whirled mockingly before my eyes. I came awake like a flash of lightning. This time also I spent the remainder of the night working out the consequences of the hypothesis.'

Sleep and the brain

We don't fall asleep. Our brains make us go to sleep. Sleep is a specialised state which has evolved in all animals to serve particular functions. If sleep serves vital functions then it is important for survival for the brain to 'make' us sleep.

Brain research has identified some of the key areas. The *hypothalamus* appears to be an important region for controlling non-REM sleep and may well keep track of how long we have been awake and how large our sleep debt is. There is a special group of cells in the hypothalamus called the *suprachiasmatic nucleus* (SCN) which receives information about light from the eyes and 'tells' the brain when it is safe to sleep. Cells in the hypothalamus are also sensitive to rises in body temperature and send a message to sleep-related cells. This explains why having a warm bath makes you feel sleepy.

The area of the brainstem known as the *pons* is important in REM sleep. During REM sleep, the *pons* sends signals to the visual system of the *thalamus* and to the cerebral cortex. The pons also sends signals to the spinal cord, causing the temporary paralysis that is part of REM sleep. Other brain sites are also important in the sleep process. For example, the thalamus generates many of the brain rhythms in non-REM sleep that we see as EEG patterns.

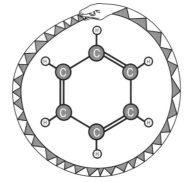

The form of the benzene ring first appeared to Friedrich Kekulé in a dream as a serpent seizing its own tail.

There are numerous other examples of how dreams have inspired people. For example, the most famous horror story of all time, *Frankenstein*, was dreamt by Mary Wollstonecraft Shelley in 1816. Musicians have also found inspiration and success with their dreams. Paul McCartney composed his hit song 'Yesterday' following a dream in 1965.

Slow wave sleep disorders
Sleepwalking

Some of the most puzzling sleep disorders are associated with slow wave sleep (also known as deep sleep, stages 3 and 4), the most notable being sleepwalking and night terrors (which are different from the nightmares of REM sleep). They mainly occur in childhood and tend to have some hereditary basis. Sleepwalking peaks in adolescence, but declines rapidly by the late teens. Episodes are often triggered by anxiety; in susceptible children, the worry can be trivial – the loss of a favourite toy, or just a frustrating day.

Sleeptalking

Some people talk in their sleep. Fortunately for many of them they only talk nonsense. Sleeptalking, like sleepwalking, can't normally occur in REM sleep because of the general paralysis at this time. Sleeptalking is common in adults and even more so in children. In fact, almost all children will do this if they are talked to during light sleep. Then there is some sort of confused reply that has little relevance to what was originally said. If two or more children share a bedroom, and one starts sleeptalking, then the other might well join in and create a bizarre meaningless conversation that we have come to know and love from the *Big Brother* house.

The core study

Remarkably, when Dement and Kleitman carried out this study, they were testing for the first time the idea that the observed physical response of rapid eye movement during sleep was connected to the almost mystical state of dreaming. The physiology of sleep was only just beginning to be unravelled and all of a sudden the world of dreams seemed to be coming into the domain of science.

William Dement and Nathaniel Kleitman (1957) The relation of eye movements during sleep to dream activity: An objective method for the study of dreaming. *Journal of Experimental Psychology*, 53 (5), 339–346.

Abstract

Method

Nine adults were studied, five of them intensively. Participants were awoken in REM and NREM sleep, and asked to record the details of any dreams on tape. In some instances the experimenter interviewed them further.

Results

On average REM activity lasted 20 minutes and occurred every 92 minutes. The frequency was characteristic for each individual. Episodes tended to be longer later on in the night. REM activity was accompanied by a relatively fast EEG pattern.

Three approaches to investigating dreams were used:

1 *Eye movement periods and dream recall*: high incidence of recall of dreaming during REM periods, and a low incidence during NREM periods. Most of recall in NREM periods was within eight minutes of the end of an REM episode.

2 *Length of REM periods and subjective dream-duration estimates*: Participants were 82% correct in estimating whether REM activity lasted for 5 or 15 minutes. There was also a significant correlation between the duration of REM activity and the number of words used to describe a dream.

3 *Eye movement patterns and visual imagery of the dream* were linked, for example horizontal REM linked to a dream about two people throwing tomatoes.

Effects of practice. Participants didn't report more dreams in the second half of the series.

Discussion

There appears to be a clear and exclusive relationship between dream states and REM activity, providing an objective means of studying dream states.

ACTIVITY

People have very different, and quite characteristic, dreams. Work out a system to record the kind of dreams experienced by members of your class. There is a 'Dream questionnaire' on page 216 which you might use. Or use one from the web (e.g. look at http://www.rpi.edu/~verwyc/DREAMA1.html).

You could even do this as one of your practical investigations.

COREstudy

Introduction

In order to be able to study dream activity it is necessary to have an objective means of knowing when someone is dreaming. This is possible if a link can be established between dreaming and some specific physiological activity. Aserinsky and Kleitman (1955) observed that periods of rapid eye movements during sleep were associated with a high incidence of dream sleep.

This study further investigated the relationship between eye movements and dreaming to demonstrate that dream experiences and REM activity are two facets of the same thing. Three approaches were used to study REM activity, as outlined in the abstract.

Method

Participants

These were nine adults, seven adult males and two females. Five of them were studied intensively.

Procedure

The experimental sessions were repeated many times. Typically the participant reported to the sleep laboratory just before their usual bedtime. They had been told to eat normally but abstain from alcohol or drinks containing caffeine on the day of the experiment.

Electrodes were attached around the participant's eyes to measure electrical activity and hence eye movement (using EOG), and attached to the participant's scalp to record brain waves (using EEG) as a measure of depth of sleep. The participant then went to sleep in a quiet darkened room.

At various times during the night participants were woken by a bell, placed by their bed. The awakenings were done either during an REM period or at varying time periods after REM activity had stopped (i.e. during NREM sleep). On average the participants were awoken 5.7 times a night and slept for six hours.

The investigators used various different patterns for awakening the five most intensively studied participants to avoid any unintentional pattern. For example, with two participants they used a table of random numbers, one participant was awoken during three REM periods and then three NREM periods, and one was told he would only be awoken during REM sleep but in fact was awoken randomly during REM and NREM sleep.

None of the participants were not told whether they had just been having REM activity when they were awoken.

The participant was instructed to speak into a recording machine near their bed, (a) stating whether they had been dreaming and (b) describing, if they could, the content of the dream. Recording their answers in this way was done because direct contact might mean that the experimenter would 'cue' certain responses from the participant.

An experimenter was listening outside the room and occasionally entered the room to further question the participant on some particular point of the dream. The participants usually fell back to sleep within five minutes.

Results

The occurrence of REM activity

- All participants had REM activity every night.

- REM activity was accompanied by a relatively fast EEG pattern.

- When REM activity was absent there were periods of deeper sleep, indicated by either slow wave activity or sleep-spindles.

- No REM activity occurred during the initial onset of sleep.

- REM periods lasted between 3 and 50 minutes, with a mean of about 20 minutes. The REM period tended to get longer the later in the night it occurred. The eyes were not constantly in motion during REM activity, instead there were bursts of between 2 and 100 movements.

- REM periods occurred at fairly regular intervals. The frequency was characteristic for each individual. WD averaged one REM period every 70 minutes, for KC it was once every 104 minutes. The average was an REM episode every 92 minutes.

- Despite the disturbance of being regularly awakened the REM periods were as frequent as those recorded in a previous study of uninterrupted sleep.

- If a participant was awakened during an REM period during the final hours of sleep, when such periods tended to be quite long, they often went back into REM sleep as if the heightened brain activity had not run its course.

Qs

1 Name **two** characteristics of REM sleep.

2 Write a suitable hypothesis for this study.

3 Would it matter if participants knew the purpose of the study? Why or why not?

4 Does the size of the sample matter?

5 Did all participants show a similar ratio of recall/no recall in REM sleep? How might this be important?

6 Why might the sleep patterns and eye movements of the participants have differed from sleep in their own beds?

7 Were participants most likely to report that they had been dreaming early on in the night or later?

8 What might suggest that reports of dreaming during NREM sleep were actually 'leftovers' from REM sleep?

Three approaches

1 Eye movement periods and dream recall

Participants were considered to be dreaming only if they could relate a coherent, fairly detailed description of dream content.

The table below shows how many dreams were recalled after being awoken in REM or NREM sleep in the five most intensively studied participants.

- For all participants there was a high incidence of recall of dreaming during REM periods, and a low incidence of recall during NREM periods (see pie charts), regardless of the patterns used to determine awakenings.

Participant	No. of dreams recalled in REM sleep out of times awakened		No. of dreams recalled in NREM sleep out of times awakened	
DN	17/26	65 %	3/24	12.5%
IR	26/34	76 %	2/31	6 %
KC	36/40	90 %	3/34	9 %
WD	37/42	88 %	1/35	3 %
PM	24/30	80 %	2/25	8 %

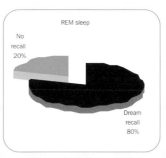

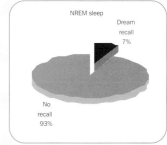

- However, there were times when REM activity was not associated with a coherent dream and times when NREM sleep did produce a coherent dream recall.

- There were individual differences – some participants were better able to recall their dreams.

- If participants were awoken more than eight minutes after the end of an REM period, very few dreams were recalled (6 dreams in 132 awakenings) whereas if participants were awoken within eight minutes of an REM period the proportion recalled rose (5 dreams in 17 awakenings).

- When participants were awoken during deep NREM sleep they sometimes were rather bewildered and reported that they must have been dreaming but couldn't remember the dream. They recalled a mood, such as anxiety or pleasantness, but no specific content.

- Most of the instances when dreams could not be recalled during REM sleep occurred during the early part of the night (only 9 of the 39 cases of no dreams in REM sleep were reported in the last four hours of sleep).

Results continued

2 Length of REM periods and subjective dream duration

A further way to establish the link between REM sleep and dreaming would be to show that the length of REM activity was proportional to the estimated duration of a dream. This was done by awakening participants either 5 or 15 minutes after the onset of REM activity and asking them to decide which was the correct duration. Some but not all of the participants were very accurate in their estimations.

A different way of assessing duration of REM activity in relation to length of dream was to calculate a correlation between how long the REM episode lasted and the number of words the participant used to describe the dream. The correlations were all significant and ranged between 0.40 and 0.71 for each participant.

3 Eye movement patterns and visual imagery of the dream

There was great variation in eye movements during REM periods and it was proposed that the movements might correspond to where and at what the dreamer was looking. To investigate this the participants were woken when their eye movements were mainly vertical or horizontal or both or neither, as shown in the table below:

Type of eye movement	Example of content of dream reported by participants
Mainly vertical *There were 3 such dreams reported*	Standing at bottom of cliff and looking at climbers at different levels.
Mainly horizontal *1 dream*	Two people throwing tomatoes at each other.
Both vertical and horizontal *10 dreams*	Looking at things close to them, e.g. talking to a group of people, fighting with someone.
Very little or no movement *21 dreams*	Watching something in the distance or just staring fixedly at some object.

Effects of practice

Participants didn't recall more dreams as they got more practised.

Discussion

This study showed that dreaming is accompanied by REM activity. It cannot be stated with complete certainly that dreaming doesn't occur at other times. The few instances of NREM dreaming can be best explained by assuming that the memory for a dream persisted for some time and thus appeared to occur during NREM sleep.

Previous research had found REM activity to be absent in some participants but Dement and Kleitman suggest that this may have happened because REM periods occurred between when the samples were taken or that REM activity was minimal because the dreams were about distant activities.

It seems reasonable to conclude that an objective measurement of dreaming may be accomplished by recording REMs during sleep.

Biographical notes on Dement and Kleitman

William Dement's career started in the 1950s as a medical student in Kleitman's lab. Today he is a Professor at Stanford University where he also runs a sleep disorders clinic. He has researched sleep disorders, circadian rhythms, sudden infant death syndrome, jet lag, sleep loss and sleep hygiene. He has been feted with a long list of awards including 'Profound Thinkers of the Bay Area Award' and 'Man of the Year of the Société de Distinction Internationale'.

Nathaniel Kleitman

Nathaniel Kleitman died in 1999 at the age of 104. He was born in Russia and immigrated to the US at the age of 20. He has been described as 'the father of modern sleep research'. Before him, few scientists had systematically investigated the intricacies of sleep, dismissing it as a state of quiescence. Kleitman's discovery, with Eugene Aserinsky, of REM sleep was the beginning of a whole new area of study. Their subjects for this study were their own children. He was no stranger to the role of subject himself. Kleitman and an associate spent more than a month 150 feet underground in Mammoth Cave, Kentucky to investigate the 'free-running' sleep–wake cycle.

Q s

1 When people are deprived of REM sleep they suffer REM rebound – they need more REM sleep. How do you think this may have affected the results in this study?

2 Dement and Kleitman offered an explanation for why dreams sometimes were reported in NREM sleep. How could one explain why dreams were not always reported in REM sleep?

3 Identify a conclusion for each of the three approaches identified in the aims.

EVALUATING THE STUDY BY DEMENT AND KLEITMAN

The research method

This study could be considered a laboratory experiment – because the experimenter controlled when the participants woke up. It could also be considered to be a natural or quasi-experiment because the IV (REM/NREM sleep) wasn't controlled by the experimenter. *What are the strengths and limitations of a lab or quasi-experiment in the context of this study?*

The research techniques

One of the techniques used in this study was self-report measures. *What are the strengths and limitations of this research technique in the context of this study?*

The sample

In what way are the participants in this sample unique? To what extent were the participants different in terms of their recall in REM sleep? How does this affect the conclusions drawn from the study?

Qualitative and quantitative

Both quantitative and qualitative data were collected in this study. *What are the strengths and limitations of producing each kind of data in the context of this study?*

Ecological validity

Participants slept in a lab with electrodes on their head and were awakened throughout the night. *To what extent does the behaviour in this study reflect 'normal' sleep and dreaming? How might this affect the conclusions drawn from the study?*

Applications/usefulness

How valuable was this study?

DEBATE

How valuable is this study? Find out more about sleep research in general and consider all the benefits (or not) of this landmark study.

What next? (?)

Describe **one** change to this study, and say how you think this might affect the outcome.

Multiple choice questions

1. REM stands for:
   (a) Random eye movements.
   (b) Random eye motion.
   (c) Rapid eye motion.
   (d) Rapid eye movements.

2. How many participants were studied intensively?
   (a) 3   (b) 5
   (c) 7   (d) 9

3. Which of the following are characteristics of REM activity:
   (a) No EEG activity.
   (b) Different kinds of EEG activity.
   (c) Relatively fast EEG activity.
   (d) Relatively slow EEG activity.

4. Which of the following procedures acted as a 'control' in this study?
   (a) Participants reported their dreams without direct contact with the experimenter.
   (b) Participants were not told if they had been woken from REM activity or not.
   (c) The study was conducted in a laboratory.
   (d) All of the above.

5. In this study, the recall of dreams was:
   (a) The DV.
   (b) The IV.
   (c) An extraneous variable.
   (d) A confounding variable.

6. Almost all of the dreams reported in NREM sleep were reported within how many minutes of REM activity?
   (a) 2   (b) 4
   (c) 6   (d) 8

7. At what time of the night were REM episodes absent?
   (a) At the beginning.
   (b) In the middle.
   (c) Towards the morning.
   (d) REM episodes were always present.

8. At what time of the night were REM episodes longest?
   (a) At the beginning.
   (b) In the middle.
   (c) Towards the morning.
   (d) The duration of REM did not differ during the night.

9. On average REM episodes lasted
   (a) 10 minutes.
   (b) 20 minutes.
   (c) 30 minutes.
   (d) 40 minutes.

10. The most unusual form of REM activity was:
    (a) Mainly vertical movement.
    (b) Mainly horizontal movement.
    (c) A mixture of horizontal and vertical.
    (d) Little or no movement.

Answers are on page 121.

Exam questions

1. (a) Identify **two** controls used in the study on sleep and dreaming by Dement and Kleitman. [2]

   (b) Explain why **one** of these controls was used. [OCR AS Psy, May 2004, paper 1] [2]

2. In the study on sleep and dreaming by Dement and Kleitman, it is suggested that REM only occurs during dreaming. Give **one** piece of evidence which supports this suggestion and **one** piece of evidence that challenges it. [OCR AS Psy, May 2003, paper 1] [4]

3. (a) In their study on sleep and dreaming, Dement and Kleitman found some participants recalled dreams following NREM sleep. How did they explain this? [2]

   (b) What evidence is there in the study to support this explanation? [2]
   [OCR AS Psy, Jan 2003, paper 1]

4. (a) From the study by Dement and Kleitman on sleep, what does an electroencephalogram (EEG) record? [2]

   (b) Outline **one** problem with using an EEG to investigate dreaming. [2]
   [OCR AS Psy, June 1999, paper 1]

Dream on

World record

So how long do you think you can stay awake? The world record was set in 1964 by Randy Gardner in San Diego USA. He wanted to enter a science fair and decided to make a project of a world record attempt at sleep deprivation. His attempt attracted a lot of attention and after a week William Dement (yes the very same) got in touch.

'I immediately called Randy's home, explained to him and his parents who I was, and asked if I could observe him attempt to break the record.' (Dement, 2001).

Gardner had to be watched all the time to make sure he did not fall asleep and Dement took his turn in keeping him awake.

'If [Gardner] began to fall asleep, I would hustle him outside to the small basketball court in his backyard or drive him around the deserted San Diego streets in a convertible with the top down and the radio playing loudly.'

Dement spent the tenth day of the attempt walking around the town with Gardner and records how the teenager was able to beat him on arcade games and also at basketball. On the eleventh day Gardner hosted a press conference where he spoke without slurring or stumbling over his words and appeared to be in excellent health. At 6:04 a.m. he finally fell asleep having set a world record for sleeplessness that has never been broken.

The remarkable aspect of this achievement is Gardner's apparent good health throughout the time without sleep. This has not been observed on other attempts where people quickly show severe psychological effects including hallucinations. One possible explanation is that he was able to indulge in *'microsleep'* – small periods of sleep during the day which allow some physiological recovery to take place.

Sleep debt

Surveys in the UK find that young adults report sleeping about 7–7.5 hours each night. A hundred years ago the average person slept nine hours each night. This means that today's population sleeps one to two hours less than people used to sleep (Webb and Agnew, 1975).

The key change is probably artificial light which triggers wakefulness. People probably sleep 500 hours less each year than they used to and this might well be less sleep than evolution intended. When people go out of their daily routine, for example on holiday, they tend to sleep longer. In fact, in less industrialised societies, the total daily sleep time tends to still be around nine to ten hours (Coren, 1996).

A group of researchers spent a summer above the arctic circle where there is continuous light 24 hours a day (Palinkas *et al.,* 1995). All their watches, clocks and other timekeeping devices were taken away, and they chose when to sleep or wake according to their 'body time'. At the end of the study, the participants' overall average daily sleep time was 10.3 hours. Every member of the team showed an increase in sleep time, with the shortest logging in at 8.8 hours a day, and the longest at almost 12 hours a day.

People who are living with a sleep debt are less efficient and the common effects of a large sleep debt are lapses in attention, reduced short-term memory capacity, impaired judgement and having 'microsleeps' which the sleeper is commonly unaware of – obviously not good if you're driving.

There is now evidence that many major disasters have been due to sleep-debt effects. The evidence shows that these include the oil spill of the *Exxon Valdez*, the nuclear accidents at Chernobyl and Three Mile Island, and the loss of the space shuttle *Challenger* (Coren, 1996).

Sleep and torture

Sleep deprivation has been used by many countries as an interrogation technique. For example, prisoners in Iraq have been deprived of sleep by playing them loud heavy metal music for long periods of time. The US Psychological Operations Company (PsyOps) reports that their aim was to break a prisoner's resistance through sleep deprivation and playing music that was culturally offensive to them (BBC, 2003).

To say this is controversial is to understate the issue. Amnesty International, for example, says these techniques may well be psychological torture and therefore breach the Geneva Convention.

Sergeant Mark Hadsell, of PsyOps, comments *'These people haven't heard heavy metal. They can't take it. If you play it for 24 hours, your brain and body functions start to slide, your train of thought slows down and your will is broken. That's when we come in and talk to them.'*

Sgt Hadsell's favourites are said to be 'Bodies' from the XXX film soundtrack and Metallica's 'Enter Sandman'. The theme tune from the US children's programme *Sesame Street* and songs from the purple singing dinosaur Barney are also on his hit list.

One US serviceman said *'In training, they forced me to listen to the Barney "I Love You" song for 45 minutes. I never want to go through that again.'* (BBC, 2003).

Barney the purple dinosaur sings 'I Love You'. But how would you feel if you had to listen to it for 24 hours?

LINKS TO OTHER STUDIES

This core study makes an interesting link to **Freud**'s approach to dreaming. In the Little Hans study he makes use of some dreams that Hans has to interpret the boy's feelings for his parents. This core study also links to the work of **Rosenhan** because of the well-established connection between sleep deprivation and symptoms of mental disorder. This core study has a methodological simplicity used to look at the seemingly very complex phenomenon of dreaming. This same methodological simplicity can be seen in the Sally-Anne test of **Baron-Cohen, Leslie and Frith**, and the experiment on eyewitness testimony by **Loftus and Palmer**.

keyISSUE

Experiments

Many people use the word 'experiment' quite loosely, as if an experiment was just another word for an investigation. It isn't. In an experiment, the experimenter:

- Alters the levels of one variable (called the **independent variable** – IV).
- Observes the effects of the IV on another variable (the **dependent variable** – DV).

Only by doing this can we discover a *causal relationship* because the experimenter can claim that any change in the DV must be due to the changes made to the IV – except if there are **confounding variables** (see page 11 for a discussion of control).

Different kinds of experiment

All experiments have an independent variable and a dependent variable.

Laboratory experiment

An experiment conducted in a *special environment* where variables can be *carefully controlled*. Participants are aware that they are taking part in an experiment though they may not know the true aims of the study.

Field experiment

An experiment conducted in a participant's *natural environment*, which means they may behave more like they do ordinarily. As with the laboratory experiment, the independent variable is still *deliberately manipulated* by the researcher. Participants are *often not aware* that they are participating in an experiment which again means they may behave more naturally. NB a field *study* is a study conducted in a natural environment where no IV has been manipulated.

Natural or quasi-experiment

The study by Dement and Kleitman could be considered to be a natural experiment. In a natural experiment, the experimenter does not manipulate the IV but takes advantage of a *naturally* varying IV. The reason for this is that there are some IVs that cannot be manipulated for practical or ethical reasons. The effects of the IV on the DV can be observed by the experimenter. Strictly speaking an experiment involves the deliberate manipulation of an IV by an experimenter, therefore natural experiments are not 'true experiments' (they are quasi-experiments) because no one has *deliberately* changed the IV to observe the effect on the DV.

An example of a natural experiment

The residents of the tiny island of St Helena (47 square miles) received television for the first time in 1995. This enabled researchers to see whether the introduction of television would produce an increase in anti-social behaviour as found in other studies (Charlton *et al.*, 2000).

The vast majority of the measures used to assess pro- and anti-social behaviour showed no differences after the introduction of television. This outcome may be explained in terms of social norms. In St Helena there was a community with a strong sense of identity and no reason to be aggressive whereas this is not the case in other communities where TV has been introduced and more anti-social behaviour was displayed.

KEY TERMS

Laboratory experiment To investigate causal relationships under controlled conditions.

Field experiment To investigate causal relationships in more natural surroundings.

Natural experiment To investigate causal relationships in situations where IV varies naturally.

You actually conduct experiments without thinking. For example, when you start a class with a new teacher you might make a joke or hand in your homework on time (both IVs) to see if the teacher responds well (the DV). You are experimenting with cause and effect.

Exam-style question

One of the most common research methods used in psychological research is the experimental method.

Take any **one** core study that is an experiment and answer the following questions.

(a) Outline the procedure that was used in your chosen study. [6]

(b) Briefly discuss **two** advantages and **two** disadvantages of the experimental method, using examples from your chosen study. [12]

(c) Describe **one** change to your chosen study, and say how you think this might affect the outcome of the study. [8]

ACTIVITY

List the core studies you have covered. For each, state the kind of experiment and identify the IV and DV, or if it is not an experiment try to identify the method. Answers given at www.a-levelpsychology.co.uk/ocr/ascorestudies

Laboratory experiment	
Well controlled, confounding variables are minimised, thus higher validity.	Artificial, a contrived situation where participants may not behave naturally (low representativeness).
Field experiment	
A more natural environment and less awareness of being studied, thus higher representativeness and ecological validity.	Less control of extraneous variables, so you can't be sure that changes in the DV are due to changes in the IV; reduces validity.
Natural experiment	
Enables psychologists to study 'real' problems such as the effects of disaster on health (increased representativeness and ecological validity).	Cannot demonstrate causal relationships because IV not directly manipulated. Participants may be aware of being studied, reduces naturalness.

One brain or two?

Sperry's research on the brain

The brain is a truly remarkable organ. Think about it. The brain creates our world for us every time we wake up. Roger Sperry said, 'Before brains there was no color or sound in the universe, nor was there any flavor or aroma and probably little sense and no feeling or emotion.' (Sperry, 1964). All these qualities only exist in our brains. I know you think a tree is green and the sky is blue and Rudolf's nose is red but it isn't so. The world is full of radiation of different wavelengths and it is our brain that senses that radiation and creates the colours we use to interpret our surroundings. It's almost too amazing to think about.

During his career Sperry made some startling discoveries about the brain, none more so than the ones described in this core study. I think this study challenges what we know about ourselves and what we can become.

A lot was already known about the brain before Sperry's study and some of that is summarised on this spread. There is also a summary of the development of brain research on pages 86–87. Every year sees our knowledge of the brain growing with the promise of finding out more about why we do the things we do. Brain scientist Wilder Penfield (see right) believed that the brain represented the most important unexplored field in the whole of science and it is hard to argue with him. We have only scratched the surface in our understanding of the brain.

Epilepsy in history

The split brain operation used in this study was performed as a means of treating severe epilepsy. Epilepsy has been recognised as a condition for many centuries and people have tried to explain it in a number of ways. In the fourteenth and fifteenth centuries seizures were commonly seen as being a curse or the work of demonic forces. People with seizures made pilgrimages to the Priory of St Valentine, a monastery on the border between France and Germany, for spiritual healing. They went there because, as well as being the patron saint of lovers, Valentine moonlights as the patron saint of people with epilepsy.

In the Middle Ages epileptics were pointed in the direction of medical 'cures' ranging from blood-letting to burning.

Treatments and attitudes are much better today but it is fair to say that people with epilepsy still experience discrimination and negative responses in the UK.

 If you are interested to find out more about the brain then you might start your exploration at the whole brain atlas (www.med.harvard.edu/AANLIB/home.html)

Sperry's animal experiments

It is an uncomfortable part of medical science that many advances come from research on animals. Pictures of animals in painful apparatus illustrate one side of the story and life-saving medicines illustrate the other.

It can be no surprise that Sperry carried out a lot of research on animal brains before he operated on people. Those of a nervous disposition should stop reading now.

Sperry was able to show that a number of functions are 'hard-wired' into the nervous system and can not be learned. For example he swapped wiring round on a rat's foot so that when it tried to move its left foot the right foot moved instead. The rat was not able to adapt to this new arrangement. He also cut the optic nerves of salamanders and then rotated them before allowing the nerves to regenerate and reconnect to the eye. The salamander then saw the world upside down and it was not able to adapt to this. And of course, the split brain technique of severing the corpus callosum was tried out on cats and monkeys before being used on people.

The full gory details of the animal work does not make good reading and many readers might object to the zoo full of animals who had their brains rearranged by Sperry. On the other hand, the patients with epilepsy who had the split brain operation were better able to live an ordinary life and so might disagree. It's a moral maze.

Wilder Penfield (1891–1976)

Penfield was interested in finding cures for epilepsy and other brain disorders. With his colleagues, Penfield developed a new surgical approach in which he was able to examine the exposed brain of a conscious patient using just a local anaesthetic. As the patient described what they were feeling, Penfield pushed a probe into sections of the brain and located the damaged tissue that was the source of the epileptic seizures. The damaged tissue was removed and many patients then had relief from their seizures.

Of course, once you have an open brain in front of you, it is only natural to poke about a bit to see what is going on. This is exactly what Penfield did and he made some astounding discoveries. For example, he found that careful administration of a mild electric shock to one of the temporal lobes could make the patient recall precise personal experiences that had long been forgotten. Penfield's research into the structure and function of the brain was prompted by his desire to discover a physical basis for the belief in the human soul.

ACTIVITY

Right eyed or left eyed?

Which is your dominant eye? Test it out for yourself. Look at a distant object such as a clock on a wall or a tree on a hill. Now line up one finger with the object so that the finger is blocking it. Then close one eye and then the other. What happens? When you close one of your eyes the object will still be blocked, only even more so. When you close the other eye the finger will appear to jump.

What the brain does

The brain has two relatively symmetrical halves (left and right). The illustration shows a brain that has been cut down the middle. You can see that the top third of the brain is not joined to its other half: the only part that has been cut through is where the two halves are joined – at the commissural fibres, which include the corpus callosum.

Cerebral cortex

This is the clever bit of the human brain and the largest part. The cerebral cortex actually covers the brain like a tea cozy and is highly wrinkled which increases the surface area and probably increases its power. Structures that are 'sub-cortical' lie under the tea cozy. Such sub-cortical structures are concerned with more basic processes like emotion and are present in all animals, whereas the cortex is specific to higher animals such as mammals.

The cortex is divided into four lobes which are believed to control different functions:

*   **Frontal lobe** (front of the brain, above the eyes): reasoning, planning, parts of speech, movement, emotions, and problem solving.

*   **Parietal lobe** (top, towards the back): movement, orientation, recognition, perception of stimuli.

*   **Occipital lobe** (back): visual processing.

*   **Temporal lobe** (sides): perception of auditory stimuli, memory, and speech.

Thalamus

The simple story is that the thalamus (a sub-cortical structure) is a 'relay station' for signals from the senses (skin, stomach, eyes, ears but not the nose) to the cerebral cortex. The real story is more complicated, because the thalamus does more than just send the signals on – it also does some initial analysis of the signals.

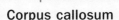

Hypothalamus

This is located below the thalamus (hence *hypo*-thalamus). It is the size of half a baked bean but plays a very important role as the major control centre for a range of essential functions. For example it controls body temperature, hunger and thirst. It also appears to be involved in emotional and sexual activity. A lot of work for a baked bean.

Cerebellum

The cerebellum, or 'little brain', is similar to the cerebral cortex in that it has two hemispheres and has a highly folded surface or cortex. This structure is associated with regulation and coordination of movement, posture, and balance.

Corpus callosum

The corpus callosum connects the left and right cerebral hemispheres and carries most of the communication between the two halves of the brain. A number of claims have been made about sex and racial differences in the corpus callosum. The idea is that the greater the traffic across the two halves the greater the person's intelligence (favouring women and white people). Such claims are made in popular magazines but they have little scientific support (Bishop and Wahlsten, 1997).

Brain stem

The brain stem is the stalk of the brain below the cerebral hemispheres. It is the major route for communication between the forebrain and the spinal cord and peripheral nerves. It also controls various functions including respiration and regulation of heart rhythms.

The core study

The idea of splitting a person's brain in half is shocking and fascinating. You just have to know what happens. If your personality is merely something in your brain, rather than in a mystical idea like a soul, then maybe cutting the brain in half will create two personalities. Of course you can't do this to people just for the sake of investigating this question but sometimes extreme surgery is the only option. In this study the split brain operation was done to relieve epilepsy, but also afforded scientists the ideal opportunity to assess the psychological effects of splitting the brain.

Cross-wired

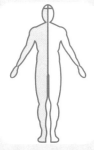

The left side of the body and the left visual field are controlled by the right hemisphere, and the right side of the body and the right visual field by the left hemisphere.

Control of the auditory fields is more complex, while our sense of smell, the most neurologically ancient of the senses, is not crossed over at all, each nostril being 'wired' to the hemisphere on the same side of the body.

Roger Wolcott Sperry (1968) Hemispheric disconnection and unity in conscious awareness. *American Psychologist, 23, 723–733.*

Abstract

The study demonstrates some interesting things about the way the human brain is organised by comparing the performance of split-brain patients with normal behaviour. Specially designed apparatus was used which:

- Presents information to left and right visual fields (LVF and RVF) for very brief periods (0.1 seconds).

- Allows hands to examine objects while out of sight.

- Relays visual and manual information to left and right hemispheres (LH and RH).

Example results	Conclusion that can be drawn
If a $ sign is flashed to the *LVF* and ? sign flashed to *RVF* the patient will draw (using his right hand) the figure ($) shown to *LVF* but will tell you that he saw the sign shown to *RVF* (?).	LVF linked to RH and RVF linked to LH.
	Left hand linked to RH (and LVF), right hand linked to LH (and RVF).
	The corpus callosum enables communication between RH and LH.
If visual material is projected to the *LVF* the participant says he did not see anything or there was just a flash of light on his left side.	Language centres are in LH.
Patients can select objects that are related to a pictured item presented to *LVF*, e.g. selecting a wrist watch when wall clock was shown.	RH is not completely 'word blind'; shows language comprehension.
If a pin-up picture is shown to the *LVF* there is an emotional reaction (such as a giggle).	The right hemisphere has some special functions such as emotion.
If two objects are placed simultaneously one in each hand and then hidden in a pile of objects, both hands then search through the pile and can select their own object but will ignore the other hand's objects.	We effectively have two minds.
	Split-brain patients are two rather than one individual.
Patients continue to watch TV or read books with no complaints; intellect and personality are unchanged.	Split-brain patients cope relatively well with everyday life.

Qs

1 Why do you think Sperry projected the slides at such a fast rate?

2 Why can normal individuals say what they see in the left visual field?

3 Why couldn't participants recognise material presented to the left visual field with their left hand?

4 Why was it important that participants couldn't see their hands?

SPERRY : SPLIT BRAIN

CORESTUDY

Aim

To study the psychological effects of hemispheric disconnection in split-brain patients, and to use the results to understand how the right and left hemispheres work in 'normal' individuals.

Previous split-brain studies with humans (e.g. Akelatitis, 1944) found that there were no important behavioural effects whereas split-brain studies with animals produced many behavioural effects (e.g. Myers, 1961).

Method

Participants

The participants were a group of patients who suffered from severe epileptic seizures which could not be controlled by medication. The split-brain operation is a possible remedy; it involves cutting through the cerebral commisures which connect the left and right hemispheres of the brain. Note that the operation was not done for the purpose of this experiment, which would have been unethical. For most patients the operation reduced the frequency and severity of their seizures.

Procedure

The main setup for testing the behavioural effects of hemispheric deconnection is shown below. It means that right and left halves of the visual field can be tested separately or together, whilst excluding the right and left arms.

The participant has one eye covered and is asked to gaze at a fixed point in the centre of a projection screen. Visual stimuli are back-projected onto the screen, either to the right or left of the screen, at a very high speed – one picture every 0.1 second or less. This means that the eye only has time to process the image in the visual field where it was placed (i.e. if the image was shown to the left visual field there is not time for the participant to move their eye or head so that the right visual field might also receive the image). Below the screen there was a gap so that the participant could reach objects but not see his or her hands.

1 Role play

Two right-handed people should sit next to each other (on one chair if possible) in front of a table with a screen on it, divided into left and right with an X in the middle. The volunteer on the left (Person A) represents the left hemisphere and the one on the right (person B) represents the right hemisphere.

The two volunteers should put their outer hands behind their back. They should place their inner hands on the table and cross them over (ideally under the screen). The two hands represent the split-brain patient's left and right hands.

Members of the class should act as experimenters and conduct Sperry's mini-experiments. The volunteers should try to react as a split-brain patient.

[Adapted from http://www.rrcc-online.com/~psych/RLExpire.htm]

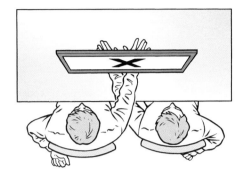

2 Right brain left brain

It is possible to demonstrate right and left field advantages in normal individuals (without split brains).

Present two words (one on the right and one on the left) on a computer screen for less than 100 milliseconds. Participants should show a preference for reporting the word on the right. If you present two pictures (one left and one right), there should be a preference to report the picture on the left because the right hemisphere is better at analysing pictures.

Results

Baseline results

- If a projected picture is shown and responded to in one visual field, it is only recognised again if it appears in that visual field.

- If visual material appeared in the *right* visual field (processed by left hemisphere), the patient could describe it in speech and writing as normal.

- If the same visual material is projected to the *left* visual field (right hemisphere) then the participant says he did not see anything or there was just a flash of light on his left side. (Language centres are in the left hemisphere.)

- If you then ask the same participant to use his *left* hand (right hemisphere control) to point to a matching picture or object in a collection of pictures/objects, then he points to the item he just insisted he couldn't see.

These results confirm that the right hemisphere cannot speak or write (called *aphasia* and *agraphia*).

$ and ? signs

If a $ sign is flashed to the left visual field (LVF) and ? sign flashed to RVF the participant will draw (using his left hand out of sight) the figure ($) shown to LVF but will tell you that he saw the sign shown to RVF (?). Sperry says *'the one hemisphere does not know what the other hemisphere has been doing'* (p. 726).

Composite words

When words are flashed partly to the LVF and partly to the RVF, the letters are responded to separately. For example if 'keycase' is projected ('key' to the LVF and 'case' to the RVF) then a participant would

- Select a key from the collection of objects with his left hand (LVF goes to right hemisphere which controls the left hand).

- Spell out the word 'case' with his right hand (RVF goes to left hemisphere which controls the right hand).

- Say 'case' if asked what word was displayed (RVF goes to left hemisphere which controls speech).

Using touch

Objects placed in the right hand (left hemisphere) can be named in speech and writing. If an object is placed in the left hand participants can only make wild guesses and may seem unaware that they are holding anything. However, if the same object is placed in a grab bag with other objects, the participant can find the original object with his left hand. They cannot retrieve the object with their right hand if it was first sensed with the left hand.

When asked to name objects held in their left hand participants frequently said something like 'This hand is numb' or 'I don't get messages from that hand'. If they successfully identified an object with their left hand they would comment 'Well, I was just guessing' or 'I must have done it unconsciously'. In other words, they had developed a way of explaining their rather strange behaviour to themselves.

Dual processing task

If two objects are placed simultaneously one in each hand and then hidden in a pile of objects, both hands can select their own object from the pile but will ignore the other hand's objects. Sperry said *'It is like two separate individuals working over a collection of test items with no cooperation between them'* (p. 727).

Everyday effects

In everyday life split-brain patients don't usually notice that their mental functions are cut in half. They continue to watch TV or read books unaware of the separate visual input. This is because all the problems described in the study only arise when visual material is displayed very briefly. In everyday life deconnection can be overcome by moving the eyes or saying an answer out loud so information is shared between right and left hemisphere.

However this doesn't mean split-brain patients are better off in their 'deconnected' state. It is true that their IQ scores and personality were little changed; however, in most complex activities people with cooperating hemispheres appear to do better, for example all the patients had some problems with short-term memory and had limited attention spans.

On the other hand, there are some tasks that are actually performed better by split-brain patients. They could carry out a double reaction-time task as fast as they could carry out a single task. In normal patients the introduction of a second task causes interference.

Results continued

Abilities of the right (minor) hemisphere

Before Sperry's research little was known about what the right, 'silent' hemisphere could do. Tests with the split-brain patients revealed a range of higher-order mental abilities, including some verbal comprehension. These capacities are described on the right. In fact there are some abilities that are dominant in the right hemisphere, such as spatial awareness and emotion.

Closing statements

Patients appear to have two independent streams of consciousness, each with its own separate memories, own perceptions, own impulses to act; in a sense two minds in one body.

Sperry ends the article by saying *'The more we see of these patients and the more of these patients we see, the more we become impressed by their individual differences'* (p. 733). Such differences might explain the contrasting results collected by different investigators. For example some patients display some ipsilateral control (right hemisphere can communicate with right hand, i.e. same side of the body). Such patients would not display some of the behavioural effects described here.

Understanding of general categories	Patients can select objects that are related to a pictured item presented to LVF, a task that requires mental processing. For example, if a picture of a wall clock was shown to the right hemisphere (LVF), the left hand will select a toy wrist watch. This shows that the right hemisphere has grasped the general category (timepiece) and is not just searching for a physical match.
Simple arithmetic problems	For example, if numbers are shown to the LVF, the left hand (held out of sight) can signal the correct answer.
Responding to spoken cues	If an object is named out loud, the left hand (right hemisphere) can locate the object because hearing is partially bilateral (about 10% goes to same side and 90% goes to opposite hemisphere). For example, if verbally instructed to find a piece of silverware the left hand (right hemisphere) may pick up a fork – but the patient cannot name the object.
Spatial awareness	On some tests the right hemisphere was found to be superior to the left (major) hemisphere – on tests that involve drawing spatial relationships and performing block design tests.
Emotion	If a pin-up picture is shown in a series of geometric figures to the LVF there is an emotional reaction (such as a giggle) whereas if the picture appears in the RVF the patient usually says he saw nothing or just a flash of light. The patient who saw the picture with his LVF cannot explain why he giggled.

Odours to right nostril (right hemisphere) can't be named but can be identified as pleasant or unpleasant – the patient might grunt or turn away. The patient can also identify the correct object with his left hand which shows that the right hemisphere can identify the smell-object. |

Q_s

1 Identify three things controlled by the left hemisphere.

2 Identify three things controlled by the right hemisphere.

3 Why is the right hemisphere referred to as the 'minor' hemisphere?

4 Sperry pointed out the fact that there were important individual differences. What is the importance of this for interpreting the study's results?

5 What does 'lateralised' mean?

Biographical notes on Roger Sperry

Roger Sperry, who was one of the premier neurobiologists of his time, started out as an English undergraduate and only later took an interest in psychology. Like many remarkable people he had a range of interests and talents: he was a star athlete in javelin and played basketball at University, an avid fisherman, and an exceptionally talented sculptor, painter and ceramicist. He also was a keen paleontologist who collected prehistoric molluscs from around the world and, according to one colleague, known for hosting great parties where he served his special 'split brain' punch.

Sperry had a profound effect on the progress of physiological psychology specifically and brain science generally. He revolutionised neuroscience. In later years he turned more and more to philosophy and formulating a non-reductionist view of consciousness. He proposed that consciousness emerges from the activity of cerebral networks as an independent entity.

'The great pleasure and feeling in my right brain is more than my left brain can find the words to tell you.'
Roger Sperry (1913–1994)

Sperry received the Nobel Prize in Medicine in 1981, one of only a few psychologists to receive the award.

 Try the split-brain game: http://nobelprize.org/medicine/educational/split-brain/index.html

EVALUATING THE STUDY BY SPERRY

The research method

This study can be described as a natural or quasi-experiment because the IV (presence or absence of split brain) varied naturally. The DV is the participant's performance on a variety of tests. However, as each of these people are described in detail it could also be argued that Sperry's work is a series of case studies. *What are the strengths and limitations of these research methods in the context of this study?*

The sample

We do not know to what extent the split-brain patients had brain damage caused by the severe epileptic fits (or the fits may have been caused by brain damage in the first place). *How does this affect the conclusions drawn from the study?*

Ethical issues

What ethical issues should have concerned the researchers in this study, and how might they have dealt with these issues?

Reductionist

What are the strengths and limitations of reductionism in the context of this study?

Qualitative or quantitative?

What kind of data were collected in this study? What are the strengths and limitations of producing this kind of data in the context of this study?

Ecological validity

To what extent can we make generalisations about human behaviour on the basis of this study?

Applications/usefuless

How valuable was this study?

DEBATE

Was this a 'landmark study'? Did Sperry produce results of major significance? Divide your class into groups; each group should produce one argument for and one argument against Sperry. You might do some further research first. What does your class conclude?

What next? (?)

Describe **one** change to this study, and say how you think this might affect the outcome.

Multiple choice questions

1. The split-brain operation was performed:
   (a) To conduct this experiment.
   (b) For patients with mild epilepsy.
   (c) For patients with severe epilepsy.
   (d) Both (a) and (c).

2. Visual stimuli were flashed on the screen for:
   (a) 1 second.   (b) 0.1 seconds.
   (c) 0.01 seconds.   (d) 0.001 seconds.

3. The right hand and right nostril are:
   (a) Both connected to the right hemisphere.
   (b) Both connected to the left hemisphere.
   (c) Connected to the right and left hemisphere respectively.
   (d) Connected to the left and right hemisphere respectively.

4. When a $ sign was flashed to the left visual field, the patient could:
   (a) Draw the $ sign with his left hand.
   (b) Draw the $ sign with his right hand.
   (c) Tell you he saw a $ sign.
   (d) Both (a) and (c).

5. When the word 'keycase' is flashed so that 'key' is processed by the LVF and 'case' by the RVF, the patient can
   (a) Spell out the word 'case' with his right hand.
   (b) Spell out the word 'case' with his left hand.
   (c) Say the word 'key'.
   (d) None of the above.

6. When a patient held an object in their left hand, they could:
   (a) Say what it was.
   (b) Find a similar object with their right hand.
   (c) Find a similar object with their left hand.
   (d) Both (a) and (b).

7. Split-brain patients had:
   (a) Personality changes.
   (b) Problems with short-term memory.
   (c) Short attention spans.
   (d) Both (b) and (c).

8. The right hemisphere was found to be:
   (a) The main language centre.
   (b) Word blind.
   (c) Able to engage in some verbal functions.
   (d) Lower in IQ.

9. The patient gave an emotional response (a giggle) if a photograph of a pin-up was displayed to the:
   (a) Right visual field.
   (b) Left visual field.
   (c) Either field.
   (d) The patients never giggled.

10. Sperry ended his article by highlighting the fact that:
    (a) His patients were essentially abnormal.
    (b) The study was unethical.
    (c) There were important individual differences in what the split brain patients could do.
    (d) All of the above.

Answers are on page 121.

Exam questions

1. (a) From Sperry's split-brain study, outline **one** difference between the ability of split-brain patients and 'normal' people to identify objects by touch alone. [2]

   (b) Give **one** explanation for this difference. [2]
   [OCR AS Psy, Jan 2003, paper 1]

2. (a) From the study by Sperry, outline the major function of the corpus callosum. [2]

   (b) Sperry suggested that we effectively have two minds. Outline **one** piece of evidence from the study that shows this. [2]
   [OCR AS Psy, Jan 2002, paper 1]

3. (a) What technique did Sperry use to present information to only one side of the brain? [2]

   (b) Why does this technique not present a problem to people with 'normal' brains? [2]
   [OCR AS Psy, June 1998, paper 1]

4. From the paper by Sperry on split-brain patients, outline evidence which indicates that language is processed in the left hemisphere of the brain. [OCR AS Psy, June 1999, paper 1] [4]

More brains

Left brain	Right brain
Linear	Intuitive
Symbolic	Holistic
Abstract	Concrete
Verbal	Nonverbal

One of the legacies of Sperry's research was to elevate the role of the right hemisphere from being the 'minor' hemisphere to one with special functions. This has led to the 'cult' of right versus left brained thinking. In 1972 Robert Ornstein suggested that society had placed too much emphasis on left-brained thinking and that we should liberate the creative powers of the right brain. Right-brain education programmes have been developed and tapes sold to develop 'whole-brain learning'. The right side was seen as the more intuitive, feminine side of human nature which was a feather in the cap of feminists. However, Corballis (1999) concludes that the differences between the hemispheres are minor and the right brain left brain movement should be regarded as little more than commercial exploitation.

Here's looking at you kid

'I used to think that the brain was the most interesting part of the body. Then I thought, "What part of my body is telling me that?"'
Emo Philips

LINKS TO OTHER STUDIES

The most striking connection is to the multiple personality study of **Thigpen and Cleckley**. Both studies look at split consciousness. In the case of Sperry, some of his patients appeared to have two consciousnesses that were not always aware of each other. In the case of Eve, there are more than two consciousnesses, but could this have a biological cause like Sperry's patients? Both studies challenge us to consider what we understand about identity and personality.

Sniff your way to success

Can breathing through one nostril affect how well your brain works? Not as silly as it sounds, perhaps. We know that the two hemispheres of the brain control different parts of the body and different cognitive functions. Add to this the nasal cycle in which each nostril takes turns to do the heavy breathing over a two hour cycle (Gpnotebook, 2005) and finish it off with the idea of a mental cycle where the left and right brains take it in turns to do the heavy thinking and you see where we are heading with this. Sniff your way to genius!

In an ingenious set of studies where people performed mental tests with tissue paper stuffed up one nostril Buebel *et al.* (1991) were able to show that forced breathing through one nostril had an effect on cognitive performance. For this outstanding finding the scientists were awarded the 1995 IgNobel Prize for Medicine (like the Nobel prizes but not quite).

Interestingly, the technique of breathing through one nostril at a time is an exercise in yoga called *Anuloma Viloma*. In this breathing technique, you inhale through one nostril, retain the breath, and inhale through the other nostril in a ratio of 2:8:4. Don't ask!

The right hemisphere after Sperry

Before Sperry's split-brain patients were studied, the scientific view doubted whether the right hemisphere was even conscious. Sperry's ingenious studies allowed him to communicate with the right hemisphere and conclude that: *'indeed a conscious system in its own right, perceiving, thinking, remembering, reasoning, willing, and emoting, all at a characteristically human level, and … both the left and the right hemisphere may be conscious simultaneously in different, even in mutually conflicting, mental experiences that run along in parallel'* (http://nobelprize.org).

When people carry out research into the brain what is doing the research? A brain looking at a brain?

Hemispherectomy

If one part of the brain is damaged perhaps it would be best to remove it. One radical way to do this is the removal of one hemisphere of the brain (i.e. half the brain). Hemispherectomy was first attempted in 1928 by US neurosurgeon Walter E. Dandy as a treatment for brain cancer. In the 1950 the technique was first used for epilepsy and it continues to be used today.

It is most commonly used on children and only those with serious conditions that do not respond to other treatments. Sometimes the surgeons remove a large part of the hemisphere but more commonly they just disconnect the damaged part from the rest of the brain. Children appear to have remarkable powers of recovery and hospital stays are commonly less than a week. The operation is remarkably successful in that patients commonly stop having seizures yet are able to regain the ability to walk.

The modern use of the hemispherectomy was pioneered by Benjamin Carson who performed his first operation in 1985 in the USA. He specialises in child brain surgery. Talking about hemispherectomy he said: *'you can't get away with that in an adult, but a child has the ability to actually transfer functions to other parts of the brain. So you can take out half of the brain of a kid, and you'll see the kid walking around, you'll see him using the arm on the opposite side, and in many cases even engaging in sporting activities.'*

'The human brain is the thing that makes you who you are. I never get over my awe of the brain' (Carson, 2002).

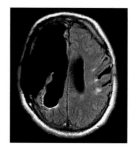

The brain of a hemispherectomy patient

keyISSUE

Reductionism

Reductionism is the idea that complex things can always be reduced to (or explained by) simpler things. This is applied to objects, phenomena, explanations and theories.

So if we look at the subject of chemistry we can see that all the chemical elements are made up of the physical particles as described by physicists. If we look at biology we can see that all life is made up of chemical elements, and if we look at psychology we can see that all behaviour is carried out by biological systems. Follow the argument back and we can hope to explain everything in terms of their basic particles and everything then becomes physics. Reductionists believe that psychology can only become a genuine science if it bases itself on biology.

The problem of reductionism

Baking cakes

Can we explain everything by breaking it down into its constituent parts? Think about a cake (turn this into a practical activity if you like). A cake is made up of a number of ingredients which you can put out on the table. They don't look much, but put together in a particular way they create some new qualities that none of the ingredients has by itself.

Cracking cheese, Gromit

Will we ever be able to explain human phenomena such as laughter in terms of our atomic structure?

Wallace and Gromit illustrate the problem of reductionism. We know that they are not really alive and in fact their movements are painstakingly created by Aardman Animations who move the models bit by bit. The story can be reduced to a series of simple movements but that does not describe everything about the characters. The final result of all these small movements is a film that brings laughter (and a few tears) to millions. It has extra ingredients that can't be described in terms of the simple movements. Sometimes people refer to this by saying 'the whole is greater than the sum of the parts'. Reductionism takes us so far, but it doesn't seem to give us the whole picture.

Holistic approaches

Such approaches focus on systems as a whole rather than on the constituent parts. The holistic view is that you can't predict how the whole system will behave from a knowledge of its components; that reductionist explanations can only play a limited role in helping us to understand behaviour and may even prevent us from discovering some useful explanations. However, holistic approaches don't provide simple answers. It is a line of argument that is sometimes useful and sometimes not.

Exam-style question

Reductionism is an approach to understanding human behaviour and experience. It aims to increase understanding by breaking complex behaviour into smaller components.

Take any **four** core studies (e.g. those in this chapter or Tajfel or Freud) and answer the following questions.

(a) Describe the basic components identified in each of these studies.
[12]

(b) Briefly discuss **two** advantages and **two** disadvantages of reductionism, using examples from these studies.
[12]

Reductionism

SOCIOLOGY can be explained by ...

PSYCHOLOGY can be explained by ...

BIOLOGY can be explained by ...

CHEMISTRY can be explained by ...

PHYSICS.

Examples of reductionist explanations in psychology

Behaviourism

Behaviourists attempt to explain all learning in terms of simple associations (see page 35). What looks like clever and thoughtful behaviour in an animal is, according to behaviourists, just a series of responses learnt by trial and error. For example, some hamsters can learn to climb upside down along the top of their cage to make a bold escape attempt. They haven't planned it out, they have learnt what is successful and what isn't.

Theory of evolution

The theory of evolution is used to explain human behaviour in terms of adaptiveness and genetics. The theory assumes that everything we do must in some way enhance our reproductive success and hence the survival of our genes. In subsequent generations only the genes for adaptive behaviours will survive.

Medical model of mental disorders

The belief that complex psychological events are caused by simple chemical changes is reductionist. An example of this is the condition known as GPI (general paresis of the insane) in which a person suddenly develops a degenerative mental condition. At the beginning of the twentieth century it was believed to be a mental illness; however, it was found to be the final stage of the sexually transmitted disease, syphilis. GPI is now rare because syphilis can be successfully treated before it attacks the brain. What if all mental disorders can be reduced to a simple answer like this? The reductionist approach says this will happen when we know more about the brain.

See page 87 for a discussion of the use of drugs to change complex moods like depression.

Scanning the brain

A new technology

In the final quarter of the twentieth century, scanning technology stimulated a dramatic breakthrough in brain research. Before scans, the only way to investigate brains was to deal with the real thing. This meant operations where the brain was altered in some way by the use of surgery or chemicals or electrical stimulation. The work of Sperry and also Penfield (see page 104) was part of this. There were also studies that were carried out on people with brain injuries though, in such cases, the final analysis often had to wait until the person died and their brain could be fully examined. Phineas Gage (see page 86) and the Texas tower murderer (see page 89) are examples of this evidence. This type of early research on brain function is clearly limited because it can't really see the brain at work.

Scanning allows scientists to view the brain while it is working. The advent of such techniques meant that scientists could now study the brain without cutting it open. A whole new world appeared to be available to them. But things are never so simple and the issue is to be able to interpret what the scans tells us and recognise what they can't tell us.

Different kinds of scanning technique

Types of scan include:

CAT (computerised axial tomography)

CAT scans are built up from taking a series of x-rays 180 degrees around the head. The images show areas of damage and will highlight, for example, the area where a person has experienced a cerebral haemorrhage (a type of stroke).

MRI (magnetic resonance imaging)

People are slid into a machine looking like a giant pencil sharpener and subjected to a strong magnetic field which is turned on and off rapidly in the presence of a radio wave. The atoms of the brain change their alignment (spin) because of the magnetic field when it is on and produce characteristic radio signals when it is turned off. A detector reads those signals and, using a computer, can map the structure of the tissue. There are no radioactive materials used in an MRI.

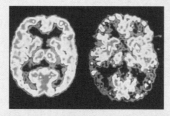

The images above show two PET scans. The normal brain on the left shows a lot of activity throughout the scanned area; the one on the right is the scan of a person with Alzheimer's Disease, showing far less activity.

fMRI (functional magnetic resonance imaging)

fMRI scans are the most recently developed forms of brain imaging and the scan of choice for psychologists. The scans use MRI technology to measure the changes in the blood oxygen levels that are connected to neural activity in the brain or spinal cord.

PET (positron emission tomography)

This is the scanning technique used in the Raine *et al*. study. Patients are injected with slightly radioactive glucose (sugar). The most active brain tissue uses the glucose and so attracts the radioactive substance. Radiation sensors detect where the radiation is greatest and so build up a picture of activity in the brain. The scans take between 10 and 40 minutes to complete and are painless. Mind you, there is the slight issue of radioactive substances in your brain.

The data from the scan is usually presented as a coloured picture where the 'hot' colours such as orange and red are used to represent the areas where there is greatest activity and the 'cold' colours such as green and blue represent the areas with least activity. The scans tell us which bits are busy but not what they are doing.

The 10% myth: 'Scientists say we use only 10% of our brains'

The 10% brain myth is one of the most persistent and most puzzling errors that people make about the brain. For a start we don't seem to be able the find the scientists who say this, if it was ever said it at all. A bit of logic is called for here along with some findings from brain studies:

- If 90% of the brain is unused then many parts of the brain could be damaged without causing any problems. This is not the case, and damage anywhere in the brain is likely to cause problems.

- If we only used 10% then brain scans would show a lot of quiet areas, but in fact most of the brain appears to be active most of the time.

- Research has built up a complex picture of what different parts of the brain do (localisation of function). There are few, if any areas that are not associated with any activity.

Early studies of the visual system (e.g. Riesen, 1950) found that if you don't use it you lose it. To put it more technically, when animals were kept in the dark for several months after birth their visual system did not develop and when they were later allowed into the light they had restricted vision.

All in all there is no scientific evidence to support the idea that we only use 10% of the brain. The writers who have bought into this myth tend to be trying to sell us something that will help us use the missing 90% and so turn into geniuses.

I had a neurologist in the back of my cab ...

To be a black cab taxi driver in London you have to pass 'the knowledge'. This tests the driver on all the possible routes in the maze of streets in a six-mile radius of Charing Cross. It takes up to three years to pass the test and three-quarters of those who start the course end up dropping out.

Malcolm Linskey, who prepares cabbies for the test, says, *'Most people learn by visualisation but we do have a few tricks which we teach them, for example "little apples grow quickly" gives you the order of the theatres on the north side of Shaftesbury Avenue: Lyric, Apollo, Gielgud, Queen's.'*

A team of neuroscientists scanned the brains of London taxi drivers to see whether they were different to those of the general public (Maguire *et al.*, 1997). They concentrated their observations on a small area in the brain called the *hippocampus*. They found that the posterior (rear) portion of this structure was larger in taxi drivers, and this effect was most pronounced in drivers who had been in the job for 40 years.

The researchers believe that this change is due to the map learning required on the job and shows that the brain can develop and grow when we are adults. This has implications for the treatment of people with brain damage. Mind you, it might not be due to map learning but to the other skills a taxi driver has to develop. An alternative explanation is suggested by taxi driver David Cohen who said, *'You do have to have a retentive memory but you also need a placid temperament to drive in London traffic.'*

Whatever the explanation, there appears to be a clear relationship between brain structure and being a black cab driver in London.

In the Wizard of Oz *the scarecrow wants to get a brain but when he gets to Oz the wizard says,* 'Why, anybody can have a brain. That's a very mediocre commodity. Every pusillanimous creature that crawls on the earth, or slinks through slimy seas has a brain!'

The Mozart effect

The idea for the Mozart effect originated in 1993 with work by Gordon Shaw (a physicist) and Frances Rauscher (a concert cellist and an expert on cognitive development) (Rauscher *et al.*, 1993). They studied the effects of listening to the first 10 minutes of the Mozart Sonata for Two Pianos in D Major (K.448) on college students. They claimed to find a temporary improvement in spatial-temporal reasoning, as measured by the Stanford–Binet IQ test.

This sounds like a technique for boosting IQ. Unfortunately, the many attempts to replicate the findings have found no effect of the music on IQ (Steele *et al.*, 1999). However, this scientific evidence has done little to dampen the enthusiasm for the Mozart Effect; the website www.mozarteffect.com makes many claims about the mind-enhancing and healing properties of the music. The website also has a range of products you can buy.

Early attempts to spot the criminal

Cesare Lombroso (1835–1909) is an important figure in the development of the science of criminology. In brief, Lombroso was impressed by Darwin's theory of evolution, which primarily described the evolution of biological traits, but was extended by Social Darwinists to describe the development of social behaviour (such as criminality) and institutions (such as marriage). In the first half of the twentieth century the theory was used to justify social inequality and the capitalist economic system. Some used it to justify racism: some of the ideas still surface today in race science (see the paper by Gould, page 174).

Lombroso argued that criminality was inherited, and that the born criminal could be identified by physical defects, which confirmed a criminal as savage, or atavistic (a genetic throwback). He suggested that criminals have particular physical features or deformities. If criminality was inherited then Lombroso thought we would be able to spot them by their large jaws, high cheekbones, handle-shaped ears, hawk-like noses, or fleshy lips. This idea sounds absurd today but maybe we still buy into it. Look at the standard film or television crime show. The criminals are most likely to be the strange-looking ones and the hero is likely to be the good-looking one.

Lombroso's theory has some similarities to phrenology (see page 86) which tried to match personality to the shape of the head. His theory is seen today in much the same way as phrenology, which is an amusing dead-end in science.

Modern criminologists and psychologists are likely to dismiss Lombroso's theories, but you can't help but wonder whether the study by Raine *et al.* is an updated version of Lombroso.

One of Lombroso's drawings of a criminal type (Lombroso, 1876). Although his theory seems quite cruel, Lombroso was an advocate for the humane treatment of criminals by arguing for rehabilitation and against capital punishment.

The core study

Once you have some fancy equipment you just have to use it. Many psychology departments now have access to brain scanners so they are looking for ideas to explore. One recurrent idea in psychiatry and criminology has been that people do bad things because they have something wrong with their brains. Raine applied the modern technology to deal with an old question about brains and crime.

Adrian Raine, Monte Buchsbaum and Lori LaCasse (1997) Brain abnormalities in murderers indicated by positron emission tomography. *Biological Psychiatry*, 42 (6), 495–508.

Abstract

Murderers who plead NGRI (not guilty by reason of insanity) are thought to have brain dysfunction but this has not been demonstrated directly by measuring brain activity.

Method

This study used PET scanning to assess brain activity during a continuous performance task (CPT). The participants were 41 NGRI murderers (experimental or E group) and 41 age- and sex- matched controls (C group). In addition 6 participants were matched for schizophrenia.

Results

1 Looking at brain structures that were previously linked to violence, differences were found between the E and C groups – the murderers had:

- Reduced activity in the *prefrontal region*, *left angular gyrus* and *corpus callosum*.

- Asymmetries in the *amygdala*, *hippocampus*, *thalamus* (left hemisphere lower activity than right).

2 Looking at the structures that were associated with mental illness but not violence, no differences were found.

Discussion

The results do *not* demonstrate that:

1 Violent behaviour is determined by biology alone.

2 Murderers pleading NGRI are not responsible for their actions.

3 Brain dysfunction causes violence.

4 All violent offenders have such brain dysfunctions.

5 Violence can be explained by the results.

The results do suggest a link between brain dysfunction and a *predisposition* towards violence in this specific group NGRI murderers, which should be further investigated.

CoreSTUDY

Aims

Previous research has suggested that brain dysfunction may predispose individuals to violent behaviour but no one has tried to confirm which particular areas might be involved. There are clues as to which areas might be involved from animal research and studies of people with brain damage. The advent of brain imaging techniques means that it is possible to directly assess brain functioning in violent individuals.

The hypothesis is proposed that seriously violent individuals:

- Have brain dysfunction in the prefrontal cortex, angular gyrus, amygdala, hippocampus, thalamus and corpus callosum (all implicated in previous research).

- Do not have brain dysfunction in other brain areas (caudate, putamen, globus pallidus, midbrain, cerebellum) which have been implicated in psychiatric conditions but not previously related to violence.

Areas of the brain discussed in this study

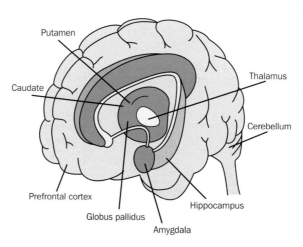

The limbic system is associated with emotion and includes the prefrontal cortex, amygdala, hippocampus, and thalamus. These structures have been linked to violent behaviour in previous research.

Biographical notes on Adrian Raine

Adrian Raine started out as an airline accountant with British Airways, but then did a degree in psychology. His first job was as a prison psychologist in top-security prisons in England. Then, in 1987, he immigrated to the US were he works now at the University of Southern California.

He has been involved for many years in the Mauritius Child Health project, a longitudinal study investigating the effects of various factors on mental health. In contrast to the findings of this study, the Mauritius Project has identified the importance of environmental rather than physiological influences on development.

Use a cauliflower to label the key areas of the brain just to get a 'feel' for it! Later you can attach new labels showing what the study found for each of these key areas. Finally, you can add a few onions and make a stir fry – education and nutrition!

Method

Participants

Murderers (experimental group) There were 41 murderers (39 men and 2 women) who had a mean age of 34.3 years. They had all been charged with murder or manslaughter and all pleaded not guilty by reason of insanity (NGRI) or incompetence to stand trial. The participants were referred to the University of California for examination to obtain proof of their diminished capacity. The reasons for referral were that the murderers had some form of mental impairment, namely:

Mental disorder	No.
schizophrenia	6
history of head injury or organic brain damage	23
history of psychoactive drug abuse	3
affective disorder	2
epilepsy	2
history of hyperactivity and learning disability	3
personality disorder	2

The participants were instructed to be medication-free for two weeks prior to brain scanning, which was checked with a urine test.

Control group The control group was formed by matching each murderer with a normal individual of the same sex and age. The six schizophrenics were matched with six schizophrenics from a mental hospital. The other controls had no history of psychiatric illness, nor was there a history of psychiatric illness in any close relatives, and no significant physical illness. None were taking medication.

Procedure

A PET scan was used to study the active brain.

All participants were given an injection of a 'tracer' (flurodeoxygluscoe or FDG). This tracer is taken up by active areas of the brain.

All participants were given a continuous performance task (CPT) which specifically aims to activate areas of the brain so the investigators could see how the different areas functioned.

1 Participants were given a chance to practise the CPT before receiving the FDG injection.

2 Thirty seconds before the FDG injection participants started the CPT so that the initial task novelty wouldn't be FDG labelled.

3 Thirty-two minutes after the FDG injection a PET scan was done of each participant. Ten slices (pictures) were recorded using the cortical peel and box techniques. The article provides precise details of the scanning techniques so that the study could be replicated.

Results

Brain differences

The table below shows the results. In summary, murderers had:

- *Reduced activity* (i.e. reduced glucose metabolism) in some areas, notably the areas previously linked to violence.

- *Abnormal asymmetries:* reduced activity on left, greater activity on the right. This applied to some of the areas identified in the hypothesis as being linked to violence (the amygdala, thalamus and hippocampus).

- *No differences* in some areas, notably those structures that were associated with mental illness but not violence.

Reduced activity	Areas previously linked to violence: prefrontal cortex, left angular gyrus, corpus callosum	Left side: amygdala, thalamus, hippocampus (previously linked to violence)
Increased activity	Area not previously linked with violence: cerebellum	Right side: amygdala, thalamus, hippocampus
No difference	Areas not previously linked with violence: Caudate, putamen, globus pallidus, midbrain	

Other differences not controlled for:

- *Handedness* Six of the murderers were left-handed but in fact they had less amygdala asymmetry and higher medial prefrontal activity than right-handed murderers.

- *Ethnicity* Fourteen of the murderers were non-white but a comparison between them and white murderers showed no significant difference.

- *Head injury* Twenty-three of the murderers had a history of head injury, but they didn't differ from murderers with no history of brain injury.

Q_S

1 Explain why the participants were required to do a 'continuous performance task' before the PET scans were carried out.

2 Why was a control group necessary?

3 Identify the IV and DV in this study.

4 Explain why the participants started the CPT task before the injection.

5 Why is it desirable to be able to replicate a study?

6 Outline **one** difference between the brain scans of the murderers and of the control group.

Discussion

Past research

Past research (animal and human studies) has identified links between areas of the brain and aggression as shown in the table. These findings are supported by this study. However, there are certain drawbacks:

- Generalisations from animal research are necessarily limited.

- Neural processes underlying violence are complex and can't be reduced to a single brain mechanism.

- Violent behaviour can be probably best explained by the disruption of a *network* of interacting brain mechanisms rather than any single structure.

- Such disruption would not *cause* violent behaviour but *predispose* an individual to violent behaviour.

- This study cannot provide a complete account because certain brain sites, which have previously been implicated (e.g. septum and hypothalamus) could not be imaged.

Conclusion
- The study provides preliminary evidence that murderers pleading NGRI have different brain functioning from normal.

- The study identifies some specific processes which may predispose some criminals to violent behaviour.

Potential confounds

Raine *et al.* claim that the results were not due to chance factors because:

1 The sample size was large.

2 Most of the effects were significant.

3 The areas affected were previously linked to violence (except one case).

4 Two-tailed tests were used throughout, preventing the erroneous rejection of a null hypothesis (called a Type I error).

5 Those brain areas that were *not* previously linked to violence (but were linked to other mental disorders) did not show group differences, which suggests that a different brain deficit underlies violent behaviour.

Brain structure	Behaviours associated with damage
Limbic system	Abnormal emotional responses, deficits in learning, memory and attention, reduced sensitivity to conditioning, might explain failure of violent offenders to learn from experience.
Prefrontal cortex	Impulsivity, loss of control, might explain aggressive behaviour.
Amygdala	Aggressive behaviour and lack of fear, might explain fearlessness.
Hippocampus	Lack of inhibition of aggression.
Angular gyrus	Deficits in verbal and arithmetic abilities, might explain low verbal IQs and poor school performance, which might predispose to a life of crime.
Corpus callosum	Poor transfer of information between hemispheres, might explain reduced processing of linguistic information.
Right hemisphere	Less regulation by left hemisphere inhibitory processes, negative emotions, inappropriate emotional expression, might explain lack of control.

However, both head injury and IQ have not been ruled out as contributory factors.

Specificity of the findings

Could violent behaviour be due to psychiatric illness?

Schizophrenia was ruled out because schizophrenics in the experimental group differed from schizophrenics in the control group. Other conditions were ruled out because the murderers did not have any of the brain characteristics typical of other mental disorders, e.g. depression is associated with abnormal left hemisphere functioning.

However, reduced prefrontal activity has been observed in a variety of psychiatric conditions.

Conclusion
Mental illness may contribute to violent behaviour but it seems that it cannot account for the brain dysfunction observed in the violent group.

Qs

1 How do we know that psychiatric illness can't explain the violent behaviour of the murderers?

2 What explanation is offered by this study for the violent behaviour of the murderers?

3 How else might you explain the violent behaviour of the murderers?

Conclusions

Raine *et al.* emphasise that it is important to recognise what these results do *not* demonstrate:

1 They do not show that violent behaviour is determined by biology alone; clearly social, psychological, cultural and situational factors play important roles in predisposing to violence.

2 They do not show that murderers pleading NGRI are not responsible for their actions, nor that PET can be used as a means of diagnosing violent individuals.

3 They do not show that brain dysfunction causes violence. It may even be that brain dysfunction is an effect of violence.

4 They do not show that all violent offenders have such brain dysfunctions; the study can only draw conclusions about this kind of violent offenders.

5 They do not show that violence can be explained by the results; the results relate to criminal behaviour.

Conclusion
Nevertheless, the findings do suggest a link between brain dysfunction and a predisposition towards violence in this specific group (NGRI murderers), which should be further investigated.

EVALUATING THE STUDY BY RAINE, BUCHSBAUM AND LACASSE

The research method

This study was a natural (quasi) experiment because the IV was not controlled by the experimenter. *What are the strengths and limitations of this research method in the context of this study?*

The research technique

What are the strengths and limitations of PET scans in the context of this study?

The sample

The murderers were not typical of all violent individuals. *In what way are the participants in this sample unique? How does this affect the conclusions drawn from the study?*

Determinist

What are the strengths and limitations of determinism in the context of this study?

Ethical issues

What ethical issues should have concerned the researchers in this study, and how might they have dealt with these issues?

Nature or nurture?

What evidence is there from this study to support the nature or nurture side of the debate?

Applications/usefulness

How valuable was this study?

What next?

Describe one change to this study, and say how you think this might affect the outcome.

DEBATE

What are the implications of this study? Some people take the view that criminals are made, not born, i.e. they become criminal because of social factors like poverty and unemployment, or because of their upbringing. One of the implications of this study is that criminals are 'born not made'. What do you think? Divide your class into groups to prepare arguments for and/or against the view that criminals are born, not made.

 Read Raine's arguments and Steven Rose's counterarguments at http://news.bbc.co.uk/1/hi/programmes/if/4102371.stm

Multiple choice questions

1. **What does NGRI stand for?**
    (a) Not guilty but requires injection.
    (b) No guilt really insane.
    (c) Not guilty by reason of insanity.
    (d) Not gifted but reasonably insane.

2. **A PET scan is different to a CAT scan because only PET scans can:**
    (a) Detect tumours.
    (b) Show specific structure.
    (c) Build a 3D picture.
    (d) Show the brain in action.

3. **Which of the following was not a reason for referral of the murderers?**
    (a) Epilepsy.
    (b) Substance abuse.
    (c) Hyperactivity.
    (d) Phobia.

4. **Participants were matched on**
    (a) Age.
    (b) IQ.
    (c) Violence.
    (d) Both (a) and (b).

5. **One group of mentally ill individuals took part in this study, those with**
    (a) Schizophrenia.
    (b) Depression.
    (c) Bulimia nervosa.
    (d) Obsessive-compulsive disorder.

6. **Which areas of the brain were previously linked to violent behaviour?**
    (a) Amygdala.
    (b) Caudate.
    (c) Corpus callosum.
    (d) (a) and (c).

7. **Which areas of the brain were previously not linked to violence?**
    (a) Cerebellum.
    (b) Hippocampus.
    (c) Amygdala.
    (d) Both (a) and (b).

8. **In which area of the brain were asymmetries found?**
    (a) Prefrontal cortex.
    (b) Putamen.
    (c) Thalamus.
    (d) Corpus callosum.

9. **The right hemisphere might be linked to violent behaviour because:**
    (a) People are right handed.
    (b) The left hemisphere has language centres.
    (c) The left hemisphere inhibits behaviour.
    (d) All of the above.

10. **Which of the following conclusions about brain dysfunction is justified?**
    (a) Causes violent behaviour.
    (b) Predisposes individuals to be violent.
    (c) Predisposes this specific group to be violent.
    (d) Causes this specific group to be violent.

Answers are on page 121.

Exam questions

1. In the study by Raine, Buchsbaum and LaCasse (brain scanning) referrals to the imaging centre were pleading not guilty of murder for reasons of insanity (NGRI).

    (a) Give **two** reasons for insanity that were being claimed. [2]

    (b) Suggest how one finding from this study might be used. [2]
    [OCR AS Psy, Jan 2002, paper 2]

2   Briefly outline the major ideas of the physiological approach to psychology that are in the study by Raine, Buchsbaum and LaCasse (brain scans). [OCR AS Psy, specimen paper] [4]

3   Outline **one** control that was used in the study on brain scanning by Raine, Buchsbaum and LaCasse. [OCR AS Psy, Jan 2004, paper 1] [2]

4   (a) In the study by Raine, Buchsbaum and LaCasse on brain scanning what is the advantage of using PET scans compared to earlier techniques? [2]

    (b) Outline **one** of the findings of this study that shows this advantage. [2]
    [OCR AS Psy, Jan 2002, paper 1]

More scans

Scanning race

Scanning techniques are now being used to investigate social issues and social judgement. Which parts of our brain are being used when we laugh or when we are attracted to someone or when we meet someone different to us? Jennifer Eberhardt is a prominent researcher in racial stereotyping, prejudice, and stigma imaging race. Recently she has been examining brain scans to see what they tell us about racism and racial differences (Eberhardt, 2005).

Working in the USA, Eberhardt's research team have used fMRI to study the face recognition of people of the same and different race to the viewer. Previous studies have shown that people find it easier to recognise faces from the same race as themselves and that this effect is stronger for European American than African American participants. The researchers were able to identify differences in brain activity that correlated with the race of the face they were identifying (Golby *et al.*, 2001).

Other work (Richeson *et al.*, 2003) found a relationship between frontal lobe activity and racial prejudice, and that the greater the brain differences in the face recognition task the greater the level of prejudice.

This work sounds very interesting if difficult to interpret but there are dangerous issues that can be raised by scanning studies on race. For example, what if you looked for differences in the average scans of different racial groups? There is little doubt that any scientific argument would soon be drowned under the weight of social prejudice. The history of brain science is littered with attempts to prove one group superior to another.

Decade of the brain

In 1990 President George Bush (the first) designated the 1990s as the Decade of the Brain: 'to enhance public awareness of the benefits to be derived from brain research'. In so doing he gave a lift to brain research in the USA. It is not known which body organ his son designated this decade to.

The two President Bushes enjoy the joke about the decade of the brain.

Adrian Raine's conclusions

'There are now 71 brain imaging studies showing that murderers, psychopaths, and individuals with aggressive, antisocial personalities have poorer functioning in the prefrontal cortex – that part of the brain involved in regulating and controlling emotion and behaviour.

'More dramatically, we now know that the brains of criminals are physically different from non-criminals, showing an 11% reduction in the volume of grey matter (neurons) in the prefrontal cortex.

'Violent offenders just do not have the emergency brakes to stop their runaway aggressive behaviour. Literally speaking, bad brains lead to bad behaviour ... One of the reasons why we have repeatedly failed to stop crime is because we have systematically ignored the biological and genetic contributions to crime causation.'

(Raine, 2004)

You will not be surprised to know that a lot of people do not agree with Raine and think he is greatly overstating the case.

The man with no brain

It's a great headline and even though it is not quite true it does describe one of the remarkable findings of the brain scan revolution. John Lorber was a neurosurgeon in Sheffield who was interested in people who had survived hydrocephalus as a child. This condition (hydro = water, cephalus = head) can be fatal if not treated as the ventricles (spaces) in the brain fill up with cerebro-spinal fluid.

A young man in perfect health was referred to Lorber because he had a slightly larger than average head which can be a sign of hydrocephalus. When Lorber looked at the CAT scans he found that the man's brain was a thin smear around the skull and the bulk of his head contained spinal fluid. According to all theories of brain structure the man should not have been alive, but not only was he alive but he had a degree in maths and economics. Lorber went on to scan more than 600 people with hydrocephalus and found numerous cases where the ventricles were filling more than 50% of the head with fluid (Lewin, 1980).

Lorber liked to give dramatic talks and entitled his paper on this topic 'Is your brain really necessary?' Partly because of his style of presentation and partly because the results are difficult to explain the work does not appear in many textbooks.

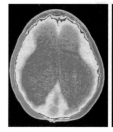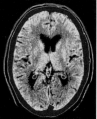

Scan of a hydrocephalus patient (left) and a normal brain (right). The dark areas are fluid and the grey areas are the brain.

LINKS TO OTHER STUDIES

This study gives us a view about why people behave badly. Raine is suggesting a biological explanation. Some of the other core studies give other explanations, for example **Bandura, Ross and Ross** suggest that bad behaviour develops by imitation, **Freud** says it develops from frustrations that arise during early life conflict, **Haney, Banks and Zimbardo** suggest it comes from the roles we play and **Milgram** says it is the situations we find ourselves in.

keyISSUE

Determinism and free will

Determinism is the idea that every event including human thought and behaviour is causally determined by an unbroken chain of prior events. According to this idea there are no mysterious miracles and no random events.

Newton's cradle is a demonstration of the idea. The movement of one ball has an effect on the others. Their motion is determined by the movement of the first ball. It is cause and effect.

The idea of determinism appears to contradict the personal experience we have of free will. We experience ourselves as making choices and deciding what to do rather than just responding like automatons to previous events. Our choices are obviously limited but we feel as if we are making choices about what we do, what we say, what we wear and so on.

The issue with determinism is that if our behaviour is a response to previous events then we have little or no control over it. In which case we can not be held responsible for the things that we do.

Freud and Skinner

Freud and Skinner said that free will was an illusion.

Sigmund Freud claimed that most of the causes of our behaviour are largely hidden from us and unconscious, thus we may think we are acting freely but in fact our behaviour is determined by unconscious forces and is predictable.

The behaviourist B.F. Skinner argued that we think we are free but that is because we are not aware of how our behaviour is determined by reinforcement.

Humanistic psychologists

Humanistic psychologists believe that behaviourists and Freudians overlooked the important role of free will in human behaviour, and the drive of humans to be self-determining.

Carl Rogers, one of the founders of humanistic psychology and also the 'inventor' of counselling, proposed a very simple personality theory, in contrast with Freud's very complex theory. The theory is built on the *actualising tendency* – the tendency in each individual to develop his/her potentials to the fullest extent possible. Rogers suggested that taking responsibility for oneself is the route to healthy self-development. As long as you remain controlled by other people or other things, you cannot take responsibility for your behaviour and therefore cannot begin to change it.

Determinism versus responsibility

In the study by Raine *et al.* described in this text, Raine says that brain dysfunction does not determine violent behaviour, but in other work he has gone a step further. In another brain-scanning study he found that men who had antisocial personality disorder (APD) had a deficiency in the frontal lobe of their brains. Raine poses the question: *'Assuming these people are not responsible for their own brain damage, should we hold then responsible for their criminal acts?'* (Raine, 2000).

This argument has already been taken to court in the USA (for example Stephen Mobley, see right) where people charged with serious offences have argued their behaviour was determined by inherited tendencies and so therefore was not their fault.

Among the arguments against Raine are first, the diagnosis of APD is controversial with the suggestion being that it is no more than giving badly behaved people a label, and the things we judge to be bad behaviour change with each generation. Second, the abnormalities are very individual and it is not possible to look at a scan and predict whether someone will be antisocial or not.

Born to kill

Stephen Mobley killed a pizza shop manager in 1981. His lawyers argued that he was not accountable for his aggressive tendencies because he 'born to kill' as evidenced by a family history of violence. He should not be sentenced to death for the crime because, in effect, he was not responsible for his actions. His lawyers' argument was rejected, and Mobley was sentenced to death.

Chaos theory

Chaos theory proposes that very small changes in initial conditions can subsequently result in major changes, sometimes called 'the butterfly effect'. A butterfly flapping its wings in Bristol can, in theory, produce a tornado in Kansas. Although this does not look like a determinist explanation it is because you can trace the hurricane back through an unbroken chain of events to the butterfly. Find that butterfly, I say, and stop the tornadoes.

ACTIVITY

Try using determinist arguments to get yourself out of tricky situations. For example, 'I couldn't help myself, I was born that way', or 'I was just responding to the flux of neurochemicals washing around my brain'. If you get a response that is anything other than a two-word sentence where the second word is 'off' then let us know. That's how much people believe in determinism.

Exam-style question

Determinism is the idea that every human behaviour is causally determined by something else, such as the action of your nervous system or events in the environment.

Select **four** core studies and use them to answer the following questions.

(a) Describe what each study tells us about how we are influenced in everyday life. [12]

(b) Briefly discuss **two** advantages and **two** disadvantages of studying determinism, using examples from these studies. [12]

Physiological Core Study 9: Schachter and Singer (emotion)

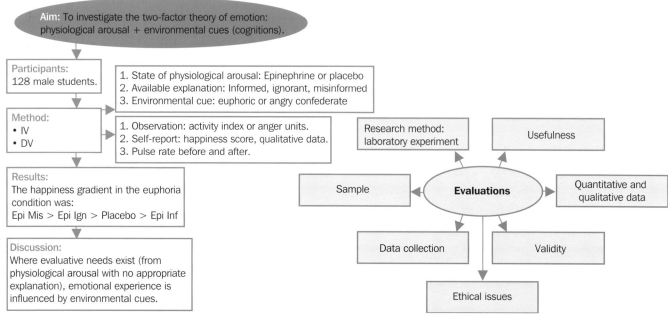

Aim: To investigate the two-factor theory of emotion: physiological arousal + environmental cues (cognitions).

Participants:
128 male students.

Method:
• IV
• DV

1. State of physiological arousal: Epinephrine or placebo
2. Available explanation: Informed, ignorant, misinformed
3. Environmental cue: euphoric or angry confederate

1. Observation: activity index or anger units.
2. Self-report: happiness score, qualitative data.
3. Pulse rate before and after.

Results:
The happiness gradient in the euphoria condition was:
Epi Mis > Epi Ign > Placebo > Epi Inf

Discussion:
Where evaluative needs exist (from physiological arousal with no appropriate explanation), emotional experience is influenced by environmental cues.

Research method: laboratory experiment

Usefulness

Sample

Evaluations

Quantitative and qualitative data

Data collection

Validity

Ethical issues

Physiological Core Study 10: Dement and Kleitman (sleep and dreaming)

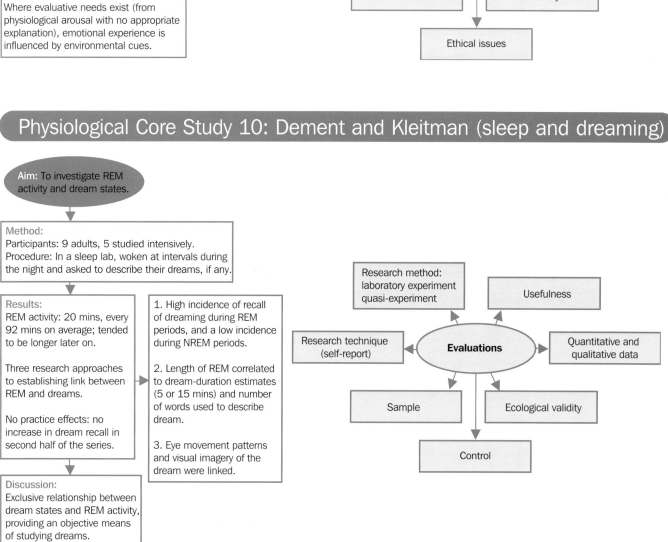

Aim: To investigate REM activity and dream states.

Method:
Participants: 9 adults, 5 studied intensively.
Procedure: In a sleep lab, woken at intervals during the night and asked to describe their dreams, if any.

Results:
REM activity: 20 mins, every 92 mins on average; tended to be longer later on.

Three research approaches to establishing link between REM and dreams.

No practice effects: no increase in dream recall in second half of the series.

1. High incidence of recall of dreaming during REM periods, and a low incidence during NREM periods.

2. Length of REM correlated to dream-duration estimates (5 or 15 mins) and number of words used to describe dream.

3. Eye movement patterns and visual imagery of the dream were linked.

Discussion:
Exclusive relationship between dream states and REM activity, providing an objective means of studying dreams.

Research method: laboratory experiment quasi-experiment

Usefulness

Research technique (self-report)

Evaluations

Quantitative and qualitative data

Sample

Ecological validity

Control

Physiological Core Study 11: Sperry (split brain)

Aim: To understand the capabilities of the left and right hemispheres

Participants:
Patients with severe epilepsy underwent split-brain surgery.

Procedure:
Patients tested on various tasks:
- Visual stimuli displayed to left and right visual field (LVF and RVF) for 0.1 sec.
- Participant asked to state what they saw.
- Or identify object with hand (out of sight).

Tests e.g.
- $ and ? to LVF and RVF.
- Composite word e.g. keycase.
- Object placed in hand.
- Simple arithmetic.
- Pin-up picture

Result:
LVF or object in left hand (right hemisphere).
- No verbal response, or flash of light seen.
- Left hand could identify.
- Might give emotional response.

RVF or object in right hand (left hemisphere).
- Can speak or write (with right hand) name of object.
- Right hand could identify.

Conclusions:
- Left hemisphere contains language centres.
- Right hemisphere produces emotional response, shows language comprehension.
- Patients cope with normal life, despite having two rather than one mind.
- Some individual differences e.g. ipsilateral control.

Evaluations
- The sample
- Qualitative or quantitative?
- Research method: natural experiment case studies
- Usefulness
- Ethical issues
- Reductionist
- Ecological validity

Physiological Core Study 12: Raine, Buchsbaum and LaCasse (brain scanning)

Aim: To see if the brains of murderers (NGRI) showed signs of physical dysfunction.

Participants:
41 NGRI murderers, 41 age- and sex-matched controls.

Method:
PET scans while participants engaged in CPT.

Result:
1. Reduced activity in *prefrontal region, left angular gyrus* and *corpus callosum* of murderers.
2. Asymmetries in the *amygdala, hippocampus, thalamus* (left hemisphere lower than right).
3. No differences in the structures (e.g. caudate) that were associated with mental illness but not violence.

Conclusions:
Brain dysfunction may predispose individuals in this specific group towards violence.
BUT findings don't show that (1) biology alone is the answer, (2) murderers are not responsible for their actions, (3) brain dysfunction causes violence, (4) all violent offenders have such brain dysfunctions, (5) violence can be explained by the results.

Evaluations
- The sample
- Research technique (PET scans)
- Research method: natural (quasi) experiment
- Usefulness
- Ethical issues
- Determinist
- Nature or nurture?

MCQ answers

Schachter and Singer (MCQs on page 93)	1c 2a 3d 4d 5b 6d 7c 8d 9c 10d
Dement and Kleitman (MCQs on page 101)	1d 2b 3c 4d 5a 6d 7a 8c 9b 10b
Sperry (MCQs on page 109)	1c 2b 3d 4a 5a 6c 7d 8c 9b 10c
Raine, Buchsbaum and LaCasse (MCQs on page 117)	1c 2d 3d 4a 5a 6d 7a 8c 9c 10c

1 (a) What are the **two** factors in Schachter and Singer's two factor theory of emotion? [2]

(b) How was each factor manipulated in the study? [2]
[OCR AS Psy, June 1994, paper 1]

Stig's answer

(a) The two factors are how the experimenter explained the effects of the injection and, the second factor was, the mood of the confederate.

(b) The factors were manipulated by the experimenter who read the instructions and told the confederate what to do.

Chardonnay's answer

(a) The two factors are physiological arousal and social cues.

(b) The physiological arousal was created by the injection of adrenalin. The social cues were delivered by the confederate who was either euphoric or angry.

Examiner's comments

Stig, you've made a common mistake here in part (a), talking about the experiment rather than the theory. Consequently, you have also missed out in part (b).

Chardonnay, you have clearly understood the two factors in the theory (part a) and how they relate to the procedure (part b). Strictly speaking, the second factor of the theory is 'cognitive appraisal', which does of course depend on social cues, but benefit of the doubt here means you will receive full credit.

Stig (0+0) Chardonnay (2+2)

2 From the study by Schachter and Singer (emotion),

(a) What did the researchers do to the subjects (participants) in the 'epi-misinformed' condition? [2]

(b) What explanation can you give for the behaviour of subjects in this condition? [2]
[OCR AS Psy, June 1999, paper 1]

Stig's answer

(a) In the epi-misinformed condition the participants were misinformed.

(b) This would be that the participants had some unexpected side effects which they needed to explain. So they would have explain these effects in some way.

Chardonnay's answer

(a) The researchers told the subjects in the epi mis condition that they would experience effects such as itching and numbness in their feet. These weren't the real effects of adrenalin thus they were misinformed.

(b) The participants in this condition had to find someone to explain their feelings of physiological arousal and they would be influenced by the confederate's social cues.

Examiner's comments

Part (a) Stig, very informative – not! Part (b), you would get something for the idea that the Epi Mis participants would have needed some explanation, but need more detail for the full two marks.

Chardonnay, you evidently understand how they were misinformed regarding the side-effects of the injection in part (a) and in part (b) adequately explain their behaviour in terms of the theory.

I think both questions 1 and 2 show how it really is important for candidates to understand both theory and study for Schachter and Singer.

Stig (0+1) Chardonnay (2+2)

3 From the study by Dement and Kleitman on sleep, give **four** characteristics of REM sleep. [OCR AS Psy, June 2000, paper 1] [4]

Stig's answer

They are rapid eye movements, faster brain activity, having dreams and can't remember another.

Chardonnay's answer

The four characteristics are that people have random eye movements. Fast EEG activity which shows that the brain is very active. The research by Dement and Kleitman showed that people very frequently have dreams in REM sleep and it is more likely to occur later in the night.

Examiner's comments

Tough question, but you've had a good stab at it Stig, identifying three characteristics.

Chardonnay, you are on sparkling form! You have correctly identified four characteristics of REM.

Stig (3) Chardonnay (4)

4 The study by Dement and Kleitman (sleep and dreaming) involved participants' self-reports of dreams and the use of equipment to measure REM and NREM.

(a) Outline **one** finding of the relationship between sleep and dreaming. [2]

(b) Give **one** reason why the conclusions of this study might not be valid. [2]
[OCR AS Psy, Jan 2002, paper 2]

Stig's answer

(a) They found that dreaming occurred in one particular kind of sleep – REM sleep. Participants reported dreams almost every time they were woken from REM sleep but rarely at other times.
(b) One reason why this conclusion may not be valid is that the study only looked at adults and even then it was only a few adults so we can't be certain that this is representative.

Chardonnay's answer

(a) There was a correlation between the length of REM activity and the number of words a participant used to describe a dream.
(b) One problem with the study was that it lacked ecological validity. It was conducted in a laboratory.

Examiner's comments

Stig, a good answer and I am glad you conveyed the idea that whilst dreaming mostly occurred in REM sleep, it did also occur on a few occasions (11/160 wakings) in NREM.

In part (b) you are referring to population validity and this is fine!

Chardonnay, spot on. You have reported a finding related to Dement and Kleitman's second hypothesis and this answers the question well.

Part (b) is brief, but sufficient for 2 marks.

Stig (2+2) Chardonnay (2+2)

---

5 In the paper by Sperry on split brain patients, he writes: 'the second hemisphere does not know what the first hemisphere has been doing'.

(a) Give **one** piece of evidence to support this statement. [2]

(b) Explain why this problem does not matter in the everyday activity of the patients in this study. [2]
[OCR AS Psy, June 2000, paper 1]

Stig's answer

(a) When they showed a dollar sign to the RVF and a question mark to the LVF, the split brain patient could recognise the dollar sign with his left hand but couldn't say what it was. (b) In everyday life people don't see things for a split second so they have time for the thing to be seen by both hemispheres.

Chardonnay's answer

(a) Patients who were given two objects to hold in each hand then could recognise the objects but only using the hand that had originally held the object. (b) This doesn't matter in everyday life because you usually can look at an object using both eyes rather than just touching it.

Examiner's comments

Stig, you have got a bit confused … easily done in this study. Remember, Left Visual Field is processed by the Right Hemisphere (no language) which, in turn, controls the left hand. But Stig, you have got part (b) right …

…which is more than Chardonnay who has lost her fizz! Your part (a) is fine, but your part (b) is not clear. Be careful in this study not to confuse eyes with visual fields. They are not the same thing!

Stig (0+2) Chardonnay (2+0)

---

6 (a) Give **one** piece of evidence that shows the language limitations of the right hemisphere of the brain. [2]

(b) Give **one** piece of evidence that shows that the right hemisphere is not completely 'word-blind'. [2]
[OCR AS Psy, Jan 2004, paper 1]

Stig's answer

(a) The right hemisphere doesn't have any language because if something is shown to the left visual field it can't be named.
(b) The right hemisphere is not totally word blind because, in some patients, they could identify an object with their left hand if the word was shown to their right hemisphere.

Chardonnay's answer

(a) In one of the studies that Sperry did, they showed the word 'keycase' to the patient. The patient only reported the word 'case' because this was in the right visual field (left hemisphere).
(b) The right hemisphere isn't completely word blind because it can sometimes respond to words.

Examiner's comments

Stig, you've got it right now in part (a) and your part (b) is spot on too.

Chardonnay, your part (a) is on the right track, though really you should have explained why the patients could not report the word 'key', as this relates to the lack of language ability in the right hemisphere. This would have given you better question focus. In part (b) you would get one mark for the word 'respond', but for the second mark you would need to say how e.g. by pointing/picking up an object with the left hand.

Stig (2+2) Chardonnay (1+1)

7 (a) Briefly describe the experimental group and the control group in the study on brain scanning by Raine, Buchsbaum and LaCasse. [2]

(b) Why are control groups used in experimental research? [2]
[OCR AS Psy, May 2002, paper 1]

Stig's answer

(a) The experimental group was the murderers. The control group was normal people.

(b) You have to use control groups to act as a comparison, to control for the results.

Chardonnay's answer

(a) The experimental group were 41 murderers (39 men and 2 women) who had pleaded NGRI. The control group were a group of 41 people matched to the murderers. Six of the experimental group were schizophrenic so 6 of the control group were too.

(b) A control group means you have something to compare the experimental group to. If you found that one participant had a higher activity in the right hemisphere you don't know if this is abnormal or not unless you have something to compare this with.

Examiner's comments

Stig, your part (a) needs a bit more detail (look at Chardonnay's answer) to really show the examiner what you know. Part (b) is fine, but to ensure the full marks you need to communicate the idea of a control group acting as a benchmark or point of reference i.e. 'comparing against the norm'.

Chardonnay, you are flaunting your knowledge in part (a) with bags of detail, more than sufficient for two marks.

Your part (b) communicates to the examiner a good understanding of the idea of the control group acting as a benchmark for normal brain activity.

Stig (1+1) Chardonnay (2+2)

---

8 (a) From the study by Raine, Buchsbaum and LaCasse, identify **two** of the characteristics that were used to match the murderers pleading not guilty by reason of insanity, with the control group. [2]

(b) Outline **one** difference between the brain scans of these two groups. [2]
[OCR AS Psy, June 2001, paper 1]

Stig's answer

(a) The murderers were matched on age and gender.

(b) One difference was that the murderers' brain scans showed more activity in the right hemisphere.

Chardonnay's answer

(a) Raine used age and sex to match the participants.

(b) The murderers had contrasting findings in the right and left structures in some areas – the amygdala, the thalamus and the hippocampus.

Examiner's comments

Part (a) is fine for both Stig and Chardonnay! What a giveaway question!

For part (b) Chardonnay clearly outstrips Stig in terms of detail. Stig your answer is a bit vague … so only one mark here. The examiner needs to know which part of the brain had more activity in the right. And is it more activity compared to the left hemisphere? Or more activity compared to the controls?

If you think you might get yourself confused, choose a simpler bit of the brain to talk about, e.g. the corpus callosum or pre-frontal cortex.

Stig (2+1) Chardonnay (2+2)

9 Some of the core studies take a physiological approach to understanding psychological processes. This approach considers how the nervous system can explain human behaviour and experience. Using the **four** core studies in this chapter answer the following questions:

(a) Describe what each study tells us about physiological psychology. [12]

(b) Briefly discuss **two** strengths and **two** weaknesses of the physiological approach, using examples from the named studies. [12]

Stig's answer

(a) The study by Schachter and Singer tells us about emotion. It tells us about how emotion is not just physiology. It isn't just adrenalin that creates an emotional experience, the cognitive cues are important too because without these people say their experience was 'as if' they were having an emotional experience. **[3]**

Sperry's study focused on the functions of the right and left hemisphere. This study was very focused on physiology and really just looked at what the brain could and couldn't do. It did show us the right brain isn't entirely useless, that it has important specialties such as emotion. It also isn't entirely word blind. **[2]**

Dement and Kleitman's study looked at sleep and dreaming. They showed that we could associate the experience of dreaming with a distinct and measurable physiological state – REM activity. Though there is a bit of doubt about whether this is really an exclusive link. One problem is that we can't generalise from this small sample of participants in an artificial setting. The second problem is that people have dreams in NREM sleep. **[3]**

The study by Raine showed us that there appear to be distinct physiological differences between people who are violent and people who aren't. This means that their behaviour is caused by the way their brain is when they are born. **[1]**

Examiner's comments

Stig, you have got good question focus here, talking about the studies and what they tell us about physiological psychology, and you haven't just written about the procedures or the findings (which some candidates do …).

Your paragraph on Schachter and Singer is quite sophisticated and demonstrates good understanding.

The Sperry paragraph is slightly vague; you could have talked in more detail about lateralisation of brain function.

Dement and Kleitman – you are writing quite a bit about problems with this study, e.g. sampling issues, but there are no points in part (a)s for evaluating. Having said that, you obviously understand the kernel of this study.

The Raine paragraph is a bit general. There are opportunities in this study to talk about why dysfunction in different parts of the brain may be related to being a murderer (e.g. lower activity in prefrontal cortex may increase impulsive behaviour). You also suggest that the murderers were hard-wired at birth to be violent – this study does not show this. Strictly speaking, there is only a correlation between abnormalities in brain functioning and murder and so we cannot conclude cause and effect.

Part (a) = 3+2+3+1= 9

(b) Strengths:

It's an approach that lends itself to conducting research because you can do well-controlled experiments on physiology. [P]

This research can be quite useful because we can find out better ways to treat illnesses. [P]

Weaknesses:

The research means you have to reduce complex behaviour to smaller units of behaviour and these may not really represent the complexity of human behaviour. [P]

There are ethical problems with this research because you have to do things to people's physiology and this may not be allowed. [P] Then you have to rely on natural studies and they don't show cause and effect. [C]

The studies often lack ecological validity. [P]

Examiner's comments

We can apply the PEC (point, example, comment) formula to marking this answer (see page ix for an explanation of PEC).

Oh dear, Stig … you've lost all your examples from studies again.

Control is certainly a strength. Physiological psychology is the most scientific branch of psychology. All of the four core studies have lots of examples of how they were controlled.

You are right in saying that usefulness is a strength, but you need to provide examples, such as: 'Schachter's work on emotion has helped contribute to medical and psychological treatments for anxiety and anger management'.

You have also mentioned three weaknesses and can only be credited for two. An examiner would mark all of them and credit you with the best two (which is why the last [P] has been crossed out).

Part (b) = 5

Total mark = a+b=14/24

Chardonnay's answer

(a) *Schachter and Singer:* This study is about emotion. It tells us that physiological factors are not everything because the participants in Marañon's study just had adrenalin and didn't always have an emotional experience. To have an emotional experience you need to the physiological input and the cognitive cue. **[2]**

Dement and Kleitman: The study was about dreaming and REM sleep. It appears to show us that the experience of dreaming is rooted in a physiological state, suggesting that your dreams are related to REM activity, but it doesn't tell us which causes which. It could be that the mental activity caused the physiological activity or vice versa. It just shows us that there are physiological correlates of a mental experience. **[3]**

Sperry: This study was about split brain patients. It shows us that the two halves of the brain have different functions. This suggests that our brains are hardwired. The study also showed us that the corpus callosum does an important job connecting the two halves. It all shows us how our thoughts are related to brain structure. **[3]**

Raine: This study had a similar finding. That brain structures can be related to behaviour. In this case it was violent behaviour that they looked at and found that murderers had different brains than normal people, or controls. This tells us that our physiology may determine our behaviour. **[2]**

Examiner's comments

The Schachter and Singer paragraph doesn't tell us about the core study as much as it tells us about Marañon, though there are certain parallels.

You clearly have a sophisticated understanding of Dement and Kleitman, but like Stig, want to evaluate it more than describe it! You could talk about how we know the two are correlated i.e. the evidence of eye movements matching dream content/estimations of dream length generally matching REM duration etc to expand your first sentence.

Your paragraph on Sperry is nice; you have drawn out quite erudite conclusions from Sperry's very important work on split-brain patients. Certainly, the similarities or commonalities between all these patients' task performance suggest that language must be hardwired into the left hemisphere.

Your paragraph on Raine is reasonable. Be careful though when you say that the murderers 'had different brains' as Raine measured brain activity. Again, we have to be careful about saying that physiology determines our behaviour – Raine is keen to avoid this oversimplification and says that this study 'does not establish causal direction'.

Part (a) = 2+3+3+2=10

(b) One problem with many of these studies is that they don't show that the physiology caused the behaviour, it could be the other way round. They just tell us that there is a relationship between physiology and behaviour. **[P]** For example, in Dement and Kleitman, we can see that REM tends to go with an experience of dreaming. But which causes which? Does dreaming cause REM or the other way round? **[E]** As it is impossible to make someone go into REM sleep, we cannot tell. **[C]**

One strength of these studies is that they have practical applications. **[P]** For example, the lawyers of murderers in Raine's study could use their results to help support their plea of Not Guilty for Reason of Insanity and get a reduced punishment. **[E]** However, some people may disagree with this use and think that this might help people who don't deserve help. **[C]**

Another problem is ecological validity. In all of the studies the participants had to be studied in a lab so that conditions were very controlled. **[P]** For example, in Dement and Kleitman's study, the participants slept in a lab in a strange bed with electrodes on their heads. This may have affected their sleep patterns so that we can't generalise the findings to other situations. **[E]** On the other hand control is a good thing to make sure results are valid and caused by the IV. **[C]**

Another problem in these studies is samples. The samples were sometimes small and/or they weren't very typical which again means we can't generalise the findings. **[P]**

Examiner's comments

We can apply the PEC formula (point, example, comma) to marking this answer (see page ix for an explanation of PEC).

Wow, Chardonnay. You have really revised this area. You have a fantastic understanding of the strengths and weaknesses of the physiological approach. It's just a shame that you appear to have run out of time.

Each of your paragraphs follows the PEC model. You have really demonstrated to the examiner, in every paragraph what you know and not left it to chance for him/her to work out what you are getting at.

In each case, your 'comment' follows on logically and raises a useful discussion point. Sometimes lazy candidates (not you, Chardonnay!) tend to come up with attempts at comments such as 'that means the study is not valid or reliable' and tack this onto the end of all four paragraphs. This strategy is not good! The examiner is unlikely to want to give the same lame comment a mark once, let alone three times. If only you'd done a fourth one.

Well done, Chardonnay, a vintage essay!

Part (b) marks = 10

Total = a + b = 10+10 = 20/24

This chapter looks at four core studies in social psychology.

1. *Milgram's demonstration of obedience in situations requiring destructive behaviour.*

2. *Haney, Banks and Zimbardo's simulation of a prison environment to investigate the effects of situational factors.*

3. *Piliavin, Rodin and Piliavin's field experiment to study the factors that affect willingness to help in an emergency situation.*

4. *Tajfel's study of the roots of prejudice – can it be explained by social identity theory?*

Social psychology

Introduction to social psychology

What is social psychology?

Social psychology is concerned with social interaction and the phenomena of social behaviour. It looks at the behaviour of the individual within a social context. One of the most influential US psychologists of the twentieth century was Gordon W. Allport who defined social psychology as:

'With few exceptions, social psychologists regard their discipline as an attempt to understand and explain how the thought, feeling and behaviour of individuals is influenced by the actual, imagined or implied presence of others. The term "implied presence" refers to the many activities the individual carries out because of his position (role) in a complex social structure and because of his membership in a cultural group' (1968, p. 3).

This definition suggests that social psychology is mainly concerned with issues of social influence, and through the middle part of the twentieth century that was the case. Modern social psychology, however, has wider interests which we can group under the following headings:

- **Social perception and judgement** is about how we make sense of and judge people and groups.
- **Social interaction** is about how we relate to others and so includes areas like conflict, cooperation and relationships.
- **Social influence** is concerned with the ways in which our interactions with other people affect the way we think, feel and behave and covers issues such as persuasion, attitude change, obedience and conformity.
- **Self-perception and identity** is concerned with how we make sense of ourselves and how we judge ourselves.

Social psychology attracts a lot of attention because it is about the events and processes that make up our daily lives. It looks at our feelings, our thoughts and our behaviour, and tries to describe and explain aspects of the human condition such as love and hate, happiness and sadness, pride and prejudice, comedy and tragedy. It is the personal science and it is about me and you.

And what makes it even more compelling is that everyone is an amateur social psychologist and if we weren't we would not be able to function in everyday life. Just walking down the street I have to make judgements about other people. At the extreme end of the scale I might judge whether they are potentially dangerous and avoid them if I judge them to be a risk. If I couldn't judge when someone has finished talking I would always be interrupting them in conversation. I make judgements about whether people like me, or find me funny, and I also make judgements about whether someone needs some support or maybe whether they are telling lies. In daily life I am a relatively competent social psychologist. The task of academic social psychology is systematically to investigate these processes.

Social phenomena

Some social phenomena defy explanation by psychologists. This world record attempt is an example. Colombian beekeeper Marian Tellez, 35, stands with a mantle of Africanised bees covering his face in an attempt to set a new Guinness world record in Bucaramanga, Colombia, September 15, 2005.

It is remarkable that someone would choose to do this and it is even more remarkable that it is a world record attempt because this means others have done it before and there are rules for completing this task. Oh, by the way, Marian's record is an estimated 500,000 bees, beating the previous record of 350,000.

Social delusions

Published in 1841 and still in print today *Extraordinary Popular Delusions and the Madness of Crowds* by Charles Mackay is a history of popular follies. The book looks at how people come to believe in irrational ideas. At the time of writing some people believed in the 'science' of alchemy that aimed to change all metal into gold and create a medicine that would cure all disease and give eternal life. Modern versions of this delusion might be the beliefs in homeopathy or astrology. MacKay also wrote about economic bubbles where the price of a commodity rises beyond any realistic value before suddenly crashing. An example of this was the Dutch tulip mania of the early seventeenth century. During this mania, speculators from all walks of life bought and sold tulip bulbs, some of which briefly became the most expensive objects in the world, until the bubble burst in 1637. Recently, the world stockmarkets saw a similar mania over technology stocks before the dot-com crash in 2002 slashed values and put many companies out of business.

Social influence: groupthink

An example of social influence is the work of Irving Janis on *groupthink*. Janis first used the term to describe a situation where each member of a group tries to match their opinion to those that they believe are held by the rest of the group. Although this is usually not a problem, in some situations the group might end up agreeing to a decision that each individual thinks is unwise. Sometimes a group of people can talk themselves into a bad decision.

Groupthink tends to occur on committees and in large organisations and Janis originally studied a number of military decisions made by US governments. He suggested some symptoms of groupthink which are shown below.

The Butler Report looked at how the UK arrived at the decision to attack Iraq in 2003. The report commented on the informal meetings that took place between a select group of advisers to Prime Minister Tony Blair. This was referred to as a 'kitchen cabinet' to describe where the discussions and decisions took place. The suggestion is that a small group of largely unelected advisers held meetings without formal rules and were led by the charisma of Tony Blair (*The Times*, 2004). Maybe they developed a groupthink, convincing each other that going to war was the best decision.

Self perception

How do we know ourselves? A theory put forward by C.H. Cooley (1902) suggested that self-concept is influenced by an individual's beliefs about what other people think of him/her. We see ourselves reflected in the behaviour of others. If people laugh at my joke then I am funny, if they scowl at me, I am bad, and so on. People are a mirror to show me what I am like.

The mirror is not always accurate because I can misinterpret what people really think of me. Cooley says that we develop a sense of self by:

(a) assessing how people see us;

(b) assessing how people judge us;

(c) putting our own judgement on these assessments.

An example of how wrong these judgements can be was provided by Dunning and Kruger (1999). They explored the breadth and depth of human incompetence and, in particular, self-delusion. They hypothesised that incompetent people overestimate their own ability, citing the example of McArthur Wheeler, who robbed two banks in broad daylight while making no attempt to disguise himself. He was arrested that night after CCTV footage was shown on the news. When police showed him the surveillance tapes, Mr Wheeler was very surprised. He is reported to have mumbled 'But I wore the juice'. Mr Wheeler had been under the impression that rubbing his face with lemon juice would make it invisible to cameras.

Dunning and Kruger asked people to rate how funny some jokes were and also to rate how good they were at judging humour. The people who were worst at judging humour (in the jokes) believed they were actually good at it. They got similar results with logic test and law entrance exams. For this work the authors received the 2000 IgNobel Prize for Psychology.

Social perception

An example of work on social perception is *attribution theory* – the theoretical models of Fritz Heider, Harold Kelley and Edward E. Jones. It is concerned with the ways in which people explain (or attribute) the behaviour of others. For example, it distinguishes between *situational* and *dispositional* explanations. Imagine you arrange to meet someone outside a club and they arrive late. You might well blame them because they didn't leave enough time to get there (dispositional explanation) whereas they might explain it as due to the bus not turning up (situational explanation). We commonly explain our own behaviour in terms of situations while believing that other people are personally in control of theirs. This bias is called the *fundamental attribution error* and is the cause of numerous domestic arguments.

Social interaction

The start of social psychology is sometimes dated to 1897 and the experimental work of Norman Triplett into the effects of competition on performance. Triplett observed that racing cyclists achieved better times on a circuit when they had someone pacing them. In a ride of 25 miles the average times per mile were;

alone:	2 min 29.9 sec.
with a pacer:	1 min 55.5 sec.
in competition:	1 min 50.4 sec.

He went on to observe this improved performance in other tasks and found, for example, that children wound fishing reels faster when there were other children also winding fishing reels in the same room.

Connections

If psychology is about human behaviour and experience then maybe all psychology is social psychology. Without other people we cannot survive our early years and it is very rare for an individual to survive and develop as an adult without social contact with other people. In this chapter we have included examples of research from mainstream social psychology, but elsewhere in the text there are many studies that have a social aspect to them. The cognitive studies of Deregowski and Loftus and Palmer show the influence of people on perceptual judgements, and the developmental studies of Freud and Bandura *et al.* are also about our social behaviour. Even in the physiological section Schachter and Singer look at the influence of others on our judgements of emotion, and Raine *et al.* looked for physiological causes of social behaviour. In the final section on individual differences there are papers on identity (Hraba and Grant, Thigpen and Cleckley) and our social judgements of abnormality (Rosenhan).

Do as you are told

The big moral question in the middle of the twentieth century was how the horrors of the Second World War (1939–45) could have happened and how they could be prevented in the future. During that war the Nazi government in Germany initiated a policy to exterminate 'worthless' ethnic groups. This led to the deaths of millions of people of Jewish descent, and the killing also extended to the mentally ill, homosexuals, gypsies and people of Slavic descent. It is not easy to kill this number of people and so death camps were set up to increase the killing efficiency. Auschwitz was the most efficient camp established by the Nazi regime, peaking at 12,000 deaths a day. Although the total number of Jewish dead in Auschwitz will never be known for certain, estimates vary between one and two-and-a-half million.

Who could do such a thing?

How could someone go to work each day to kill thousands of people and dispose of the bodies? The first response is to think of these people as monsters. They cannot be like us because we would not do these things. But can we be so sure of our humanity? Perhaps it was not monsters but ordinary people with ordinary lives who did these things. Social psychologists set out to investigate this and find out under what circumstances people will comply to authority.

Solomon Asch (1955) Asch carried out some studies on conformity to group pressure. Subjects were recruited to take part in a test of perception. They were asked to say which line from a choice of three matched the target line. Unknown to one subject in each group the rest of the group members were confederates of the experimenter and primed to give certain responses. For most of the trials they gave the obvious and correct answers, but on a few 'critical' trials they all gave the wrong answer. The subject was the last in the group to answer and had to listen to all the others giving their wrong answers. He then had to either give a different answer to the rest of the group or conform to the group pressure by giving a wrong answer. In around 40% of the trials, the subject conformed to the group.

Stanley Milgram worked with Asch while he was a post-graduate student and devised variations of Asch's study. In particular he carried out a cross-cultural version with data gathered in Norway, Paris and the USA (Milgram, 1960). He was interested in national character and devised an elaborate hoax to investigate it. As in the Asch study, subjects had to make a judgement in a group, but in this case they made the judgement in a single cubicle where they could not see the subjects but only hear them. In fact there were no other group members and the subject just heard recorded voices. When he returned to the USA he devised plans for a new study. He wanted to make the Asch study more relevant to everyday behaviour. His moment of inspiration came when he stopped thinking about how to change the level of conformity and asked just how far a person would go under the experimenter's orders. At that moment the obedience study was born.

Milgram was of Jewish descent and the killings of the Second World War had an enduring effect on his life and his work.

'The impact of the Holocaust on my own psyche energised my interest in obedience and shaped the particular form in which it was examined' (Milgram, cited in Blass, 2004, page 62).

Atrocities

Atrocities happen in each generation. The Milgram study is commonly related to the Second World War but even as he conducted his studies a new horror was unravelling in South East Asia where the USA had started a major conflict with the people of Vietnam. It is often referred to as the Vietnam War, though not if you are Vietnamese. The USA was finally defeated by the peasant army of the Vietnamese in 1973 with a loss of 55,000 American lives. Less commonly reported are the 1.5 million Vietnamese lives lost, many of whom were civilian peasants.

The women's barracks at Auschwitz

My Lai

Milgram commented on one particular act of savagery by the US Army. On the morning of March 16, 1968 a company of soldiers moved into the peasant village of My Lai looking for armed fighters. They found only women, children and the elderly, but they treated them as insurgents and tortured, raped and finally murdered them. Somewhere between 350 and 500 villagers were slaughtered before the killing frenzy was stopped when a US Army helicopter crew famously landed between the American troops and the remaining Vietnamese hiding in a bunker. The 24-year-old pilot, Warrant Officer Hugh Thompson, Jr., confronted the leaders of the troops and told them he would open fire on them if they continued their attack on civilians. This helicopter crew are still hailed as heroes today in Vietnam (www.cnn.com/WORLD/9803/16/my.lai) but were treated by many as traitors in the USA.

The massacre was covered up and denied for a year but eventually the information became public knowledge. Just one man (William Calley) was charged and eventually served three years under house arrest before being pardoned by President Nixon.

Milgram wanted to know how this event could happen. And there are many other issues to consider, for example:

- Some of the 120 soldiers on that patrol opted out of the killing. How did they do manage to do that while the others felt they had to obey orders?

- What factors led the helicopter crew to decide to intervene against their own colleagues?

- Why did the American authorities and later the general public deny what happened?

The remarkable work of Stanley Milgram

Milgram's obedience study had such an impact that the variety and originality of his other work is often missed. He was one of the most innovative psychologists of the last century. The items on this page are just a selection of his work. If you want to know more then try his book *The Individual in a Social World* (1992).

Six degrees of separation

'It's a small world, isn't it?' we say to each other when we discover a personal connection with someone who lives miles away from us. In one of his many innovative studies, Milgram set out to test this idea in 1967. He asked some people from Kansas (in the Midwest of the USA) to send packages to a stranger in Massachusetts, on the East Coast several thousand miles away. The senders were told the stranger's name, occupation, and roughly where they lived. They were told to send the package to someone they knew on a first-name basis who they thought was most likely, out of all their friends, to know the target personally. That person would do the same, and so on, until the package was personally delivered to its target.

Milgram reported the results enthusiastically but also selectively. One of the packages got through in four days but it was one of the few that did. Most didn't make it but the ones that did were able to get there in about six hops. This led to the famous phrase *'six degrees of separation'* which commonly appears in writings on the experience of urban life. It suggests that any two people in the world can be connected by an average of six acquaintances. It is a delightful idea and may well be right but Milgram did not find the clear evidence to support this.

Modern communications allow researchers to look at the small-world hypothesis again. A recent study of over 60,000 email users (Dodds *et al.*, 2003) attempted to reach one of 18 target people in 13 countries (including Estonia, India and Norway) by forwarding email messages to acquaintances. Most of the chain messages were not completed but there are many reasons for this, including apathy on the part of the people who were contacted and also email overload which is a new stress issue for many workers in the West. Using the chains that did reach their destinations the researchers calculated that social searches can reach their target in five to seven steps. So maybe Milgram was right after all.

Familiar strangers

Milgram noticed a strange phenomenon of city life: we regularly see people we recognise but never talk to or interact with. He called these people 'familiar strangers'. They might be the person who always gets on the same bus as you, or you see in the corner shop, or who sits in the same shop doorway every day. Milgram got his students to carry out a novel study on these familiar strangers (Milgram, 1977). They chose a suburban railway platform and one morning photographed the commuters waiting for a train. The students numbered the people on the photograph and then a few weeks later gave out the pictures and a questionnaire. The students got on the train and by the time the train arrived in New York City 119 out of the 139 passengers had completed the survey.

On average the commuters reported seeing four familiar strangers in the picture but only having spoken to an average of 1.5. Other questions revealed that although 47% of the passengers had wondered about the familiar strangers, less than one-third reported feeling even a slight inclination to start a conversation.

Biographical notes on Stanley Milgram

Stanley Milgram was born in New York City in 1933 to working-class Jewish parents who had immigrated to the USA from Europe. Milgram excelled in all subjects at school where his classmate was Philip Zimbardo. His first degree was in political science but after a crash-course in psychology he started a doctorate in psychology at Harvard University in 1954.

Stanley Milgram (1933–1984)

In 1960 he moved to Yale University and carried out the obedience studies for which he is most famous. The work was acknowledged by psychologists and the public but the controversy it caused affected his career. In 1967 he returned to New York to work at the City University where he stayed for the rest of his life. Milgram preferred to take on subjects that affected ordinary people in their everyday lives. For example, his mother-in-law is reported to have asked why people no longer give up their seats on subway trains so Milgram sent out teams of students to investigate this.

The Milgram family had a history of heart disease and Stanley survived four heart attacks before succumbing to the fifth in 1981. His work still jumps off the pages of psychology books and magazine articles.

Milgram devised too many research techniques to even mention here. We have given two examples but there was also the dropped letter technique to measure prejudice and helping behaviour, the obedience requests on the subway trains, the cyranos (people saying the words written by someone else) and the mental maps of cities. Psychologists can usually retire if they develop one new method; Milgram developed many.

The core study

Milgram's background as a political scientist and his concern to explain the Holocaust meant that he was drawn to the social psychology of conformity. His initial work looked at national differences in conformity to see whether it was the structure of a society that led people to carry out atrocities. He found that rates in different societies were fairly similar so Milgram came up with another approach. How far would you go in obeying unjust authority? Now read on.

Stanley Milgram (1963) Behavioural study of obedience.
Journal of Abnormal and Social Psychology, 67, 371–378.

Abstract

Obedience to legitimate authority was tested by asking subjects ('teachers') to administer increasingly strong electric shocks to another subject (the 'learner') every time he made a mistake on a learning task. The experiment took place in a laboratory at Yale University, where 40 male volunteers were selected.

Method

The naïve subject was deceived about the true aims of the experiment (he thought it was about learning) and deceived about the identity of the learner who was in fact a confederate.

When the shock level reached 300 volts the confederate banged on the wall and stopped responding. The experimenter delivered a standard set of 'prods' if the teacher suggested he should stop.

Subjects were debriefed after the experiment.

Results

Prior to the study psychology students estimated that less than 3% would go to the maximum shock level. In fact 65% of the subjects continued to the maximum voltage; only five participants (12.5%) stopped at 300 volts.

Discussion

The extent of destructive obedience and the tension shown were unexpected. Possible explanations include prestige of institution, sense of obligation to continue with the experiment, and the subject's lack of opportunity to think about or discuss what he was doing.

The learner is strapped into an 'electric chair apparatus' and an electrode attached to his wrist so he can receive shocks if he makes a mistake on the learning task.

core STUDY

Aim

Obedience is an indispensable part of social life. In order to live in communities some system of authority is required. The issue of obedience was particularly relevant in the 1960s, when explanations were sought for the inhumane obedience of Germans who systematically slaughtered millions of innocent people during the Second World War.

Obedience may be deeply ingrained in the human character and may be thought to be destructive, but we should also remember that it serves productive functions as well, such as acts of charity and kindness.

The aim of this study was to investigate the process of obedience, to demonstrate the power of a legitimate authority even when the command requires destructive behaviour.

Method

Participants

Milgram advertised for 500 New Haven men to take part in a scientific study of memory and learning at Yale University. Everyone was to be paid $4.50 (a reasonable sum of money in those days) simply for coming to the laboratory.

The final group of subjects was selected from all those who volunteered, consisting of 40 men aged between 20 and 50, from various occupational and educational backgrounds (postal clerks, salesmen, engineers and labourers).

The part of the experimenter was played by a biology teacher, dressed in a technician's coat. The learner (or victim) was played by a 47-year-old accountant, trained for the role. Both of these men were accomplices of Milgram (confederates).

Procedure

Each subject was told that the experiment aimed to see how punishment affected learning. Each study would involve one teacher and one learner. The naïve subject was introduced to the other 'subject' (the accountant); lots were drawn for the parts of teacher and learner. The naïve subject always got the part of teacher.

Learner and teacher were taken to the experimental room where the learner was strapped into an 'electric chair apparatus' in order to prevent excessive movement when the electric shocks were delivered (see photograph). An electrode was attached to the learner's wrist and also attached to a shock generator in the next room. The experimenter advised them that, 'Although the shocks can be extremely painful, they cause no permanent tissue damage' (page 373).

Learning task The teacher was asked to read a series of word pairs to the learner, and then read the first word of the pair along with four terms. The learner had to indicate which of the four terms was originally paired with the first word.

Shock generator This machine had 30 switches each labelled with a number from 15 to 450 volts, in increments of 15 (see illustration at far right). There were also labels to describe the intensity.

In order to convince the naïve subject that the shocks were genuine, they were given a sample shock of 45 volts, on their wrist.

The teacher was told to give a shock for a wrong response and, each time, to move one level higher on the shock generator. The teacher also had to announce the voltage each time, thus reminding him of the increasing intensity.

Preliminary and regular run A pilot run of the experiment showed that it takes some time before subjects can get the procedure right so each subject was given 10 words to read to the learner. The teacher made 7 errors on this practice run and so received 7 shocks, reaching the moderate level of 105 volts.

For the regular run the teacher started again from 0 volts and was given a new list of words.

 Stanley Milgram at www.stanleymilgram.com, also http://www.ulmus.net/ace/library/obedience.cfm

Feedback from the victim The learner had a predetermined set of responses, giving approximately three wrong answers to every correct answer. The learner made no sign of protest or any other comment until a shock level of 300 volts was reached. At this point he pounded on the wall but thereafter ceased to provide any further response to questions; the subject usually turned to the experimenter for advice and was told to wait 5–10 seconds before treating the lack of response as a wrong answer. He was to continue increasing the shock levels with each wrong answer. After the 315 volt shock the learner pounded on the wall again but after that there was no further response from the learner.

Experimenter feedback If the subject turned to the experimenter for advice about whether to continue giving shocks, the experimenter was trained to give a series of standard 'prods' which were always made in sequence. Prod 2 was only used if prod 1 was unsuccessful. If the subject refused to obey prod 4 then the experiment was terminated. The sequence was begun anew on each hesitation.

Prod 1	'Please continue', or 'Please go on'.
Prod 2	'The experiment requires that you continue.'
Prod 3	'It is absolutely essential that you continue.'
Prod 4	'You have no other choice, you must go on.'
Special prods	If the teacher asked whether the learner might suffer permanent physical injury, the experimenter said: 'Although the shocks may be painful, there is no permanent tissue damage, so please go on.'
	If the teacher said that the learner clearly wanted to stop, the experimenter said: 'Whether the learner likes it or not, you must go on until he has learned all the word pairs correctly. So please go on.'

Dependent measures

Each subject was scored between 0 and 30 depending on when they terminated the experiment. An obedient subject was one who administered all the shock levels.

Further records Most sessions were taped and some photographs taken through one-way mirrors. Notes were kept on any unusual behaviour and observers wrote descriptions of subjects' behaviour.

Interview and dehoax All subjects were interviewed after the experiment and were asked various open-ended questions. They were also given some psychological tests. After this, procedures were undertaken to ensure that the subject would leave the laboratory in a state of well-being. A friendly reconciliation with the learner was arranged.

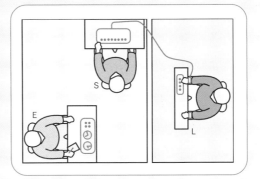

The experimenter (E) persuades the subject (S) to give what the subject believes are painful electric shocks to a 'learner' (L), seated in a separate room. The learner is strapped into his chair and an electrode placed on his wrist which is connected to the generator in order to adminsister the shocks. The learner provides answers using a four-way panel in front of him.

Qs

1 Identify five aspects of the method which were designed to increase the concern felt by the naïve subject.

2 If you felt uneasy about the experiment would you have felt able to take your money and go? Explain your answer.

3 Identify the IV and DV in this experiment.

4 Orne and Holland (1968) argued that the subjects didn't really believe the shocks were real because such things don't happen in a psychology experiment. What evidence is there that the subjects did believe the shocks were real?

Experiment or investigation?

There is some debate about whether this study is an experiment or not. We can be certain that it was conducted in a laboratory. This leads many people to assume it was an experiment but to be classed as an experiment there must be an IV and DV.

Some people say it was simply an investigation to see how willing subjects were to obey unjust authority.

However, it could be argued that the shock levels were the IV, and the DV was willingness to obey. Milgram himself described it as an experiment.

The shock generator

The labels for every group of four switches:

Slight shock	15	30	45	60
Moderate shock	75	90	105	120
Strong shock	135	150	165	180
Very strong shock	195	210	225	240
Intense shock	255	270	285	300
Extremely intense shock	315	330	345	360
Danger: Severe shock	375	390	405	420
XXX	435	450		

Results

Preliminary notions

Milgram described the experimental situation to 14 psychology undergraduates and asked them to predict how 100 hypothetical subjects would behave. They expected that no more than 3% of subjects would continue to 450 volts.

Experimental results

Subjects accept situation With few exceptions the subjects were convinced of the reality of the experimental situation. In the post-experimental briefing they were asked to indicate how painful the shocks had been. The modal response was 'extremely painful'.

Signs of extreme tension Many subjects showed nervousness and a large number showed extreme tension, '*subjects were observed to sweat, tremble, stutter, bite their lips, groan and dig their finger-nails into their flesh*'. Fourteen displayed nervous laughter which seemed bizarre and three had '*full-blown uncontrollable seizures*'.

Distribution of scores The results are shown in the graph below. The two key findings are:

- Over half of the subjects (26/40 or 65%) went all the way with the electric shocks.

- Only nine (22.5%) stopped at 315 volts.

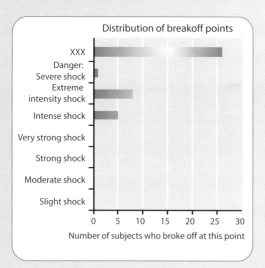

Distribution of breakoff points

Number of subjects who broke off at this point

Discussion

Two findings emerged which were surprising:

1 The sheer strength of the obedient tendencies, despite the fact that:

- People are taught from childhood that it is wrong to hurt someone.

- The experimenter had no special powers to enforce his commands.

- Disobedience would bring no material loss to the subject.

- This behaviour was not expected by the students in the pre-experiment survey, nor by the persons who observed the experiment.

2 The extraordinary tension generated, as one observer related:

'*I observed a mature and initially poised businessman enter the laboratory smiling and confident. Within 20 minutes he was reduced to a twitching, stuttering wreck, who was rapidly approaching a point of nervous collapse. He constantly pulled on his earlobe, and twisted his hands. At one point he pushed his fist into his forehead and muttered "Oh God, let's stop it." And yet he continued to respond to every word of the experimenter, and obeyed to the end*' (page 377).

Why did they obey?

1 The location of the study at a prestigious university provided authority.

2 Subjects assume that the experimenter knows what he is doing and has a worthy purpose, so should be followed.

3 Subjects assume that the learner has voluntarily consented to take part.

4 The subject doesn't wish to disrupt the experiment because he feels under obligation to the experimenter due to his voluntary consent to take part.

5 This sense of obligation is reinforced because the subject has been paid (though he was told he could leave).

6 Subjects believe that the role of learner was determined by chance; therefore the learner can't really complain.

7 It is a novel situation for the subject who therefore doesn't know how to behave. If it was possible to discuss the situation with others the subject might have behaved differently.

8 The subject assumes that the discomfort caused is minimal and temporary, and that the scientific gains are important.

9 Since the learner has 'played the game' up to shock level 20 (300 volts) the subject assumes the learner is willing to continue with the experiment.

10 The subject is torn between meeting the demands of the victim and those of the experimenter.

11 The two demands are not equally pressing and legitimate.

12 The subject has very little time to resolve this conflict and he doesn't know that the victim will remain silent for the rest of the experiment.

13 The conflict is between two deeply ingrained tendencies: not to harm someone and to obey those whom we perceive to be legitimate authorities.

'*I think he's trying to communicate, he's knocking ... Well it's not fair to shock the guy ... these are terrific volts. I don't think this is very humane ... Oh, I can't go on with this.*'

Those who continued to the end often heaved a sigh of relief, mopped their brows, some shook their heads apparently in regret, some remained calm throughout.

ACTIVITY

Before conducting this study, Milgram asked various people (psychiatrists, undergraduates and some ordinary people) to predict how the subjects would behave in this study. Try conducting a survey yourself — briefly outline the experimental procedure and ask people to predict how 100 hypothetical participants would behave.

EVALUATING THE STUDY BY MILGRAM

The research method

This study was a laboratory experiment. *What are the strengths and limitations of this research method in the context of this study?*

The sample

The subjects were US males and volunteers. *In what way are the participants in this sample unique? How does this affect the conclusions drawn from the study?*

Quantitative and qualitative data

Give examples of both kinds of data in this study. What are the strengths and limitations of quantitative and qualitative data in the context of this study?

Ecological validity

Do you think the participants would behave as they would in everyday life with an authority figure?

Personality versus situation

What does this study tell us about the relative effects of personality and situation on behaviour?

Ethical issues

What ethical issues should have concerned the researchers in this study, and how might they have dealt with these issues?

Applications/usefulness

How valuable was this study?

(See page x for note on evaluating research studies/articles)

Further details of the study were provided by Milgram in his book Obedience to Authority *(1974).*

The subjects were sent a follow-up questionnaire, which showed that 84% felt glad to have participated, and 74% felt they had learned something of personal importance.

Milgram considered abandonment when it became clear that some subjects were distressed. However he decided that 'momentary excitement is not the same as harm' (1974, page 212).

What next?

Describe **one** change to this study, and say how you think this might affect the outcome.

DEBATE

Do the ends justify the means? Work in groups and prepare two lists: one list of all the plus points of this experiment and one list of all the minus points. On balance do you think that Milgram was justified in conducting this study?

Multiple choice questions

1. Identify the sampling method used:
   (a) Volunteer sample.
   (b) Opportunity sample.
   (c) Random sample.
   (d) Nice sample.

2. Which ethical issue was not really a problem in this study?
   (a) Informed consent.
   (b) Deception.
   (c) Privacy.
   (d) Psychological harm.

3. At what shock level did the learner start banging on the wall?
   (a) 200 volts.   (b) 250 volts.
   (c) 300 volts.   (d) 350 volts.

4. How many prods did the experimenter use?
   (a) 2   (b) 4
   (c) 6   (d) 8

5. After the experiment, the subject was:
   (a) Introduced to the learner.
   (b) Dehoaxed.
   (c) Given psychological tests.
   (d) All of the above.

6. Students predicted that:
   (a) 1% would obey fully.
   (b) 3% would obey fully.
   (c) 5% would obey fully.
   (d) 10% would obey fully.

7. What percentage of participants stopped at 300 volts?
   (a) 12.5%   (b) 17.5%
   (c) 22.5%   (d) 27.5%

8. What percentage of participants stopped at 450 volts?
   (a) 50%   (b) 55%
   (c) 60%   (d) 65%

9. Milgram offered explanations for why the subject obeyed. Which of the following was not one of his reasons?
   (a) Sense of obligation.
   (b) The setting was prestigious.
   (c) Discomfort is minimal.
   (d) They didn't take the task seriously.

10. Does Milgram suggest that obedience is:
    (a) A bad thing?
    (b) A good thing?
    (c) Both bad and good.
    (d) Unusual.

Answers are on page 163.

Exam questions

1. From the study by Milgram on obedience:

   (a) Outline **one** way in which the study had low ecological validity. [2]

   (b) Outline **one** way in which the study had high ecological validity. [2]
   [OCR AS Psy, May 2005, paper 1]

2. From the Milgram study give **four** features of the study which explain the high level of obedience. [OCR AS Psy, Jan 2004, paper 1] [4]

3. Psychologists sometimes make the distinction between situational and individual explanations of behaviour. Consider the Milgram study and:

   (a) Give a situational explanation for the behaviours of the teachers. [2]

   (b) Give an individual explanation for the behaviour of the teachers. [2]
   [OCR AS Psy, specimen paper]

4. Milgram's study is often criticised for being unethical, though Milgram himself made a robust defence of it. Give **two** examples of how the ethics of this study can be defended. [OCR AS Psy, June 1999, paper 1] [4]

Obedience now

Milgram and ethics

Many text books use the obedience study as an example of lack of ethical sensitivity. We would argue that they are wrong to do so. It is true that after the study was carried out there was an ethical storm about them. For example Diana Baumrind (1964) wrote a damming critique, arguing that just because someone volunteers for a study this does not take away the researcher's responsibilities towards them. She used direct quotes from Milgram's study to illustrate the lack of regard she believed was given to the subjects. For example:

'In a large number of cases the degree of tension [in the subjects] reached extremes that are rarely seen in sociopsychological laboratory studies. Subjects were observed to sweat, tremble, stutter, bite their lips, groan, and dig their fingernails into their flesh. These were characteristic rather than exceptional responses to the experiment' (page 375).

Baumrind accepted that some harm to subjects is a necessary part of research, for example testing out new medical procedures, because the results could not be achieved in any other way. Social psychology, however, is not in the same game as medicine and is unlikely to produce life-saving results, thus does not justify harming subjects.

The case for the prosecution was very powerful. His application to join the American Psychological Association (APA) was put on hold while they investigated the study, and he was not given the post he hoped for at Yale.

The case for the defence, however, is overwhelming. At the time of study there were no ethical guidelines for psychological studies and Milgram took more care than his colleagues about such issues. His obedience study contains the first reference to *debriefing* in a psychological report and

he kept in contact with his subjects after the study to check their progress and response.

His work was eventually endorsed by the APA and he was awarded the Prize for Behavioral Science Research of the American Association for the Advancement of Science in 1964 (a prize also awarded to Stanley Schachter).

Finally, the obedience study has created a mirror for the world to see itself in. We can't look on at atrocity and comfort ourselves that we would never do it. We have to confront the fact that ordinary people can do despicable things. The Milgram study still dominates social psychology as arguably its greatest piece of work.

Obedience of soldiers

We normally think of soldiers in battle as an efficient killing machine, obediently firing their weapons on the command of their officers. The history of warfare tells another story, however, and this makes the Milgram study even more remarkable.

At the brutal Battle of Gettysburg (1863) in the US Civil War the soldiers used muskets that took a long time to load and, obviously, a short time to fire. After the battle over 27,000 muskets were recovered though surprisingly 90% were still loaded. In fact 12,000 of these were loaded more than once and one musket had 23 rounds in its barrel (Grossman, 1995).

How could this be? The only answer is that the soldiers wanted to look as if they were firing at the enemy so kept reloading their weapons even though they had not fired off the first shot.

In the Second World War (1939–45) numerous studies of US troops came to the same conclusion. Fewer than 20% would fire their guns even when they were under fire. The reason was not fear, because these men often performed acts of great heroism but they did not want to fire a gun at another human being (Grossman, 1995).

The puzzle with the Milgram study is that the majority of soldiers in fear of their lives will not fire a gun at another human being, but a man under no physical pressure will effectively electrocute another. In war the inhibitions against killing someone are still strong and that makes the Milgram study even more surprising.

The US forces learnt from previous wars and now use a range of psychological techniques to break down the inhibitions of troops against killing. Fire rates for troops have increased from 20% (Second World War) to 55% in Korea (1950s) to 90% in Vietnam (1960s and 70s). Western forces are now much more efficient killing machines.

Popular culture

Milgram's experiment and the subsequent replications have entered popular culture and are still commonly referred to outside the world of psychology. During his life Milgram made a number of scientific films on his work and advised on a made-for-TV movie about the obedience experiment called *The Tenth Level* starring William Shatner and John Travolta. It is not thought to be a masterpiece. There are numerous other references to the work in film including a scene in *Ghostbusters* where Bill Murray's character is shown as a sly professor administering electrical shocks to a college student while flirting with an attractive female. One of the film-writers, Harold Ramis, has said this parody was inspired by the Milgram study (Blass, 2004).

Peter Gabriel's 1986 album *So* has a track that was inspired by the Milgram experiment. 'We Do What We're Told (Milgram's 37)' refers to the 37 out of 40 participants who showed complete obedience in one particular experiment.

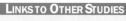
LINKS TO OTHER STUDIES

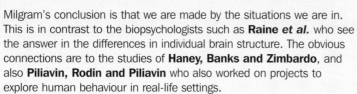
Milgram's conclusion is that we are made by the situations we are in. This is in contrast to the biopsychologists such as **Raine et al.** who see the answer in the differences in individual brain structure. The obvious connections are to the studies of **Haney, Banks and Zimbardo**, and also **Piliavin, Rodin and Piliavin** who also worked on projects to explore human behaviour in real-life settings.

KeyISSUE

Ecological validity

Ecological validity is the degree to which the behaviour observed in a study reflects the behaviour that occurs in *everyday* settings.

Ecological validity is associated with *generalisability* which is the extent to which findings can be generalised to the real world. It is also concerned with *representativeness* which is the extent to which a study mirrors conditions in the real world.

In virtually all studies there is a trade-off between experimental control and ecological validity. The greater the control the greater the danger of compromising the ecological validity. When we study people in a laboratory their behaviour is clearly affected by the laboratory environment and the tasks they are required to do are often very contrived. If we study them in their daily life it is usually impossible to do this in a controlled way.

Obedience in the lab

The business of a psychologist is to produce explanations of behaviour. For example, Milgram was challenged by events of the Holocaust (see page 130) to provide an explanation for why people obey authority when harm to another is involved. He proposed the explanation that it is a deeply ingrained behaviour tendency. A psychologist must then test this explanation by conducting research. Milgram tested how far people would go when destructive obedience was required. In order to control variables he did it in a laboratory. The question is whether the Milgram study reflects what happens in real life or whether people only behave like that in lab experiments.

- Did the participants realise it was a hoax? If they did then they may have been just pretending.

- Was the situation too contrived to have any relevance to daily life?

- Did the experimental situation mirror any features of the Holocaust?

Orne and Holland (1968) claimed that Milgram's research lacked ecological validity. If the experiment was actually measuring the experimenter–participant relationship rather than authority–subject relationships in general, then it is not reasonable to generalise the findings beyond this specific setting to obedience behaviour generally.

Milgram's response was that real life was no different. Experiments are like social situations, the experiment (being a social situation) is a reflection of life. The relationship between an experimenter and participant is no different to that between any authority figure and someone in a subservient position.

Obedience in the real world

Nurses

Hofling *et al.* (1966) conducted a study in a US hospital. Nurses were telephoned by a 'Dr Smith' who asked that they give 20mg of Astroten to a patient. This order contravened hospital regulations:

- instructions should not be given on the phone;

- nor from an unknown doctor;

- nor for a dose in excess of the safe amount (the dosage was twice that advised on the bottle);

- and especially for an unknown drug.

Nevertheless, 21 out of 22 (95%) nurses did as requested. When the nurses involved in the study were interviewed afterwards they said, in their defence, that they had obeyed because that's what doctors expect nurses to do – they behaved as nurses do in real life. Or did they?

More nurses

In another study (Rank and Jacobsen, 1977) nurses were also asked to carry out an irregular order. This time 16 out of 18 (89%) *refused*. There were important differences:

- the drug was familiar (Valium);

- the nurses could consult with peers.

Think outside the box.

Just because a study is conducted in a contrived, artificial lab doesn't mean it is low in ecological validity.

Studies conducted in the real world aren't always high in ecological validity – they may still be contrived.

Exam-style question

Ecological validity concerns whether we can generalise the findings of a research study to everyday settings. The more you control variables, the less ecological validity there may be.

Using **four** core studies, answer the questions that follow.

(a) Describe how each of the studies was different from everyday life. [12]

(b) Comment on **four** problems that psychologists may have when they study behaviour in everyday life. [12]

ACTIVITY

Look at other core studies and for each of them identify one aspect that has high ecological validity and one that has low ecological validity.

Other core studies

Many of the studies in this text have been selected because they have clear relevance to issues of everyday life. In order to carry out controlled investigations, compromises are made. For example, the memory study by Loftus and Palmer (page 6). It is clearly not possible to stage accidents, so they have to be viewed in picture format. This means there are limits to how much we can generalise the results.

The study by Tajfel (page 156) appears to be low in ecological validity because the boys are asked to carry out a very unusual (and unrepresentative) task. On the other hand, the point of the study was to demonstrate that categorisation alone was enough to produce ethnocentric behaviour and so all the other variables had to be eliminated. The study was fit for purpose because it demonstrated the principle that was being tested.

KEY TERMS

Ecological validity The ability to generalise a research finding beyond the particular setting in which it is demonstrated to other settings. It is established by considering representativeness and generalisability.

Social roles and deindividuation

Deindividuation and behaviour in crowds

Psychological research into crowds began at the end of the nineteenth century, with the work of Le Bon (1895). As with much psychological research, this work was stimulated by social conditions of the time, which included increasing unrest on the part of working people against repressive social conditions. This led to collective political action, such as mass demonstrations which frequently led to violence as police and army forces attempted to suppress them.

Le Bon proposed that the source of this violence lay in 'mob psychology' – when people were in a crowd, their individual conscience and autonomy was suppressed, and they reverted to what Le Bon described as a primeval, animalistic state in which they would commit acts of aggression which were unthinkable to the same people when they were acting as individuals.

This basic assumption is part of Zimbardo's theory of deindividuation. Zimbardo (1970) described this as a state of awareness where an anonymous individual develops a reduced sense of personal agency. This produces weakened restraints against impulsive behaviour; increased sensitivity to immediate cues of current emotional states; a lowered ability to engage in rational planning; less concern about what other people will think, and an inability to monitor or regulate personal behaviour.

Biographical notes on Philip Zimbardo

Philip George Zimbardo was born into poverty in New York City, the grandchild of Sicilian immigrants. The family were constantly on the move (31 times to be exact) because they couldn't pay the rent. Zimbardo was often ill as a child, including one spell of spending six months in a hospital aged five. This provides a link with the study by Hodges and Tizard (page 64) because Zimbardo says this was a formative experience in his development, leading him to recognise the importance of human relationships.

Professor Zimbardo has conducted research in many other areas of psychology, such as shyness, persuasion, hypnosis and most recently terrorism. He helped to create the US Public TV programme *Discovering Psychology* and acts as series host. Zimbardo has received numerous awards for his distinguished teaching, creative research, dedicated social action, and career-long contributions to psychology. He was recently president of the American Psychological Association.

The deindividuation studies

Shocking women

Zimbardo (1970) devised some studies to investigate the effects of deindividuation. In one study, young female college students did a 'learning task' which required them to give electric shocks to other members of the group. Those students who wore name tags (enhancing their identity) gave fewer shocks than those who were made to feel anonymous (no name tags or, in some conditions, wore bags on their heads). In the anonymous groups, the women increased the shock levels as the study progressed.

Surprisingly, when the study was carried out on Belgian soldiers the opposite effect was found: the group without identity tags gave fewer shocks. It may be that, for soldiers who normally wear uniforms, this did not lead to deindividuation. The results certainly show that the deindividuation effect does not apply in all situations.

Trick or treat?

Fraser (1974) set up a Halloween party to investigate the effects of costumes on children's behaviour. Half of the party games were non-aggressive in nature, and half had similar content but involved aggression. The first and third sets of games were played without costumes; the middle set was played wearing the costumes. The children were much more aggressive when wearing costumes, but interestingly, managed to win fewer rewards during this phase.

The above research was about children's games but the same effect can be seen when masks disguise identity and remove social controls on behaviour, to tragic effect. The following news report comes from the *New York Times*: *'A gang of young men wielding knives and bats went on a Halloween rampage Wednesday night, assaulting several homeless people on the footbridge to Wards Island and leaving one of them dead among the garbage-strewn weeds, his throat slashed. The group of about 10 young men, some wearing Halloween masks, apparently attacked the homeless men for thrills'* (McKinley, 1990).

Legal defence

Deindividuation has been used as a mitigating defence plea in a court of law. Colman (1991) described how expert psychological testimony given in two murder trials in South Africa had influenced the legal judgments. In the trial of eight workers found guilty of murdering non-strikers, Colman was an expert witness and used deindividuation, extreme frustration, group polarisation, bystander apathy, and learned helplessness to explain why some defendants had watched passively while others committed murders. The Court of Appeals withdrew the death penalty.

Not so shocking women

Johnson and Downing (1979) argued that the hoods and coats worn by Zimbardo's research participants were highly suggestive of violence, since they resembled Ku Klux Klan costumes, and that therefore the

Lord of the Flies (William Golding 1954)

This is a story about a group of British school boys who are marooned on a desert island after their plane is shot down. They develop their own society that becomes increasingly savage. A key feature of their transformation from civilised to savage behaviour is

research participants had gained expectations as to how they ought to behave in the study, and acted accordingly. They replicated the study, comparing a group dressed in the same way as those in Zimbardo's study with a group dressed in nurse uniforms. Johnson and Downing found that those wearing nurse uniforms, while just as anonymous, gave fewer shocks than the others. This suggests that deindividuation actually leads to conformity to group or situational norms, rather than necessarily leading anti-social behaviour.

Cues in the environment

Zimbardo (1969) left one car a block away from New York University and another a block away from Stanford University; the New York car was in a downtown area and the Stanford car in a smart middle-class area of California. Zimbardo removed the licence plates and raised the bonnets slightly to show abandonment and to act as 'releaser cues' for vandalism. Within minutes of being left unattended the New York car was vandalised and in a few days was totally stripped. In contrast the car in California stood untouched for more than a week until Zimbardo attacked it himself with a sledgehammer. Over the next few days this car was vandalised, overturned and eventually destroyed. The cues in the environment triggered the vandalism.

The experiment prompted Wilson and Kelling (1982) to develop their theory of 'broken windows' which says that one unattended broken window leads to many more. Their review of urban crime revealed that residents withdraw from an apparently neglected street. Once they go, the informal cues that provide some control over social behaviour are reduced. The level of vandalism rises and a vicious circle kicks in with the area spiralling down towards more serious crime and disorder.

The dark room

Anonymity need not lead to the anti-social deindividuation described by Zimbardo. In a study by Gergen et al. (1973) for example, people were monitored as to how they would act with strangers. In one condition, the research participants were asked to spend one hour of their time in a closed room with people they had never seen before, and were not likely to see again. Once in the room, the research participants tended to establish themselves out in the space available and carried out friendly conversations with the other person, from the same position. Most people described the experience as friendly, but not intimate.

In the experimental condition, the research participants were given the same instructions, but this time were asked to stay in a room that was completely dark. In this condition, people moved about much more, and the conversation was patchy and usually stopped after a short while. Several people reported developing intimate and deep emotional contact with other people in the room. The researchers suggested that anonymity may reduce some social inhibitions, allowing the person to experience intense positive emotion more readily which is much like the intimacy that some people can develop with a stranger, such as in conversation on a train. They concluded that this was evidence of deindividuation, although the observations are very different from the anti-social deindividuation described by Zimbardo.

Visual cues suggest an area is not cared for and so encourage further vandalism.

the change in their physical appearance. By painting themselves they are able to disinhibit their reluctance to kill a pig for food. Once these barriers are down their behaviour becomes increasingly barbaric. The paint effectively created a uniform to hide behind and allowed the new behaviour.

Prisons

A closed institution such as a hospital or prison can have an effect on the behaviour and personality of people inside. A prison environment might affect people who work there as well as those who are sent there. The uniforms of prisoners and guards might change behaviour in the way that the Halloween costume changed that of trick-or-treaters. The theory of deindividuation suggests that removing individuality will allow unfamiliar and negative behaviour.

If putting people into prisons makes their behaviour worse and the behaviour of their guards more brutal then we need to look again at our criminal justice policy. Over 9 million people are held in prisons worldwide (Home Office, 2003) with about half them being detained in just three countries (USA, Russia and China). In the UK in the summer of 2005, 76,675 people were being held in prison (70,017 men and 4,658 women) (NOMS, 2005).

Civilian prisons and prisoner of war (POW) camps

There are some key differences between the conditions of civilian prisons and POW camps as shown below. As you read the following study try to match up which one you think the mock prison is most like.

Prison
- Sent to prison after trial.
- Allowed to keep some personal items.
- Guards have strict rules.
- Referred to by name.

POW camp
- Snatched without warning.
- Depersonalised through clothes and appearance.
- Guards can often make own rules.
- Referred to by number.

The core study

Like Milgram's approach to obedience Zimbardo did not base his work in theory. They were both interested in how people will behave in extreme situations. Milgram looked at the response to commands from an individual in authority and Zimbardo wondered how that authority would develop in the social world of a mock prison.

Craig Haney, Curtis Banks and Philip Zimbardo (1973)
A study of prisoners and guards in a simulated prison.
Naval Research Reviews, 30 (9), 4–17.

Operationalisation

In order to implement a variable such as 'power' the concept must be 'broken down' into constituent operations.

Abstract

This study set out to investigate the dispositional explanation of the behaviour of guards and prisoners, by assigning these roles to 'normal' individuals living in a simulated prison environment. Would the context affect their behaviour?

Method

Twenty-two well-adjusted male students were selected from volunteers and randomly assigned to role of guard or prisoner. Guards were instructed to make their own decisions about how to maintain order but not to use physical abuse.

Prisoners and guards were given clothing which would promote feelings of anonymity (e.g. sunglasses and stockings on head), power (baton for guards) and humiliation/emasculation (smocks for prisoners). The prisoners were further dehumanised by using numbers rather than names.

The guards did shifts and went home at other times; the prisoners remained in the prison throughout.

Results

The study was ended prematurely after six days. Within two days some prisoners showed signs of extreme emotional depression and five had to be released early, one with a psychosomatic rash. There were significant individual differences. All participants expressed negative self-evaluations at the end.

Discussion

1 *Reality of simulation*: Many features of the study pointed to total role immersion (e.g. prisoners referring to themselves by number).

2 *Pathology of power*: guards appeared to relish their power and abused it.

3 *Pathological prisoner syndrome*: social disintegration, passivity, dependence and flattened mood, occurring as a result of deindividuation, arbitrary control (learned helplessness) and dependency.

coreSTUDY

Introduction

Explanations for the failure of prisons focus on the dispositional hypothesis – suggesting that failure is due to the nature of the people who administer them and/or the nature of those who populate them. Guards are viewed as sadistic, uneducated and insensitive; prisoners are characterised as having a disregard for law, order and social convention, and being impulsive and aggressive. Thus poor conditions in prisons are due to the 'bad people' not bad conditions. This draws attention away from the complex matrix of social, economic and political forces that make prisons what they are.

It is not possible to evaluate this dispositional hypothesis by direct observation of existing prison settings because the effects of environment and personality cannot be separated. In order to study the effects of context separately one must create a 'new' prison populated by 'normal' people randomly assigned to the roles of prisoner and guard.

Method

Overview

The independent variable was assignment to the role of prisoner or guard. The roles were enacted in an environment designed to be physically and psychologically like a prison.

Dependent variables were assessed using:

1 *Direct observation*: audio and video tapes.

2 *Self-report*: questionnaires, mood inventories, personality tests, daily guard reports and post-experimental interviews.

Aim

The aim of this study was to create a 'mock' prison which was sufficiently real to allow role-playing participants to go beyond the superficial demands of their assignment. To do this the researchers identified relevant variables in existing prison situations and then designed a setting in which these variables were operationalised – variables such as feelings of power and powerlessness, control and oppression, arbitrary rule and resistance, status and anonymity were operationalised, e.g. by giving the guards sunglasses and uniforms and having them strip-search the prisoners.

Hypothesis

The general hypothesis was *'assignment to the treatment of "guard" or "prisoner" would result in significantly different reactions on behavioural measures of interaction, emotional measures of mood state and pathology, attitudes toward self, as well as other indices of coping and adaptation to this novel situation'* (page 4).

Participants

Volunteers were found through a newspaper advertisement. The 75 respondents were given a series of psychological tests and interviews; the 24 men judged to be the most stable (physically and mentally) were selected. All were college students, largely middle-class and strangers to each other. There were two reserves who were not used and one who dropped out, finally leaving 10 prisoners and 11 guards (one of the prisoners was not involved from the start but stepped in when some prisoners left early).

Zimbardo's website http://www.zimbardo.com/ has a link to a website devoted to this study (http://www.prisonexp.org/) with a slide show, discussion questions and links to other sites.

Procedure

Physical aspects of the prison The prison consisted of three small cells. The doors had steel bars. In an adjacent wing of the building there were rooms for the guards, a bedroom for the 'superintendent' (Zimbardo) and 'warden' (one of the research assistants) and an interview-testing room. Finally there was the 'yard', a room which represented fenced prison grounds. This room had an observation screen at one end for video recording equipment.

Operational details The prisoners remained in prison throughout the study. The guards worked three-man eight-hour shifts, going about their normal lives at other times.

Role instructions All participants signed a contract. They were guaranteed a minimally adequate diet, clothing, housing, medical care, payment in return for their 'intention' to serve in whatever role assigned to them for the duration of the study (up to two weeks).

The contract also made it clear that they would have little privacy and their basic civil rights would be suspended with the exception of physical abuse.

The guards met at a pre-experiment briefing session and were told that they should 'maintain a reasonable degree of order within the prison necessary for its effective functioning' and decide amongst themselves how to deal appropriately with any situation that arose.

The guards believed mistakenly that the primary interest of the study was in the behaviour of the prisoners.

Uniforms Each group (guards and prisoners) was issued with identical uniforms in order to promote feelings of anonymity.

- *Guards*: khaki shirts and trousers (to convey a military attitude), a whistle and police night stick (symbols of power) and reflecting sunglasses.

- *Prisoners*: loose fitting muslin smock (emasculating) with identification number on front and back, no underclothes (all to convey humiliation, dependency and subservience), a light chain and lock on one ankle (oppression), rubber sandals and a cap made from a nylon stocking (like being shaved). The prisoners were allowed no personal belongings.

Induction procedure The prisoners were told to be at home on a particular Sunday. The Palo Alto City Police Department arrived, unexpectedly, at each prisoner's home, advised them of their legal rights, conducted a thorough search in front of curious neighbours and took them away. At the station the prisoners were fingerprinted and later transported to the mock prison where they were stripped, sprayed with delousing fluid, made to stand naked in the yard and finally placed in cells where they had to remain silent.

Administrative routine The guards only referred to the prisoners by number, to further dehumanise them. The prisoners were allowed three supervised toilet trips and given two hours for reading or letter-writing per day, and two visiting periods and movies per week.

Results

In general, as the experiment progressed:

- Guards and prisoners showed more negative feelings towards each other and towards themselves.

- Prisoners expressed more intentions to harm others.

Behaviour of the guards Guards were prevented from using physical abuse but often expressed aggression verbally. When the experiment ended one guard said he was upset at the suffering of the prisoners. However on several occasions they remained on duty for extra hours without complaint, and without additional pay.

Reactions of prisoners Five prisoners had to be released early because of extreme emotional depression, crying, rage and acute anxiety, one of whom had developed a psychosomatic rash.

Individual differences Some guards were fair and relatively passive; others went far beyond their rules to engage in creative cruelty and harassment. Some prisoners coped by becoming sick whereas others coped by being very obedient.

End of experiment The experiment was terminated early, after six days.

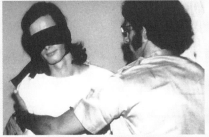

Guard dealing with blindfolded prisoner

ACTIVITY

Think of other situations which promote feelings of anonymity. In each situation describe the effects of such anonymity (or deindividuation).

How do people reduce anonymity?

Qs

1 Why couldn't they investigate their hypothesis using naturalistic observation?

2 Describe how you might 'randomly assign' participants to conditions.

3 The participants all signed a contract. Suggest what effect this may have had on their behaviour.

4 Do you think that real prisoners and guards have a sense of deindividuation? Why or why not?

Biographical notes

Prisoner No. 416, who broke down within 36 hours, got a clinical psychology Ph.D., did his internship in a California prison, and became a forensic psychologist.

Craig Haney teaches Psychology and Law courses at the University of California at Santa Cruz, and is one of the nation's leading lawyers handling prisoner litigation.

W. Curtis Banks, now deceased, was a Professor of Psychology at Howard University, specialising in psychological testing. He served for nine years as the editor of *The Journal of Black Psychology*. [Source of some data www.prisonexp.org]

Discussion

Reality of the simulation

A critical question is whether the participants were simply acting out their assigned roles or went beyond this. Certain features of prison life were necessarily absent (e.g. physical beatings) and the 'sentence' was only a short one (two weeks). The fact that profound psychological effects were observed, despite this lack of realism, makes the results even more significant.

Participants' behaviour transcended their preconceived stereotypes, as shown by situations where role demands were minimal, e.g. when they thought they weren't being observed and when in private situations:

* 90% of prisoners' private conversations related directly to the prison conditions, e.g. food, guard harassment, etc. Guards also talked about prisoner problems.

* Post-experimental interviews revealed that harassment was greater off-screen.

* The guards continued to be aggressive even when prisoners had become quite passive. For example, one guard paced around the yard while the prisoners slept, pounding his night stick into his hand.

* The guards, in post-experiment interviews, did explain their harassing behaviour as 'just playing the role' but this may have simply been a way to deny responsibility for their behaviour.

* The prisoners referred to themselves by their prison numbers when talking to a Catholic priest; some even asked him to get a lawyer to help them get out.

* When the five remaining prisoners appeared before a mock parole, they were told they could leave early if they forfeited all payment. Three of them agreed, effectively ending their contract, yet returned meekly to their cells when told to await the parole board's decision.

* The guards were willing to work overtime for no extra pay.

Guards wore sunglasses to increase their sense of deindividuation and power.

Pathology of power

Most of the guards found their sense of power was exhilarating. This was revealed in observing their behaviour and in post-experimental interviews. This sense of power was displayed in the way the guards changed prisoners' 'rights' into privileges and gave these as rewards for obedient behaviour. Also 'constructive' activities such as watching movies were cancelled.

The guards became more aggressive over the course of the study. Those guards who were most hostile were the leaders and even those guards not drawn into the power syndrome respected the norm of never contradicting an action by a more hostile guard.

The pathological prisoner syndrome

The prisoners displayed various responses to their harsh treatment:

1 *Disbelief.*

2 *Rebellion*, for example one prisoner went on hunger strike.

3 *Collective action*; they elected a grievance committee to try to work within the system.

4 *Individual self-interests*, for example siding with the guards against the prisoner on hunger strike.

This social disintegration led to feelings of isolation. In the end the model prisoner behaviour was one of passivity, dependence and flattened mood.

Processes that led to this syndrome

* *Loss of personal identity*: The prisoners lost their sense of individuality (were deindividuated).

* *Arbitrary control*: In post-experimental interviews this was the most frequently mentioned negative aspect of the prison experiment. The unpredictable decisions of the guards led the prisoners to behave like zombies, a

response similar to the *learned helplessness* phenomenon – when there is no predictable relationship between what you do and the response your action receives, you learn that it is pointless responding in the future.

* *Dependency and emasculation*: Prisoners depended on the guards for everything; this emasculated the men and increased their sense of helplessness.

Despite the fact that there were, at any time, only three guards versus nine prisoners, the prisoners never tried to directly overpower them. Interestingly, after the study was over, the prisoners said they thought the guards had initially been selected for their physical size but in fact there was no size difference.

Conclusion

The prison context creates destructive and pathological relationships between prisoners and guards.

'Pathology' refers to the nature of disease and its causes, processes, development. Something that is pathological is something caused by a mental or psychological disease. So Zimbardo is suggesting that both the guards' power and the prisoners' behaviour (syndrome) are a kind of psychological disease or abnormality.

Qs

1 Haney *et al.* say they created a situation with 'sufficient mundane realism'. What did they mean?

2 Outline **three** pieces of evidence that support the claim that participants' behaviour went beyond role-playing.

3 In what way were the prisoners' reactions 'pathological'?

4 What evidence is there to support the dispositional hypothesis in relation to the guards' behaviour?

5 Considering the initial hypothesis, suggest a conclusion that can be drawn from this study.

The research method

This study might be regarded to be a field experiment. *What are the strengths and limitations of this research method in the context of this study?*

The research technique

Observation and self-report were used as methods of data collection. *What are the strengths and limitations of these techniques in the context of this study?*

The sample

In what way are the participants unique? How does this affect the conclusions drawn from the study?

Personality versus situation

According to this study, which has the greater influence on behaviour: personality or the situation?

Ethical issues

What ethical issues should have concerned the researchers in this study, and how might they have dealt with these issues?

Ecological validity

The prison was just a simulation and the roles played by prisoners and guards were based on their social perceptions of what prison life should be like. In real life people may draw on personal norms of behaviour. *How much does this study tell us about real prisons?*

Applications/usefulness

How valuable was this study?

What next?

Describe **one** change to this study, and say how you think this might affect the outcome.

DEBATE

Do the ends justify the means?

Zimbardo justified the psychological harm to participants in terms of the importance of this study for prison reform. However, if anything US prisons have become less rather than more humane. You should work in groups to prepare evidence for a debate.

Multiple choice questions

1. How many men were involved, in the end, in the actual experiment?
    (a) 20
    (b) 21
    (c) 22
    (d) 23

2. Zimbardo took the part of:
    (a) A prisoner.
    (b) A guard.
    (c) The superintendent.
    (d) The warden.

3. The decision about who was to be a guard was made:
    (a) Randomly.
    (b) On the basis of physique.
    (c) A volunteer sample.
    (d) Using psychological tests.

4. Which of the following items was *not* part of the guards' uniform?
    (a) Sunglasses.
    (b) Whistle.
    (c) Hand gun.
    (d) Wooden baton.

5. What aspect of the prisoners' uniform was meant to 'emasculate' them?
    (a) Chain around ankle.
    (b) Stocking on their head.
    (c) Loose-fitting muslin gown.
    (d) ID number.

6. How many prisoners had to be released early?
    (a) 2
    (b) 3
    (c) 4
    (d) 5

7. One prisoner developed:
    (a) Blistered arms.
    (b) Frequent headaches.
    (c) Amnesia.
    (d) Psychosomatic rash.

8. The prisoners responded to the guards harsh treatment with:
    (a) Rebellion.
    (b) Collective action.
    (c) Passivity.
    (d) All of the above.

9. What word is used to describe a loss of individuality?
    (a) Deindividuation.
    (b) Reindividuation.
    (c) Unindividuation.
    (d) Individuation.

10. The results of this study support what explanation of prison behaviour?
    (a) Dispositional.
    (b) Situational.
    (c) Interactional.
    (d) Both a and b.

Answers are on page 163.

Exam questions

1. From the prison simulation study by Haney, Banks and Zimbardo explain what is meant by the terms:

    (a) 'pathological prisoner syndrome'; [2]

    (b) 'pathology of power'. [2]
    [OCR AS Psy, Jan 2005, paper 1]

2. From the prison simulation study by Haney, Banks and Zimbardo:

    (a) Outline **one** feature of the simulation that was fairly true to life. [2]

    (b) Outline **one** feature that was not very true to life. [2]
    [OCR AS Psy, Jan 2004, paper 1]

3. (a) From the prison simulation study by Haney, Banks and Zimbardo describe **two** features of the uniform given to the prisoners. [2]

    (b) Identify **two** effects that this uniform was intended to have on the prisoners. [2]
    [OCR AS Psy, Jan 2003, paper 1]

4. (a) Identify **two** of the self-report measures used in the prison simulation study by Haney, Banks and Zimbardo. [2]

    (b) Describe **one** advantage of using self-report measures in the study. [2]
    [OCR AS Psy, Jan 2002, paper 1]

Going straight

Zimbardo and ethics

The prison simulation has been subjected to sustained attack by psychologists about its ethical nature. It may be harder to defend than the Milgram studies. We'll look at three charges here.

1 Zimbardo encouraged the guards' brutal behaviour

Look at his instructions to the guards. *'You can create in the prisoners feelings of boredom, a sense of fear to some degree, you can create a notion of arbitrariness that their life is totally controlled by us, by the system, you, me and they'll have no privacy … They have no freedom of action, they can do nothing, say nothing that we don't permit. We're going to take away their individuality in various ways. In general what all this leads to is a sense of powerlessness. That is, in this situation we'll have all the power and they'll have none'* (Zimbardo, 1989 quoted in Haslam and Reicher, 2003).

2 He prevented the prisoners from withdrawing

There is video evidence of the prison simulation, though only a limited amount has ever been made available by Zimbardo for public scrutiny . On the bits available it is evident that the prisoners want to leave at one point. In fact one of the prisoners can be heard screaming *'I want out! I want out!'* In another harrowing segment where the prisoners are engaged in a physical struggle with the guards a prisoner can be heard screaming *'F*** the experiment and f*** Zimbardo!'*, while another voice screams *'It's a f****** simulation'*. Zimbardo refused to let the prisoners out after this outburst and gave them the impression that they could not get out.

3 Zimbardo misrepresents the data from the study

In the video clip described above there is a clear impression that the prisoners want to get out of the study, and that they understand it is a role play. This goes against Zimbardo's interpretation that the prisoners internalised the prison and believed in it, and that even when given the opportunity to leave they did not. Zimbardo continues to put forward this damaging and degrading picture of human behaviour while arguing that the prison simulation must not be replicated. It can be argued that the study is the creation of Zimbardo's expectations of a prison rather than the social roles in our society.

Response to terror

Zimbardo has written extensively on the psychology of terror, including examples of torture by US forces, for example in the Abu Ghraib prison in Iraq. The behaviour of the guards has been compared to the behaviour of the guards in the prison simulation, but perhaps the key issue is the instructions given to them. In Zimbardo's prison, he gave the instructions and set the tone for the guard's behaviour. In Abu Ghraib, psychologists also gave instructions as the prison was run by a PsyOps (Psychological Operations) unit.

Private Lynndie England (below), who was charged with abusing the prisoners insisted she was acting on orders: *'I was instructed by persons in higher rank to "stand there, hold this leash, look at the camera", and they took pictures for PsyOps [psychological operations]'* (Ronson, 2004).

LINKS TO OTHER STUDIES

The prison simulation is an extreme example of the categorisation effect shown by **Tajfel**. The guards, in particular, came to identify with each other during the study. The reworking of the study by Haslam and Reicher was based on the social identity theory of Tajfel. There are also links to the study by **Rosenhan** on the behaviour of people in institutions.

Zimbardo has personal links to other core study authors Stanley **Milgram** (school mate, page 131), Stanley **Schachter** (colleague, page 92) and Judith **Rodin** (colleague, page 149).

'The Experiment'

In 2002 the BBC broadcast a social psychology experiment that reworked some of the ideas from the Stanford Prison Experiment. Zimbardo tried to prevent the study taking place, arguing that because his study was unethical this new study would inevitably be unethical as well. In fact, The Experiment had a large ethical committee, with clinical psychologists on hand much of the time in case anyone became distressed. They also removed the key problem with the original study which was the involvement of the research staff, or in other words the unintentional cruelty of Zimbardo.

Unlike Zimbardo's study, The Experiment had a theoretical base. It was designed to test social identity theory (Tajfel and Turner, 1979), which argues that people only behave according to social roles after they have identified with the social group, challenging Zimbardo's view of people as being controlled by social roles. Zimbardo's view concentrates on tyranny but ignores resistance. It stresses the negative side of group behaviour and overlooks the positive side, for example how collective action can overcome inequality (Reicher, 1996; Tajfel, 1978).

The results provided support for social identity theory, but also produced some unexpected outcomes. For example, the guards failed to identify with their high status position in the same way as Zimbardo's guards. This failure paved the way for their authority to be overthrown, so a tyrannical regime emerged.

The results give a much more positive view of human behaviour and our ability to co-operate and resist authority. It flatly contradicts Zimbardo's interpretation of the prison simulation.

Zimbardo on 'The Experiment'

'This alleged replication should never be considered as an "experiment" or even as serious social science. This "replication" is one fat, million dollar plus experiment to demonstrate the power of "demand characteristics" to elicit desired behaviour. The researchers were clueless about the psychology of imprisonment – they interfered between any dynamic relationship between guards and prisoners with silly reality TV confessionals, with TV style contests of which prisoner could win the prize of becoming a guard, with everyone always aware that what they were doing would be shown eventually on the telly' Zimbardo (2005, personal communication).

keyISSUE

Measurement: quantitative and qualitative

Qualitative data

Qualitative data are about 'qualities' of things. They are descriptions, words, meanings, pictures, texts, and so forth. They are about what something is like, or how something is experienced. Good examples of studies included in this book which are based on the collection of qualitative data are Freud's case study of Little Hans (page 72) and Haney, Banks and Zimbardo's prison simulation. Studies which mainly deal with qualitative data are in the minority in this book and this reflects the dominance of quantitative data in psychological research.

Quantitative data

Quantitative data are about 'quantities' of things. They are numbers, raw scores, percentages, means, standard deviations, etc. They are measurements of things, telling us how much of something there is. Most of the studies in this book deal with quantitative data. For example the memory study by Loftus and Palmer (page 6) records estimates of speed and Samuel and Bryant's study of children's judgements (page 48) records the number of children who make a particular judgement.

Exam-style question

The data collected in a study may be quantitative (numbers or measurements) or qualitative (descriptions, words, meanings). In some studies both quantitative and qualitative data is collected.

Using **four** core studies, answer the questions which follow.

(a) Describe the quantitative and/or qualitative measures used in each study.   [12]

(b) Give **two** advantages to using quantitative data and **two** advantages to using qualitative data.   [12]

Using the terms correctly

People sometimes refer to research methods as being either qualitative or quantitative. This is misleading, however, because it implies that certain methods always produce certain kinds of data. For example, experiments are usually referred to as 'quantitative' and textual analysis is usually described as 'qualitative'. Experiments, however, can sometimes produce both kinds. Milgram (1963) described the behaviour of his participants in some detail (qualitative), as well as measuring the extent to which they were prepared to comply with the demands of the experimenter (quantitative). On the other hand, textual analysis can be 'quantitative'. For example, the Washoe study (page 30) is largely about the signs that Washoe makes but the headline figures in summaries of the study often refer to the number of signs. For this reason it is more accurate to use the terms qualitative and quantitative to refer to 'data', rather than 'research method'.

The core study of multiple personality by Thigpen and Cleckley (page 198) is a good example of both measures.

Quantitative measures:

- Scores on personality tests.
- IQ scores.
- Memory test scores.
- EEG measures of brain activity.

Qualitative measures:

- Clinical interviews with patient(s).
- Interviews with family members.
- Observations of therapists.
- Letter sent to therapists.
- Responses to Rorschach test.

Idiographic and nomothetic

The debate over the relative merits of qualitative and quantitative data has a long history in psychology. There has been a tension between those who put most value on studying individuals and those that look for common features in groups of people. The study of the individual is called the idiographic approach whereas nomothetic is more the study of a cohort of individuals.

Nomothetic is a tendency to *generalise*, and *is* expressed in the natural sciences. It describes the effort to develop laws that explain objective phenomena, for example, in physics we have laws of motion. An example in psychology is the attempt to identify and measure underlying features in personality and cognition.

Idiographic is a tendency to *specify*, and is expressed in the humanities. It describes the effort to understand the meaning of accidental and often subjective phenomena. In psychology, first-hand accounts of personal experience are a good example of this approach.

To quant or qual?

Look at the terms on the right and figure out which applies best to qualitative or quantitative data.

The answers are not as straightforward as you might think and in some cases they are a matter of opinion. The debate between advocates of the two types is very fierce and often insulting. Maybe people use qualitative measures to cover up for not being able to

You can't explain the magic of the Ronettes in just numbers.

Never mind the quality, feel the width

It is hard to see how we can understand anything without using a combination of qualitative and quantitative measures. Think about music, for example. You might want to know who the best-selling artist was but you also need to know how someone feels. You can measure brain waves (quantitative) but you cannot capture the full response to the greatest song ever performed which is 'Be My Baby' by the Ronettes (what do you mean you've never heard of it?).

use statistics, or do people use quantitative measures to avoid difficult questions and personal experience?

Good, and not so good, Samaritans

At first sight the city is a lonely and alien place. Buildings hover over the streets and cast long shadows over the faceless and nameless people who scurry beneath them. Many people only experience the city when they commute into work or to shop. To them it can be a dangerous and unfriendly place.

Every so often a news story captures the public imagination and turns into a modern parable of city life. The case of James Bulger in Liverpool is one of these stories (see page 152) and so was the case of Kitty Genovese, a young woman murdered in a New York street in 1964. This murder made the news because of the reported behaviour of the residents of the neighbourhood in which the attack took place.

Social psychologists including Stanley Milgram became interested in the newspaper accounts of the murder. John Darley and Bibb Latané devised a number of laboratory studies that demonstrated the *bystander effect*.

The *bystander effect* (also known as *bystander apathy*) is a phenomenon where persons are less likely to intervene in an emergency situation when others are present than when they are alone.

There have been numerous attempts to explain this effect by psychologists and some of them are outlined here.

Pluralistic ignorance

Imagine this, you are walking down the street and you see some smoke coming out of a building. You are not sure it's smoke, it might be steam. It could be a fire but it might not be. How can you tell? The most obvious thing to do is to look at the reaction of other people. As you look around they seem to be relaxed about it and just walking on. It must be steam you think, so you walk on too. But maybe those other people were also unsure and they walked on because they saw you looking relaxed. Between all of you, and without saying a word, you have negotiated that the situation is not an emergency. This effect is called *pluralistic ignorance.*

In a laboratory study, participants were directed to a room to fill in questionnaires. They were either alone or with two other people. While they were in the room steam started to come through a vent in the wall. The question was how many people would report this. Seventy-five per cent of people left on their own reported the steam but only 38% of people in a group did so (Latané and Darley, 1968).

Kitty Genovese

The assault

Kitty Genovese drove home from her bar job arriving at 3.15 a.m. When she got out of the car she was approached by Winston Moseley who stabbed her. She screamed and her cries were heard by several neighbours but on a cold night with the windows closed only a few of them recognised the sound as a cry for help. When one of the neighbours shouted at the attacker, Moseley ran away, and Genovese made her way towards her own apartment around the end of the building. She was seriously injured but now out of view of those few who may have had reason to believe she was in need of help.

Other witnesses observed Moseley enter his car and drive away, only to return five minutes later. He searched the apartment complex, following the trail of blood to Genovese, who was lying in a hallway at the back of the building. Out of view of the street and of those who may have heard or seen any sign of the original attack, he proceeded to rape her, rob her, and finally murder her. The time from the first assault until her death was about half an hour.

Later investigation revealed that at least 38 individuals nearby had heard or observed portions of the attack, though none could have seen or been aware of the entire incident. Many were entirely unaware that an assault or homicide was in progress; some thought that what they saw or heard was a

lovers' quarrel or a group of friends leaving the bar outside which Moseley first approached Genovese.

The *New York Times* ran the story under the headline *'Thirty-Eight Who Saw Murder Didn't Call the Police'* which was not exactly true. The article began, *'For more than half an hour thirty-eight respectable, law-abiding citizens in Queens watched a killer stalk and stab a woman in three separate attacks in Kew Gardens'*. It is from this semi-correct article that the murder became famous and the local residents were damned.

The Genovese family

It was a difficult call for us to know whether to describe the case of Kitty Genovese in this book. It appears in many psychology articles and most introductory texts and, remarkably, she is probably more famous with psychology students than most of the psychologists they study. She is famous, however, for the way she died and we doubt this is how she would have wanted to be remembered. She had family and friends and a full and interesting life. She was much more than a gruesome headline.

Then there is her family. There can be no closure for the families of murder victims, especially for the Genovese family. The story still surfaces from time to time and still appears in psychology texts like this one. About 40 years after the murder yet another television programme was made. Kitty's brother Bill said *'I was consulted in a project for the History Channel not long ago. See, they're going to do the story anyway, so we may as well cooperate. At least we have some measure of control if we cooperate'* (Gado, 2005).

Diffusion of responsibility

It's such a relief when someone else sorts out an emergency. The more people there are in a group the less chance that it will be you, you hope. Experimental studies show that adding people to a group reduces the chance of an individual stepping up to help in an emergency (Darley and Latané, 1968)..

In another experiment students were recruited to take part in some discussions via an intercom. Each student had to talk for two minutes, then comment on what the others said, though in fact there was only one real person taking part. The other 'students' were pre-recorded. As the student listened to one of the other voices the person appeared to have a seizure and started choking before lapsing into silence. If the student believed they were the only person to hear this emergency then 85% tried to help, but if they thought that the other people could also hear it the intervention rate dropped as low as 30% (Darley and Latané, 1968).

The tradition with firing squads is to leave one of the guns without a bullet but not say which one has the blank. This allows everyone in the firing squad to believe they did not shoot at the victim. This helps to diffuse their responsibility for the execution.

The picture shows the painting Execution of the Emperor Maximilian *by Edouard Manet (1867).*

Calling the police

Although the residents are always given the blame in the Kitty Genovese story, their perception of the local police contributed to the social climate. At the time of the attack one local resident commented;

'Shortly after moving in I heard screaming on the street several times, called the police and was politely told to mind my own business' (Rosenthal, 1999, page 46).

Parables

A parable is a story that is told to illustrate a religious, moral or philosophical idea. It is possible to see some psychology studies, such as the Milgram experiment and the Stanford Prison Simulation, as parables.

The good Samaritan is a famous Christian parable (Luke: 10: 25–37), told by Jesus to illustrate the idea that it is important to show compassion for all people regardless of race. The parable tells of a man attacked, robbed and left for dead at the side of the road. He is ignored by two passers-by, both religious men. A third man, however stops and helps. He is a Samaritan and therefore of a different race from the man who was robbed. He would have less reason to stop than the first two men but his compassion was such that he could not pass by and do nothing. This story produces the term 'good Samaritan' to describe someone who helps a stranger. The charity group 'the Samaritans' in this country provides free support to people contemplating suicide.

The somebody else's problem (SEP) field

In an ironic take on the bystander effect The Hitchhiker's Guide to the Galaxy *(by Douglas Adams) describes the somebody else's problem field (SEP field). This fictional technology is a cheaper and more practical alternative to an invisibility field. A SEP field can be created around a bizarre and unbelievable scene so that the unconscious mind of an observer defines it as 'somebody else's problem', and therefore doesn't see it at all.*

An example of this was given in Adam's third book Life, the Universe and Everything, *when a UFO landed in the middle of a cricket ground during a match, and the crowd didn't notice it. The SEP field requires much less energy than a normal invisibility field and a single flashlight battery can run it for over a hundred years.*

The idea of the SEP field has some grounding in real life, in that people may not notice things that don't fit their view of the world: when people look at branded goods they see attractive design and not the sweat shop conditions in which many of them are made.

The Good Samaritan study

Students at a theological college were asked to present a sermon on helping; on their way to the sermon, they passed a man slumped and groaning in a doorway. If the students thought they were late 10% helped, compared with 63% who thought they were early. Some of those who didn't help said they didn't notice the victim (Darley and Batson, 1973).

Stimulus overload

People living in cities are bombarded every day with stimuli and with social interactions. Some days it is just too much. Milgram (1970) suggested that people have stimulus overload and so restrict their attention to the events that they believe are most important. These are likely to be things that are personally relevant or connected to people they know. The lives of strangers will inevitably come way down the list.

When do you help and when do you walk by? Not an easy decision.

The core study

The moral panic that arose in the 1960s about the alienation of people in cities stimulated a lot of laboratory experiments related to helping behaviour. There will always be questions over how far these studies can be applied to everyday life. A small number of brave researchers took their studies out into the city. This is one example.

One of the issues to consider as you read the study is the view that is taken of people in the city. In particular they are seen as relatively passive with the most important variable being the number of other people near to them.

Irving M. Piliavin, Judith Rodin and Jane Allyn Piliavin (1969)
Good samaritanism: an underground phenomenon? *Journal of Personality and Social Psychology*, 13 (4), 289–299.

Abstract

A field experiment was conducted to observe the effect of several variables on helping behaviour. The experiment was staged on the New York subway during the middle of the day (11 a.m. to 3 p.m.) and the 4,500 participants were the passengers on the train.

Method

Four teams of students, each team consisting of a victim, model and two observers, staged a standard collapse. The IVs were:

- Victim drunk or ill (carried a cane).

- Victim black or white.

- Model intervened or not.

- Group size.

Main results

The frequency of helping was considerably higher than found in lab experiments. The main findings were:

(a) An apparently ill person is more likely to receive help than one who appears drunk, and help is forthcoming more quickly.

(b) The race of the victim has little effect except when the victim is drunk and then they are more likely to be helped by someone of the same race.

(c) The longer the emergency continues without help being forthcoming, the more likely that someone will leave the critical area.

(d) The 'diffusion of responsibility' effect was not found in this situation, i.e. helping was greater in seven-person groups than in three-person groups.

Conclusion

The results can be explained in terms of a cost–reward model.

COReSTUDY

Introduction

Since the murder of Kitty Genovese psychologists have conducted many studies in order to find explanations for bystander behaviour, such as Latané and Rodin's study (1969) which showed that assistance was more likely if bystanders were acquaintances rather than strangers. Much of this work has been conducted in laboratories which is not a problem *if* some research is also conducted in the field to provide confirmation from a more natural setting.

Aims

The main aim of this study was to consider the effect of type and race of victim on speed (latency) and frequency of response. In addition the impact of modelling and group size was also investigated.

Type of victim (drunk or ill) Research suggests that people who are seen as partly responsible for their plight receive less help (Schopler and Matthews, 1965). In addition, bystanders might be reluctant to help a drunk because he/she may behave embarrassingly and/or become violent.

Race of victim (black or white) Research suggests that people would be more likely to help someone of their own race.

Impact of modelling Past research (Bryan and Test, 1967) shows that people are more likely to help in an emergency situation if they have seen someone else displaying the behaviour.

Group size Darley and Latané (1968) found that increases in group size led to decreases in frequency of responding and an increase in latency (how long it takes to offer help).

Method

Subjects

About 4,450 men and women who were travelling on the 8th Avenue express subway train in New York City weekdays between 11 a.m. and 3 p.m. over a two-month period. There were slightly more white people than blacks, and on average there were 43 people in a compartment on any one trial and, on average, 8.5 people in the 'critical area'.

Procedure

On each trial, a team of four General Studies students boarded the train separately. There were four different teams. Two girls acted as observers and took seats outside the critical area. The male model and victim remained standing. After approximately 70 seconds the victim staggered forward and collapsed, and remained lying on his back staring at the ceiling until receiving help. The express train does not stop for $7\frac{1}{2}$ minutes between 59th and 125th Street, the start and stopping points for this study. If no help was forthcoming when the train stopped the model helped the victim to his feet.

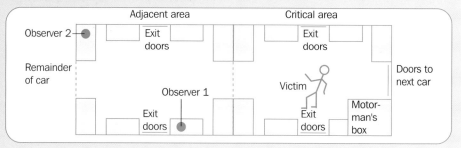

Layout of subway carriage showing the critical area and position of the victim

Victim The four victims (one in each team) were aged 26–35, one was black. All were dressed identically. Each victim participated in both cane and drunk trials.

On 38 trials the victim was drunk and 65 trials the victim was sober.

- *The 'drunk' condition* The victim smelled of alcohol and carried a bottle wrapped in a brown paper bag (as they do in New York).

- *The cane condition* The victim appeared sober and had a black cane.

Model Four white males aged between 24 and 29 played the models. There were three possibilities:

- *No model* The model didn't help at all.

- *Early model* helped after 70 seconds.

- *Late model* helped after 150 seconds.

The point of this was to see if a 'model' (someone offering help) affected the behaviour of other passengers.

Measures On each trial one observer noted:

- Race, sex and location of every person seated or standing in the critical area.

- Total number of persons in the carriage.

- Total number who helped the victim.

- Race, sex and location of every helper.

The second observer noted:

- Race, sex and location of every person in the adjacent area.

- Time when help was first offered.

Both observers noted any comments made by nearby passengers.

Results

The frequency of helping was impressive compared with previous lab experiments.

Amount of help offered Piliavin et al. report that the cane victim received spontaneous help 95% of the time (62/65 trials) whereas the drunk victim was spontaneously helped 50% of the time (19/38 trials).

- On 60% of the 81 trials when the victim was given help, the help was given by two or more helpers.

- On 21 out of the full 103 trials (with and without a model) 34 people left the critical area after the victim collapsed.

Time taken to help Results are shown in the graph. Help was slower to be forthcoming in the drunk condition. Only 24% of the drunk victims were helped before the model stepped in and 'encouraged' others to help, whereas 91% of the cane victims were helped before the model stepped in. The median latency for cane trials (nonmodel condition only) was 5 seconds whereas it was 109 seconds for drunk trials.

Gender 90% of the first helpers were males.

Race Black victims received less help less quickly especially in the drunk condition. Also in the drunk condition there was a slight 'same race' effect – whites were slightly more likely to help whites than to help blacks.

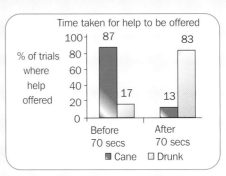

Time taken for help to be offered

Comments More spontaneous comments were made in the drunk condition and also made mainly on the trials where no help was given within the first 70 seconds. Many women made comments such as *'It's for men to help him'* or *'You feel so bad when you don't know what to do'* (p. 295).

Group size The more passengers who were in the immediate vicinity of the victim the more likely help was to be given. This appears to be the reverse of Darley and Latané's 'diffusion of responsibility' effect. This may be because the original effect was produced in lab experiments where all helpers bar one were confederates. In a field experiment the greater number of potential helpers may have counteracted any diffusion effect. Second, the fact that potential helpers could see the victim may have reduced the tendency to diffuse responsibility.

Qs

1 Was the sample a random, volunteer or opportunity sample?

2 Why was a subway train a good place to conduct the experiment?

3 State **two** hypotheses for this study.

4 Why do you think the results differ from those of Latané and Darley? (You should think of at least two explanations.)

Biographical notes

Irving and **Jane Piliavin** are both retired professors of sociology at the University of Wisconsin at Madison. Irving is a keen poker player and they both like watching American football. Jane tells the story of how the Samaritan study came about: *'[Irv] was working with Bibb Latané on a post-doc designed to give people in other fields (his is social work) the opportunity to retrain. He was riding on the subway himself … when a drunk rolled off his seat and fell to the floor. Nobody did anything for a long time (until he did). By the time he got [home] a few hours later he had designed the study'* (personal communication).

Judy Rodin has recently completed ten years as President of the University of Pennsylvania and was also given an award for outstanding lifetime contribution to psychology from the American Psychological Association. She began her career studying attribution and applied this to the control of eating and the importance of control (and lack of control) among the elderly. Her mentor was Stanley Schachter.

ACTIVITY

Try role-playing this experiment. Arrange your classroom to look like the subway carriage. Make a list of all the different conditions and have a go trying them out while the observers keep a record of all data.

Conclusions

This study explains helping behaviour in situations where escape is not possible and where bystanders are face-to-face with their victims. Piliavin *et al.* proposed a model to explain people's response to such emergency situations.

- The observation of an emergency situation creates a sense of arousal in the bystander.

- This arousal is interpreted differently in different situations, e.g. fear, disgust, etc. (Schachter, 1964).

- The arousal is heightened (a) the more one empathises with the victim, (b) the closer one is to the emergency, (c) the longer the emergency continues.

- The arousal can be reduced by (a) helping directly, (b) getting help, (c) leaving the scene, (d) rejecting the victim as undeserving of help (Lerner and Simmons, 1966).

- The response that is chosen will be a function of the cost–reward matrix outlined below:

	Helping	Not helping
Cost	e.g. effort, embarrassment, possible physical harm.	e.g. self blame, perceived censure from others.
Reward	e.g. praise from self, victim and others.	e.g. continuation of other activities.

Note that this model suggests that helping is motivated by a selfish desire to rid oneself of an unpleasant emotional state rather than being a positive 'altruistic' model of helping.

This model can be used to explain the conclusions from the study, as shown in the table below.

Re-analysis of data from this study

It is interesting to examine the original data more carefully. We have included this data on our website (www.a-levelpsychology.co.uk/ocr/ascorestudies). If one only considers the trials where help was offered spontaneously (no model) then cane victims were helped 100% of the time and drunk victims 86% (not 50%) of the time. In addition, the data for spontaneous help shows that the only person who was not helped was the one black confederate who was acting drunk. So the entire result depends on this one person!

Qs

1 Do you think it matters that there were more cane than drunk trials? Why or why not?

2 Why do you think that the early model elicited more help than the later model?

3 Identify two explanations as to why underground passengers will be more likely to help an ill rather than a drunk victim?

4 One interesting finding showed that people were more likely to move from areas in the drunk condition than the cane condition. Use the cost–reward model to explain why this happened.

5 Use the cost–reward model to try to explain the behaviour of one bystander during the Kitty Genovese murder.

Conclusions	Interpretation of each conclusion based on the cost–reward model of response to emergency situations	
	Costs of helping	Costs of not helping
1 A person who is ill is more likely to be given aid than one who appears drunk.	Drunk: high (greater disgust).	Drunk: low (less censure because victim to blame for own plight).
2 Men are more likely to help.	Women: high (danger).	Women: low (not a woman's role).
3 Some tendency for same-race helping, especially in the drunk condition.	Opposite race: high (more fear if different race).	Same race: higher (censure for not helping your own).
4 The amount of help did not decrease as group size increased.	Cane trials: low	Cane trials: high (more self-blame)
5 The longer the emergency continued: (a) The less impact the model had. (b) The more likely it was that individuals left the immediate vicinity. (c) The more observers made spontaneous comments.	(a) Arousal already reduced by another means therefore help less likely. (b) As arousal increases, there is more need to reduce it and leaving the area is one way to do this. (c) Reduces self-blame by discussing reason for not helping.	

EVALUATING THE STUDY BY PILIAVIN, RODIN AND PILIAVIN

(See page x for note on evaluating research studies/articles)

The research method

This study was a field experiment. *What are the strengths and limitations of this research method in the context of this study?*

The sample

How representative was this sample? How does this affect the conclusions drawn from the study?

DEBATE

Why *don't* people help? Why *do* they help? Construct a list of the factors that increase or decrease rates of helping. Then consider how such information might be applied in everyday life.

Ethical issues

What ethical issues should have concerned the researchers in this study, and how might they have dealt with these issues?

Reliability

There were two observers involved in this study. How confident can we be about the reliability of their observations?

Personality versus situation

What does this study tell us about the relative effects of personality and situation on behaviour?

Qualitative or quantitative?

What kind of data were collected in this study? What are the strengths and limitations of producing this kind of data in the context of this study?

Ecological validity

To what extent can we make generalisations about human behaviour on the basis of this study?

Applications/usefulness

How valuable was this study?

What next?

*Describe **one** change to this study, and say how you think this might affect the outcome.*

Multiple choice questions

1. Which of the following was an IV that was *not* manipulated by the experimenters?
   - (a) Race.
   - (b) Drunk.
   - (c) Group size.
   - (d) Model.

2. The subjects were:
   - (a) Psychology students.
   - (b) General studies students.
   - (c) Passengers on the subway.
   - (d) Both b and c.

3. The victims were:
   - (a) All male and white.
   - (b) All male, black and white.
   - (c) All white, some men and some women.
   - (d) Black and white, men and women.

4. The model intervened:
   - (a) 70 seconds after the victim collapsed.
   - (b) 70 seconds after the train left the station.
   - (c) 150 seconds after the victim collapsed.
   - (d) Both a and c.

5. Which of the following is a DV in this experiment?
   - (a) Willingness to help.
   - (b) Race of helper.
   - (c) Time taken to offer help.
   - (d) All of the above.

6. Passengers were more willing to help:
   - (a) Women.
   - (b) Drunks.
   - (c) Victims with a cane.
   - (d) Black victims.

7. Passengers in the critical area who did not help dealt with their arousal by:
   - (a) Asking someone to help the victim.
   - (b) Turning away from the victim.
   - (c) Making a comment about why they weren't helping.
   - (d) Leaving the critical area.

8. The diffusion of responsibility effect predicts that:
   - (a) Helping increases when group size increases.
   - (b) Helping decreases when group size increases.
   - (c) Helping decreases when group size decreases.
   - (d) Group size has no effect on rates of helping.

9. The results of this study showed that the diffusion of responsibility effect:
   - (a) Occurred.
   - (b) Didn't occur.
   - (c) May have occurred but was counteracted by the number of potential helpers.
   - (d) The study did not consider this effect.

10. Piliavin *et al.* proposed that the first thing that happens in an emergency situation is
    - (a) Rewards.
    - (b) Costs.
    - (c) Arousal.
    - (d) Both (a) and (b).

Answers are on page 163.

Exam questions

1. According to Piliavin, Rodin and Piliavin diffusion of responsibility has been demonstrated in laboratory studies on helping behaviour,
   - (a) What is meant by the term diffusion of responsibility? [2]
   - (b) Why did it not occur in Piliavin, Rodin and Piliavin's study on 'subway Samaritans'? [2]

   [OCR AS Psy, June 1995, paper 1]

2. (a) According to the model of response to emergencies proposed by Piliavin, Rodin and Piliavin, what are the **two** factors that influence a person's decision to help or not? [2]
   - (b) Give an example of the results from the study and explain it in terms of the **two** factors. [2]

   [OCR AS Psy, June 1998, paper 1]

3. (a) Outline how **one** ethical guideline was broken by Piliavin, Rodin and Piliavin. [2]
   - (b) Outline **one** way in which ethical guidelines were upheld by Piliavin, Rodin and Piliavin. [2]

   [OCR AS Psy, May 2005, paper 1]

4. (a) In the Subway Samaritan study by Piliavin, Rodin and Piliavin, some of the researchers acted as victims and some as models. Identify **one** of the model conditions. [2]
   - (b) Outline **one** conclusion that was drawn from the model conditions. [2]

   [OCR AS Psy, Jan 2001, paper 1]

Deciding to help

James Bulger

The event in the UK that provoked a similar moral panic to the murder of Kitty Genovese was the murder of toddler James Bulger. One Friday in February 1993 James Bulger, a two-and-a-half-year-old boy, was abducted from his mother in a shopping centre by two ten-year-old boys. The three boys walked around Liverpool for over two hours before James was tortured and murdered next to a railway line. The haunting image of the time was from cctv cameras in the shopping centre that captured the moment of abduction.

In a strange coincidence with the Genovese murder, 38 witnesses appeared at the trial of the two ten-year-olds. These people had seen or, in some cases, had contact with the boys during their journey across the city. None of them had intervened decisively enough to save the toddler.

Were these witnesses an example of the bystander effect? Such an interpretation is probably neither helpful nor accurate. Another view (for example, Levine, 1999) suggests they can be seen in terms of the sense they made of an ambiguous situation and the social categories they used to interpret it. In particular they assumed the boys were brothers and this category of 'family' prohibited any intervention. We don't interfere in 'domestics' and we don't tell other people how to treat their children.

The following witness quotes come from the trial (cited in Levine, 1999): *'I saw a little boy apparently two and a half to three years of age ... [...]. He was holding, it looked to be a teenager's hand, which I presumed was his older brother.'*

One witness reported this exchange with one of the boys, *'"I'm fed up of having my little brother." He says, "It's always the same from school" and he said, "I'm going to tell me mum, I'm not going to have him no more."'*

Group membership and bystanders

The studies that followed the Kitty Genovese attack dealt with bystanders as if they were isolated individuals. Recent research has looked at the social identity of bystanders and the groups they have allegiance to. For example, Dovidio *et al.* (1997) found evidence that people were more likely to help members of their own social group (the 'ingroup'). In their study, students were asked to volunteer to help a student distribute questionnaires for their research project. They were more likely to offer help if they thought the student was an ingroup member. This work connects to the Tajfel study concerning group behaviour described on page 156.

Levine *et al.* (2002) reworked one of the early bystander studies (the 'good Samaritan' experiment on page 147) and looked at the effect of group identity. They advertised for fans of Premier League football teams to take part in a study. Some Manchester United fans were selected and put together to create a sense of group identity. The fans were directed as a group across the college campus to another room. On the way they witnessed a runner having an accident where he fell over and appeared to hurt himself. In one condition he was wearing neutral clothes and in the other two conditions he wore either a Manchester United shirt or a Liverpool (despised rivals) shirt. The injured runner was usually helped when he wore a Manchester United shirt, but he was rarely helped when he wore the other shirts.

Football fans might look like muppets but they'll help their fellow fans.

The London bombs, July 2005

What happens in a real emergency? Do people help or do they look the other way? The London bomb attack produced numerous cases of personal heroism that challenge the view of the uncaring city. If you look, for example, at the pictures of the No. 30 bus that was bombed you can see almost as many people going to help as there are running away. We have remarkable first-hand footage of the events taken by people on their camera phones. In fact the news made the internet blog sites before it was broken on the BBC, which is a new way that people can communicate and help each other.

What follows are some accounts of people involved in the London bombs. Although we selected the quotes we have not tried to put our own explanation on the events. We think they show the remarkable variation of human behaviour and the complexity of human experience.

A woman who was seriously injured in one of the trains commented, *'There was nobody around. There were people talking across from me – people trying to calm each other – but I felt that my experience was quite lonely. It feels like there were lots of lonely individuals in one setting.'*

A man on one of the other trains describes the horror in the carriage then says, *'Your humanity strikes in, you think is there anyone you can save here or take out with me? A right hand came out and held onto my leg and I tried to see where they were and you couldn't see anything. It was just a mass of bodies and I thought instinctively I've got to get that person out.'*

A former firefighter was widely pictured shepherding a bomb victim to safety as she clutched a surgical mask to her burnt face. He was hailed a hero in the press but he commented, *'I was filled with a certain level of guilt that I was made out to be a hero – the real heroes were the people who lost their lives.'*

And a woman on the Piccadilly line train said *'... people so often comment on the arrogance of Londoners and how unfriendly we are – yesterday there was none of that. We all rallied together helping one another get through it – holding hands, sharing water, calming those who were panicked.'*

(BBC, 2005; Yahoo news, 2005)

LINKS TO OTHER STUDIES

This study was looking for imitative responses of the people on the train so there is a link to the work of **Bandura, Ross and Ross**. There is also a link to the categorisation work of **Tajfel** as shown in the selective way that people help some victims but not others.

key**ISSUE**

Personality versus situation

KEY TERMS

A situational factor is anything in the environment, including the behaviour of other people.

A dispositional factor is an enduring aspect of an individual's behaviour – their disposition or personality.

'The social psychology of this century reveals a major lesson: often, it is not so much the kind of person a man is as the kind of situation in which he finds himself that determines how he will act.' (Milgram, cited in Blass, 2004, page 101).

Some situations make strange behaviours look ordinary.

'Would you sit in a vat of baked beans please?'

'You must be kidding.'

'It's for charity.'

'When do I start?'

Exam-style question

Some psychologists are interested in the question of whether it is one's personality or the situation which determines our behaviour.

Using **four** core studies, answer the questions which follow.

(a) Describe what each study tells us about how situations or personality affect behaviour.   [12]

(b) Discuss **four** problems psychologists may have when they study the effect of situations on behaviour.   [12]

Not my fault

When we make a judgement about someone's behaviour we have to decide how responsible they are for it. It's the difference between saying 'it was an accident' and 'it was your fault'. It we think they are responsible then we make *dispositional* (personality) explanations (for example, she's late because she doesn't think it matters to get here on time) and if we think they are not responsible we make *situational* explanations (for example, she's late because the bus didn't turn up).

We have a tendency to overestimate how much control someone has, and we tend to make dispositional explanations when a situational one would be more appropriate. This is called the *fundamental attribution error*. When we judge our own behaviour, however, we are more likely to see ourselves as a victim of circumstances and not so responsible.

The issue of assigning responsibility for behaviour is an important question in social psychology. Why are we obedient? Why do we choose to help? Why do we behave differently when we are given power? The studies in this chapter all look at such questions and seem to point to the answer being more to do with the situation we are in rather than the personality we have.

The Milgram study

The Milgram study illustrates the two sides of this question. One of the initial aims of the study was to test whether there was something in the character of some nations that made them more prone to extreme obedience or, alternatively, whether anyone can be made to behave obediently in the 'right circumstances'. On first analysis of the Milgram study we might well take the situational approach and suggest that people obeyed because certain features of the situation led them to suspend their sense of autonomy (acting independently) and become an agent of the authority figure. The situational factors that lead to such obedience include the proximity of the authority figure and the distance from the victim. This would suggest that it is not evil people who commit evil crimes but ordinary people who are just obeying orders.

It is not that simple, however, and when you look further into the study you find

individual differences of behaviour that are due to personal choice. To start with, not all the participants obeyed, and 35% stopped before the highest shock. For example one participant, Gretchen Brandt, was a 31-year-old medical technician involved in the female-only experiment. When the shock level reached 210 volts she said *'Well, I'm sorry, I don't think we should continue'*. In response to the various prods she said, *'I think we are here of our own free will'* and refused to go further. It transpired that she had spent her youth in Germany before the Second World War (1939–45) and said *'Perhaps we have seen too much pain'* (Milgram, 1974).

Demand characteristics

One way that situations affect us is by giving us cues on how we should behave. Depending on where we are we will behave differently. For example if someone bumps into you in a shop you might feel offended and say something, but at a football match you probably won't think anything of it. Different situations demand different behaviours, so as a student you sit relatively quietly and listen, but as a member of the public outside the *Big Brother* house you jump up and down and shout nonsense at the top of your voice. You are the same person but behaving as the situation demands.

Orne (1962) described these cues to behaviour as demand characteristics and showed how powerful they can be in a number of studies. One of these involved a psychologist asking a few friends for a favour. When they agreed they were asked to do five press-ups. Their reaction tended to be to ask 'why?', with a degree of puzzlement. Another group of friends were asked if they would take part in an experiment. When they agreed they were asked to do five press-ups. Their reaction tended to be to ask 'where?'. This suggests that people are prepared to do things as research participants that they would not normally be prepared to do in other social contexts.

The implication for psychology is that the laboratory and the experience of being a participant creates demand characteristics. If this is so then the behaviour we observe might be due to the participant being in a psychology study rather than solely the variable being tested.

Prejudice and discrimination

Psychology and prejudice

Psychology is the study of people carried out by people. Inevitably, the problems psychologists investigate also form part of their own experience. Psychologists study prejudice but they also have to struggle to deal with it. Early research in the first part of the twentieth century was based on US and European theories of racial superiority. As ever, the person who carries out the studies finds that the group they belong to is the best. For example a review of 73 studies on race and intelligence in 1925 came to the conclusion that the *'studies taken all together seem to indicate the mental superiority of the white race'* (Garth, 1925, p. 359). This work would not stand up to any scientific scrutiny today (or then to be fair) but it reflected the views of some psychologists at that time (see also the core study by Gould, page 174).

The rise of anti-Semitism in the 1930s in the Western world and the progress of the civil rights movement in the 1960s in the USA changed the mainstream approach to prejudice in psychology. After the horror of the Holocaust (see the core study by Milgram, page 132) some psychologists saw prejudice as a sign of sickness and they looked for features in someone's personality that were part of this sickness. The theory of the *authoritarian personality*, for example, put forward by Adorno *et al.* (1950), described prejudice as a consequence of a failure to resolve childhood conflicts between children and their parents. Adorno *et al.* described authoritarian people as rigid thinkers who wanted to enforce strict adherence to social rules. These people were believed to hold prejudices towards people from low-status groups. Adorno's work has been heavily criticised but there is general agreement that he was correct in pointing out that rigid categorical thinking is a central ingredient of prejudice.

Some of the other approaches to the study of prejudice are shown on this page. Work goes on to understand the nature of prejudice so that we can try to reduce the worst excesses of this very human behaviour. The work shown here concentrates on racism because it has been a major concern of psychologists and because it stimulated the study by Tajfel. There are, of course, many other ways in which one person will show their prejudice towards another, such as sexism, ageism, anti-Semitism and also religious prejudice.

Prejudice

Prejudice is the process of pre-judging something. In psychology prejudice generally refers to bias towards people often based on social stereotypes. Prejudice is an *attitude* – it is what you think and feel, it has a cognitive and emotional component.

Discrimination

To *discriminate* is to make a distinction. There are several meanings of the word, including statistical discrimination, or the actions of a circuit called a 'discriminator'. This core study addresses the most common colloquial sense of the word, *invidious* discrimination. That is, irrational social, racial, religious, sexual, disability, ethnic and age-related discrimination of people. Discrimination is the *behaviour* that arises out of prejudice.

Religious prejudice

Hunter (1991) investigated how people interpret the behaviour of others who belong to different groups. In Northern Ireland there are still very strong divisions between Catholics and Protestants. Catholic and Protestant participants were shown television scenes in which Protestants and Catholics were in violent conflict with each other. The viewers were then asked to explain why the violence was taking place. In general, the two groups attributed their own group's violence to external (situational) factors suggesting it was provoked by circumstances, whereas they attributed the opposite group's violence to internal (dispositional) factors such as they are 'bad' or 'unfair'. This principle seems to be helpful in explaining why intergroup violence can escalate so much. A situation of intergroup hatred evolves, not simply from opposing points of view, but from a long history of events that have been perceived very differently.

Conflict model

Sherif (1966) proposed a conflict model of prejudice. This model suggests that when groups interact they inevitably develop attitudes about each other. If the groups are 'positively independent' (in other words working towards common goals) then good intergroup relations develop and the intergroup attitudes are positive. On the other hand, if the groups are 'negatively independent' (in other words in competition for scarce resources) then group conflict develops and ethnocentric attitudes appear. Sherif and his associates tested this theory in a number of field studies. The basic idea they were testing was whether they could take a group of people without any hostile attitudes towards each other, divide them into groups, create conflict between the groups through introducing competition, and thus create ethnocentric attitudes and behaviour.

The research is commonly referred to as the Robber's Cave studies. Sherif and his associates (1961) set up a summer camp for boys between the ages of 11 and 12. To start with they were divided into two groups but largely played and worked together. During this time they got on fine, but when competition was introduced the social relationships between the groups deteriorated rapidly.

Having created hostility between the two groups the researchers set out to test whether working on a common project would promote harmony. This was trickier than they thought as the hostility ran very deep, but they eventually engineered a situation in which the boys had to cooperate. They claim that the boys became friends again after this.

A teenage boy walks past territorial markers of Protestant loyalists in Belfast.

explanations of prejudice

Just-world hypothesis

The *just-world effect* (Lerner, 1980) refers to the tendency of some people to believe the world is 'just' and people 'get what they deserve'. They believe that good things do (or should) happen to good people and bad things should happen to bad people. The National Lottery is a good example of this: winning is a complete lottery (the clue is in the name) but the press seem to think that the prizes should go to the 'deserving poor'. There are a lot of negative comments when someone with a criminal record wins the big prize. For example, Michael Carroll from Norfolk has been relentlessly vilified in the press since his big win in 2002.

Psychological studies have found that people who believe in a just world are more likely to believe that rape victims contributed to the assault by their behaviour, that sick people caused their illness and the poor deserve to have no money. The big problem with this type of thinking is the world is not just and the bastards sometimes win.

Rather surprisingly, it has been shown that belief in a just world has some benefits. Believers are likely to have less depression, less stress and greater life satisfaction (Bègue, 2005).

Competition takes a lot of forms, but does it lead to prejudice and discrimination? In the UK Premier League Arsenal and Manchester United have been rivals for 10 years but their managers Sir Alex Ferguson and Arsene Wenger are known to be the best of friends.

In Jane Austen's novel Pride and Prejudice, *the heroine forms a strong opinion of a man's character before she hears his side of the story. When the balance of the facts is finally made known to her, they challenge her preconceptions and ultimately overturn this prejudice.*

Frustration–aggression

Dollard *et al.* (1939) proposed a model of prejudice as the displacement of social frustration. They suggested that groups which were economically frustrated by, for example, unemployment, impoverished housing conditions, or other forms of social inequality, would use another group as the scapegoat for their frustrations. In support of this, Hovland and Sears (1940) found that the number of lynchings of black Americans in rural areas of the southern United States correlated negatively with the price of cotton – the lower the price of cotton, the more lynchings had taken place. The term lynching refers to a brutal form of 'mob justice' where a group of people takes the law into its own hands and hangs someone they believe is guilty of a crime. They argued that the economic frustration experienced by white farmers was vented on the black population.

Ingroup favouritism

Ingroup favouritism develops very easily. For example, a study found that people were more likely to cooperate with someone when they found they shared birthdays (Miller *et al.*, 1998). In other studies (Pelham *et al.*, 2002) it has been found that:

- Women are more likely to marry men who share the first letter of their family name.

- People are more likely to live in cities that include their birthday number (e.g. people born on March 3 are more likely than others to live in Three Rivers, Michigan).

- People named Louis are more likely to live in St Louis, people named Paul in St Paul, people named Helen in St Helen, and people named Raine in Manchester!

Social identity theory

Social identity theory was developed by Henri Tajfel. It states that the social groups and categories to which we belong are an important part of our self-concept, and therefore a person will sometimes interact with other people, not as a single individual, but as a representative of a whole group or category of people. A simple example of this is the common experience of doing something to make your family proud of you and you feel as if you are representing your family and don't want to let them down.

Sometimes you act as an individual and sometimes as a group member and during one conversation you might change between these two identities. In business meetings people sometimes suggest that they are wearing 'a different hat' to convey the idea that they are adopting a social identity.

There are three basic psychological processes underlying social identification. The first of these is *categorisation* which is a basic tendency to classify things into groups. This commonly leads to an exaggeration of the similarities of those items in the same group, and an exaggeration of the differences between those in different groups. This means that when we categorise people, we accentuate the similarities to ourselves of people in the same group (the ingroup), and exaggerate the differences from ourselves of people in other groups (outgroups).

The second psychological process is that of *social comparison*. Social groups do not exist in isolation but in a social context in which some groups have more prestige, power or status than others do. Once a social categorisation has been made, the process of social comparison means that the group is compared with other social groups, and its relative status is determined. This comparison has an inbuilt bias in favour of ingroups because we know more about them.

The third psychological mechanism underlying social identity concerns the way that membership of a social group affects our *self-concept*. According to Tajfel and Turner (1979), people want to belong to groups which will reflect positively on their self-esteem. If the group does not compare favourably with others, and membership of it brings about lowered self-esteem, people will try to leave the group, or to distance themselves from it. If leaving the group is impossible, then they may look for ways that group membership may provide a positive source of self-esteem.

The core study

Each generation has to deal with prejudice. It appears to be a common feature in groups and societies and very easy to whip up. Perhaps it does not take very much at all to make people feel part of one group and hostile to another. Tajfel stripped this down to its very basic component to see whether just telling someone they were in a team was enough to make them discriminate against people in other teams.

Henri Tajfel (1970) Experiments in intergroup discrimination. *Scientific American*, 223, 96–105.

This experiment is often described as the 'minimal group experiment' because group membership had very limited justification.

Abstract

Aim

To see if group membership is all that is required for discrimination to occur in intergroup situations.

Experiment 1

Sixty-four schoolboys completed a visual estimating task and were then assigned to groups on the basis of their performance (over/underestimators or more/less accurate). In fact group assignment was done randomly.

Each boy was asked to make choices about what rewards to give participant pairs on 18 different matrices when the choices were ingroup only, outgroup only or intergroup.

In the intergroup choice, most participants gave more money to members of their ingroup. In the ingroup and outgroup choices, selections were closely distributed around the point of fairness.

Experiment 2

Forty-eight schoolboys were assigned to the Klee or Kandinsky group ostensibly because of expressed liking for the paintings.

Each boy was asked to make reward choices, but this time the matrices were designed to separate certain factors:

- *Maximum joint profit* (MJP).

- *Maximum ingroup profit* (MIP).

- *Maximum difference* (MD).

When making intergroup choices:

- MIP and MD exerted a strong effect against MJP (type A matrix).

- MD alone exerted a strong effect against MIP and MJP (type B matrix).

When choosing between ingroup members choice was near MJP; this was less the case when choosing between outgroup members.

Conclusion

Outgroup discrimination is created easily by developing a sense of group belonging, which triggers the social norms of groupness and fairness.

CORESTUDY

Introduction

One of the social norms we learn relates to intergroup behaviour. We have various means of reducing the cognitive complexity of our social world and one strategy is to classify groups as 'we' or 'they' (ingroups and outgroups). There are social norms about how we behave towards ingroup members and towards outgroups (i.e. intergroup behaviour). This view of intergroup behaviour leads to several predictions:

1. An individual may discriminate against an outgroup even when he personally will gain nothing.

2. Such discrimination may occur even if the individual feels no hostility towards the outgroup.

3. This norm may be expressed even before any attitudes of prejudice or hostility have been formed.

This means that discriminatory intergroup behaviour may occur without any social/economic explanations. This study, conducted with Claude Flament, R.P. Bundy and M. Billig, aimed to test the prediction that group membership is all that is required for discrimination to occur.

Experiment 1

Method

Participants

64 boys, aged 14 and 15, from a comprehensive school in Bristol.

Procedure

Participants were tested in groups of eight at a time.

Part 1: Establish intergroup categorisation The boys were taken to a lecture theatre and told that the study was investigating visual judgements. The boys were then shown 40 different dot clusters on a screen and asked to estimate the number of dots in each cluster.

After the boys completed their estimates they were divided into two experimental conditions:

1. *Estimator group* were told that in tasks of this kind it has been found that some people consistently overestimate and some consistently underestimate the number of dots, but this is not related to accuracy.

2. *Accuracy group* were told that some people are consistently more accurate than others.

Biographical notes on Henri Tajfel

Henri Tajfel has been described as the most influential social psychologist in post-war Britain (Billig, 2005). He was born in Poland, and studied chemistry in Paris at the outbreak of the Second World War. His experiences as a prisoner of war led him to have an abiding interest in prejudice and group identity.

Tajfel came to Britain in the 1950s and studied psychology. He was a strong critic of the simplified and reductionist explanations that psychologists produced, explanations that failed to relate to what people really knew about human behaviour. Given his dislike for such reductionist approaches, it was ironic that Tajfel often found the minimal group studies were taken out of context and social identity theory was interpreted in reductionist terms.

Henri Tajfel (1919– 1982)

Part 2: Measuring effects of categorisation on intergroup behaviour The boys were then asked to take part in a further investigation on other kinds of decision-making. To make coding easier, the boys were told that they would be assigned to groups based on performance on the visual task. In fact the assignment to groups was made at random: boys in experimental condition 1 were designated 'underestimators' or 'overestimators'; those in condition 2 were split into 'better' and 'worse' accuracy groups.

All the boys were told that the second decision task would consist of giving rewards or penalties in real money to the other boys. They would be told the code number of the individuals who they were rewarding/penalising, and they would be told which group the boy was in. They would be taken to work on their own in separate cubicles. In each cubicle there would be a booklet containing 18 pages of ordered numbers. They were told that after they had finished the task they would return to the original room and receive the amount of money the other boys had awarded them. Each point was worth 0.1 pennies (pre-decimalisation, when a pint cost 15 pennies!).

The matrix booklet On each page in the booklet there were 14 boxes containing two numbers in each box (as shown in the matrix). The numbers were the rewards and penalties to be awarded to the individual identified at the start of the row. The participant had to indicate his choice by ticking one column in each matrix. There were three different kinds of matrix:

1 *Ingroup choices:* the boys in the top and bottom row were members of the participant's own group.

2 *Outgroup choices:* the boys in the top and bottom row were members of the outgroup.

3 *Intergroup choices:* one row identified a member of the ingroup (apart from the boy himself) and the other row was from the outgroup.

Scoring Scoring the intergroup matrix: A rank of 1 was given if the participant had awarded their ingroup member the lowest possible number of points in that matrix. A rank of 14 was given if the participant had awarded their ingroup member the highest possible number of points.

Comparable (but more complex) methods were used to score the other two kinds of choice, the ingroup and outgroup choices.

Results

For intergroup choices, Tajfel found that the large majority of participants gave significantly more money to members of their ingroup. In contrast the results for the ingroup and outgroup choices were closely distributed around the point of fairness (a rank of 7.5, which would be 0 and −1 in the matrix example below).

Conclusion

A review of the situation:

• The boys knew each other well.

• Groups were defined by 'flimsy and unimportant criteria'.

• The boys' individual interests were not much affected since no one knew what their actual choices were.

• The amount of profit was not trivial – each left the experiment with the equivalent of about a US dollar.

The boys could have gone for *maximum joint profit* (all the boys would then end up with most money), or choose the point of maximum fairness. As we have seen they did choose *maximum fairness* when their choices were not intergroup ones. In order to analyse their choices further a second experiment was conducted.

An example of a matrix. Each participant had to tick one column on each matrix e.g. 12 and −25, or −9 and 4. The numbers represent rewards for the member identified. There were 14 matrices on each page of the 18-page booklet. Some matrices had ingroup choices, some had outgroup choices and some (like this one) had intergroup (or 'differential') choices.

Member no. 74 of overestimators group	12	10	8	6	4	2	0	1	5	9	13	17	21	25
Member no. 44 of underestimators group	25	21	17	13	8	5	1	0	2	4	6	8	10	12

ACTIVITY

Conduct your own mini-study. In the first experiment there were six matrices.

Matrix	Top row numbers
1	−19, −16, −10, −7, −4, −1, 0, 1, 2, 3, 4, 5, 6
2	12, 10, 8, 6, 4, 2, 0, −1, −5, −9, −13, −17, −21
3	1, 2, 3, 4, 5, 6, 7, 8, 9, 10, 11, 12, 13, 14
4	18, 17, 16, 15, 14, 13, 12, 11, 10, 9, 8, 7, 6, 5
5	−14, −12, −10, −8, −6, −4, −2, −1, 3, 7, 11, 15, 19, 23
6	17, 14, 11, 8, 5, 2, −1, −2, −3, −4, −5, −6, −7, −8

For bottom row numbers, reverse top row numbers. Each matrix appeared three times, once for each type of choice (ingroup, outgroup and intergroup).

1 Produce a booklet with all 18 matrices.

2 Select a 'naïve' participant (i.e. someone who doesn't know about this experiment) and (a) show them some dots briefly and ask them to estimate how many there are, (b) tell them they are an overestimator, (c) give them the booklet to fill in.

3 Score the results for the intergroup choices as described in the study and pool your class data.

Qs

1 Summarise the **three** predictions which follow from the principle of there being a social norm for behaviour towards outgroups.

2 Why do you think it was a good idea to have two experimental conditions (estimators and accuracy groups)?

3 Identify the IV and DV in experiment 1.

4 In terms of social identity theory, explain why you think the boys acted in the way they did.

5 Can you think of an alternative explanation for their behaviour in this experiment?

6 In what way may 'demand characteristics' explain the outcome of this experiment?

Experiment 2

Method

Participants

Three new groups of 16 boys (48 boys in total).

Procedure

This time the groups were divided on the basis of aesthetic preference (liking for art). The boys were shown 6 reproductions of paintings by Klee and 6 by Kandinsky. The boys were asked to express their preference for one of these 'foreign painters'.

Matrices

Tajfel used different matrices (see right) in the same three choice situations: ingroup, outgroup and intergroup choices. These matrices made it possible to study the effect of relative weight of some of the variables in pulling decisions one way or the other. Specifically he wanted to assess three things:

1 *Maximum joint profit* (MJP): the largest possible award for two people.

2 *Maximum ingroup profit* (MIP): largest possible award to member of the ingroup.

3 *Maximum difference* (MD): largest possible difference in gain between a member of ingroup and a member of outgroup, in favour of ingroup.

Results

When boys made intergroup choices Tajfel found that:

- The MJP exerted hardly any effect at all; boys did not make their choices on the basis of trying to give both parties their best joint deal.

- On the other hand, MIP and MD exerted a strong effect against MJP (type A matrix). Participants always tried to give their ingroup members the best deal at the cost of the outgroup member, maximising the profit of their own group.

- In addition MD alone exerted a strong effect against MIP and MJP (type B matrix); when profits for both ingroup and outgroup could be maximised, participants were most concerned with maximising the difference in their group's favour.

When the choice was between two ingroup members, participants' choices were nearer the MJP then when the choice was between two outgroup members (despite the fact that making outgroup choices presented no conflict with the ingroup's interest).

Subsequent experiments

Further experiments found that fairness was an important factor; most choices were a compromise between fairness and favouring one's own group. Tajfel also found that discrimination actually increased when the situation became more familiar.

Conclusions

The experiments demonstrated that outgroup discrimination is extraordinarily easy to trigger. Other studies (e.g. Sherif et al., 1961) have had to use direct competition based on existing hostility in order for such discrimination to occur.

Participants managed to achieve a neat balance between the two social norms: groupness and fairness. In real life, however, it may be that fairness sometimes 'goes out the window', since ingroup identity is usually based on more weighty issues than, for example, overestimation. Being socialised into 'groupness' has many positive effects but also negative ones – such as reinforcing intergroup tensions. Given this outcome, perhaps educators might give some thought to the potential side effects of encouraging 'team spirit'.

Type A matrices used in Experiment 2

- Outgroup-over-ingroup choice (top row outgroup, bottom row ingroup) the MJP, MIP and MD are all at the far right (in black) i.e. choosing column 7 & 25 is the MJP, MIP and MD.

- Ingroup-over-outgroup choice: MIP and MD are at the far left, the MJP is at the far right (in orange). This meant that MIP and MD were in conflict with MJP.

												MJP, MIP, MD
MIP, MD												MJP

19	18	17	16	15	14	13	12	11	10	9	8	7
1	3	5	7	9	11	13	15	17	19	21	23	25

23	22	21	20	19	18	17	16	15	14	13	12	11
5	7	9	11	13	15	17	19	21	23	25	27	29

Type B matrices used in Experiment 2

- Outgroup-over-ingroup choice: the MJP, MIP and MD are all at the far right.

- Ingroup-over-outgroup choice (in orange): the MD is at the far left, the MIP and MJP are at the far right.

												MJP, MIP, MD
MD												MIP, MJP

7	8	9	10	11	12	13	14	15	16	17	18	19
1	3	5	7	9	11	13	15	17	19	21	23	25

11	12	13	14	15	16	17	18	19	20	21	22	23
5	7	9	11	13	15	17	19	21	23	25	27	29

Qs

1 In the matrix below identify the MJP, MIP and MD if you were (a) a member of the Klee group, (b) a member of the Kandinsky group.

Klee	19	18	17	16	15	14	13	12	11	10	9	8	7
Kandinsky	1	3	5	7	9	11	13	15	17	19	21	23	25

2 How does this study support social identity theory?

3 Tajfel found that increased familiarity between participants led to increased discrimination. Why might this be?

EVALUATING THE STUDY BY TAJFEL

The research method

This study was a laboratory experiment. *What are the strengths and limitations of this research method in the context of this study?*

The sample

The target population was male English schoolboys (aged 14–15). *How does this affect the conclusions drawn from the study?*

Qualitative or quantitative?

What kind of data were collected in this study? What are the strengths and limitations of producing this kind of data in the context of this study?

Reductionist

To what extent is this study reductionist? What are the strengths and limitations of reductionism in the context of this study?

Ethnocentrism

The issue of ethnocentrism is described on the next spread. *What can this study tell us about ethnocentricism?*

Personality versus situation

What does this study tell us about the relative effects of personality and situation on behaviour?

Ecological validity

To what extent can we make generalisations about human behaviour on the basis of this study?

Applications/usefuless

How valuable was this study?

 DEBATE

How much does this study tell us about **prejudice and discrimination in the real world?** Divide your class into groups and designate some groups 'pro-Tajfel' and other groups 'anti-Tajfel'. Each group should try to find further evidence to support their arguments and present their best arguments to the class.

?

What next?

Describe **one** change to this study, and say how you think this might affect the outcome.

Multiple choice questions

1. In experiment 1 the boys were placed in groups:
   (a) Based on how they did on the visual task.
   (b) Based on their preference for the two types of painting.
   (c) Using random methods.
   (d) Both (a) and (c).

2. The two conditions in the first experiment were:
   (a) Estimator and accuracy.
   (b) Ingroup and outgroup.
   (c) Klee and Kandinsky.
   (d) All of the above.

3. In experiment 1, each booklet contained:
   (a) 12 matrices.
   (b) 14 matrices.
   (c) 16 matrices.
   (d) 18 matrices.

4. Which of the following was not one of the types of matrix used in experiment 1?
   (a) Intergroup choices.
   (b) No group choices.
   (c) Ingroup choices.
   (d) Outgroup choices.

5. The results for intergroup choices for experiment 1 showed that:
   (a) All boys favoured ingroup members.
   (b) Most boys favoured ingroup members.
   (c) Some boys favoured ingroup members.
   (d) Very few boys favoured ingroup members.

6. In both experiments:
   (a) The participants were the same group of boys.
   (b) The same set of matrices was used to test discrimination.
   (c) The same visual task was used to assign boys to groups.
   (d) None of the above.

7. In the second experiment, for the ingroup-over-outgroup choice, matrices Type A and B differed in terms of the location of the:
   (a) MJP.   (b) MIP.
   (c) MIP and MD. (d) MD.

8. In the intergroup choices the strongest effect was due to:
   (a) MJP.   (b) MIP.
   (c) MIP and MD. (d) MD.

9. In the intergroup choices there was little effect from:
   (a) MJP.   (b) MIP.
   (c) MIP and MD. (d) MD.

10. Tajfel suggests that two social norms were applied, but in real life one may go 'out the window', this is:
    (a) Groupness.
    (b) Ingroup favouritism.
    (c) Conformity.
    (d) Fairness.

Answers are on page 163.

Exam questions

1. In the second experiment by Tajfel, the majority of the participants opted for 'maximum difference' rather than 'maximum ingroup profit' when making their intergroup choices. Explain how this finding demonstrates discrimination. [OCR AS Psy, Jan 2005, paper 1]   [2]

2. From the study by Tajfel on discrimination, outline what is meant by the term 'intergroup discrimination'. [OCR AS Psy, May 2004, paper 1]   [2]

3. In his study on intergroup discrimination Tajfel suggests that belonging to one group and awareness of another causes discriminatory behaviour.

   (a) Outline **one** way in which the boys were categorised in the study.   [2]

   (b) Describe how Tajfel's approach may be considered to be reductionist.   [2]
   [OCR AS Psy, May 2002, paper 2]

4. (a) In the study on ethnocentrism by Tajfel, how did the boys believe they had been allocated to groups?   [2]

   (b) Give **one** real-life example of allocation to groups that produces ethnocentricism.   [2]
   [OCR AS Psy, June 1998, paper 1]

5. In Tafjel's study participants were randomly allocated to groups. Outline the task that they were then asked to carry out. [OCR AS Psy, Jan 2004, paper 1]   [2]

Reducing prejudice

Describing how intergroup prejudice occurs is one thing: working out how it can be changed is quite another. Cook (1978) described five main criteria which need to be met if social prejudice is to be seriously challenged, and these are listed in the box below. Looking at them, we can see that one of the necessary conditions for getting rid of social prejudice is to have a society in which all people and all groups of people have equal status. This is obviously difficult to achieve in any society where status goes with wealth and wealth is unequally distributed.

Criteria for reducing prejudice

- *Equal status for participants.*
- *Potential for members of the two groups to make personal acquaintance.*
- *Contact with non-stereotypical individuals.*
- *Social support for contact between the groups.*
- *Some occasion for co-operative effort.*

(Cook, 1978)

A much-quoted study of equal-status contact was carried out by Deutsch and Collins (1951), who compared two kinds of housing projects. One project was thoroughly integrated, with black and white residents being assigned to houses regardless of their race. The other housing estate was segregated (i.e. black and white residents were separated). The researchers interviewed residents in both projects and found, not surprisingly, that casual and neighbourly contact between the racial groups was higher in the integrated estate. They concluded also that this contact was accompanied by a decrease in racial prejudice, and therefore supported the equal-status contact hypothesis.

Nothing is ever that simple and there is some evidence which challenges this

approach. Stephan (1978) evaluated the short-term consequences of school desegregation policies in the United States where children were bussed across towns so that the schools had a racial mix in them. He noted that the prejudice towards black pupils showed very little reduction, while black prejudice towards white pupils had actually increased. The only positive consequence of the desegregation, Stephan argued, was the improved academic performance of the black pupils which in fairness is an important consequence.

Anti-racism

Research on the effectiveness of anti-racism campaigns suggests that they have limited effect and can sometimes backfire and make matters worse. Research studies found that people in two minds about their attitudes towards ethnic minority groups become more unfavourable when exposed to anti-racism advertising (Maio, 2002). Commenting on the findings, Maio said:

'It is important to develop messages that elicit more positive attitudes toward ethnic minority people among recipients who are initially ambivalent toward them. At the very least, it is important to design messages that do not increase prejudice among people in this category, as was found in this research.'

A campaign in Scotland to promote anti-racism using posters and TV advertisements was found to be unsuccessful. After four years of a campaign costing over one million pounds a survey in 2005 showed that attitudes had not changed. The survey found, for example, that 10% of Scots believe there is nothing

The picture shows a football fan supporting his national team. Is national pride just a step away from racism? Are the two inevitably connected or can people be proud of their nationality without having racist attitudes?

racist about attacking non-white people, and almost half feel that using racially abusive terms is acceptable.

A slightly more optimistic view is put on this by Brewer (1999) who wrote,

'Ultimately, many forms of discrimination and bias may develop not because outgroups are hated, but because positive emotions such as admiration, sympathy, and trust are reserved for the ingroup.'

Stephen Lawrence

One evening in April 1993 two black teenagers, Stephen Lawrence and Dwayne Brooks, were rushing to catch a bus home in the southeast London suburb of Eltham. They were confronted by a gang of white youths. Brooks was able to get away but Lawrence was assaulted and murdered. The police investigation that followed – or rather the lack of it – sparked an outrage that led six years later to a major inquiry into police methods in London.

Institutional racism

The Macpherson Report into the murder and the police response put the term 'institutional racism' on the agenda for the first time. This means that we should look to the culture of an organisation and the social identity of police officers rather than trying to root out a few individuals with prejudice.

When the report was published Dwayne Brooks summed it up succinctly. *'Racism killed my best friend Stephen. Racism also stopped officers from administering first aid whilst he was lying on the pavement. Racism also allowed the officers investigating this case to treat me like a suspect and not a witness. Racism also rubbished our chances of convicting those killers of the murder of Stephen Lawrence'* (BBC, 1999).

LINKS TO OTHER STUDIES

Discrimination and racism are fault lines that seem to run through every society. These issues are explored in the study by **Gould** which shows how they can intrude into scientific explanations. The consequences of racism are shown in the identity studies of **Hraba and Grant**. On a more general level, Tajfel's social identity theory was used as a basis for the design on the reworking of **Haney, Banks and Zimbardo**'s prison simulation by Haslam and Reicher and the recent bystander studies by Levine.

key**ISSUE**

Ethnocentricism

One source of bias in psychology is egocentrism, the tendency to see things from our own viewpoint and that of people like us. In our everyday lives we are asked to make judgements about people and events. We have a range of opinions that we are prepared to offer to other people when asked, and sometimes when not asked. Another bias that can affect judgements is ethnocentrism (seeing things from the point of view of the group).

Is it a matter of balance?

Psychologists pretend to be objective (free from bias and value judgements). But this cannot be so: work on ethnocentrism shows that you inevitably view the world from the perspective of yourself and the various groups to which you belong.

Sometimes psychologists attempt to take a balanced view and put both sides of an argument. The problem with this attempt is that it presumes that we all agree where the middle of two opposing arguments, and hence the balance, should lie. To take an extreme example, imagine taking a balanced approach to racism where we put the views for peaceful coexistence and balance it with an argument for ethnic cleansing. This is clearly impossible. So we have to accept that the choice of the balancing point is not a matter of detached objectivity, but a matter of opinion.

Support the team

With an ethnocentric standpoint we tend to see our own team as the best. Also, we underestimate the failings of our own team and exaggerate those of the opposing team. There are a number of reasons for this, including our access to evidence. We are likely to know far more about the behaviour and opinions of contemporaries. Also, if we support similar people, we are likely to receive reciprocal support back from them. We expect our friends to support us and not to do us down, particularly in the company of strangers. It is all to do with social cohesion and a sense of belonging.

ACTIVITY

Here are some examples of ethnocentric thinking. Spot the bias (answers below).

• Europeans drive on the wrong side of the road.

• Japanese people read their books back to front.

• America lost the Vietnam War.

Can you think of your own examples?

Scientific racism

Psychology has a history of not challenging race science. There might well be questions to consider about the differences between groups of people but a reasonable enquiry is difficult to make because of *scientific racism*, which we can define as the attempt to justify racial politics through the use of bogus scientific arguments.

One of the problems with studies of racial difference is that it is very difficult to define race, and the idea that there are biologically different races of people is controversial to say the least. There are other problems (Jones, 1991) including:

• Social movement has meant that many people have ancestors from many parts of the world.

• The differences between people of the same race are much greater than the differences between people of different races.

• It is near impossible to get reliable comparisons between people from different ethic groups because you can't use the same measures.

The greatest footballer (Stuart Pearce) at the greatest football club (Nottingham Forest). No sign of ethnocentrism here.

Bias in psychology

Ethnocentrism creates two possible sources of bias:

1 Researchers mainly study their own culture: many of the studies in this text are about young Western white people.

2 Researchers find it difficult to interpret the behaviour and experience of people from other cultures: this is illustrated in some of the anecdotal evidence in the Deregowski study (page 14).

Exam-style question

Ethnocentricism is the tendency to overvalue one's own group and undervalue other groups.

Using **one** core study, answer the questions which follow.

(a) Describe how the data were collected in your chosen study.   [8]

(b) Give **two** advantages and **two** disadvantages of studying ethnocentricism from your chosen study.   [12]

(c) Suggest **one** other way that data could have been collected in your chosen study and say how you think this might affect the results.   [6]

Social Core Study 13: Milgram (obedience)

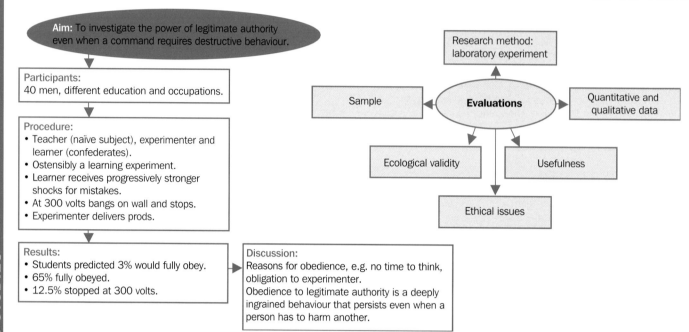

Aim: To investigate the power of legitimate authority even when a command requires destructive behaviour.

Participants:
40 men, different education and occupations.

Procedure:
• Teacher (naïve subject), experimenter and learner (confederates).
• Ostensibly a learning experiment.
• Learner receives progressively stronger shocks for mistakes.
• At 300 volts bangs on wall and stops.
• Experimenter delivers prods.

Results:
• Students predicted 3% would fully obey.
• 65% fully obeyed.
• 12.5% stopped at 300 volts.

Discussion:
Reasons for obedience, e.g. no time to think, obligation to experimenter.
Obedience to legitimate authority is a deeply ingrained behaviour that persists even when a person has to harm another.

Evaluations
Research method: laboratory experiment
Sample
Quantitative and qualitative data
Ecological validity
Usefulness
Ethical issues

Social Core Study 14: Haney, Banks and Zimbardo (prison simulation)

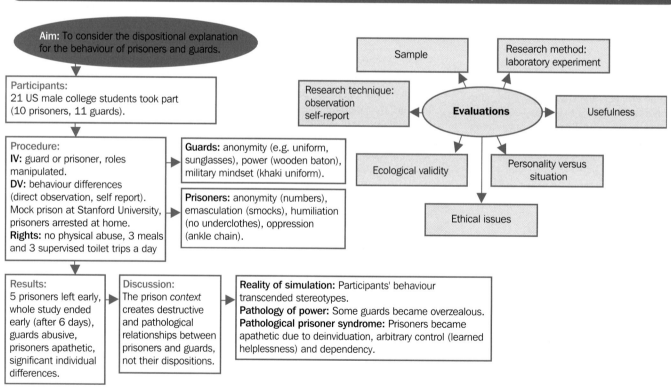

Aim: To consider the dispositional explanation for the behaviour of prisoners and guards.

Participants:
21 US male college students took part (10 prisoners, 11 guards).

Procedure:
IV: guard or prisoner, roles manipulated.
DV: behaviour differences (direct observation, self report).
Mock prison at Stanford University, prisoners arrested at home.
Rights: no physical abuse, 3 meals and 3 supervised toilet trips a day

Guards: anonymity (e.g. uniform, sunglasses), power (wooden baton), military mindset (khaki uniform).

Prisoners: anonymity (numbers), emasculation (smocks), humiliation (no underclothes), oppression (ankle chain).

Results:
5 prisoners left early, whole study ended early (after 6 days), guards abusive, prisoners apathetic, significant individual differences.

Discussion:
The prison *context* creates destructive and pathological relationships between prisoners and guards, not their dispositions.

Reality of simulation: Participants' behaviour transcended stereotypes.
Pathology of power: Some guards became overzealous.
Pathological prisoner syndrome: Prisoners became apathetic due to deinviduation, arbitrary control (learned helplessness) and dependency.

Evaluations
Sample
Research method: laboratory experiment
Research technique: observation self-report
Usefulness
Ecological validity
Personality versus situation
Ethical issues

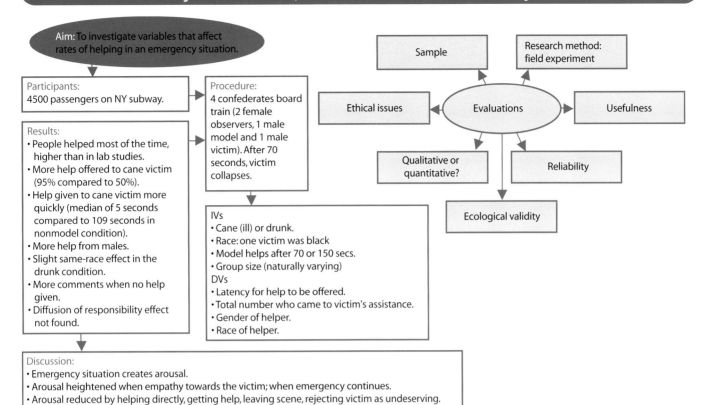

Aim: To investigate variables that affect rates of helping in an emergency situation.

Participants:
4500 passengers on NY subway.

Procedure:
4 confederates board train (2 female observers, 1 male model and 1 male victim). After 70 seconds, victim collapses.

Results:
- People helped most of the time, higher than in lab studies.
- More help offered to cane victim (95% compared to 50%).
- Help given to cane victim more quickly (median of 5 seconds compared to 109 seconds in nonmodel condition).
- More help from males.
- Slight same-race effect in the drunk condition.
- More comments when no help given.
- Diffusion of responsibility effect not found.

IVs
- Cane (ill) or drunk.
- Race: one victim was black
- Model helps after 70 or 150 secs.
- Group size (naturally varying)

DVs
- Latency for help to be offered.
- Total number who came to victim's assistance.
- Gender of helper.
- Race of helper.

Evaluations
- Sample
- Research method: field experiment
- Ethical issues
- Usefulness
- Qualitative or quantitative?
- Reliability
- Ecological validity

Discussion:
- Emergency situation creates arousal.
- Arousal heightened when empathy towards the victim; when emergency continues.
- Arousal reduced by helping directly, getting help, leaving scene, rejecting victim as undeserving.
- = cost-reward model.

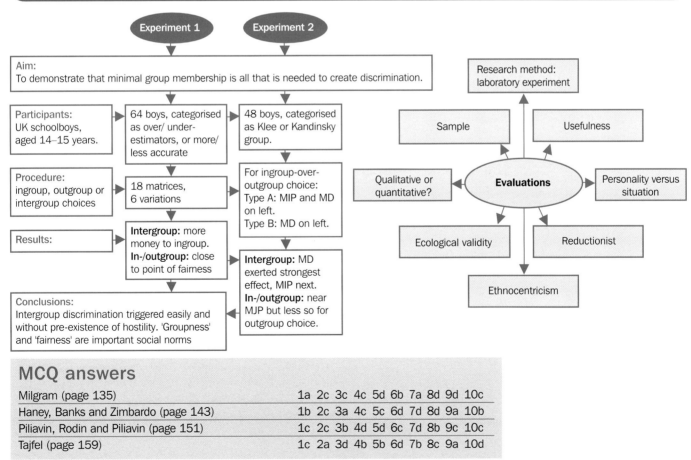

Experiment 1   Experiment 2

Aim:
To demonstrate that minimal group membership is all that is needed to create discrimination.

Participants:
UK schoolboys, aged 14–15 years.

64 boys, categorised as over/ under-estimators, or more/ less accurate

48 boys, categorised as Klee or Kandinsky group.

Procedure:
ingroup, outgroup or intergroup choices

18 matrices, 6 variations

For ingroup-over-outgroup choice:
Type A: MIP and MD on left.
Type B: MD on left.

Results:

Intergroup: more money to ingroup.
In-/outgroup: close to point of fairness

Intergroup: MD exerted strongest effect, MIP next.
In-/outgroup: near MJP but less so for outgroup choice.

Conclusions:
Intergroup discrimination triggered easily and without pre-existence of hostility. 'Groupness' and 'fairness' are important social norms

Evaluations
- Research method: laboratory experiment
- Sample
- Usefulness
- Qualitative or quantitative?
- Personality versus situation
- Ecological validity
- Reductionist
- Ethnocentricism

MCQ answers

Milgram (page 135)	1a 2c 3c 4c 5d 6b 7a 8d 9d 10c
Haney, Banks and Zimbardo (page 143)	1b 2c 3a 4c 5c 6d 7d 8d 9a 10b
Piliavin, Rodin and Piliavin (page 151)	1c 2c 3b 4d 5d 6c 7d 8b 9c 10c
Tajfel (page 159)	1c 2a 3d 4b 5b 6d 7b 8c 9a 10d

1 In his study of obedience, Milgram encouraged the participants to continue with the electric shocks.

(a) Outline **one** way in which Milgram encouraged his participants to continue. [2]

(b) Describe **one** way in which the findings of the Milgram study can be applied to social control in everyday life. [2]
[OCR AS Psy, Jan 2002, paper 2]

Stig's answer

(a) He told them 'The experiment demands that you continue'. This was one of a series of prods.

(b) You could use this to help training soldiers to obey officers especially in the heat of battle when it is important to obey. This study shows that small steps lead people to obey.

Chardonnay's answer

(a) The participants were encouraged to continue by the prods given by the experimenter.

(b) You could use the findings to help train policemen in how to effectively tell people what to do for their own safety.

Examiner's comments

Stig, in part (a) you have identified the prods and given an example of them; clearly two marks. Your answer in part (b) identifies a real-life situation where, arguably, social control is legitimate. The 'small steps' is a nice touch.

Chardonnay, you have identified the prods, but the question asks you to outline a way in which the participants were encouraged to continue i.e. you need a bit more detail. One way to achieve this would be an example of a prod. In part (b), you identify a legitimate situation for social control, but again, a bit more detail for the second mark.

Stig (2+2) Chardonnay (1+1)

2 (a) In the study by Milgram on obedience, how were the subjects recruited? [2]

(b) Outline **one** advantage of recruiting subjects in this way. [2]
[OCR AS Psy, June 1998, paper 1]

Stig's answer

(a) The subjects answered an ad that was placed in a newspaper.

(b) One advantage of this is you get people who are very willing.

Chardonnay's answer

(a) The subjects were recruited by volunteering because they read an advertisement in the newspaper and volunteered to take part.

(b) This is a good way to get subjects because you can get access to a wide range of different people so you get a more varied sample than, for example, an opportunity sample.

Examiner's comments

Stig, a bit more detail required for two marks in part (a), for example, something about the contents of the advert. Again, in part (b) you need to slightly expand your point, perhaps by saying that volunteers are more likely to engage with the experiment.

Chardonnay, part (a) is fine as you have got advert + volunteering; so 2 marks here. In part (b) you make a nice comparison with a standard opportunity sample.

Stig (1+1) Chardonnay (2+2)

3 In the prison simulation study by Haney, Banks and Zimbardo features of the procedure led to the prisoners becoming dependent on the guards.

(a) Identify **two** behaviours for which the prisoners were dependent on the guards. [2]

(b) Describe **one** psychological effect this dependency had on the prisoners. [2]
[OCR AS Psy, Jan 2001, paper 2]

Stig's answer

(a) They were dependent on the guards for their food and for their general care.

(b) This dependency made them vulnerable to the guards and made them feel depressed.

Chardonnay's answer

(a) They depended on the guards for food and letting them exercise in the yard.

(b) This dependency increased their sense of helplessness making them passive because they couldn't improve the situation.

Examiner's comments

In part (a) Stig would get one mark for food; but 'general care' is a bit vague. Part (b) is short but you have identified a psychological effect (often candidates supply a behavioural effect with no reference to prisoner's psychology).

Chardonnay – part (a) gives two clear behaviours in answer to the question. Part (b) demonstrates an excellent understanding of the psychological effects of dependency.

Stig (1+2) Chardonnay (2+2)

4 (a) In the study by Haney, Banks and Zimbardo, the researchers refer to the guards developing a pathology of power. What does this term mean? [2]

(b) Give an example of the guards' behaviour that illustrates their pathology of power. [2]
[OCR AS Psy, specimen paper]

Stig's answer

(a) It means that the guards got into the swing of having power. It became like a disease for them.

(b) For example one of them paced back and forth in the yard while the prisoners were sleeping, hitting his baton against his hand.

Chardonnay's answer

(a) The guards quickly began to enjoy the power but they could not stop – it became self-perpetuating – even if they wanted to. Too much power makes people behave badly.

(b) Early on, the guards abused their power status by cancelling all prisoner 'rights', e.g. watching movies, eating and even sleeping and controlled when prisoners could do these things.

Examiner's comments

Yes Stig, pathology does indicate 'disease' and some of the guards did rapidly make the most of this power. Just enough for two marks. Your answer for part (b) is really an answer to another question i.e. 'Describe one piece of evidence to show that the guards were not just role playing' and does not really indicate pathology of power i.e. abuse of their power status.

Chardonnay, a clear definition of pathology of power in part (a), followed with examples of guard's behaviour demonstrating their abuse of their power.

Stig (2+1) Chardonnay (2+2)

---

5 Piliavin, Rodin and Piliavin's Subway Samaritan study was a field study. Describe **one** advantage and **one** disadvantage of conducting field studies and relate them to this study. [OCR AS Psy, Jan 2002, paper 1] [4]

Stig's answer

One advantage of a field study is it is a more natural environment and this was a natural environment.

One disadvantage is that you can't ask for informed consent.

Chardonnay's answer

Advantage of a field study: this study looked at helping behaviour in a natural environment where people might have to help someone.

Disadvantage: you can't control variables as clearly so it is more difficult to be sure that the DV was changed due to the IV, e.g. in this study that helping was due to crowd size.

Examiner's comments

Both your points are true, Stig, but you have forgotten to relate them to the Piliavin study. Don't forget to read the question carefully to make sure you haven't left anything out.

Chardonnay, you have successfully described both an advantage and disadvantage and linked them to the Piliavin study. Well done.

Stig (1+1) Chardonnay (2+2)

---

6 (a) Referring to the subway study by Piliavin, Rodin and Piliavin, state **two** of the variables which were manipulated and studied by the researchers. [2]

(b) Describe the effects of **one** of these variables on the behaviour of people in the subway study. [2]
[OCR AS Psy, June 1994, paper 1]

Stig's answer

(a) Race of the victim and whether he was drunk or had a cane.

(b) They didn't find much effect for race.

Chardonnay's answer

(a) One condition was whether the victim was drunk and the other condition was whether he was ill (holding a cane).

(b) They found that people on the subway were less willing to offer help to a drunk victim than one holding a cane, and if they did offer help they were much slower.

Examiner's comments

Yep, spot on for part (a), Stig. The part (b) needs more information to get the two marks.

Hmmm, Chardonnay. This is a common mistake. Whether the victim was drunk or ill is just one variable, i.e. the 'type of victim' (though two conditions).

Nice detail in part (b) referring to frequency and latency of helping.

Stig (2+1) Chardonnay (1+2)

7 (a) In his study into intergroup discrimination, Tajfel used a set of matrices to try to find out whether the participants' choices when awarding points would be influenced by one of three factors: 'maximum ingroup profit', 'maximum joint profit' and 'maximum difference'. Using the matrix below, identify the pair of numbers that indicate 'maximum joint profit'. [2]

Matrix 1

20	19	18	17	16	15	14	13	12	11	10	9	8
2	4	6	8	10	12	14	16	18	20	22	24	26

(b) When allocating points to an in-group and an out-group member the participants mostly used 'maximum difference'. Outline what this tells us about their behaviour. [2]
[OCR AS Psy, June 2001, paper 1]

Stig's answer

(a) 14 and 14 would be the maximum joint profit.

(b) It tells us that they preferred to have a bigger difference.

Chardonnay's answer

(a) 8 and 26.

(b) It tells us that the most important thing was not getting the maximum but making sure that the difference between ingroup and outgroup was maximised. So this means not simply getting the best.

Examiner's comments

Stig, you are not alone in writing this answer. About 90% of candidates gave the same answer but, unfortunately all 90% were wrong! MJP is the pair of numbers that when added exceeds all other pairs. Part (b) does not enlighten me much!

Chardonnay, you have obviously revised MJP. A lovely explanation of what Maximum Difference means.

Stig (0+0) Chardonnay (2+2)

8 In the experiments on categorisation by Tajfel, the boys favoured their own group even though they did not know who was in it. Give **two** explanations for this. [OCR AS Psy, June 1996, paper 1] [4]

Stig's answer

One explanation would be that this increases their own self-esteem. The second explanation is that it makes them feel superior to the outgroup.

Chardonnay's answer

The two explanations are that favouring your own group increases the value of that group and this would increase your social esteem because your group has got more rewards. Also, Tajfel says that just by putting people into groups creates ingroup favouritism because we are 'socialised into groupness' by our upbringing and school experience.

Examiner's comments

Stig, I'm not clear how your first point is different to your second… I might understand if you had given me a bit more detail. It is perhaps not the most obvious question about this study and so is quite difficult.

Chardonnay, you have identified two distinct reasons and explained both clearly.

Stig (1+0) Chardonnay (2+2)

9 Psychologists often conduct research studies as a response to real-life events, to try to find out why people behaved as they did. This is referred to as the 'context' of the study.

Select any **one** study from this chapter and answer the following questions.

(a) Describe the context against which your chosen study was carried out. [8]

(b) Briefly discuss **two** advantages and **two** disadvantages of carrying out psychological research in relation to real-life events or changes in society, using examples from your chosen study. [12]

(c) Describe **one** change to your chosen study and discuss how this change may affect the results. [12]

Stig's answer

(a) Milgram: the study was carried out in a lab at a University in America. The participants were all men and volunteers who answered an ad in the newspaper. When they came to the study they were told there were two roles – the teacher or learner. The other participant was in fact a confederate and got the role of learner. The real participant would have to deliver shocks to the learner everytime he made a mistake on a learning task, and these shocks progressively became stronger.

Examiner's comments

Stig, you have answered a different question here… you have answered 'describe the procedure of your chosen study' but really the question is about the context. Make sure you read the question carefully. Otherwise all your time may be wasted.

Part (a) 0/6

(b) When psychologists want to investigate real-life events they often have to create experiments to represent them. This is partly because in real life there are so many variables that affect behaviour that you wanted clearly see which is the critical IV. [P] So in an experiment like the one by Milgram he controlled for lots of variables (e.g. feedback from the victim) so we can just see the influence of the experimenter on their obedience. [E] This means that conducting research about a real life context but in a laboratory probably has more validity (i.e. is measuring what it claims to). [C]

Another advantage of conducting research about real life situations is that it can be very useful and relevant to society. [P] For example, Milgram's study shows us that even Americans (and not just Germans) have high levels of obedience. [E] This study probably helped reduce prejudice and negative stereotypes against Germans as the study shows us that they are not so different from Americans. [C]

One problem with conducting research about real life contexts is that it can be really controversial. [P] For example, Milgram's research was thought to be very controversial at the time because it was not what anyone expected. No one expected 65% of Americans to be so obedient that they might kill someone. [E] However, some people might think that it is good to be controversial as it means that everyone has to think about the issues more, rather than just accepting them. I mean, after studying Milgram, I had to think more about whether such atrocities like Auschwitz could have happened here. [C]

Another disadvantage of conducting research about a real life situation is that people might use the findings of the research for the wrong reasons in real life. [P]

Examiner's comments

We can apply the PEC formula (point, example, comment) to marking this answer (see page ix for an explanation of PEC).

This is a good answer Stig, for a number of reasons. You have addressed the question and written about two advantages and two disadvantages of carrying out research in relation to real-life events. You have followed the ideal format (Point–Example–Comment) for each paragraph. You have expanded your points and examples to really show the examiner that you understand.

You first advantage is fine. You have related your point about control of variables in experiments well to the issue of real-life changes and followed this through with an example from your chosen study. Your comment is good, showing that you understand the concept of validity.

Again, your second and third paragraphs are clear and well related to the question, following PEC throughout.

In your fourth paragraph, you make a valid point and linked example. However, perhaps you ran out of time and so there is no mark for example and comment here.

Part (b) = 10/12

(c) Milgram's study could be redone by having subjects face-to-face with the learner which would make it harder to give the shocks and should reduce obedience. Trying things like this would show us more about the factors that increase or decrease obedience.

Examiner's comments

This is OK, Stig, but you need more detail. You have identified a change on the results, but you should explain why.

Part (c) = 3/8

Total mark = a+b+c=0+10+3 = 13/26

Chardonnay's answer

(a) The prison simulation study was set against the context of prison riots in the US. Prisons were failing. Connected with this, when Zimbardo was writing, the reoffending rates were very high. In other words, prisoners were released and then committed a crime within 1 year. People blamed this on the disposition of the guards and prisoners. They were 'bad' people and that's why there was such trouble. Prisoners are dishonest and immoral, guards choose the job because they are brutal. Zimbardo wanted to investigate this because he thought it was the prison situation that made the people behave like this and if you wanted to change prisons then you need to change the way they are organised, but people don't want to do this because it would involve a major overhaul of the system.

Examiner's comments

Chardonnay, this is quite a tough question, but you have given a reasonably clear account of the background of Zimbardo's study. It is perhaps worth noting that this research was funded by the US Navy as they too were also interested in the experience of imprisonment and its effects due to some of their personnel being imprisoned during the Korean war.

Part (a) = 5/6

EXAM QUESTIONS AND ANSWERS

b) One advantage of conducting research in relation to real life events is that a proper piece of research e.g. an experiment can be the only way to really understand what it going on e.g. disentangle the factors which influence the behaviour of interest. **[P]** For Zimbardo, in order to look at situation versus disposition you have to set up a mock prison. The strength of this approach is that you can be sure that the people allocated to one or the other role are the same, thus you can control the important variable of disposition. **[E]** This helped to make the research more valid, rather than Zimbardo just going into real prisons and looking around and guessing whether it was the situation or the disposition causing all the problems. **[C]**

The downside of this is that sometimes research about real life is controlled so much that it stops being like real life. **[P]** In Zimbardo, everyone knew it was just for 2 weeks so they may not have behaved like real prisoners or guards. **[E]** Also they were really just play-acting even though they got very aggressive it wasn't the same as real life.

One advantage of conducting research in relation to real life situations or changes is that it can educate the public and people in government so they can make better decisions about how things in the country should be run. **[P]** For example, Zimbardo was good because it tells people in charge of the prison set up in this country that the situation is very negative for both prisoners and guards and that the ways prisons are organised should be more positive, so that guards cannot abuse their power. **[E]** Without research into real life situations, the people in charge of the country cannot make informed decisions about how to run prisons; they can only guess. **[C]**

One problem of researching real life situations is that in order to create an experimental situation or simulation close to real life, you have to break some ethical guidelines. **[P]** For example, in Zimbardo, the study was not ethical. But some people would say that this doesn't matter if he finds out something worthwhile and important to society. **[C]**

Examiner's comments

We can apply the PEC formula (point, example, comment) to marking this answer (see page ix for an explanation of PEC).

Chardonnay, this is quite a strong answer, clearly structured into two advantages and two disadvantages.

Your first paragraph is spot on, following the PEC format throughout, with appropriate detail and explanation.

Your second paragraph would get the Point mark for making a generic point (disadvantage) about such research, as well as the Example mark. However, your final sentence does not really take the example further forward; it is just another example.

Your third paragraph is very good – a nice point about how research informs the public and decision makers, followed through with an apt example and comment.

The final paragraph has a relevant point; often ethics and realism are at odds with one another. You would need more detail to get the example mark – briefly explain how Zimbardo was unethical (in order to give the prison some realism).

Part (b) = 10/12

(c) Zimbardo's study could be changed so that if you tried out some changes to the prison routine you could see if that reduced aggression. This would be a more positive study. Once you set up the prisoners and guards and started the aggression you could, for example, let the prisoners wear their own clothes, so they were not wearing the smocks and their ID numbers. This would give the prisoners a sense of identity and they may not feel so depersonalised. Also, they may not feel so emasculated (like a woman). This might affect the results a lot. The prisoners may not become so depressed so rapidly as they may feel a bit more in control. Also, the guards would not be able to take the mickey out of the prisoners because they were wearing dresses (like they did in the original study). Though perhaps they might ridicule/bully the prisoners for their normal clothes. It is possible that the study may not have to be stopped so soon. However, I do think that because the guards are still in their uniforms and that they started off in the prison being aggressive, that this would probably still continue, especially as Zimbardo says that pathology of power is self-perpetuating.

Examiner's comments

This is a full answer, Chardonnay. You have described your suggested change (change of prisoner clothes) and implications that this would have on the prisoners (less depersonalisation) with some understanding of the psychological processes at play. You have then suggested ways this might alter the overall results (change of length of study, change in amount of aggression) with some discussion around this.

Part (c) = 8/8

Total =a+b+c = 5+10+8=23/26

This chapter looks at four core studies in individual differences.

1. Gould's review of IQ testing during the First World War and the effects this had on social policy.

2. Hraba and Grant's experiment that revealed the attitudes of black children towards black people.

3. Rosenhan's astonishing demonstration of the unreliability of psychiatric diagnosis.

4. Thigpen and Cleckley's case study of a woman with three different personalities.

5

Individual differences

Introduction to individual differences

What are individual differences?

Much of psychology is concerned with how groups of people behave and their typical or 'average' behaviour. For example if we were looking at the effectiveness of a new happiness drug we could give the drug to one group of people and a sugar pill to another group, and then consider the average score for each group to see if the drug had any effect on happiness. Most psychologists are interested in these average or mean scores. In contrast, the study of *individual differences* focuses on the differences within each group, how individual people differ in their behaviour and personal qualities, and what this tells us about human behaviour.

Francis Galton

The study of individual differences can be traced back to the work of Francis Galton. He invented and defined the field. In 1884 Galton created a mental testing laboratory – the anthropometric lab for testing data about people, such as visual acuity, strength of grip, colour vision, hearing acuity, hand preference, etc. He hoped to use these measures to estimate people's hereditary intelligence.

Before Galton, psychology had been looking for general principles of experience. By contrast, Galton's anthropometric laboratory looked for individual differences and operated within his cousin Darwin's ideas of individual variability and selection. Although we would not recognise Galton's tests as measures of mental abilities today they do mark the beginning of mental testing.

Galton is also credited with developing a staggering range of techniques and concepts that define the field even today (see Fancher, 1996).

- *Self-report questionnaires:* in 1873 Galton wrote to all the Fellows of the Royal Society (eminent scientists) with a lengthy questionnaire to discover the common features of people who are successful in science.

- *Nature and nurture:* he invented this term to describe the difference between environmental and inherited influences.

- *Twin studies:* he devised the first of these, as well carrying out the first comparisons of natural and adopted children to their parents.

Evolution

If you had to pick one scientific idea that had the greatest effect on modern thought then you might well pick the theory of evolution. This theory has transformed the way we look at ourselves and continues to exert an influence on psychology particularly with the growing interest in genetic explanations of behaviour. Darwin argued that human beings were descended from animal ancestors and demonstrated the similarities in the physical structures of people and animals, even down to the structure of the brain.

Natural selection

The two key ideas of Darwin's theory are

- *genetic variation:* all individuals are genetically unique, and

- *selection:* the individuals who breed are the ones who are better adapted to the environment they are living in.

The features that make some individuals survive and reproduce are likely to be passed on to the next generation. This is a process of selective breeding where the selection is done by the environment (i.e. 'natural selection'). The issue this raises for humans is that we are able to tamper with natural selection by the development of medicine that keeps people alive, and by the development of laws that prevent murderous disputes, or regulate fertility through the conventions of marriage. Maybe this will have an effect on how the species develops. If so then what should we do about it?

Hope for us all: Charles Darwin (1809–1882) did not do very well at school, and in his autobiography he said of his education that 'Nothing could have been worse for the development of my mind ...' *(Darwin, 1969, page 27).*

- *Eugenics:* the term describing the attempt to breed a superior group of people was also invented by Galton.

- *Scatterplots:* Galton wanted to find ways to present his data on family resemblances and he devised the scatterplot.

- *Statistics:* Galton developed regression lines and the correlation coefficient.

The above is a phenomenal list but it is only a selection of his output and you can add *word association* to it. Galton devised a word association technique; his paper on this was read by Freud and contributed to the development of one of the major techniques of psychoanalysis. And if you're still not impressed then he also invented the weather map, and hence weather forecasting.

Measuring differences

The research areas in individual differences are limited by whether we can measure those differences. We are able to measure qualities such as *aptitude* (for example, a airline pilot requires qualities such as concentration, awareness, problem solving, etc.), *intelligence* (commonly measured by IQ tests), *personality* (commonly measured by questionnaires but also by projective tests and interviews), *creativity* (commonly measured by tasks that require original thinking but difficult to evaluate because of disagreement on its true definition), and *attitudes* (cognitive judgements we make about the world). Other qualities such as imagination, ambitions and inspirations might be important differences between us, but are harder to measure.

Personality

A major area of individual differences is the study of personality. Personality is a collection of emotional, cognitive and behavioural patterns that are unique to a person. It is an interesting observation that we easily recognise an individual's personality but have great difficulty in describing it. One way that psychologists have attempted to describe personality is to define common traits that we all share and then measure individuals on these dimensions. So, for example, if we say that sociability is a trait then we would devise a sociability test and give everyone a score on that scale. In this way we can build up a picture of an individual (and their individual differences).

According to trait theory, a sociable person is likely to be sociable in any situation because of the traits in their personality. The counter argument is that people behave as the situation demands and it is *where* someone is rather than *who* someone is that best predicts how they will behave (see the social psychology studies and also the notes on demand characteristics on page 53).

Psychologists have proposed several models of personality traits and the one most commonly cited at the moment is Costa and McCrae's (1992) *Five Factor Model*, which proposes five key dimensions of personality: extraversion, agreeableness, conscientiousness, neuroticism, and openness to new experiences.

Personality types

'Let me have men about me that are fat, sleek-headed men and, such as sleep o'nights. Yond Cassius has a lean and hungry look. He thinks too much, such men are dangerous.'
William Shakespeare, *Julius Caesar*, Act I, scene ii.

Caesar is making judgements about individual differences in personality from observations of body shape, This approach was also used by Sheldon in his twentieth-century descriptions of three major body types and matching personalities: the *endomorph* is physically quite round, and is typified as the 'barrel of fun' person. By contrast, the *ectomorph* is lean and hungry with little body fat. He/she is intense, thoughtful and private. The *mesomorph* has a more athletic body and tends to be assertive, adventurous and courageous.

Although this typology is intuitively appealing there is very little evidence to support the connection between body shape and personality.

Rorschach inkblot test

Most psychological tests ask direct questions that require little interpretation. In contrast projective tests require a lot of interpretation. In such tests a neutral stimulus is used; it is presumed that an individual will project thoughts and feelings onto this stimulus when describing it. Sometimes these thoughts and feelings will have been hidden from the individual themselves.

The most famous of these tests is the Rorschach inkblot test which is named after Hermann Rorschach (1884–1922) who developed the inkblots, though he did not use them for personality analysis. The individual is shown ten standard abstract designs, and responses are analysed to give a measure of emotional and intellectual functioning and integration.

The rationale for the test sounds very plausible (and they are used in the Thigpen and Cleckley study on page 198) but there is little evidence to support the analyses derived from these tests. One fundamental problem is that analysis has to be carried out by another person whose own inner thoughts and feelings may be projected onto their interpretations.

Some surprising variables predict differences in individual experience. For example, people with red hair are more sensitive to pain (New Scientist 15.10.02). A group of red haired and dark haired women were given an anaesthetic and then subjected to an electric shock. The process was repeated until the women said they felt no pain. The researchers found that red heads required 20 per cent more anaesthetic to dull the pain.

More pain for Chris Evans?

Is it mad to be happy?

In a gentle parody of psychiatric diagnosis Richard Bentall (1992) proposed that happiness should be classed as a mental disorder and referred to under the new name of major affective disorder, pleasant type. He suggested that the relevant literature shows that happiness is statistically abnormal, is made up of a discrete cluster of symptoms, is associated with a range of cognitive abnormalities, and probably reflects the abnormal functioning of the central nervous system. You would think that an article like this would contribute to the sum of human happiness but sadly some people took it seriously and it made them sad. Humour is a serious business.

Connections

The psychology of individual differences sparks more heated debate than any other area, because attempts to measure differences between people have been inextricably linked to the idea that psychological characteristics are inherited. Research on individual differences has created an industry of testing that quantifies all imaginable human characteristics. These tests appear in many studies, for example Schacter and Singer (page 90) and Hodges and Tizard (page 64). Techniques of regression, first developed by Galton, are used widely in applied areas of psychology such as health.

Intelligence testing

The testing of intelligence is probably the most controversial issue in psychology. It attracts extreme opinions, for example,

'The measurement of intelligence is psychology's most telling accomplishment to date' (Herrnstein, 1973).

'The IQ test has served as an instrument of oppression against the poor' (Kamin, 1977).

The reasons why intelligence testing is so controversial will become obvious as you work your way through this chapter.

Binet's pioneering tests

The first tests that we can recognise as IQ tests were developed in France by Alfred Binet who started his scientific studies by examining the relationship between head size and intelligence. He discovered that there was little connection between size of head and intelligence. He was later commissioned by the minister of public education to develop a technique to identify children in need of special education, and from this the intelligence test was born. The test was used to give an estimate of a child's mental age by comparing the child's performance on various tasks with the performance of children of various ages. It was later suggested that the mental age of the child should be divided by the chronological age to give an index of intelligence and so the notion of IQ was developed. This is an example of norm referencing.

Intelligence quotient / Chronological age

$$(IQ) = (MA) / (CA) \times 100$$

Mental age

Binet believed that children who were in need of extra help could be identified by these tests, but he vigorously argued against the idea that intelligence is a fixed quantity that cannot be improved by further help. This approach got sadly lost in the translation of tests into English and in their transportation to America. In contrast to the approach of Binet, the fiercest supporters of intelligence testing in the English-speaking world were scientists, who believed that individual differences are mainly due to genetic factors, and those who proposed eugenic solutions to the perceived problems of society. For example, Lewis Terman, who introduced the IQ test to America while he was professor of psychology at the American Stanford University, wrote:

'If we would preserve our state for a class of people worthy to possess it, we must prevent, as far as possible, the propagation of mental degenerates' (Lewis Terman, 1921, cited in Kamin, 1977).

The big words disguise the sentiments of the quote. To paraphrase Terman, he is saying we must stop poor and uneducated people from having children. All this would seem unpleasant but unimportant were it not for that fact that over half of the states in America brought in sterilisation laws for the 'feeble minded' and carried out tens of thousands of operations (Kamin, 1977).

What is intelligence?

Intelligence is commonly defined in terms of mental abilities such as reasoning, problem solving, thinking abstractly, comprehending language, and learning. In psychology we usually see intelligence as being distinct from creativity or personality. Having said that, there is no agreed definition or theory of intelligence.

The first thing to say is that just because we have a word for something it doesn't mean it exists. For example, Father Christmas is a fantasy idea used to keep young children in check, and some people argue that intelligence is a similar fantasy. It is clear we act *intelligently* (and not so intelligently on occasions) but is there a *thing* called intelligence?

There are three important issues of debate around the idea of intelligence.

1 *One intelligence or many?* It is clear that we are better at some tasks than others. At school we might be very good at English and average at maths. Does this mean there is an 'English intelligence' and a 'maths intelligence'? IQ testers argue that there is an underlying factor of general intelligence (called 'g') that affects all our performance. If we can show that this general factor exists then we can go on to discuss intelligence as a single ability, but if there are several intelligences then the discussion stops here. The jury is still out on whether g exists.

2 *Can intelligence be reliably measured?* The first problem here is to define what it is you want to measure. IQ tests are the main way to estimate intelligence and the questions are clearly limited to things that can be put on paper, so many of the intelligent things we do in everyday life cannot be included.

3 *Is intelligence an inherited quality?* On one level the answer is yes because we all need to have bodies and brains to be intelligent, but the underlying question is whether the differences between people can best be explained by genetic or social factors. It is this question that is so controversial.

Eugenics

Eugenics refers to the attempt to improve the quality of human beings through selective breeding, so for example, if we wanted to improve the general level of intelligence in the country we would encourage intelligent people to have lots of children and unintelligent people to have none. Of course this only works if the factors that lead to differences in intellectual performance can be inherited.

There are many problems with the eugenics approach to intelligence including the controversial assumptions that:

- *there is a single human quality that we can call intelligence rather than many different types of intelligent behaviour;*
- *intelligence can be reliably and validly measured;*
- *intelligence is a fixed quantity and cannot be improved;*

It is a well-rehearsed argument that the idea of eugenics leads to destructive and brutal social policies. The article by Gould gives some examples of how this evidence has been used.

A game for all the family. Make a list of all the words you know that refer to intelligent behaviour. You might divide the list into the words that are positive judgements and those that are negative. Here's a few to get you started. Give prizes for the longest list.

clever	stupid
brainbox	idiot
bright	cretin
gifted	dipstick
???	???

The most remarkable thing about this exercise is just how many words there are. This illustrates how important intelligence is for us in this country, just as the importance of snow to Eskimos is revealed by the enormous number of words for it in their language.

Performance and ability

Performance is what you actually do, and *ability* is what you are capable of. You might have heard a teacher say 'You have the ability, but you are not doing the work.' They mean that the reason you got a Grade E in your examinations was due to poor performance and not poor ability (and obviously not the teacher's fault either). Any test we give to someone can only measure their performance on that test, and not their ability. We can only infer their ability from that performance. So when we are measuring intelligence, we are, in fact, measuring *performance* on the particular test and not the underlying *intellectual ability*.

The problem here is that there are all manner of factors that affect our performance, for example:

- The *language* of the test: words mean different things to different people.

- The test *situation*: some people work well in quiet environments with few distractions, whereas others can only concentrate if the television is on in the background.

- *Expectations:* if you expect that you will not be able to answer the questions you will be more likely to give up easily.

- *Motivation:* if you are competitive and want to win everything then you will try harder to do well.

Anne Robinson Testing the Nation *in the popular BBC programme. The show attracts large audiences and shows our remarkable interest and trust in IQ testing. The show also panders to our various prejudices about intelligence by comparing teams such as blonde women and nurses. In the December 2005 test, men scored higher than women, the Royal Navy team did better than the dinner ladies team and Londoners scored higher than Glaswegians.*

Measuring people

To measure something you have to compare it against something else. If we want to measure a table, it is easy because we can use a ruler, but if we are measuring people what can we use? There are three ways in which psychologists use tests to measure people;

1 *Direct measurement:* where we use a physical measure such as grip strength or reaction time. Although these measures can be useful, there are only a limited number of direct measures we can make of the psychological aspects of people.

2 *Criterion referenced measurement:* where we compare the performance of an individual against an ideal performance (the *criterion*).

3 *Norm referenced measurement:* where we compare the performance of an individual against performance of other people, most commonly the peer group. This is far and away the most common way of using psychological tests.

An example of norm referenced measurement can be seen in IQ testing. As children get older, they develop their educational skills and so get more answers correct on an IQ test. This is not taken to mean that their IQ is getting better even though their intellectual skills are improving. The individual is compared against children of the same age, so their IQ score represents their ranking in their own age group. This measure has a number of benefits in that it tells you how well you are doing compared to people like you.

Statistical techniques and intelligence testing

The need to interpret mental tests led to the development of a range of statistical techniques; for example Karl Pearson developed the technique of *correlational analysis* while working with mental tests.

Charles Spearman also produced a test of correlational analysis (see page 229) and developed another very important statistical technique. Like many other intelligence testers of his time, Spearman favoured eugenic solutions and so was looking to establish that intelligence had a single innate characteristic. He developed the technique of *factor analysis* which looks at a large number of correlations and seeks to distinguish underlying factors. He took the data from a range of mental tests and showed that there was one factor that explained the variations in scores on most of the tests. He called this factor 'g'.

The core study

This study is a review article of past research. Stephen Jay Gould looks back at the early testing of IQ and illustrates some of the problems with testing and some of the political consequences that can follow from misinterpreting the results. It is not meant to be a balanced account and Gould made no secret of his view that intelligence cannot be reduced to a single number and that the differences between people can not be explained by genetics.

Stephen Jay Gould (1982)
A nation of morons. *New Scientist*, May, 349–353.

Abstract

Yerkes pioneered early mental tests as a means of providing objective numerical data for human behaviour. The tests were intended as measures of innate mental ability and were in two forms (Alpha and Beta), one written and the other pictorial so that men who couldn't read or write could still be tested. If a man failed the Alpha test he would be given the Beta test and if he failed that he would be given an individual examination.

In reality the system didn't work like this. For example, there were long queues for the Beta tests so men who should have done the Beta test had to do the Alpha test and ended up with zero scores. The result was to produce a systematic bias which lowered the mean scores of blacks and immigrants.

Data analysis

Boring's analysis of some of the data produced three facts:

1 The average mental age of *whites* was equivalent to a moron.

2 *Immigrants* from southern and eastern Europe had lower scores than those from northern and western Europe.

3 *Negroes* had the lowest mental age.

Yerkes acknowledged certain problems. For example there was a positive correlation between average test scores and length of residence in the US. This would suggest that the mental tests were assessing familiarity with American ways and not innate intelligence.

The effect of the tests

1 *Screen 1.75 million recruits* for officer training.

2 *Establish the first mass-produced intelligence tests*, which were of great interest to business and educational institutions.

3 *Inform social policy* – the US Immigration Restriction Act (1924) was framed to severely restrict immigration from southern and eastern Europe (but less so from northern and western Europe) which had a profound effect in the years leading up to the Second World War.

Biographical notes on Stephen Gould and Robert Yerkes

Stephen Jay Gould (1941–2002)

The main interest of both men lay in comparative psychology and evolutionary theory. Neither specialised in the field of mental testing.

Stephen Jay Gould was Professor of Comparative Zoology at Harvard University. Gould challenged Darwin's view of evolution as a gradual process and instead suggested it was better described as 'punctuated equilibrium' – evolution occurs relatively quickly with long periods of little change.

Robert Mearns Yerkes was most famous for his research with gorillas and chimpanzees, and later was director of the Yale Laboratories of Primate Biology. He was heavily influenced by Darwin's theory of evolution and used this to argue that humankind could benefit from selective interbreeding – a eugenic view.

core**study**

Introduction

This article is different from the other core studies because it does not describe a research study. It is a critical account of early IQ testing and the effect of these tests on American social policy. It is an edited extract from Gould's book *Mismeasure of Man* (1981).

In the period before the First World War, psychology was regarded by many as a 'soft' science. Psychologists wanted their subject to be taken seriously and viewed as a rigorous science like physics. One way to achieve this would be to find more objective methods of representing human behaviour, for example using methods which produced objective numerical data. The field of mental testing offered a way to do this. At that time mental testing had a poor reputation – poorly trained amateurs were producing absurd and unreliable results.

Robert M. Yerkes, a psychologist at Harvard University, had one of those *'big ideas that propel the history of science'*. Could he persuade the US army to allow him to test all their recruits? This would enable him to develop the science of mental testing and enable the army to identify the most able recruits. He obtained funding from the army and Colonel Yerkes ended up overseeing the testing of 1.75 million recruits during the First World War.

Method

The new army mental tests were devised by Yerkes, working with other prominent psychologists such as Lewis Terman. They were all hereditarians, believing that intelligence was inherited and generally unaffected by the environment.

Their scheme included three types of test:

- The **Army Alpha** test, a written exam for literate recruits.

- The **Army Beta** test, a pictorial test for illiterates and men who failed the Alpha test.

- **Individual examination** for those who failed the Beta.

Army psychologists would grade each man from A plus to E minus and offer suggestions for military placement. Yerkes suggested C minus should be equivalent to 'low average intelligence – ordinary private'; D and E men could not be expected to read and understand written instructions.

ACTIVITY

Try an online intelligence test. There are many of them; for example, http://www.iqtest.com tests your performance in 13 different areas of intelligence. http://www.iqtest.com/profileexplain.html?p=2 presents a breakdown of how a question relates to different aspects of intelligence.

Was the Army test fair?

Yerkes claimed that the tests measured 'native intellectual ability' (cited by Gould page 349), in other words an ability that was innate and not affected by educational opportunities and cultural experiences. However, the examples shown for both the Alpha and Beta tests (on far right) suggest otherwise. It is true that some aspects of the test cannot be criticised for cultural bias, such as filling in the next number in a series – though even this relies on knowledge of numbers. However, it is clear that other parts have a heavy cultural bias. *'How could Yerkes and company attribute the low scores of recent immigrants to innate stupidity when the multiple choice test consisted of questions like [those shown on the right]?'* (page 149).

Problems with administering the tests

Ideally the men who were illiterate should have been given the Beta test. Yerkes' corps tried hard to do this but …

- The standards varied from camp to camp – in some camps schooling to Grade 3 was the criteria for taking the Alpha test whereas at other camps anyone who said he could read took the Alpha. The result was that many men got zero (or nearly zero) on the Alpha test not because they were innately stupid but because they were only semi-literate.

- Yerkes had not anticipated that so many recruits would be illiterate so queues for the Beta began to lengthen. To reduce congestion men who were not suitable for the Alpha test nevertheless had to do it.

- The pressure for results meant that the individual examination of men who failed the Beta test was not possible. This was especially true for the black 'failures' that were treated with less concern. When such individuals *were* recalled their scores improved dramatically. For example, at one camp 86% of those who had scored D minus obtained a higher grade on retesting.

- These problems led to a systematic bias in the test results because it was immigrants and Negroes who had a poor grasp of English and poor schooling. The outcome was an artificially low mean score for immigrants and blacks.

Results

Yerkes' aim had been to produce statistics and he did. His lieutenant E.G. Boring (later a famous psychologist himself) worked out all sorts of statistics including one which showed that the average mental age for Alpha was 10.775 and for Beta was 12.158 – the men who took the Beta test were brighter! This didn't make sense, so the Alpha scores were ignored.

The trouble with such numerical data is that it may fail to represent experience. *'Some things have to be seen, touched and tasted. What was it like to be an illiterate black or foreign recruit, anxious and befuddled at the novel experience of taking an examination, never told why, or what would be made of the results; expulsion, the front lines? In 1968, an examiner recalled his administration of the Beta: "It was touching to see the intense effort … put into answering the questions, often by men who never before had held a pencil in their hands." Most of the men must have ended up utterly confused or scared shitless. I believe that [this] makes it ludicrous to believe that Beta measured any internal state of intelligence'* (page 350).

Q s

1 What are 'hereditarians'?

2 Identify the **three** kinds of IQ tests devised for army recruits and, for each one give a brief description.

3 What skills did Yerkes claim his mental tests were assessing?

4 What skills do you think the army tests were assessing?

5 What is meant by 'culture bias'?

6 Explain in what way the army tests were culture biased.

7 Outline the problems with the way the tests were administered.

The army tests
Each test took less than an hour.

Examples from the Alpha test
There were 8 parts in this test, such as:

- *Analogies, such as 'Washington is to Adams as first is to …' [Second, because Washington was the first US president and Adams was the second.]*
- *Multiple choice: 'Crisco is a: patent medicine, disinfectant, tooth paste, food product?' [It is a food product.]*
- *'The number of a Kaffir's legs is: 2, 4, 6, 8? [2, because a Kaffir is a tribesman.]*

Examples from the Beta test

There were 7 parts containing pictures and symbols. One part (picture below) required recruits to spot what was missing in each picture. In case you were wondering a rivet is missing from the knife in picture 10 and the ball is missing from the man's right hand in picture 15.

In the picture below Test 1 involves running a maze, Test 2 is to count the number of cubes, Test 3 is to find the next number in the series, and Test 4 involves translating the numerals into symbols.

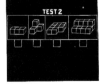

More numerical data

From the ocean of numbers, three 'facts' emerged which continued to influence social policy in America long after their source in the tests had been forgotten.

Fact 1. White Americans had a declining mental age. The average mental age was found to be only 13 years, just above being a 'moron'. It had previously been set at 16 years by Lewis Terman. This led to predictions of doom for the declining American intelligence caused by unconstrained interbreeding with Negroes and immigrants.

Fact 2. European immigrants could be graded by their country of origin. They were all 'morons' but some were worse than others – the darker people of southern Europe and the Slavs of eastern Europe were less intelligent than the fair people of northern and western Europe. The average IQ for Russians was 11.34, Italians 11.01 and Poles 10.74.

Fact 3. The Negroes had the lowest mental age. The Negroes scored an average of 10.41. A further analysis showed that those with the lighter skins scored higher than those with darker skins.

'A Study of American Intelligence'

These facts were used to by Carl Brigham, a disciple of Yerkes, to argue in his book *A Study of American Intelligence* (1923) that Yerkes' research did measure innate intelligence and thus demonstrated the innate inferiority of immigrant groups such as Jews despite the fact that *some* Jews might be especially able.

Jews came out badly in the tests. Notable exceptions, such as Einstein, were explained by the fact that the public noticed the few great ones because they were so rare.

Some doubts

The data showed that the average mental age of Latin and Slavic immigrants was almost two years below English, Scandinavian and Teutonic immigrants. Yerkes acknowledged a potential problem – that most Latins and Slavs had recently arrived whereas the wave of Teutonic immigration had passed long before. Thus test finding might be explained by familiarity with the language and culture of America. Yerkes had to admit *'There are indications to the effect that individuals handicapped by language difficulty and illiteracy are penalized to an appreciable degree in Beta as compared with men not so handicapped'* (cited by Gould page 351).

There was another inexplicable finding – the average score for foreign-born recruits rose consistently with years of residence in America. This suggested that familiarity with American culture, and not innate intelligence, regulated the scores. Yerkes refuted this point by claiming that recent immigrants were the dregs of Europe.

Despite such doubts, Yerkes' results were taken at face value.

Impact of the tests

Screening recruits

The tests helped to select men suitable for officer training. At the start of the war there were 9,000 officers; at the end there were 200,000, two-thirds of whom started their careers because of success on the tests.

IQ testing after the war

Once the war was over and Yerkes' tests became widely known, enquiries flooded in from schools and businesses, who recognised the potential value of the tests for ranking and streaming students and employees – the era of mass testing had begun.

The immigration debate

The ultimate triumph of eugenics was the impact of Yerkes' data on immigration. Eugenics is the science that seeks to improve human genetic quality through social intervention such as selective breeding, or in this case, screening out undesirable genetic strains. In the 1920s this scientific evidence greatly assisted the 1924 Immigration Restriction Act. In fact Yerkes' data did more than that: his evidence was used to determine which immigrants should be kept out. The 1924 act set quotas at 2% of the people from each nation recorded in the 1890 census. Why the 1890 census instead of the 1920

Henry Fairfield Osborn, president of the American Museum of Natural History, wrote in 1923:

'I believe those tests were worth what the war cost, even in human life, if they served to show clearly to our people the lack of intelligence in our country, … We have learned once and for all that the Negro is not like us. So in regard to many races and sub-races in Europe we learned that some which we had believed possessed of an order of intelligence perhaps superior to ours [read Jews] were far inferior.' Brackets inserted by Gould.

Qs

1   Yerkes claimed that the army tests assessed innate intelligence. Outline **two** pieces of evidence against this.

2   How did Yerkes explain the high correlation between IQ and years spent at school?

3   How could this data have been used to improve the lives of those with low scores?

4   The 'Immigration Restriction Act' was passed in the USA in 1924. In what way was this Act related to Yerkes' IQ tests?

5   How could the IQ test data be used in eugenics?

6   Do you think that this article presents a balanced view of the use of early intelligence tests?

one? Because in 1890 there were few immigrants from southern and eastern Europe. The effect was to slow immigration from these parts of Europe down to a trickle. President Coolidge proclaimed *'America must be kept American'*.

In the years between 1924 and the outbreak of the Second World War it is estimated that these quotas barred six million people from southern, central and eastern Europe from entering the US even when the quotas for northern and eastern Europeans were not filled.

Gould ends his article by saying *'We know what happened to many who wished to leave but had nowhere to go. The paths to destruction are often indirect, but ideas can be agents as sure as guns and bombs'* (page 352).

EVALUATING THE STUDY BY GOULD

The research technique

This core study reviewed other research by Yerkes and Boring. Their data were collected using mental tests, a psychometric technique. *What are the strengths and limitations of such techniques in the context of this study?*

Quantitative or qualitative

What kind of data were collected in this study? What are the strengths and limitations of producing this kind of data in the context of this study?

The sample

The data for this study were collected from American army recruits. *In what way is this group of participants unique? How does this affect the conclusions drawn from the study?*

Validity and reliability

In what way might the army IQ tests be said to lack validity and reliability?

Ethnocentrism

What does this study tell us about ethnocentrism?

Nature or nurture?

What evidence is there from this study to support the nature or nurture side of the debate?

Applications/usefulness

How valuable was Yerkes' research? How valuable was this review?

DEBATE

What is frightening is not that intelligent men devised such stupid tests but that others believe the results without questioning the method by which they were obtained.

Multiple choice questions

1. **Which test was for illiterates?**
   (a) Army alpha.   (b) Army Beta.
   (c) Army gamma.   (d) All of the above.

2. **If a recruit failed the Army Alpha test, what was supposed to happen?**
   (a) He could retake the test.
   (b) His IQ was scored as zero.
   (c) He was not allowed to serve in the army.
   (d) He should be given the Army Beta test.

3. **The number of a Kaffir's legs is:**
   (a) 2   (b) 4
   (c) 6   (d) 8

4. **Nordics were more intelligent than:**
   (a) Italians.
   (b) Poles.
   (c) Negroes.
   (d) All of the above.

5. **The least intelligent immigrants were from:**
   (a) Northern Europe.
   (b) Southern Europe.
   (c) Eastern Europe.
   (d) Both (b) and (c).

6. **Average test scores and years of residence in America were:**
   (a) Negatively correlated.
   (b) Positively correlated.
   (c) Uncorrelated.
   (d) Not considered.

7. **Which of the following was *not* one of the 'facts' produced in this review?**
   (a) Negroes had the lowest mental age.
   (b) White American mental age is declining.
   (c) European immigrants can be graded by their country.
   (d) Immigration policy was changed.

8. **The Beta tests weren't always given because Yerkes did not anticipate:**
   (a) That so many recruits would be illiterate.
   (b) How long it would take to do each test.
   (c) Yerkes wanted to show that Negroes were inferior.
   (d) Both (a) and (b).

9. **The Restriction Act (1924) restricted immigrants mainly from:**
   (a) Western and northern Europe.
   (b) Eastern and northern Europe.
   (c) Western and southern Europe.
   (d) Eastern and southern Europe.

10. **Eugenics is:**
   (a) A method of increasing intelligence.
   (b) A health movement.
   (c) A movement that seeks to improve human genetic quality through social intervention.
   (d) All of the above.

Answers are on page 205.

Exam questions

1. From the study by Gould suggest how the use of IQ tests may actually have been a form of social control. [OCR AS Psy, Jan 2005, paper 1]   [4]

2. (a) From the review of IQ testing by Gould identify **one** of the three 'facts' created from the data gathered by Yerkes.   [2]

   (b) Outline **one** use that was made of Yerkes' data by politicians.   [2]
   [OCR AS Psy, Jan 2004, paper 1]

3. (a) From the report by Gould, why did Yerkes use three types of IQ tests on the army recruits?   [2]

   (b) Outline **one** problem with the Beta tests described in this study.   [2]
   [OCR AS Psy, Jan 2003, paper 1]

4. According to Gould (IQ testing), Yerkes believed that his IQ tests measured 'native intellectual ability'.

   (a) What did Yerkes mean by 'native intellectual ability'?   [2]

   (b) Identify **two** criticisms of the test as a measure of native intellectual ability.   [2]
   [OCR AS Psy, June 1997, paper 1]

Specialised intelligences

In our country we concentrate on a few cognitive skills to measure intelligence but around the world people show intelligence by developing a range of skilled behaviours.

Musical intelligence

Some people can develop advanced musical intelligence if it is adaptive in their community. Lord (1960) studied how singers of oral verse in a rural Balkan community became singers of epic songs. This requires a high level of linguistic and musical intelligence because the singer has to learn musical and linguistic formulae that allow them to construct appropriate songs. This is no mean feat as each song lasts a whole evening, and a different song is sung on each of the 40 days of the holy month of Ramadan. The singer has to learn the skill by observing these events for many years, practise in private and then perform.

Navigational intelligence

Many of us are capable of getting lost in a shop so the idea that some people can navigate across thousands of miles is almost unimaginable. This is an essential skill, however, in island communities like Micronesia where islands can be thousands of miles apart. Gladwin (1970) studied how men in the Puluwat Islands of Micronesia train to become master navigators. This position is achieved by very few individuals because it demands an extremely high aptitude, involving a combination of different kinds of intelligence. The master navigators must memorise vast amounts of factual information such as the identities and locations of all the islands, the names and paths of all of the stars, and the techniques for using this information to devise a route. They also have to develop exceptional practical skills involved with sea travel such as reading currents, the weather and the waves.

Footballers are often caricatured as being unintelligent, against the evidence of their clearly expert skill. Wayne Rooney, for example, shows great football intelligence in being able to see opportunities, make decisions quickly and read the actions of other players to say nothing of his great physical agility.

Intelligence testing and race

Early IQ tests were used to suggest there are differences between different racial groups; this is an argument that has not gone away. There are many problems with any exploration of racial differences. This argument is particularly controversial in intelligence because differences between one group and another are often presented as differences in ability rather than differences in performance. In truth, the only evidence we have are performance scores, and we have to explain why groups perform differently. This could be due to a range of cultural, educational and motivational factors, which are more plausible that any genetic explanations for the reasons described by Jones (see the key issue on ethnocentrism, page 161).

There is also the matter of how the genetic effect is calculated; the statistic that is commonly cited is heritability. This statistic estimates how much the variation within any given population is due to genetic factors. It does not, however, tell us why two populations differ and so contributes nothing to our understanding of this issue (see Rose *et al.*, 1984). It also fails to tell us anything about how much genetics affect the characteristics of individuals.

Problems like these make assertions about racial differences very difficult and, in fact Kline (1991), a leading psychometrician, suggested that:

'The only advantage in setting out the different scores on IQ tests of racial groups is to give ammunition to those who wish to decry them. It adds nothing to theoretical understanding or to the social or educational practice' (Kline, 1991, p. 96).

The bell curve

In case you think the debate about whether differences in intelligence are inherited has gone away then look no further than *The Bell Curve*. The book gets its name from the bell-shaped normal distribution of scores that all IQ tests are designed to produce. This controversial book by Richard J. Herrnstein and Charles Murray, published in 1994, made the authors notorious for their discussion of race and intelligence.

Herrnstein and Murray argue that differences between people are largely due to genetics. They argue that intelligence is not much affected by changing environmental circumstances (such as better schooling) so we'd better get used to some groups being intellectually superior to others.

One of the most prominent critics of *The Bell Curve* was Stephen Jay Gould who released a revised edition of *The Mismeasure of Man* to challenge the ideas in it. He argues that the current evidence about the heritability of intelligence does not suggest that genetics provide the best explanation of differences in group scores.

This argument will run and run.

LINKS TO OTHER STUDIES

This study links into the debate about ethnocentrism, and so connects to **Hraba and Grant** and also **Tajfel**. There are a number of studies that use IQ measures including **Baron-Cohen, Leslie and Frith**, **Thigpen and Cleckley**, and **Hodges and Tizard**. The work of **Piaget** is also on intelligence though he was interested in the qualities that we all share rather than trying to quantify any differences between us.

The study also links into the methods part of this course because the correlation test that we use was developed by **Spearman** specifically to describe mental abilities, and to provide evidence for arguments about eugenics.

KeyISSUE

Psychometrics

The term psychometric means 'measuring the mind', though many psychometricians would be very uncomfortable with a term such as 'mind'. A psychological test is a task or set of tasks that can be given in a standard format to an individual or group of people, and which produces a score that can be represented as a number (or a category). It can involve almost any activity though most commonly it involves filling in a questionnaire. Tests are used to measure a range of qualities including:

- cognitive functions (e.g. IQ tests);
- personality (e.g. Eysenck's EPI);
- mood (e.g. The Beck Depression Inventory);
- attitudes (e.g. political opinion polls);
- aptitude for various jobs (e.g. The Comprehensive Ability Battery);
- illness behaviour (e.g. the McGill Pain Inventory).

Psychometric tests are extensively used in everyday life and you are likely to come into contact with them on a fairly regular basis.

Psychometric methods produce quantitative data which are straightforward to analyse. The issue with such numerical data is that they may not capture the richness of experience and ability, as Gould said. *'Some things have to be seen, touched and tasted.'* The issue of quantitative versus qualitative measurement is discussed on page 145.

The issue of quantitative versus qualitative measurement is discussed on page 145.

Exam-style question

Psychologists use many different methods to measure psychological abilities such as IQ tests, questionnaires, EEG machines and PET scans.

Choose **one** core study and answer the following questions.

(a) Describe the way in which the equipment was used to collect data in your chosen study. [6]

(b) Give **two** advantages of using this equipment in your chosen study and give **two** disadvantages of using this equipment in your chosen study. [12]

(c) Suggest **one** way in which data could have been gathered for your chosen study without the use of this equipment and say how you think this might affect the results. [8]

The technology of psychometric tests

Reliability

Does the test give you a consistent score?

If you use a ruler to measure the height of a chair today and check the measurement tomorrow, you expect the ruler to give you the same result. It is unlikely that the height of the chair has changed very much though you might make an error in reading the scale.

Any tool used to measure a psychological quality must be able to give the same result time after time. This is a problem with most psychometric measures such as an IQ test because the second time you do the test you are likely to do better just through practice. This means that we have to have a range of very similar tests to measure the same quality.

Standardisation

How does your score compare to the average?

The score on a psychometric test is calculated by working out a 'standard' – the test is given to a large sample of people to find out what 'typical' people get on the test. Then when we give someone the test we can say where they sit in the distribution, whether they are above or below average. The accuracy of the standard will depend on how well we chose our sample, and how representative it is.

Validity

Does the test measure what it aims to measure?

I could produce a test of creativity which required people to identify different uses for a brick. But does this actually measure creativity? If it doesn't then a person's score on my test is meaningless. We can use tests to estimate a psychological quality like intelligence but we cannot get a valid measure unless we can define precisely and ensure that measurement techniques match the definition.

ACTIVITY

Design a psychometric test to measure either (a) stupidity (not necessarily the opposite of intelligence) or (b) charmingness.
- Identify five items for your test
- How will you check its reliability?
- How will you assess its validity?

Issues

- *Acquiescence:* people have a tendency to agree with items on a test.
- *Social desirability:* people have a tendency to respond in a way that makes them look good.
- *Middle categories:* many questionnaires ask people to respond on a five-point scale, and there is a tendency for people to use the middle value (Kline, 1993).
- *Coaching:* people can be coached to do well and so mask their true score.
- *Cultural differences:* most tests are designed in one culture and tested on people from that culture to establish standards. These tests, and standards, are then used in different cultural settings (an imposed etic).

KEY TERMS

Validity, in general, is about the 'meaningfulness' of results. It is a measure of the extent to which something tests or measures what it aims to test/measure.

Reliability refers to whether a measuring device or assessment is consistent.

Racial identity

An American story

Many of the core studies were carried out in America but none is more drenched in the American story than the doll study of Hraba and Grant. It comes out of the racial divisions in the USA and is a landmark in the Civil Rights movement of the twentieth century.

In the USA at the start of the twentieth century slavery was banned, but a new method of oppression had been developed. Following a court ruling (*Plessey* v. *Ferguson*, 1896) it became legal to create a segregated society under the principle of 'separate but equal'. Many states in the USA used this principle to have separate buses, drinking fountains and schools for whites and blacks.

The long legal battle against this law was led by the National Association for the Advancement of Coloured People (NAACP). One of the obvious challenges was that the 'separate but equal' principle clearly did not apply because although black people had separate facilities they were worse than those provided for white people. This was particularly true in basic schooling for black children. Lawyers used evidence from psychologists Kenneth Clark and Mamie Phipps Clark on identity and esteem in black children. They devised the doll test (described in the core study) and found that young black children in 1940s USA had a sense of racial inferiority. They repeated their tests in the states where the court cases were being brought including South Carolina, Delaware and Virginia. The psychological evidence was brought into the courtroom and is believed to have had an important impact on the eventual decision of the courts. Clark and Clark were able to show scientifically something that is blindingly obvious today: if you treat people like crap for long enough they end up feeling like crap. Not many psychological studies have had such an impact on social policy and the lives of ordinary people.

The anti-segregation cases were eventually taken to the American Supreme Court (the highest available court): the Clarks prepared evidence on the effects of segregation. The Supreme Court acknowledged the work presented by the Clarks:

'To separate them from others of similar age and qualifications solely because of their race generates a feeling of inferiority as to their status in the community that may affect their hearts and minds in a way unlikely ever to be undone...' (Clark in O'Connell and Russo, 2001, p. 271).

On May 17, 1954 (*Brown* v. *Topeka Board of Education*) the principle of 'separate but equal' was ruled illegal.

Civil rights struggle

The issue of segregation did not end in 1954 and years of struggle were required to remove the worst excesses of segregation policies. One famous example of this struggle is shown in the photograph. In September 1957 nine black students enrolled at Central High School in Little Rock, Arkansas. Local white opposition threatened violence and social disorder, and the State Governor ordered the Arkansas National Guard to surround Central High School to keep the nine students from entering the school in order to defuse social unrest and to maintain law and order. The photo shows Elizabeth Eckford, a 17-year-old black woman facing the taunts of the crowd as she tried to find a way through the lines of troops taunted by white students such as Hazel Massery behind her shouting with hostility. Elizabeth was not allowed through and had to make her way home alone.

The photograph taken was circulated all over the world, illustrating the ugliness of the event. Eckford recalled her experience:

'I stood looking at the school – it looked so big! Just then the guards let some white students through. The crowd was quiet. I guess they were waiting to see what was going to happen. When I was able to steady my knees, I walked up to the guard who had let the white students in. He too didn't move. When I tried to squeeze past him, he raised his bayonet and then the other guards moved in and they raised their bayonets. They glared at me with a mean look and I was very frightened and didn't know what to do. I turned around and the crowd came toward me.

'They moved closer and closer. Somebody started yelling, "Lynch her! Lynch her!"

'I tried to see a friendly face somewhere in the mob – someone who maybe would help. I looked into the face of an old woman and it seemed a kind face, but when I looked at her again, she spat on me. They came closer, shouting, "No nigger bitch is going to get in our school. Get out of here!" I turned back to the guards but their faces told me I wouldn't get any help from them.' (http://www.atimes.com/atimes/Front_Page/GC11Aa01.html)

In one of those remarkable stories that illustrate how individuals can rise above the divisions in our societies, the two women met 40 years later and are reported to have developed a friendship. For more information read J. Haskins (1998) *The Dream and the Struggle: Separate but not Equal*.

Self and identity

Who am I? is a question we all face sometimes. One way of exploring this sense of self is to ask people to give 20 answers to this seemingly simple question. We might put down our family associations and the groups we belong to or even the things we own. Some people will put down their religion or their ethnicity or their nationality. They will also put down some personal qualities.

But how do we know who or what we are? One source of evidence is the reaction of other people to us. If people laugh at me then I am funny (or ridiculous) and if people smile at me then I am friendly. These reactions act as a mirror to my personality telling me what other people think of me.

These reactions might also affect how much I value myself. My self-image describes how I see myself and my self-esteem refers to how much I approve of or like myself. A number of techniques have been used to get information on self-concept and self-esteem such as the doll studies and also asking people to draw self-portraits. These drawings inevitably disclose something of what we think about ourselves.

Malcolm X

Following the *Brown* v. *Topeka Board of Education* ruling, the Civil Rights Movement in the USA gained strength and brought about real change. Among the major figures were Martin Luther King Jr and Malcolm X. Although this is mainly an American story the oppression of minority peoples is a worldwide issue.

It is a little-known fact that Malcolm X visited Birmingham, UK on 12 February 1965. He chose Birmingham because at that time parts of Smethwick in Birmingham were full of racial conflict which was being made worse by local and national politicians using race to try to get elected in the area. During his visit he drank in a local pub, walked down Marshall Street and gave several interviews. Only nine days later on his return to the USA, Malcolm X was murdered in Harlem, New York City at the Audubon Ballroom.

Despite his murder, Malcolm X remains one of the world's most revered and controversial civil rights activists. His teachings and speeches are still influential, even though it is 40 years since his death.

Malcolm X was born Malcolm Little in 1925 in Omaha, Nebraska. He considered the name 'Little' to be a slave name and chose 'X' to signify his lost tribal name. The family's home was burned to the ground by the white supremacist organisation The Black Legion in 1929. Malcolm was a good student but dropped out of school and worked in a variety of odd jobs. He was sentenced to ten years for burglary in 1946 but paroled after seven years.

Malcolm X became a member of the Nation of Islam and wrote extensively about human rights. He was a gifted and charismatic orator and among his most famous quotes is this statement about human rights:

'Human rights are something you were born with. Human rights are your God-given rights. Human rights are the rights that are recognised by all the nations of this earth' (BBC, 2005a).

If you are interested in Malcolm X then you can pick up the very readable *Autobiography of Malcolm X*, or watch the Spike Lee film.

Biographical notes on Mamie and Kenneth Clark

Mamie Phipps was born in Hot Springs, Arkansas, USA, where although she was from a middle-class family, she was not protected from the social policies of the time and attended a segregated school and used facilities that were reserved for 'Coloreds Only'. She began studying self-perception in black children as a graduate student at Howard University, where she met and married Kenneth Clark. Between 1939 and 1940, the two published three major articles on this subject. Mamie continued her work at Columbia University where, in 1943, she became the first African-American woman and the second African American (after her husband) in the University's history to receive a psychology doctorate. Even after conducting, publishing and presenting significant research and earning her Ph.D., Mamie had difficulty finding work as a psychologist. Dr Clark explained her frustration: *'Although my husband had earlier secured a teaching position at the City College of New York, following my graduation it soon became apparent to me that a black female with a Ph.D. in psychology was an unwanted anomaly in New York City in the early 1940s'* (O'Connell and Russo, 2001, p. 271).

Mamie Phipps Clark (1917–83) with some of her students

Kenneth Clark was the first African-American to earn a doctorate in psychology at Columbia, to hold a permanent professorship at the City College of New York, to join the New York State Board of Regents and to serve as president of the American Psychological Association. In addition to his work as a psychologist and educator, he assisted corporations in developing racial policies and minority hiring programmes.

Even the rat was white

In 1955, when Robert Guthrie enrolled in a master's programme at the University of Kentucky, he was the only black face in a sea of white. *'I remember one of my white professors eyeing me as if I were an anthropological specimen and remarking, "You are from one of our Negro schools"'* Guthrie recalls (APA 2005).

After serving in the US army Guthrie returned to psychology and wrote the classic text *Even the Rat Was White*. In the book he describes the role of racial bias in the history of psychology, in the development of divisive theories and also in the failure to value the work of black psychologists. The book describes the biographies of early African-American psychologists and their scientific contributions, as well as their problems, views, and concerns of the field of social psychology. He uses research documents that are not often found in the mainstream by referring to journals and magazines such as the *Journal of Black Psychology*, the *Journal of Negro Education*, and *Crisis*.

The second edition published in 1998 reviews the progress of the last 25 years and discusses the new challenges for black psychologists. Guthrie argues that the 'myth of mental measurement' and eugenicist philosophy continue to exist and create negative stereotypes of oppressed peoples.

The core study

The original research on which this core study was based probably had more influence on the lives of ordinary people than any other study in the history of psychology. The Clark and Clark study gave scientific weight to the humanitarian arguments against racial segregation in the USA. Hraba and Grant revisited the study at the end of the 1960s to see whether there had been a change in black identity in the intervening years. Had the real improvement in the situation of black people in the USA led to a more positive self-identity?

You can read the original study by Clark and Clark here: http:/psychclassics.yorku.ca/Clark/Skin-color

Joseph Hraba and Geoffrey Grant (1970) Black is beautiful: A re-examination of racial preference and identification. *Journal of Personality and Social Psychology*, 16 (3), 398–402.

Abstract

Aim

This study aimed to repeat an earlier study by Clark and Clark (1939) to see if children in interracial settings behave differently in 1970.

Method

Eighty-nine black and 71 white children aged 4–8 years were selected from five state schools in Lincoln, Nebraska – an interracial community. Each child was interviewed individually using a set of eight instructions and four dolls, identical except that two were black and two were white.

The instructions measured racial preference (e.g. 'Give me the doll that you want to play with'), racial awareness or knowledge (e.g. 'Give me the doll that looks like a white child') and racial self-identification ('Give me the doll that looks like you').

The children were also asked to name and indicate the race of their best friends.

Results

The main findings were:

- The majority of black children in this study, unlike those in the Clark and Clark study, preferred the black doll.
- Same-race preference increased with age.
- Black children with light coloured skin were at least as strong in their preference for a black doll as other black children, a result that again differed from the Clark and Clark study.
- There was no relationship between doll preference and race of friends, even with those children who were totally racially consistent in their doll choices.

Discussion

The change in findings since the earlier study suggests that interracial contact and acceptance may increase black pride.

The fact that there was little relationship between doll choice and friendship choice may be explained as an effect of 'black is beautiful' (acceptance of and by whites) and/or may be because doll choice does not correspond to friendship choice and/or because race is not an important criteria for children of this age.

CoreSTUDY

Aim

Kenneth and Mamie Clark first investigated the negative self-attitudes held by black children in 1947, using dolls. Since that time there have been a number of further investigations of this topic. One finding has been that black children who had little experience of white 'outgroups' (e.g. through living in all black communities) showed a preference for black rather than white dolls (Gregor and McPherson 1966). Clark and Clark also had found that black preference for white dolls was stronger in interracial schools then in segregated ones.

However, another study (Morland 1966) found the opposite using a picture technique. And Johnson (1966) found that black youths rated black and white equally, concluding that *'not all Negroes have negative self-attitudes'* (page 273).

The present study aims to test the hypothesis that black children growing up in an interracial setting prefer white rather than black dolls.

Method

Procedure

The procedures used by Clark and Clark were followed as closely as possible. The participants in this study were interviewed individually. Four dolls were used which were identical except that two were black and two were white dolls. The participants were instructed to hand over the doll that:

1 they wanted to play with.
2 was a nice doll.
3 looked bad.
4 was a nice colour.
5 looked like a white child.
6 looked like a coloured child.
7 looked like a Negro child.
8 looked like you.

Clark and Clark claimed that:

- Items 1–4 measure racial preference.
- Items 5–7 measure racial awareness or knowledge.
- Item 8 measures racial self-identification.

Hraba and Grant collected further data by asking the participants to name and indicate the race of their best friends. They also asked the teachers for the same information. Choice of friend is an example of a 'behaviour'.

The sample

The sample was obtained from five state schools in Lincoln, Nebraska ('middle America'). A total of 160 children aged 4–8 years were used. The sample consisted of all 89 black children in the school. The 71 white children were drawn randomly from those classrooms containing the black participants. Thus the sample was 60% black and 40% white. The interviewers were both black and white.

Setting

The population of Lincoln was 1.4% black. Three of the schools had 3% black students while the rate was higher in the remaining two (7% and 18%). Seventy per cent of the sample reported they had white friends.

ACTIVITY

After you have read the whole study, try to produce your specially 'reduced' version – maximum 30 words! Can anyone do it in less and preserve the key features?

Results

Racial preference (items 1–4)

On all measures of racial preference (items 1–4) there was a significant difference from the Clark and Clark findings.

- Both black and white children preferred their own race doll.

- The white children were significantly more ethnocentric on items 1 and 2 and the black children were significantly more ethnocentric on item 4.

Age All children showed an increasing ethnocentric preference with age (except for the white children and item 4). Clark and Clark had also found that black preference for white dolls decreased with age.

Skin colour The Clarks classified the black children by skin colour: light, medium, dark, and found that those with light skin colour showed greatest preference for the white dolls and those with the darkest skin showed the least preference. This trend was not found in this study; the light-skinned children expressed as strong a preference for the black dolls as their darker-skinned peers.

Racial identification (items 5–8)

In the Clark and Clark study most of the children correctly identified the dolls as white and 'coloured' (90% and 94% respectively). The 1969 black sample was similar: 90% correctly identified the white doll and 94% correctly identified the black doll.

With regard to item 7, slightly more children in this study correctly identified the Negro doll than in the Clark and Clark study (86% as compared to 72%).

Age Like the Clarks, this study found an inverse relationship between misidentification and age, i.e. misidentification decreased with age.

Skin colour There were again no differences in terms of the participants' skin colour except for item 8. In the Clarks' study 80% of the light-skinned black respondents misidentified themselves as white; this was reduced in this study to 15%.

Race of interviewer The race of interviewer had no effect on the doll choices.

Race of respondents' friends For both black and white children there was no apparent relationship between choice of doll and race of friend. This was even true amongst those children who were totally consistent in their doll preferences on items 1–4 (i.e. the black children who chose the black doll all four times and the white children who chose the white doll all four times). One might have expected this group of children (23 black and 20 white) to show a preference for same-race friends. However, 87% of the 23 black children had white friends and 60% of the 20 white children had all white friends.

ACTIVITY

Students could try to role play this activity. One student plays the experimenter and another plays the role of child. The child should be given a card in private that says 'white' or 'black' and should make choices appropriate to that role. The class can be asked to guess whether the child is black or white. (Note that many of the children did not make consistent choices.)

Table showing percentage of choices made by black and white children in this study and Clark and Clark's study.

Measure of racial preference	Clark and Clark (1939) blacks %	Lincoln (1969) blacks %	Lincoln (1969) whites %
1 Which doll do you want to play with?			
White doll	67	30	83
Black doll	32	70	16
Don't know or no response	1		1
2 Which is the nice doll?			
White doll	59	46	70
Black doll	38	54	30
Don't know or no response	3		
3 Which doll looks bad?			
White doll	17	61	34
Black doll	59	36	63
Don't know or no response	24	3	3
4 Which doll is the nice colour?			
White doll	60	31	48
Black doll	38	69	49
Don't know or no response	4		3

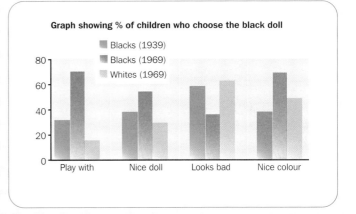

Graph showing % of children who choose the black doll

- Blacks (1939)
- Blacks (1969)
- Whites (1969)

Qs

1 Describe **one** control that was used in this study.

2 Identify the **two** dependent variables in this study.

3 How do you think the order of the questions might have affected the results?

4 How can you explain the fact that not all the children were able to accurately identify the race of the dolls?

5 Which group was the most ethnocentric? Explain your answer.

6 What explanation would you offer for the changes in the findings between 1939 and 1969?

Discussion

Doll preference

The results suggest that black children in interracial communities are not white-oriented, in contrast with the results from Clark and Clark's earlier study of a segregated community. There are various explanations for this change:

* Times may have changed. It may be that blacks are now prouder of their race and therefore more likely to identify with it.

* It might be that 30 years ago black youngsters in Lincoln, unlike those in other cities, would have responded in this way, i.e. they may have always had a more positive racial identity.

* It might be that Lincoln is an example of a place where the black movement has had a strong impact. There had been a black pride campaign, sponsored by local groups. Thus the children in Lincoln may have a more positive racial identity than elsewhere.

* It could be, as proposed at the start of the study, that interracial contact does increase black pride. Hraba and Grant found that 70% of the black children in this study and 59% of the white children had interracial friends. Pettigrew (1967) proposed that interracial contact brings acceptance and this enhances academic performance; it may similarly increase black pride.

Biographical notes on Joseph Hraba

Professor Hraba writes *'We did the doll study as graduate students. First was a pre-test as a class project in the summer and then the study the following spring. After the study was published, a man then at Makerere in Kampala wrote to me requesting that I ship the dolls. I then asked why and he replied that he could not find black dolls in Uganda. The doll manufacture was monopolised by East Asians, making dolls in their image. Bad idea for a tiny middleman minority, I thought, and Big Daddy Amin subsequently engaged in genocide'* (personal communication).

Joseph Hraba is Emeritus Professor at Iowa State University.

Doll preference and friendship

The four explanations on the left all *assume* that doll choice corresponds to interracial behaviour. However, the fact that there was no relationship between doll preference and friendship suggests that this assumption may not be justified.

There are three ways of explaining the lack of relationship between doll preference and friendship choice.

Explanation 1 If we assume that the children use the same criteria for doll choice and for friendship, and if we assume that 'black is beautiful' means a rejection of whites, then we would expect those black children who consistently choose black dolls also to have all black friends.

This explanation was shown to be incorrect (because the consistent black children choose some white friends). However, it is possible that the black pupils may have preferred to have black friends but this is not possible in a predominantly white school.

Explanation 2 If we assume that the children use the same criteria for doll choice and for friendship, and if we assume that 'black is beautiful' means an acceptance of and by whites, then we

would expect those black children who consistently choose black dolls to also have both black and white friends.

This explanation was nearly realised as the black children who had both black and white friends tended to have a stronger preference for the black dolls than those children who had all black friends.

Explanation 3 If we assume that doll choice does not correspond to friendship choice, and that 'black is beautiful' is not an important criteria for children of this age, then we would expect there to be no relationship between doll choice and friendship choice.

This is what happened. Hraba and Grant point to psychological research that indicates (a) that race may not be an important criteria for friendship at this age (Criswell, 1937) and (b) children of this age may not detect conceptual self-contradictions (Piaget, 1954). This explanation is further supported by the fact that 73% of all the children were not consistent when answering questions 1–4.

Table summarising the three explanations when the black child consistently chooses the black doll.

	Doll choice ...	Black pride ...	Predicted outcome ...	Actual outcome
1	Shows racial preference.	Means rejection of whites.	Total preference for black friends.	Didn't happen possibly because not possible in a predominantly white school.
2	Shows racial preference.	Means acceptance of and by whites.	Have both black and white friends.	Describes what occurred *most* but not all of the time.
3	Other criteria important in making friendships.	Children not affected by race and/or conceptual self-contradictions.	Doll choice not related to friendship choice.	This is what occurred.

Qs

1 What social changes took place between 1939 and 1969?

2 In what other ways was this study different to Clark and Clark's study?

3 How can Piaget's views be used to explain the lack of relationship between doll choice and friend choice?

EVALUATING THE STUDY BY HRABA AND GRANT

The research method

This study was a natural (quasi) experiment because the IV were not controlled by the experimenter. *What are the strengths and limitations of this research method in the context of this study?*

The sample

To what extent does the target population in this study differ from other US communities? How does this affect the conclusions drawn from the study?

Ethical issues

What ethical issues should have concerned the researchers in this study, and how might they have dealt with these issues?

Qualitative or quantitative?

What kind of data were collected in this study? What are the strengths and limitations of producing this kind of data in the context of this study?

Ethnocentricism

What does this study tell us about ethnocentrism?

Validity and ecological validity

To what extent were the researchers testing what they intended to test? To what extent can we generalise the findings from this study to everyday situations?

Applications/usefulness

How valuable was this study?

DEBATE

'Black is beautiful'. Hraba and Grant suggest that the black pride movement has increased the self-esteem of blacks and also led to acceptance of and by whites; discuss this claim with respect to the UK instead of America. Divide into small groups, each of which should collect evidence to support their views about social changes in interracial attitudes in the last 30 years.

? What next?

Describe **one** change to this study, and say how you think this might affect the outcome.

Multiple choice questions

1. Why did the researchers choose to use schools in Lincoln in this study?
   (a) They worked in Lincoln.
   (b) Clark and Clark's study was set in Lincoln.
   (c) It was an interracial community.
   (d) All of the above.

2. What age were the children who were tested?
   (a) 3–8 years old. (b) 4–8 years old.
   (c) 3–7 years old. (d) 4–7 years old.

3. Which one of the following assesses racial preference?
   (a) The doll you want to play with.
   (b) The doll that is like your own dolls.
   (c) The doll that looks like a white child.
   (d) The doll that looks like you.

4. Which one of the following assesses racial awareness?
   (a) The doll you want to play with.
   (b) The doll that is like your own dolls.
   (c) The doll that looks like a white child.
   (d) The doll that looks like you.

5. Approximately what percentage of black children wanted to play with a black doll in the 1939 study?
   (a) 30 (b) 40 (c) 60 (d) 70

6. What percentage of black children wanted to play with a black doll in the 1969 study?
   (a) 30 (b) 40 (c) 60 (d) 70

7. The black children's preference for same-race dolls:
   (a) Increased with age.
   (b) Decreased with age.
   (c) There was no relationship with age.
   (d) Was not shown in this study.

8. In the study by Hraba and Grant, the black children who had light skin colour tended to show:
   (a) A preference for white dolls.
   (b) A preference for black dolls.
   (c) No preference for black or white dolls.
   (d) Their preferences were not reported.

9. Hraba and Grant found that the *black* children who consistently showed a preference for the black dolls had:
   (a) All black friends.
   (b) All white friends.
   (c) Black and white friends.
   (d) Mainly white friends.

10. The findings from the 1939 study were different to the 1969 study. Four reasons were given for the difference. Which of the following was *not* one of them?
    (a) Times may be changing.
    (b) The black pride movement has enhanced black identity.
    (c) Interracial contact may enhance black pride.
    (d) The interviewers may have been more friendly.

Answers are on page 205.

Exam questions

1. From the Hraba and Grant study on doll choice
   (a) Outline **one** similarity with the Clark and Clark study. [2]
   (b) Outline **one** difference from the Clark and Clark study. [2]
   [OCR AS Psy, May 2004, paper 1]

2. The study by Hraba and Grant on doll choice found evidence of ethnocentric bias, one feature of which is to overestimate the worth of people in the same group.
   (a) Outline **one** way in which the white children were ethnocentric. [2]
   (b) Suggest **one** problem that psychologists face when they study ethnocentric bias. [2]
   [OCR AS Psy, Jan 2001, paper 2]

3. (a) Hraba and Grant studied the changes that have occurred in the way that black Americans perceive themselves. Name **two** of the factors measured in this study. [2]
   (b) What social changes had taken place between the carrying out of the original study and the replication? [2]
   [OCR AS Psy, specimen paper]

4. Hraba and Grant found that black children in 1969 showed a greater preference for black dolls than black children did in 1939. Give **two** explanations for this change. [OCR AS Psy, June 1999, paper 1] [4]

Modern identity is not all black or white

Racial identity is not a binary issue. In the USA there was a time where some issues of race did come down to black or white issues, but in the UK today the picture is much more diverse. Our major cities are a rich ethnic mix and many families have mixed roots. Some schools in London can have as many as 40 different languages registered as the first tongue of the pupils. Our sense of identity can be a mix of skin colour, religion and country of origin. We might feel that this identity is given to us or we can adopt some features of it when we become aware of other ethnic groups or are attracted to them.

Data from the 2001 census found that Britain has one of the highest rates in the world of inter-ethnic relationships and, consequently, mixed race people. By 1997 half of black men and a third of black women in relationships had a white partner, according to a study by the Policy Studies Institute (PSI), which also showed that interracial relationships were common in the Asian communities: up to 20% of Asian men and 10% of Asian women had a white partner.

Ethnic monitoring means we are often asked to tick a box to show our racial identity but this does not work for everyone and we are all more than a label. Raphael Mozades described his own mixed ethnicity upbringing.

'My mum was white and my dad was brown. My mum's relatives lived here, and the old ones had German accents. My dad's relatives lived in Israel and mostly couldn't speak English. When we went there, they said things in a funny language and pinched our cheeks. They smelled of garlic. And they came, originally, from exotic-sounding places like Bukhara and Isfahan [in today's Uzbekistan and Iran respectively].'

'At about 14, I started playing basketball seriously. The Harlesden Cougars basketball club was 99% black. The other 1% was me. I wasn't black, and couldn't understand the patois into which the other guys sometimes lapsed. I was basically the white kid, or the whitest they had.'

'And then came university. Where Harlesden had been black, Oxford was white. I went from being the only white kid on the team to the only black kid on the team. The blackest they had, anyway. They even told me that I had natural athleticism but lacked control and shouldn't shoot the ball.'

(*Guardian* 29.12.05)

Identity and football

For many, a key affiliation that contributes to their identity is their football team. The Birmingham poet Benjamin Zephaniah has been a lifelong supporter of Aston Villa though his support on the terraces has been well tested in the past.

He says, *'When I was a teenager, I used to come here every other week. It was a lot different then – 25,000 people stood here on the famous Holte End, I was almost the only black face.'*

Benjamin Zephaniah

'I always remember one game when I came here with my uncle and Villa were winning 2–0 and everybody was happy.'

'And then the other team, I forget who they were, started to come back and beating Villa. The mood changed and suddenly the crowd noticed I was the only black kid and they took it out on me. It was terrible.' (BBC, 2005b)

Despite these experiences he is now patron of Aston Villa Supporters' Club. In his poem 'Knowing Me', he expresses his passion for the club and shows how it is part of his wider sense of identity.

*With my Jamaican hand on my Ethiopian heart
The African heart deep in my Brummie chest,
And I chant, Aston Villa, Aston Villa, Aston Villa,
Believe me I know my stuff.*

'Race is an important part of my identity, but I wish it wasn't. I'd like to identify myself as a martial artist, an Aston Villa supporter, or a hip-hop reggae person; but when a policeman stops me on the street it has nothing to do with that.'

(*Guardian* 21.03.05)

LINKS TO OTHER STUDIES

This study contributes to our understanding of developmental processes and so fits in with the other studies on child development such as **Samuel and Bryant** and **Freud**.

The study also contributes to the methodology of psychology by inventing a technique for measuring identity. This innovation is shared by many of the core studies including **Bandura, Ross and Ross**, and **Baron-Cohen, Leslie and Frith**. Further studies on adoption can be found in extra material for **Hodges and Tizard**. This study also links into the social identity theory put forward by **Tajfel**.

Trans-racial adoption

A modern concern about racial identity centres on trans-racial adoption. Trans-racial adoption became common after the Second World War (1939–45). Children from war-torn countries without families were adopted by families in the wealthy Western countries. In this country there has been concern about white families adopting or fostering black children. The question is whether the children are harmed or disturbed by being brought up in a home from a different ethnic group to the one they were born in. As with most issues around race and ethnicity there are a lot of strong opinions though evidence is hard to come by.

A number of studies have used the Clark Doll Test to examine the racial awareness and preferences of the adopted children (e.g. Shireman and Johnson, 1986). These studies found little or no difference in responses of black children brought up in either black or white families as both groups expressed similar levels of racial awareness and preference. Of course, it has to be noted that the Doll Test is a limited technique to explore such a complex quality as racial identity.

keyISSUE

Promoting human welfare

Why do we study our psychology? What will we do with all the information that we find out? J.B. Watson set the agenda for modern psychology when he wrote the following:

'The interest of the behaviorist in man's doings is more than the interest of the spectator – he wants to control man's reactions as physical scientists want to control and manipulate other natural phenomena. It is the business of behaviourist psychology to be able to predict and to control human activity' (Watson, 1930, page 11).

This is all fine and dandy if we can all agree what is good for us and what needs to be controlled and who is going to do the controlling. If psychology can produce facts about people which allow us (the psychologists) to control them (the rest) then we need to be very sure that we are doing the right thing.

This is one of those debates that can never go away because every generation has to puzzle out how much control an individual should have and how much the society should have.

Psychology and war

Psychologists have been active in military actions for over a century. Some of their interventions have been to help soldiers deal with the traumas of combat and get them ready to go back into action, some interventions have been in propaganda to increase the confidence of our troops or undermine the morale of the enemy, and they have also developed interrogation techniques. If you believe a prisoner has information that could save the lives of others how far should you go to get that information from them? These are not easy questions for anyone but the involvement of PsyOps (Psychological Operations) at Abu Ghraib prison in Iraq and at Guantanamo Bay has moved these techniques outside the internationally agreed rules for the treatment of prisoners.

A different point of view to Watson's was put forward by George Miller (1969) in his Presidential Address to the American Psychological Association (APA). Miller pointed out that the aim of the APA is to promote human welfare. But what does this mean? Whose welfare is being promoted, and at whose expense? He said,

'Understanding and prediction are better goals for psychology and for the promotion of human welfare because they lead us to think, not in terms of coercion by a powerful elite, but in terms of the diagnosis of problems and the development of programmes that can enrich the lives of every citizen' (page 1069).

'Our responsibility is less to assume the role of experts and try to apply psychology ourselves than to give it away to the people who really need it' (page 1070).

> ### You decide
>
> Miller suggests that psychology should try and tell us about *'what is humanly possible and humanly desirable'* (page 1067). It is clear that some psychology lives up to this ambition and that some falls short. We leave you to judge where to put the line. Look at the examples and core studies on this page and think where you stand.

Consumer psychology

Advertising campaigns and shopping centres benefit from psychological input. Shopping centres such as the Victoria Centre in Nottingham are designed to make you lose your sense of time and to keep you in the centre. The entrances are large and well signposted but the exits are much smaller and less easy to find. The aim is to encourage you to spend more.

> **Exam-style question**
>
> One of the aims of psychology is to promote human welfare.
>
> Select **four** core studies and use them to answer the following questions.
>
> (a) Describe how each study is useful. [12]
>
> (b) Using examples from these studies, discuss **four** problems psychologists have when they try to carry out useful investigations. [12]

Several of the studies mentioned in this book have made particular contributions to human welfare. The **Milgram** study gives us a clearer view of what we are capable of, the **Rosenhan** study highlights the poor way that psychiatric patients were being treated in mental hospitals, the doll studies of **Clarke** and **Clarke** (page 180) contributed to the Civil Rights movement in the USA, the work of **Loftus** on false memories (page 4) has helped families make sense of conflicting evidence, and the work of **Hodges** and **Tizard** has contributed to understanding the effects of residential care. You wouldn't expect a text like this to select studies that damaged human welfare, but cases can be made against the brain scanning work of **Raine**, for example, or the mass IQ testing of **Yerkes** (page 174).

Psychobabble

Media psychologists popularise the subject and bring basic ideas to public attention. The accusation against them is that they simplify and distort what we know and on occasions actually tell lies. Psychologists can't read minds, intentions or body language any better than members of the general public. These tricks belong with clairvoyance and fortune telling.

Therapy

Psychologists have devised many therapies over the last hundred years which have had some success. The therapies range from the lengthy psychoanalysis of Freud to the more focused cognitive therapies such as Rational Emotive and Behaviour Therapy (REBT). Some of the core studies consider therapy issues, such as Little Hans.

Madness and schizophrenia

The concept of madness has been around for a long time, but the diagnosis of specific mental disorders only dates back around 100 years. The way a society deals with people who are different tells you a lot about that society. Sometimes people are revered for their differentness and sometimes they are persecuted. In the Western world, people who have been categorised as mad have been subjected to an unimaginably wide range of brutal and cruel treatments. They have been feared, ignored, beaten, chained, locked up and tranquilised. In the twenty-first century when we have discovered so much about health, the causes of mental disorders remain largely unknown and the treatments are still very controversial.

Schizophrenia is perhaps one of the most misunderstood and feared conditions. A literal translation of the term is 'shattered mind' which gives rise to the common misconception that it refers to a split personality. The condition was first described by Kraepelin in 1887 and further defined and named by Bleuler in 1911.

Symptoms

Schizophrenia is a serious mental disorder in which the person has persistent problems in perception or reality testing. The symptoms are divided into *positive symptoms* (those that are additional to normal experience and behaviour) and *negative symptoms* (reduction in normal experiences or behaviour). The positive symptoms include delusions, hallucinations and thought disorder. The negative symptoms include unusual emotional responses and lack of motivation.

Diagnosis is inevitably based on self-reports from the patient and observations from expert witnesses such as a psychiatrist. There is no biological test for schizophrenia, so the judgement depends on the expertise of the diagnostician. This makes the condition very different from medical conditions such as measles or meningitis and is one reason why it is difficult to see schizophrenia as a disease.

Categorising people

People find it easy to make judgements of 'oddness' in other people. 'He's never been quite right, you know' they might nudge someone and say, but we find it hard to say what it is that is so odd about the person. Psychological diagnosis is an attempt to classify oddness in people.

Diagnosis

The psychological diagnosis of personality has a long history. The Greeks, for example, recognised such diagnoses as senility, alcoholism, mania, melancholia and paranoia. The first comprehensive system of psychological disorders was created in 1896 by Emil Kraepelin. He believed that mental disorders have the same basis as physical ones, and that the same diagnostic principles should be applied – the careful observation of symptoms. The advantages of introducing a diagnostic system include:

- diagnosis is a communication shorthand;
- it suggests which treatments are likely to be successful;
- it may point out the cause;
- it aids scientific investigation by collecting together people with similar symptoms.

In 1952, the *Diagnostic and Statistical Manual of Mental Disorders (DSM)* was developed and approved by the American Psychiatric Association. A revised version, *DSM IV*, is widely used today in the USA. In the UK and the rest of the world it is more common to use the *International Statistical Classification of Diseases and Related Health Problems* (ICD) which is published by the World Health Organisation.

A diagnosis is arrived at using family resemblances. If you think of a big family that you know, then you will notice that most of the family members have some similar physical features, yet each member of the family is different from the others. It is a similar recognition process with mental disorders. Each person who has a particular condition has some similar features in their behaviour to other people with the same condition.

'The cause of lunacy?' The term lunatic (also loony, lunacy) comes from the Latin word 'luna' meaning moon. It highlights the commonly believed link between madness and the phases of the moon. Modern science has not established a link between the moon and madness but the connection might have arisen from the increased level of light at the full moon. This might have kept people awake and so made them susceptible to sleep deprivation symptoms.

Mad

We use the term madness in a number of ways.

- *Feelings of anger: 'she makes me so mad!' we snarl between gritted teeth.*
- *Senseless or laughable behaviours: we might say 'that was a mad idea'.*
- *Showing enthusiasm: 'I'm mad for it'.*
- *Showing irrational behaviour or being mentally unsound.*

All these definitions overlap each other but they are all very distinct as well. The madness we are talking about in this chapter is the fourth definition. Perhaps because we fear this condition we have many different words we use other than mad, for example, crazy, daft, demented, distraught, insane, lunatic, bonkers, cracked, daffy, gag, fruitcake, nuts, wacky. These words have very flexible meanings and can refer to the other definitions mentioned above. This shows how we tend to blur the boundaries between acceptable and unacceptable behaviours.

Visual and auditory hallucinations

Drugs

People have been aware of hallucinations for centuries. Some have seen them as a gift that provides special visions of life. One way of inducing hallucinations is to take certain drugs, for example LSD or mescaline. These have sometimes been referred to as mind-expanding drugs because of the feeling that the user has of seeing new things that they were not previously aware of. Mescaline is made from South American cacti such as the peyote cactus. It has been used in religious rituals for centuries. Users typically experience visual hallucinations and altered mental states which are often described as pleasurable and illuminating but occasionally there are feelings of anxiety or revulsion.

The dangers with hallucinogens come from the dramatic effect they have on the chemistry of the brain. The unwanted effects can include dizziness, sickness, anxiety, feelings of dying or not being able to return to normal consciousness. None of these are pleasant but the major concern is hallucinogen persisting perception disorder (HPPD) which occurs with a number of drugs and leaves the user experiencing hallucinations even when the drug has left their system.

Could it be that people with schizophrenia are having similar altered states?

What is it like to hear voices?

Hearing voices is a relatively common experience. Many people can have internal conversations with their family and friends

Joan of Arc was a French heroine of the 100 Years War who inspired the French to many victories over the English. From the age of 12 she heard voices which initially encouraged her in her religious observance, but later told her to do battle with the English. She was eventually captured, tried and burnt by the English who believed her voices came from the Devil. The French, however, believed the voices came from God and after her death she was made a Catholic saint.

even when they are alone. People who have recently been bereaved often report hearing the voice of the deceased person. Sometimes, however, the voices appear to be more distanced and often more troubling. The voices might be present all day and have the effect of preventing the voice-hearer from doing things in their daily life. The experience of hearing voices is very varied and difficult to describe.

Are voices a symptom of illness?

People who hear voices often find it disturbing, and dealing with someone who is hearing voices can also be quite disturbing. In recent times hearing voices has been seen as a symptom of mental disturbance and treated with major tranquillisers. Not everyone responds to this treatment and some people can learn to live with their voices without serious medication. In fact some people regard their voices as positive and there are numerous accounts of people finding their voices inspirational or comforting. Perhaps hearing voices should not always been seen as a symptom of mental disturbance but merely as a variation in human experience.

Mental health in the UK

There is still a lot of stigma attached to mental distress which means that it is often hidden. In its broadest definition, mental distress touches most people during their lives.

- It is estimated that as many as one in six adults in the UK are affected by mental distress at any one time.

- The most common conditions are mixed anxiety and depression which affect about 9% of adults every year.

- Up to 670,000 people in the UK have some form of dementia – 5% of people over 65 and 10–20% of people over 80.

- One in four consultations with a GP concern mental health issues. Up to 630,000 people are in contact with specialised mental health services at any one time.

Schizophrenia

The rate of schizophrenia is declining in this country but it is estimated that around 1% of the population will experience episodes during their lifetime and the prevalence of the disorder in any one year is between 2 and 4 in 1000. The prevalence rates are similar for men and women but it tends to show earlier in men with the prevalence in men aged 15–24 twice that of women.

Chemical treatments

The most common treatment for schizophrenia in the UK for the last 50 years has been anti-psychotic medication such as chlorpromazine, which is relatively successful in reducing symptoms (WHO, 2001) but has damaging side effects, such as:

- *Parkinson-like symptoms* Characterised by muscle rigidity and tremor, people with symptoms of drug-induced Parkinsonism may appear to have fixed facial expressions and speak in a slow manner with a monotonous tone.

- *Tardive dyskinesia (TD)* Abnormal facial movements, smacking lips, chewing, sucking, and twisting the tongue are characteristic signs. TD often persists after the treatment has stopped and cannot be treated.

Sources: ONS 2000, MIND website, Sainsbury Centre for Mental Health website.

The core study

What do we mean by the terms 'sane' and 'insane'? Does insanity exist in the individual or the society that judges them? These are the questions that Rosenhan is looking at in this study. At the time of the study there was growing unease with the medical approach to mental disorders and growing scepticism at the claims of psychiatrists to be able to diagnose and treat these disorders.

David L. Rosenhan (1973) On being sane in insane places. *Science*, 179, 250–258.

Abstract

Is abnormality a characteristic of certain individuals or is it something that is perceived because of the context they are seen in?

Study 1

Rosenhan arranged for 8 pseudopatients (men and women) to present themselves to 12 different US psychiatric hospitals. Their only symptom was hearing voices, all other details of their life history were honest except their name. All bar one were diagnosed as schizophrenic. They endeavoured to behave normally and recorded their observations in a notebook. The average stay was 19 days (range 7–52 days).

It may be that psychiatrists are more inclined to call a healthy person sick (a false positive, type 2 error) than a sick person healthy (a false negative, type 1).

Study 2

A further study was conducted to see if this error would persist. Staff at a psychiatric hospital were told the results of this study and warned that pseudopatients would present themselves over the next 3 months. No pseudopatients sought admission yet 41 real patients were suspected by at least one staff member and 23 by at least one psychiatrist. This is a type 1 error.

The results from these studies suggest that psychiatric diagnosis is highly unreliable.

Other results

- The label 'schizophrenia' is sticky – when discharged the pseudopatients were labelled 'schizophrenia in remission'.

- The label of abnormality changes the way the individual is perceived – 'normal' behaviours in an abnormal setting are seen as abnormal.

- Patients are depersonalised – staff ignored direct questions and avoided eye contact (study 3).

- Patients are powerless – many human rights were taken away, e.g. personal privacy.

Conclusion

It is not possible to distinguish the sane from the insane when they are labelled 'abnormal' because this creates expectations. One solution would be to place abnormal individuals in community health care to avoid the institutional context and/or focus on behavioural diagnoses rather than global labels such as 'schizophrenia'.

ROSENHAN : SANE IN INSANE PLACES

ACTIVITY

This is a lengthy report. After you have read through the whole report construct a mobile or some other work of art to illustrate the various strands. This will help you process the various different themes. Note that Rosenhan's article can be read at http://courses.ucsd.edu/fall2003/ps163f/Rosenhan.htm#_ftn1

corestudy

Introduction

'If sanity and insanity exist, how shall we know them?'

We may be convinced that we can tell the normal from the abnormal, but the evidence for this ability is not quite as compelling:

- It is common to read about murder trials where the prosecution and defence each call their own psychiatrists who disagree on the defendant's sanity.

- There is much disagreement about the meaning of terms such as 'sanity', 'insanity', 'mental illness' and 'schizophrenia'.

- Normality and abnormality are not universal; what is considered normal in one culture may be seen as quite aberrant in another.

This is not to suggest that there is no such thing as deviant or odd behaviours, nor that 'mental illness' is not associated with personal anguish. Murder and hallucinations are deviant. Depression is linked to psychological suffering.

Is the diagnosis of insanity based on characteristics of the patients themselves or the context in which the patient is seen? Many distinguished researchers have presented the view that the diagnosis of mental illness is *'useless at best and downright harmful, misleading, and pejorative at worst'* (page 251).

The question of personality versus situation can be investigated by getting 'normal' people (that is people who do not have, and have never had serious psychiatric symptoms) to seek to be admitted to a psychiatric hospital. If such 'pseudopatients' were diagnosed as sane this would show that the sane individual can be distinguished from the insane context in which he is found.

On the other hand, if such pseudopatients were diagnosed as insane then this suggests that it is the context rather than the individual's characteristics that determine the diagnosis, that the psychiatric diagnosis of 'insanity' has less to do with the patient and more about the (insane) environment in which they are found.

Biographical notes on David Rosenhan

David Rosenhan is Emeritus Professor of Law and Psychology at Stanford University, a post he has held since 1970 – thus his interest in the legal definition of abnormality discussed at the start of this core study. Slater (2005) informs us that Rosenhan recruited his pseudopatients by ringing friends up and asking if they were doing anything in October. This included his friend Martin Seligman with whom he wrote one of the classic textbooks for Abnormal Psychology. Slater also reports that he recently has been afflicted by a paralysing condition as yet undiagnosed: *'this renegade researcher, one who devoted the better part of his career to the dismantling of psychiatric diagnosis. Now here he was, a diagnostic question himself.'* (page 65)

Study 1

Aim

To see if sane individuals who presented themselves to a psychiatric hospital would be diagnosed as insane.

Method

Pseudopatients

The 'pseudopatients' were five men and three women of various ages and occupations (graduate student, psychologist, pediatrician, psychiatrist, painter and housewife). They did not give their real names or occupations. Rosenhan was one of the pseudopatients.

Setting

Twelve different hospitals were used which were located in five different states across America. The hospitals represented a range of different kinds of psychiatric institutions – modern and old, well-staffed and poorly staffed. Only one was a private hospital.

Procedure

The pseudopatient called the hospital and asked for an appointment. On arrival (s)he told the admissions officer that (s)he had been hearing voices. When asked what the voices said, the pseudopatient reported that they were often unclear but included the words 'empty', 'hollow', and 'thud' spoken in an unknown voice. These symptoms were chosen because they represented an existential crisis ('My life is empty and hollow, who am I?'), a symptom of schizophrenia not previously reported.

Beyond the description of auditory hallucinations, each pseudopatient stated the facts of their lives as they actually were. None of their life histories were pathological (i.e. abnormal) in any way.

Pseudopatients admitted to the psychiatric ward ceased to show any symptoms of abnormality. There was some nervousness because of the shock of being admitted so easily, and also because they were afraid of being detected as a fraud, and afraid of being on a psychiatric ward.

The pseudopatients secretly did not take their medication but otherwise followed the ward routine. They spent their time making notes about their environment. The reports from the nurses showed that the patients were friendly, cooperative and 'exhibited no abnormal indications'.

They did not know when they would be discharged, as one of the conditions of taking part in the study was that they would have to get out by their own devices.

Results

All pseudopatients were admitted and, bar one, diagnosed as schizophrenic; each was eventually discharged with a diagnosis of schizophrenia 'in remission'. This diagnosis shows the 'stickiness' of the label – once a schizophrenic always a schizophrenic albeit in remission (i.e. symptoms not present at the moment).

Length of hospitalisation varied from 7 to 52 days, with an average of 19 days.

Explanation

The failure to detect the pseudopatients' sanity cannot be due to:

- The quality of the hospitals (several were considered to be excellent).

- The time available to observe them (they were in hospital for a reasonable time).

- Their behaviour, which was sane (many of the real patients recognised this, saying 'You're not crazy. You're a journalist or a professor.').

The failure to detect sanity may be because doctors have a strong bias towards the 'type 2 error' – they are more inclined to call a healthy person sick (a false positive, type 2 error) than a sick person healthy (a false negative, type 1 error). It is clearly more dangerous to misdiagnose illness than health, and err on the side of caution.

However, what holds for medicine may not hold for psychiatry, especially because psychiatric diagnoses carry personal, legal and social stigmas.

Study 2

Aim

To see if the tendency toward diagnosing the sane as insane could be reversed.

Method

The staff in one psychiatric hospital were informed of the results of the first study (which they found hard to believe) and told that at some time during the next three months, one or more pseudo-patients would try to be admitted to the hospital. Each member of staff was asked to rate all patients who sought admission using a 10-point scale where 1 reflected high confidence that the patient was a pseudopatient.

Results

Over the three months 193 patients were admitted for treatment. None of them were actually pseudo-patients but:

- 41 were judged to be pseudopatients by at least one staff member.

- 23 were suspected by at least one psychiatrist.

- 19 were suspected by a psychiatrist and one other staff member.

Explanation

The hospital staff were now making more type 1 errors (calling a sick person healthy) because they were trying to avoid making type 2 errors. *'One thing is certain: any diagnostic process that lends itself so readily to massive errors cannot be a very reliable one'* (page 252).

Qs

1 What hypothesis was Rosenhan testing?

2 What was demonstrated in studies 1 and 2?

3 Explain the term 'schizophrenia in remission' in your own words.

4 Doctors prefer to err on the side of caution. Rosenhan gave the example that it is better to call a healthy person sick – but some people might think it was more cautious to call a sick person healthy. Which view do you prefer and why?

5 Rosenhan points out that it may be OK to make a type 2 error when diagnosing physical illness but the same is not true for mental illness. Why?

6 Explain whether you would have volunteered to be a pseudopatient. Why or why not?

More results

Stickiness of psychodiagnostic labels

The results show the profound effect of a 'label' on our perceptions of people. Many studies in psychology have demonstrated the same thing. For example, Asch (1946) showed that central personality traits (such as 'warm' and 'cold') have a powerful effect on how we perceive someone's total personality. In the same way, once a person is labelled 'abnormal', this means that all subsequent data about them are interpreted in that light. For example, one pseudopatient who described a warm relationship with his mother but distant one with his father, and good relationships with his wife and children apart from occasional angry exchanges was described by a psychiatrist:

'39-year-old male ... manifests a long history of considerable ambivalence in close relationships, which begins in early childhood ... Affective stability is absent. His attempts to control emotionality with his wife and children are punctuated by angry outbursts ... And while he says he has several good friends, one senses considerable ambivalence ...' (page 253).

In another example a psychiatrist suggested that a group of patients sitting outside the cafeteria before lunch were exhibiting the oral-acquisitive nature of their illness – in reality they didn't have much else to do except turn up for lunch early.

Labels are self-fulfilling for psychiatrists and for the patients themselves. There is a considerable overlap between sane and insane – the sane are not 'sane' all of the time, nor are the insane insane all of the time. It makes no sense to label oneself permanently depressed on the basis of occasional depression. It seems more useful to focus on behaviours.

The experience of psychiatric hospitalisation

The term 'mental illness' is of recent origin. It was coined to promote more humane behaviour towards those who were psychologically disturbed; instead of diagnosing such individuals as witches they were seen to be suffering from a physical illness. However, it is doubtful that people really regard mental illness in the same way as they regard physical illness. You can recover from a broken leg but not from schizophrenia (you remain 'in remission').

The mentally ill are society's lepers. That such attitudes are held by the general population is not surprising; what is surprising is that the professionals (nurses, doctors, psychologists, social workers) hold similar attitudes. Or perhaps it is not surprising given the very limited contact between staff and patients that was observed in this study. For example, the average amount of time that attendants spent 'out of the cage' (the glassed quarters where professional staff had their offices) was 11.3% of their total time at work and much of this was spent on chores rather than mingling with patients. Psychiatrists were rarely seen on the wards.

Powerlessness and depersonalisation

The staff treated the patients with little respect: punishing them for small incidents, beating them and swearing at them. Such treatment is depersonalising and creates an overwhelming sense of powerlessness, further exacerbated by the living conditions in a psychiatric hospital: minimal personal privacy (e.g. no doors on toilets) and lack of confidentiality (their records were open for anyone to see).

Conclusion

How many people, one wonders, are sane but not recognised as such in our psychiatric institutions? Once hospitalised the patient is socialised by the bizarre setting, a process Goffman (1961) called 'mortification'.

One solution might be to use other approaches to the treatment of mental illness: community mental health facilities to avoid the effects of the institutional setting, or to use behaviour therapies which avoid psychiatric labels.

A second solution is to increase the sensitivity of mental health workers and recognise that their behaviour is also controlled by the situation.

Study 3

Aim

To investigate patient–staff contact.

Method

In four of the hospitals pseudopatients approached a staff member with the following question 'Pardon me, Mr/Mrs/Dr X, could you tell me when I will be eligible for grounds privileges?' (or '... when will I be presented at the staff meeting?' or '... when am I likely to be discharged?'). The pseudopatient did this as normally as possible and avoided asking any particular person more than once in a day.

Results and conclusion

The most common response was a brief reply as the member of staff continued without pausing and making no eye contact. Only 4% of the psychiatrists and 0.5% of the nurses stopped; 2% in each group paused and chatted.

In contrast, as a control, a young lady approached staff members on the Stanford University campus, and asked them six questions. All of the staff members stopped and answered all questions, maintaining eye contact.

The avoidance of contact between staff and patients serves to depersonalise the patients.

Qs

1 In what way is the label 'schizophrenia' a 'central trait'?

2 How did one psychiatrist interpret a pseudopatient's report that he had occasional fights with his wife?

3 Rosenhan suggests that some mental health professionals have negative attitudes towards the mentally ill. Identify **two** pieces of evidence for this view.

EVALUATING THE STUDY BY ROSENHAN

The research method

The studies were controlled participant observations. (It was not an experiment even though various IVs were tested, as there were no alternate IVs tested.) However, study 3 was a field experiment. *What are the strengths and limitations of these research methods in the context of this study?*

The sample

There were two samples: pseudopatients and hospitals. *In what way are the samples unique? How does this affect the conclusions drawn from the study?*

Quantitative or qualitative?

Give examples of each kind of data. What are the strengths and limitations of each kind of data in the context of this study?

Ethical issues

What ethical issues should have concerned the researchers in this study, and how might they have dealt with these issues?

Personality versus situation

What does this study tell us about the relative effects of personality and situation on behaviour?

Ecological validity

To what extent can we generalise the findings from this study to everyday situations?

Applications/usefulness

How valuable was this study?

DEBATE

'There is nothing to be gained by a diagnosis of schizophrenia.'

Divide your class into groups and prepare a case for the prosecution or defence and then conduct a class debate. Whichever view you support, make sure you are also prepared to answer the claims of the opposition.

What next?

*Describe **one** change to this study, and say how you think this might affect the outcome.*

Multiple choice questions

1. Which of the following symptoms of schizophrenia did the pseudopatients describe?
   (a) Having visual hallucinations.
   (b) Being controlled by outside forces.
   (c) Hearing voices.
   (d) Having two minds.

2. How many patients were admitted with a diagnosis of schizophrenia?
   (a) 8   (b) 7
   (c) 6   (d) 5

3. The mean number of days the pseudopatients spent in hospital was:
   (a) 7   (b) 12
   (c) 19   (d) 26

4. A type 2 error is calling a:
   (a) Healthy person sick.
   (b) Healthy person healthy.
   (c) Sick person sick.
   (d) Sick person healthy.

5. The pseudopatients were discharged with a diagnosis of:
   (a) Schizophrenia in reverse.
   (b) Lapsed schizophrenia.
   (c) Schizophrenia existential.
   (d) Schizophrenia in remission.

6. In the second study, how many real patients were

wrongly identified as pseudopatients by at least one psychiatrist?
   (a) 19   (b) 23
   (c) 41   (d) 63

7. When the pseudopatients approached a staff member with a question, the psychiatrists stopped and answered the question:
   (a) 0.5% of the time. (b) 1.5% of the time.
   (c) 2% of the time. (d) 4% of the time.

8. Who recognised that the pseudopatients were not real patients?
   (a) Some nurses. (b) Some doctors.
   (c) Some patients. (d) All of the above.

9. Which of the following is *not* true about the label 'schizophrenic'?
   (a) It creates expectations.
   (b) It is 'sticky'.
   (c) It may not be accurate.
   (d) It is Russian.

10. Behaviour therapies might be preferable to hospitalisation because:
   (a) They don't involve labels.
   (b) The patient is not viewed as normal or abnormal.
   (c) They focus on behaviours.
   (d) All of the above.

Answers are on page 205.

Exam questions

1. Rosenhan in his study on 'being sane in insane places' refers to 'type 1' errors as calling a sick person healthy and 'type 2' errors as calling a healthy person sick.

   (a) Suggest why health professionals made type 2 errors in their diagnosis of the pseudopatients in the first experiment. [2]

   (b) Describe how the health professionals made type 1 errors in the second experiment. [2]
   [OCR AS Psy, May 2005, paper 1]

2. From the study by Rosenhan:

   (a) Identify **two** behaviours displayed by the pseudopatients which were labelled as abnormal by the hospital staff. [2]

   (b) Outline **one** reason why it is difficult to define abnormality and normality. [2]
   [OCR AS Psy, Jan 2005, paper 1]

3. (a) Give **two** examples of powerlessness and depersonalisation experienced by the pseudopatients in Rosenhan's study (sane in insane places). [2]

   (b) Outline **one** possible explanation for the behaviour of staff in this study. [2]
   [OCR AS Psy, Jan 2002, paper 1]

4. (a) In his study 'On being sane in insane places' what does Rosenhan mean when he writes about 'the stickiness of psychodiagnostic labels'? [2]

   (b) Give **one** example of how the label 'schizophrenic' affected how hospital staff interpreted the pseudopatient's behaviour. [2]
   [OCR AS Psy, June 2001, paper 1]

Reaction to Rosenhan's study

Rosenhan's article created a major storm when it was published. On the one hand there was a barrage of criticism about psychiatrists and their diagnoses; on the other hand the psychiatric profession fought back against Rosenhan, arguing that since psychiatric diagnosis mainly relies on self-reports from patients, the study no more demonstrates problems with psychiatric diagnosis than lying about other medical symptoms. Psychiatrist Robert Spitzer (1975) claimed:

'If I were to drink a quart of blood and, concealing what I had done, come to the emergency room of any hospital vomiting blood, the behaviour of the staff would be quite predictable. If they labelled and treated me as having a peptic ulcer, I doubt I could argue convincingly that medical science does not know how to diagnose that condition.'

Spitzer had a key role in the development of the DSM (below) and hence increased the number of people defined as mentally disordered.

Making us crazy

One of the biggest controversies about psychiatric diagnosis is whether disorders are real. The current version of the Diagnostic and Statistical Manual (DSM) *runs to 900 pages, describing more than 300 mental disorders. The DSM defines many sorts of behaviour as mental disorders, some of which do not seem to deserve the label. For example, you or I might call Oppositional Defiant Disorder 'awkwardness'.*

A diagnosis can be worth a lot of money: it may enable a patient to sue an employer for causing illness; it allows the pharmaceutical industry to produce medication for each one. You might not be surprised that some of the main funders of DSM development are pharmaceutical companies. The world thinks it is going mad because the drug companies tell it so, and psychologists collude in this nonsense because it is good for our business as well (Kutchins and Kirk, 1997).

Madness at the movies

For most people their only direct observation of people with serious mental disturbance is at the movies. Sometimes these films can give us a meaningful insight into these altered mental states and films like *The Madness of King George* and *A Beautiful Mind* show the pain in a compassionate way. Other films play on our stereotypes of madness to make great drama. The classic *Psycho* taps into our fears of madness to create one of the most iconic horror films. The risk of violence from people with mental disorders is, however, very low, but many people derive their fears from fictional stories.

One flew over the cuckoo's nest

Ken Kesey's 1962 cult book of life in a mental hospital in the USA was turned into a film in 1975 starring Jack Nicholson. The film was awarded all five major Oscars and has recently been cited as 'culturally significant' by the US Library of Congress. In the film, Randle P. McMurphy, a serial petty criminal who has been sentenced to a fairly short prison term decides to have himself declared insane so he'll be transferred to a mental institution which he thinks will be more comfortable than prison. In the asylum McMurphy's ward is run by the tyrannical Nurse Ratched, who has crushed the patients into submission.

Jack Nicholson as McMurphy

As McMurphy takes on Nurse Ratched in a series of power games he becomes a hero to the patients and starts to empower them. All the time the viewer is challenged to question just how sane or insane the inmates are.

McMurphy destabilises the culture of the asylum and he is eventually pacified by a lobotomy after he responds violently to one of Nurse Ratched's psychological power games.

The myth of mental illness

What is the difference between a medical and mental disorder? We go to see medical doctors for both conditions and they use similar treatments (e.g. drugs) but is this the best approach? In his critique of the medical model Thomas Szasz (1960) raised some general points about the problems of diagnosis and the view we have of mental disorders. He argued they are not the same as physical illnesses.

Szasz suggests that the idea of mental *illness* is used to obscure the difficulties we have in everyday living. Not long ago it was witches and devils that were held responsible for problems in social living. The belief in mental illness is no more sophisticated than a belief in demonology. Mental illness, according to Szasz, is 'real' in exactly the same way as witches were 'real'.

LINKS TO OTHER STUDIES

This study is one of a select group that had a dramatic effect on public perceptions and continues to have a lasting influence. Other studies in this text to have such an effect include **Haney, Banks and Zimbardo**, **Milgram** and **Bandura, Ross and Ross**. These studies are all still cited many years after the research was conducted and provide moral stories for the understanding of human behaviour. By looking at unusual (or abnormal) behaviour we gain some clues as to what we mean by normality. Other studies that give us insights about this include **Baron-Cohen, Leslie and Frith** and **Freud**.

keyISSUE

Observation

Observation is the starting point for all research. We observe and try to make sense of our observations. Often we move beyond our observations to make research hypotheses which we test using other methods. Sometimes, however, psychologists use observational techniques to gather the bulk of their data.

In this text the Rosenhan study gathers the bulk of its data from observational techniques and so is commonly referred to as an observational study. The study by Bandura, Ross and Ross also uses observational techniques but the main question of the study is answered using an experimental hypothesis and so this study is commonly referred to as an experiment. If you think people are splitting hairs then you may well be right. It is probably best to think of observation as a technique for gathering data rather than as a research method.

Observing everyday life

John Trinkaus is a giant in observational research. When something annoys him enough he takes the time and trouble to categorise and record it. He has published nearly 100 brief reports of observations of everyday life. For example, one study in 1993 looked at the number of shoppers in the express checkout line who had more than the permitted number of items. In his 1990 paper 'Exiting a Building: An Informal Look' he calculated the percentage of people who chose a door that was already open rather than one that was closed. In his 2003 paper 'Snow on Motor Vehicle Roofs: An Informal Look' he calculated the percentage of drivers who don't bother to brush the snow off their cars. For his careful appreciation of the little things in life, Professor Trinkaus was awarded the 2003 IgNobel Prize.

An example of a participant observation

In the 1950s the social psychologist Leon Festinger read a newspaper report about a religious cult that claimed to be receiving messages from outer space predicting that the end of the world would take place on a certain date in the form of a great flood. The cult members were going to be rescued by a flying saucer so they all gathered with their leader, Mrs Keech. Festinger was intrigued to know how the cult members would respond when they found their beliefs were unfounded. In order to observe this at first hand Festinger and some colleagues posed as converts to the cause and were present on the expected eve of destruction. One of those colleagues was Stanley Schachter (see page 92). When it was apparent that there would be no flood, the group initially became disheartened but Mrs Keech announced that she had received a new message from the aliens saying that the group's efforts had saved the day. Although some cult members soon left the cult others took this as proof of the cult's beliefs and became even more enthusiastic evangelists. The question of just how involved the psychologists were, and how much they contributed towards the false beliefs, remains (Festinger et al., 1956).

Advantages of observation	Disadvantages of observation
A means of conducting preliminary investigations in a new area of research, to produce hypotheses for future investigations.	The observer may 'see' what he/she expects to see. This is called observer bias. This bias may mean that different observers 'see' different things, which leads to low inter-observer reliability.
What people say they do is often different from what they actually do so observations can give a different take on behaviour.	If participants don't know they are being observed there are ethical problems such as deception and invasion of privacy. If participants do know they are being observed they may alter their behaviour.
Able to capture spontaneous and unexpected behaviour.	

Multiple personalities

Multiple personality disorder (MPD)

Multiple personality disorder (MPD) is a psychiatric condition characterised by having at least one 'alter' personality that controls behaviour. The 'alters' are said to occur spontaneously and involuntarily, and function more or less independently of each other. In the USA the condition is referred to as Dissociative Identity Disorder (DID).

MPD is defined as the occurrence of two or more personalities within the same individual, each of which is able to take control sometime in the person's life. In the popular imagination it is commonly confused with schizophrenia because of the split personality aspect of it (see page 188). There are very striking differences between the two conditions, most critical of which is the reality testing of the individual. People with schizophrenia commonly have problems testing reality and do not see things in the same way as people without the condition. In everyday speech they are experiencing a period of insanity. In the case of multiple personality, none of the personalities have difficulty with reality testing.

The symptoms are:

- The patient has at least two distinct identities or personality states. Each of these has its own, relatively lasting pattern of sensing, thinking about and relating to self and environment.
- At least two of these personalities repeatedly assume control of the patient's behaviour.
- Common forgetfulness cannot explain the patient's extensive inability to remember important personal information.
- This behaviour is not directly caused by substance use or by a general medical condition.

What is the cause of MPD?

It is commonly believed that MPD is a response to extremely traumatic situations from which there is no physical means of escape. The traumatic situations might involve physical or emotional pain or anticipation of that pain. If the person 'goes away in their own head' they can remove themselves from the pain and function as if it had not occurred.

Readers beware

Whenever you come across symptoms, either medical or psychiatric, there is a tendency to think they describe something about you. This is because they do. In this case we all experience some forms of dissociation in our daily lives. We are all a bit different in different situations. You behave in one way with your friends and another way with your parents; believe me, they are grateful for this. (See also the Barnum Effect on page 213.)

The controversy: does MPD exist?

One view suggests that MPD is real and commonly a response to childhood sexual abuse. The other view suggests that MPD is created in the therapist's office by the use of hypnotism and guided imagery. Look at the information here and come to your own opinion though it is only fair to say that we (the authors) remain sceptical about the existence of MPD.

What is dissociation?

Your perception of yourself and your experience of the world depend on a number of factors including feelings, thoughts, memories and sensations. You make sense of these inputs to create your view of reality. If some of these information sources become disconnected then it can change your sense of identity or your perceptions of the world. This is what happens in dissociation.

Dissociation is common enough in everyday life. Maybe you are driving somewhere on a familiar route and when you arrive at your destination you realise you can't recall the entire journey. It is almost as if you went into automatic pilot mode. Or maybe you have to give a talk or a performance to a large group of people. You are nervous about it but you keep control of yourself and almost watch yourself doing the performance as if you are in the audience. It almost feels as if someone else is doing it. 'Is that really me?' you ask yourself. In this way we can use dissociation to help us deal with stressful events. Dissociation is also sometimes experienced as a side effect of drugs or alcohol.

Types of dissociation

Amnesia: A loss of memories of specific events or experiences, or sometimes not remembering personal information.

Depersonalisation: This can include out-of-body experiences like seeing yourself as part of a movie, or feeling that your body is not real.

Identity confusion: A sense of uncertainty about who you are and maybe a struggle inside to define who you are.

Iraqis carry the body of a man in a Baghdad street following airstrikes. People in extreme situations like war zones often experience dissociation. It is seen as a symptom of post traumatic stress disorder which is a diagnosis that was invented to describe the experience of US veterans of the war in Vietnam.

Dissociation as a response to trauma

The following survivor account of the July 2005 bombs in London was reported in *The Observer* and shows how one person used dissociation to deal with the initial crisis. She experiences the event as surreal and like a movie.

'It was about three minutes after we left King's Cross when there was a massive bang and there was smoke and glass everywhere. The lights went out, and with the smoke, we couldn't breathe. We sort of cushioned each other during the impact because the compartment was so full. It felt like a dream, it was surreal. The screaming from the front carriage was terrible. It was just horrendous, it was like a disaster movie, you can't imagine being somewhere like that. You just want to get out. I kept closing my eyes and thinking of outside.'

[http://www.guardian.co.uk/attack onlondon/story/0,,1525460,00. html]

Altered states and popular delusions

Mesmerism

In the eighteenth century Viennese doctor and showman Anton Mesmer developed a technique that eventually took his name – mesmerism. Mesmer discovered that if he could create the right atmosphere he could influence the behaviour of suggestible people. In a theatrical performance he would wear brightly coloured clothes and move around people, waving a magnetised stick and playing the part of a healer. He was able to induce people to dance or fall asleep. The act was similar to the modern day stage hypnotist and circus tent evangelist. With royal patronage from Louis XVI, Mesmer set up a Magnetic Institute but he was eventually found out and exposed as a fraud.

A caricature of Mesmer's animal magnetism

Hypnosis

'When using hypnosis, one person (the subject) is guided by another (the hypnotist) to respond to suggestions for changes in subjective experience, alterations in perception, sensation, emotion, thought or behaviour' (APA, 2005).

Hypnosis commonly involves (a) intense concentration, (b) extreme relaxation, and (c) high suggestibility. It is a versatile phenomenon and can be used for entertainment, personal development and therapy. The patients of hypnotherapists are usually people looking for such things as pain relief or a way of giving up smoking. More controversially, some therapists use hypnosis to recover repressed memories of sexual abuse or memories of past lives. Freud started the work into repressed memories (see page 70) and he initially used hypnosis, though wisely moved away from it quite quickly.

Altered states?

Hypnosis is commonly believed to be a trance-like altered state of consciousness. This view sees hypnosis as a route to hidden parts of the mind. An alternative and more plausible view sees hypnosis as a response to social demands where people who are especially suggestible respond to cues from the hypnotist (Wagstaff, 1981). In other words, hypnosis is an extreme example of social conformity where the person behaves as they think they are expected to. Connections are made between hypnotism and mesmerism, and also with a belief in demonic possession and exorcism.

Another popular delusion is that we can contact the dead by joining hands and wearing gothic clothes.

Demonic possession

There are different ways of explaining similar phenomena. The idea of demonic possession sees the victim as having other entities, in this case demons, inside them. The way to remove the demons is through exorcism. This has been carried out in ceremonies such as those caricatured in movies such as *The Exorcist* and more commonly in the USA today at mass religious meetings where the preacher will cast out demons in a dramatic show. Maybe the phenomenon of multiple personality is a different way of explaining a similar experience.

Postscript: people who don't believe in hypnotism can't be hypnotised.

Repressed memory therapy (RMT)

The assumption behind RMT is that psychological problems such as eating disorders, depression and extreme anxiety are caused by repressed memories. Repressed memories are not in conscious awareness and cannot be recalled without help from a therapist, but is the therapist helping the patient recall something they have forgotten or are they helping them to invent a memory? The repressed memories are commonly of shocking childhood experiences such as sexual abuse. RMT therapists believe that psychological health can only be restored by recalling and dealing with the repressed memories.

RMT is so controversial that in the UK The Royal College of Psychiatrists has banned members from using therapies designed to recover repressed memories of childhood abuse. In the USA a report for The American Psychological Association in 1996 noted that *'there is a consensus among memory researchers and clinicians that most people who were sexually abused as children remember all or part of what happened to them although they may not fully understand or disclose it. At this point it is impossible, without other corroborative evidence, to distinguish a true memory from a false one.'*
[http://www.apa.org/pubinfo/mem.html]

References to multiple personality go back a long way and appear in The Bible, for example in the Gospel of St Mark 5: 8–10: 'He ... said to him, "Come out of the man, you unclean spirit!" And Jesus asked him, "What is your name?" He replied, "My name is Legion; for we are many." And he begged him not to send them out ....'

The core study

We take it for granted that we have one personality that is relatively consistent and predictable. We ask someone 'How are you today?' and not 'Who are you today?'. The revelation of this study was that, for at least one person, this second question was more appropriate. The therapists described an unusual phenomenon and set a pattern for how we would describe this type of experience. They were also at the beginning of the celebrity psychiatrist circus where psychological problems and even individual cases are given a public airing not only for information but also for entertainment. Read the study and decide for yourself whether MPD is real or a creation of therapists.

THIGPEN AND CLECKLEY : MULTIPLE PERSONALITY DISORDER

Corbett H. Thigpen and Hervey Cleckley (1954) A case of multiple personality.
Journal of Abnormal and Social Psychology, 49, 135–151.

Abstract

Eve White (EW) was referred to a psychiatrist, Dr Thigpen, because she experienced severe headaches and blackouts that had no physical cause. Therapy revealed some fairly unexceptional emotional problems.

The ordinariness of this case changed when the therapist received a letter from EW, with some strange handwriting at the bottom. At her next visit a new 'person' emerged – Eve Black (EB), a very different physical presence, flirtatious and confident whereas EW was demure and retiring.

EB was aware of all EW did but the same was not true in reverse. When EB was 'out' she often behaved mischievously and would leave EW to be punished. This explained events in EW's past where she could not account for things she did. This was substantiated by her husband and parents.

Psychometric and projective personality tests were used to show a difference between the two Eves. EW had a higher IQ and memory function but EB was psychologically healthier – regressed rather than repressed. In some ways they were one personality at two stages of life. EB's role was to embody all the angry feelings thus enabling EW to maintain a nice, loving persona.

After eight months of therapy a third personality, Jane, emerged, who was superficially a compromise between EW and EB. An EEG showed that EB was different to EW and Jane. The solution lay in some integration of the three personalities but the therapists recognised that it would be morally wrong for them to 'kill off' any one personality.

The film The Three Faces of Eve *staring Joanne Woodward (who won an Oscar for her performance of Eve) was based on a book of the same name by Thigpen and Cleckley, both released in 1957.*

CORESTUDY

Introduction

Multiple personality disorder was reasonably well known in the 1950s, based on a few detailed case histories which were viewed with some suspicion.

The patients

Eve White

Dr Thigpen had treated a 25-year-old married woman for several months, called 'Eve White' for the purposes of this article. Eve White (EW) was referred to the psychiatrist because of 'severe and blinding headaches', and said that 'blackouts' often followed the headaches. During early interviews EW discussed her emotional difficulties and personal conflicts. Thigpen regarded the case as relatively normal but was puzzled by a recent trip for which she had no memory. Hypnotism enabled them to clear up this amnesia.

Several days later a letter was received. The letter was unsigned but clearly from EW because of the handwriting. The final paragraph was puzzling. Had EW inserted this paragraph as a prank? It was hard to imagine the *'matter-of-fact … meticulously truthful and consistently sober'* EW becoming playful. She denied sending the letter at her next visit though she remembered starting such a letter. At this time she started to become rather agitated and asked if hearing voices was a sign of insanity. At that moment a strange look came over her face and she put her hands to her head as if seized by a sudden pain. After a tense moment of silence, her hands dropped and with a quick smile and bright voice said *'Hi there, Doc!'*.

The appearance of Eve Black

EW was transformed from a retiring and conventional figure, lacking attractiveness, into a novel feminine apparition.

'The newcomer [had] a childishly daredevil air, an erotically mischievous glance, a face marvellously free from the habitual signs of care, seriousness and underlying distress, so long familiar in her predecessor. This new and apparently carefree girl spoke casually of Eve White and her problems, always using "she" or "her" in every reference, always respecting the strict bounds of separate identity. When asked her own name she immediately replied, "Oh, I'm Eve Black"' (page 137).

Biographical notes on Corbett Thigpen and Hervey Cleckley

Both men and their patient were from Augusta, Georgia in the southern USA. Dr Cleckley was chief of psychiatry and neurology at University Hospital of Georgia. His book, *The Mask of Sanity*, can be read http://www.cassiopaea.com/cassiopaea/psychopath.htm

Dr Thigpen retired as a clinical professor of psychiatry at the Medical College of Georgia in 1987. He treated Margaret Mitchell, the author of *Gone with the Wind* (another Georgian), in hospital and became a close friend. He was a life-long amateur magician, but this case was probably his best 'trick'.

Thumbnail sketches

Eve White

Demure, retiring, in some respects almost 'saintly', face often looks sad, reads and composes poetry, steadfast, lacking boldness, spontaneity and initiative, industrious worker, competent housekeeper, not self-righteous but seldom playful or joking, voice softly modulated, dresses in a simple way, devoted to her daughter.

Eve Black

Party girl, childishly vain, egocentric, enjoys taunting and mocking, does things 'on a whim', immediately amusing and likeable, voice a little 'coarse', uses slang, dresses a little provocatively, posture and gait light-hearted, developed a skin rash when wearing nylon stockings, could never be hypnotised.

Case study

Thigpen and Cleckley spent the next 14 months (approximately 100 hours) interviewing Eve White (EW) and Eve Black (EB), collecting material about their behaviour and inner lives.

Initially, in order to interview EB, EW had to be hypnotised. Soon it became possible to simply ask to speak to EB and she would come forth. This complicated EW's life because it meant that EB was able to pop out more easily at other times too.

Eve Black's life history

It appeared that EB had enjoyed an independent life since EW's early childhood. EW had no knowledge of her existence until some time after EB emerged unbidden in the psychiatrists' office. When EB was 'out' EW was completely oblivious of what EB did and was apparently unconscious. In contrast EB had some awareness of what EW did when EB was not out. She could report what the other did and thought but didn't participate in these thoughts and actions. EB regarded EW's distress about her failing marriage as silly. EB was not cruel but like a *'bright-feathered parakeet who chirps undisturbed while watching a child strangle to death'* (page 138).

EB claimed that during childhood she often emerged to play pranks, though she also lied easily so that it was difficult to take her account as reliable evidence. However, EW provided indirect support for EB's reports because she could remember punishments and accusations for things she didn't know she had done but which were described by EB. EW's parents and husband also confirmed EB's stories. For example, EW was punished when, aged six, she wandered off through the woods to play with some other children. Her denials were not believed at the time and she was severely punished. EB had separately reported this incident, saying that she enjoyed the adventure and enjoyed being able to withdraw and leave EW to be punished.

Another incident was reported by EW's husband who lost his temper with EW when he found she'd spent a lot of money on new clothes and hidden them away. EB confessed to being the culprit in this shopping spree.

EB denied any association with EW's child or the husband, whom she despised. She had never made herself known to them nor EW's parents. There would be no reason for them to suspect that EW was really two people and, in any case, EB was able to pass herself off as EW, imitating her tone of voice and gestures. However EW's parents were aware of unexplained changes in her, which they described as her 'strange little habits'.

Therapy

It was difficult to proceed with the therapy because EB was unwilling be involved. However a bargain was struck where she would be allowed more time 'out' if she cooperated more and avoided serious misbehaviour – otherwise the psychiatrists suggested they would limit the extent to which EB was 'allowed out'.

EB reported that she had caused the severe headaches and imaginary voices. She also claimed to be able to wipe EW's memory if she thought very hard about it. One example of this was a report (from a distant relative) that a previous marriage had occurred. EB eventually confessed that when EW was working away from home for a while EB had gone to a dance and ended up marrying a man she scarcely knew. She lived with this man for several months though EW had no recollection of this.

The aim of therapy was to achieve reintegration of the two personalities. They tried to call out both personalities at once but EW experienced a violent headache and became very distressed; EB tried once and said it gave her *'such a funny, queer, mixed-up feeling that I ain't gonna put up with it no more'* (page 122).

During the course of therapy EW decided to leave her husband and, at that time, her daughter went to live with EW's parents. The headaches, blackouts and voices disappeared and she managed to do well at her job and achieve some stability. EB had been causing less trouble and seldom 'came out', though she did occasionally go on dates with 'bad company'. Fortunately EW was spared the knowledge of this.

Psychological tests

Psychological tests were conducted on the two Eves by a clinical psychologist, who reported that the basic behaviour pattern was similar in both personalities.

	EW	EB
Psychometric tests:		
IQ test	110	104
Memory scale	Above IQ.	On a par with her IQ.
Projective personality tests: Rorschach test and drawings of human figures	Rigid and not capable of dealing with her hostility. Conflict in role as wife and mother, resulting in anxiety. Result indicates **repression**.	Able to conform to the environment; a healthier profile than EW. Result indicates **regression** – a wish to return to an earlier period of life.

The projective tests (see page 171) suggested that the existence of dual personalities was due to a wish to return to an earlier stage of life (EB in fact used EW's maiden name). EW's hostility towards her roles as wife and mother made her feel guilty which activated the defence mechanism of repression, removing the conflict from her conscious awareness. Playing the role of EB permits her to discharge her feelings of hostility towards EW and others. The problem started earlier in life. EW felt rejected by her parents when her twin sisters were born; EW loved them dearly, EB despised them. In a sense EB's role was to embody all the angry feelings thus enabling EW to maintain a nice, loving persona.

Qs

1 Describe **one** example of something EB did which got EW into trouble.

2 How did Thigpen and Cleckley test EB's claim that she could erase items from EW's memory?

3 What are psychometric and projective tests?

4 Describe what you think may have caused EW's problem.

Eight months into therapy

After eight months the situation changed for the worse again. EW's headaches and blackouts returned. EB was questioned but denied any part in this new development and said she too was experiencing blackouts. During one session of hypnosis EW stopped talking, her eyes shut and her head dropped. After a silence of two minutes, she blinked, looked around the room as if to work out where she was and, in a husky poised voice, said to the therapist 'Who are you?'. It was immediately apparent that this was neither EW nor EB. This new person, Jane, was more mature and bold than EW but not difficult like EB. In a superficial way she could be described as a compromise between the two Eves.

EEG test

A study was done of the brain waves of the three patients using an electroencephalogram (EEG). Tenseness was most pronounced in EB, next EW and then Jane. EW and Jane had a fairly similar alpha rhythm whereas EB's was a little bit faster. This difference was significant. Slightly fast records are sometimes associated with psychopathic personality (i.e. a personality disorder characterised by a lack of social conscience). There was also evidence of restlessness and generalised muscle tension in EB's tracings but not in the others.

The three personalities

Jane was aware of everything the other two did but could not fully access their memories prior to her emergence. Jane was able to report when EB was lying. She felt free from EW's responsibilities and didn't identify with her role as wife and mother, though she felt compassion towards the child. Jane gradually took over more and more from EW, though she felt she shouldn't come between a distressed mother and her child. Jane only emerged through EW and could not displace EB.

The therapists hoped that Jane might become the fully integrated and healthy personality but they did not wish to 'order euthanasia for the heedlessly merry and amoral but nevertheless unique Eve Black' (page 146). This raises the question of the therapists' responsibility. They believed that they had some choice about which personality to reinforce but ultimately the choice lay with the patient.

Jane showed her compassion for EW in a letter to the therapists: 'Today [EW] did something that made me know and appreciate her as I had not been able to do before. I wish I could tell her what I feel but I can't reach her. She must not die yet... She saved the life of a little boy today. .. she darted out in front of a car to pick him up ... but instead of putting him down again, the moment his baby arms went round her neck, he became her baby – and she continued to walk down the street carrying him in her arms ... There seemed only one solution to prevent her possible arrest for kidnapping. That was for me to come out and find the child's mother' (page 147).

ACTIVITY

Try a role play with two actors – one the therapist, the other the patient who switches between the different personalities.

Discussion

Possible explanations for Eve's behaviour:

- She was a skilful actress, though this seems unlikely because it would be hard to see how she could have maintained this act over such a long period of time.

- It could be that Eve was suffering from a hysterical disorder or schizophrenia, though many of the appropriate symptoms were absent.

- The therapists' observations were not objective.

How does disintegration occur? Identical twins start as one cell but divide at the very outset. The same could be true of a multiple personality. Can it be reintegrated? Jane appeared to be some sort of fusion of the other personalities, not a mere addition of different traits. Like the fusion of hydrogen and oxygen to make water, Jane was a product genuinely different from both ingredients from which it was formed.

What is personality?

In order to understand multiple personality, we need to understand 'personality'. We hear people say things like 'John Doe has become a *new man* since he stopped drinking' or 'a friend was *not himself* the other night' or that 'a woman's absorption in her home resulted in her losing her *entire personality*'. In psychiatry the term implies a unified total. Dictionaries define it as 'individuality', 'personal existence or identity'. Bearing this in mind Thigpen and Cleckley felt it was appropriate to speak of Eve White, Eve Black and Jane as three 'personalities'.

However, the *physical* evidence for this was weak. The differences in EEGs and in psychometric and projective tests were not particularly impressive. A handwriting expert concluded that, even though the handwriting of each personality superficially appeared to be by a different person, they all were clearly written by the same individual.

Final word

Thigpen and Cleckley finished their article with a plea for psychiatry to avoid explanations which offer little real insight. They recognised that they had not been able to propose any new explanation for multiple personalities but found the case very thought-provoking and suggest that further research may yield understanding of this disorder.

Q s

1 How do you think the psychiatrists' personal involvement in the case may have affected their ability to report the facts?

2 Suggest **two** pieces of evidence which support the claim that this patient did have MPD.

3 Why did the psychiatrists think that schizophrenia was an unlikely diagnosis?

4 Freud's concepts of id, ego, and superego – which of these goes with each of the three personalities?

EVALUATING THE STUDY BY THIGPEN AND CLECKLEY

(See page x for note on evaluating research studies/articles)

The research method

This was a case study. *What are the strengths and limitations of this research method in the context of this study?*

The research technique

How were the data gathered in this study? List the different techniques and for each give strengths and limitations.

The sample

In what way is the participant in this study unique? How does this affect the conclusions drawn from the study?

Qualitative and quantitative

Give examples of both quantitative and qualitative data from this study. What are the strengths and limitations of each kind of data in the context of this study?

Ethical issues

What ethical issues should have concerned the researchers in this study, and how might they have dealt with these issues?

Nature or nurture?

What evidence is there from this study to support the nature or nurture side of the debate?

Applications/usefulness

How valuable was this study?

WWW You might look at various websites to collect evidence about the nature of MPD or dissociative identity disorder (DID) e.g. www.dissociation.com

DEBATE

Was Eve suffering from multiple personality disorder? *Or was it something else? After this case Thigpen and Cleckley saw lots more people supposedly with MPD but they felt that almost all the cases were the result of therapists' suggestions. When a disorder is not 'real' but is caused by a therapist planting ideas in a patient's head it is called 'iatrogenic'. Have a look at the next page for some further discussion of this.*

What next? (?)

*Describe **one** change to this study, and say how you think this might affect the outcome.*

Multiple choice questions

1. Which of the following was *not* one of Eve White's symptoms?
   (a) Hearing voices.
   (b) Headaches.
   (c) Trouble sleeping.
   (d) Blackouts.

2. Approximately how many hours were spent interviewing the patients?
   (a) 100
   (b) 120
   (c) 150
   (d) 200

3. Which of the following is true?
   (a) EB had access to EW's memories.
   (b) EW had access to EB's memories.
   (c) Neither (a) nor (b).
   (d) Both (a) and (b).

4. Eve Black was described as:
   (a) Reversed.
   (b) Repressive.
   (c) Regressive.
   (d) Reintegrated.

5. Which of the following is a projective personality test?
   (a) Wechsler–Bellevue.
   (b) Rorschach.
   (c) Cattell.
   (d) Snoopy Scale.

6. What score did Eve White get on the IQ test?
   (a) 102   (b) 104
   (c) 106   (d) 110

7. Who was Jane most similar to?
   (a) EB.
   (b) EW.
   (c) Neither EB or EW.
   (d) Tarzan.

8. The EEG test showed that the alpha rhythms were similar in:
   (a) EW and Jane.
   (b) EW and EB.
   (c) EB and Jane.
   (d) EW, EB and Jane.

9. Why is it unlikely that the patients were simply acting?
   (a) They said they couldn't act.
   (b) The therapy took place over a long period of time.
   (c) They didn't change their story when hypnotised.
   (d) All of the above.

10. What other diagnosis, aside from multiple personality disorder, might have been possible?
    (a) Schizophrenia.
    (b) Split personality.
    (c) Depression.
    (d) Obsessive-compulsive disorder.

Answers are on page 205.

Exam questions

1. (a) Identify **two** psychological tests that were carried out on Eve White and Eve Black in the case study of multiple personality disorder by Thigpen and Cleckley. [2]

   (b) Outline the findings of **one** of these tests. [2]
   [OCR AS Psy, May 2003, paper 1]

2. Explain **one** problem with using the evidence from the study by Thigpen and Cleckley to support the diagnosis that Eve had multiple personality disorder. [OCR AS Psy, Jan 2005, paper 1] [2]

3. The Thigpen and Cleckley study looks at the controversial diagnosis of 'multiple personality'. It is controversial because some people do not believe there is such a condition as 'multiple personality'. Suggest **two** pieces of evidence from the case study that suggest that the patient really did have a multiple personality. [OCR AS Psy, specimen paper] [4]

4. In the study by Thigpen and Cleckley on multiple personality the therapist described the first time he encountered Eve Black. He described how she crossed her legs and the 'therapist noted from the corner of his awareness something distinctly attractive about them and also this was the first time he had received such an impression'.

   (a) How does the therapist interpret this observation? [2]

   (b) Give **one** other interpretation of this observation. [2]
   [OCR AS Psy, June 2000, paper 1]

The real Eve

Christine Sizemore (Eve's real name) always wanted to tell her own story. She was discouraged from doing this by Thigpen because of the possible harm it would do her if she revealed herself to the world. A less charitable interpretation would be that he was also protecting his control over the story. According to Sizemore she agreed to Thigpen and Cleckley preparing academic reports about her for discussion in scientific seminars, but she was not aware they were writing a book for publication to the general public. She was also not aware that Thigpen filmed some of the filmed therapy sessions. The resulting film *Case Study in Multiple Personality* was made available from his university library. When she found about this, after 20 years, she took legal action to ban its use.

The battle for control of her story was lost before it started as Thigpen and Cleckley published their book and then sold the rights to Hollywood. When *The Three Faces of Eve*, starring Joanne Woodward, was premiered, Thigpen and Cleckley were

the stars of the event, but Sizemore was advised to leave town to avoid distress and not to see the film. Joanne Woodward got an Oscar for playing Chris Sizemore, who got nothing, not even any recognition of her existence. The book and the film told of a successful therapy and a happy ending, but this bore little relationship to the truth. Some time later when she tried to write her own account she discovered that Thigpen claimed to have a document signed by her giving him full rights over her story. In an ironic twist, Christine Sizemore's identity and life story had been taken over by her psychiatrists.

Eventually in 1977 she collaborated with her cousin Elen Pitillo to reveal her identity(ies) to the world with the book *I'm Eve*. This text tells a very different story to that told by Thigpen and Cleckley, a story which starts much earlier in her life, has many more identities and goes on much longer. By the time the book was published she describes herself as being adjusted to her problems and able to live a full and rewarding life.

Sybil

Bennett Braun was a leading researcher and therapist in MPD in the USA. In 1980 Braun helped establish an MPD facility at the hospital he worked at and by 1984 he was president of the International Society for the Study of Multiple Personality and Dissociation. Within 20 years he had been expelled from the American Psychiatric Association and can no longer treat anyone for MPD, the condition for which he was considered an expert. How did it get to this?

The best way to answer this is to look at just one of his patients, Patricia Burgus. After a difficult birth of her second child in 1982, Burgus began to experience depression and received conventional therapy. After a while she came in contact with Braun who suggested she and her son should be hospitalised. He suggested that she had MPD and had therefore almost certainly survived some childhood trauma.

In hospital she had a range of therapies including hypnosis and mind altering drugs, sometimes being woken up in the middle of the night to have her treatment. During the

sessions Braun told her about a satanic cult dating back to the seventeenth century, that she had experienced sexual abuse as a child and that she had given birth to several children who had been sacrificed by the cult. Eventually she described herself as a high priestess who ran the affairs of the cult without her husband or her everyday self knowing anything about it. The lack of any corroborating evidence for these activities or pregnancies did not deter the therapist. Other patients started to incorporate Burgus into their stories and her role of high priestess became established in the collective fantasy of the psychiatric facility.

Burgus's condition got worse and she was transferred to a regular psychiatric ward where she was taken off the medication and started to recover. The multiple personalities quickly disappeared and the satanic cult was shown to be a sham. Several lawsuits were brought against Bennett Braun and his colleagues. Patricia Burgus and her family eventually accepted a settlement of $10.6 million.

A cautionary tale of psychiatric treatment

The public view of MPD has been heavily influenced by films such as *The Three Faces of Eve* and *Sybil*. The story of Sybil (Schreiber, 1973) tells of a woman with 16 personalities, created as a response to childhood sexual abuse. Before the publication of the book and the subsequent movie of the same name there were only 75 reported cases of MPD. Since then the diagnosis rate in the USA has gone through the roof as has the number of personalities believed to exist in the patients.

Sybil was eventually identified as Shirley Mason, who died in 1998 at the age of 75. Her therapist was Cornelia Wilbur, who died in 1992. It is now known that Mason had no symptoms of MPD before she began having therapy with Wilbur. The magazine *Newsweek* (January 25, 1999) reported that, according to historian Peter M. Swales (who first identified Mason as Sybil), *'there is strong evidence that [the worst abuse in the book] could not have happened.'*

During her therapy that included hypnosis and mind-altering drugs, Mason read the literature on MPD including the book *The Three Faces of Eve*. It is commonly believed that the case of Sybil is an example of an *iatrogenic* disorder (that is, one caused by the doctor). A different view is put forward by Philip M. Coons who supports the MPD diagnosis and points out that *'the relationship of multiple personality to child abuse was not generally recognised until the publication of Sybil'* (http://www.healthy place.com/communities/personality_ disorders/wermany/reading_room/abuse.htm).

LINKS TO OTHER STUDIES

This study has direct links to **Rosenhan**'s question about how we can distinguish sanity from insanity. It also links with **Sperry**'s account of split-brain surgery. In this work he talks about split consciousness and two people in the same body. There is also a strong link to the work of Elizabeth **Loftus** on memory. She has been prominent in the recovered memory / false memory debate which is central to any evaluation of multiple personality. Finally, there is a link to **Freud** in the use of hypnosis and also the belief in repressed memories of childhood sexual abuse.

keyISSUE

Case studies

KEY TERMS

A case study is a research investigation that involves the detailed study of a single individual, institution or event. It uses information from a range of sources, such as interviews and observations, to obtain data. These findings are then selected and organised, for instance to represent the individual's thoughts and emotions.

Case studies provide some of psychology's best stories. In this text we have looked at a number including the story of Little Hans by Freud who used detailed case studies as the main evidence for his theories, the multiple personalities of Eve described by Thigpen and Cleckley, and the development of language in Washoe recorded by Gardner and Gardner. These case studies give us detailed information on Hans, Eve and Washoe and they provide some unique insights into behaviour and experience. Freud uses the story of Hans to support the existence of the Oedipus complex in boys, and Thigpen and Cleckley used Eve's story to support their view of multiple personality. The study of Washoe provides evidence that animals can use abstract signs to communicate.

All the stories are engaging and have stood the test of time. There is still considerable interest in all of them and they commonly appear in introductory psychology textbooks. Their appeal goes beyond the boundaries of psychology and several case studies have become well known to the general public. There is no doubt that they have contributed to our understanding of ourselves and others but it is also important to look at the scientific value and personal consequences of these studies.

Whose story is it anyway?

One of the issues concerns authorship. If my life story was going be told in a book or a scientific paper then I would like to have some say in it. Apart from anything else it is my story and I ought to be able to tell it. This is the position Eve (Christine Sizemore) was in but her attempts to tell her own story were impeded and discouraged by her therapists who had authored papers and a book about her. And if you were Hans wouldn't you like to contribute to the story? The therapists took control of their patients' life stories and in some cases made money out of it. We don't know about Washoe.

Biography and autobiography

The story I would tell about myself is bound to be different to the stories that other people would tell about me. Autobiographies are very different to biographies; you can see the contrast if you pick up the autobiography of Malcolm X (see page 181) which also contains a biography of him by Alex Haley. This is not to say that we tell lies about ourselves or others but just that seeing a story from the inside is very different to seeing it from afar. Case studies are most commonly biography rather than autobiography and so have that outsider view of the events.

Recovery from early blindness

Richard Gregory read a report in the newspapers of a man (SB) who had been blind since he was an infant and was given his sight at the age of 52. Gregory wondered what someone sees when they open their eyes for the first time and how they learn to make sense of sensations. The case study is available on the internet at the author's website (http://www.richardgregory.org/) and gives a fascinating account of a very rare experience.

Exam-style question

A case study is a detailed investigation of a single individual, institution or event and is usually conducted over a period of time.

Select **one** core study and answer the following questions.

(a) Describe how the data were gathered in your chosen study.   [6]

(b) Briefly discuss **two** strengths and **two** weaknesses of the case study method with examples from your chosen study.   [12]

(c) Suggest **one** other way data could have been gathered for your chosen study and say how you think this might affect the results.   [8]

The ethics of case studies

Some case study participants became part of major scientific debates and there are question marks about whether the welfare of these subjects was sometimes placed behind the drive for research. Consider the cases of HM and Genie, described below.

HM

HM is very famous in psychology and *'...he has probably had more words written about him than any other case in neurological or psychological history'* (Ogden and Corkin, 1991, page 195). HM had a brain operation in 1953 to reduce the number of seizures he was experiencing. A side effect of the procedure was that HM lost 10 years of his memory and also the ability to remember anything new. Time stopped for HM in 1953, and he woke in a Groundhog Day experience every 90 seconds. A tragedy for HM but an opportunity for scientists who used him as a research subject for over 40 years. The issue here is how consent was ever gained from HM as he had no knowledge of where he was or commonly who he was talking to.

Genie

Genie was brought up in terrible conditions for the first 13 years of her life, during which she was continually restrained by her father, often strapped to a chair, and never spoken to. When she was discovered she was unable to speak. She seemed to be an ideal case to use to answer a number of scientific questions about the development of language.

Her subsequent care and exploitation by psychologists is a matter of some dispute (Rymer, 1993). For years she lived with the family of one of the psychologists who was studying her and she was well-cared for. But when the research money ran out, Genie was abandoned back into abusive environments. Genie's mother successfully sued some of the psychologists involved for 'extreme, unreasonable, and outrageously intensive testing, experimentation, and observation'. It is argued that concern for psychological research was placed before compassion for the child. See page 63 for more details of this case study.

Individual differences Core Study 17: Gould (IQ testing)

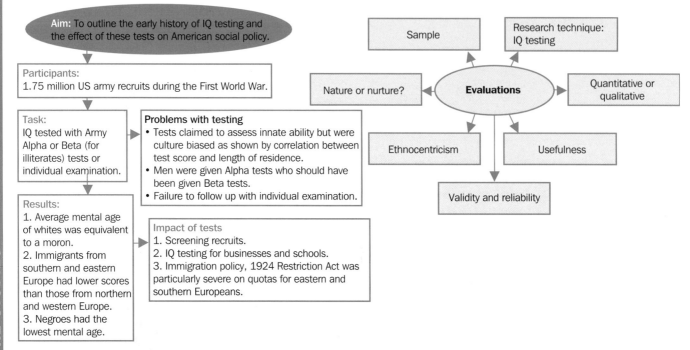

Aim: To outline the early history of IQ testing and the effect of these tests on American social policy.

Participants:
1.75 million US army recruits during the First World War.

Task:
IQ tested with Army Alpha or Beta (for illiterates) tests or individual examination.

Results:
1. Average mental age of whites was equivalent to a moron.
2. Immigrants from southern and eastern Europe had lower scores than those from northern and western Europe.
3. Negroes had the lowest mental age.

Problems with testing
• Tests claimed to assess innate ability but were culture biased as shown by correlation between test score and length of residence.
• Men were given Alpha tests who should have been given Beta tests.
• Failure to follow up with individual examination.

Impact of tests
1. Screening recruits.
2. IQ testing for businesses and schools.
3. Immigration policy, 1924 Restriction Act was particularly severe on quotas for eastern and southern Europeans.

Evaluations
- Sample
- Research technique: IQ testing
- Nature or nurture?
- Quantitative or qualitative
- Ethnocentricism
- Usefulness
- Validity and reliability

Individual differences Core Study 18: Hraba and Grant (doll choice)

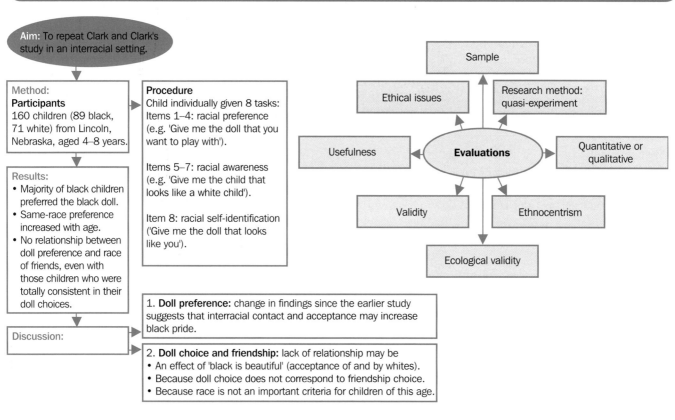

Aim: To repeat Clark and Clark's study in an interracial setting.

Method:
Participants
160 children (89 black, 71 white) from Lincoln, Nebraska, aged 4–8 years.

Results:
• Majority of black children preferred the black doll.
• Same-race preference increased with age.
• No relationship between doll preference and race of friends, even with those children who were totally consistent in their doll choices.

Discussion:

Procedure
Child individually given 8 tasks:
Items 1–4: racial preference (e.g. 'Give me the doll that you want to play with').

Items 5–7: racial awareness (e.g. 'Give me the child that looks like a white child').

Item 8: racial self-identification ('Give me the doll that looks like you').

1. **Doll preference:** change in findings since the earlier study suggests that interracial contact and acceptance may increase black pride.

2. **Doll choice and friendship:** lack of relationship may be
• An effect of 'black is beautiful' (acceptance of and by whites).
• Because doll choice does not correspond to friendship choice.
• Because race is not an important criteria for children of this age.

Evaluations
- Sample
- Ethical issues
- Research method: quasi-experiment
- Usefulness
- Quantitative or qualitative
- Validity
- Ethnocentrism
- Ecological validity

Individual differences Core Study 19: Rosenhan (sane in insane places)

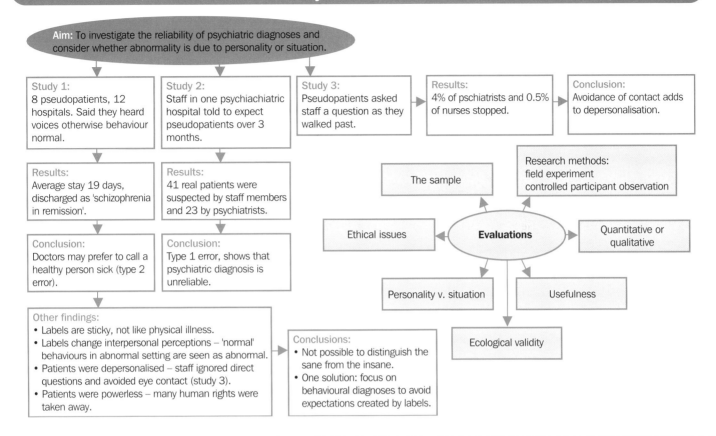

Aim: To investigate the reliability of psychiatric diagnoses and consider whether abnormality is due to personality or situation.

Study 1:
8 pseudopatients, 12 hospitals. Said they heard voices otherwise behaviour normal.

Study 2:
Staff in one psychiachiatric hospital told to expect pseudopatients over 3 months.

Study 3:
Pseudopatients asked staff a question as they walked past.

Results:
4% of pschiatrists and 0.5% of nurses stopped.

Conclusion:
Avoidance of contact adds to depersonalisation.

Results:
Average stay 19 days, discharged as 'schizophrenia in remission'.

Results:
41 real patients were suspected by staff members and 23 by psychiatrists.

Conclusion:
Doctors may prefer to call a healthy person sick (type 2 error).

Conclusion:
Type 1 error, shows that psychiatric diagnosis is unreliable.

Other findings:
- Labels are sticky, not like physical illness.
- Labels change interpersonal perceptions – 'normal' behaviours in abnormal setting are seen as abnormal.
- Patients were depersonalised – staff ignored direct questions and avoided eye contact (study 3).
- Patients were powerless – many human rights were taken away.

Conclusions:
- Not possible to distinguish the sane from the insane.
- One solution: focus on behavioural diagnoses to avoid expectations created by labels.

Evaluations
- The sample
- Research methods: field experiment controlled participant observation
- Ethical issues
- Quantitative or qualitative
- Personality v. situation
- Usefulness
- Ecological validity

Individual differences Core Study 20: Thigpen and Cleckley (multiple personalities)

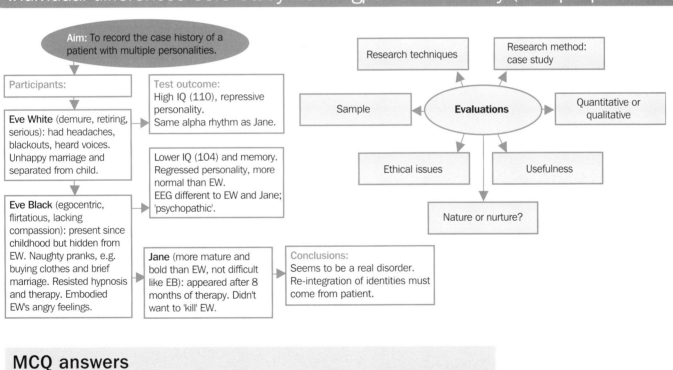

Aim: To record the case history of a patient with multiple personalities.

Participants:

Eve White (demure, retiring, serious): had headaches, blackouts, heard voices. Unhappy marriage and separated from child.

Eve Black (egocentric, flirtatious, lacking compassion): present since childhood but hidden from EW. Naughty pranks, e.g. buying clothes and brief marriage. Resisted hypnosis and therapy. Embodied EW's angry feelings.

Jane (more mature and bold than EW, not difficult like EB): appeared after 8 months of therapy. Didn't want to 'kill' EW.

Test outcome:
High IQ (110), repressive personality.
Same alpha rhythm as Jane.

Lower IQ (104) and memory. Regressed personality, more normal than EW.
EEG different to EW and Jane; 'psychopathic'.

Conclusions:
Seems to be a real disorder.
Re-integration of identities must come from patient.

Evaluations
- Research techniques
- Research method: case study
- Sample
- Quantitative or qualitative
- Ethical issues
- Usefulness
- Nature or nurture?

MCQ answers

Gould (MCQs on page 177)	1b 2d 3a 4d 5d 6b 7d 8a 9d 10c
Hraba and Grant (MCQs on page 185)	1c 2b 3a 4c 5a 6d 7a 8b 9c 10d
Rosenhan (MCQs on page 193)	1c 2b 3c 4a 5d 6b 7d 8c 9d 10d
Thigpen and Cleckley (MCQs on page 201)	1c 2a 3a 4c 5b 6d 7c 8a 9b 10a

1 From the article by Gould on IQ testing,

(a) Describe **one** of the practical problems experienced by Yerkes when he attempted the mass testing of army recruits for the First World War. [2]

(b) Give **one** use that was made of the data by politicians. [2]
[OCR AS Psy, June 2000, paper 1]

Stig's answer

(a) There were too many illiterates so they couldn't give them all the Beta test.

(b) It was used to help pass the Immigration Act in 1923.

Chardonnay's answer

(a) Different camps applied different criteria so that in some camps recruits with above 3rd grade schooling were given the Alpha test whereas in other camps people with no schooling were given the Alpha tests.

(b) It was used to decide which immigrants would be allowed in, i.e. not the Eastern and Southern Europeans because they were less intelligent.

Examiner's comments

Stig, part (a) is true. To make sure you got the second mark it would be good if you say how these illiterates had to take the Alpha test (and scored 0 or near to 0).

Similarly, for part (b), you are spot on, but a little bit of extra detail would be useful, e.g. about who this immigration act limited.

Chardonnay, you have given accurate detail for both question parts.

Stig (1+1) Chardonnay (2+2)

2 This is an example of a test item similar to those found in the Army Beta test described in Gould's study of IQ testing.

(a) Identify **one** problem with this test example and explain why it is a problem. [2]

(b) Outline **one** effect of such test items on Yerkes' conclusions. [2]

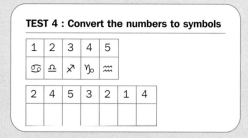

[OCR AS Psy, Jan 2002, paper 1]

Stig's answer

(a) You have to read the instructions to do the test and the pictorial test was intended for illiterates.

(b) Yerkes concluded that some groups of people were less intelligent e.g. the Negroes but the reason they didn't do well was not because of low innate intelligence but because they couldn't read the test items.

Chardonnay's answer

(a) The test example requires some skills of reading and writing. It wouldn't be very good as a test of intelligence for people who couldn't read or write.

(b)The effect was that the people doing the Beta test didn't do very well because they couldn't understand the test items.

Examiner's comments

Stig, your part (a) is just enough for the full two marks. For part (b) you have referred to Yerkes' conclusions (i.e. answered the question) and related his faulty conclusion to the test item. Good!

Chardonnay, your answer to part (a) is good. However, your part (b) response does not really answer the question as you have not referred to Yerkes' conclusions.

Stig (2+2) Chardonnay (2+0)

3 (a) Outline **one** way in which the social and political context of Hraba and Grant's study on doll choice differed from Clark and Clark's original study. [2]

(b) In what way might the change in context have caused the difference in results found between the two studies? [2]
[OCR AS Psy, Jan 2002, paper 1]

Stig's answer

(a) The political context was different because between the studies, there had been the black pride ('black is beautiful') movement.

(b) The effect of this movement was to increase the positive identity of black people so that children would prefer black dolls.

Chardonnay's answer

(a) One difference was that Hraba and Grant studied the children around the time of the Civil Rights movement and Martin Luther King, when people were more aware of black rights etc.

(b) The effect of this was that the civil rights movement had a positive effect on self-esteem and therefore the black children felt better about themselves and their race and so were more likely in the second study to choose the black doll (racial preference).

Examiner's comments

Stig, part (a) is fine – just enough for 2 marks. In part (b) you have successfully related the movement to a result but need slightly more explicit detail for the full 2 marks, e.g. describing how in Clark and Clark's study black kids generally favoured the white doll for racial preference questions, whilst in Hraba and Grant's study the black participants favoured the black doll.

Chardonnay, in part (a) you identify the civil rights movement and briefly what it was about. This is enough for two marks. Part (b) is also good, relating the political movement to self-esteem and racial preference measured in the two studies.

Stig (2+2) Chardonnay (2+2)

---

4 (a) Describe **one** way Hraba and Grant measured racial identification and preference in their study. [2]

(b) Outline **one** problem with Hraba and Grant's use of dolls to measure racial identification and racial preference. [2]
[OCR AS Psy, Jan 2005, paper 1]

Stig's answer

(a) To ask the children which doll they would like to play with.

(b) Doll choice doesn't really reflect friendship choice because there are many more factors involved in friendship choice than colour. The doll choice lacks ecological validity.

Chardonnay's answer

(a) They measured it by asking children to choose which doll they preferred, choosing between black and white dolls.

(b) One problem is that dolls aren't the same as real people so choosing a doll isn't the same as choosing a friend.

Examiner's comments

Stig, part (a) is ok, but you need to be a bit more explicit and say that the dolls were black and white. Your part (b) is spot on as you have identified ecological validity and explained this with reference to doll choice versus real life choices in the study.

Chardonnay, your part (a) is spot on. For part (b) what you have given is just not quite enough for the full two marks: you draw a distinction between doll choice and friendship choice without saying how they are different.

Stig (1+2) Chardonnay (2+1)

---

5 The study by Rosenhan (sane in insane places) broke a number of ethical guidelines.

(a) Outline **one** way in which the hospital staff were treated unethically. [2]

(b) If the study had been ethical, suggest what effect this would have had on the results. [2]
[OCR AS Psy, June 2001, paper 2]

Stig's answer

(a) The staff didn't know they were part of a study.

(b) If the staff knew the truth the study would have been pointless.

Chardonnay's answer

(a) The staff were deceived: not aware that pseudopatients would be presenting themselves and, in the second study, didn't know that really there weren't any pseudopatients.

(b) One way would be to debrief all staff afterwards and offer them the opportunity to withdraw their data. However then the results would be biased because of attrition.

Examiner's comments

Stig, you're right in part (a) but it would be a good idea to identify the ethical guideline. Similarly in part (b) you are probably right in speculating that the study would have been pointless – but why? More specifically, to answer the question you need to refer to the actual results of the study!

Chardonnay, you have given a very clear answer in part (a), over and above the requirements of the question. Your part (b) is an excellent answer showing quite a sophisticated understanding of ethical issues.

Stig (1+0) Chardonnay (2+2)

6 (a) From the Rosenhan study 'sane in insane places' give **one** example of how the pseudopatients' requests for information were dealt with by the staff. [2]

(b) Identify **two** effects of this on the pseudopatients. [2]
[OCR AS Psy, May 2003, paper 1]

Stig's answer

(a) Most of them gave a brief answer without eye contact and just walked on.

(b) It depersonalised them.

Chardonnay's answer

(a) The staff largely ignored the patients and spent little time with them.

(b) The effects were that the patients didn't feel they counted and were not real people. They were depersonalised and it lowered their self-esteem.

Examiner's comments

Stig, to the point and spot on in (a). A good example of getting full credit without waffling. In part (b) the question asks for 2 effects. Thus only 1 mark here.

Chardonnay, this is fine in part (a). In part (b), you have given 2 effects – depersonalisation and reduction in self-esteem so fine for 2 marks.

Stig (2+1); Chardonnay (2+2)

---

7 From the study by Thigpen and Cleckley on multiple personality disorder:

(a) Identify **two** tests completed by Eve. [2]

(b) Explain why an independent tester analysed the results of the tests carried out on Eve. [2]
[OCR AS Psy, May 2005, paper 1]

Stig's answer

(a) Eve did an IQ test and a personality test.

(b) It was better to have an independent tester so that he wouldn't affect how she performed.

Chardonnay's answer

(a) Eve did an IQ test and a projective personality test (the Rorschach test).

(b) They employed an independent tester so that the tester was not biased in how they interpreted Eve's responses or that she didn't act up to him how she might have done with Thigpen and Cleckley who she knew quite well.

Examiner's comments

Stig, 1 mark for IQ test, but 'personality test' is a bit vague. For part (b) you need a bit more by way of explanation – so just 1 mark again.

Chardonnay, spot on for part (a). In part (b) you provide a full answer.

Stig (1+1) Chardonnay (2+2)

---

8 Thigpen and Cleckley used a case study to investigate multiple personality disorder. Give **one** advantage and **one** disadvantage of the case study method used in this study. [OCR AS Psy, Jan 2001, paper 1] [4]

Stig's answer

One advantage of the case study method is that it allows you to study one individual case of multiple personality or other abnormal disorder. Such cases are very rare so it is really the main way to study the disorder while giving sufficient detail.

A disadvantage is that any individual is unique, there were special things about Eve's case which are unique and therefore the conclusions drawn from this may not apply to other cases.

Chardonnay's answer

Advantage: Case studies allow us to gain rich detail about one individual case.

Disadvantage: The problem is that the individual is likely to be unique in some way and we can't generalise from this case.

Examiner's comments

Stig, your advantage and disadvantage are excellent, well described and effectively related to Thigpen and Cleckley's study.

Chardonnay, you are right about the advantage and disadvantage of a case study but you need to connect each of these to the Thigpen and Cleckley study.

Stig (2+2) Chardonnay (1+1)

9 One approach to understanding 'normal' behaviour and experience is to study the behaviour and experience of 'abnormal' individuals. Select **four** studies that have involved some abnormal behaviour.

(a) Outline the abnormal features of behaviour described in each of these studies. [12]

(b) Using examples from these studies, discuss **two** advantages and **two** disadvantages of studying abnormal behaviour. [12]

Stig's answer

(a) Thigpen and Cleckley: The lady in this study had multiple personality disorder. This meant she had three different personalities who came out at different times. This is not normal because you do things you didn't know you were doing. [2]

Rosenhan: This study looked at the way abnormal people are treated in mental hospitals and suggested that one reason we see them as abnormal is because we see them in the context where we interpret their behaviours as abnormal. [2]

Sperry: This was a study of split brain patients who had been epileptic, both of which are abnormal. Normally the two halves of the brain are connected and communicate with each other. The epilepsy may have caused brain damage. [2]

Freud: This study was about Little Hans who was a little boy who developed various phobias about horses – about white horses and about horses pulling laden carts. The phobias expressed his repressed feelings about his mother, father and sister. [2]

Examiner's comments

In general, Stig, your response is accurate but quite thin. You need a bit more detail in your answer to attract the third mark for each study.

For Thigpen and Cleckley you have said just enough (though in quite a basic way) to get 2 marks. Your final comment, though not well phrased, referring to Eve White's lack of knowledge of Eve Black's behaviour, helps you get 2 marks here.

Your comment on Rosenhan shows very good understanding of the study. For the third mark you could have used an example (such as the hospital worker pathologising pseudopatient's normal behaviour waiting for lunch) or reference to the difficulty/unreliability of diagnosis of mental illness.

Sperry – some examples of the patients' problems, such as not being able to say what was flashed in the left visual field, are needed here.

Freud – some reference to Oedipal complex, or examples of Hans's dreams/fantasies, would help gain the third mark.

Part (a) = 2+2+2+2 = 8/12

(b) Advantage 1: We can find out things about normal behaviour by studying abnormal behaviour. **[P]** For example, Sperry's study showed us about the functions of the two halves of the brain. In normal individuals the right, silent hemisphere is difficult to study but this could be done when the two hemispheres were deconnected. **[E]** Sperry showed, for example, that the right hemisphere does have some linguistic abilities.**[C]**

Advantage 2: We can find better ways to treat abnormal individuals. **[P]** For example, Rosenhan showed that putting people in mental hospitals creates more abnormality rather than help **[E]** it so it would be better to have community treatment centres. **[C]**

Disadvantage 1: It may not be appropriate to generalise from abnormal to normal individuals. **[P]** For example, Freud's study might be about a unique individual who was disturbed from the beginning. **[E]** So it may not tell us much about normal development.

Disadvantage 2: The samples are often very small so we can't really generalise from them. **[P]** For example, Freud's study was only about one boy and he may have unique characteristics. **[E]**

Examiner's comments

We can apply the PEC (point, example, comment) formula to marking this answer (see page ix for an explanation of PEC).

Generally you have adopted a good, strong approach, deploying accurate information relevant to the question.

Paragraph 1 is spot on, following the P-E-C formula.

Paragraph 2 is slightly thinner, but in each case just enough to gain each of the marks. To be safe, it is best to provide more by way of explanation and back up your assertions.

In paragraph 3 you make an appropriate point, linked to an appropriate example. Your final sentence does not get the comment mark because it does not really add anything beyond your original point.

Again, in paragraph 4 you have a clear point and example. Although it is also about generalisation, it is sufficiently different from the previous point to get the mark. How could you get the comment mark? Well, if a study cannot be generalised, it will have limited usefulness!

Counting up the Ps, Es and Cs …

Part (b) = 10/12

Total = a+ b = 8+10 = 18/24

10 People are different. This is referred to as 'individual differences' Such differences may be due to culture or to personality or to experience. Select **four** studies that tell us about individual or cultural differences.

(a) Describe the findings of each of these studies. [12]

(b) Briefly discuss **two** advantages and **two** disadvantages of studying individual or cultural differences giving examples from any of these studies. [12]

Chardonnay's answer

(a) Deregowksi's study found that perception was related to culture rather than simply being innate. Deregowski looked at lots of different studies to reach this conclusion, for example one that used pictures, and the native Africans didn't interpret the 3D cues correctly because they didn't know them.

Gould's study found that early IQ tests were culturally biased but were used to change social policy such as the immigration laws.

Tajfel's study could be related to prejudice between different cultural groups and tells us that discrimination can occur just because you think you belong to a group. It doesn't need any more than this to create ingroup behaviour.

Hraba and Grant's study found that black children in 1969 had a stronger black identity than black children did in 1939. They also found that this might be related to the fact that the children lived in an interracial setting.

Examiner's comments

Chardonnay, the information you give is accurate, but often lacking detail; general conclusions rather than specific findings.

For Deregowski you could talk about any anecdotal evidence or more experimental evidence e.g. results on the ambiguous trident test.

For Gould, you could give examples of items of the tests were culturally biased and be more specific about how the immigration laws were changed.

The Tajfel paragraph shows good understanding, but reference to some more specific results would help e.g. in the first study ingroup–outgroup choices were less likely to show fairness.

For Hraba and Grant you could talk about racial preference and racial awareness as well as racial self-identity. (Strictly speaking, there was not a significant change in racial self-identity when comparing the two studies.)

Part (a) = 2+1+2+2 + 7/12

(b) It is important to study individual and cultural differences to understand the ways that people differ rather than assuming that all people are the same. **[P]** For example, Gould's study showed that the people who designed the IQ tests assumed that everyone had the same knowledge and weren't aware of their cultural biases. **[E]** This led to false conclusions about the intelligence of immigrants. **[C]**

Another advantage is that cross-cultural studies mean we can see what is due to nature and what is due to nurture, **[P]** which is what Deregowski's study was about. He showed that perception is due to nurture and not just nature. **[E]**

A disadvantage of studies on cultural differences is that when we study people from other cultures we use tools developed in our own culture **[P]** and people in another culture may not do so well, so the reason they don't do well is that they found the test confusing not because they lacked certain abilities. **[C]** This could have been true in Deregowksi's study.

A second disadvantage is that people from other cultures also don't always understand what they are expected to do **[P]**, so this is another reason they don't come out well when studied by Western psychologists **[C]**. This again could have been true in Deregowski's study.

We can apply the PEC (point, example, comment) formula to marking this answer (see page ix for an explanation of PEC).

Chardonnay, a decent answer. All your points are very clearly made and genuinely answer the question – well done. You just fall down in detail in places.

Paragraph 1 is lovely!

Paragraph 2 you need to make a 'comment' – perhaps explaining how this helps us understand that cultural experience and socialisation is more powerful than any 'cultural genes'.

Paragraph 3 – this is a very good point, and you clearly see the implication of this, giving you a comment mark. However, you need to relate it to some specifics of Deregowski to get the example mark (such as the use of Western material like paper and pencil rather than more familiar [at the time] sand and sticks).

You have lost the Example mark in Paragraph 4 for the same reason.

Counting up the Ps, Es and Cs …

Part (b) = 9/12

Total = a+b= 7+9 = 16/24

This chapter looks at research methods in psychology. Research methods are the techniques that scientists use in order to conduct systematic studies and produce facts about the world.

Psychological research

Practical investigations folder

You are required to conduct four activities (as listed below) and record certain details in a practical investigations folder. You do not hand this folder in to the exam board but you do use it in one of your AS exams, *Psychological Investigations* (Unit 2542). In this exam you will be asked questions related to four activities that you have conducted. Some of the questions simply require you to copy material from your psychological investigations folder, other questions are more general.

Activity A

Activity B

Activity C

Activity D

Data analysis

End of chapter

Introduction to research methods

Evaluating research

Replicable

If a result is sound it ought to be possible to repeat it. If it is not possible to get the same result again it raises a question mark about the original study. Sometimes studies are not repeated because of ethical issues, for example the study by Schachter and Singer, but the question still remains.

Sensible

Research needs to be based on theory and make sense. For example, the science of phrenology was based in the idea that the shape of the brain, and hence the head, determined personality. This is not supported by any evidence and so can not make sense even though it sounds plausible.

Objective

If we are objective then we try to remove as much bias as possible from our study (the opposite is to be subjective and personal). We can do this by using controls and by, for example, recording exactly what we observe rather than our interpretations. Freud's study is a very subjective account of Little Hans's fears.

Valuable

Psychological research doesn't have to have direct benefit to the general public but many people think it should make a contribution to our understanding of ourselves and others. In other words it should be useful. Whatever criticisms are made of Milgram's study, it has provided a valuable insight into human behaviour.

We use research methods to find out information about the world. We try to collect information that will help understand our world a bit better. The alternative is to make information up, in other words just to guess why certain things happen; this is less likely to help our understanding.

The first way to find out things is to look at what is happening around you and record it. To start with we tell a story about what we see and then we try put it in categories. This is the process of **observation**; we all use it in everyday life to make sense of our world. This intuitive method of 'research' has been developed by psychologists to increase our knowledge of the world. Sometimes they record things that are usual in everyday life, such as the way people perceive depth, and sometimes they record rather unusual things that are rarely experienced, such as hallucinations.

The main subject for psychological research is the behaviour and experience of people, and if you want to know what someone thinks, feels or does the first thing to do is to ask them. This gives us first-hand accounts that we call **self-reports**. These are excellent sources of data but not necessarily accurate. We are not always the best witnesses of ourselves because we forget what we did, or we want to put over a good impression of ourselves, or because sometimes we just don't know why we do things.

As we build up our evidence (from observations and self-reports) we start to develop theories which we want to test to see if they are right or not. For example, observations of autistic children led to the theory that children with this condition had a specific deficit in their way of interpreting the world. The study by Baron-Cohen, Leslie and Frith (page 22) tested this theory using the Sally-Anne test. They compared the judgements of children with autism against the judgements of other children. Psychologists use **tests of difference** to see whether there is a measurable difference between the two sets of scores. These results can then be used to challenge or support their theories.

Some issues can be explored by looking at differences between groups and some are better explored by looking for associations between scores. For example we might measure a person's level of stress and also their sense of control over their behaviour (locus of control). Our hypothesis might be that the more control we feel we have over our lives the less stress we will experience. We can examine this hypothesis using a test of **correlation**.

In this chapter we look at these four ways of collecting data and comment on the relative strengths and weaknesses of them.

ACTIVITY

Play with psychological methods

Why not use your phone or iPod to carry out your studies? If you haven't got an iPod then just make one out of pink cardboard and white string; nobody will notice. You can observe people's behaviour with an iPod: do they make less eye contact in the street? Do they hum out loud, or move in rhythm? You can experiment whether people do better at simple tests when listening to the iPod than when not listening. Or you can compare the effects of different types of music on performance. You can make a questionnaire about iPod playlists or colours or attitudes to people who have iPods. And you might correlate the amount of time people use shuffle (compared to listening to whole albums) with some personality variable (such as extraversion – find a questionnaire on the web).

The mobile phone has pushed us to develop a whole new range of behaviours. Do people use hand gestures when they are on the mobile phone? Why? You could compare the gestures and facial expressions of mobile phone users with the gestures and expressions of face-to-face conversation. And what about asking people about how and when they use it, how many texts they send, and whether they save any texts, if so from whom? You could send the same message to males and females and look at the different answers. People love to talk about their phones so a questionnaire should be easy enough.

Science and pseudoscience

Science is a way of collecting knowledge about the world we live in that uses objective, verifiable methods and builds up coherent theories. It rolls back the clouds of superstition and ignorance to give us understanding and control of the world. Pseudoscience appears to use the techniques of science but does not produce verifiable evidence. Pseudoscience can be identified because it:

- Makes claims that cannot be verified.
- Makes claims that are not connected to previous research.
- Does not submit the data for review by other scientists.

Unfortunately, psychology is not free of pseudoscience though it is sometimes a matter of opinion as to which category some research falls into. For example, some suggest that Neuro-Linguistic Programming (NLP) has absolutely nothing to do with theories of biology (neuro), language (linguistic) or computers (programming), however NLP claims to be scientific and sells a lot of books. We leave it for you to decide, but beware of the fakers and charlatans.

Examples of pseudoscience include:

- *Graphology: interpreting personality from samples of handwriting (see the Barnum Effect on this page).*
- *Reiki therapy: the healing massage of spiritual energies without ever touching the body.*
- *Phrenology: reading personality by examining bumps on the head (see page 86).*
- *Clairvoyance: predicting future events, though failing to spot who will win the 3.30 at Kempton Park.*
- *Astrology: predicting personality and future events from the relative position in the sky of stars which are millions of light years away.*

The Barnum Effect

We love to hear information about ourselves. It is maybe our top topic of conversation and we pay good money for people to tell us things about ourselves. Unfortunately we are not good at distinguishing sense from nonsense in this information. The *Barnum Effect* (named after P.T. Barnum, the famous North American hoaxer and showman) refers to a powerful tendency to believe information given to us about our personal qualities. This is used to good effect by fortune tellers, astrologers, handwriting 'experts' and various other contemporary shamans. If the 'expert' can say what people are prepared to accept, and can phrase it in such a way that it implies some intimate insight, then there is a good, if dishonourable, living to be made.

Our gullibility to personality statements was tested by Forer (1949). This is an excellent example of scientific enquiry and it also gives us some insight into the appeal of the pseudosciences. Some of Forer's students filled in a personality questionnaire and agreed to give their opinion of the results when they received their personal profile. When each student received their profile they believed it was a unique description of their personality. Most of the students endorsed most of the statements as being true about them. All in all they were very impressed with the description about them.

In fact the students all received the same 13 statements shown on the right. When you look at them, try to imagine that you are being told this about you in a sincere voice by someone who claims to have knowledge of these matters. Better still, try saying these statements to someone else after reading their tea leaves.

Barnum statements

1 You have a great need for other people to like and admire you.
2 You have a tendency to be critical of yourself.
3 You have a great deal of unused capacity which you have not turned to your advantage.
4 While you have some personality weaknesses, you are generally able to compensate for them.
5 Your sexual adjustment has presented problems for you.
6 Disciplined and self-controlled outside, you tend to be worrisome and insecure inside.
7 At times you have serious doubts as to whether you have made the right decision or done the right thing.
8 You prefer a certain amount of change and variety and become dissatisfied when hemmed in by restrictions and limitations.
9 You pride yourself as an independent thinker and do not accept others' statements without satisfactory proof.
10 You have found it unwise to be too frank in revealing yourself to others.
11 At times you are extroverted, affable, sociable, while at other times you are introverted, wary, reserved.
12 Some of your aspirations tend to be pretty unrealistic.
13 Security is one of your major goals in life.

Connections

To understand any evidence you have to understand how the data were collected. You might ask the question 'How do you know that?', and throughout this text we have tried to answer that question. The 20 core studies illustrate a wide range of data collection techniques in psychology. We have our own views on which evidence is the strongest and which should be taken with a pinch of salt. We hope that by studying how the evidence was collected you can make up your own mind about which you think is most valuable.

The psychological investigations exam

The **psychological investigations exam** is a one-hour exam. It is divided into four sections, one related to each of your four practical activities.

For each practical activity you may be asked **three** types of question:

- Questions that require you to **copy** out of your practical investigations folder.

- Questions about your practical activity that do not involve copying out of your folder that require you to **evaluate** what you did.

- General questions on **research methods**.

Examples of white questions (copying out of your practical investigation folder)

1. Explain the aim of your activity. [2]
2. Describe the procedure that you followed for this activity. [4]
3. Describe your questionnaire, including an example of one of the questions. [2]
4. Outline **two** findings from your observation. [4]
5. How did you select the participants for your study? [2]
6. (a) Name the statistical test that was used to analyse your data. [1]
   (b) Write down your statement of significance. [2]
   (c) Explain what this means in relation to your investigation. [3]
7. (a) Sketch an appropriately labelled graph or table or chart summarising your findings. [3]
   (b) Outline **two** conclusions that can be drawn from this graph or table or chart. [4]

Examples of evaluation questions (evaluating your practical investigation)

On ethics
Describe **one** ethical issue you considered when planning your own activity. [4]
How did you deal this ethical issue? [3]

On strengths and weaknesses
Describe **one** strength and **one** weakness in the way you conducted your investigation. [4]

On reliability and validity
Explain **one** way you could make your observation more reliable. [4]
Outline **one** way that your measurements may have lacked reliability. [3]

On the sampling method
Identify **one** strength and **one** weakness of the sampling method you choose. [6]
Suggest one improvement to the way you selected your sample. [3]

On measures of central tendency and dispersion
What is the best measure of central tendency to describe your results? Explain your answer. [2]

On improvements
For your activity, suggest **two** improvements that could be made. [4]
Suggest **one** effect that each of these improvements might have on the validity of your results. [6]
For your activity, suggest an alternative way of finding out the same information. [4]
Outline **one** problem with the way you measured each of your variables. [3]
Suggest an alternative way of measuring each of your variables and explain the effect these changes may have on your results. [6]

Examples of research methods questions

On ethics
Outline **one** reason why it would be considered unethical to conduct an experiment using electric shocks. [3]
What ethical issues arise when using self-report methods? [6]
Describe **one** ethical issue that a researcher should consider before conducting an observational study. [3]

On strengths and weaknesses
Describe **one** strength and **one** weakness of observational methods. [4]
Identify **two** strengths of self-report methods. [4]
Outline **one** advantage and **one** disadvantage of experimental methods. [4]
Outline **one** advantage and **one** disadvantage of the experimental design you used. [4]

On reliability and validity
What is meant by reliability? [2]
What is meant by the validity of a questionnaire? [2]

On the sampling method
Outline **one** strength and **one** weakness with the way you selected your sample. [6]
Describe **two** sampling methods that might be used when using self-report. [2]

On certain methods
Explain what is meant by a positive correlation. [2]
Briefly outline **one** way that gender differences could be investigated. [3]
When is it appropriate to use tests of correlation? [2]

The practical investigations folder

The exam board provides you with a **practical investigations folder**. You use this to record details relating to each of the four practical activities. You are permitted to take this folder into the exam. The following pages contain:

Guidance on conducting a practical investigation

1 **Decide on your aim(s) and/or hypothesis**

2 **Design decisions** will include

- For **Activity A** (self-report): the number and type of questions (5–10 questions is fine, best to use closed questions to collect quantitative data). You may use an existing questionnaire.

- For **Activity B** (observation): select a method for recording observations and a sampling technique.

- For **Activity C** (difference between two conditions): identify and operationalise the IV and DV, decide on an experimental design and how to allocate participants to conditions.

- For **Activity D** (correlational analysis): identify co-variables.

  For all activities:

- Write brief and debrief (see page 217).

- Write down the standardised procedure.

- Decide on a sampling technique (see page 27).

- Discuss potential ethical issues and how to deal with them (see page 95).

3 **Pilot study** (see right)

4 **Conduct the study**

5 **Summary of results**

- You do not have to analyse everything, e.g. every question asked or task done by participants.

- For quantitative data you can use descriptive statistics such as measures of central tendency and dispersion (see page 224) or graphs (bar chart or pie chart, or a scattergraph for correlations).

- For Activities C and D you must use an inferential statistical test.

- For qualitative data (e.g. comments made by respondents, or answers to open-ended questions) you can identify some trends in the answers and summarise these.

6 **Fill in your folder**

   Details are given for each activity of what needs to go in your folder and what you might include under each heading.

Key tips for your investigations

- Do something simple.

- You do not need lots of participants – 10 are enough.

- Your design doesn't have to be perfect – problems provide you with more to evaluate.

- Design it yourself – that way you will understand it better. If you try to repeat an existing study you will probably do something much more complicated than necessary.

- Spend as much time completing your practical investigations folder and evaluating the investigation as you spent conducting it.

Key tips for the exam

- Make your folder as clear as possible (use bullet points so it is easy to use the information in the exam).

- Make sure your practical investigations folder is correct (respond to suggestions from your teacher).

- Prepare the evaluation and research methods questions in an separate folder (not to be taken into the exam).

A **pilot study** is a small-scale trial run of a research design before doing the real thing. It is done in order to find out if certain things don't work. For example, participants may not understand the instructions or may guess what the experiment is about. They may get very bored because there are too many tasks or questions.

Ethics

You must not conduct research that involves any risk, distress or embarrassment to participants or which deceives them except in a minor way. You must not use participants under the age of 16.

Activity A: Questions, self-reports and questionnaires

The most obvious way to find out what a person feels, thinks or does is to ask them. The term 'self-report techniques' refers to any data collection method that involves asking people to report on their thoughts, feelings or behaviour. This data can be collected by asking people to write about themselves (a questionnaire) or talk about themselves (an interview). Questionnaires/interviews can be structured which means that there are a set of pre-determined questions. Or they can be unstructured which means that questions are developed as the interview goes along. On this course we concentrate on structured techniques, and in particular on questionnaires. Commonly, questionnaires require short responses and allow us to easily compare the results between one person and another, and also to calculate average responses.

The advantages and disadvantages of questionnaires and interviews, structured and unstructured, are given on page 77.

Open and closed questions

Open questions invite respondents to provide their own answers and tend to produce qualitative data. They are more difficult to analyse than closed questions. Closed questions provide limited choices, are easy to analyse (quantitative data) but may not permit people to express their precise feelings.

Examples of open questions

1 What factors contribute to making work stressful?

2 When do you feel most stressed?

Examples of closed questions

1 Which of the following factors at work makes you feel stressed? (You may tick as many answers as you like)
   - ❏ Noise at work   ❏ Lack of control
   - ❏ Too much to do   ❏ Workmates
   - ❏ No job satisfaction

2 How many hours a week do you work?
   - ❏ 0 hours   ❏ 1 to 10 hours
   - ❏ 11 to 20 hours   ❏ More than 20 hours

Likert scale

1 Work is stressful

   Strongly agree Agree Not sure Disagree Strongly disagree

2 How much stress do you feel in the following situations? (Circle the number that best describes how you feel.)

   At work: A lot of stress 5 4 3 2 1 No stress
   At home: A lot of stress 5 4 3 2 1 No stress
   Travelling to work: A lot of stress 5 4 3 2 1 No stress

Semantic differential technique

Complete the statement 'People who are bosses are usually...'

   Hard _ _ _ _ _ _ _ Kind
   Small _ _ _ _ _ _ _ Large
   Passive _ _ _ _ _ _ _ Active
   Beautiful _ _ _ _ _ _ _ Ugly

Ethics

You should obtain the informed consent of all respondents.

Example activity: investigating dreams

Aim

To find out about people's dreams. *Research questions:* What do people dream about? Do people dream in colour? How often do people have nightmares?

Method: structured questionnaire/interview

Brief all participants about the purpose of questionnaire and what will be involved; hand out the questionnaire (or record the answers for interviewee); debrief the participant.

Results: possible ways to deal with the answers:

- For each question work out the mode. (The data from this questionnaire are nominal (in categories) therefore the mode is the appropriate measure of central tendency).
- Show results for each question in a bar chart.
- Compare the content of male and female dreams.

Questionnaire: what are your dreams like?

Think of a recent dream and answer the following questions related to your dream (you may tick more than one answer to each question):

1 What characters were in the dream?
   - ❏ Known (e.g. family, friends)
   - ❏ Generic (e.g. a policeman or a teacher rather than a specific teacher)
   - ❏ Animals
   - ❏ Fantasy figure (e.g. angel, dragon)
   - ❏ Other (please specify) _____

2 What kind of dream was it?
   - ❏ Emotional   ❏ Not emotional
   - ❏ Positive   ❏ Negative

3 How meaningful was your dream?
   - ❏ Can you remember a lot of details?
   - ❏ Was the dream just fragments?
   - ❏ Was it related to specific daytime events?

Ideas for investigations

Collect data, then compare boys and girls, or older and younger respondents or any two groups.

1 Use existing questionnaires

Conduct an IQ test or other psychological test. There are many tests you can use on the web, for example http://www.queendom.com

2 Design your own questionnaire

- How obedient are you?
- Attitudes towards violence on TV.
- Views on the cause and treatment of mental illness.

Briefing and debriefing

A brief is given to each participant prior to a study to explain to them what they will be required to do (standardised instructions) and inform participants of their right to withdraw from the study at any time. It should contain sufficient detail about the study for the participant to be able to provide informed consent.

Even with informed consent participants may not fully understand what is involved and only realise this once the study has started. That is why they also should be told that they have the right to withdraw at any time.

A debrief is conducted after the experiment for two reasons.

1 *Ethical*: If any deception took place then participants are told the true aims of the study and offered the opportunity to discuss any concerns they may have. They may be offered the opportunity to withdraw their data from the study.

2 *Practical*: The experimenter may ask for further information about the researcher topic. For example: they may ask why the participant found one condition more difficult, or may ask whether the participant believed the set-up.

Guidance on filling in the practical investigations folder

State the aim of this activity

Every study has an aim or aims – an aim is what it is that the researcher wants to find out, such as 'to investigate dreaming', and may include one or more research questions, such as 'what do people dream about?' and 'how long do dreams last?'

It is a good idea to include the phrase '... using a questionnaire' as part of your aims for this study. You might also explain why you thought of doing this investigation, and make reference to any previous research.

Give examples of the questions used, including any rating scales, etc.

- State how many questions there were and include a few examples.
- Explain how you dealt with the answers: If the data are quantitative, say how you scored the answers and what the different totals meant (e.g. 'A score of 20 indicates ...')

Details of the sample

- Type of sampling method (i.e. how you selected participants, discussed on page 27).
- Number of participants and description of them (e.g. sex, age).
- The target population (i.e. the group of people from whom you selected your sample such as 'My school' or 'the sixth form at my school').

Outline the procedure you used for collecting data

Record sufficient detail for your study to be replicated (i.e. repeated by someone else following exactly the same steps). You should:

- State the source of your questions (are they your own or from an established questionnaire?).
- Record where and when the respondents answered the questions.
- Say what briefing and debriefing you gave respondents.

Summarise your results

For quantitative data, you could include:

- Descriptive statistics: These are explained on page 224.
  - Measures of central tendency (mean, median and/or mode as appropriate)
  - Measures of dispersion (range).
  - Graphical representation e.g. a bar chart of mean score(s).
- Verbal summary of results, i.e. 'looking at the bar chart I can see that...'

State the conclusions which you drew from your findings

Try to state two conclusions* about your results. These could refer to:

- Any patterns in the results, e.g. differences between younger and older.
- Any questions which produced consistently similar responses.

*Note that conclusions are generalisations made from the results – they are about people rather than about the participants. For example, saying 'people seem to dream more about events in their lives' rather than 'the participants dreamt more about events in their lives'.

Reliability and validity: self-report techniques

Reliability: if the same questionnaire/interview/test is repeated it should produce the same outcome. This is tested via the test–retest method, i.e. giving participants a test and then giving the same participants the same test a month later to see if the same result is obtained. The two scores can be compared by calculating a correlation coefficient (see page 229).

Validity: the validity of a questionnaire or interview is related to the question of whether it really measures what you intended to measure. One way to assess this is concurrent validity, which can be established by comparing the current test with a previously established test on the same topic. Participants take both tests and then you compare their scores on the two tests.

Activity B: An observation

The starting point for scientific enquiry is observation. We observe what is going on and then we develop some research questions for further studies. For example, we might observe that some children have difficulty adapting to their new school when they move from primary to secondary. We observe this and then devise research techniques to find out more about this.

The issue with collecting data through observation is to make it as objective as possible so that it is not just the personal view of the observer. Observational studies can vary in design on a number of dimensions, for example how naturalistic or controlled they are, how much the observer participates in the behaviour, how aware people are of being observed and whether the observation is direct or indirect (content analysis). These dimensions are explained on page 195, along with a consideration of the advantages and disadvantages of observations.

Making observations

You might think that making observations is easy but if you tried the example activity (on the right), you should now realise it is difficult:

1   To work out what to record and what not to record.

2   To record everything that is happening even if you do select what to record and what not to record.

Observational research, like all research, aims to be objective and rigorous. For this reason it is necessary to use observational techniques either in an observational study or, for example, as a way of measuring the DV in an experiment.

Unstructured observations

The researcher records all relevant behaviour but has no system. The behaviour to be studied is largely unpredictable. An example of this was in Rosenhan's study when pseudopatients observed behaviour on the wards in mental hospitals.

One problem with unstructured observations is that the behaviours recorded will often be those which are most visible or eye-catching to the observer but these may not necessarily be the most important or relevant behaviours.

Structured observations

One of the hardest aspects of the observational method is deciding how different behaviours should be categorised. This is because our perception of behaviour is often seamless; when we watch somebody perform a particular action we see a continuous stream of action rather than a series of separate behavioural components.

In order to conduct systematic observations one needs to break up this stream of behaviour into different categories. What is needed is operationalisation – breaking the behaviour being studied into a set of components. For example when observing infant behaviour have a list such as smiling, crying, etc.

Using a coding system means that a code is invented to represent each category of behaviour. A behaviour checklist is essentially the same thing, though a code for each behaviour may not be given. In the study by Bandura, Ross and Ross a behaviour checklist was used.

A behaviour checklist/coding system is developed after first making preliminary observations. It should:

Example activity: observing anxiety

Aim: To consider individual differences in anxiety when speaking in public. You could compare males and females.

Method

1.   *Pilot study: Unstructured observation.* Ask several volunteers (males and females) to stand up in front of your class and deliver a one-minute talk on any topic. The rest of the class should make a note of any nonverbal behaviours for example: scratching nose, licking lips, waving hands, saying 'um'.

2.   *Create a behaviour checklist.* Work out a suitable behaviour checklist from your preliminary observations and construct a table to record observations, for example:

	Person 1	Person 2	Etc.
Extraneous vocalisation e.g. 'um'			
Hand touches face			
Etc.			

3.   *Structured observations.* Repeat your observations using the behaviour checklist to score behaviours in a more structured way. Make a record for each speaker.

Results

•   Summarise your findings in a table showing totals for each behavioural category for each speaker.

•   Show results in a bar chart.

Indirect observation: content analysis

Indirect observations can be made of text. This includes published texts such as books or films or TV programmes, and personal texts such as diaries or drawings or even text messages. Such observations are 'indirect' because they are observations of the communications produced by people.

The process involved is similar to any observational study:

1   Decisions about a sampling method (what material to sample and how frequently).

2   Decisions about coding units/behaviour checklist.

•   *Be objective*: the observer should not have to make inferences about the behaviour and should just have to record explicit actions.

•   Cover *all possible component behaviours* and avoid a 'waste basket' category.

•   Make each category *mutually exclusive*, meaning that you should not have to mark two categories at one time.

Ideas for investigations

1 Use existing coding systems

Facial Action Coding System (FACS)

[www.2.cs.cmu.edu/afs/cs/project/face/www/facs.htm] Ekman and Friesen (1978) designed this for observing facial expressions.

2 Devise your own coding system

Use of mobile phones (direct observation)

Observe people in a shopping centre or other public place. You might consider mobile phone use in relation to age and gender, whether they were texting or phoning, whether they were on their own or in a group, and whether they ignored or included the other people in the group.

Mating preferences (content analysis)

Evolutionary theory predicts that males and females will seek different qualities in a partner. Men should seek attractiveness in a mate because they can maximise successful reproduction by mating as often as possible with fertile partners, and attractiveness is an indicator of fertility. Women should offer attractiveness and seek resources because each reproduction has a greater physiological cost for them than for a man and therefore they want to ensure the success of each pregnancy by having a mate who can support them. Waynforth and Dunbar (1995) analysed nearly 900 lonely hearts ads from 400 newspapers to see if there was support for evolutionary predictions about mating preferences. The study looked at three behaviours: individuals seeking resources, seeking attractiveness and offering attractiveness.

Reliability and validity: observational studies

Reliability: observations should be consistent which means that ideally two observers should produce the same record. The extent to which two (or more) observers agree is called inter-observer reliability. See page 223 for calculating this. Low reliability can be dealt with by training observers in the use of a coding system/behaviour checklist.

Validity: observations will not be valid (or reliable) if the coding system/behaviour checklist is flawed. For example some observations may belong in more than one category, or some behaviours may not be codeable.

The validity of observations is also affected by observer bias – what someone observes is influenced by their expectations. This reduces the objectivity of observations. This can be dealt with by using more than one observer and averaging data across observers (balances out any biases).

Guidance on filling in the practical investigations folder

State the aim of this activity

The aim is what it is that the researcher wants to find out, such as 'to investigate gender stereotypes', and may include one or more research questions, such as 'what behaviours are associated with male and female gender stereotypes?.'

It is a good idea to include the phrase '... *using an observation*' as part of your aims for this study.

Describe the categories of behaviour that you observed and the rating or coding system that you used

Record sufficient detail for your study to be replicated (i.e. repeated by someone else following exactly the same steps). You should:

- State the categories of behaviour that you used.
- Show the table that you used to collect data in.

Details of the sample that you observed

Type of sampling method (i.e. how you selected participants, discussed on page 27).

Number of participants and description of them (e.g. sex, age).

The target population (i.e. the group of people from whom you selected your sample such as 'My school' or 'the sixth form at my school').

Outline the procedure that you followed for your observation.

Record sufficient detail for your study to be replicated (i.e. repeated by someone else following exactly the same steps). You should:

- State the location of where your observation took place – where, when (time of day), how long?
- Did the participants know they were being observed?
- How many observers were involved?

Summarise your results

If you have coded behaviour you will have quantitative data, and could present:

- A table summarising your observations.
- Descriptive statistics, such as a bar chart or a measure of central tendency (these are explained on page 224).
- A verbal summary of results, i.e. 'looking at the bar chart I can see that...'

If you have conducted an unstructured observation you will have qualitative data, and could:

- Summarise the data by identifying repeated themes (thematic analysis).
- Use themes to produce quantitative data and then you can produce bar charts, etc.
- Present a verbal summary of results.

Give your conclusions

Try to state two conclusions about your results. These could refer to:

- Any patterns in the results such as differences depending on the time of day observations were made.
- Generalisations that can be made about human behaviour on the basis of your study.

Ethics

You should not observe people without their informed consent unless it is in a public place where people would normally expect to be observed by others.

Activity C: Investigating the difference between two conditions

When psychologists want to investigate the difference between two conditions they commonly use the experimental method. They control as much as they can, manipulate just one variable (IV) and measure its effect on behaviour (DV). For example we might want to see whether listening to music helps students study. We have some students listening to music and some not (these are the two conditions) and then give them a test. It is logical and simple. There are two basic experimental designs:

1 *Repeated measures:* you test each individual in both conditions comparing their performance in both parts of the experiment.

2 *Independent groups:* you test one group of people in the first condition and a different group of people in the second condition, and then compare the two sets of scores.

Example activity: investigating memory

Aim

To investigate the effects of organisation on the recall of information.

Method 1: independent groups

1 Generate a list of 100 words in categories (e.g. food is one category) and then think of four food items (produces five words: the category name plus four words in the category). Ideally all the words should be relatively common and about the same length.

2 Divide the list in half and arrange 50 words in categories and 50 words in random order.

3 Give some participants the organised list and some participants the random word list. Allow them five minutes to study the words and then test their recall.

Method 2: repeated measures

1 Create one list of 50 words composed of 25 in category order followed by 25 random order words.

2 Give this list to participants, allowing them five minutes to study the words and then test their recall of the words.

Results

- Calculate the mean number of words remembered in the organised condition and the random condition.

- Represent this information in a bar chart.

- Calculate the appropriate inferential statistic to determine whether your results are significant.

Ethics

You should gain the informed consent of all participants, ensuring that they do understand what will be involved. After the study you should debrief participants fully.

Repeated measures: order effects and counterbalancing

The order of the conditions may affect performance (an order effect). Participants may do better on the second condition because of a practice effect OR may do worse on the second condition because of being bored with doing the same test again (boredom effect).

One way to control order effects is to use counterbalancing which ensures that each condition is tested first or second in equal amounts. For example:

Group 1: The participants do the organised words first and then the random words.

Group 2: The participants do the random words first and then the organised words.

Hypotheses

The alternate hypothesis (H_1)

A alternate hypothesis states what you believe to be true. It is a precise and testable statement of the relationship between two variables.

The alternate hypothesis for the experiment on the left is:
'People remember more words in the organised condition rather than the random condition.'

The alternate hypothesis for an experiment states the expected relationship between the IV and DV. In a correlational study you state the expected relationship between the co-variables.

The null hypothesis (H_0)

The null hypothesis is a statement of no difference or no relationship between the variables.

For example:
'There is no difference between recall in the organised and random conditions.'
'There is no relationship between age and intelligence.'

Operationalisation

A 'good' hypothesis should be written in a testable form, i.e. a way that makes it clear how you are going to design an experiment to test the hypothesis.

'Operationalisation' means to specify a set of operations or behaviours that can be measured or manipulated. For example:

Hypothesis *'People work better in quiet than noisy conditions.'*

What precisely do we mean by 'work better' and 'quiet' and 'noisy'? We need to define the operations:
- 'work better' = obtain a higher score on a memory test
- 'quiet' = no sound
- 'noisy' = radio playing.

Operationalised hypothesis *People obtain a higher score on a memory test when tested in quiet (no sounds) rather than noisy (radio playing) conditions.*

Guidance on filling in the practical investigations folder

State the hypothesis and null hypothesis for this activity

(Alternate) Hypothesis: state the expected relationship between the IV and DV, and ensure that they are fully operationalised (see below).

Null hypothesis: is a statement that no difference is expected.

Identify the variables

See page 103 for details about IV and DV.

The independent variable (IV) is the variable that you manipulated; there will be two conditions of the IV.

The dependent variable (DV) is the variable that was measured, state exactly how it was measured.

Both variables should be clearly operationalised.

Describe the two conditions

- Describe the exact treatment given to the participants in each condition; this may include a description of the materials used (such as word lists), the instructions to each group, and any other differences between conditions.

Details of the sample that you used for your observation

- Type of sampling method (i.e. how you selected participants, discussed on page 27).
- Number of participants and description of them (e.g. sex, age).
- The target population (i.e. the group of people from whom you selected your sample such as 'My school' or 'the sixth form at my school').

Outline the design/procedure

Identify the research design: repeated measures, matched participants (which is a repeated measures design) or independent measures (see page 11 'Control by research design').

Record sufficient detail for your study to be replicated (i.e. repeated by someone else following exactly the same steps). You should:

- State the location of where your observation took place – where, when (time of day), how long?
- Details of the brief (standardised instructions) and any debrief.

Name the statistical test used to analyse the data.

Use either:

- the Mann–Whitney test (for independent groups), see page 227.
- the Wilcoxon test (for repeated measures or matched participants), see page 228.

What were the results of your analysis?

Write down (see page 225 for further explanation)

- The observed value.
- The number of participants.
- The required significance level (p)
- Whether the hypothesis was one-tailed (directional) or two-tailed (non-directional).
- The critical value.

State your conclusions including statements of significance relating to the hypothesis

State whether you can accept or reject the null hypothesis; use the phrase given at the end of the statistical test on page 227 or 228.

Use this space to present data using tables, visual displays and verbal summaries

- Tables: showing appropriate measures of central tendency (mean, median, mode) and dispersion (range and/or box plot). Make sure that tables are clearly labeled.
- Visual display: a bar chart showing the means for each condition/group. Again make sure this is clearly labelled.
- Verbal summaries: write a description of your conclusions, e.g. 'from the bar chart you can see that'. Focus on any interesting results.

You may attach a computer print-out to this practical folder, or record your calculations here.

You can attach a sheet of your raw data plus any workings.

Ideas for investigations

- **Replicate the study by Loftus and Palmer** (independent groups).
- **Compare performance on a memory task (independent groups)** with or without music playing.
- **Right brain left brain** (repeated measures): If you perform two tasks that occupy your left hemisphere you should be slower than when doing two tasks that involve separate hemispheres. Participants should tap their right finger while reading a page from a book (both involve left hemisphere) and repeat the same task without reading. Count the number of taps in 30 seconds. You should counterbalance conditions.

Reliability and validity: measurements

The **reliability** of measurements can be checked using the test–retest method described on page 217.

The **validity** of measurements concerns whether you are testing what you intended to test. For example, you might decide to measure helping behaviour by dropping your handkerchief and seeing how long it took for people to pick it up in two different situations. Would this really test helping behaviour?

Activity D: Independent measures and a test of correlation

A correlation is a way of measuring the relationship between two variables.

Age and beauty co-vary. As people get older they become more beautiful. This is a positive correlation because the two variables *increase* together.

You may disagree and think that as people get older they become less attractive. You think age and beauty are correlated but it is a negative correlation. As one variable increases the other one decreases.

Or you may simply feel that there is no relationship between age and beauty. This is called a zero correlation.

Example activity: assertiveness and watching TV

Aim: To see whether watching TV is related to assertiveness (because many programmes encourage such behaviour).

Method

You need to obtain two pieces of data from everyone in your class:

1 The number of hours they watched TV in the last 48 hours (presuming that the more TV watched, the more 'assertive' programmes watched).

2 An 'assertiveness' score – each person should rate themselves (or be rated by someone else) on a scale of 1 to 10 where 10 is very assertive. Alternatively there's a short quiz at http://www. therapy now.com/TherapyNowASSERT.htm

Results

* Plot the scores for each person on a scattergraph.

* Calculate a correlation coefficient using Spearman's test on page 229.

(If you have access to a computer you can use Excel to plot the scattergraph and calculate the correlation coefficient.)

Scattergraphs

A scattergraph is a graph that shows the correlation between two sets of data (or co-variables) by plotting dots to represent each pair of scores. For each individual we obtain a score for each co-variable – in our case the co-variables are age and beauty.

The top graph illustrates a positive correlation. The middle graph shows a negative correlation. The bottom graph is a zero correlation.

The extent of a correlation is described using a correlation coefficient – this is a number between +1 and −1 that is calculated using a statistical test (Spearman's test on page 229). +1 is a perfect positive correlation and −1 is a perfect negative correlation.

The correlation coefficients for the graphs are 0.76, −0.76 and 0.002

The plus or minus sign shows whether it is a positive or negative correlation. The coefficient (number) tells us how closely the co-variables are related. −0.76 is just as closely correlated as +0.76, it's just that −0.76 means that as one variable increases the other decreases (negative correlation), and +0.76 means that both variables increase together (positive correlation).

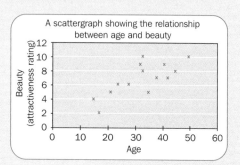

A scattergraph showing the relationship between age and beauty

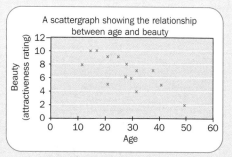

A scattergraph showing the relationship between age and beauty

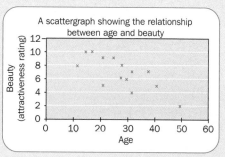

A scattergraph showing the relationship between age and beauty

The strengths and weaknesses of investigations using correlational analysis

Strengths	Weaknesses
• Can be used when it would be unethical or impractical to conduct an experiment. • If correlation is significant then further investigation is justified. • If correlation is not significant then you can rule out a causal relationship.	• People often misinterpret correlations and assume that a cause and effect have been found whereas this is not possible. • There may be other, unknown (intervening) variable(s) that can explain why the co-variables being studied are linked.

Ethics

You should have the informed consent of all participants.

If you are using pre-existing data you should respect confidentiality and be aware of the possible social sensitivity of such data.

Guidance on filling in the practical investigations folder

State the hypothesis and null hypothesis for this activity

Hypothesis: state the expected relationship between the co-variables, and ensure that they are fully operationalised.

Null hypothesis: is a statement that no relationship is expected.

[See page 220 for a description of hypotheses.].

Describe the two variables and how they are measured

Provide clear details of each variable.

Give details of the sample you used

- Type of sampling method (i.e. how you selected participants, discussed on page 27).
- Number of participants and description of them (e.g. sex, age).
- The target population (i.e. the group of people from whom you selected your sample such as 'My school' or 'the sixth form at my school').

Summarise the procedure you used in this investigation

Record sufficient detail for your study to be replicated (i.e. repeated by someone else following exactly the same steps). You should:

- State the location of where your observation took place – where, when (time of day), how long?
- Give exact details of the task(s) the participants had to carry out.
- Give details of the brief (standardised instructions) and any debrief.

Name the statistical test used to analyse the data

Use either

- Spearman's rank correlation for ordinal or interval data, see page 229.
- Chi-square test for frequency data, see page 226.

Present your data using tables, visual displays and verbal summaries

- Tables: showing appropriate measures of central tendency (mean, median, mode) and dispersion (range and/or box plot). Make sure that tables are clearly labelled.
- Visual display: a scattergraph. Again make sure this is clearly labelled. A hand-drawn one is possibly better than a computer one because it is easier to copy in the exam.
- Verbal summaries: a description of the scattergraph i.e. is it positive, negative or zero, weak or strong?

State the results of the statistical analysis

Write down (see page 225 for further explanation):

- The observed value.
- The number of participants.
- The required significance level (*p*).
- Whether the hypothesis was one-tailed (directional) or two-tailed (non-directional).
- The critical value.

State your conclusions including statements of significance relating to the hypothesis

State whether you can accept or reject the null hypothesis, use the phrase given at the end of the statistical test on page 226 or 229.

You may attach a computer print-out to this practical folder, or record your calculations here

You can attach a sheet of your raw data plus any workings.

Ideas for investigations

IQ and memory (1) Take an IQ test on the internet (for example see http://www.queendom.com). (2) Give participants a word list to learn and test recall the next day.

IQ and reaction time Test reaction time using a metre ruler. One person stands on a chair holding the ruler in the air while the second person loosely holds the lower end. When person 1 drops the ruler, person 2 has to grab it. The point at which the ruler is clasped equals reaction time. Alternatively go to http://mindbluff.com/reaction.htm

Using chi-square (page 226) One might predict, from Freudian theory, that women would prefer long thin chocolates (e.g. a flake) because it represents a penis rather than oval ones (e.g. a wagon wheel) which represent a womb. Collect data in this 2×2 frequency table:

	Men	Women	Total
Flake			
Wagon wheel			
Total			

Alternatively you can collect other data about men and women, for example when men and women pass each other in a crowded corridor or street do they face towards (open pass) or away (closed pass)?

Or collect data about older and younger people.

Reliability and validity: correlational studies

Correlation can be used to assess reliability, for example correlating the observations of two or more observers. A general rule is that if (Total agreements) / (Total observations) > 0.80, the data have inter-observer reliability.

The **reliability** and **validity** of any study can be assessed through replication: a study is repeated using the same standardised procedures to see if the findings are the same.

Descriptive statistics

Descriptive statistics are used to **describe** and **summarise** the data that you found from your research.

Measures of central tendency

Measures of central tendency inform us about central (or middle) values for a set of data. There are different ways you can calculate an 'average':

1   The **mean** is calculated by adding up all the numbers and dividing by the number of numbers.

It can only be used with interval or ratio data (see right).

2   The **median** is the middle value in an ordered list.

It can be used with ordinal data.

3   The **mode** is the value that is most common.

Used when the data are in categories (such as number of people who like pink) i.e. nominal data.

Measures of dispersion

A set of data can also be described in terms of how dispersed or spread out the numbers are. The easiest way to do this is to use the **range**.

Consider the two data sets below:

3, 5, 8, 8, 9, 10, 12, 12, 13, 15
mean = 9.5   range = 12 (3 to 15)

1, 5, 8, 8, 9, 10, 12, 12, 13, 17
mean = 9.5   range = 16 (1 to 17)

The two sets of numbers have the same mean but a different range, so the range is helpful as a further method of describing the data. If we just used the mean the data would appear to be the same.

The range is the difference between the highest and lowest number.

Something a little more sophisticated

Another way to show dispersion is to identify the interquartile range and a *box plot*. This is the spread of the middle section of the data which is obviously less affected by outlying extremities.

For example, there are 20 numbers below. The interquartile range is the middle 50%. In this case the middle 10 numbers: 8 to 13.

3, 3, 5, 7, 8, **8, 9, 9, 10, 10, 10, 11, 12, 12, 13**, 15, 17, 19, 20, 25

A box plot shows the median, the interquartile range and the full range, as shown on the right.

What are nominal, ordinal, interval and ratio data?

Nominal. *The data are in separate categories, such as grouping people according to their favourite football team (e.g. Nottingham Forest, Inverness Caledonian Thistle, etc.).*

Ordinal. *Data are ordered in some way, e.g. asking people to put a list of football teams in order of liking. Nottingham might be first, followed by Inverness, etc. The 'difference' between each item is not the same; i.e. the individual may like the first item a lot more than the second, but there might be only a small difference between the items ranked as second and third.*

Interval. *Data are measured using units of equal intervals, such as when counting correct answers or using any 'public' unit of measurement. Many psychological studies use **plastic interval scales** in which the intervals are arbitrarily determined so we cannot actually know for certain that there are equal intervals between the numbers. However, for the purposes of analysis, such data may be accepted as interval.*

Ratio. *There is a true zero point and equal interval between points on the scale, as in most measures of physical quantities.*

Graphs

A picture is worth a thousand words! Graphs provide a means of 'eyeballing' your data and seeing the results at a glance.

*   **Bar chart:** the height of the bar represents frequency. You can exclude empty categories, unlike the histogram. No true zero, and data are not continuous. Suitable for words and numbers.

*   **Pie chart, pictograms:** illustrating frequency of data using slices of a pie or pictures.

*   **Histogram:** essentially a bar chart except that the area within the bars must be proportional to the frequencies represented and the horizontal axis must be continuous. There should be no gaps between the bars.

Don't draw meaningless graphs

Imagine that you did a study where there were two groups of ten participants. One group were given a list of words organised into categories (items of food, precious metals, etc.), the other group were given the same list of words in random order. The recall scores are shown in the two graphs below.

The participant-by-participant graph (top) is meaningless, yet many students do this kind of graph.

A bar chart showing the means for both groups (bottom) is all you need.

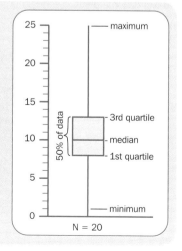

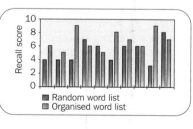

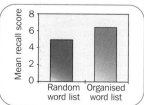

Inferential statistics

Inferences

When we carry out a psychological investigation we usually have two hypotheses:

- The **null hypothesis,** predicting that the results will be due to chance effects
- The **alternate hypothesis,** predicting that the results are due to the variable that is being studied.

Which one offers the best explanation for our results? We cannot prove one hypothesis to be correct, but we can make an intelligent guess about which one is the most likely explanation. This intelligent guess is called an **inference**. We want to know the probability that our results could be due to chance effects before we make our intelligent guess. To assess this probability we use inferential statistical tests.

Inferential statistical tests

We use statistical tests to tell us the probability of the results occurring by chance. If we carried out the same study several times, we would obtain slightly different results on each occasion. Could we explain these differences as being due to chance variation?

For example, if we carry out a study on the effect of alcohol on reaction time, we might obtain the following results:

- Average time taken to sort a pack of playing cards into suits without alcohol = 34 seconds

- Average time taken to sort a pack of playing cards into suits after drinking three measures of alcohol = 38 seconds

We want to know whether this 4-second difference in performance between conditions is due to the effect of the alcohol, or whether it is due to the variation caused by chance effects.

Statistical tests tell us the probability that the null hypothesis can explain our results.

Significance

It is an academic convention that we accept the null hypothesis as the best explanation of the results unless there is only a 5% probability (or less) of the results being due to chance factors (this is written as $p < 0.05$). In our example, if the statistical test tells us that there is less than 5% probability of the results occurring due to chance effects, then we *reject* the null hypothesis, and conclude that alcohol has affected reaction time. It is important to note, however, that we have *not proved* that the alcohol *caused* a drop in performance. We have *inferred* a causal link, and there is a 5% chance that we are wrong.

Sometimes the 5% chance of error is just a bit too high. For example, it is not very reassuring to be told by the doctor that there is a 5% chance that the tablets will make you turn green. In this case we would use a more stringent significance level, and only reject the null hypothesis if there is less than a 1 in 100 chance of error ($p < 0.01$), or even 1 in 1,000 ($p < 0.001$). This chosen value of 'p' is called the significance level.

Interpreting statistical tests

If you carry out your statistical test on a computer then it will most likely give you the answer as p-value. This tells you the probability of your results occurring by chance and this is precisely what you want to know.

If, however, you calculate the test by hand you will not get a p-value straight away. You will end up with a test statistic such as a 'U' if you calculate the Mann Whitney U. Each inferential test produces a single number, the test **statistic** or observed value (so called because it is based on the *observations* made). To decide if this **observed value** is significant this figure is compared to another number, found in a table of critical values; this is called the **calculated** or **critical value**. There are different tables of critical values for each different inferential test on the next four pages. To find the appropriate critical value in a table you need to know several pieces of information about the data:

- *The degrees of freedom*: in most cases you get this value by looking at the number of participants in the study (N).

- Whether the hypothesis was one-tailed (directional) or two-tailed (non-directional).

- The desired significance level, usually $p \leqslant 0.05$.

Some tests are significant when the observed value is equal to or exceeds the critical value, for others it is the reverse (the size of the difference between the two is irrelevant). You need to know which, and you will find it is stated underneath each table of critical values.

When you look at a one-tailed cat you know which way it is going. A two-tailed cat could be going either way.

One-tailed or two-tailed?

When you look up the critical value for your data you need to know whether your hypothesis was one-tailed or two-tailed:

- A **one-tailed** (directional) hypothesis states the kind of difference between two conditions or two groups of participants, e.g. 'People given the critical word "smashed" give a *higher* speed estimate than those given the critical word "contacted"'.

- A **two-tailed** (non-directional) hypothesis predicts simply that there will be a difference between two conditions or two groups of participants, e.g. 'People given the critical word "smashed" give a *different* speed estimate than those given the critical word "contacted"'.

Inferential statistics

Chi-square (χ^2)

When to use the chi-square test

The hypothesis predicts a *difference* between two conditions or an *association* between variables.

The sets of data must be *independent* (no individual should have a score in more than one 'cell').

The data are in frequencies (*nominal* – see page 224 for an explanation).

Note

This test is unreliable when the expected frequencies fall below 5 in any cell. i.e. you need at least 20 participants for a 2 × 2 contingency table.

Critical values of chi-square (χ^2) at the 5% level

df	One-tailed test *	Two-tailed test *
1	2.71	3.84
2	4.60	5.99
3	6.25	7.82
4	7.88	9.49
5	9.24	11.07

* The critical values table shows values for one- and two-tailed tests. However, statisticians argue that you can only test one-tailed hypotheses with a chi-square test.

The observed value of χ^2 must be equal to or exceed the critical value in this table for significance to be shown.

Source: abridged from P.A. Fisher and F. Yates (1974) Statistical tables for biological, agricultural and medical research (6th edition), Longman

How to do the chi-square test: Example 1

Alternative hypothesis: People who have a high score on the Belief in the Paranormal scale are less able correctly to assess coincidence (directional, one-tailed).

Null hypothesis: There is no association between belief in the paranormal and correct assessment of coincidence.

Step 1 Draw up a contingency table (right)
In this case it will be 2 × 2 (rows first, then columns)

Assessment of chance	Belief in the paranormal High	Low	Totals
Right	5 (cell **A**)	12 (cell **B**)	17
Wrong	10 (cell **C**)	9 (cell **D**)	19
Totals	15	21	36

Step 2 Find the observed value by comparing observed and expected frequencies for each cell

	Row x column/ total = expected frequency (E)	Subtract expected value from observed value, ignoring signs $\lvert(E - O)\rvert$	Square previous value $(E - O)^2$	Divide previous value by expected value $(E - O)^2/E$
Cell A	17 × 15/36 = 7.08	5 – 7.08 = 2.08	4.3264	0.6110
Cell B	17 × 21/36 = 9.92	12 – 9.92 = 2.08	4.3264	0.4361
Cell C	19 × 15/36 = 7.92	10 – 7.92 = 2.08	4.3264	0.5463
Cell D	19 × 21/36 = 11.08	9 – 11.08 = 2.08	4.3264	0.3905
Adding all the values in the final column gives you the observed value of χ^2				1.984

Yates's correction appears for some books but is no longer regarded as necessary.

Step 3 Find the critical value of chi-square
* Calculate degrees of freedom (*df*): calculate (rows – 1) × (columns – 1) = 1
* Look up the critical value in a table of critical values (on the left)
* For a one-tailed test, *df* = 1, and the critical value of χ^2 ($p \leq 0.05$) = 2.71
* As the observed value (1.984) is less than the critical value (2.71), we must retain the null hypothesis and conclude that there is no association between belief in the paranormal and the correct assessment of coincidence.

How to do the chi-square test: Example 2 (a larger contingency table)

Alternative hypothesis: certain parental styles are associated with greater turmoil in adolescence (non-directional, two-tailed).

Null hypothesis: There is no association between parental style and greater turmoil in adolescence.

Step 1 Draw up a contingency table (right)
In this case, it will be 3 × 2 (rows first, then columns)

Parental style	Adolescent turmoil High	Low	Totals
Authoritarian	10 (cell **A**)	4 (cell **B**)	14
Democratic	5 (cell **C**)	7 (cell **D**)	12
Laissez-faire	8 (cell **E**)	2 (cell **F**)	10
Totals	23	13	36

Step 2 Find the observed value of χ^2 by comparing observed and expected frequencies for each cell

	Row × column/ total = expected frequency (E)	Subtract expected value from observed value, ignoring signs $\lvert(E - O)\rvert$	Square previous value $(E - O)^2$	Divide previous value by expected value $(E - O)^2/E$
Cell A	14 × 23/36 = 8.94	10 – 8.94 = 1.06	1.1236	0.1257
Cell B	14 × 13/36 = 5.06	4 – 5.06 = –1.06	1.1236	0.2221
Cell C	12 × 23/36 = 7.67	5 – 7.67 = –2.67	7.1289	0.9294
Cell D	12 × 13/36 = 4.33	7 – 4.33 = 2.67	7.1289	1.6464
Cell E	10 × 23/36 = 6.39	8 – 6.39 = 1.61	2.5921	0.4056
Cell F	10 × 13/36 = 3.61	2 – 3.61 = –1.61	2.5921	0.7180
Adding all the values in the final column gives you the observed value of χ^2				4.0472

Step 3 Find the critical value of chi-square
* Calculate degrees of freedom (*df*): calculate (rows – 1) × (columns – 1) = 2
* Look up the critical value in a table of critical values (on the left)
* For a two-tailed test, *df* = 2, and the critical value of χ^2 ($p \leq 0.05$) = 5.99
* As the observed value (4.0472) is less than than the critical value (5.99), we must retain the null hypothesis and therefore conclude that there is no association between parental style and turmoil in adolescence.

The Mann–Whitney *U* test

When to use the Mann–Whitney test

The hypothesis predicts a *difference* between two sets of data. The two sets of data are from separate groups of participants – *independent* groups. The data are *ordinal* or *interval* (see page 224 for an explanation).

How to do the Mann–Whitney test

Alternative hypothesis: male participants interviewed on a high bridge give higher attractiveness ratings of a female interviewer than those interviewed on a low bridge (directional, one-tailed).

Null hypothesis: There is no difference in the ratings of attractiveness between those interviewed on a high or low bridge.

Step 1 Record the data and allocate points

Participant no.	High-bridge group	Points	Participant no.	Low-bridge group	Points
1	7	1.5	1	4	10.0
2	10	0	2	6	8.5
3	8	1.0	3	2	10.0
4	6	3.5	4	5	9.5
5	5	7.0	5	3	10.0
6	8	1.0	6	5	9.5
7	9	0.5	7	6	8.5
8	7	1.5	8	4	10.0
9	10	0	9	5	9.5
10	9	0.5	10	7	7.0
			11	9	3.0
			12	3	10.0
			13	5	9.5
			14	6	8.5
$N_1 = 10$		16.5	$N_2 = 14$		123.5

- To allocate points, consider each score one at a time
- Compare this score with all the scores in the other group
- Give 1 point for every higher score
- Give $\frac{1}{2}$ point for every equal score.

Step 2 Find the observed value of *U*
U is the lowest total number of points

Step 3 Find the critical value of *U*
- N_1 = number of participant in one group
- N_2 = number of participant in other group
- Look up the critical value in the table on the right
- For a one-tailed test, $N_1 = 10$ and $N_2 = 14$, and the critical value of $U = 41$
- As the observed value (16.5) is less than critical (41), we can reject the null hypothesis and conclude that the participants interviewed on a high bridge give higher ratings of attractiveness of a female interviewer than those interviewed on a low bridge.

Critical values of *U* at the 5% level for a one-tailed test

N_1

N_2	2	3	4	5	6	7	8	9	10	11	12	13	14	15
2				0	0	0	1	1	1	1	2	2	2	3
3		0	0	1	2	2	3	3	4	5	5	6	7	7
4		0	1	2	3	4	5	6	7	8	9	10	11	12
5	0	1	2	4	5	6	8	9	11	12	13	15	16	18
6	0	2	3	5	7	8	10	12	14	16	17	19	21	23
7	0	2	4	6	8	11	13	15	17	19	21	24	26	28
8	1	3	5	8	10	13	15	18	20	23	26	28	31	33
9	1	3	6	9	12	15	18	21	24	27	30	33	36	39
10	1	4	7	11	14	17	20	24	27	31	34	37	41	44
11	1	5	8	12	16	19	23	27	31	34	38	42	46	50
12	2	5	9	13	17	21	26	30	34	38	42	47	51	55
13	2	6	10	15	19	24	28	33	37	42	47	51	56	61
14	2	7	11	16	21	26	31	36	41	46	51	56	61	66
15	3	7	12	18	23	28	33	39	44	50	55	61	66	72

For any N_1 and N_2, the observed value of *U* must be **equal to** or **less than** the critical value in this table, for significance to be shown.

Critical values of *U* at the 5% level for a two-tailed test

N_1

N_2	2	3	4	5	6	7	8	9	10	11	12	13	14	15
2							0	0	0	0	1	1	1	1
3			0	1	1	2	2	3	3	4	4	5	5
4		0	1	2	3	4	4	5	6	7	8	9	10
5		0	1	2	3	5	6	7	8	9	11	12	13	14
6		1	2	3	5	6	8	10	11	13	14	16	17	19
7		1	3	5	6	8	10	12	14	16	18	20	22	24
8	0	2	4	6	8	10	13	15	17	19	22	24	26	29
9	0	2	4	7	10	12	15	17	20	23	26	28	31	34
10	0	3	5	8	11	14	17	20	23	26	29	33	36	39
11	0	3	6	9	13	16	19	23	26	30	33	37	40	44
12	1	4	7	11	14	18	22	26	29	33	37	41	45	49
13	1	4	8	12	16	20	24	28	33	37	41	45	50	54
14	1	5	9	13	17	22	26	31	36	40	45	50	55	59
15	1	5	10	14	19	24	29	34	39	44	49	54	59	64

For any N_1 and N_2, the observed value of *U* must be **equal to** or **less than** the critical value in this table, for significance to be shown.

Source: R. Runyon and A. Haber (1976) Fundamentals of Behavioural Statistics, 3rd edition. Copyright 1976. Reproduced with kind permission from McGraw-Hill Education

The Wilcoxon matched pairs signed ranks test (*T*)

When to use the Wilcoxon test

The hypothesis predicts a *difference* between two sets of data.

The two sets of data are pairs of scores from one person (or a matched pair) = *related*.

The data are *ordinal* or *interval* (see page 224 for an explanation).

How to do the Wilcoxon test

Alternative hypothesis: There is a difference in the score on a short-term memory test when it is taken in the morning or in the afternoon (non-directional, two-tailed).

Null hypothesis: There is no difference in the score on a short-term memory test whether it is taken in the morning or in the afternoon.

Step 1 Record the data, calculate difference between the scores and rank them

- Rank the numbers from low to high, ignoring the signs (i.e. the lowest number receives the rank of 1)

- If there are two or more of the same number (tied ranks), calculate the rank by working out the mean of the ranks that would have been given

- If the difference is zero, omit this from the ranking and reduce *N* accordingly

Participant	Score on test taken in the morning	Score on test taken in the afternoon	Difference	Rank
1	15	12	+3	8
2	14	15	−1	2
3	6	8	−2	5.5
4	15	15	omit	
5	14	12	+2	5.5
6	10	14	−4	9
7	8	10	−2	5.5
8	16	15	+1	2
9	17	19	−2	5.5
10	16	17	−1	2
11	10	15	−5	10
12	14	8	+6	11

Step 2 Find the observed value of *T*

- *T* = the sum of the ranks of the less frequent sign

- In this case, the less frequent sign is plus, so T = 8 + 5.5 + 2 +11 = 26.5

Step 3 Find the critical value of *T*

- N = 11

- Look up the critical value in the table of critical values (on the right)

- For a two-tailed test, *N* = 11, and the critical value of *T* = 10

- As the observed value (26.5) is greater than the critical value (10), we can retain the null hypothesis and conclude that there is no difference in the score on a short-term memory test whether it is taken in the morning or in the afternoon.

Critical values of *T* at the 5% level

N	One-tailed test	Two-tailed test
5	T≤ 0	
6	2	0
7	3	2
8	5	3
9	8	5
10	1.1	8
11	13	10
12	17	13
13	21	17
14	25	21
15	30	25
16	35	29
17	41	34
18	47	40
19	53	46
20	60	52
21	67	58
22	75	65
23	83	73
24	91	81
25	100	89
26	110	98
27	119	107
28	130	116
29	141	125
30	151	137
31	163	147
32	175	159
33	187	170

The observed value of *T* must be **equal to** or **less than** the critical value in this table for significance to be shown.

Source: R. Meddis (1975) Statistical Handbook for non-statisticians. London: McGraw-Hill

Spearman's rank correlation test (*rho*)

When to use Spearman's rank correlation test

The hypothesis predicts a *correlation* between two variables.

The two sets of data are pairs of scores from one person or thing.

The data are *ordinal* or *interval* (see page 224 for an explanation).

Charles Edward Spearman (1863–1945)

How to do Spearman's rank correlation test

Alternative hypothesis: Participants recall on a memory test is positively correlated to their GCSE exam performance (directional, one-tailed).

Null hypothesis: There is no correlation between recall on a memory test and GCSE exam performance.

Step 1 Record the data, rank each co-variable and calculate the difference

Rank A and B separately, from low to high (i.e. the lowest number receives the rank of 1).

If there are two or more scores with the same number (tied ranks), calculate the rank by working out the mean of the ranks that would have been given.

Participant	Memory score (A)	GCSE score (B)	Rank A	Rank B	Difference between Rank A and B (d)	d²
1	18	8	10	2.5	7.5	56.25
2	14	16	5.5	9	–3.5	12.25
3	17	10	9	5	4.0	16.0
4	13	9	4	4	0	0
5	10	15	3	8	–5.0	25.0
6	8	14	1	7	–6.0	36.0
7	15	12	7	6	1	1.0
8	16	8	8	2.5	5.5	30.25
9	9	17	2	10	–8.0	64.0
10	14	5	5.5	1	4.5	20.25

N = 10 Σd^2(sum of differences squared = 261.0)

Step 2 Find the observed value of *rho*

$$rho = 1 - \left(\frac{6\Sigma d^2}{N(N^2 - 1)} \right)$$

$$= 1 - \left(\frac{6 \times 261.0}{10 \times (100 - 1)} \right) = 1 - \frac{1566}{990} = 1 - 1.58 = -0.58$$

Note that this is a negative correlation – when comparing this figure to the critical value, only the value (not the sign) is important. The sign does, however, tell you whether the correlation is positive or negative. If the prediction was one-tailed and the sign (and therefore the correlation) is not as predicted, then the null hypothesis must be retained.

Step 3 Find the critical value of *rho*

- N = 10
- Look up the critical value in the table of critical values (on the right)
- For a one-tailed test, N = 10, and the critical value of *rho* = 0.564
- As the observed value (0.58) is greater than the critical value (0.564), we should be able to reject the null hypothesis; *however* the sign is in the wrong direction – it is negative whereas a positive correlation was predicted. Therefore we must retain the null hypothesis and conclude that there is no correlation between recall on a memory test and GCSE exam performance.

Critical values of *rho* at the 5% level

N	One-tailed test	Two-tailed test
4	1. 000	
5	0.900	1. 000
6	0.829	0.886
7	0.714	0.786
8	0.643	0.739
9	0.600	0.700
10	0.564	0.648
11	0.536	0.618
12	0.503	0.587
13	0.484	0.560
14	0.464	0.539
15	0.443	0.521
16	0.429	0.503
17	0.414	0.485
18	0.401	0.472
19	0.391	0.460
20	0.380	0.447
21	0.370	0.435
22	0.361	0.425
23	0.353	0.415
24	0.344	0.406
25	0.337	0,398
26	0.331	0.390
27	0.324	0.392
28	0.317	0.375
29	0.312	0,368
30	0.306	0.362

The observed value of *rho* must be **equal to** or **greater than** the critical value in this table for significance to be shown

Source: J.H. Zhar (1972) Significance testing of the correlation coefficient. Reproduced from the Journal of the American Statistical Association, 67, 578–80

1 Outline the procedure you used for collecting data. [4]

Stig's answer

I used a dream questionnaire from the internet. I printed 20 copies of this questionnaire and added some instructions for the participants about what to do, asking for their consent.

I then gave the questionnaires out to a range of people I know so that I got a good range of ages and both males and females. I asked people to return the questionnaire when they finished. I thanked them for taking part and asked if they had any further questions.

Chardonnay's answer

For this study I interviewed people about their attitudes to mental illness. I used a structured questionnaire containing 10 questions, some open and some closed. I only interviewed students at my college. I approached people during the lunch hour and asked them if they could spare 10 minutes for my psychology project. I then further explained the aim of the project to respondents so they could give their informed consent.

It took about 5–10 minutes to complete the interview. I noted down all the answers I was given and at the end gave interviewees a chance to read through the notes and sign a form to say it was OK for me to use this data. I thanked them for their time.

Examiner's comments

Stig, you have covered the basics of your procedure, but there are some details which would prevent me from replicating your study. Incidentally, a good way of checking your procedure is to get a friend to read it and see if they feel they could conduct a perfect replication of your study. If not, there is something missing and you will not get full marks. Here, I do not know where your respondents filled in the questionnaire, whether they were on their own or in groups, whether you gave them a time limit or not. As I do not have access to the questionnaire, it also might be useful if you gave a quick summary of the instructions!

Chardonnay, this is a good answer, covering all the main details to allow replication. You have included information given to the participants, location, time taken as well as the step-by-step information.

Stig (2) Chardonnay (4)

2 Suggest **one** strength and **one** weakness of the sampling method you chose. [3+3]

Stig's answer

The strength of an opportunity sample is that it is easy to obtain because you just go out and get whoever is available at the time. The weakness is that you may get a biased sample because you only ask certain kinds of people (those who are around you).

Chardonnay's answer

I used a volunteer sample. The strength of choosing this method was to get those people who would really want to take part and not just answer the questionnaire as quickly as possible, but would think about the questions. This is quite important when asking participants to reveal their attitudes towards mental illness. The weakness of choosing this method is that volunteers are not typical of all other people, they are possibly more highly motivated and more willing to please so the students who volunteered in my study might have tried to please me and tell me the answers they thought I was expecting.

Examiner's comments

Stig, this is quite a short answer. You have essentially *identified* one strength and one weakness but you have not elaborated or explained further. Also, the question requires you to relate the strength and weakness to *your* study.

Chardonnay, for each strength and weakness you have identified it, explained it a little bit further and also, crucially, related it to your own study. Generally speaking, if the question mentions 'your study', you do have to ensure the answer is framed within the context of your study and not just any study!

Stig (1+1) Chardonnay (3+3)

3 Describe what psychologists mean by the term validity. [2]

Stig's answer

It means that the psychologist found out what he was hoping to find out. The results were what he had predicted.

Chardonnay's answer

Validity means how true the results are. Are they really what happens in everyday life or did some aspect of the study mean that the results are meaningless. Validity is about whether you are testing what you meant to test.

Examiner's comments

Stig, this is not the right answer at all!

Chardonnay, you have got round to the right answer in the end (validity refers to whether you are measuring what you claim to be). Also, you have also referred to a form of validity (ecological validity), by way of expansion. Thus, you have done (just) enough for two marks.

Stig (0) Chardonnay (2)

4 Suggest **one** way that you could assess the validity of your questionnaire. [4]

Stig's answer

You could give the questionnaire to someone several times and see if they gave the same answer.

Chardonnay's answer

You could see if the questionnaire was really testing what you meant to test by using another questionnaire on the same topic and see if you got similar results. For example, if you were doing a questionnaire on dreams you could compare what people said with another questionnaire about dreams and see if the results were similar because if both questionnaires produce the same data then it shows that it is more likely that they are getting something real.

Examiner's comments

Hmmm, Stig, this technique (test–retest) is a way of checking out the *reliability* and not validity.

Chardonnay, you clearly understand what validity is and you have given a detailed account of concurrent validity. However, you have not related your answer to *your* questionnaire. Consequently, you cannot get full marks.

Stig (0) Chardonnay (3)

---

5 State the null hypothesis for your activity.

Stig's answer

The null hypothesis is that there is no difference in the recall of participants with the critical word 'smashed' or the critical word 'contacted'.

Chardonnay's answer

There is no correlation between IQ and age.

Examiner's comments

Stig – you have good detail here, but I don't know what the participants are trying to recall (speed, whether they saw glass, colour of car…). Even in a null hypothesis you should give clear (though brief) operationalisation of the DV.

Chardonnay, you need to also operationalise your variables (e.g. did you measure age in months via self-report?)

Stig (2) Chardonnay (1)

---

6 (a) Suggest an alternative way of measuring each of your variables. [3]

(b) Explain the effect these changes may have on your results. [3]

Stig's answer

(a) The two variables in my study were stress score and health score. I could have measured both of these variables using a different questionnaire. I could have used a stress scale for adolescents instead of one for adults which would have been more valid. I could have measured health by asking more detailed questions than just asking how many times people had been off school.

(b) The effect might have been to produce a different result. I might have found a correlation between the two variables because stress was measured more validly and because health was assessed more exactly.

Chardonnay's answer

(a) I could have measured IQ using a different IQ test. Perhaps one that is better known. Age could be measured in months instead of years.

(b) It is possible that a better known test would be more reliable but it shouldn't really affect the outcome. Individual scores might be different but overall there would be the same trend. The change in measuring age wouldn't make any difference.

Examiner's comments

Stig – the two alternatives you suggest in (a) are plausible and in sufficient detail for the marks available. Your part (b) answer is fine, just not quite sufficient for three marks as you have not referred to how your changes might impact on the results.

Chardonnay, your part (a) is fine, though presumably you are measuring age by self-report (and not guessing age by observation). Your part (b) is a little bit vague and shows some lack of thought. When you say that individual score changes might not impact upon the trend, I am not entirely convinced. Such changes may change the rank order of the scores and therefore change the results of the correlational statistical test, especially on a small sample.

Stig (3 + 2) Chardonnay (2+2)

References

Adorno, T.W., Frenkel-Brunswick, E., Levinson, D. and Sanford, N. (1950) *The Authoritarian Personality*. New York: Harper. ▸page 154

Aitchison, J. (1983) *The Articulate Mammal* (2nd edition). London: Hutchinson. ▸page 28

Akelatitis, A.J. (1944) A study of gnosis, praxis and language following section of the corpus callosum and anterior commisure. *Journal of Neurosurgery*, 1, 94–102. ▸page 106

Allport, G.W. (1968) The historical background of modern psychology. In G. Lindzey and E. Aronson (eds) *Handbook of Social Psychology* (2nd edition, vol. 1, pp. 1–80). Reading, MA: Addison-Wesley. ▸page 128

APA (2005) http://www.apa.org/divisions/div30/define_hypnosis.html (accessed Jan 2006). ▸page 197

Asch, S.E. (1946) Forming impressions of personality. *Journal of Abnormal and Social Psychology*, 41, 258–290. ▸page 192

Asch, S.E (1955) Opinions and social pressure. *Scientific American*, 193, 31–5. ▸page 130

Aserinsky, E. and Kleitman, N. (1955) Two types of ocular motility occurring in sleep. *Journal of Applied Physiology*, 8 (1), 1–10. ▸page 98

Bandura, A. (2004) Swimming against the mainstream: the early years from chilly tributary to transformative mainstream. *Behaviour Research and Therapy*, 42, 613–630. ▸page 54

Bandura, A., Ross, D. and Ross, S.A. (1961) Transmission of aggression through imitation of aggressive models. *Journal of Abnormal and Social Psychology*, 63, 575–582. ▸pages 56–58

Banyard, P. and Kagan, G. (2002) *Pre-degree Psychology: a Challenge to the Profession*. Psychology Learning and Teaching Conference, York University. ▸page 76

Baron, R.A. and Byrne, D. (1991) *Social Psychology: Understanding Human Interaction* (6th edition). London: Allyn and Bacon. ▸page 19

Baron-Cohen, S., Leslie, A.M. and Frith, U. (1985) Does the autistic child have a 'theory of mind'? *Cognition*, 21, 37–46. ▸pages 22–24

Baron-Cohen, S., Leslie, A.M. and Frith, U. (1986) Mechanical, behavioural and intentional understanding of picture stories in autistic children. *British Journal of Developmental Psychology*, 4, 113–125. ▸pages 18, 26

Bartlett, F.C. (1932) *Remembering*. Cambridge: Cambridge University Press. ▸page 5

Baumrind, D. (1964) Some thoughts on ethics of research: After reading Milgram's behavioural study of obedience. *American Psychologist*, 19, 421–423. ▸page 136

BBC (1999) Racism killed my best friend. http://news.bbc.co.uk/1/hi/uk/285644.stm ▸page 160

BBC (2000) Cherie Blair 'bad role model'. http://news.bbc.co.uk/1/hi/uk/660867.stm ▸page 54

BBC (2003) Sesame Street breaks Iraqi POWs. http://news.bbc.co.uk/1/hi/world/middle_east/3042907.stm ▸page 102

BBC (2004) Builder survives nailgun accident. http://news.bbc.co.uk/1/hi/health/3685791.stm (accessed October 2005). ▸page 86

BBC (2005) Reliving the London bombing horror. http://news.bbc.co.uk/1/hi/uk/4346812.stm; London explosions: Your accounts http://news.bbc.co.uk/1/hi/talking_point/4659237.stm (accessed December 2005). ▸page 152

BBC (2005a) Malcolm X. http://www.bbc.co.uk/insideout/west midlands/series8/week_three.shtml (accessed Jan 2006). ▸page 181

BBC (2005b) Benjamin Zephaniah. http://www.bbc.co.uk/birmingham/content/articles/2005/05/11/picture_of_birmingham_benjamin_zephaniah_feature.shtml (accessed Jan 2006). ▸page 186

BBC website (2005) http://news.bbc.co.uk/1/hi/world/europe/4630855.stm ▸page 68

Bègue, L. (2005) Self-esteem regulation in threatening social comparison: The role of belief in a just world and self-efficacy. *Social Behaviour and Personality*. See http://www.findarticles.com/p/articles/mi_qa3852/is_200501/ai_n9520808/pg_3 (accessed December 2005). ▸page 155

Bentall, R.P. (1992) A proposal to classify happiness as a psychiatric disorder. *Journal of Medical Ethics*, 18, 94–98. ▸page 171

Billig, M. (2005) http://www.lboro.ac.uk/departments/ss/depstaff/staff/bio/billig.htm (accessed September 2005). ▸page 156

Bishop, K. and Wahlsten, D. (1997) Sex differences in the human corpus callosum: Myth or reality? *Neuroscience and Biobehavioral Reviews*, 21, 581–601. ▸page 105

Blass, T. (2004). *The Man who Shocked the World: The life and legacy of Stanley Milgram*. New York: Basic Books. ▸page 130

Bleuler, E. (1911 trans. 1950) *Dementia Praecox*. New York: International University Press. ▸page 188

Bowlby, J. (1953) *Child Care and the Growth of Love*. Harmondsworth: Penguin. ▸page 62

Brazelton, T.B., Koslowski, B. and Tronick, E. (1976) Neonatal behavior among urban Zambians and Americans. *Journal Academy of Child Psychiatry*, 15, 97–108. ▸page 63

Brewer, M.B. (1999). The psychology of prejudice: ingroup love or outgroup hate? *Journal of Social Issues*, 55 (3), 429–444. ▸page 160

Brigham, C. (1923) *A Study of American Intelligence*. Princeton, NJ: Princeton University Press. ▸page 176

British Crime Survey (2004) http://www.homeoffice.gov.uk/rds/crimeew0304.html ▸page 60

Broadcasting Standards Commission (2002) *Briefing Update: Depiction of Violence on Terrestrial Television*. ▸page 60

Bryan, J.H. and Test, M.A. (1967) Models and helping: naturalistic studies in helping behaviour, *Journal of Personality and Social Psychology*, 6, 400–407. ▶page 148

Bryant, P. (2006) Expert interview. *Psychology Review*, 12 (3), 131–154. ▶page 49

Bushman, B.J. and Anderson, C.A. (2001) Is it time to pull the plug on the hostile versus instrumental aggression dichotomy? *Psychological Review*, 108, 273–279. ▶page 55

Cannon, W.B. (1927) The James-Lange theory of emotion: A critical examination and an alternative. *American Journal of Psychology*, 39, 106–24. ▶page 88

Carson, B.S. (2002) Gifted hands that heal (interview by Academy of Achievement). http://www.achievement.org/auto doc/page/car1int-1 (accessed October 2005). ▶page 110

Chwalisz, K., Diener, E. and Gallagher, D. (1988) Autonomic arousal feedback and emotional experience: evidence from the spinal cord injured. *Journal of Personality and Social Psychology*, 54, 820–828. ▶page 88

Charlton, T., Gunter, B. and Hannan, A. (eds) (2000) *Broadcast Television Effects in a Remote Community*. Hillsdale, NJ.: Lawrence Erlbaum. ▶page 103

Clark, K.B. and Clark, M.P. (1939) *The Development of Consciousness of Self in Negro Pre-school Children. Archives of Psychology*. Washington, DC: Howard University. ▶pages 180, 181, 182

Clarke, A.M. and Clarke A.D.B. (1998) Early experience and the life path. *The Psychologist*, 11, 433–36. ▶page 62

Colman, A.M. (1991) Crowd psychology in South African murder trials. *American Psychologist*, 46, 1071–1079. ▶page 138

Cook, S.W. (1978) Interpersonal and attitudinal outcomes in cooperating interracial groups. *Journal of Research and Development in Education*, 12 (1), 97–113. ▶page 160

Cooley, C.H. (1902) *Human Nature and the Social Order*. New York: Scribner. ▶page 129

Corballis, M.C. (1999) Are we in our right minds? In S. Della Salla (ed.) *Mind Myths: Exploring Popular Assumptions about the Mind and Brain*. Chichester: John Wiley and Sons. ▶page 110

Coren, S. (1996) *Sleep Thieves*. New York: Free Press. ▶page 102

Costa, P.T., Jr. and McCrae, R.R. (1992) Normal personality assessment in clinical practice: The NEO Personality Inventory. *Psychological Assessment*, 4, 5–13. ▶page 171

Criswell, J.H. (1937) Racial cleavage in Negro–white groups. *Sociometry*, 1, 81–89. ▶page 184

Daly, M. and Wilson, M. (1998) *The Truth About Cinderella*. London: Weidenfeld & Nicolson. ▶page 68

Damasio, A. (1999) *The Feeling of What Happens*. New York: Harcourt Brace. ▶page 88

Darley, J.M. and Batson, C.D. (1973) 'From Jersualem to Jericho': A study of situational and dispositional variables in helping behavior. *Journal of Personality and Social Psychology*, 27, 100–108. ▶page 147

Darley, J.M. and Latané, B. (1968) Bystander intervention in emergencies: Diffusion of responsibility. *Journal of Personality and Social Psychology*, 8, 377–383. ▶pages 147, 148

Darwin, C. (1969) *The Autobiography of Charles Darwin: With Original Omissions Restored, edited with appendix and notes by his grand-daughter, Nora Barlow*. New York: W.W. Norton. ▶page 170

Dement, W.C. (2001) *The Promise of Sleep*. London: Pan. ▶page 102

Dement, W.C. and Kleitman, N. (1957) The relation of eye movements during sleep to dream activity: An objective method for the study of dreaming. *Journal of Experimental Psychology*, 53, 339–346. ▶pages 98–100

Deregowski, J. (1972) Pictorial perception and culture. *Scientific American*, 227, 82–88. ▶pages 14–16

Deregowski, J.B. (1996) A man is a difficult beast to draw: the neglected determinant in rock art. NEWS'96, Swakopmund, Namibia [full text at http://cogweb.ucla.edu/ep/Art/Deregowski_96.pdf]. ▶page 18

Deutsch, M. and Collins, M.E. (1951) *Interracial Housing: A Psychological Evaluation of a Social Experiment*. Minneapolis, MiN.: University of Minnesota Press. ▶page 160

DeVries, R. (1969) Constancy of generic identity in the years three to six. *Monographs of the Society for Research in Child Development*, 34 (3, Serial No. 127). ▶page 47

Dodds, P., Muhamad, R. and Watts, D. (2003) An experimental study of search in global social networks. *Science*, 301, 827–829. ▶page 131

Dollard, J., Doob, L.W., Miller, N.E., Mowrer, O.H. and Sears, R.R. (1939) *Frustration and Aggression*. New Haven, CT: Yale University Press. ▶pages 55, 155

Dovidio, J.F., Gaertner, S.L., Validzic, A., Matoka, A., Johnson, B. and Frazier, S. (1997) Extending the benefits of recategorization: Evaluations, self-disclosure, and helping. *Journal of Experimental Social Psychology*, 33, 401–420. ▶page 152

Dunn, J. and Deater-Deckard, K. (2001) *Children's Views of their Changing Families*. York (UK): York Publishing Services/Joseph Rowntree Foundation. ▶page 68

Dutton, D.G. and Aron, A.P. (1974) Some evidence for heightened sexual attraction under conditions of high anxiety. *Journal of Personality and Social Psychology*, 30, 510–517. ▶page 89

Eagly, A.H. (1978) Sex differences in influenceability. *Psychological Bulletin*, 85, 86–116. ▶page 11

Ekman, P. and Friesen, W.V. (1978) *Manual for the facial action coding system*. Palo Alto, CA: Consulting Psychology Press. ▶page 219

Eberhardt, J.L. (2005) Imaging race. *American Psychologist*, February–March, 181–190 (available online at http://www.apa.org/journals/features/amp602181.pdf). ▶page 118

Fancher, R.E. (1996). *Pioneers of Psychology* (3rd edition). New York: W.W. Norton. ▶page 170

Festinger, L., Riecken, H.W. and Schachter, S. (1956) *When Prophecy Fails.* Minneapolis: University of Minnesota Press. ▸pages 92, 195

Fisher, R.A. and Yates, F. (1974) *Statistical Tables for Biological, Agricultural and Medical Research* (6th edition). Longman. ▸page 226

Forer, B.R. (1949) The fallacy of personal validation: A classroom demonstration of gullibility. *Journal of Abnormal Psychology*, 44, 118–121. ▸page 213

Fraser, S.C. (1974) 'Deindividuation: effects of anonymity on aggression in children'. Unpublished report. Los Angeles: University of Southern California. ▸page 138

Freud, A. (1946) *The ego and the mechanisms of defense.* New York: International University Press. ▸page 58

Freud, S. (1909) Analysis of a phobia in a five-year-old boy. In J. Strachey (ed. and trans.) *The Standard Edition of the Complete Psychological Works: Two Case Histories (vol. X)*, pages 5–147. London: The Hogarth Press. ▸pages 72–74

Freud, S. (1925) cited at http://www.loc.gov ▸page 71

Freud, S. (1933) *New Introductory Lectures on Psycho-Analysis.* London: Hogarth. ▸page 71

Frith, U. and Happe, F. (1999) Theory of mind and self-consciousness: What is it like to be autistic? *Mind and Language*, 14 (1), 1–22. ▸page 21

Gado, M. (2005) A cry in the night: the Kitty Genovese murder. http://www.crimelibrary.com/serial_killers/predators/kitty_genovese/11.html (accessed December 2005). ▸page 147

Gardner, R.A. and Gardner, B.T. (1969) Teaching sign language to a chimpanzee, *Science*, 165, 664–672. ▸pages 30–32

Garth, T.R. (1925) A review of racial psychology. *Psychological Bulletin*, 22 (June), 343–364. ▸page 154

Gergen, K.J., Gergen, M.M. and Barton, W.H. (1973) Deviance in the dark. *Psychology Today* (October), 129–130. ▸page 139

Gladwin, T. (1970) *East is a Big Bird: Navigation and Logic on Puluwat Atoll.* Cambridge, MA: Harvard University Press. ▸page 178

Goffman, E. (1961) *Asylums.* Garden City, NY: Doubleday. ▸page 192

Golby, A.J., Gabrieli, J.D.E., Chiao, J.Y. and Eberhardt, J.L. (2001) Differential responses in the fusiform region to same-race and other-race faces. *Nature Neuroscience*, 4, 845–850. ▸page 118

Golding, W. (1954) *Lord of the Flies.* London: Faber and Faber. ▸page 138

Goleman, D. (1995) *Emotional Intelligence.* New York: Bantam. ▸page 94

Gould, S.J. (1981) *Mismeasure of Man.* London: Penguin. ▸page 174

Gould, S.J. (1982) A nation of morons. *New Scientist*, May, 349–353. ▸pages 174–176

Gpnotebook (2005) http://www.gpnotebook.co.uk/simplepage.cfm?ID=-1127219150 (accessed October 2005). ▸page 110

Gregor, A.J. and McPherson, D.A. (1966) Racial preference and ego-identity among white and Negro children in a deep south standard metropolitan area. *Journal of Social Psychology*, 68, 95–106. ▸page 182

Gross, R. (2003) *Key Studies in Psychology.* London: Hodder. ▸page 66

Grossman, D. (1995) *On Killing: The Psychological Cost of Learning to Kill in War and Society.* Boston, MA: Little, Brown. ▸page 136

Guthrie, R.V. (1998) *Even the Rat was White: A Historical View of Psychology* (2nd edition). Boston: Allyn and Bacon. ▸page 181

Haney, C., Banks, C. and Zimbardo, P. (1973) A study of prisoners and guards in a simulated prison. *Naval Research Reviews*, 30 (9), 4–17. ▸pages 140–142

Harlow, H.F. (1959) Love in infant monkeys. *Scientific American*, 200 (6), 68–74. ▸page 63

Haskins, J. (1998) *The Dream and the Struggle: Separate but not Equal.* New York: Polaris. ▸page 180

Haslam, A. and Reicher, S. (2003) A tale of two prison experiments. *Psychology Review*, 9 (4), 2–5. ▸page 144

Hawthorne, J., Jessop, J., Pryor, J. and Richards, M. (2003) *Supporting Children through Family Change: A Review of interventions and services for children of divorcing and separating parents.* York (UK): York Publishing Services/Joseph Rowntree Foundation. ▸page 68

Hayes, K.J. and Hayes, C. (1952) Imitation in a home-raised chimpanzee. *Journal of Comparative Physiological Psychology*, 45, 450–459. ▸page 28

Hayes, K.J. and Nissen, C.H. (1971) Higher mental functions of a home raised chimpanzee. In A.M. Schrier and F. Stollinz (eds) *Behaviour of Nonhuman Primates* (vol. 4, pp. 59–115). New York: Academic Press. ▸page 28

Heerman, J.A., Jones, L.C. and Wikoff, R.L. (1994) Measurement of parent behavior during interactions with their infants. *Infant Behavior and Development*, 17, 309–319. ▸page 62

Herrnstein, R.J. (1973) *I.Q. in the Meritocracy.* Boston, MA: Little, Brown. ▸page 172

Herrnstein, R.J. and Murray, C.A. (1994). *The Bell Curve: Intelligence and Class Structure in American Life.* New York: Free Press. ▸page 178

Hewstone, M., Stroebe, W., Codol, J.-P. and Stephenson, G.M. (1988) *Introduction to Social Psychology: A European Perspective.* Oxford: Blackwell. ▸page 19

Hobson, R.P. (1984) Early childhood autism and the question of egocentrism. *Journal of Autism and Developmental Disorders*, 14, 85–104. ▸page 24

Hodges, J. and Tizard, B. (1989) Social and family relationships of ex-institutional adolescents. *Journal of Child Psychology and Psychiatry*, 30 (1), 77–97. ▸page 64

Hodges, J. and Tizard, B. (1989a) IQ and behavioural adjustment of relationships of ex-institutional adolescents. *Journal of Child Psychology and Psychiatry*, 30, 53–75. ▸page 64

Hofling, K.C., Brontzman, E., Dalrymple, S., Graves, N. and Pierce, C.M. (1966) An experimental study in the nurse–physician relationship. *Journal of Mental and Nervous Disorders*, 43, 171–178. ▸page 137

Hohmann, G.W. (1966) Some effects of spinal cord lesions on experienced emotional feelings. *Psychophysiology*, 3, 143–156. ▸page 88

Home Office (2003) *World Prison Population List*, http://homeoffice.gov.uk/rds/pdfs2/r188.pdf (accessed December 2005). ▸page 139

Hovland, C.I. and Sears, R.R. (1940) Minor studies of aggression: Correlation of lynchings with economic indices. *Journal of Psychology*, 9, 301–310. ▸page 155

Hraba, J. and Grant, G. (1970) Black is beautiful: A re-examination of racial preference and identification. *Journal of Personality and Social Psychology*, 16 (3), 398–402. ▸pages 182–184

Hughes, H. (1992) Impact of spouse abuse on children of battered women. *Violence Update*, August 1, 9–11. ▸page 60

Hunter, J.A. (1991) Intergroup violence and intergroup attributions. *British Journal of Social Psychology*, 30, 261–265. ▸page 154

James, I. (1988) Medicine and the performing arts, the Stage Fright Syndrome, *Trans Med Soc Lond*, 105, 5–9. ▸page 94

James, W. (1884) What is an emotion? *Mind*, 9, 188–205. ▸page 88

Johnson, D.W. (1966) Racial attitudes of Negro freedom school participants and Negro and white civil rights participants. *Social Forces*, 45, 266–272. ▸page 182

Johnson, R.D. and Downing, L.L. (1979) Deindividuation and valence of cues: effects on pro-social and anti-social behavior. *Journal of Personality and Social Psychology*, 37, 1532–1538. ▸page 139

Jones, R.L. (ed.) (1991) *Black Psychology* (3rd edition). Berkeley, CA: Cobb & Henry. ▸page 161

Kamin, L.J. (1977) *The Science and Politics of IQ*. Harmondsworth, Middlesex: Penguin. ▸page 172

Kanner, L. (1943) Autistic disturbances of affective contact. *Nervous Child*, 2, 217–250. ▸page 20

Keller, K.L. (1987) Memory factors in advertising: The effect of advertising retrieval cues on brand evaluations. *Journal of Consumer Research*, 14, 316–333. ▸page 4

Kline, P. (1991) *Intelligence: The Psychometric View*. London: Routledge. ▸page 178

Kline, P. (1993) *The Handbook of Psychological Testing*. London: Routledge. ▸page 179

Koluchová (1976) The further development of twins after severe and prolonged deprivation: A second report. *Journal of Child Psychology and Psychiatry*, 17, 181–188. ▸page 62

Koluchová, J. (1991) Severely deprived twins after twenty-two years' observation. *Studia Psychologica*, 33, 23–28. ▸page 62

Kraepelin, E. (1887) *Psychiatrie. Ein kurzes Lehrbuch für Studirende und Aerzte. Zweite, gänzlich umgearbeitete Auflage*. Leipzig: Abel Verlag. ▸page 188

Kruger, J. and Dunning, D. (1999) Unskilled and unaware of it: How difficulties in recognizing one's own incompetence lead to inflated self-assessments. *Journal of Personality and Social Psychology*, 77, 1121–1134. ▸page 124

Kunzig, R. (2004) Autism: what's sex got to do with it? *Psychology Today*, Jan/Feb [full text at http://cms.psychology today.com/articles/pto-3207.html]. ▸pages 23, 26

Kutchins, H. and S.A. Kirk. (1997) *Making us Crazy: DSM – the Psychiatric Bible and the Creation of Mental Disorder*. New York: Free Press. ▸page 194

Latané, B. and Darley, J.M. (1968) Group inhibition of bystander intervention in emergencies. *Journal of Personality and Social Psychology*, 10, 215–221. ▸page 146

Latané, B. and Rodin, J. (1969) A lady in distress: inhibiting effects of friends and strangers on bystander intervention. *Journal of Experimental Social Psychology*, 5, 189–202. ▸page 148

Le Bon, G. (1895) *The Crowd: A Study of the Popular Mind*. Translated 1898. London: Transaction. ▸page 138

Lerner, M.J. (1980) *The Belief in a Just World: A Fundamental Delusion*. New York: Plenum. ▸page 155

Lerner, M.J. and Simmons, C.H. (1966) Observer's reaction to the 'innocent victim': Compassion or rejection? *Journal of Personality and Social Psychology*, 4, 203–210. ▸page 150

Levine, M., Cassidy, C., Brazier, G. and Reicher, S. (2002) Self-categorisation and bystander non-intervention: two experimental studies. *Journal of Applied Social Psychology*, 7, 1452–1463. ▸page 152

LeVine, R.A. and Campbell, D.T. (1972) *Ethnocentrism: Theories of Conflict, Ethnic Attitudes, and Group Behavior*. New York: Wiley. ▸page 161

Levine, R.M. (1999) Rethinking bystander non-intervention: social categorisation and the evidence of witnesses at the James Bulger murder trial. *Human Relations*, 52, 1133–1155. ▸page 152

Lewin, R. (1980) Is your brain really necessary? *Science*, 210, 1232–1234. ▸page 118

Loftus, E. (1979) *Eyewitness Testimony*. Cambridge, MA.: Harvard University Press. ▸page 10

Loftus, E. (1997) Creating false memories. *Scientific American*, 277(3), 70–75. [full text at http://faculty.washington.edu/eloftus/Articles/sciam.htm]. ▸page 10

Loftus, E. and Palmer, J.C. (1974) Reconstruction of automobile destruction. *Journal of Verbal Learning and Verbal Behaviour*, 13, 585–589. ▸pages 6–8

Loftus, E. and Pickrell, J. (1995) The formation of false memories. *Psychiatric Annals*, 25, 720–725. ▸page 10

Lombroso, C. (1876) *L'Uomo Delinquente*. Milan: Horpli. ▸page 113

Lord, A.B. (1960) *The Singer of Tales*. Cambridge, MA: Harvard University Press. ▸page 178

Lorenz, K.Z. (1966) *On Aggression*. New York: Harcourt, Brace & World. ▸page 55

Mackay, C. (1841) *Extraordinary Popular Delusions and the Madness of Crowds*. Reprinted in Wordsworth Reference collection 1995. ▸page 128

Maddox, B. (1998) The Grimms got it right – renowned Grimm's Fairy Tales authors, Jakob and Wilhelm Grimm; stepfamily horror stories and step parents, *New Statesman*, October 16. ▸page 68

Maguire, E.A., Frackowiak, R.S. and Frith, C.D. (1997) Recalling routes around London: activation of the right hippocampus in taxi drivers. *Neuroscience*, 17, 7103–7110. ▸page 113

Maio, G. (2002) How anti-racism advertising can backfire, http://www.esrc.ac.uk/ESRCInfoCentre/PO/releases/2002/december/antiracismadv.aspx ▸page 160

Manchester Evening News (2005) manchesteronline.co.uk, 3 May. ▸page 54

Marañon, G. (1924) Contribution a l'etude de l'action emotive de l'adrenaline. *Revue Française Endocrinologie*, 2, 301–25. ▸page 88

Matsumoto, D. (1994). *People: Psychology from a cultural perspective*. Pacific Grove, CA: Brooks/Cole. ▸page 52

McGarrigle, J. and Donaldson, M. (1974) Conservation accidents. *Cognition*, 3, 341–50. ▸page 52

McKinley, J.C., Jnr. (1990) Gang kills homeless man in Halloween rampage. *New York Times*, A1, B3, November 2. ▸page 138

Meddis, R. (1975) *Statistical Handbook for Non-statisticians*. London: McGraw-Hill. ▸page 228

Milgram, S. (1960) Conformity in Norway and France: an experimental study of national characteristics. Dissertation: Harvard University. ▸page 130

Milgram, S. (1963) Behavioural study of obedience. *Journal of Abnormal and Social Psychology*, 67, 371–378. ▸pages 132–134, 135

Milgram, S. (1967) The small world problem. *Psychology Today*, May, 60–67. ▸page 131

Milgram, S. (1970) The experience of living in cities: a psychological analysis. *Science*, 167, 1461–1468. ▸page 147

Milgram, S. (1974) *Obedience to Authority: An Experimental View*. New York: Harper & Row. ▸page 153

Milgram, S. (1977) The familiar stranger: An aspect of urban anonymity. In S. Milgram, *The Individual in a Social World* (pp. 51–53). Reading, MA: Addison-Wesley. ▸page 131

Milgram, S. (1992) (edited by J. Sabini and M. Silver). *The Individual in a Social World: Essays and Experiments* (2nd edition). New York: McGraw-Hill. ▸page 131

Miller, D.T., Downs, J.S. and Prentice, D.A. (1998) Minimal conditions for the creation of a unit relationship: The social bond between birthdaymates. *European Journal of Social Psychology*, 28, 475–481. ▸page 155

Miller, G.A. (1969) Psychology as a means of promoting human welfare. *American Psychologist*, 24 (12), 1063–1075. ▸page 187

Miller, N.E. and Dollard, J. (1941) Social learning and Imitation. New Haven, CT: Yale University Press. ▸page 54

Milner, P. (1970) *Physiological Psychology*. New York: Holt, Rinehart and Winston. ▸page 87

MIND factsheets (http://www.mind.org.uk/Information/) accessed Jan 2006. ▸page 189

Moore, C. and Frye, D. (1986) The effect of the experimenter's intention on the child's understanding of conservation. *Cognition*, 22, 283–298. ▸page 52

Morland, K.J. (1966) A comparison of race awareness in northern and southern children. *American Journal of Orthopsychiatry*, 36, 22–31. ▸page 182

Mowrer, O.H. (1947) On the dual nature of learning – A reinterpretation of 'conditioning' and 'problem-solving.' *Harvard Educational Review*, 17, 102–148. ▸page 76

Muir, H. (2003) www.newscientist.com/article.ns?id=dn3676 ▸page 21

Myers, R.E. (1961) Corpus callosum and visual gnosis. In J.R. Delafresnaye (ed.), *Brain Mechanisms and Learning*. Oxford: Blackwell. ▸page 106

Neimark, J. (1996) The diva of disclosure, memory researcher Elizabeth Loftus. *Psychology Today*, 29 (1), 48. ▸page 19

Neisser, U. (1982) *Memory Observed*. New York: Freeman. ▸page 4

Neisser, U. and Harsch, N. (1992) Phantom flashbulbs: False recollections of hearing the news about the Challenger. In E. Winograd and U. Neisser (eds) *Affect and Accuracy in Recall: Studies of 'flashbulb' memories* (vol. 4, pp. 9–31). New York: Cambridge University Press. ▸page 5

Nelson, L.D. and Norton, M.I. (2005) From student to superhero: situational primes shape future helping. *Journal of Experimental Social Psychology*, 41, 423–430. ▸page 55

Nickerson, R.S. and Adams, J.J. (1979) Long-term memory for a common object. *Cognitive Psychology*, 11, 287–307. ▸page 4

Nobel Prize website (2005) http://nobelprize.org/medicine/articles/sperry/index.html (accessed October 2005). ▸page 110

NOMS (2005) http://www.homeoffice.gov.uk/rds/pdfs05/hosb 1005.pdf (accessed December 2005). ▸page 139

O'Connell, A.N. and Russo, N.F. (ed.) (2001) *Models of Achievement: Reflections of Eminent Women in Psychology*. New York: Columbia University Press. ▸page 180

Ogden, J.A. and Corkin, S. (1991) Memories of H.M. In W.C. Abraham, M.C. Corballis and K.G. White (eds) *Memory Mechanisms: A Tribute to G.V. Goddard*. Hillsdale, NJ: Erlbaum. ▸page 203

ONS (Office for National Statistics) (2000) *Psychiatric morbidity among adults living in private households*. London: HMSO. ▸page 189

Orne, M.T. (1962) On the social psychology of the psychological experiment: with particular reference to demand characteristics and their implications. *American Psychologist*, 17, 776–783. ▸page 153

REFERENCES

Orne, M.T. and Holland, C.C. (1968) On the ecological validity of laboratory deceptions. *International Journal of Psychiatry*, 6 (4), 282–293. ▸page 137

Ornstein, R.E. (1972) *The Psychology of Consciousness*. San Franciso: Freeman. ▸page 110

Palinkas, L.A., Suedfeld, P. and Steel, G.D. (1995) Psychological functioning among members of a small polar expedition. Aviation, *Space and Environmental Medicine*, 66, 943–950. ▸page 102

Papert, S.A. (1999) *Mindstorms: Children, Computers and Powerful Ideas* (2nd edition). New York: Basic Books. ▸page 47

Papez, J.W. (1937) A proposed mechanism of emotion. *Journal of Neuropsychiatry and Clinical Neuroscience*, 7(1), 103–112. ▸page 89

Pelham, B.W., Mirenberg, M.C. and Jones, J.T. (2002) Why Susie sells seashells by the seashore: Implicit egotism and major life decisions. *Journal of Personality and Social Psychology*, 82(4), 469–487. ▸page 155

Pettigrew, T.F. (1967) Social evaluation theory: Convergences and applications. *Nebraska Symposium on Motivation*, 15, 241–319. ▸page 184

Piaget, J. (1954) *The Construction of Reality in the Child.* New York: Basic Books. ▸page 46

Piliavin, I.M., Rodin, J. and Piliavin, J.A. (1969) Good samaritarianism: An underground phenomenon? *Journal of Personality and Social Psychology*, 13, 289–299. ▸pages 148–150

Pinker, S. (1994) *The Language Instinct: How the Mind Creates Language*. New York: William Morrow. ▸page 34

Premack, D. and Premack, A.J. (1966) *The Mind of an Ape.* New York: W.W. Norton. ▸page 28

Premack, D. and Woodruff, G. (1978) Does the chimpanzee have a theory of mind? *The Behavioral and Brain Sciences*, 4, 515–526. ▸page 20

Raine, A. (2000) Brain size linked to violence. http://news.bbc.co.uk/1/hi/health/630929.stm (accessed October 2005). ▸page 119

Raine, A. (2004) Unlocking Crime: The Biological Key, BBC News, December http://news.bbc.co.uk/1/hi/programmes/if/4102371.stm (accessed October 2005). ▸page 118

Raine, A., Buchsbaum, M. and LaCasse, L. (1997) Brain abnormalities in murderers indicated by positron emission tomography. *Biological Psychiatry*, 42 (6), 495–508. ▸page 114–116

Ramachandran, V.S. and Rogers-Ramachandran, D. (1996) Synaesthesia in phantom limbs induced with mirrors. *Proceedings of the Royal Society of London*, 263, 377–386. ▸page 18

Rank, S.G. and Jacobsen, C.K. (1977) Hospital nurses' compliance with medication overdose orders: a failure to replicate. *Journal of Health and Social Behaviour*, 18, 188–193. ▸page 137

Rauscher, F.H., Shaw, G.L. and Ky, K.N. (1993) Music and spatial task performance. *Nature*, 365, 611. ▸page 113

Reicher, S.D. (1996) Social identity and social change: Rethinking the context of social psychology. In P. Robinson (ed.) *Social Groups and Identities: Developing the legacy of Henri Tajfel*. Oxford: Butterworth-Heinemann. ▸page 138

Richeson, J.A., Baird, A.A., Gordon, H.L., Heatherton, T.F., Wyland, C.L., Trawalter, S. and Shelton, J.N. (2003). An fMRI investigation of the impact of interracial contact on executive function. *Nature Neuro-science*, 6, 1323–1328. ▸page 118

Riesen, A.H. (1950) Arrested vision. *Scientific American*, 408, 16–19. ▸page 112

Ronson, J. (2004) The road to Abu Ghraib – part two. *The Guardian*, October 30. ▸page 138

Rose, S., Kamin, L.J. and Lewontin, R.C. (1984) *Not in our Genes: Biology, Ideology, and Human Nature.* Harmondsworth: Penguin. ▸page 178

Rose, S.A. and Blank, M. (1974) The potency of context in childrens' cognition: An illustration through conservation. *Child Development*, 45, 499–502. ▸page 48

Rosenhan, D.L. (1973) On being sane in insane places. *Science*, 179, 250–258. ▸pages 190–192

Rosenthal, A.M. (1964) *Thirty-Eight Witnesses: The Kitty Genovese Case, Part 2*. Berkeley, CA.: University of California Press. ▸page 146

Rosenthal, A.M. (1999) *Thirty-Eight Witnesses: The Kitty Genovese Case*. Berkeley: University of California Press. ▸page 146

Rosenthal, R. (1966) *Experimenter Effects in Behavioural Research*. New York: Appleton-Century-Crofts. ▸page 11

Rosenthal, R. and Fode, K.L. (1963) The effect of experimenter bias on the performance of the albino rat. *Behavioural Science*, 8 (3), 183–189. ▸page 53

Rosenthal, R. and Jacobsen, L. (1966) Teacher expectations. *Psychological Reports*, 19, 115–118. ▸page 53

Ross, J.M. (1999) Once more onto the couch. *Journal of the American Psychoanalytic Association*, 47, 91–111. ▸page 70

Rubenstein, S. and Caballero, B. (2000) Is Miss America an undernourished role model? *JAMA*, 283 (12), 1569.

Rumbaugh and Lewin (1994) *Kanzi: The Ape at the Brink of the Human Mind.* New York: Doubleday. ▸page 34

Runyon, R. and Haber, A. (1976) *Fundamentals of Behavioural statistics* (3rd edition). Reading, Mass.: McGraw-Hill. ▸page 227

Rutter, M. (2005) The adoption of children from Romania/The social and intellectual development of children adopted into England from Romania. *The Research Findings Register*, summary number 55. http://www.ReFeR.nhs.uk/ViewRecord.asp?ID=5 (accessed 18 April 2006). ▸page 68

Ryan, J. (2004) Army's war game recruits kids. *San Francisco Chronicle*, 23 September. ▸page 60

Rymer, R. (1993) *Genie: Escape from a Silent Childhood*. London: Michael Joseph.

Sacher, W. (1993). Jugendgefährdung durch Video- und Computerspiele? [Is there a danger to youth from video and computer games?] *Zeitschrift für Pädagogik*, 39, 313–333. ▸page 60

Sainsbury Centre for Mental Health. http://www.scmh.org.uk (accessed Jan 2006). ▸page 189

Samuel, J. and Bryant, P. (1983) Asking only one question in the conservation experiment. *Journal of Child Psychology*, 22 (2), 315–318. ▸pages 48–50

Schachter, S. (1959) *The Psychology of Affiliation*. Stanford, CA: Stanford University Press. ▸page 90

Schachter, S. and Singer, J.E. (1962) Cognitive, social and physiological determinants of emotional state. *Psychological Review*, 69, 379–399. ▸pages 90–92

Schachter, S. and Wheeler, L. (1962) Epinephrine, chlorpromazine and amusement. *Journal of Abnormal and Social Psychology*, 45, 121–128. ▸page 92

Schaffer, H.R. and Emerson, P.E. (1964) The development of social attachments in infancy. *Monographs of the Society for Research in Child Development*, 29 (3 Serial No. 94). ▸page 62

Schacter, S. (1964) The interaction of cognitive and physiological determinants of emotional state. In L. Berkowitz (ed.) *Advances in Experimental Social Psychology, Vol. 1*. New York: Academic Press. ▸page 150

Schopler, J. and Matthews, M.W. (1965) The influence of the perceived causal locus of partner's dependence on the use of interpersonal power. *Journal of Personality and Social Psychology*, 4, 609–612. ▸page 148

Schreiber, F.R. (1973) *Sybil*. New York: Warner Books.

Senate Intelligence Committee (2004) *Report on the U.S. Intelligence Community's Prewar Intelligence Assessments on Iraq*. ▸page 129

Shannahoff-Khalsa, D.S., Boyle, M.R. and Buebel, M.E. (1991) The effects of unilateral forced nostril breathing on cognition. *International Journal of Neuroscience*, 57, 239–249. ▸page 110

Shayer, M., Demetriou, A. and Perez, M. (1988) The structure and scaling of concrete operational thought: Three studies in four countries and only one story. *Genetic Psychology Monographs*, 114. 307–376. ▸page 52

Sherif, M. (1966) *In Common Predicament: Social Psychology of Intergroup Conflict and Cooperation*. Boston: Houghton-Mifflin. ▸page 154

Sherif, M., Harvey, O.J., White, B.J., Hood, W.R. and Sherif, C.W. (1961) *Intergroup Co-operation and Conflict: The Robbers Cave Experiment*. Norman, OK: University of Oklahoma Press. ▸page 154

Shireman, J.F. and Johnson, P.R. (1986). A longitudinal study of Black adoptions: single parent, transracial, and traditional. *Social Work*, 31 (3), 172–176. ▸page 18~6

Sidoli, M. (1996) Farting as a defence against unspeakable dread. *Journal of Analytical Psychology*, 41 (2). ▸page 76

Sizemore, C.C. and Pitillo, E.S. (1977) *I'm Eve*. New York: Doubleday. ▸page 202

Slater, L. (2005) *Opening Skinner's Box*. London: Bloomsbury. ▸pages 63, 190

Smith, L.T. (1999) *Decolonizing Methodologies: Research and Indigenous Peoples*. University of Otago Press, Dunedin. ▸page 19

Smith, P. and Bond, M.H. (1993) *Social Psychology across Cultures: Analysis and Perspectives*. New York: Harvester Wheatsheaf. ▸page 19

Sperry, R.W. (1964) from 'James Arthur Lecture on the Evolution of the Human Brain'. Quoted on http://faculty.washington.edu/chudler/quotes.html (accessed October 2005). ▸page 104

Sperry, R.W. (1968) Hemispheric deconnection and unity in conscious awareness. *American Psychologist*, 23, 723–733. ▸pages 106–108

Spitzer, R.L. (1975). On pseudoscience in science, logic in remission, and psychiatric diagnosis: a critique of Rosenhan's 'On being sane in insane places.' *Journal of Abnormal Psychology*, 84, 442–452. ▸page 194

Steele, K.M., Bass, K.E. and Crook, M.D. (1999). The mystery of the Mozart effect: failure to replicate. *Psychological Science*, 10 (4), 366–369. ▸page 113

Stephan, W.G. (1978). School desegregation: an evaluation of predictions made in *Brown* vs. *Board of Education*. *Psychological Bulletin*, 85, 217–238. ▸page 160

Stratton, G.M. (1896) Some preliminary experiments on vision without inversion of the retinal image. *Psychological Review*, 3, 611–617. ▸page 13

Szasz, T.S. (1960) *The Myth of Mental Illness*. London: Paladin. ▸page 194

Tajfel, H. (1970) Experiments in intergroup discrimination. *Scientific American*, 223, 96–105. ▸page 156–158

Tajfel. H. (1978) The achievement of group differentiation. In H. Tajfel (ed.), *Differentiation between social groups: Studies in the social psychology of intergroup relations*. London: Academic Press. ▸page 144

Tajfel, H. and Turner J.C. (1979) An integrative theory of intergroup conflict. In: S. Worchel and W.G. Austin (eds) *The Social Psychology of Intergroup Relations (S. 33–47)*. Monterey, CA: Brooks/Cole Publishers. ▸pages 138, 155

Terrace, H.S. (1979) *Nlm*. New York: Alfred A. Knopf. ▸page 34

Terrace, H.S., Petitto, L.A., Sanders, R.J. and Bever, T.G. (1979) Can an ape create a sentence? *Science*, 206, 891–902. ▸page 34

The Times (2004) Blair promises to end 'kitchen cabinet' government, www.timesonline.co.uk/article/0,,15629-1185343,00.html ▸page 129

Thigpen, C.H. and Cleckley, H. (1954) A case of multiple personality. *Journal of Abnormal and Social Psychology*, 49, 135–151. ▸pages 198–200

Thigpen, C.H. and Cleckley, H. (1957) *The Three Faces of Eve*. New York: McGraw-Hill. ▸page 202

Tizard, B. (1986) *The Care of Young Children: Implications of Recent Research*. London: Thomas Coram Research Unit Working Paper No. 1. ▸page 62

Tizard, B. and Phoenix, A. (2002). *Black, White or Mixed Race? Race and Racism in the Lives of Young People of Mixed Parentage* (revised edition). London: Routledge. ▸page 68

Trinkaus, J. (1990) Exiting a building: An informal look. *Perceptual and Motor Skills*, 71 (October), 446. ▸page 195

Trinkaus, J. (1993) Compliance with the item limit of the food supermarket express checkout lane: An informal look. *Psychological Reports*, 73 (1), 105–106. ▸page 195

Trinkaus, J. (2003) Snow on motor vehicle roofs: An informal look. *Psychological Reports*, 92 (3.2), 1227–8. ▸page 195

Triplett, N. (1897) The dynamogenic factors in pacemaking and competition, *American Journal of Psychology*, 9, 507–533. ▸page 129

Turnbull, C.M. (1961) *The Forest People*. New York: Simon & Schuster. ▸page 19

Valins, S. (1966) Cognitive effects of false heart-rate feedback. *Journal of Personality and Social Psychology*, 4, 400–408. ▸page 88

Wagstaff, G.F. (1981) *Hypnosis, Compliance and Belief*. New York: St Martins Press. ▸page 197

Watson, J.B. (1930) *Behaviorism* (revised edition). New York: W.W. Norton. ▸page 187

Watson, P. (1980) *War on the Mind*. Harmondsworth: Penguin. ▸page 19

Waynforth, D. and Dunbar, R.I.M. (1995) Conditional mate choice strategies in humans: Evidence from 'lonely hearts' advertisements. *Behaviour* 132: 755–779. ▸page 219

Webb, W.B. and Agnew, H.W. (1975) Are we chronically sleep deprived? *Bulletin of the Psychonomic Society*, 6, 47–48. ▸page 102

Wells, G.L. and Bradfield, A.L. (1998) 'Good, you identified the suspect': Feedback to eyewitnesses distorts their reports of the witnessing experience. *Journal of Applied Psychology*, 83, 360–376. ▸page 10

Wells, G.L. and Olson, E.A. (2003). Eyewitness testimony, *Annual Review of Psychology*, 54, 277–295. ▸page 10

WHO (2001) *Mental health: New understanding, new hope*. ▸page 189

Wilson, J. and Kelling, G. (1982) Broken windows. *The Atlantic Monthly*, March, 29–38. ▸page 139

Women's Aid (2002) http://www.womensaid.org.uk/landing_page. asp?section=0001000100050001 ▸page 60

Yagyu, T., Wackermann, J., Kinoshita, T., Hirota, T., Kochi, K., Kondakor, I., Koenig, T. and Lehmann, D. (1997) Chewing-gum flavor affects measures of global complexity of multichannel EEG. *Neuropsychobiology*, 35 (1), 46–50. ▸page 87

Yahoo news (2005) The Queen, prime minister join in memorial service for London bomb victims. http://news.yahoo.com/s/cpress/20051101/ca_pr_on_wo/britain_bombings;_ylt=AuoCq Dje_Etd3tsTcZH54Bhs9L4F;_ylu=X3oDMTBjMHVqMTQ4BHNIY wN5bnN1YmNhdA— (accessed December 2005). ▸page 152

Zhar, J.H. (1972) Significance testing of the Spearman rank correlation coefficient. *Journal of the American Statistical Association*, 67, 578–580. ▸page 229

Zimbardo, P.G. (1969) The human choice: individuation, reason and order versus deindividuation, impulse and chaos. *Nebraska Symposium on Motivation*, 17, 237–307. ▸page 138

Zimbardo, P.G. (1970). The human choice: individuation, reason, and order versus deindividuation, impulse, and chaos. In W.J. Arnold and D. Levine (eds), *1969 Nebraska Symposium on Motivation* (pp. 237–307). Lincoln, NE: University of Nebraska Press. ▸page 139

Index

INDEX